DOMINUS ILLUMINATIO MEA

DOMINUS ILLUMINATIO MEA

DENIS THE CARTHUSIAN

COMMENTARY
on the
DAVIDIC
Psalms

VOLUME II
[PSALMS 26–50]

Which are most learnedly explained, to the degree able, in their multiple senses, namely LITERAL, ALLEGORICAL, TROPOLOGICAL, & ANAGOGICAL, with nothing except the most sound Scriptures of both Testaments.

Translation & Introduction by
ANDREW M. GREENWELL

Commentary in Latin taken from
Doctor Ecstaticus D. Dionysius Cartusianus,
Opera Omnia, Vol. 5 (Psalms 26–43)
(Montreuil: Typis Cartusiae S. M. de Pratis 1896)
Opera Omnia, Vol. 6 (Psalms 44–50)
(Montreuil: Typis Cartusiae S. M. de Pratis 1898)
English Translation & Introduction © Andrew M. Greenwell
Copyright Volume Two © Arouca Press 2021

All rights reserved:
No part of this book may be reproduced or transmitted,
in any form or by any means, without permission

ISBN: 978-1-989905-44-9 (pbk)
ISBN: 978-1-989905-45-6 (hardcover)

Arouca Press
PO Box 55003
Bridgeport PO
Waterloo, ON N2J3G0
Canada
www.aroucapress.com
Send inquiries to info@aroucapress.com

Book and cover design by
Michael Schrauzer

DEDICATION

To my children,
Elizabeth Grace, Mary Abigail, and Christopher Michael

Ecce haereditas Domini, filii; merces, fructus ventris.
Sicut sagittae in manu potentis, ita filii excussorum.
Beatus vir qui implevit desiderium suum ex ipsis:
non confundetur cum loquetur inimics suis in porta.
— Psalm 126:3–5

Nocte surgentes vigilemus omnes,
Semper in psalmis meditemur, atque
Voce concordi Domino canamus
Dulciter hymnos.

Ut pio Regi pariter canentes,
Cum suis Sanctis mereamur aulam
Ingredi caeli, simul et perennem
Ducere vitam.

Praestet hoc nobis Deitas beata
Patris, ac Nati, pariterque Sancti
Spiritus, cuius resonat per omnem
Gloria mundum.

— Hymn, Roman Breviary
(ascribed to St. Gregory the Great).

CONTENTS

Abbreviations x
Introduction to Denis the Carthusian's
 Commentary on the Psalms, Volume 2 xi
Acknowledgments xxxviii
COMMENTARY ON THE PSALMS, VOLUME 2 1
PSALM 26 3
PSALM 27 27
PSALM 28 41
PSALM 29 53
PSALM 30 75
PSALM 31 105
PSALM 32 117
PSALM 33 133
PSALM 34 151
PSALM 35 189
PSALM 36 203
PSALM 37 231
PSALM 38 253
PSALM 39 275
PSALM 40 305
PSALM 41 329
PSALM 42 349
PSALM 43 359
PSALM 44 385
PSALM 45 413
PSALM 46 429
PSALM 47 439
PSALM 48 453
PSALM 49 469
PSALM 50 489

ABBREVIATIONS

DS Heinrich Denziger, *Enchiridion Symbolorum Definitionum et Declarationum de Rebus Fidei et Morum* (*Compendium of Creeds, Definitions, and Déclarations on Matters of Faith and Morals*) (P. Hünerman, ed.) (Robert Fastiggi and Anne Englund Nash, eds., Eng. ed.) (43rd ed.) (San Francisco: Ignatius Press 2012).
PG *Patrologiae cursus completus. Series Graeca.* Ed. J.-P. Migne. Paris: Migne, 1857–1886.
PL *Patrologiae cursus completus. Series Latina.* Ed. J.-P. Migne. Paris: Migne, 1844–1864.
ST St. Thomas Aquinas, *Summa Theologiae* (corpusthomisticum.org)
CCC Catechism of the Catholic Church

INTRODUCTION
to
DENIS THE CARTHUSIAN'S
Commentary on the Psalms

PART 2
[PSALMS 26–50]

THE PSALMS: *THE VOICE OF THE WHOLE CHRIST*

> [T]he book of Psalms... principally speaks of... Christ... [f]or it is about Christ, and not... only of the person of Christ, but of the whole Christ.[1]
>
> —Denis the Carthusian

IN THE INTRODUCTION TO THE FIRST VOLume of Denis's *Commentary on the Psalms*, I emphasized the form of Denis's *Commentary*, pointing out its ecstatic nature, its Christological focus, its reliance on Scripture to explain Scripture, its Thomistic nature, and its emphasis on the Christian manner of life and praxis. These qualities, of course, are found as amply in this second volume as they were in the first.

In this Introduction to the second volume of Denis's *Commentary*, however, I want to reflect upon Denis's understanding of Christ's presence in the Psalms, specifically, Christ's voice in the Psalms. Following St. Augustine who fleshed out this concept out in his *Enarrationes in Psalmos*, Denis believes the Psalms contain the voice of the whole Christ, *vox totius Christi*. There are distinctions in Christ's voice in the Psalms, so Denis identifies the various voices of Christ, the *voces Christi*: the voice about Christ (*vox de Christo*), the voice of Christ to the Father (*vox Christi ad Patrem*), and the voice of Christ to us (*vox Christi ad nos*).[2]

---

[1] Denis the Carthusian, *Commentary on the Davidic Psalms: Beatus Vir* (Waterloo, ON: Arouca Press, 2020), 17-18 (herein *Beatus Vir*).

[2] The focus on the "person" who is speaking in the Psalm is called prosopological

Now, for the Psalms to contain Christ's voice in any real sense implicitly says something about Christ. It presupposes that Christ could say "before David was made, I am."[3] There is therefore a Christology underlying Denis's *Commentary on the Psalms*. In reflecting upon this Dionysian Christology, I want to consider two things. First, I want to provide a short reflection on what I would call Denis's *ontologically high* Christology which leads to an *epistemologically robust* Christ. Second, I want to address briefly what implications arise out of the Psalms being the *vox totius Christi*; namely, the significance of the Psalms being a *theological source* (what theologians call the *locus theologicus*) of Christology.

WHO IS CHRIST AND WHAT DOES HE KNOW?

Let us start off with Denis the Carthusian's Christology. Much of Christology comes down to the answer to two questions Christ asks of us: *Who do you say that I am?* and the related question *What do you say that I know?* For Denis, these two questions are intertwined. The first question asks how ontologically *high* we think of Christ. The second question asks how epistemologically *robust* we think him. Actually, St. Peter answered both those questions for us. To the first, Peter answered, "You are the Christ, the Son of the living God."[4] To the second, Peter answered, "Lord you know all things."[5] But these statements of Peter's faith deserve a little elaboration.

Tu es Christus, Filius Dei vivi.

"You are the Christ, the Son of the living God." Denis understands this Petrine statement of faith in accordance with the Council of Chalcedon.[6] Denis accepts the dogma that the eternal and only begotten Son of God, the Word of God and second Person of the Blessed Trinity, is consubstantial with the Father, the first Person of the Blessed Trinity. In his divine Person and nature therefore, Christ pre-existed the Incarnation; in fact,

---

exegesis (from the Greek word for "face" or "person," πρόσωπον (*prosōpon*). Also found in the Psalms are the voices of the Mystical Body of Christ. There is the *vox de ecclesia*, the voice about the Church, the *vox ecclesiae*, the voice of the Church, and the voice of the Church to Christ, *vox ad Christum*. See generally Michael Fiedrowicz, *Psalmus Vox Totius Christi: Studien zu Augustins* enarrationes in Psalmos (Freiburg: Herder 1977).
3   *Cf.* John 8:58: *Jesus said to them: Amen, amen I say to you, before Abraham was made, I am.*
4   Matt. 16:15.
5   John 21:17.
6   DS 301-02.

Jesus, viewed from the vantage point of his divine Person, existed eternally with the Father and the Holy Spirit with whom he shares the same divine nature. Moreover, at the Incarnation, the only begotten Son of God assumed the nature of man, and so became — uniquely — the God-man Jesus. This is the bedrock of Denis's understanding of who Jesus is. Such a divine person would have no problem speaking to us in the Psalms before he assumed human nature, since "before David was made, he was."

Now, this union of God and man in Jesus Christ is called the "grace of union" or the "hypostatic union," which is a grace unique to Christ. In his *Commentary on the Psalms* Denis makes express mention of it.[7] Indeed, Denis invokes it at the very outset in his allegorical exposition of Psalm 1:1, a Psalm which he applies allegorically to Christ. "Blessed is the man" Jesus, Denis says, because he enjoyed the grace of union.

There is great theological and practical significance in this grace of union. To believe in the hypostatic union means to believe that Jesus was not a human person. Jesus had no human personality.[8] His personality was a divine one. Jesus was a divine Person who assumed a human nature. So, with respect to Jesus' two natures, we can say he was fully man and fully God. With respect to his personhood, however, his "I," his "ego," — the "I" to whom he referred to when he said, "before Abraham was made, I am," in John 8:58 — is one of the eternal Persons of the Blessed Trinity. This reality informs the question of Christ's *human* knowledge. One might say *scire sequitur esse*: what one knows follows from what one is.

Domine, tu omnia nosti.

"You know all things." This follows from the statement, "you are the Christ, the Son of the living God." So, as a necessary concomitant of that grace of union, Denis states the following: "It is clear... that the soul of Christ from its inception was granted the beatific vision of God, as the

---

7 Articles IX (Psalm 1:1); XXI (Psalm 5:1).
8 In using the word "personality," I use the word in a strict ontological sense; when "personality" is used in a loose, non-ontological sense and in reference only to Christ's human nature (*i.e.*, personality = assemblage of human characteristics that make one human distinct from another), one can say Jesus has a personality. But because of the possibility of confusion it may cause and corrosive effect it might have on the Chalcedonian dogma, it is preferable not to use such a term. The same is true for the word "being." Jesus was not a human "being" in any ontological sense; he was a divine Being, namely, the Son of God, that assumed a human nature. Again, if "being" is used loosely in a non-ontological sense in reference to the human nature of Jesus, meaning a human existence, then it might be used. But confusion arises from using two identical words in such equivocal matters in an issue of such importance.

Damascene [St. John of Damascus] attests and also Thomas [Aquinas]."[9] So along with the grace of union, from the first instant of his human life, that is, from the first moment of the Incarnation, Jesus' human soul was graced, in a superlative way,[10] with the beatific vision.[11] "For those things which are, which were, and which will be, and especially that which pertains to the mystery of human redemption, Christ [in his human nature] knew and always saw in the Word, even has he does now."[12]

The beatific vision is the vision of "divine essence by an intuitive vision and face to face, so that the divine essence is known immediately, showing itself plainly, clearly and openly, and not mediately through any creature."[13] Those with the beatific vision "clearly behold God, one and triune, as He is."[14] "It is called vision in the mind by analogy with bodily sight, which is the most comprehensive of the human sense faculties; it is called beatific because it produces happiness in the will and the whole being."[15] So Denis's belief is that while *in via* on earth, Jesus in his human soul saw God face-to-face as do the blessed in heaven, and saw all things in God. Moreover, at the same instant that he was graced with the beatific vision, Jesus in his human nature was also graced with infused knowledge.[16] Like St. Thomas Aquinas, Denis also understands that Christ, in his human nature, acquired knowledge experientially, and so in this sense "increased

---

9 *Beatus Vir*, 37 [Article IX (Psalm 1:1)]. One should note the implication of relying on the 8th century John of Damascus and the 13th century St. Thomas as authorities. Authorities five centuries apart and representing both the Latin and the Eastern "lungs" of the Church held the same doctrine. The reference to St. John of Damascus (*ca.* 675–*ca.* 749) is likely a reference to his *Expositio Fidei Orthodoxa*, III, 21-22, where he addresses the lack of ignorance (ἄγνοια) in Christ. For example: "[W]e declare him... at the same time God and man, and all-knowing (*et qui sciat omnia*/πάντα εἰδέναι). *For in him are all the treasures of wisdom and knowledge, the hidden treasures.* (Col. 2:3)." PG 94, 1085-88.

10 I say superlative because it flows naturally, substantially, from the hypostatic union and so differs from the beatific vision of the blessed in heaven, since the vision of the saints is not based directly on the hypostatic union, but rather, on a union based upon adoption and grace. ST IIIa, q. 10, art. 4. This is one reason Denis and others call Jesus the Saint of Saints: because of the grace of union, which is unique to him, he is a leap above all others.

11 Article XLVIII (Psalm 20:4) ; *see also* Article LIV (Psalm 22:1); Article LX (Psalm 26:1); Article LXI (Psalm 27:2); Article LXXI (Psalm 33:2); Article LXXII (Psalm 34:9) ; Article LXXVIII (Psalm 39:6).

12 *Beatus Vir*, Article IX (Psalm 1:2), p. 39.

13 DS 1000-02 (Benedict XII, *Benedictus Deus*) (1336 AD).

14 DS 1305 (*Laetentur caeli*) (1439 AD).

15 John A. Hardon, S. J., *Catholic Dictionary* (New York: Image 1980), 49-50 (s.v. "beatitude").

16 Article LX (Psalm 26:1).

in wisdom and stature, and in favor with God and man."[17] In summary, Denis's underlying conception is that, as a consequence of the hypostatic union or the grace of union, Jesus' human nature while on earth enjoyed an unrivaled human knowledge through three sources: the beatific vision, infused knowledge, and acquired or experiential knowledge.[18] Thus, uniquely, Jesus was *simul viator et comprehensor*, both a wayfarer and one with the beatific vision of the blessed. This is the classic formulation.

Now this was not a novel theory when Denis subscribed to it. In fact, it was—and is—the received teaching as to Christ's fonts of knowledge.[19] Because of its importance in understanding Denis's *Commentary*, it behooves us to look more closely at this teaching's development and the consensus that, until recently, existed with respect to it.

Christ's Human Knowledge.

> When it is inquired whether Christ knows all things in the Word, 'all things' may be said in two ways: The first way, properly, so that it encompasses all things that in any way are, will be, or were—whether they be things done, said, or thought, by whomsoever, and at whatever time. And in this fashion it must be said that the soul of Christ knows all things in the Word.... [T]he soul of Christ knows in the Word all things existing in whatever time, and also the thoughts of men, of which He is the Judge, so that what is said of him in John 2:25 'For he knew what was in man,' can be understood not merely of the Divine knowledge, but also of his soul's knowledge, which it had in the Word.[20]
> — St. Thomas Aquinas

Denis, like St. Peter and like St. Thomas, understands Christ to "know all things in the Word." Christ in his human nature knows "all that in any way whatsoever is, will be, or was done, said, or thought." During the 900 years following Chalcedon theologians reflected upon the issue

---

17 Luke 2:25.
18 Article LX (Psalm 26:1). Additionally, in his human nature, Jesus also received in their fulness the virtues—except, in a very limited sense, faith and hope—and all the gifts of the Holy Spirit, which include those intellectual gifts of wisdom, understanding, and knowledge. Because of the beatific vision Denis concedes only a limited "hope" in Christ, accidental in nature only, and pertaining only to the anticipation of the resurrection of the body, glorification of his body, and his ascension into heaven.
19 ST IIIa, q. 1, art. 2; qq. 8-12; q. 15, art. 2.
20 ST IIIa, q. 10, art. 2.

of Christ's knowledge, and their reflections ultimately reached a polished form by the labors of the Scholastic theologians of the Middle Ages. By the time Denis drew from St. Thomas Aquinas's *Summa Theologiae* in the 1430s, the doctrines in the main were settled for almost two hundred years. As St. Thomas himself observed, "it is possible for a created intellect seeing the essence of God, to know all things which God knows with his knowledge of vision, and *all hold this [to be true] of the soul of Christ.*"[21] By the time Denis draws from St. Thomas in the 1430s, the doctrine was in all its significant parts universally held by all theological and philosophical schools, by theologians throughout the world.[22] It was even held by heretics who had split from the Church with respect to other teachings.[23] As Bernard Leeming, S. J., professor of dogmatic theology at Heythrop College, Oxford, summarized it in a 1952 article in the *Irish Theological Quarterly* entitled "The Human Knowledge of Christ," by the twelfth century that doctrine was "unanimous, certain and constant" and held by all. The only disputed question, it seems, was what theological note it ought to receive.[24] Leeming summarizes:

> They [all theological and philosophical schools, nations, even heretics] agree, moreover, that the matter is not open to discussion: "it is part of the faith" (Toletus), "the contrary would practically be heresy" (Petavius, the Salamanca theologians, Janssens), "theologically certain" (Medina, Pesch, Lercher, Lépicier), "the contrary would be erroneous, or rash, or unsound in faith" (Suarez, Alvarez, Platin, Billuart, Lugo, Hurter), "taught as certain in all Catholic schools" (Galtier), "common and certain in theology"(Solano); Stentrup sums it up: "No Catholic theologian has a right to depart from this doctrine which touches the faith and which has been received by the unanimous and constant agreement of approved theologians and writers."[25]

---

21   *De veritate*, q. 8 a. 4 co. (*ut de anima Christi ab omnibus tenetur*). "And so, to the soul of Christ, which above all other creatures sees God more perfectly, is attributed the knowledge of all things, present, past, and future."
22   "Nominalist, Realists, Scotist, Thomists, Baconians, Augustinians, Molinists" all agreed upon the doctrine. Bernard Leeming, S. J., "The Human Knowledge of Christ," 19 *Irish Theological Quarterly* 3 (July 1962), 235.
23   "Wyckliff, Huss, the Jansenists, and Hooker, — all are in perfect accord that Christ in His humanity saw God face to face." Leeming, 235.
24   "A theological note is a judgment of the dogmatic or theological value of a proposition according to its relation with the norms of faith." *New Catholic Encyclopedia* (New York: Thomson-Gale 2003, Vol. X, 453 (s.v. "Notes, Theological").
25   Leeming, "Human Knowledge of Christ," 235.

Leeming was not exaggerating. Indeed, the doctrine was expressly mentioned by Pope Pius XII as the Church's ordinary,[26] uncontested, uncontroversial, and received teaching in his encyclical *Mystici Corpus Christi* (1943) and again in his encyclical *Haurietis Aquas* (1956).

The received orthodox doctrine which underlies Denis's understanding of our Lord was gracefully summarized by Pius XII in his encyclical *Mystici Corporis Christi*:

> But the knowledge and love of our Divine Redeemer, of which we were the object from the first moment of His Incarnation, exceed all that the human intellect can hope to grasp. For hardly was He conceived in the womb of the Mother of God, when He began to enjoy the Beatific Vision, and in that vision all the members of His Mystical Body were continually and unceasingly present to Him, and He embraced them with His redeeming love. O marvelous condescension of divine love for us! O inestimable dispensation of boundless charity! In the crib, on the Cross, in the unending glory of the Father, Christ has all the members of the Church present before Him and united to Him in a much clearer and more loving manner than that of a mother who clasps her child to her breast, or than that with which a man knows and loves himself.[27]

Both the beatific vision and knowledge of Jesus as well as his infused knowledge were the subject matter of the Pian encyclical *Haurietis Aquas* on the Sacred Heart:

> [The Sacred Heart] is, besides, the symbol of that burning love which, infused into His soul, enriches the human will of Christ and enlightens and governs its acts by the most perfect knowledge derived both from the beatific vision and that which is directly infused.[28]

---

26 As Leeming noted: "Indeed, the agreement of theologians upon this matter has been regarded as almost a classical case of theologians representing the mind of the whole Church: such a judgment, so universal and so long-continued, upon a question of revealed truth, effectively involves the mind of the Church, and were that judgment mistaken, the implication would be that the Holy Ghost was not with the Church." Leeming, 235.
27 DS 3812 (*Mystici Corporis*, No. 75).
28 DS 3924 (*Haurietis Aquas*, No. 56).

The Chalcedonian dogma thus has a direct bearing on informing our understanding of the *human knowledge* of Christ. As the Church reflected upon the implications of the Chalcedonian dogma to the human knowledge of Jesus over the centuries, a unanimous consensus was reached among pope, bishops, the theologians, and the faithful regarding Christ's knowledge. At the heart of Denis's *Commentary on the Psalms* is this fully-developed orthodox Christological position regarding the human knowledge of Christ while he was a wayfarer, a *viator*, on earth.

So, it would seem, the matter was settled.

The Slobification of Christ

Ah, but matters are never settled. "For there must also be heresies."[29] And there were, and are, such heresies that have arisen with respect to the beatific vision and the three-fold human knowledge of Christ. Thankfully, Denis was spared from their infection. As I wrote in the Introduction to the first volume of the *Commentaries*, part of its merits was that "Modernism tinges it utterly nowhere."[30] Nowhere is this assertion truer than in Denis's *high* and *robust* Christology.

Nihil sub sole novum. There is nothing new under the sun. So there have always been detractors of Christ's human knowledge;[31] however, these errant voices had by and large been overcome until modern times. The first modern concerted attack upon this doctrine arose in the late 19th and early 20th centuries, when liberal and modernist theologians took aim at it and the Church responded with prudent yet forceful vigor to defend it. The sallies against the doctrine started small. For example, some theologians began by denying that Jesus was always aware of his Messianic dignity. Such views and others like them were roundly condemned by the Church's *Magisterium* acting through the Holy Office in 1917, with the publication of *Lamentabili sane*.[32] Shortly later, in a subsequent decree by the Holy Office promulgated in 1918, collateral positions relating to Christ's human knowledge were held unsafe to hold and teach. That is, to teach these positions was dangerous to the Faith.

---

29 1 Cor. 11:19.
30 *Beatus Vir*, xxxiii-xxxiv.
31 These errors with respect to Christ's knowledge followed upon the errors relating to Christ's divine nature or person. For example, the Arians held that Christ — being a creature — was ignorant of things. The Monophysite heretics known as the Agnotae also attributed ignorance to the human soul of Christ. See A. Mass, "Knowledge of Christ," *Catholic Encyclopedia* (New York: Encyclopedia Pres., 1913), Vol. VIII, 675.
32 DS 3435 (*Lamentabili*, 35)

Thus, the Church through its magisterial organs taught that it was a danger to the Faith to state that it was not certain "in the soul of Christ, while living among men," there existed "the knowledge possessed by the blessed or those who have the beatific vision."[33] Similarly dangerous was it to state that it was not certain that "the soul of Christ not only was ignorant of nothing, but also from the beginning [of his Incarnation] knew all things past, present, and future in the Word, that is, all things that God knows by knowledge of vision." Finally, it was a danger to the Faith to teach that the soul of Christ had "limited knowledge," and not "universal knowledge."[34]

Heresies, however, as John Cassian reminds us, "bear some likeness to that hydra which the poets' imagination invented; for they too hiss against us with deadly tongues; and they too cast forth their deadly poison, and spring up again when their heads are cut off."[35] And about five decades after the Modernist's rumblings had been squelched by the Holy Office, and not long after Pope Pius XII penned his Encyclical *Haurietis Aquas*, the attacks against the received doctrine that Christ enjoyed the beatific vision while on earth began again, particularly in the post-conciliar theological confusion after Vatican II.[36]

But in the contemporary attack upon the received doctrine we see something new. These attacks are now largely *intramural*, and, what is more, the guardians of doctrine appear to suffer from some sort of doctrinal enervation. Although the *Magisterium* of the Church may not have outrightly conceded ground and capitulated, it certainly has offered a lackadaisical defense of the received doctrine once considered monolithic.[37] It is almost as if, to follow the thought of St. John Henry

---

33 DS 3645.
34 DS 3647.
35 John Cassian, *On the Incarnation of the Lord*, I, 1 Nicene and Post-Nicene Fathers (2nd Series) (New York: The Christian Literature Company, 1894), Vol. XI, 511. (eds. Philip Schaff and Henry Wallace).
36 Though the teaching was not expressly part of its documents, "virtually all of the bishops who spoke on the matter during the [Second Vatican] Council took the traditional doctrine [regarding Christ's three-fold human knowledge] for granted as a matter of faith or at least theologically certain." Jeremy Wilkins, "Love and Knowledge of God in the Human Life of Christ," Pro Ecclesia XXI:1 (2012), 82 (citing J. A. Riestra, "La scienza di Cristo nel Concilio Vaticano II: Ebrei 4, 14 nella constituzione dogmatici *Dei Verbum*," Annales Theologici 2 (1988): 99-119.
37 As William Chami observes, the three most recent documents issued by the International Theological Commission do not even mention the beatific vision. More notably, it is conspicuously absent *in haec verba* from the current Catechism of the Catholic Church. William Chami, *How Did Jesus Know He Was God?*

Newman, there has been a "temporary suspense of the functions of the *Ecclesia docens*,"[38] the teaching Church, in this regard. Here again, Denis may prove useful. As I stated in the Introduction to the first volume, Denis's *Commentary* "is free of the theological and moral dissent which has plagued and dissipated and mollified and enervated Catholicism since Vatican II."[39]

The modernist and unclean spirit ousted in the early 20th century, like the unclean spirit of the Gospel of Luke, returned to the Church from where it had been cast out and brought with it seven other spirits some more evil than itself.[40] It is now quite common to find detractors of Christ's knowledge and rejectors of the received teaching, even by some theologians of notable repute and some even touted for their "orthodoxy." Pope Pius XII complained of this "enemy of the faith Chalcedon" in 1951, who, "in their arduous pursuit [of studying Christ from a psychological point of view,] desert the ancient teachings more than is right." But Pius XII was still able to say that this error was "widely diffused outside the fold of the Catholic religion,"[41] and not necessarily within the Catholic fold. But it is now widely diffused inside the fold of the Church. So widely diffused is it that in 1966 the Congregation of the Doctrine of the Faith under Cardinal Ottaviani warned of those within the Church who called into question the "venerated Person of our Lord Jesus Christ," particular with respect to a "certain Christological humanism [that] is twisted such that Christ is reduced to the condition of an ordinary man."[42]

So it is now quite common for theologians to challenge the received doctrine Denis relied upon in crafting his *Commentary*, and to do so with practical impunity. It seems that the world groaned and found itself to be filled with slobifiers of Christ.[43] As Raymond Brown summarized

---

Self-Consciousness and Human Knowledge of Christ: Maritain, Rahner, and Weiandy (Eugene, OR: Wipf & Stock, 2020), 9.

38   John Henry Newman, *The Arians of the Fourth Century*, Works New York: Longmans, Green & Co., 1897), 466.

39   *Beatus Vir*, xxxiv.

40   Fr. Most traces the return of this spirit to 1939, when the Jesuit Pierre Galtier published his book *L'Unité du Christ — Être, Personne, Conscience* (Beauchesne: Paris, 1939).

41   Pius XII, *Sempiternus Rex Christus*, 28-29.

42   CDF, *Circular Letter to the Presidents of Episcopal Conferences regarding some sentences and errors arising from the interpretation of the decrees of the Second Vatican Council* (July 24, 1966).

43   I ought to explain the term. Joan Osborne popularized a song written by Eric Bazilian which asked, "What if God was one of us? Just a slob like one of us?" The

the straws blowing in the post-conciliar wind: "all modern Christology is based on the theory that the human knowledge of Jesus was limited."[44]

In effect, the same threat is presented by these novel theories of Christ's human knowledge as was presented by the Modernists a century earlier. What solvent is dissolving a solute is not particularly important if one wants to preserve the solute. So whether the solvent is called "neo-modernism," or "liberalism," or "liberation theology," or "theology from below," or "theology of the people," or *"nouvelle théologie,"* or anything else is not particularly relevant. The focus should be on preserving the traditional doctrinal solute from *any* doctrinal solvent whatever its theological chemistry might be.

Notably, some of those associated with the now-mainstream *nouvelle théologie* school are among those who raised doubts regarding the received teaching, and proffer their own competing theories.[45] Ostensibly, they

---

modern effort to make Christ more like us is the theological slobification of him. Etymologically, the word slob comes from the Irish *slaba*, meaning "mud, mire dirt." Certainly, the word has derogatory connotations; however, in each instance that theologians seek to tamper with the traditional doctrine they in fact derogate from Christ's grace of union and its concomitant, the beatific vision.

44 R. Brown, *Biblical Reflections on Crises Facing the Church* (New York: Paulist 1975), 35, n. 28. *Pace* Brown's triumphalism, there are theologians that defend the traditional view. E.g., William G. Most, *The Consciousness of Christ* (Front Royal, VA: Christendom Press, 1980); For recent efforts at advancing or defending the traditional Thomistic doctrine, *see* Simon Francis Gaine, O. P., *Did the Savior See the Father? Christ, Salvation, and the Vision of God* (Bloomsbury: T & T Clark, 2015); Thomas Joseph White, O. P., *The Incarnate Lord* (Washington, DC: CUA Press, 2015). For a traditional presentation see Reginal Garrigou-Lagrange, *Christ the Savior: A Commentary on the Third Part of St. Thomas' Theological Summa* (B. Herder, 1957), Chps. XII-XIV, Questions 10-12.

45 Chami, 9. "Alternative theories offered include a kind of mission-consciousness (Balthasar), unobjectified filial consciousness (Rahner, Weinandy), "abba experience" (Schillebeeckx), and an infused prophetic insight existing with authentic human knowledge of the father (Galot)." Of course, there are many outside of the *nouvelle théologie* tag that are even more adverse to the received doctrine, and have actually been condemned by Church authorities, for example, the liberation theologian Jon Sobrino, S. J., whose works, because of "imprecisions and errors," even "dangerous propositions," were subject to *Notification* by the Congregation of the Doctrine of the Faith. Sobrino argued that Jesus had "faith," identical to all wayfarers, thereby denying the beatific vision, since the possession of the beatific vision is inconsistent with having "faith." The Congregation for the Doctrine of the Faith noted: "Jesus, the Incarnate Son of God, enjoys an intimate and immediate knowledge of his Father, a 'vision' that certainly goes beyond the vision of faith. The hypostatic union and Jesus' mission of revelation and redemption require the vision of the Father and the knowledge of his plan of salvation." Significantly, however, the CDF did not use the word "beatific vision," and, moreover, put the word vision in scare quotes.

want to "return to the sources," and so they use the word *ressourcement*. But one gets the strange feeling that by *ressourcement* they mean to go back to a time before the doctrine that Christ had a beatific vision was the consensus so that they could reject that consensus. They juke Pius XII by calling his comments about Christ's beatific vision and infused knowledge *obiter dicta*, and then make an end run around the centuries-old development and consensus by "going to the sources." The feeling that this is their strategy is not baseless, for the more honest of these theologians concede that their proposals contradict the "traditional teaching" as Denis recites it and as found in St. Thomas's *Summa Theologiae* and in Pope Pius XII's Encyclicals and everywhere in between.[46]

Now, one might think that this sort of intramural skirmish is about as important as how many angels dance on the head of a pin. Aren't we venturing into theological dialectics, and should we not keep in mind the exhortation of St. Ambrose and St. Paul: "[I]t was not in dialectics that God is pleased to save his people, 'for the kingdom of God is not in speech, but in power.'"[47] But this would be mistake. Capitulating on the traditional doctrine augurs massive theological, pastoral, and devotional change. It would mean a different Christ. It seems, to paraphrase Tertullian, that our modern theologians invent a new Jesus, as if we were ashamed of the old Jesus![48]

The doctrinal and moral implications associated with whether Christ has the beatific vision are enormous, for any doctrine that detracts from Christ's knowledge asserts some modicum of ignorance or at least nescience in Christ.[49] That implies a rejection of Chalcedon.[50] Moreover,

---

This suggests some reticence in defending the received doctrine regarding Christ's beatific vision. However, the CDF did cite to Pius XII's *Mystici Corporis Christi* and *Haurietis Aquas*, and it did appear to construe the language in the Catechism of the Catholic Church §§ 473-74 (which do not use the words "beatific vision," but only the more vague "vision," as equivalent to the "beatific vision" used by Pius XII).
46 Thomas G. Weinandy, O. F. M., "Jesus' Filial Vision of the Father," *Pro Ecclesia* XIII: 2 (2004), 189.
47 St. Ambrose, *Exposition of the Christian Faith*, I, 5, 42, PL 16, 537 (quoting 1 Cor. 4:20).
48 *Cf.* Tertullian, *Adv. Marcionem*, I, 8, PL 2, 254.
49 "Ignorance differs from nescience, in that nescience denotes mere absence of knowledge; wherefore whoever lacks knowledge about anything, can be said to be nescient about it.... On the other hand, ignorance denotes privation of knowledge, i.e. lack of knowledge of those things that one has a natural aptitude to know." ST IaIIae, q. 76, art. 2, c. (trans. English Dominican Province)
50 For example, the Arians and the Nestorians—both of whom would reject Chalcedon—ascribed ignorance to Christ's human nature. Pope Vigilius (500—555

just like nature abhors a vacuum—and so something always rushes in its place—religion abhors ignorance. If ignorance or even nescience is admitted of Christ's human nature, the Word of God made flesh, then there is a vacuole that will become filled with the word of man. Moreover, if Christ could err or be ignorant about God and man, then how can his word be trusted? And if there is ignorance in Christ, does not that mean that modern man can correct it? This sort of doctrine is a trapdoor to hubris.

The devotional effect of scuttling this doctrine in its developed fullness is likewise enormous. Did Christ become incarnate and suffer and die only generically "for us" (*pro nobis*), "for us men" (*propter nos homines*) only? Or did also become incarnate and suffer and die "for me" (*pro me*) as also St. Paul insists?[51] As the Christ child lay swaddled in a manger, as the adult Christ sweat blood at the Garden of Gethsemane, or as he suffered on the Cross, did his human mind behold—as a result of the beatific vision—each of us by face, by name: past, present, and future? If the soul of Jesus did not have the beatific vision and infused knowledge from the first moment of his Incarnation, then classic prayers and indulgenced devotions like the following, which hail back to Christ when *in via*, are pious frauds, to be scrapped as products of sophomoric piety, or the feverish phantasms of senilic widows, that we moderns have outgrown.

> *Domine Iesu, Per vagitus Tui in praesepio pro me nascentis,*
> *Per lacrimas Tui in cruce pro me morientis,*
> . . . .
> *Miserere mei et salva me.*
>
> Lord Jesus, by Your infant cries when you were born for me in the manger
> By the tears when you did die for me on the Cross,
> . . . .
> Have mercy on me and save me.[52]

No. Such prayers are not pious frauds; they are grounded, like Denis's *Commentary*, on a theological truth that the fullness of Catholic truth requires us to accept: Jesus, from the first moment of his Incarnation had the beatific vison, "and in that vision all the members of His Mystical Body were continually and unceasingly present to Him, and He

---

AD) certainly saw a link between one's belief about Christ's ontological constitution and Christ's knowledge. DS 416-420.
51 Gal. 2:20
52 *Enchiridion Indulgentiarum* (1952), No. 93, p. 38

embraced them with His redeeming love." There is no room for ignorance in the Jesus of Denis, which is the Jesus of the Gospels, and the Jesus preached by the Church, and who is the Jesus of history. Along with the disciples who knew Jesus, along with the medieval Schoolmen, along with all the Catholic theologians until the modern skeptical age, Denis says regarding Jesus's human knowledge, "we know that you know all things" in the Word, *nunc scimus quia scis omnia in Verbo*.[53]

THE PSALMS AND THE PROPHETS AS A *LOCUS THEOLOGICUS* OF THE VOX CHRISTI

The other point I want to address relates to how the voice of Christ in the Psalms and the Prophets affects our knowledge of Christ, and therefore also our relationship with him. We tend to draw the teachings of Jesus exclusively from the Gospel, as if those were the only words that the Son of God spoke to us. And it is true, as the author of the epistle to the Hebrews states, that "God ... in these days has spoken to us by his Son."[54] To be sure the human words spoken by Jesus, the Word made flesh, have a certain preeminence, as is clearly expressed in the ritual of our Liturgy by the way we handle the Gospels. But the epistle to the Hebrews also acknowledges that "at sundry times and diverse manners," God "spoke in times past to the fathers by the prophets."[55] This includes the Psalms and the Prophetic books. The Word speaks to us here also. In fact, Christ does so in particular in those Psalms where we find the voice of Christ to us, the *vox Christi ad nos*. And in those Psalms wherein we find the voice of Christ to the Father, *vox Christi ad Patrem*, we are made privy to the internal thoughts, the internal prayer life, of Christ. Viewed in this manner, the Psalms are a theological mother lode of Christology.

The notion that the Word spoke to us before he assumed flesh seems to be largely lost to us, and this is something that I hope Denis may allow us to recover. The epistle to the Hebrews does not deprecate, much less abrogate, the witness of the prophets or the Davidic psalms: "God ... at sundry times and diverse manners, spoke in times past to the fathers by the prophets."[56] Jesus himself noted that the Old Testament is riddled with information about him: "These are the words which ... are written in the law of Moses, and in the prophets, and in the Psalms concerning

---

53 John 16:30.
54 Heb. 1:2.
55 *Id.*
56 Heb. 1:1.

me."⁵⁷ The New Testament is virtually awash with quotes or references to the Psalms. This belief finds its echo in our Creed, where we say that God *locutus est per prophetas*: he has spoken through the prophets. Since Denis sees David as a prophet, indeed, as the preeminent prophet of Christ, this means he sees the words of the Psalms as words of Christ. So likewise for the other prophets. Accordingly, Christ's voice speaks in at least three registers—evangelical, psalmic, and prophetic—all of which must be kept in mind to understand the whole Christ. Robbing Christ of his voice in any one or both of these two latter registers results in a skewed view of Christ: it risks foisting upon us a neo-Marcionite Christ.

The Marcionites were a Christian sect founded by one Marcion of Sinope (*ca.* 85–*ca.* 160 AD). At the heart of this heresy was the belief that the teachings of Jesus were at odds with the teachings of the Old Testament. The result was a battle of Gods, a *theomachy*, a loving, forgiving, merciful, compassionate God wearing white trunks in one corner and a legalistic, vengeful, jealous, and punitive God wearing black trunks in the other. There is an incipient or functional Marcionism, I would suggest, in the common modern rejection, based on the supposed teachings of Jesus, of the Old Testament prescriptions against homosexual relations or adultery as intrinsically evil and involving exceptionless moral norms. Similarly, a neo-Marcionism seems to be behind modern efforts to oppose the moral liceity of capital punishment in certain cases, the moral liceity of which is clearly revealed the Old Testament.

Does not Tertullian's rhetoric seem apropos of the modern insipid kerygma?

> Listen, you sinners; and you who have not yet come to this, hear, that you may attain to such a pass! A better god has been discovered, who never takes offense, is never angry, never inflicts punishment, who has prepared no fire in hell, no gnashing of teeth in the outer darkness! He is purely and simply good. He indeed forbids all delinquency, but only in word. He is in you, if you are willing to pay him homage, for the sake of appearances, that you may seem to honor God; for your fear he does not want. And so satisfied are the Marcionites with such pretenses, that they have no fear of their god at all.⁵⁸

---

57 Luke 24:44.
58 Tertullian, *Adv. Marc.* I, 27. *Ante-Nicene Christian Library* (Edinburgh: T & T Clark 1878), Vol. 7, 52-53 (eds. Alexander Roberts and James Donaldson).

I think an indication of our loss of this sense is the sort of surprise engendered in us when reading sentences such as the following in Denis's *Commentary*: "As you said through Samuel,"[59] "This is what the Lord says through Isaiah,"[60] "for I know, O Lord, what you through holy Ezekiel stated,"[61] "the Lord speaks through Hosea,"[62] "This is what the Savior said through Jeremiah,"[63] "The Lord speaking through Malachi,"[64] "and again through another [of your prophets Zechariah],"[65] "And the Lord says through Zephaniah,"[66] "the Lord says through the prophet Amos,"[67] When Christ said ... through the prophet Micah,"[68] "and through Amos."[69] Christ speaking through the prophets peppers the *Commentary*. A particularly rich example of this can be found in Denis's *Commentary* on Psalm 40:2:

> For Christ lovingly regarded needy and poor mankind when he predicted through Jeremiah: *I think ... thoughts of peace, and not of affliction*; and through Zechariah: *Behold I come, and I will dwell in the midst of you*; and through Micah: *Your salvation is close, I will save you, do not fear*; and Isaiah, *I myself that spoke, behold I am here*.[70]

Now this considerably broadens the words of Christ given that there are the books of four major prophets—Isaiah, Jeremiah, Ezechiel, and Daniel—and twelve minor prophets with their respective books—Hosea, Joel, Amos Obadiah, Jonah, Micah, Nahum, Habakkuk, Zephaniah, Haggai, Zechariah, and Malachi—to draw from. And this does not include those prophets whose prophecies are found elsewhere—such as Samuel, Baruch, Elijah, and Elisha.

There is great merit in this expansive *locus theologicus*, the theological source, for our knowledge of Christ. For one, we have a Christ here speaking with his full, harmonious voice—the Old and the New.

---

59 Article XXIV (Psalm 7 :9)
60 Article IX (Psalm 1:3)
61 Article XXII (Psalm 6:5)
62 Article XXXVIII (Psalm 15:4)
63 Article LXVII (Psalm 30:3)
64 Article LXXI (Psalm 33 :6)
65 Article LX (Psalm 26 :9)
66 Article LXVII (Pslam 30:24)
67 Article LXXVI (Psalm 36:19)
68 Article LXXVI (Psalm 37:21)
69 Article XCII (Psalm 49:3)
70 Article LXXX (Psalm 40:2)

Moreover, reliance on the Old Testament prophets and Psalms as part of the *locus theologicus* in informing our Christology has the added merit of inoculating the Christian reader against any neo-Marcionism that may have reared its head in a world laden with theological liberalism.

ACKNOWLEDGMENTS

Once again, I would like to thank Alex Barbas and Arouca Press for the confidence they placed in this work, and their dedication to seeing it published. Again, I thank my wife, Betsy, for her patience during this project, my legal assistant, Cindi, for her eagerness to proofread this text. Finally, I appreciate the continued recommendations of Bishop Daniel Flores of Brownsville, Texas, Deacon Keith Fournier of Tyler, Texas, Dom Hugh Knapman, OSB, of Douai Abbey, Dom Pius Mary Noonan, OSB, of Notre Dame Priory, Abbot Philip Anderson, OSB, of Clear Creek Abbey, and I am humbled to include Dom Alcuin Reid, Prior of Monastère Saint-Benoît in Brignoles, France, now among their ranks.

O clementissime Iesu, gratias ago tibi ex toto corde meo.
Propitius esto mihi vilissimo peccatori.
Ego hanc actionem offero divino Cordi tuo
Emendandam atque perficiendam,
Ad laudem et gloriam sanctissimi Nominis tui
Et beatissimae Matris tuae,
Ad salutem animae meae totiusque Ecclesiae tuae.
Amen.

— Feast of the Holy Innocents (MMXX)

COMMENTARY on the DAVIDIC Psalms

PART 2
[PSALMS 26–50]

Psalm 26

ARTICLE LIX

EXPOSITION OF CHRIST OF THE TWENTY-SIXTH PSALM:
DOMINUS ILLUMINATIO MEA, &c.
THE LORD IS MY LIGHT, &c.

> 26{27}[1] *Unto the end, the Psalm of David before he was anointed. The Lord is my light and my salvation, whom shall I fear? The Lord is the protector of my life: of whom shall I be afraid?*
>
> *In finem, Psalmus David, priusquam liniretur. Dominus illuminatio mea et salus mea; quem timebo? Dominus protector vitae meae; a quo trepidabo?*

PLACED BEFORE THIS PSALM IS THIS TITLE: 26{27}[1] *In finem, Psalmus David, priusquam liniretur; In the end, the Psalm of David, before he was anointed.* By this we understand that David in the Books of Samuel is described as being anointed three times. The first, in the house of his father, as a sign of his future reign.[1] The second, in Hebron over the tribe of Judah.[2] The third, over the entire people of Israel.[3] Similarly, a Christian is anointed three times. The first, in Baptism, through which he receives the pledge (*pignus*) of the Holy Spirit. The second, in Confirmation. The third, in Extreme Unction. But this Psalm is entitled *of David, before he was anointed* the second time: for his second anointment is what this Psalm relates to. Therefore, the sense of the title of this Psalm is this: *the Psalm*, directing us *unto the end*, that is, the beatific consummation and Christ, is *of David*, that is, it applies to any member of the faithful, *before he was anointed* the second time, that is, [any member of the faithful] prior to the time he comes into the presence of the heaven of the blessed in which all the blessed are perfectly anointed by the Holy Spirit. For in the manner David after his first anointing encountered the greatest persecutions from Saul,[4] and sometime after his second anointment under the son of Saul,

---

[1] 1 Sam. 26:13.
[2] 2 Sam. 2:4.
[3] 2 Sam. 5:3.
[4] 1 Sam. 18–27.

Ish-boseth,[5] and also some after his third anointing from his own son, namely, Absalom,[6] so a Christian after the anointing of Baptism undergoes many tribulations from demons, the world, and the flesh, until he receives the anointing of Confirmation, which though obtained, he still is vexed by various tribulations from the followers of the devil, the sons of pride, even until the end of his life, which is the ultimate anointing. And so, he assuredly does not lack tribulations until he reaches the heavenly anointing. Thus in this Psalm is demonstrated how necessary it is for a man of God to suffer in the present exile. As a remedy against this in the beginning of the Psalm we are introduced to the most strong weapons, namely, the elevation of the mind unto God, confidence in his goodness, and the memory of the benefits of God.

Therefore it says: *Dominus illuminatio mea, the Lord is my light*, that is, the illuminator of my soul, illuminating me with natural light and the light of grace, or the gifts of nature and of grace, illuminating the reason lest it err, lest it be deceived, lest it sin. Hence, Micah says: *When I sit in darkness, the Lord is my light.*[7] *Et salus mea, and my salvation*, that is, the Lord himself is the object and the cause of my salvation, the giver and the preserver of all my perfection and my grace. Therefore, *quem timebo? Whom shall I fear?* This as if saying, "No one, except the Lord my God," because, as the Apostle [Paul] says, *If God be for us, who is against us?*[8] If he illumines, who is able to darken? If he saves me, who is able to condemn me? Thus Solomon says: *The just, bold as a lion, shall be without dread.*[9]

Dominus protector vitae meae, the Lord is the protector of my life, that is, the defender from those things that are contrary to the spiritual life of my soul. He also protects us through guardian angels from the adversities of the mind and of the body, and if not from all [adversities] on account of our demerits, still from many on account of his clemency. Since, therefore, it is so, *a quo trepidabo? Of whom shall I be afraid?* It is as if saying "I will fear the attacks of neither demons, nor the world, nor the flesh." But this must not be understood as referring to an inordinate fear, namely, carnal, human, and purely servile. For he whose mind is affixed upon God, and is strengthened in him by the gift of fortitude, fears nothing, knowing with greatest certainty God is everywhere present to him, and ready to sustain him in all things which God orders, or allows to befall

---

5   2 Sam. 2:8 *et seq.*; 2 Sam. 3:1.
6   2 Sam. 15–18.
7   Micah 7:8b.
8   Rom. 8:31b.
9   Prov. 28:1b.

him, or inflicts upon him. Indeed, in all adversities he will rejoice, as the Apostles, *who went from the presence of the council, rejoicing that they were accounted worthy to suffer reproach for the name of Jesus.*[10] And no wonder, since great is the gift of the Most High to suffer for justice's sake, as the Apostle [Paul] attests: *Unto you it is given for Christ, not only to believe in him, but also to suffer for him.*[11] Therefore, let us not sorrow in adversity and reproach and injury.

26{27}[2] *While the wicked draw near against me, to eat my flesh. My enemies that trouble me, have themselves been weakened, and have fallen.*

Dum appropiant super me nocentes, ut edant carnes meas, qui tribulant me inimici mei, ipsi infirmati sunt et ceciderunt.

26{27}[2] *Dum appropiant super me nocentes, while the wicked draw near against me,* that is while the evildoers are insurgent against me, *ut edant carnes meas, to eat my flesh,* that is, invading me so invidiously and powerfully and as if they were intending to devour my flesh. Whence the Apostle [Paul] said to the Galatians: *If you bite and devour one another; take heed you be not consumed one of another.*[12] And so I will not be afraid then, if *the wicked draw near against me*: and this because: *qui tribulant me, they who trouble me,* namely, *inimici mei, my enemies,* namely, demons and unjust men, *ipsi infirmati sunt, have themselves been weakened* by the power of the Passion of Christ and the assistance of the angels, who hinder the demons, so that they may not attack as much as they would like. Also, the more that evil men are strengthened against justice, the more their hearts are weakened in grace, and the more they are subject to vice and to demons and weakened in all good. *Et ceciderunt, and have fallen,* that is, the aforementioned enemies of mine have been vanquished by me through grace, for I resisted temptations, and I did not withdraw from God on account of adversity. This verse can be said (and ought to be said) to the glory of God by him who recognizes that he emerged victorious over temptations and the snares of the adversaries of his salvation by the grace of God. And from the triumph over the former [enemies], more strongly hoping in the Lord, he is not in fear of other attacks in the way of justice; but with the Lord's aid, confident of prevailing over that which tempts him and those who persecute him, he says what follows:

---

10 Acts 5:41.
11 Phil. 1:29.
12 Gal. 5:15.

26{27}[3] *If armies in camp should stand together against me, my heart shall not fear. If a battle should rise up against me, in this will I be confident.*

Si consistant adversum me castra, non timebit cor meum. Si exsurgat adversum me praelium, in hoc ego sperabo.

26{27}[3] *Si consistant adversum me castra, if armies in camp should stand together against me*, that is, if a battle array of demons [should set themselves against me,] tempting and persecuting me, *non timebit cor meum, my heart shall not fear* of being vanquished by them, or of being separated from Christ, because the firmness of hope and faith that I have in Christ. This is what the Apostle says: *I am sure that neither death, nor life, nor angels, nor principalities, nor powers, [nor things present, nor things to come, nor might, nor height, nor depth, nor any other creature,] shall be able to separate us from the love of God, which is in Christ Jesus our Lord.*[13] But by angels and by the remainder of those [things mentioned by St. Paul] it is certain that we are to understand them as demons. And so here the word *camp* (*castra*) is understood in sacred Scripture as demons; but sometimes, by the word *camp* is understood the holy angels. Whence, in another place is written: *the angels of God met Jacob, and when he saw them, he said: These are the camps* (*castra*) *of God.*[14] And the prophet Joel said: *for* the Lord's *armies* (*castra*) *are exceedingly great, for they are strong and execute his word*. Of which camps (*castris*) a later Psalm says: *Bless the Lord, all you his angels: you that are mighty in strength, and execute his word, hearkening to the voice of his orders.*[15] *Si exsurgat adversum me proelium, if a battle should rise up against me*, that is, the persecution of men, *in hoc ego sperabo, in this I will be confident*, that is, in such a case I will not desert my post, but I will have confidence in God. And so also Job says to the Lord: *Set me beside you, and let any man's hand fight against me.*[16] And in the Gospel, Christ says: *When you shall hear of wars and seditions, be not terrified.*[17]

26{27}[4] *One thing I have asked of the Lord, this will I seek after; that I may dwell in the house of the Lord all the days of my life. That I may see the delight of the Lord, and may visit his temple.*

---

13 Rom. 8:38–39. E. N. The words in bracket replace the "*etc.*" of Denis.
14 Gen. 32:1b–2a.
15 Ps. 102:20.
16 Job 17:3.
17 Luke 21:9a.

Unam petii a Domino, hanc requiram, ut inhabitem in domo Domini omnibus diebus vitae meae, ut videam voluptatem Domini, et visitem templum eius.

26{27}[4] *Unam petii a Domino, one thing I have asked of the Lord.* In accordance to an idiomatic property of Hebrew, adjectives and pronouns are substantivated (*substantivantur*) in the feminine gender, in the manner with Latin in the neuter gender.[18] Where, therefore, *one* (*unam*) is said, the sense is "one something" (*unum aliquid*), or "one thing" (*unam rem*). And so, *One thing* (*unam*) *I have asked of the Lord*, from whom all good things come, *hanc requiram, this will I seek after*, that is, I will not cease to beg for, until he opens to the one knocking.[19] And what is this one thing so highly preferred is exposited in the words that come next: *ut inhabitem in domo Domini omnibus diebus vitae meae, that I may dwell in the house of the Lord all the days of my life*, that is, that both in reality and in name I may be a member of the Church militant, and I may remain living well among the faithful, persevering even until the end. *Ut videam voluptatem Domini, that I may see the delight of the Lord*,[20] that is, that I may understand and may observe his precepts; *et visitem templum eius, and may visit his temple*, that is, Mother Church, hearing the Divine Office.[21] Or [another explanation], *that I may visit his temple*, that is, that my soul may be by hope and desire in heaven: as the Apostle [Paul] says, *Our conversation is in heaven*.[22] Or [alternatively] thus: *that*

---

18 E. N. An adjective or pronoun is substantivated (nominalized or nounified) when it is used so that it acts as a noun. For example, the adjective *homeless* can be substantivated to mean *homeless person*, or the pronoun "one" can be substantivated (nounified) to mean one *person*, or one *man, woman, and child*. When this is done in Hebrew the substantivated adjective/pronoun becomes feminine in gender (whereas in Latin is treated as neuter). All this has already been taken into consideration by the Douay-Rheims translators who translated *unam* as "one thing."
19 Cf. Luke 11:10: *For every one that asks, receives; and he that seeks, finds; and to him that knocks, it shall be opened.*
20 E. N. Here, Denis goes with a variant reading: *voluntatem Domini*, *the will of the Lord*, and not *voluptatem Domini, the delight of the Lord.* Since there is no real significance in terms of Denis's argument as to which version is used, I have chosen the Douay-Rheims's reading.
21 E. N. The Divine Office is the prayer of the Church (outside of the Mass) during fixed (canonical) hours — Matins, Lauds, Prime, Terce, Sext, None, Vespers, Compline, which the founder of Western monasticism, St. Benedict (*ca.* 480–550 A. D.), called the *Opus Dei*, the *Work of God.* "Nothing is to be placed before the work of God," *nihil operi Dei praeponatur*, insisted St. Benedict in his acclaimed Rule. *Reg. Ben.*, No. 43, PL 66, 675.
22 Phil 3:20a. E. N. The English word conversation translates the Latin *conversatio*, which might broadly be understood as "manner of living" or way of life. The Greek

I may dwell in the house of the Lord, that is, in the Kingdom of Heaven after this present exile; *that I may see the delight of the Lord*, that is, that I may know perfectly, and may see without peril that which pleases the Lord, so that in all things I may perfectly obey his will, as also the holy angels now do; *and may visit his temple*, that is, may unceasingly approach towards God himself, and I may see him, speak to him, and without end possess him as a most dear friend. For God is the temple of the heavenly Jerusalem, in the manner that John says: *I saw no temple therein. For the Lord God Almighty is the temple thereof, and the Lamb.*[23]

26{27}[5] *For he has hidden me in his tabernacle; in the day of evils, he has protected me in the secret place of his tabernacle.*

Quoniam abscondit me in tabernaculo suo; in die malorum protexit me in abscondito tabernaculi sui.

And these things I pray for confidently: **26{27}[5]** *Quoniam abscondit me in tabernaculo suo in die malorum; for he has hidden me in his tabernacle in the day of evils*: that is, during the time of tribulations and temptations now occurring, he has hidden me from adversaries in the faith and the unity of the Church, since — however much they may have found me bodily so as to persecute me — they did not find me consenting to their works or being found to belong to the number of the reprobate. And so it adds: *protexit me, he has protected me* from the snares of these rivals, namely, of the evil devils and men, *in abscondito tabernaculi sui, in the secret place of his tabernacle*, that is, the communion of the Church, namely, in the mutual prayer of the faithful on behalf of themselves and each other, proceeding from internal charity, which with merit is called *the secret place of the tabernacle* of God because it flows from the affection realized only in God; and it should be in a hidden manner, because Christ taught: *You*, he said, *when you shall pray, enter into your chamber, and having shut the door, pray to your Father in secret.*[24] And this prayer [of the Church available to those in communion with it] defends and provides help to many faithful. For which reason it is to be strongly

---

word used is πολίτευμα (*politeuma*) which implies membership in a πόλις (*polis*) or city, thus citizenship. The Revised Standard Version (Catholic Edition) translates it as "commonwealth." Thus, the concept here is not one of "talking" — engaging in conversation — but of engaging in living a life in common in Christ with those of the same Faith, including the Saints in heaven.

23   Rev. 21:22.
24   Matt. 6:6a.

abhorred to be excommunicated and certainly also to be in mortal sin, because only charity puts one in the communion of saints.[25]

26{27}[6] *He has exalted me upon a rock: and now he has lifted up my head above my enemies. I have gone round, and have offered up in his tabernacle a sacrifice of jubilation: I will sing, and recite a Psalm to the Lord.*

In petra exaltavit me, et nunc exaltavit caput meum super inimicos meos. Circuivi, et immolavi in tabernaculo eius hostiam vociferationis; cantabo, et Psalmum dicam Domino.

26{27}[7] *Hear, O Lord, my voice, with which I have cried to you: have mercy on me and hear me.*

Exaudi, Domine, vocem meam, qua clamavi ad te; miserere mei, et exaudi me.

26{27}[6] *In petra, upon a rock,* that is, upon the faith of Christ, of which the Apostle [Paul] said *the rock was Christ,*[26] *exaltavit me, he has exalted me,* giving me by faith in, and the grace of, Christ to despise this earth, and to desire heavenly things, and faithfully to adhere to divine things; *et nunc, and now,* in the present life, *exaltavit caput meum, he has lifted up my head,* that is, my reason, which is the principal power of the soul, *super inimicos meo, above my enemies,* giving me victory over temptations, and [the strength] to vanquish invisible and visible enemies. This applies to all good faithful, but especially those who have given up all things for Christ and who wage war in the cloister of the King of glory, as also the Lord says: *If any man will come after me, let him deny himself, and take up his cross daily, and follow me.*[27] Indeed, Christ again

---

25   E. N. Either excommunication or mortal sin will sever one from the communion of Saints which is the Church. For this reason, sacramental confession (or the lifting of excommunication) is needed to reconcile an excommunicate or sinner in mortal sin to God and thus also to re-instate his communion into the fellowship of Saints and obtain its benefits. In particular, this must be done prior to participating the Eucharist (Communion), which is the sign, symbol, and perfecter of that communion. With respect to the Eucharist, St. Augustine in one of his sermons ingeniously plays on the verb *estote* (which can mean either *eat* or *be*) and *estis* (which can mean *you eat* or *you are*). *Estote quod videtis, et accipite quod estis,* he says: "Become (or eat) what you see, and receive what you are (or you eat)." Sermon 272, PL 38, 170. Thus, one who partakes in the Eucharist without being in communion with the Church lies to himself, to those about him, and to the Lord. Hence its sacrilegious nature.
26   1 Cor. 10:4b.
27   Luke 9:23.

says to such persons: *Fear not, little flock, for it has pleased your Father to give you a kingdom.*[28]

Circuivi, I have gone round. An earlier Psalm says, *The wicked walk round about;*[29] but now in the person of a just man, he says, *I have gone round.* There is, therefore, a kind of evil circuit and there is a kind of good circuit. For a circuit is a certain circling around of created things. But the evil turn toward created things often circling around them so that they rest in them, fixing their love, delight, and end in them. But the good travel around these things, referring their love and knowledge of these to the glory of the Creator, to whom alone they finally direct their attention to and love. Therefore, in this way he now asserts: *I have gone round*, that is, I have seen all these visible things I see around me in order that I may perceive from them the invisible things of God.[30] Indeed, I have considered all things as created for men, so that from them they may attain to the knowledge of God. *Et immolavi in tabernaculo eius, and I have offered up in his tabernacle*, that is, in the chamber of my soul, or in the Church, *hostiam vociferationis, a sacrifice of jubilation*, that is, a sacrifice of affection or of high prayer, as we find said in a later Psalm: *Offer to God the sacrifice of praise.*[31] And in Hosea: *Say to the Lord: Take away all iniquity, and receive the good: and we will render the calves of our lips*,[32] that is, we will offer (*immolabimus*) to you the prayers and public cries of our mouths. *Cantabo, I will sing*, that is, I will praise with my mouth, *et psalmum dicam Domino, and recite a Psalm to the Lord*, that is, I will glorify him and confess him by my deeds. For to sing (*cantare*) is only to praise with the voice; but to recite a Psalm (*psallere*) is to venerate and proclaim God with good deeds.

Finally, after the bringing to mind all of the benefits of God and his good intentions, he returns again to the imploration of divine kindness, because it behooves to pray without ceasing.[33] And the more a man

---

28 Luke 12:32.
29 Ps. 11:9a.
30 *Cf.* Rom. 1:20: *For the invisible things of him, from the creation of the world, are clearly seen, being understood by the things that are made; his eternal power also, and divinity: so that they are inexcusable.*
31 Ps. 49:14a.
32 Hosea 14:3b. E. N. In his *Commentary on Hosea*, Denis says that this expression "the calves of our lips" stems from the fact that calves were victims of sacrifice in the Old Law, and so they represent sacrifice. Accordingly, the term "calves of our lips" should be understood as "the sacrifice of praise, the action of giving thanks, and prayer." Doctoris Ecstatici D. Dionysii Cartusiani, *Opera Omnia*, Vol. 10 (Montreuil: 1900), 317.
33 *Cf.* Luke 18:1: *And he spoke also a parable to them, that we ought always to pray, and not to faint.* E. N. The parable is the parable of the importunate widow, Luke 18:2–8.

makes progress [in the spiritual life], the more he desires to make greater progress, and the more frequently and with more sweetness will he pray: indeed, praying unceasingly is an enkindling toward prayer. Therefore he says: **26{27}[7]** *Exaudi, Domine, vocem meam qua clamavi ad te; hear, O Lord, my voice, with which I have cried to you,* that is, the prayer which with ardent affection I have dispatched to you; *miserere mei, have mercy on me,* removing from me all sins, *et exaudi me, and hear me,* granting the desired perfection.

26{27}[8] *My heart has said to you: My face has sought you: your face, O Lord, will I still seek.*

Tibi dixit cor meum, exquisivit te facies mea; faciem tuam, Domine, requiram.

26{27}[8] *Tibi dixit cor meum, my heart has said to you,* that is, my intellect has spoken to you offering to you my soul's desire. It does this in the manner recalled of the most holy Anna: *Now Anna spoke in her heart, and only her lips moved, but her voice was not heard at all.*[34] Whence also Christ says: *The true adorers shall adore the Father in spirit and in truth.*[35] *Exquisivit te facies mea, my face has sought you,* that is, you alone have I sought, and above all things my mind — or perhaps better, my faith, which is the face and the eye of my soul — has chosen to find you and to possess you: for I dispose and refer all the knowledge of created things and all of my works to you as my final end. Hence there is added: *faciem tuam, your face,* that is, a clear knowledge of you, indeed, contemplating your very self through species (*per speciem*),[36] *Domine, requiram, O Lord, will I still seek,* that is, incessantly will I endeavor to attain to it. Moses — who said to the Lord: *If therefore I have found favor in your sight, show me your face, that I may know you*[37] — sought his face.

---

34   1 Sam. 1:13a.
35   John 4:23a.
36   E. N. Denis is referring here to the limited knowledge that we have of God while *in via*. The knowledge of God *in via* is not, as it is in heaven when we see God "face to face," direct or immediate knowledge of his essence. This sort of knowledge was referred to as knowledge by essence (*intellectus per essentiam*) or in itself (*per seipsam*), or, in the words of St. Paul, we shall know even as we are known. *Cf.* 1 Cor. 13:12. On earth, while we see God "through a glass in a dark manner," we derive all our knowledge of God mediately through our senses, either by means of a species (or a likeness or a form or an idea) (*per speciem* or *per ideam*) or through acts (*per actus*). Our knowledge of God is, therefore, analogical. *See, e.g.,* St. Thomas's *Compendium theologiae*, lib. 1 cap. 105.
37   Ex. 33:13a.

We are unable to see in this present life this most superlatively blessed face,[38] in which there is the immense plenitude of all delights, as God also responding to Moses said: *You cannot see my face: for man shall not see me and live.*[39] Accordingly, we ought to seek and always desire this face, and with a pure mind minister to the Lord so that, after the course of this life, we might be found worthy to see God as he is: who so seen, nothing will be that can possibly be more desired.

26{27}[9] Turn not away your face from me; decline not in your wrath from your servant. Be you my helper, forsake me not; do not you despise me, O God my Savior.

Ne avertas faciem tuam a me; ne declines in ira a servo tuo. Adiutor meus esto; ne derelinquas me, neque despicias me, Deus salutaris meus.

26{27}[10] For my father and my mother have left me: but the Lord has taken me up.

Quoniam pater meus et mater mea dereliquerunt me; Dominus autem assumpsit me.

But in order that I might obtain this, O Lord, I pray, 26{27}[9] *Ne avertas*, turn not away now *faciem tuam*, your face, that is, the kindness of your appearance, or the presence of your grace, *a me*, from me; *ne declines in ira a servo tuo*, decline not in your wrath from your servant, that is, do not withdraw from me, denying me grace, because of my sins, whose denial is called *wrath* in this place. *Adiutor meus esto*, be my helper, O Lord, cooperating with me so that I might ultimately acquire beatitude; *ne derelinquas me*, forsake me not in tribulation and in distress; *neque despicias me, Deus salutaris meus*; do not despise me, O God my Savior, that is, God saving me.[40] See how fiery and fervent these words are, wherein one includes the other, indeed, the fervor of one inflames the mind to an affectionate increase of the other.[41] 26{27}[10] *Quoniam*

---

38 L. *superbeatissimam*. For more on Denis's use of superlatives, see footnote 17-128 in Volume 1.
39 Ex. 33:20.
40 L. *Deus salvans me*. The equivalent of *Deus salutis meae auctor*, "God, the author of my salvation," or *Deus salutis*, "God of my salvation."
41 E. N. There is a sort of stacking up of pleas and *pari passu* a commensurate rise in affection and fervor: don't avert your face, don't leave in anger, be my helper, forsake me not, do not despise, the words being but shades and phases of the same plea.

pater meus et mater mea, for my father and my mother, that is, my carnal progenitors, *dereliquerunt me, have left me,* being indignant with me, because I was following you, and I was leaving them. Or [alternatively]: my father and my mother, that is, the first parents, namely Adam and Eve,[42] abandoned me, introducing upon me original sin and the various punishments following from that sin. *Dominus autem assumpsit me, but the Lord has taken me up,* by his mercy hearing me and preserving [me] in him. Or [it may be thus understood], *the Lord has taken me up,* clothing himself with my nature, when he became man.

26{27}[11] *Set me, O Lord, a law in your way, and guide me in the right path, because of my enemies.*

Legem pone mihi, Domine, in via tua, et dirige me in semitam rectam, propter inimicos meos.

26{27}[12] *Deliver me not over to the will of them that trouble me; for unjust witnesses have risen up against me; and iniquity has lied to itself.*

Ne tradideris me in animas tribulantium me, quoniam insurrexerunt in me testes iniqui, et mentita est iniquitas sibi.

26{27}[11] *Legem pone mihi, Domine; set me, O Lord, a law in your way.* Why is this asked for? Is there not already a law, both natural and divine, proposed for us which we might observe? What else therefore is being asked for when he says, *set me, O Lord, a law* other than that the divine law—which is proposed for all—might be put in place in him, before the eyes of his heart, so that by the grace of God he may actually think and fulfill it? Therefore, he says: *Set me, O Lord, a law,* that is place your law in my memory, so that I might walk *in via tua, in your way; et dirige me in semita recta, and guide me in the right path,* that is, in the observation of your precepts, which are just and right: and this do *propter inimicos meos, because of my enemies,* that is, the occasion of my enemies, namely so that I might evade the snares that they have prepared for me. 26{27}[12] *Ne tradideris me in animas tribulantium me, deliver me not over to the will of them that trouble me,* that is, into the power and the evil will of the devil or of evildoing men, lest I conform or consent to them. And this I pray, *quoniam insurrexerunt in me testes iniqui, for unjust witnesses have risen up against me,* namely, the troublemakers already mentioned, who rise up against me, endeavoring

---

42 Gen. 3:6.

to cause me to fall. These are the evil witnesses, for they falsely affirm and take counsel, and strive to deceive me under the guise of good. And if I do not consent to them, they nevertheless strive to accuse me falsely. However, that iniquity of theirs trips them, not me: for it harms them: but to me, so long as I do not consent to them, it works together toward glory.[43] This is why it continues, *et mentita est iniquitas sibi, and iniquity has lied to itself*, that is, their own depravity has made them fall.

26{27}[13] *I believe to see the good things of the Lord in the land of the living.*

Credo videre bona Domini in terra viventium.

26{27}[13] *Credo, I believe* with a formed and unshaken faith,[44] *videre bona Domini, to see the good things of the Lord*, which *eye has not seen, nor ear heard*, nor heart conceived,[45] *in terra viventium, in the land of the living*, that is, in the Kingdom of Heaven, which is called *land* because it is a place of quiet and permanent, as *land* down here below is not moved,

---

43 E. N. "[W]hen you observe the law of God and do His will in a way that is displeasing to [your] nature, you acquire a double claim to reward: first, you have obeyed, and secondly, you have obeyed with difficulty and against resistance and combat. The sacrifice you have made ... is rewarded here by new graces and hereafter by an increase of eternal glory and happiness. Following up on this reasoning, what an immense treasure of merit that person accumulates who, assailed by all kinds of temptations, is steadfast in clinging to God! ... If the contest is severe, the crown is brilliant; one minute of pain and an eternity of glory!" P. J. Michel, S. J., *Temptations* (Manchester, N. H. Sophia Institute 2016), 97–98. (F. P. Garesché, S. J., trans.).
44 E. N. When Denis says *with a formed faith (fide formata)*, he is referring to a faith informed by charity, a *fides formata caritate. See* Gal. 5:6. As St. John Henry Newman described the distinctiveness of a faith formed by charity: "The safeguard of Faith is a right state of heart.... This it is what gives it birth; it also disciplines it. This is what protects it from bigotry, credulity, and fanaticism. It is holiness, or dutifulness, or the new creation, or the spiritual mind, however we word it, which is the quickening and illuminating principle of true faith, giving it eyes, hands, and feet. It is Love which forms it out of the rude chaos into an image of Christ; or, in scholastic language, justifying Faith ... is *fides formata charitate*." John Henry Newman, Sermon 12, *Fifteen Sermons Preached before the University of Oxford* (London: Longman, Green and Co., 1918), 234. A naked faith, a *fides nuda*, a faith unformed by charity, a *fides informata*, does not save. The Council of Trent was preemptory about it. "If anyone says that the sinner is justified by faith alone in the sense that nothing else is required by way of cooperation in order to obtain the grace of justification and that it is not at all necessary that he should be prepared and disposed by the movement of his will, let him be anathema." DS 1559. "Therefore, nobody should flatter himself with faith alone." DS 1538.
45 1 Cor. 2:9a.

but (Scripture attesting) *stands forever.*[46] On account of this hope and on account of this faith I bear all things with equanimity, knowing *that the sufferings of this time are not worthy to be compared with* that *glory.*[47] But no one fully subdues the difficulties in reaching this beatitude. Hence it adds in a consoling fashion:

26{27}[14] *Expect the Lord, do manfully, and let your heart take courage, and wait you for the Lord.*

Expecta Dominum, viriliter age, et confortetur cor tuum, et sustine Dominum.

26{27}[14] *Expecta Dominum, expect the Lord,* patiently hoping in him; *viriliter age, do manfully,*[48] whatever you know is pleasing to God, because your works will be rewarded;[49] *et confortetur cor tuum, and let your heart take courage,* against all the adverse temptations of this world and of demons by the virtues and the gifts of the Holy Spirit; *et sustine Dominum, and wait for the Lord,* in both prosperity and adversity, let not your spirit be fatigued. This most sweet verse ineffably consoles and strengthens every soldier of Christ, certainly every laborer, who with fear and reverence strives to serve God. And so, O servant of Christ, *expect the Lord.* The Lord *shall appear at the end, and shall not lie: if* he *make any delay, wait for* him, *for he shall surely come.*[50] Whence James admonishes: Take . . . *for an example* of longanimity, *labor, and patience, the prophets.* . . . *Behold, we account them blessed who have endured. You have heard of the patience of Job, and you have seen the end of the Lord.*[51] Finally, act manfully, because the Apostle [Paul] exhorts: *My beloved brethren, be steadfast and unmovable; always abounding in the work of the Lord, knowing that your labor is not in vain in the Lord.*[52] Let your hearts be comforted, in the manner that the Lord commanded Joshua: *Behold I command you, take courage, and be strong. Fear not and be not*

---

46 Eccl. 1:4.
47 Rom. 8:18.
48 E. N. On "manly virtues" not excluding women, see Article VIII (Psalm 1:1) in Volume 1.
49 Jer. 31:16b: *There is a reward for your work, says the Lord.*
50 Hab. 2:3. Denis adapts this verse which refers to Habakkuk's vision and applies it to the Lord.
51 James 5:10–11. In James 5:10, Denis's reading deviates from the Sixto-Clementine's Vulgate's "suffering evil" (*exitus malis*). Denis's text reads "of longanimity" (*longanimitatis*).
52 1 Cor. 15:58.

dismayed: because the Lord your God is with you in all things whatsoever you shall go to.⁵³ Finally, wait upon the Lord, so that you may be able to say with holy Job: *Although he should kill me, I will trust in him.*⁵⁴ This verse makes sloth (*acediam*) flee, inflames charity, builds longanimity, induces steadfastness, and expels all torpor, diffidence, pusillanimity, negligence, and desperation.

ARTICLE LX

EXPOSITION OF THE SAME TWENTY-SIXTH PSALM OF CHRIST

26{27}[1] *The Psalm of David before he was anointed. The Lord is my light and my salvation, whom shall I fear? The Lord is the protector of my life: of whom shall I be afraid?*

Psalmus David, priusquam liniretur. Dominus illuminatio mea et salus mea; quem timebo? Dominus protector vitae meae; a quo trepidabo?

EXPOSITING THE ABOVE PSALM OF CHRIST, the sense of its title will be: **26{27}[1]** *In finem, psalmus David; in the end, the Psalm of David,* that is, this Psalm is befitting to Christ, *priusquam*, before that same Christ, *liniretur, was anointed* the second time, that is, before he was glorified in the body.⁵⁵ For the first anointing is the glorification of his soul, which he had from the beginning of the conception in the Virgin. But the second anointing of his is the glorification of his body, when he received it in the Resurrection, of which glorification John says, *For as yet the Spirit was not given, because Jesus was not yet glorified.*⁵⁶

Therefore, Christ as man, thus says: *Dominus*, the Lord, that is, God, the Trinity, is *illuminatio mea, my light*, that is, the cause of all my created wisdom; and from the first moment of the creation of my soul he illumined it with the light of glory and the beatific vision.⁵⁷ When

---

53 Joshua 1:9.
54 Job 13:15a.
55 For the three types of anointing, *see* Article LIX (Psalm 26:1).
56 John 7:39b.
57 E. N. For the notion that Christ was both a *comprehensor* (enjoyed the direct vision of God) and a *viator see* footnotes P-91 and 1-46 and Article IX (Psalm 1:3)

considering that in Christ was the uncreated Wisdom, which is the same as the divine essence and the person of the Word, and by this Christ actually and eternally knew whatever the Father and the Holy Spirit [knew]; indeed, this Wisdom is one in three Persons. There was also in Christ [as man a] created wisdom, and this [created wisdom] was multiple.[58] For he had the wisdom of the heavenly homeland or of the blessed in heaven, knowing all things in the Word through the union of the divine essence with his intellect, by means of coupling of intelligible form.[59] From the beginning of his conception in his Mother, he also had an inserted or infused knowledge by which he knew all things in their proper nature by intelligible species concreated with them.[60] Besides these, some attribute to Christ as man an acquired or experimental knowledge in which he advances, not, however, by learning in any way from others, but by his own discovery.[61] So that by the natural light of the agent intellect, he abstracts from phantasms intelligible species, and these are stored in the possible intellect, and by this means he acquired knowledge. For no natural perfection or operation was seen to be lacking

---

in Volume I.

58 Christ as man had three levels, as it were, of knowledge of God and created things: *scientia beata, scientia indita vel infusa*, and *scientia acquisita* (blessed knowledge, infused or inserted knowledge, and acquired knowledge). Denis will elaborate on these in this part of the Article.

59 The mode of Christ's human knowledge Denis speaks of here—the *scientia beata*—was the knowledge obtained through the beatific vision, where Jesus, in his human nature, saw God face-to-face, directly, *per essentiam* in the light of glory, without mediation. DS 3812, 3645–57. In this knowledge, God himself (by a supernatural act) becomes the "intelligible form" of the human intellect. "The glory of God has enlightened it." Rev. 21:23. See IIIa, q. 9, art. 2, q. 10, arts. 1–4. While this knowledge of God and created things was direct, supernatural, and as perfect as human knowledge can ever be, since the "receptacle" is a created intellect, it was and is not comprehensive and infinite as was and is the knowledge that Jesus, in his divine nature as the Word, has and had of the Godhead (which was infinite *simpliciter*). ST, IIIa, q. 10, art. 2 ad 2; *see also* Session XX (Oct. 15, 1435) of the synod of Basel where it condemned the proposition: *Anima Christi videt Deum tam clare et intense quantum clare et intense Deus videt se ipsum*. "The soul of Christ sees God as clear and as intensely as the clarity and intensity with which God sees himself."

60 This is the *scientia indita* or the *scientia infusa*. See ST IIIa, q. 9, art. 11, arts. 1–6. Denis uses the word concreated (*concreatas*) to distinguish the fact that the knowledge of the thing is not subsisting in a thing, and so it is not a created thing since created things—strictly speaking—are subsisting things, whereas this knowledge of the thing does not subsist in the thing but in the mind of Christ. ST IIIa, q. 9, art. 3; q. 11, arts.1–6.

61 *See* ST IIIa, q. 12, arts. 1–4.

in the soul of Christ. For, as the Damascene[62] instructs, none of those things God planted in our nature was lacking in Christ.[63]

On account of all of these kinds of knowledge united in the soul of Christ, the Savior says: *Dominus illuminatio mea, et; the Lord is my light, and* he is *salus mea, my salvation,* that is, the object of my created happiness; *Quem timebo? Whom shall I fear?* Certainly no one, unless I freely will to assume the passion of fear, as I did at the approach of the Passion when I began to grow sorrowful and to be sad:[64] which passions I imperiously cast off just as I voluntarily had assumed them. *Dominus protector vitae meae, The Lord is the protector of my life,* in a most singular and most excellent way keeping me from the evils of fault and the dangers of the soul within, so that such were unable to be in me;[65] and outside from wounds of the body other than those that were required so as to suffer for the redemption of the human race. For when the Jews sought him to cast him down headlong [from a hill] or to stone him, Jesus concealed himself, the Lord protecting him.[66] When also the devil left him at the highest mountain, the angels immediately approached and ministered to him.[67] *A quo trepidabo? Of whom shall I be afraid?* It is as if he were saying, in the way previously explained, "Neither the Jews nor the Gentiles nor the temptations of the Devil will I fear"

---

62 St. Thomas himself changed his mind on this topic and believed that Jesus had an acquired or experiential knowledge. See ST IIIa, q. 9, art. 4; q. 12, arts. 1–4.
63 *E. N.* This is perhaps a cite to St. John of Damascus's *Expositio de Fide Orthodoxa*, I, 11, PG 94, 842, where he states that the Word assumed the whole nature of man for our salvation, and that included all the properties of that human nature, that is, all the faculties of the soul and of the body, including the "blameless passions" (ἀδιάβλητα πάθη / *adiablēta pathē*), in other words, those which were not reprehensible or punishable. St. John of Damascus condemned those that asserted that Christ was ignorant of the day of his return (the Agnotae) as "impiously teaching Christ not to know of the day of judgment." *De Haeresibus,* VII, 85, PG 94, 756.
64 Matt. 26:37b.
65 *E. N.* A reference to the impeccability of Christ. It was absolutely impossible for Christ to sin. Christ was free from original sin and was free of any actual sin whatsoever. "From the Hypostatic Union there arises a physical impossibility of sinning and from the Beatific Vision a moral impossibility that is, it involves such a close connection with God in knowledge and love that a turning away from God is actually excluded." Ludwig Ott, *Fundamentals of Catholic Dogma* (North Carolina: TAN Books 1974), 169 (trans., Patrick Lynch, ed. James Canon Bastible). Ott gives this doctrine a theological note of *sententia fidei proxima,* a teaching proximate to the faith.
66 Luke 4:29–30; John 8:59.
67 Matt. 4:11.

26{27}[2] *Whilst the wicked draw near against me, to eat my flesh. My enemies that trouble me, have themselves been weakened, and have fallen.*

Dum appropiant super me nocentes, ut edant carnes meas, qui tribulant me inimici mei, ipsi infirmati sunt et ceciderunt.

26{27}[3] *If armies in camp should stand together against me, my heart shall not fear. If a battle should rise up against me, in this will I be confident.*

Si consistant adversum me castra, non timebit cor meum. Si exsurgat adversum me praelium, in hoc ego sperabo.

26{27}[2] *Dum*, while, that is, during that time, that *appropriant super me nocentes, the wicked draw near against me*, that is, the Jews with the pagans, seizing me and binding me at the night before the Passion, *ut edant carnes meas, to eat my flesh*, that is, so that they might kill me, *qui tribulant me inimici mei, ipsi infirmati sunt, et ceciderunt; my enemies that trouble me, have themselves been weakened and have fallen.* This we already see fulfilled in the Jewish enemies of Christ. For they are weakened, lost to faith and grace; and they have fallen, losing authority, dominion, and all the honor of the law. **26{27}[3]** *Si consistant adversum me castra, if armies in camp should stand together against me*, that is, the armies of the Jews, who stood before Herod and Pilate vigorously yelled, *Crucify him, crucify him;*[68] *non timebit cor meum, my heart shall not fear* them who are able to kill the body, but are not powerful enough to render damage to the soul.[69] *Si exsurgat adversum me praelium, if a battle should rise up against me*, that is, the attack of the persecutors endeavoring to crucify me, *in hoc sperabo, in this will I be confident*, that is, at such a point in time I will confide in the Lord that I am going to be the victor, namely, that I am going to destroy death, to take away sin, to redeem the world, to cast down devils, to rise again on the third day, and to judge unbelievers.

26{27}[4] *One thing I have asked of the Lord, this will I seek after; that I may dwell in the house of the Lord all the days of my life. That I may see the delight of the Lord, and may visit his temple.*

Unam petii a Domino, hanc requiram, ut inhabitem in domo Domini omnibus diebus vitae meae, ut videam voluptatem Domini, et visitem templum eius.

---

68 Luke 23:21; *Cf.* Matt. 27:23.
69 *Cf.* Matt. 10:28.

26{27}[4] *Unam, one thing,* that is, one above all others, *petii a Domino: hanc requiram; I have asked of the Lord, this will I seek after,* praying perseveringly; and this one thing is, *ut inhabitem in domo Domini omnibus diebus vitae mae, that I may dwell in the house of the Lord all the days of my life,* that is, that I might rule by grace in the hearts of men and in the Church militant through faith. For Christ as man frequently prayed for the salvation of the world, namely, that God would open the hearts of men so that they might receive the indwelling of Christ through faith. Indeed, it is for this reason that he suffered: so that he might dwell in us. Therefore, Christ also said to Peter, *I have prayed for you, that your faith fail not.*[70] For we are the house of God, and of Christ, his Son, in which [house] Christ desires to dwell. It is for this reason that the Apostle [Paul] says: *Christ as the Son in his own house: which house are we, if we hold fast the confidence and glory of hope unto the end.*[71] *Ut videam voluntatem Domini, that I may see the will of the Lord,*[72] that is, so that I may see the faithful obedient to the divine will, therefore, I ask to dwell in the house of the Lord. For often by the phrase "divine will" is understood the effects and sign of the divine will, as when the Apostle [Paul] states: *For this is the will of God, your sanctification.*[73] And in the Lord's Prayer we say: *Thy will be done,*[74] that is, may your precept be fulfilled. *Et visitem templum eius, and I may visit his temple,* that is, I will enter into men's souls by grace and the consolations of the Holy Spirit, and I will remain with men through the Sacraments. Whence, speaking of the Church, Christ said, *Behold I am with you all days, even to the consummation of the world.*[75]

Or [we might understand it] thus: *That I may dwell in the house of the Lord,* that is, that I may ascend to heaven and sit at the right hand of the Father. For as is known, Christ sometimes prayed for his bodily glorification and exaltation. *That I may see the delight of the Lord* to be fulfilled by all the citizens of heaven who desire in all things to submit to the will of God; *and may visit his temple,* that is, that I might send holy angels from heaven to visit and guard the militant Church; or, so

---

70 Luke 22:32a.
71 Heb. 3:6. For Denis's belief that St. Paul was the author of Hebrews, *see* footnote 8-34 in Volume 1.
72 *E. N. See* footnote 26-20 as to Denis's variant reading (using *voluntatem* "will," instead of *voluptatem*, "delight"); however, here the use of "will" is required to make sense of Denis's argument, so I have departed from the Douay-Rheims and replaced "delight" with "will."
73 1 Thess. 4:3a.
74 Matt. 6:10.
75 Matt. 28:20b.

that I might send the Paraclete, the Holy Spirit, to the Apostles and the other disciples, which I cannot send unless I first ascend: in the way that is written by John: Unless I go, *the Paraclete will not come to you.*[76]

> **26{27}[5]** *For he has hidden me in his tabernacle; in the day of evils, he has protected me in the secret place of his tabernacle.*
>
> *Quoniam abscondit me in tabernaculo suo; in die malorum protexit me in abscondito tabernaculi sui.*
>
> **26{27}[6]** *He has exalted me upon a rock: and now he has lifted up my head above my enemies. I have gone round, and have offered up in his tabernacle a sacrifice of jubilation: I will sing, and recite a psalm to the Lord.*
>
> *In petra exaltavit me, et nunc exaltavit caput meum super inimicos meos. Circuivi, et immolavi in tabernaculo eius hostiam vociferationis; cantabo, et psalmum dicam Domino.*

Accordingly, I reasonably pray this, **26{27}[5]** *Quoniam, For,* the Lord himself *abscondit me in tabernaculo suo, has hidden me in his tabernacle,* that is, in the shadow and the custody of his divinity in which all the blessed in heaven abide as if in a tabernacle not made with human hands; *in die malorum, in the day of evils,* that is, during the time that the Jews persecuted me in the way that we see expressed in the Gospel: *But Jesus hid himself, and went out of the temple.*[77] And Luke: *But he passing through the midst of them, went his way.*[78] For at those times his very divinity made his body invisible to those who were seeking to injure him. *Protexit me in abscondito tabernaculi sui, he has protected me in the secret place of his tabernacle,* that is, in himself, and in the intimate contemplation of himself. For the person of the Word himself protected in all things the man which he assumed. But God is fittingly said to be secreted [or hidden] in the tabernacle because of what we read of him in Isaiah: *Verily you are a hidden God, the God of Israel.*[79] **26{27}[6]** *In petra, upon a rock,* that is, upon the immovable[80] charity of God and neighbor, and upon the certain trust in his name, *exaltavit me, he*

---

76 John 16:7b.
77 John 8:59b.
78 Luke 4:30.
79 Is. 45:15.
80 *E. N.* As to the "immovable" nature of charity, *see* footnote 20-8 and Articles XLVIII (Psalm 20:4) and LIV (Psalm 22:5) in Volume I.

has exalted me from all defect and vice, confirming me in himself — and to be confirmed in him is to be in the highest degree exalted; *et nunc, and now,* that is, in the day of the Resurrection, *exaltavit caput meum, he has lifted up my head,* that is, [he has lifted up] my very self — for he has used a part to express the whole;[81] *super inimicos meos, above my enemies,* that is, above all aerial powers,[82] which I have vanquished, and above all the Jews, who sought to keep me in the sepulcher.

Circuivi, I have gone round, Judea and many other lands when I was conversing with men, preaching the Gospel of the Kingdom of God and healing the sick: in the way that Peter testified about Christ: *He went about doing good, and healing all that were oppressed by the devil.*[83] *Et immolavi in tabernaculo eius, and I have offered up in his tabernacle,* that is, in the synagogues and in the temple of Jerusalem, *hostiam vociferationis, a sacrifice of jubilation,* that is, [a sacrifice] of a stern and great rebuke against evil men, of devoted prayer for their conversion, and divine praise. Christ most frequently offered this to God. *Cantabo, et psalmum dicam Domino; I will sing, and recite a Psalm to the Lord,* through myself and through my ministers, praising and venerating God. For which reason, the Savior also says in [the Gospel of] John: *I seek not my own glory,*[84] *but I honor my Father.*[85]

26{27}[7] Hear, O Lord, my voice, with which I have cried to you: have mercy on me and hear me.

Exaudi, Domine, vocem meam, qua clamavi ad te; miserere mei, et exaudi me.

26{27}[8] My heart has said to you: My face has sought you: your face, O Lord, will I still seek.

Tibi dixit cor meum, exquisivit te facies mea; faciem tuam, Domine, requiram.

26{27}[7] *Exaudi, Domine, Hear, O Lord* Father, *vocem meam qua clamavi ad te, my voice with which I have cried to you,* offering you the *sacrifice of jubilation* just mentioned, and saving the world through unceasing

---

81 E. N. Meaning that he has used the word "head" synecdochally, i.e., he has used a part to refer to the whole. Denis explains this feature in Article IV in Volume 1 as being the fifth rule of Tyconius.
82 E. N. *aeries potestates,* aerial powers. Cf. Eph. 2:2. A reference to demonic powers.
83 Acts 10:38b.
84 John 8:50a.
85 John 8:49a.

grace; *miserere mei, have mercy on me*, delivering me from the troubles of this present world, *et exaudi me, and hear me* for the salvation of the world. **26{27}[8]** *Tibi dixit cor meum, my heart has said to you*, that is, my mind has always spoken to you interiorly, contemplating and praising you unceasingly; *exquisivit te facies mea, my face has sought you*, that is, all my exertion always sought the honor and glory of your name. *Faciem tuam, your face*, that is, the clear and blessed vision of your essence, *Domine, requiram, O Lord, will I seek*: not that you will show it to me [sometime in the future], for from the very beginning I saw it by species[86] as a perfect *comprehensor*;[87] but so that you may show it to the elect for whose salvation you sent me. This is what Christ said: *Father, . . . they also whom you have given me* I will *that they may see my glory which you have given me, because* you have loved me *before the creation of the world.*[88]

26{27}[9] *Turn not away your face from me; decline not in your wrath from your servant. Be you my helper, forsake me not; do not you despise me, O God my Savior.*

Ne avertas faciem tuam a me; ne declines in ira a servo tuo. Adiutor meus esto; ne derelinquas me, neque despicias me, Deus salutaris meus.

26{27}[10] *For my father and my mother have left me: but the Lord has taken me up.*

Quoniam pater meus et mater mea dereliquerunt me; Dominus autem assumpsit me.

26{27}[9] *Ne avertas faciem tuam a me, turn not away your face from me*, rejecting these prayers which I pour out before you; *ne declines in ira a servo tuo, decline not in your wrath*, that is, do not delay on account of man's sin to fulfill that which I ask for them: I who am your servant in accordance with that form of a servant that I accepted, about which you said through the prophet Isaiah: *Behold my servant, I will uphold him*;[89] and again through another [of your prophets]: *Behold, I will bring my servant the Orient . . . and I will take away the iniquity of that*

---

86   E. N. On knowledge by species (*per speciem*), see footnote 26-36.
87   E. N. *Comprehensor*, one of the blessed in heaven.
88   John 17:24. Denis has this verse as *because I have loved you* (*quia dilexi te*) and not *because you have loved me* (*quia dilexisti me*). I suppose it to be a mistake and have followed the Sixto-Clementine Vulgate and not Denis's *Commentary*.
89   Is. 42:1a.

land in one day,[90] namely, in the day of his Passion. *Adiutor meus esto, be you my helper,* O Lord Father, working together with me in all things; *ne derelinquas me, forsake me not* to the hands of the ungodly, or in the sepulcher, *neque despicias me, do not despise me,* that is, my Mystical Body, namely, the Church, for which I have suffered, *Deus salutaris meus,* O *God my Savior,* that is, my salvation insofar as I am man. **26{27}[10]** *Quoniam pater meus et mater mea, for my father and my mother,* that is, the people of the Hebrews, out of whose seed I was born, *dereliquerunt me, have left me,* because they did not want to receive me: as is stated in the Gospel, *He came unto his own, and his own received him not.*[91] *Dominus autem assumpsit me, but the Lord has taken me up,* raising me up to an immortal status, and converting the Gentiles to me.

26{27}[11] *Set me, O Lord, a law in your way, and guide me in the right path, because of my enemies.*

Legem pone mihi, Domine, in via tua, et dirige me in semitam rectam, propter inimicos meos.

26{27}[12] *Deliver me not over to the will of them that trouble me; for unjust witnesses have risen up against me; and iniquity has lied to itself.*

Ne tradideris me in animas tribulantium me, quoniam insurrexerunt in me testes iniqui, et mentita est iniquitas sibi.

26{27}[13] *I believe to see the good things of the Lord in the land of the living.*

Credo videre bona Domini in terra viventium.

26{27}[11] *Legem pone mihi, Domine, [in via tua, et dirige me in semitam rectam, propter inimicos meos]; Set me, O Lord, a law [in your way, and guide me in the right path, because of my enemies].*[92] Christ prays for his Mystical Body in this verse, since he loves it as he loves himself. **26{27}[12]** *Ne tradideris me in animas tribulantium me, deliver me not over to the will of them that trouble me,* that is, over to the power of the Jews, not so that I might not fully die, but so that I may not be detained in death; *quoniam insurrexerunt in me testes iniqui, for unjust witnesses have risen up against me.* In the time of Christ's Passion this was fulfilled as the evangelists all record, in the way that is written by

---

90 Zech. 3:8b–9.
91 John 1:11.
92 E. N. The matter in brackets is supplied in lieu of Denis's "etc."

one of them: *Whereas many false witnesses had come in. And last of all there came two false witnesses,* saying: We heard this man declaring, *I am able to destroy the temple of God, and after three days to rebuild it.*[93] *Et mentita est iniqitas sibi,* and iniquity has lied to itself, that is, their falsehood entrapped them and damned them, and it did not harm me, but was the cause of great merit.

26{27}[13] *Credo videre bona Domini, I believe to see the good things of the Lord,* that is grace and the gifts of the Holy Spirit, *in terra viventium, in the land of the living,* that is, in the Church militant. Since I suffered, I am worthy [to ask God the Father] that men participate in the heavenly goods, and that they might be led to a heavenlike life in the world. Or [we could understand it] thus: *I believe to see the good things of the Lord,* that is, to receive the accidental reward,[94] in the *land of the living,* that is, in the heavenly homeland, and also with the bodily eye to enter upon the glory of God in its effects. In this verse, therefore, Christ touches upon the fruits and the rewards of his Passion. Not however that it is appropriate for Christ to believe by faith, which is a theological virtue, because such a kind of faith he did not have;[95] but we can take the word "to believe" in this place, for a certain kind of knowledge, so that it could be understood in this sense: *I believe to see,* that is, I know I will see.

26{27}[14] *Expect the Lord, do manfully, and let your heart take courage, and wait for the Lord.*

Expecta Dominum, viriliter age, et confortetur cor tuum, et sustine Dominum.

Finally, Christ consoles and enlivens his faithful imitators, and says: **26{27}[14]** *Expecta Dominum, viriliter age, [et confortetur cor tuum, et sustine Dominum]; expect the Lord, do manfully, [and let your heart take courage, and wait for the Lord].*[96] This verse with the others just gone over is satisfactorily discussed in the prior exposition.

Observe how most beautiful this Psalm is, how from the beginning it raises the mind of the reciter to the Lord, excites confidence, and

---

93 Matt. 26:60, 61.
94 E. N. On accidental rewards as distinguished from essential rewards, *see* footnote 1-48 in Volume 1.
95 E. N. In his human nature, Christ did not have faith in the ordinary sense, since he saw God face to face as a result of the beatific vision. For more on this topic, *see* footnote 1-46 in Volume 1.
96 E. N. The matter in brackets is supplied in lieu of Denis's "etc."

excludes inordinate fear. Let us most devoutly sing this Psalm, therefore, so as to obtain these goods. And so that many becoming and fruitful and befitting things be enjoyed, let it be sung by anyone at evening devoutly and intently against the darkness, fears, and the snares of the night.

PRAYER

ALMIGHTY GOD, HELPER AND PROTECTOR of our lives, protect us from the snares of our enemies and from all dangers of soul and body, so that through your gift of piety, we might, through perseveringly insistent works pleasing to you, be found worthy to see your goodness in the land of the living.

Deus omnipotens, adiutor et protector vitae nostrae, protege nos ab hostium insidiis, et ab omnibus periculis animae et corporis: ut tuae pietatis dono, placitis tibi operibus peserveranter insistentes, bona tua in terra viventium videre digni inveniamur.

Psalm 27

ARTICLE LXI

LITERAL EXPOSITION OF THE TWENTY-SEVENTH PSALM:
AD TE, DOMINE, &c.
UNTO YOU WILL I CRY, O LORD, &c.

27{28}[1] *A Psalm for David himself. Unto you will I cry, O Lord: O my God, be not you silent to me: lest you be silent to me, I become like them that go down into the pit.*

Psalmus ipsi David. Ad te, Domine, clamabo; Deus meus, ne sileas a me: nequando taceas a me, et assimilabor descendentibus in lacum.

NOW THE TITLE OF THIS PSALM HAS ALREADY been explained:[1] 27{28}[1] *Psalmus ipsi David*, a Psalm for David himself. When the word "himself" is used in this title, it is understood as literally referring to Christ. Therefore, the sense of the title is this: This Psalm is attributed and relates to David himself, that is, Christ, whom the holy prophets frequently call David, as is quite apparent. To which we can add at this time that which Amos wrote: *In that day I will raise up the tabernacle of David, that is fallen.*[2] In the Acts of the Apostles, the apostle James, full of the Holy Spirit, set forth this scripture using variant words, namely according to the interpretative translation of the Septuagint,[3] thus saying: *I will return, and will rebuild the tabernacle of David, which is fallen down*, that is, I will repair the Church militant of

---

1 E. N. See Article XXXVIII (Ps. 15:1) in Volume 1.
2 Amos 9:11a.
3 E. N. The reference is to Acts 15:16 and its divergence from Amos 9:11 in the Latin text. This comes from the fact that Acts 15:16 (written in Greek) quotes Amos from the Septuagint—a Greek translation of the Hebrew Scriptures. In quoting Amos 9:11, Acts 15:16 has the word ἀναστήσω, which means to "rebuild," and it is translated as *ræedificabo* in the Vulgate. The Greek word translates the Hebrew אקים (*'ā-qîm*). However, St. Jerome viewed the Hebrew word to mean "raise up" (and so he translated it in Amos 9:11 into Latin as *suscitabo*). The Vulgate however translates Acts which quotes Amos from the Septuagint Greek version. So in the Vulgate Amos 9:11 (translated from the Hebrew) reads *raise up* (*suscitabo*), whereas in Acts the quotation from Amos (translated from the Greek of the Septuagint) reads *rebuild* (*ræedificabo*).

Christ. So here this Psalm fittingly refers to Christ at his Passion.

Therefore, Christ the man says: *Ad te, Domine; unto you, O Lord,* eternal Father, *clamabo, I will cry,* that is, I will with great affection pray while hanging on the gibbet of the Cross — upon which Christ with greatest affection said, *Forgive them, for they know not what they do.*[4] And many other things he prayed while he was on the Cross silently within himself which are not written about: indeed, it is believed that at no time did he more lovingly pray for the salvation of the world than when he hung on the Cross. *Deus meus, ne sileas a me; O my God, be not silent to me,* that is, do not be silent, holding yourself out as if you were not listening, but respond to me by internal inspirations with good words, with consolatory words; *nequando, lest,* that is, lest at any time, *taceas a me, you be silent to me,* delaying that which I seek, *et assimilabor descendentibus in lacum, and I become like them that go down into the pit,* that is, I will be similar to those descending into the grave and into hell, of which the body is held in the earth and the soul in Gehenna.[5] For Christ, as Isaiah said, *was reputed with the wicked;*[6] and he (according to the Apostle [Paul]) was *made a curse for us,* so that he might deliver us *from the curse of the law.*[7] For it is written: *He is accursed of God that hangs on a tree.*[8] From this, therefore, Christ asserted himself *to become like them that go down into the pit,* not that this would happen truly in fact, but according to the estimation of the wicked, as a later Psalm says: *I am counted among them that go down to the pit.*[9] Or [one can understand it] thus: *I become like them that go down into the pit,* that is, the Holy Fathers, who before my Passion descended into the infernal limbo. This Christ became in a very true way, for his soul descended into this limbo immediately when it departed from the body. For which reason, the Apostle [Paul] said: *it behooved him in all things to be made like unto his brethren.*[10]

---

4 Luke 23:34a.
5 E. N. Gehenna (from the Hebrew word meaning "valley of the sons of Hinnom") was a gorge south of Jerusalem where children sacrificed to Moloch and which later became a place of refuse. This refuse — including dead bodies, among other filth — was constantly being burned. It was used as an image of eternal hell, the hell of the damned.
6 Is. 53:12b.
7 Gal. 3:13. *Christ has redeemed us from the curse of the law, being made a curse for us: for it is written: Cursed is every one that hangs on a tree.*
8 Deut. 21:23a.
9 Ps. 87:5a.
10 Heb. 2:17a.

27{28}[2] Hear, O Lord, the voice of my supplication, when I pray to you; when I lift up my hands to your holy temple.

Exaudi, Domine, vocem deprecationis meae, dum oro ad te, dum extollo manus meas ad templum sanctum tuum.

27{28}[2] *Exaudi, Domine, vocem depecationis meae;* Hear, O Lord, the voice of my supplication, that is, the heartfelt clamor of my prayers and of fervent affection, *dum oro ad te,* when I pray to you, that is, when I pray that I may obtain your very self, insofar as the receiving of accidental rewards. But insofar as it relates to the beatific vision, Christ as man from the beginning of his Incarnation possessed God, and in this way he did not pray to obtain him.[11] And I direct my intention to you finally, *dum extollo manus meas, when I lift up my hands,* my bodily hands on the altar of the Cross, *ad templum sanctum tuum,* to your holy temple so as to rebuild it, that is, to the redemption of the human race, which is the temple of the living God. This is what the Savior says: *I, if I be lifted up from the earth, will draw all things to myself.*[12] Or [alternately] thus: *When I lift up my hands,* that is, I raise up the desires of my heart to your holy temple, that is, to the heavenly homeland, since I, in short, after the Passion will ascend there; and my elect, for whom I here suffer, may attain it through the merits of my death.

27{28}[3] Deliver me not away together with the wicked; and with the workers of iniquity destroy me not: Who speak peace with their neighbor, but evils are in their hearts.[13]

Ne simul tradas me cum peccatoribus, et cum operantibus iniquitatem ne perdas me; qui loquuntur pacem cum proximo suo, mala autem in cordibus eorum.

27{28}[3] *Ne simul tradas me,* deliver me not away together into the power of evil men, *cum peccatoribus,* with the wicked, that is, in the manner that you deliver them over, who you permit not only to die

---

11 For the difference between accidental rewards and essential rewards in Christ, *see* footnote 1-48 in Volume 1. Since Christ as man had the beatific vision from the first moment of the Incarnation (which is the *essential* award for the blessed in heaven), it follows he could not be praying for what he already possessed; accordingly, Denis argues that the prayer in Ps. 27:1, if understood as Christ's prayer, must be limited to accidental rewards such as the Resurrection and the glorification of his body.
12 John 12:32.
13 The Sixto-Clementine Vulgate has *trahas* (drag, haul, draw off); Denis has *tradas* (hand over, deliver, transmit), consistent with the *Codex Amiatinus*. I have adopted Denis's reading since it fits his commentary.

bodily, but also to putrefy in the grave, and to be held fast in hell. *Et cum operantibus iniquitatem ne perdas me*, *and with the works of iniquity, destroy me not*. Christ who was a comprehensor and was confirmed in all good, by no means prayed that he might not be damned or might not sin. What else, therefore, could *And with the works of iniquity, destroy me not*, mean other than, "Do not permit my body to corrupt in the earth or to be separated from the soul for a long while but immediately resurrect me?" And so, *Draw me not away together with the wicked*, that is, with the Pharisees and the Scribes and the other false Jews: *quo loquuntur pacem*, *who speak peace*, that is, [who speak] fraudulently with words of peace, *cum proximo suo*, *with their neighbor*, that is, with me who am their brother and their neighbor, for I was born of their nature; *mala autem*, *but evils*, that is, envy, guile, and the desire to kill me, *in cordibus eorum*, *are in their heart*. For frequently, as the Evangelists report, the Jews gathered together to ensnare Jesus while he was speaking, bringing forth adulatory words, but intending deceit in their hearts.[14]

27{28}[4] *Give them according to their works, and according to the wickedness of their inventions. According to the works of their hands give you to them: render to them their reward.*

Da illis secundum opera eorum, et secundum nequitiam adinventionum ipsorum. Secundum opera manuum eorum tribue illis, redde retributionem eorum ipsis.

27{28}[4] *Da illis*, *give them*, Lord of all, just Judge, *secundum opera eorum, et secundum nequitiam adinventionum ipsorum*, *according to their works, and according to the wickedness of their inventions*, that is, according to that which their evil counsel may deserve. *Secundum opera manuum eorum tribue eis*, *according to the works of their hands give to them*, that is, according to their actions both interior and exterior compensate them, *redde tributionem eorum ipsis*, *render to them their reward*, delivering them over into the hands of the emperor of the Romans, and to a *reprobate sense*,[15] and unto final ire. He often repeats the same judgment (*sententiam*) to declare his heart's affection for observing justice. Now Christ says this, not wishing simply vengeance, but so as to foreannounce that which will be in store for them in the future. Or he says this also optatively (*optative*),[16] conforming the affection of his heart to the divine justice, in the

---

14 Matt. 22:15, *and elsewhere.*
15 Rom. 1:28.
16 *E. N.* Optative (from Latin *opto*, "I opt") means a verbal mood expressive of a

manner that the saints in heaven do. Christ says this in accordance with the understanding in Jeremiah: *Let them be confounded that persecute me, and let not me be confounded:... bring upon them the day of affliction, and with a double destruction, destroy them,*[17] O Lord, our God. And with Isaiah: *For the day of vengeance is in my heart, the year of my redemption is come.*[18]

27{28}[5] *Because they have not understood the works of the Lord, and the operations of his hands: you shall destroy them, and shall not build them up.*

Quoniam non intellexerunt opera Domini et in opera manuum eius; destrues illos, et non aedificabis eos.

Therefore they will also so perish, 27{28}[5] *Quoniam non intellexerunt opera Domini, because they have not understood the works of the Lord,* that is, the divine miracles of Christ, those things which Christ did in the name of the Lord, *et in opera manuum eius, and the operations of his hands,* that is, the human works of Christ, namely, the sanctity of his manner of living and the truth of his doctrine. For they wrote off his miracles to *Beelzebub, the prince of the devils.*[19] But they also censured his life, calling him: *a man that is a glutton and a wine drinker, a friend of publicans and sinners,*[20] a transgressor of the law, not keeping the Sabbath.[21] And they ridiculed his teachings saying: *He is mad, why hear you him?*[22] and *We have found this man perverting our nation.*[23] Therefore, O Lord Father, *destrues illos, you shall destroy them* with sword, hunger, thirst, and the selling out of and their expulsion from, the land of their birth, all of which was done to them by Titus.[24] *Et non aedificabis eos, and you shall not build them up*: that is, you

---

wish or desire. Denis states in Article LVI (Psalm 24:4) in Volume 1 that prophets such as David assert the coming judgments of God in a prophetic sense, not in an optative sense (*i.e.,* not affirmatively willing or desiring the threatened doom and divine vengeance); however, Christ—like the blessed in heaven—can will punishment optatively because of the love of, and its agreement with, the divine justice.

17 Jer. 17:18.
18 Is. 63:4.
19 Matt. 12:24b.
20 Matt. 11:19b.
21 John 9:16.
22 John 10:20.
23 Luke 23:2.
24 E. N. The Roman emperor Titus (39–81 AD). Titus was responsible for destroying Jerusalem and its Temple (70 AD) during the First Jewish-Roman War during the Siege of Jerusalem, where the Romans were led by Titus who would then become emperor after Vespasian.

will not interiorly mend them, building up their hearts into your dwelling by faith and grace; nor will you restore them outside, returning them to the land of their fathers, but even until the end of time you will desert them.

27{28}[6] *Blessed be the Lord, for he has heard the voice of my supplication.*

Benedictus Dominus, quoniam exaudivit vocem deprecationis meae.

27{28}[7] *The Lord is my helper and my protector: in him has my heart confided, and I have been helped. And my flesh has flourished again, and with my will I will give praise to him.*

Dominus adiutor meus et protector meus; in ipso speravit cor meum, et adiutus sum: et refloruit caro mea, et ex voluntate mea confitebor ei.

Thereafter Christ gives thanks that he has been heard, and says: 27{28}[6] *Benedictus Dominus, Blessed be the Lord* Father, or God the Trinity, *quoniam exaudivit vocem deprecationis meae, for he has heard the voice of my supplication* just aforementioned where I prayed for my actual and my Mystical Body. 27{28}[7] *Dominus adiutor meus, the Lord is my helper,* cooperating with me in all things by his grace, and giving me the fitness and the efficacious means of making satisfaction [for the sins] of the whole world. For Christ as man was able to merit; and his humanity itself united with the Word received an effective reward deserving of such merit as to be boundless. *Et, and* the Lord is *protector meus, my protector* in adversities: as has already often been said. *Et in ipso speravit cor meum, and in him has my heart confided,* that is, my soul has always confided in his goodness and help knowing all good comes from him.[25] The confiding will not be groundless, for as it says next: *et adiutus sum, and I have been helped,* that is, I efficaciously pursued all that which was necessary for the redemption of humanity. *Et refloruit caro mea, and my flesh has flourished again:* which at the third day is resuscitated and glorified, and is made impassible and unchangeable; *et ex voluntate mea confitebor ei, and with my will I will give praise to him,* that is, as man, from all the good that I have collected from taking the form of a servant, I will praise my heavenly Father with all my heart, and I will give thanks to the God three and one.

---

25 *Cf.* James 1:17: *Every best gift, and every perfect gift, is from above, coming down from the Father of lights, with whom there is no change, nor shadow of alteration.*

27{28}[8] *The Lord is the strength of his people, and the protector of the salvations of his Anointed.*

Dominus fortitudo plebis suae, et protector salvationum Christi sui est.

27{28}[8] *Dominus fortitudo plebis suae,* the Lord is the strength of his people, that is, their preserver in good and the one who is the cause in them of whatever virtues and perfections and fortitude they may have; *et protector salvationum Christi sui est,* and the protector of the salvations of his Anointed. The salvations[26] of Christ are the saving effects of his most blessed Passion, namely delivery from sin, the infusion of grace, the opening of the gates of the Kingdom of Heaven. God the Father is the protector of these salvations of Christ his son, for he defends the elect, that they not be despoiled from these effects by the tempter, and he protects them to the end so that they might be saved.

27{28}[9] *Save, O Lord, your people, and bless your inheritance: and rule them and exalt them forever.*

Salvum fac populum tuum, Domine, et benedic haereditati tuae; et rege eos, et extolle illos usque in aeternum.

In addition, the man Christ, *mediator of God and men,*[27] prays for the Church which he redeems, and says: **27{28}[9]** *Salvum fac populum tuum, Domine;* save, O Lord, your people, that is, your faithful people, or all people — even the unfaithful — converting them to the faith: for all people are yours through creation; *et benedic,* and bless, that is, grant in many ways the gifts of your graces, *hereditati tuae, your inheritance,* that is, the Christian people whom you especially care for, possess, and make fruitful. *Et rege eos,* and rule them, directing to eternal life, *et extolle illos, and exalt them,* that is, keep them in a sublime manner of life and high

---

26 E. N. *Salvationes Christi.* Denis uses the plural "salvations of Christ," identifying them as delivery from sin, infusion of grace, and the admission into heaven of the elect. Psalm 27:8 uses the word *salvationum* (plural genitive), so Denis is consistent with the text. The Douay-Rheims, however, translated the Latin plural into a singular; so I have pluralized it here. In his book *Summa of All Councils* the doctor of the Sorbonne and the *curé* of Montmartre, Louis Bail (1610–1669 AD), on the authority of Ps. 27:8, identifies "three salvations" or "three redemptions" of Christ: redemption against our impotence in obtaining our salvation by sufficient means and aid, redemption from sin itself through justification, and redemption from all misery by our glorification. These roughly align with Denis's divisions.
27 1 Tim. 2:5.

merit in this life, *usque in aeternum, even for ever,* that is, rule them and raise them up until such time that they reach eternal felicity.

See, why do you fear? Why are you faint of heart? Why do you not most fully hope, O Christian? Attend to that which Christ prays for you. Attend to the fact that your Creator has become your Savior, your God has become your Brother, your Judge has become your Advocate. He who with the Father and the Holy Spirit hears [you] is he who entreats the Father and the Holy Spirit on your behalf. *Let us go therefore with confidence to the throne of grace: that we may obtain mercy and find grace in seasonable aid.*[28]

ARTICLE LXII

TROPOLOGICAL OR MORAL EXPOSITION OF THE SAME TWENTY-SEVENTH PSALM

27{28}[1] *A Psalm for David himself. Unto you will I cry, O Lord: O my God, be not you silent to me: lest you be silent to me, I become like them that go down into the pit.*

Psalmus ipsi David. Ad te, Domine, clamabo; Deus meus, ne sileas a me: nequando taceas a me, et assimilabor descendentibus in lacum.

NOW, FROM A MORAL POINT OF VIEW THIS Psalm fittingly refers to any member of the faithful afflicted in soul, or in body, or in both, who cries out to the Lord to obtain relief: 27{28}[1] *Ad te, Domine, clamabo; unto you will I cry, O Lord* in all tribulation and distress, and not to anyone else: because you alone are God, the whole of my salvation, in whom alone I finally and steadfastly trust, so that even if you were to slay me,[29] I would nevertheless trust in you, knowing it is more possible for heaven and earth to be annihilated than it is for those placing hope in your goodness to be defrauded. Therefore, *Deus meus, ne sileas a me; O my God, be not silent to me,* ignoring or repelling my desires; but *speak, Lord, for your servant is listening.*[30] Speak to me by internal inspiration, by the exhortation of holy Scripture, by the explanations of your devoted servants. Console, O Lord, my soul;

---

28 Heb. 4:16.
29 *Cf.* Job. 13:15.
30 1 Sam. 3:10.

remove from it the disquiet caused by worldly things and speak to and illumine the soul so quieted in the manner attested of a pious soul: *Behold I will allure her, and will lead her into the wilderness: and I will speak to her heart.*[31] *Et assimilabor descentibus in lacum*, and *I become like them that go down into the pit*: that is, I am tormented by so many tribulations, I am afflicted by so many evils, that I may appear similar to *them that go down into the pit*, in which is the fullness of misery. Or [it can be understood] thus: And I will be similar to *them that go down into the pit*, that is, unless you kindly hear my prayers, I will descend and I will be with others in the pit, that is, in the depth of vices, in the chasm of danger, and in the snare of infernal prison.

27{28}[2]   *Hear, O Lord, the voice of my supplication, when I pray to you; when I lift up my hands to your holy temple.*

Exaudi, Domine, vocem deprecationis meae, dum oro ad te, dum extollo manus meas ad templum sanctum tuum.

27{28}[2] *Exaudi, Domine, vocem deprecationis meae, dum oro ad te; Hear, O Lord, the voice of my supplication, when I pray to you*, that is, when I adore you, *dum extollo manus meas, when I lift up my hands*, both my corporal and spiritual hands, *ad templum sanctum tuum, to your holy temple*, that is, to the heavenly homeland of the blessed, lifting my bodily hands with ardent desires of the mind toward the Church triumphant, calling upon it, and praying to be led to it: in the manner that Jeremiah admonished: *Let us lift up our hearts with our hands to the Lord in the heavens.*[32] Whence the Apostle [Paul] said: *I will therefore that men pray in every place, lifting up pure hands, without anger and contention.*[33] See how frequently a holy man repeats the same sentence while praying. An ardent affection truly ignores measure: he is not wearied of praying, but he is unceasingly enkindled, and flame produces flame, and the fire of love of affectionate prayer nourishes and increases the fire. For he is never fully filled of divine things, but the more that he may taste them, the more they increase the appetite, in the manner that is written: *They that eat me, shall yet hunger: and they that drink me, shall yet thirst.*[34]

---

31   Hosea 2:14.
32   Lam. 3:41.
33   1 Tim. 2:8.
34   Ecclus. 24:29.

27{28}[3] *Deliver me not away together with the wicked; and with the workers of iniquity destroy me not: Who speak peace with their neighbor, but evils are in their hearts.*[35]

Ne simul tradas me cum peccatoribus, et cum operantibus iniquitatem ne perdas me; qui loquuntur pacem cum proximo suo, mala autem in cordibus eorum.

27{28}[3] *Ne simul tradas me cum peccatoribus, deliver me not away together with the wicked*, that is, do not permit me to be yoked to sin and to be subject to the servitude of the devil to whom sinners are subject, as we see contained in the Gospel, *Whosoever commits sin, is the servant of sin*;[36] and he who is defeated by the devil in temptation is subjected to an unhappy dominion.[37] *Et cum operantibus iniquitatem, and with workers of iniquity*, that is, with those persevering in evil, *ne perdas me, destroy me not*, removing from me grace in the present and glory in the future. *Qui loquuntur pacem cum proximo suo, mala autem in cordibus eorum*; they *who speak peace with their neighbor, but evils are in their heart*, that is, who bless with their mouth, but curse with their heart, as are flatterers, liars, fraudfeasors. Such men — Alas! — are many; indeed, few people come upon faithful and honest friends. For this reason, this [observation regarding the wicked] is very well stated: now if only it would be effectively pondered. For the Prophet says: *The holy man is perished out of the earth, and there is none upright among men... Everyone hunts his brother to death.... Keep the doors of your mouth from her that sleeps in your bosom. For the son dishonors the father... and a man's enemies are they of his own household.*[38] For as the Apostle [Paul] said: *All seek the things that are their own.*[39]

27{28}[4] *Give them according to their works, and according to the wickedness of their inventions. According to the works of their hands give you to them: render to them their reward.*

Da illis secundum opera eorum, et secundum nequitiam adinventionum ipsorum. Secundum opera manuum eorum tribue illis, redde retributionem eorum ipsis.

---

35 The Sixto-Clementine Vulgate has *trahas* (drag, haul, draw off); Denis has *tradas* (hand over, deliver, transmit), consistent with the *Codex Amiatinus*. I have adopted Denis's reading since it fits better with his *Commentary*.
36 John 8:34b.
37 *Cf.* 2 Pet. 2:19. *Promising them liberty, whereas they themselves are the slaves of corruption. For by whom a man is overcome, of the same also he is the slave.*
38 Micah 7:2, 5, 6.
39 Phil 2:21.

27{28}[5] *Because they have not understood the works of the Lord, and the operations of his hands: you shall destroy them, and shall not build them up.*

Quoniam non intellexerunt opera Domini et in opera manuum eius; destrues illos, et non aedificabis eos.

27{28}[4] *Da illis secundum opera eorum,* give them according to their works. The verse with the one that follows is clear from the preceding exposition.[40] So render unto them due punishment, O Lord, 27{28}[5] *quoniam non intellexerunt opera Domini,* because they have not understood the works of the Lord, that is, the example of Jesus Christ, whose entire life is to inform ours; *et in opera manuum eius,* and the operations of his hands, that is, [the operations] of Christ, they have not understood; that is, they have not considered the judgment of Christ, in which he gives eternal life to the good and perpetual punishment to the wicked. The wicked do not understand these *works of the Lord,* for though they may assert they know them, they deny them by their deeds, and they exhibit themselves as not knowing them, in the manner that is written: *They are wise to do evil, but to do good they have no knowledge.*[41] *Destrues illos,* you shall destroy them, O Lord, depriving them of spiritual being,[42] and depriving their will of the desire for good when you cast them down unto eternal punishment; *et non aedificabis eos,* and shall not build them up, interiorly through the illumination and grace of the Holy Spirit, and you will not set in order nor will you confirm their interiors,[43] but they will be miserable and inclined to fail.

---

40 *E. N. See* Article LXI (Psalm 27:4-5).
41 Jer. 4:22b.
42 *E. N.* By "spiritual being" (*esse spirituale*), Denis means sanctifying grace, a supernatural existence, and so by saying there will be a deprivation of spiritual being he does not mean the actual destruction of the spiritual soul. For example, St. Thomas states: *Infunditur igitur divinitus homini ad peragendas actiones ordinatas in finem vitae aeternae primo quidem gratia, per quam habet anima quoddam spirituale esse, et deinde fides, spes, et caritas.* "Therefore, so that he might perform actions ordered to the end of eternal life, there is divinely infused in man a first grace, by which the soul has a kind of spiritual existence, and then faith, hope, and charity." *De virtutibus,* q. 1 a. 10 co. And in his *Summa Theologiae* IIIa, q. 73 art. 5 ad. 1, he says *per Baptismum, qui est spiritualis regeneratio, accipimus esse spirituale.* "By Baptism, which is a spiritual regeneration, we receive spiritual being."
43 *E. N.* Denis refers to the *interioria,* the things interior to man, the interior principles which include the powers of the soul such as the intellect, will, and so forth. [A]*d beatitudinem homo ordinatur per principia interiora, cum ad ipsam naturaliter ordinetur.* "Man is ordered to happiness through interior principles, since he is ordained to it by nature." ST, IaIIae, q. 2, art. 4, c. Since the Fall, the *interiora* in

27{28}[6] *Blessed be the Lord, for he has heard the voice of my supplication.*
Benedictus Dominus, quoniam exaudivit vocem deprecationis meae.

27{28}[7] *The Lord is my helper and my protector: in him has my heart confided, and I have been helped. And my flesh has flourished again, and with my will I will give praise to him.*
Dominus adiutor meus et protector meus; in ipso speravit cor meum, et adiutus sum : et refloruit caro mea, et ex voluntate mea confitebor ei.

27{28}[6] *Benedictus Dominus, blessed be the Lord,* that is, blessed be the Lord himself, and may he be blessed by all,[44] *quoniam exaudivit vocem deprecationis meae, for he has heard the voice of my supplication,* as I may now perceive out of interior inspiration, or may experience through [the prayer's or God's] effects. For sometimes devoted servants of God, before they have finished their prayer, then and there sense that they have been heard. On account of this the Lord says: *And it shall come to pass, that before they call, I will hear; as they are yet speaking, I will hear.*[45] **27{28}[7]** *Dominus adiutor meus, the Lord is my helper* in doing those things that are good, *et protector meus, and my protector,* in turning away from those things that are evil; *et ipso speravit cor meum, in him has my heart confided,* without whom I am able to think, to speak, or to do nothing good, *et adiutus sum, and I have been helped* by his grace not to submit to the enemies of my soul. *Et refloruit caro mea; and my flesh has flourished again*: that is, my body, which before was subject to sin, which was stained with various kinds of defilement, and which devoted itself to iniquities, this [body], by means of the help of God is subject to the empire of reason,[46] to the obedience of charity.[47] The

---

man are disturbed and they must be set aright, correctly ordered, and confirmed in grace so as to attain the happiness of heaven.

44 E. N. "There is not a better grammar to learn, than to learn how to bless God, and therefore it may be no levity, to use some grammar terms herein. God blesses man *dative* (datively), he gives good to him; man blesses God *optative* (optitatively), he wishes well to him; and blesses him *vocative* (vocatively), he speaks well of him. For, though towards God, as well as towards man, real actions are called blessings ... yet the word here, εὐλογία (*eulogia*), is properly a blessing in speech, in discourse, in conference, in words, in praise, in thanks." John Donne, *Sermon 36: Preached on Trinity Sunday, The Works of John Donne,* Vol. 2 (London: John W. Parker 1839), 129–30.

45 Is. 65:24.

46 E. N. "The virtuous life is the empire of reason." Marie-Dominique Chenu, O. P., *Aquinas and His Role in Theology* (Collegeville: The Liturgical Press 2002), (trans. Paul Philibert, O. P.), 105.

47 Denis says *caritatis obsequio,* which is redolent of the *obedientia caritatis,* the

bloom of continence already shines, and the odor of chastity now emits its fragrance in the way that the divine Apostle [Paul] commands: *Let no sin therefore reign in your mortal body.... Neither yield you your members as instruments of iniquity unto sin.*[48] *Et ex voluntate mea*, and with my will, that is, spontaneously and promptly, *confitebor ei, I will confess to him*,[49] namely, the Lord. *I will confess to*, I say, *to him* all my evils and all my vices, judging, condemning, and punishing myself. And I will confess to him his goodness and benefits, praising him, venerating him, and loving him.

27{28}[8] *The Lord is the strength of his people, and the protector of the salvations of his Anointed.*

Dominus fortitudo plebis suae, et protector salvationum Christi sui est.

27{28}[8] *Dominus fortitudino plebis suae*, the Lord is the strength of his people, that is, the cause of the strength of his servants, in the manner that Moses said: *Fear not.... The Lord your God, who is your leader, himself will fight for you*;[50] *et protector salvationum*, and the protector of the salvations, that is, he is the preserver of saving virtues *Christi sui, of his Annointed*: that is, the Lord himself is the defender and preserver of the virtue and the grace of every single Christian anointed with the sacred chrism and the Holy Spirit. For the virtues and the grace of God

---

obedience of charity, in St. Peter's epistle. See 1 Pet. 1:22: *Purifying your souls in the obedience of charity, with a brotherly love, from a sincere heart love one another earnestly.* In his *Exposition on the Song of Songs*, the Benedictine Abbot William of St. Thierry (ca. 1085–1148) expressed it thus: "The soul converted to God, and married to the Word of God, is first taught to know the riches of prevenient grace, and is permitted to taste how sweet is the Lord; but thereafter taught by returning into the house of its conscience, purified in the obedience of charity (*castificanda in obedientia caritatis*), and perfectly cleaned of vices, and adorned with virtues, so that it is worthy to possess the spiritual grace of godliness (*pietatis*) and affection for virtues which is the bridechamber of the Bridegroom." *Exp. alt. sup. Cantica canticorum*, 10, PL 180, 477.

48 Rom. 6:12–13.
49 The word *confitebor* has two senses: praise or confess. As St. Augustine puts it in his *Expositions on the Books of Psalms*: "[I]n Scripture, when we confess to God, it is customarily said in two senses, either of sin, or of praise. The confession of sin all know about, but the confession of praise few heed to." *Enarrationes in Psalmos*, Psalm 137, PL 37, 1774. When used of Christ in the Article LXVI above, Denis used the meaning of praise. When used of this article of the Christian faithful, he uses it in the sense of confession of sins and praise. I therefore have departed from the Douay-Rheims translation to accommodate this.
50 Deut. 1:29–30.

are our salvations, which are necessary to be defended by God, so that they may not be driven out or perish by the entrance of vices.

> **27{28}[9]** *Save, O Lord, your people, and bless your inheritance: and rule them and exalt them forever.*
>
> *Salvum fac populum tuum, Domine, et benedic haereditati tuae; et rege eos, et extolle illos usque in aeternum.*

Finally, the faithful man, forgetful of self, and lit with love for the common good, prays out of fraternal charity for all men: **27{28}[9]** *Salvum fac populum tuum, Domine; save, O Lord, your people*: the explanation of which is clear from the prior Article. Truly beautiful and sweet is this Psalm, which begins from a singular charity and it ends in a common love: in which a devout man first prays for himself, and then glorifying in the fact that he is heard, and praising God, he prays, as is proper, for all the Christian people. And the prayer of this verse is in full measure both succinct and fervid: which [prayer] we ought daily to pour forth with a mind most intent, as also the whole Psalm in due time, because it contains such great fruits and consolations.

PRAYER

WITH WEAK HANDS RAISED TOWARD your holy temple, we beseech you on our knees,[51] O Lord, do not consign our souls with sinners who do not know you; do not desert us, do not destroy us with workers of evil; but, ruling us, lift us up with you into the heavenly kingdom.

> *Ad templum sanctum tuum manus cum genibus levantes invalidas, quaesumus, Domine, ne tradas cum peccatoribus non te agnoscentibus animas nostras: non nos deseras, non nos cum operantibus iniquitatem perdas; sed nos regendo, tecum in caelisti regno extollas.*

---

51 Alternative reading *gemitibus*, with tears.

Psalm 28

ARTICLE LXIII

EXPOSITION OF THE TWENTY-EIGHTH PSALM:
AFFERTE, DOMINO, FILII, &c.
BRING TO THE LORD, O CHILDREN OF GOD, &c.

28{29}[1] *A Psalm for David, at the finishing of the tabernacle. Bring to the Lord, O you children of God: bring to the Lord the offspring of rams.*

Psalmus David, in consummatione tabernaculi. Afferte Domino, filii Dei, afferte Domino, filios arietum.

THE TITLE OF THIS PSALM IS: 28{29}[1] *PSALmus David, in consummatione tabernaculi; a Psalm for David, at the finishing of the tabernacle.* In the first book of Chronicles we read that the ark of the Lord brought back from the land of the Philistines remained at the temple in Shiloh.[1] But after some time, David built for it a tabernacle, and people were urged to sacrifice victims when he introduced it [into the tabernacle or temple]. Therefore, from this historical incident the present Psalm takes its title, and one is literally able to apply to it that history. But it is much more agreeable to explain the thing that is figured than the figure.[2] For it is evident that David is a figure of Christ, and the ark is a type of the Church;[3] and also the completion of the tabernacle designates the perfection of the Church. Just as David led the

---

1 *Cf.* 1 Chr. 13. E. N. The ark found its home in Shiloh after the Jews entered the promised land. Joshua 18:1. Subsequently, the ark was captured by the Philistines during battle. 1 Sam. 4:10–11. It was later returned to the people of Israel. 1 Sam. 6:10–15. Only later did David build a tabernacle in Shiloh to house the ark until the temple of Jerusalem was completed. 2 Sam. 6:1-2; 1 Chr. 13:6–14; 2 Sam. 6:17–18. After the ark was placed into the tabernacle, David offered holocausts (burnt offerings) and peace offerings. The ark remained under the tabernacle for forty years until it was moved to the temple in Jerusalem. 1 Kings 8:1–6.
2 On how the things that are signified or figured are more pleasing than the things signifying or figuring, *see* footnote 7-2 in Volume 1.
3 E. N. A "type of the Church": The word type, coming from the Greek noun *typos* (τύπος), means a figure or impression caused by stamping or molding, which refers to a corresponding original or antitype (ἀντίτυπος). The Jewish ark of the covenant is the type, and the antitype is the Church founded by Christ.

ark into its tabernacle, so Christ leads the Church into the Kingdom of Heaven. This, therefore, is the sense of the title: *Psalmus David, a Psalm for David*, that is, this Psalm is ascribed to the David here speaking, *in consummatione tabernaculi, at the finishing of the tabernacle*, that is, is written looking forward to the perfection of the Church. For David in the Holy Spirit foreknowing the whole world would be converted to the faith of Christ by the Apostles, speaks here of the universal Church, since it offers a worthy sacrifice to God. For he says:

Afferte, bring, that is, carry something to the glory of the Creator, *Domino, to the Lord*, whose are all things, *O filii Dei, O children of God*, by adoption, *to whom Christ gave... power to be made the sons of God.*[4] Of whom is written: *Dearly beloved, we are now the sons of God; and it has not yet appeared what we shall be.*[5] And again: *Behold what manner of charity the Father has bestowed upon us, that we should be called, and should be the sons of God.*[6] And so, O all you faithful, in testimony of all that you might have received from God, *bring* to him, that is, offer something up to him. For in the manner that we have received from God all that we have, so offer to God all that we are, all that we are able, all that we do, and all that we have; that is, we are obliged to deliver over to him this service, because it is he who created us, and not we ourselves. For this reason, the Apostle [Paul] says: *For none of us lives to himself.*[7] And again: *All whatsoever you do in word or in work, do all in the name of the Lord Jesus Christ, giving thanks to God and the Father by him.*[8] Whence regarding that which the Psalmist says here — *Bring, to the Lord, O children of God* — Moses so leads us: *No one shall appear with his hands empty before the Lord: but every one shall offer according to what he has.*[9] For the exterior oblation is a sign of the interior oblation whereby the spirit [of a man] immolates himself to God by obedience and reverence. Of this interior oblation we read in Ecclesiasticus: *It is a wholesome sacrifice to take heed to the commandments.*[10]

Then he declares that which the children should bring to God. *Afferte Domino filios arietum, bring to the Lord the offspring of rams*, that is, [bring] yourselves, you who are sons of the Apostles, who are called *rams* because they are leaders of the sheep of Christ, and the most

---

4 John 1:12.
5 1 John 3:2a.
6 1 John 1:1a.
7 Rom. 14:7a.
8 Col. 3:17.
9 Deut. 16:16b-17a.
10 Ecclus. 35:2a. E. N. The verse continues: *and to depart from all iniquity.*

strong protectors of them, leading them into the sheepfold of Christ. For no one is able to bring to God anything greater in his possession than himself. Therefore, bring yourselves, that is, with your heart and your deeds get close to him, adhere to him, and serve him.

28{29}[2] *Bring to the Lord glory and honor: bring to the Lord glory to his name: adore you the Lord in his holy court.*

Afferte Domino gloriam et honorem; afferte Domino gloriam nomini eius; adorate Dominum in atrio sancto eius.

But lest anyone understand wrongly in what manner he ought to offer himself to God, and wishes to kill himself, or foolishly to offer cattle, therefore it goes on to show what it means to offer one's self: **28{29}[2]** *Afferte Domino gloriam et honorem, bring to the Lord glory and honor*: that is, so bring yourselves to God so that you might glorify and honor the Lord, to the degree in your power, both as to yourself and to others. As the Savior says in the Gospel: *So let your light shine before men, that they may see your good works, and glorify your Father who is in heaven.*[11] This is what we pray for daily in the Lord's Prayer when we pray: *Hallowed be thy name* (in us),[12] that is, give us the grace to be able to so serve you, so that from the purity and holiness of our manner of living, all may know how truly holy you are, O Lord God, to whom such service is pleasing. Therefore, *Bring to the Lord glory and honor* in the manner that the Apostle [Paul] did saying: *Now to the king of ages, immortal, invisible, the only God, be honor and glory for ever and ever.*[13] And David: *Yours, O Lord, is magnificence, and power, and glory, and victory: and to you is praise . . . yours are riches, and yours is glory. For all things are yours: and we have given you what we received of your hand.*[14]

Afferte Domino gloriam nomini eius, bring to the Lord glory to his name. Glory is clear knowledge together with praise.[15] What else therefore is, *Bring to the Lord glory to his name?* except "By mouth and deeds manifest

---

11 Matt. 5:16.
12 Matt. 6:9.
13 1 Tim. 1:17.
14 1 Chr. 29:11a, 12a, 14b.
15 E. N. *Gloria est clara cum laude notitia.* The definition is Augustinian and it is a gloss, as it were, of Rom. 16:27: See *Against Maximinum the Heretical Bishop of the Arians*, 2.13.2, PL 42, 770: *Restat ergo ut soli sapienti Deo gloria sit per Iesum Christum, hoc est, clara cum laude notitia.* "It stands firm, therefore, that glory, that is, clear knowledge together with praise, is due God who alone is wise, through Jesus Christ." St. Thomas mistakenly attributes this definition in various of his works to St. Ambrose.

to others the knowledge of God, so that they may know how holy and just the Lord is, and how all our goods and all our merits are his gifts, and through this they may apply themselves in holiness and justice to serve God, and with unceasing praise to ascribe to him all good things."[16] This is the pleasing sacrifice to God, that he most exactingly requires from us, in the manner that Micah most beautifully wrote: *What shall I offer to the Lord that is worthy? wherewith shall I kneel before the high God? ... May the Lord be appeased with thousands of rams? ... I will show you, O man, what is good, and what the Lord requires of you: Verily, to do judgment, and to love mercy, and to walk solicitous with your God.*[17] *Adorate Dominum in atrio sancto eius*, adore *the Lord in his holy court*, that is, in ecclesiastical unity, or in the chamber of your heart, praying to *your Father in secret*[18] and in spirit and truth. For *God is a spirit; and they that adore him, must adore him in spirit and in truth.*[19] And our spirit is the atrium of God, for in it is the Most High detained and given banquet, in the manner that is attested to in Revelation: *Behold, I stand at the gate, and knock. If any man shall hear my voice, and open to me the door, I will come into him, and will sup with him, and he with me.*[20]

28{29}[3] *The voice of the Lord is upon the waters; the God of majesty has thundered; The Lord is upon many waters.*

Vox Domini super aquas; Deus maiestatis intonuit; Dominus super aquas multas.

Additionally, the holy David describes the constitution of the Church, saying: **28{29}[3]** *Vox Domini, the voice of the Lord*, that is the preaching of Christ, *super aquas, is upon the waters*, that is, upon the people of the Jews, of whom Christ in the Gospels says, *I was not sent but to the sheep that are lost of the house of Israel.*[21] For Christ was especially promised and sent to them, and he first preached to them either by himself or through his disciples. *Deus maiestatis, the God of majesty*, that is, Christ, the King of glory, *intonuit, has thundered*, that is, showed forth the most high example, teaching by it that which transcends all reason, namely, God to be one and three, him to be God and man, his flesh to be true

---

16 Cf. Luke 1:75: *In holiness and justice before him, all our days.*
17 Micah 6:6–8.
18 Matt. 6:6b.
19 John 4:24b.
20 Rev. 3:20.
21 Matt. 15:24.

food indeed.²² He also *thundered*, that is, he taught terrible things (*terribilia*) of the future judgment and the punishments of hell. And in all this he spoke most excellently, as the Jews that were sent him returned saying: *Never did man speak like this man.*²³ *Dominus super aquas multas, the Lord is upon many waters*: that is, the preaching of Christ also was poured upon the Gentiles: for (as the evangelists testify) Christ at times went through and preached in Tyre and Sidon and other Gentile lands.²⁴ But the people is described by the term waters, because in Revelation it says: *The many waters ... are peoples.*²⁵ And Solomon: *Cast your bread upon the running waters*, which represents the peoples who beg. Or [alternatively] thus: *The voice of the Lord*, namely of the eternal Father, *upon waters*. For when Christ was baptized in the Jordan, the voice of the Father was heard (that is, *the God of majesty*, that is, the heavenly Father, *thundered*), saying: *This is my beloved Son.*²⁶ *The Lord is upon many waters*, that is, the power of Christ capable of cleansing sin that from that time is conferred upon all waters. For Christ by the touch of his most pure flesh conveyed to all waters regenerative power.²⁷

28{29}[4] *The voice of the Lord is in power; the voice of the Lord in magnificence.*

Vox Domini in virtute; vox Domini in magnificentia.

28{29}[4] *Vox Domini in virtute*, *the voice of the Lord is in power*; that is, the preaching of the Gospel done by Christ and his disciples with a

---

22 E. N. Denis, of course, is referring to the mysteries of the Trinity, the Incarnation, and Transubstantiation of the Eucharist. "Though faith is above reason, there can never be any real discrepancy between faith and reason. Since the same God who reveals mysteries and infuses faith has bestowed the light of reason on the human mind, God cannot deny himself, nor can truth ever contradict truth." CCC § 159.
23 John 7:46.
24 Matt. 15:21; Mark 7:24.
25 Rev. 17:15.
26 Matt. 3:17; 17:5. E. N. The first cite is to Christ's Baptism at the Jordan. The second cite is to Christ's Transfiguration.
27 E. N. A reference, of course, to the waters used in the sacrament of Baptism. The Catechism of the Council of Trent states that Baptism "was instituted by our Lord when, having been baptized by John, He gave to water the power of sanctifying." (trans., John A McHugh, O. P. and Charles J. Callan, O. P.) *Catechism of the Council of Trent for Parish Priests* (New York: Joseph F. Wagner 1947), 170. Among other authorities, the Catechism cites to one of St. Augustine's sermons (No. 37): "The Lord is baptized, not because He had need to be cleansed, but in order that, by the contact of His pure flesh, He might purify the waters and impart to them the power of cleansing."

great power of miracles, in the manner that is written in the Gospels: *But they going forth preached everywhere: the Lord working withal, and confirming the word with signs that followed.*[28] *Vox Domini in magnificentia; the voice of the Lord in magnificence*: that is, this preaching was done with great excellence, both because of the sanctity of the life of those preaching and because of the marvels which God worked through them, giving them *a mouth and wisdom, which all your adversaries shall not be able to resist and gainsay.*[29] Here the divine and holy Apostle [Paul] says: *We ought more diligently to observe the things which we have heard, lest perhaps we should let them slip. How shall we escape if we neglect so great salvation... which was confirmed unto us.... God also bearing them witness by signs, and wonders, and divers miracles, and distributions of the Holy Spirit?*[30] For (as elsewhere the Apostle teaches):

To one... by the Spirit, is given the word of wisdom: and to another, the word of knowledge, [according to the same Spirit; to another, faith in the same spirit;] to another, the grace of healing [in one Spirit; to another, the working of miracles;] to another, prophecy; to another, the discerning of spirits; to another, diverse kinds of tongues; [to another, interpretation of speeches].[31]

Because of these things, therefore, the *voice of the Lord* was delivered *in magnificence*.

28{29}[5] *The voice of the Lord breaks the cedars: yea, the Lord shall break the cedars of Lebanon.*

Vox Domini confringentis cedros, et confringet Dominus cedros Libani.

28{29}[6] *And shall reduce them to pieces, as a calf of Lebanon, and as the beloved son of unicorns.*

Et comminuet eas tamquam vitulum Libani: et dilectus quemadmodum filius unicornium.

---

28 Mark 16:20.
29 Luke 21:15.
30 Heb. 2:1, 3, 4.
31 E. N. Denis selected *charismata* and then finished his quotation with *"etc."* I have taken it to mean that he wanted the full recitation of the three verses; accordingly, that text in brackets is not in the Latin text, but is implicitly suggested.

28{29}[5] *Vox Domini confringentis cedros, the voice of the Lord breaks the cedars*: that is, the speech of Christ, or Christ himself, who is the voice, speech, and word of the eternal Father,[32] breaks the proud, who are similar to cedars in that they are great and sublime in their own eyes. These Christ breaks in three ways. First, by corrupting in them immoderate passions and vices, and by extinguishing pride that is in them. And this fracturing is kindly and healthy. These are cedars which learn from Christ because he is meek and humble of heart.[33] Second, Christ breaks these cedars, taking away from them or not giving to them spiritual being, but spiritually killing them.[34] Third, he breaks them in the day of judgment, when they are eternally damaged. And in this way, he broke the highest of all cedars, namely, Lucifer. Of whom we read: *The cedars in the paradise of God were not higher than he*.[35] But in this place we take the reference to cedars in a good way, because by the word cedars is understood angels, of which Lucifer was the highest. Now often Scripture uses the word cedar in a good way, in the manner the Wisdom of Ecclesiasticus did: *I was exalted like a cedar in Lebanon*.[36] For the cedar is a most high tree. And some height is good, and some is evil.

Et confringet Dominus cedros Libani; the Lord shall break the cedars of Lebanon: that is, proud prelates and princes, of fleshly eminence and splendorous fame, or with eminence of genius or knowledge, or with secular power, but glorying vainly. For "Lebanon" is to be understood as whiteness.[37] God breaks these cedars of Lebanon in the three ways

---

32   John 1:1. *Vox, sermo, et verbum*. Desiderius Erasmus wrote two extensive apologias (in 1520 and a new version in 1522) justifying his use of the word *sermo* to translate the Greek λόγος (*logos*) in John 1:1 instead of St. Jerome's *verbum* in his translation of the Gospel of John from the Greek. This stirred great controversy. Here, Denis says that Christ was all three — voice, speech, and word.
33   Matt. 11:29.
34   E. N. As to the meaning of "spiritual being," *esse spirituale* meaning sanctifying grace, see footnote 27–42.
35   Ez. 31:8a.
36   Ecclus. 24:17a.
37   E. N. *Candidatio*: whiteness or brightness. Achard of St. Victor (*ca.* 1100–1171), a canon regular and abbot at the Abbey of St. Victor of Paris, speaks of the two Lebanons, each of which has its form of whitnesses or brightnesses (*candidationes*): the whiteness (*candidatio*) of the truth and the whiteness of vanity. While the Lebanon of Christ has the true whiteness (*verum candorem*), the Lebanon of the world has the whiteness of shade (*umbratilem candorem*). The whiteness (*candidatio*) of Christ is interior, more hidden or latent, and remains in the shade (*intus magis latet et adhuc in occulto manet*), whereas the whiteness of the world is exterior, and entirely superficial (*exterior tota est et in superficie apparet*). Like whitened sepulchers of which Jesus spoke (*see* Matt. 23:27), the whiteness of the world is "like a wall

previously mentioned. Whence the most sacred and Christ-bearing virgin Mary: *He has put down the mighty from their seat*, she says, *and has exalted the humble.*[38] This accords with Ecclesiasticus: *God has overturned the thrones of proud princes, and has set up the meek in their stead.*[39] **28{29} [6]** *Et comminuet eas tanquam vitulum Libani; and shall reduce them to pieces, as a calf of Lebanon*: that is, the Lord consumes the cedars we have talked about as suckling calf consumes [milk] in Lebanon, offering [to the proud] either fault, or grace, or eternal salvation. For just as there are three ways of understanding the breaking of cedars, so also there are three ways that consuming them can be understood. *Et dilectus*, *and as the beloved*, that is, one humble, and pleasing to God, he will be *quemadmodum filius unicornium*, *as the son of unicorns*, that is, he will not be consumed as cedar, but he will be strong and secure in the Lord his God, and he will be like a young of a unicorn or of a rhinoceros,[40] who is a most strong, large, and fearless animal. Therefore, in saying this — *and as the beloved son of unicorns* — [the Psalmist] displays the distinction between the proud and those confident in their own strength and the humble who are confident in God.

28{29}[7] *The voice of the Lord divides the flame of fire.*

Vox Domini intercidentis flammam ignis.

28{29}[8] *The voice of the Lord shakes the desert: and the Lord shall shake the desert of Cades.*

Vox Domini concutientis desertum et commovebit Dominus desertum Cades.

---

that is painted on the outside white, but inside is totally dirty and unclean." "The whitening of Christ is found in goods that are spiritual and true, and the whiteness of the world in goods that are carnal and false." For this reason, Achard of St. Victor concludes, "the whitening of Christ feeds and illumines the spiritual eyes," whereas the "whiteness of the world deludes, strangles, and blinds the carnal eyes." See Achard de Saint-Victor, *Sermons Inédits* (Paris : Librairie Philosophique J. Vrin 1970), Sermo XIII , 145–46. Denis clearly has in mind the second sense of Lebanon and whiteness.
38   Luke 1:52.
39   Ecclus. 10:17.
40   E. N. The word translated as *unicornus* in the Vulgate (similarly μονοκερώτων [*monokerōtōn*]) in the Septuagint) or "unicorn" is the Hebrew word רְאֵם (*re'em*). Literally, it means "one-horned," and has no reference to the mythical horse-like animal we know as a unicorn. It has been variously translated as wild ox, oryx, wild bull, unicorn, rhinoceros. St. Jerome translated as both rhinoceros (*e.g.*, Num. 23:22, Job 39:9) and unicorn (*e.g.*, Ps. 28:6, 21:22, and Is. 34:7). Denis thus appears to understand unicorn as synonymous with rhinoceros.

28{29}[7] *Vox Domini intercidentis flammam ignis, the voice of the Lord divides the flame of fire*: that is, the Lord himself through the dew of his grace, destroys and extinguishes the fires or inflammation of anger and lust in his servants, leading them to the cool refreshment of meekness and chastity. Also — in a literal sense — Christ often extinguished and divided material fire prepared for their martyrdom and which the holy martyrs and faithful were thrown into, such as that fire of Saint Agnes that St. Ambrose wrote about.[41] Indeed, many of the saints have remained entirely unhurt in fire. Christ also divided the flames of fire when he mercifully illuminated certain Jews that were enraged against him, yet some he has left in their disbelief. 28{29}[8] *Vox Domini concutientis desertum, the voice of the Lord shakes the desert*: that is, the speech of Christ excites unfruitful hearts, those indolent and arid, rousing them to holy fear and divine love, so that they might be agile, fruitful, and fervid. For the heart of a sinner is called a desert, as it is abandoned by God, and is cut off from [spiritual] moisture and the fruits of salvation and of grace. *Et commovebit Dominus, and the Lord shall shake* to penance and a praiseworthy life, *desertum Cades, the desert of Cades*,[42] that is, the heart of the elect and those having the faith of God. For the term "Cades" is interpreted as meaning unchanged or holy. The elect, therefore, will be shaken by the Lord to salvation before they die, because they are able to go astray during this time [of pilgrimage], but finally they will not be able to be lost [when confirmed in grace by the Lord]. It is also possible to understand by "the desert of Cades," the whole of Judaea, which received the law from God, and in the end of time is to be changed to the faith. The Lord shall shake it at the end of the world, so that it may convert to Christ, as Hosea has testified to: *And after*

---

41 E. N. Denis is probably referring to St. Ambrose's work *On Virgins (De Virginibus*, I, 2, 5.) where St. Ambrose speaks of the martyrdom of the 12-year-old Agnes. *Si ad aras invita raperetur, tendere Christo inter ignes manus, atque in ipsis sacrilegis focis tropaeum Domini signare victoris.* "If she was unwillingly whisked to the [pagan] altars, [it was] to stretch her hands within the fires to Christ, and at the very sacrilegious fires to signal the trophy of victory of the Lord." PL 16, 189–90. The miracle is related in its fulness by Jacob of Voragine in *The Golden Legend*: "The deputy, Aspasius by name, had Agnes thrown into a roaring fire, but the flames divided and burned upon the hostile crowd on either side, leaving the maiden unscathed." (trans., William Granger Ryan) Jacob de Voragine, *The Golden Legend* (New Jersey: Princeton University Press 2012), 103.

42 Cades (or Kadesh), which is derived from the Hebrew word meaning "holy," refers to a site, sites, or perhaps even a region located either south of, or at the southern border of, Canaan and the Kingdom of Judah. It was apparently desert or wilderness.

this the children of Israel shall return, and shall seek the Lord their God, and David their king,[43] that is, their Messiah, and all will be explained.

28{29}[9] The voice of the Lord prepares the stags: and he will discover the thick woods: and in his temple all shall speak his glory.

Vox Domini praeparantis cervos, et revelabit condensa; et in templo eius omnes dicent gloriam.

28{29}[9] *Vox Domini praeparantis cervos*, *the voice of the Lord prepares the stags*: that is, Christ by his words disposes his fervent servants to run quickly in the way of his precepts;[44] and he prepared the Apostles, giving them the first fruits of the Holy Spirit,[45] so that they might disseminate the word of God throughout the whole world, attending quickly to the burden that was enjoined upon them, in the manner that stags are quick in their actions. *Et revelabit condensa*, *and he will discover the thick woods*, that is, he will illumine the hearts of these [fervent servants or Apostles], so that they might understand the things hidden in the Scriptures. For this Christ did to his Apostles and to many others. *Et in templo eius omnes dicent gloriam*, *and in his temple all shall speak his glory*, that is, in the Church of God all the faithful shall attribute glory and praise to God.

28{29}[10] The Lord makes the flood to dwell: and the Lord shall sit king forever. The Lord will give strength to his people: the Lord will bless his people with peace.

Dominus diluvium inhabitare facit, et sedebit Dominus rex in aeternum. Dominus virtutem populo suo dabit; Dominus benedicet populo suo in pace.

28{29}[10] *Dominus diluvium*, *the Lord . . . the flood*, that is, the plenitude or the superabundance of grace, *inhabitare facit*, *makes to dwell* in the hearts of his elect, especially during the time of the evangelical law, which — because of the supereffluent mercy of God shown to Christians — is called the time of grace. *Et sedebit Dominus rex in aeternum*, *the Lord shall sit as king forever*, that is, he will eternally preside over his faithful, and he will dwell in them by means of grace, and in the future also by glory, in the manner that Zechariah predicted of Christ: *He shall bear the glory, and shall sit, and rule upon his throne: and he shall be a*

---

43 Hosea 3:5a.
44 *Cf.* 118:32: *I have run the way of your commandments, when you did enlarge my heart.*
45 *Cf.* Rom. 8:23.

*priest upon his throne.*⁴⁶ **28{29}[10/11]**⁴⁷ *Dominus virtutem populo suo dabit, the Lord will give strength to his people,* that is, so that they might turn away from evil, and they may do good. *Dominus benedicet populo suo, the Lord shall bless his people,* that is, he will give them much grace, *in pace, with peace,* that is, so that they will be with a tranquil and quieted mind. For disturbed and unquieted hearts are not capable of divine mercy.⁴⁸ Or [one could understand it this way], *in peace,* that is, at their end, so that they might receive true and stable peace. Or [yet another way of understanding it], *in peace,* that is, in him [the Lord] himself: For Christ (as the Apostle said) *is our peace, who has made both one.*⁴⁹

PRAYER

REMOVE US, O LORD, FROM ALL EVIL, and grant to us a contrite and humble heart to offer up to you for our sins, so that by your power and magnificence you might check the scandals of those who work iniquity and you might bless your people in peace.

*A cunctis malis exime nos, Domine, et tribue nobis cor contritum
et humiliatum pro peccatis nostris tibi offerre: ut tua virtute
et magnificentia sedatis scandalis, quae operantur
iniquitatem, populo tuo benedicas in pace.*

---

46 Zech. 6:13b. E. N. The editors show a discrepancy, the text containing *in*, "on," and the Vulgate contained *super*, "upon."
47 Denis has labeled this verse as 28:11, though it appears to be numbered in the Vulgate and the Douay-Rheims as a continuation of 28:10.
48 By speaking of the *cor inquietum* as not *capax divinae benedictionis*, Denis certainly did not suggest that these hearts are not touchable by actual graces, but his point is that until these "restless hearts" return to God and find their rest in him, they are not in a state of sanctifying or justifying grace, which grace is required to have the theological virtues of faith, hope, and charity, the infused virtues, and the gifts of the Holy Spirit, the foundation to do supernatural good, obtain merit, and effectively to resist evil. As St. Augustine makes clear, the disquieted heart famously mentioned by him in his *Confessions* is not meant to remain disquieted and apart from God, but is meant to follow the prevenient promptings of actual grace so that it may ultimately find rest in God: *[F]ecisti nos ad te inquietum est cor nostrum, donec requiescat in te.* "You have us for yourself, and our heart is restless until it rests in you." *Conf.*, I, i, 1, PL 32, 661.
49 Eph. 2:14a.

Psalm 29

ARTICLE LXIV

EXPOSITON OF THE TWENTY-NINTH PSALM:
EXALTABO TE, DOMINE, &c.
I WILL EXTOL YOU, O LORD, &c.

29{30}[1] *A Psalm of a canticle, at the dedication of David's house.*
Psalmus canti, in dedicatione domus David.

HE TITLE OF THIS PSALM IS: 29{30}[1] *PSAL-mus cantici, in dedicatione domus David*; *a Psalm of a canticle, at the dedication of David's house.* The word "Psalm" means good work or praise with work; but a canticle is spiritual joy.[1] Now the dedication of David's house refers to the Resurrection of the body of Christ. For the *Wisdom of God has built itself a house*,[2] when it assumed a human body. But in the Resurrection, he dedicated that house, raising up again his body to an impassible, inviolable, and most singular state. This is therefore the sense of the title: *Psalm*, that is, a laborious praise (*laus operosa*), and one instructing us to the doing of good works. Praise, I say, *of a canticle*, that is, containing spiritual joy, *at the dedication of David's house*, that is, at the resuscitation of the body of the Lord Savior.

29{30}[2] *I will extol you, O Lord, for you have upheld me: and have not made my enemies to rejoice over me.*

Exaltabo te, Domine, quoniam suscepisti me, nec delectasti inimicos meos super me.

---

1 E. N. *Psalmus, bonam operationem vel laudem cum operatione significat; canticum vero, spiritualem laetitiam.* Defining a "Psalm" as a good operation, or work, or deed (*bonam operationem*) is commonplace, e.g., St. Thomas in his *Commentary on the Psalms* (Ps. 4) defines a Psalm as a *bonam operationem*, "a good work." *Super Psalmo 4* n. 1. But I have not been able to discover anyone other than Denis that adds the secondary component (*laudem cum operatione*), an act of praise with an operation, work, deed, or labor. Here, Denis is defining a "psalm of a canticle," *psalmus cantici*. Many of the Psalms are classified as a mere psalm (*psalmus*), others as canticles (*canticum*), others as psalms of a canticle (*psalmus cantici*), and some as canticles of a psalm (*canticum psalmi*). Denis's definition of a "psalm of a canticle," a *psalmus cantici*, is a good work or praise with labor that is also a song of spiritual joy.
2 Prov. 9:1a.

Therefore, Christ giving thanks to God the Father for his Resurrection says: **29{30}[2]** *Exaltabo te, Domine, I will extol you, O Lord*, that is, I will praise you, and I will make you well known, so that they may exalt, and venerate, and acknowledge you as boundless, and incomparably more worthy than all creatures; *quoniam suscepisti me, for you have upheld me* in the Resurrection to an impassible status, and in the Ascension to your right hand; *nec delectasti inimicos meos super me, and have not made my enemies to rejoice over me*, that is, you have not allowed them finally or for a lengthy period of time to rejoice over my afflictions. For although the Jews at the time of Christ's death rejoiced, it was not however to the extent they thought they would. For they thought to extinguish entirely his name and memory, and they reckoned his body would rot in the grave; but when they heard from the guards who oversaw the tomb what the facts were, they began to sorrow, especially because of that testimony that the dead that were raised again together with Christ witnessed the Resurrection of Christ. For they [the others rising with Christ] came (as the Gospel of Matthew relates) into the holy city, and appeared to many. This did not escape the notice of the head priests; indeed [it may be inferred] from what we read [the dead who rose again with Christ] had appeared to them.[3] But they were made sorrowful on the day of Pentecost, and thereafter, when they saw in the disciples of Christ such manifest miracles of God that many thousands converted to Christ.[4] Further, the devils rejoiced at the tribulations of Christ. For nothing less than the devil had opted to kill Jesus; and not only that, but the devil had been put in the heart of Judas the son of Simon Iscariot so that he would betray him.[5] Nevertheless, at that night seeing the admirable patience of Jesus, and some other things besides (from which he [the devil] was able to conjecture Jesus to be the true Christ), he began to fear, and to sorrow about his betrayal. Whence he disturbed the wife of Pilate at night in a dream, so that she might counsel her husband not to kill that just man.[6] Since, therefore, the demons had come to realize that Jesus whose death they had procured was the Christ, then all the delight that they had had in his persecution ceased. Here, therefore, the Savior says to the Father, *and you have not made my enemies to rejoice over me*. And according to that understanding, by enemies is designated both unbelieving Jews and devils.

---

3   Matt. 27:53. E. N. As Denis says in Article XLII (Psalm 17:8) in Volume I, this is believed, though it is not in so many words stated in Matt. 27:52–53.
4   See Acts 2:43; 4:2; etc.
5   John 13:2.
6   Matt. 27:19.

29{30}[3] *O Lord my God, I have cried to you, and you have healed me.*

Domine Deus meus, clamavi ad te, et sanasti me.

29{30}[4] *You have brought forth, O Lord, my soul from hell: you have saved me from them that go down into the pit.*

Domine, eduxisti ab inferno animam meam; salvasti me a descendentibus in lacum.

29{30}[5] *Sing to the Lord, O you his saints: and give praise to the memory of his holiness.*

Psallite Domino, sancti eius; et confitemini memoriae sanctitatis eius.

29{30}[3] *Domine Deus meus clamavi ad te;* O Lord my God, I have cried to you: at the time of the Passion, when I said, *Not my will, but yours be done;*[7] and at the Cross, when I said to the Father, *Into your hands I commend my spirit;*[8] *et sanasti me,* and you have healed me from the wound of death, by reuniting the soul with an immortal and glorified body. **29{30}[4]** *Domine, eduxisti ab inferno;* O Lord, you have brought forth from hell, that is from the limbo of the Fathers,[9] *animam meam,* my soul, in the day of the Resurrection; *salvasti me a descendentibus in lacum,* you have saved me from them that go down into the pit, that is, you have preserved me so that I not be numbered among those that have descended into the lower hell (*infernum inferiorem*).[10] Therefore, I, Christ, exhort you: **29{30}[5]** *Psallite Domino,* sing to the Lord, to God the Father, who has conferred so many goods to me, *sancti eius, et confitemini memoriae sanctitatis eius;* O you his saints, and give praise to the memory of his holiness, that is, announce and reflect again with a confession of praise

---

7   Luke 22:42b.
8   Ps. 30:6a; Luke 23:46.
9   E. N. For the limbo of the Fathers (*limbus patrum*) see Article LXI (Psalm 27:1) and *see* footnote 23-14 of Volume I.
10 Ps. 85:13. E. N. When Denis refers to the lower hell (*infernus inferior*), which is specifically mentioned by Psalm 85:13 to which he cites, he is not referring to the hell or limbo of the fathers (*limbus patrum*), the "hell" in the Apostle's creed, the *infernus superior.* The lower hell (*infernus inferior*) was not destroyed by Christ. In response to the error of the Armenians in this regard, the Church taught: *Quod Christus non destruxit descendo ad inferos inferiorem infernum.* "That Christ did not destroy the lower hell, by descending into hell [meaning the limbo of the fathers]." DS 1077. Contrary to the souls who were not in mortal sin and were awaiting Christ's redemptive death, the souls in the lower hell of the damned were neither visited nor released, and never will be released, since that hell is for eternity. DS 443; *see also* DS 76, 780, 801.

on the mercy of the divine holiness or of the holy God, by which you bring to mind his sending me, his Son, into the world, so that I might redeem you. So Christ exhorts that we sing to the Lord because of the good things that he obtained for himself, and that we might confess to him how good it is for him to have remembered us, who were forgetful of him, for the benefits which he bestowed to us in Christ.[11]

29{30}[6] *For wrath is in his indignation; and life in his good will. In the evening weeping shall have place, and in the morning gladness.*

Quoniam ira in indignatione eius, et vita in voluntate eius ad vesperum demorabitur fletus, et ad matutinum laetitia.

29{30}[6] *Quoniam ira, for wrath*, that is, the ruin of the human race or the punishment for original sin, is *in indignatione eius, is in his indignation*, that is, arises out of a just divine detestation [of sin], which sin is so detested that it cannot be remitted unless I subject myself to death; indeed, even the Father himself in a certain way (*quodammodo*) avenged that sin in me, as is attested to by Isaiah: *For the wickedness of my people have I struck him.*[12] *Et vita, and life*, that is, the redemption of human nature and my resuscitation, is *in voluntate eius, in his good will*, that is, proceeds from the kind goodness of God the Father. For God does all things freely, as the Apostle [Paul] said: *All things according to the counsel of his will.*[13] And so from the most merciful will flows forth that by the Passion of Christ the world was delivered from the death of sin and obtained the life of grace.

Ad vesperum demorabitu fletus; in the evening weeping shall have a place: that is, due to Christ on the Cross being already dead, a great weeping and vehement sorrow existed in his disciples and friends; indeed, as the Evangelist [Luke] says, that the *centurion* and *all the multitude of them that were come together to that sight . . . returned striking their breasts.*[14] *Et ad matutinum laetitia, and in the morning gladness*, that is, by Christ powerfully rising again at daybreak, consolation took hold of the previously mentioned mourners. For in the day of the Resurrection, Christ appeared five times, and their hearts rejoiced. Or [we can understand it] thus: *in the evening*, that is, during the time of this [earthly] exile,

---

11   E. N. As happens so often, Denis has switched from first person (Christ narrating) to third person (Denis narrating) in this sentence.
12   Is. 53:8b.
13   Eph. 1:11b.
14   Luke 23:47a, 48.

we who *sit in darkness, and in the shadow of death*,[15] *weeping shall have its place*, that is, being that Christ suffered great pain, it is becoming both to suffer with him and to weep for our ungratefulness; *and in the morning gladness*, that is, in the day of blessed remuneration and of celestial light there will be exultation to them who in the prior evening mourned, in the manner that the Apostle [Paul] says: *if we suffer with him, we shall also reign with him.*[16]

29{30}[7] *And in my abundance I said: I shall never be moved.*

Ego autem dixi in abundantia mea: Non movebor in aeternum.

29{30}[8] *O Lord, in your favor, you gave strength to my beauty. You turned away your face from me, and I became troubled.*

Domine, in voluntate tua praestitisti decori meo virtutem; avertisti faciem tuam a me, et factus sum conturbatus.

29{30}[7] *Ego autem dixi in abundantia mea*, *and in my abundance I said*, that is, I, Christ, existing in the plenitude of grace and the exuberance of divine consolation, said: *Non movebor in aeternum, I shall never be moved*, that is, I will not always be disturbed by the persecution of all the ungodly. Whence, in the Last Supper Christ said to his disciples: *For the things concerning me have an end.*[17] Or [we might understand it this way], *I shall never be moved*, that is, from obedience to my Father I will never deviate, nor deflect in the least bit from the rectitude of a holy manner of living, but I will be immobile in God. For because of the abundance of his grace, Christ was a comprehensor, and he was confirmed in good: for this reason, he is able to say, *I shall never be moved.* **29{30}[8]** *Domine*, O Lord, Father, *in voluntate tua*, *in your favor*, that is, in the goodness of your love and the kindliness of your favor, *praestitisti decori meo, you gave . . . to my beauty*, that is, to my holy and immaculate and splendid manner of my life, *virtutem*, *strength*, that is, the earlier-mentioned stability in you.

But *avertisti faciem tuam a me; you have turned away your face from me*; that is, at the time of your Passion you have withdrawn internal and customary consolations from the inferior powers of my soul,[18] and so

---

15 Luke 1:79a.
16 Rom. 8:17b; 2 Tim. 2:12a. Denis blends the two verses. Rom.8:17b: *And if sons, heirs also; heirs indeed of God, and joint heirs with Christ: yet so, if we suffer with him, that we may be also glorified with him.* 2 Tim. 2:12a: *If we suffer, we shall also reign with him.*
17 Luke 22:37b.
18 E. N. Denis explains this limited abeyance of the effects of Christ's beatific

you allowed me to be handled violently and to be suspended among two thieves, and [so treated me] as if I were not your beloved Son. Whence I was compelled to exclaim: *My God, my God, why have you forsaken me?*[19] *Et factus sum conturbatus*, and *I became troubled*: not with the trouble of fault (*culpae*), for I earlier stated, *I shall not be moved*; but [*I became troubled*] with the trouble of punishment (*poenae*) or of natural and violent afflictions.[20] As is written by John: *When Jesus had said these things, he was troubled in spirit; and he testified, and said: Amen, amen I say to you, one of you shall betray me.*[21] And Luke said: *And being in an agony, he prayed the longer; and his sweat became as drops of blood, trickling down upon the ground.*[22]

29{30}[9] To you, O Lord, will I cry: and I will make supplication to my God.

Ad te, Domine, clamabo, et ad Deum meum deprecabor.

29{30}[10] What profit is there in my blood, while I go down to corruption? Shall dust confess to you, or declare your truth?

Quae utilitas in sanguine meo, dum descendo in corruptionem? Numquid confitebitur tibi pulvis, aut annuntiabit veritatem tuam?

Nevertheless, following this time of trouble, **29{30}[9]** *Ad te, Domine, clamabo; to you, O Lord, I will cry*, praying while upon the Cross for those who crucified me[23] and for the salvation of the whole world. Then, Christ changing his person, says that same thing that he said to the Father, for

---

vision by the Father in Article L (Psalm 21:2) of Volume 1, when he explains the meaning of Christ's cry from the Cross: *God, my God, why have you forsaken me*. There is no suggestion of a full withdrawal of the beatific vision or severance of the grace of union. Denis maintains that even on the Cross, Christ in his humanity remained with the vision of God and hypostatically united to the Word. As Denis just stated, with respect to this vision, *I shall never be moved*. Yet Christ's suffering was real, and the limited withdrawal of the joy of vision allows for this so that Christ's suffering is not merely apparent. In fact, the real physical suffering may be more poignant because of Christ's continued vision of God while suffering it. Denis cannot be accused of any Docetism whatsoever.

19   Ps. 21:2; Matt. 27:46.
20   For the very important distinction between fault (*culpa*) and punishment (*poena*), see footnote 21-146 in Volume 1.
21   John 13:21.
22   Luke 22:43b–44.
23   Luke 23:34.

the Church, that he might inform her to do similarly, and he says: *et ad Deum meum deprecabor*, *and I will make supplication to my God*, not ceasing from the invocation of him because of any distress of tribulations or the bitterness of the Passion. And this I do reasonably: for **29{30}** [10] *Quae utitlitas in sanguine meo*, *what profit is there in my blood*, that is, what will have been the fruit of the Incarnation, and my life, and the pouring out of my Blood, *dum descendo in corruptionem*, *while I go down to corruption*, that is, if I remained in the sepulcher and was reduced to ash? For Christ was made Incarnate and suffered his Passion so that he might convert the world. But if he had not risen again from the dead, the world would not have believed in him at all, and so there would be no utility seen to have arisen from his Passion or his death. It is for this reason that the Apostle [Paul] said: *If Christ be not risen again, then is our preaching vain, and your faith is also vain.*[24] Whence, Christ suitably proved that which he said, adding: *Numquid confitebitur tibi pulvis? Shall dust confess to you, or declare your truth?* That is, shall my flesh turned to ash and corrupted be an occasion of, and a material basis for, believing and having confidence in your name? *Aut*, or would the effect of such dust *annuntiabit veritatem tuam*, *declare your truth*, my appearing to the Apostles showing to them my scars and saying, *Handle, and see;*[25] and verifying the scriptures of the Prophets, all of which in agreement prophesied my flesh forthwith to be raised again. It is for this reason, therefore, that Christ after his Resurrection told his disciples: *All things must needs be fulfilled, which are written in the law of Moses, and in the Prophets, and in the Psalms, concerning me.*[26]

29{30}[11] *The Lord has heard, and has had mercy on me: the Lord became my helper.*

Audivit Dominus, et misertus est mei; Dominus factus est adiutor meus.

29{30}[12] *You have turned for me my mourning into joy: you have cut my sackcloth, and have compassed me with gladness.*

Convertisti planctum meum in gaudium mihi; conscidisti saccum meum, et circumdedisti me laetitia.

---

24   1 Cor. 15:14.
25   Luke 24:39: *See my hands and feet, that it is I myself; handle, and see: for a spirit has not flesh and bones, as you see me to have.*
26   Luke 24:44b.

29{30}[13] *To the end that my glory may sing to you, and I may not regret: O Lord my God, I will give praise to you forever.*

Ut cantet tibi gloria mea, et non compungar. Domine Deus meus, in aeternum confitebor tibi.

29{30}[11] *Audivit Dominus,* **the Lord has heard** the prayers I have advanced, *et misertus est mei,* **and has had mercy on me,** delivering me from the universal punishment of the present life; *Dominus factus est adiutor meus,* **the Lord became my helper,** giving me all power in heaven and on earth.[27] **29{30}[12]** *Convertisti,* **you have turned,** O Lord, *planctum meum,* **my mourning,** that is, the sorrow of which I said, *My soul is sorrowful even unto death,*[28] *in gaudium mihi,* **into joy for me:** because in exchange for that temporal sorrow you have given the eternal joy of the essential reward of all the elect and to me the joy of accidental reward, conveying me from the ignominious Passion to the glory of the Resurrection. For as the Apostle [Paul] attested, Christ *with a strong cry and tears* poured out supplications to God.[29] *Conscidisti saccum meum,* **you have cut my sackcloth:**[30] that is, you permitted my body, the despised hiding place (*contemptum latibulum*) of my soul and divinity, during the Passion to be mutilated with many wounds, so that *from the sole of the foot unto the top of the head, there is no soundness therein;*[31] *et circumdedisti me laetitia,* **and have compassed me with gladness,** that is, you have restored a glorious body to my soul in the Resurrection; **29{30}[13]** *ut cantet tibi gloria mea,* **to the end that my glory may sing to you,** that is, so that I — glorified in body and soul — might praise you, *et non compungar,* **and may not regret,** that is, no longer suffer more. For Christ *rising again from the dead, dies now no more.*[32] *Domine Deus meus, in aeternum confitebor tibi;* **O Lord my God, I will give praise to you forever,** praising you inasmuch as I am man without end in the Kingdom of Heaven, where I sit with you at your right hand.[33]

---

27 Matt. 28:18b.
28 Matt. 26:38a.
29 Heb. 5:7: *Who in the days of his flesh, with a strong cry and tears, offering up prayers and supplications to him that was able to save him from death, was heard for his reverence.*
30 The Vulgate's *conscidisti* has been rendered in the Douay-Rheims as *you have cut;* however, I think it would have been better to translate it as torn or rent to pieces or (tropologically) ill-treated, mutilated.
31 Is. 1:6a.
32 Rom. 6:9a.
33 *Cf.* Heb. 1:3: Christ *being the brightness of his glory, and the figure of his substance, and upholding all things by the word of his power, making purgation of sins, sits on the right hand of the majesty on high.*

ARTICLE LXV

TROPOLOGICAL EXPOSITION OF THE SAME TWENTY-NINTH PSALM.

29{30}[1] *A Psalm of a canticle, at the dedication of David's house.*
Psalmus canti, in dedicatione domus David.

NOW MORALLY EXPOUNDING THIS PSALM, BY the *house of David* we understand the Church, or any member of the faithful, in whom God dwells by faith and grace. And by the dedication of this house, we understand the commission or exhibition which shows us to be serving the true and living God.[34] And so the sense of this title is: **29{30}[1]** *Psalmus cantici, in dedicatione domus David*, Psalm of a canticle, at the dedication of David's house, that is, for the showing of thanksgiving and obedience, wherein with heart, by mouth, and in manner of life we return thanks to the Most High for his benefits, and voluntarily show ourselves to be at his service.

29{30}[2] *I will extol you, O Lord, for you have upheld me: and have not made my enemies to rejoice over me.*

Exaltabo te, Domine, quoniam suscepisti me, nec delectasti inimicos meos super me.

Therefore, the Church or any one member of the Christian faithful seeing himself preserved and delivered by God from many dangers, gives thanks and says: **29{30}[2]** *Exaltabo te, Domine*; I will extol you, O Lord,

---

34 Denis uses the words *deputatio* and *exhibitio*. The first suggests a sort of deputation, a commission, which is what we find, *e.g.*, in Matt. 28:19-20: *Teach all nations; baptizing them in the name of the Father, and of the Son, and of the Holy Spirit, teaching them to observe all things whatsoever I have commanded you.* Exhibitio means a showing, exhibition, a holding forth, providing an example or sample. This sort of exhibition is what is suggested in Matt. 5:16: *So let your light shine before men, that they may see your good works, and glorify your Father who is in heaven*, or what is suggested by St. Paul in 1 Cor. 10:31: *whether you eat or drink, or whatsoever else you do, do all to the glory of God*. The first notion (*deputatio*) is well-rendered by the English word commission, as the notion of the "Great Commission" is common among us. The second notion, however, is hard to render into English, and the English word "exhibition" is far from conveying Denis's thought. We do not have the notion of a "Great Exhibition," and the notion of "exhibition" is tempered by the opposite warning of Matthew 6:1-6, that we should do things not to be seen by men, "in secret," not "in the synagogues and corners of the street," but "in our chamber," behind closed doors.

humbling myself, and reverently rendering service to you, acknowledging your loftiness, and attributing to you every perfection, goodness, and grace. For the more profoundly we humble ourselves, the more gloriously do we extol God. And so also *I will extol you, O Lord, quoniam suscepisti me, for you have upheld me*, that is, you have not permitted evil men and demons, who delight in my adversities, finally to glory over me; but from punishments or vices you have delivered my soul, and so you have given delight to the holy angels and the godly men because of me, *for there shall be joy before the angels of God upon one sinner doing penance.*[35]

29{30}[3]   O Lord my God, I have cried to you, and you have healed me.
Domine Deus meus, clamavi ad te, et sanasti me.

29{30}[4]   You have brought forth, O Lord, my soul from hell: you have saved me from them that go down into the pit.
Domine, eduxisti ab inferno animam meam; salvasti me a descendentibus in lacum.

29{30}[3] *Domine Deus meus, clamavi ad te*, O Lord my God, I have cried to you, for your indulgence of sins, the infusion of virtues, and the lightening of punishment or of persecutions; *et sanasti me, and you have healed me* from the interior wounds of sin, or also from external tribulation or bodily sickness. **29{30}[4]** *Domine, eduxisti ab inferno animam meam; You have brought forth, O Lord, my soul from hell*, that is, you have freed me from the guilt and stain of mortal sin by which men merit hell; *salvasti me a descendentibus in lacum, you have saved me from them that go down into the pit*, that is, you have not allowed me to persevere in evil, in the way those who cherish infernal things, or those who descend into the depths of vices. See how great this benefit of God is! And this above all is given to them who, inspired by God, forsake the world and all the things that are in the world, and faithfully serve Christ in religion.[36] They who turned away from their former way of life and the companionship of evil most truly

---

35 Luke 15:10.
36 E. N. In other words, those who answer to the call to the religious life. As St. Thomas observes (ST IIaIIae, q. 189, art. 10, co.), it is certain that, in itself, the religious life is a greater good than the secular life, and to doubt this "detracts from Christ" (*derogat Christo*). As Pope St. John Paul II stated: Jesus' "way of living in chastity, poverty and obedience appears as the most radical way of living the Gospel on this earth, a way which may be called divine, for it was embraced by him, God and man, as the expression of his relationship as the Only-Begotten Son with the Father and with the Holy Spirit. This is why Christian tradition has always spoken of the objective superiority (*concreta praestantia*) of the consecrated life." *Vita Consecrata*, 18.

are able to say this verse, indeed, they ought to do so with great and most devout joyfulness. For we who have forsaken the world, or we who have turned to true and persevering penance, ought to consider how many of our neighbors, our contemporaries, our companions — who just a short time ago were living amongst us, and who were perhaps much better than we — hell has already devoured. How much, therefore, are we bound to give thanks to God most high, who has already justly damned them, and who has so kindly spared us, and led us to a better life!

29{30}[5] *Sing to the Lord, O you his saints: and give praise to the memory of his holiness.*

Psallite Domino, sancti eius; et confitemini memoriae sanctitatis eius.

Since a holy man alone is in no manner sufficient to give worthy thanks to God for such an ineffable benefit, all the saints who are either in heaven or on earth are summoned to the praise of God and the giving of thanks, and so one finds added: **29{30}[5]** *Psallite Domino, sancti eius, et confitemini;* Sing to the Lord, O you his saints, and give praise, the confession of praise,[37] *memoriae sanctitatis eius,* to the memory of his holiness, that is, to the holy memory of God,[38] or to our holy God mercifully remembering that he who was opposed to him and forgetful of him be not forgotten, but led back to him. For this the Lord says through Isaiah: *Can a woman forget her infant, so as not to have pity on the son of her womb? And if she should forget, yet will not I forget you.*[39] Therefore, let us not be forgetful of the mercies of the Lord, who so anticipates us in all goodness and grace.[40] But say intently with Isaiah this: *I will remember*

---

37 E. N. On the difference between the confession of praise and the confession of sin, *see* footnote 27-49.
38 E. N. The notion of the memory of God (*memoria Dei*) is quite lovely, and the maternal Isaian image used to express it is a very beautiful one. "We are not unforgettable for ourselves and by ourselves," the French philosopher Jean-Louis Chrétien wrote, "[b]ut we are unforgettable for God." Jean-Louis Chrétien, *The Unforgettable and the Unhoped For* (New York: Fordham University Press 2002), 97. (trans., Jeffrey Bloechl). St. Thomas expresses it with poignant succinctness in reference to one of the central mysteries of our Faith: [C]*ausa . . . incarnationis est memoria Dei de homine,* "the cause of the Incarnation is the memory of God of man." *Super Heb.,* cap. 2 l. 2.
39 Is. 49:15.
40 E. N. The word "anticipates" translates the Latin *praevenit,* but not altogether adequately. God *praevenit,* anticipates, comes first, comes before. "In Spanish," Pope Francis has said, "there is a very expressive word that explains it well: *El nos "primerea,"* he "precedes" us. He is always first. When we arrive he is already there waiting

the tender mercies of the Lord, the praise of the Lord for all the things that the Lord has bestowed upon us... which he has given... according to his kindness.[41] And this with Jeremiah: *The mercies of the Lord that we are not consumed: because his commiserations have not failed.*[42]

29{30}[6] For wrath is in his indignation; and life in his good will. In the evening weeping shall have place, and in the morning gladness.

  Quoniam ira in indignatione eius, et vita in voluntate eius ad vesperum demorabitur fletus, et ad matutinum laetitia.

29{30}[6] *Quaniam ira, for wrath,* that is, the effect of divine justice, namely, the deprivation of grace, the vengeance of fault, the introduction of punishment, is *in indignatione eius, in his indignation,* that is, from the just judgment of God, who is indignant with the ungrateful and the ungodly; *et vita, and life,* that is, the enlivening of the soul by grace, and all the effects of the mercy of God, is *in voluntate eius, in his good will,* that is, it arises and is caused out of the good pleasure of the divine goodness. *Ad vesperum, In the evening,* that is, in adversity and in consideration of our own darkness and imperfection, *demorabitur fletus, weeping shall have place,* for sins and the exile of this present life; *et ad matutinum, and in the morning,* that is, in prosperity, and from the contemplation of the divine perfections and the benefits of God, *laetitia, joy* shall have a place, that is, the good men who wept in the evening shall rejoice.

29{30}[7] And in my abundance I said: I shall never be moved.

  Ego autem dixi in abundantia mea: Non movebor in aeternum.

29{30}[8] O Lord, in your favor, you gave strength to my beauty. You turned away your face from me, and I became troubled.

  Domine, in voluntate tua praestitisti decori meo virtutem; avertisti faciem tuam a me, et factus sum conturbatus.

---

for us." Homily of Pope Francis on the Occasion of the Feast of St. Ignatius, Church of the Gesù, Rome, July 31, 2013. http://www.vatican.va/content/francesco/en/homilies/2013/documents/papa-francesco_20130731 _omelia-sant-ignazio.html (5/19/2020). "The expression 'El nos primerea'... is in Lunfardo Porteño, or Buenos Aires street slang.... It is a term perhaps derived from soccer—*fútbol*—and means 'he gets there before you,' 'he bests you,' 'he anticipates you,' 'he beats you to it.'" "Primerea: The Spanish Slang at the Heart of Pope Francis's Theology," https://www.catholic.org/news/hf/faith/story.php?id=51946 (5/19/2020).

41 Is. 63:7. The verse finishes: *and according to the multitude of his mercies.*
42 Lam. 3:22.

29{30}[9] *To you, O Lord, will I cry: and I will make supplication to my God.*

Ad te, Domine, clamabo, et ad Deum meum deprecabor.

29{30}[10] *What profit is there in my blood, while I go down to corruption? Shall dust confess to you, or declare your truth?*

Quae utilitas in sanguine meo, dum descendo in corruptionem? Numquid confitebitur tibi pulvis, aut annuntiabit veritatem tuam?

29{30}[7] *Ego autem*, and I, after sin [now] converted to you, *dixi in abundantia*, *in my abundance I said*, that is, in the exceeding confidence of my fervor: *Non movebor in aeternum*, *I shall never be moved*, that is, I will never return to the prior sin, and never will I abandon, never will I be sad about, never will I depart from, God's narrow path.[43] For it is common for this to take hold of the newly-converted: that while they perceive unfamiliar consolations and the grace of the Holy Spirit, they are immediately incautiously presumptuous, and they display great rejoicing as if they will never lose such sweetness, not thinking sufficiently of their own weakness. But this is incautious. And so it continues: **29{30}[8]** *Domine, in voluntate tua; Lord, in your favor*, that is, according to that which is pleasing to you, *praestitisti decori meo*, *you gave to my beauty*, that is, to the interior renewal of my soul, which is renewed daily *from glory to glory*,[44] *virtutem*, *strength*, that is, the stability of grace. It is as if he were saying: "Not as I presume and reckon, but as it appears becoming and good to you, you have given me the gift of grace. Therefore, I ought not unadvisedly to presume in my abundance."

Avertisti faciem tuam, *you turned away your face*, that is, the tender refuge of your consolations and assistance, *a me, et factus sum conturbatus; from me, and I became troubled*, that is, sorrowful and indolent, as if

---

43 E. N. This refers capital sin of *acedia* or spiritual sloth, and some of its "daughters." "Flee from sins as from the face of the serpent," Ecclus. 21:2; therefore, we should never return to the prior sin. We should not be like Lot's wife and look back to sin. *Save your life: look not back.* Gen. 19:17. *No man putting his hand to the plough, and looking back, is fit for the kingdom of God.* Luke 9:62. The obligation to bear the burden of fighting against sin and pursuing spiritual wisdom means not doing so is sinful. *Bow down you shoulder, and bear her*, that is, spiritual wisdom, *and be not grieved (acedieris) with her bands.*" ST IIaIIae, q. 35, art. 1 s.c. (quoting Ecclus. 6:26). Acedia is a form of sinful sorrow (*tristitiam*), and two of the "daughters" of acedia as identified by Pope St. Gregory the Great and mentioned by St. Thomas are, faintheartedness (*pusillanimitas*), and despair (*desperatio*). ST IIaIIae, q. 35, art. 4.

44 2 Cor. 3:18b.

defrauded of that hope of which I said, *I shall never be moved*. But so as to have your face turn back to me, **29{30}[9]** *Ad te, Domine, clamabo; to you, O Lord, will I cry* with ardent affection, *et ad Deum meum deprecabor, and I will make supplication to my* God, for all things which my soul is in need of. And with merit: for, **29{30}[10]** *Quae utilitas in sanguine meo, what profit is there in my blood*, that is, in my life (for blood is the seat of the soul,[45] by which life is caused), *dum descendo in corruptionem, while I go down to corruption*, that is, while I die spiritually, and I perish in soul? It is as if he is saying, "None."[46] Indeed, it would be better not to be than to be without grace, for without grace I have no means to please you. Therefore follows this: *Numquid confitebitur tibi pulvis; shall dust confess to you*, that is, inconstant, proud, and impenitent man: of whom has previously been treated in the first Psalm, that he is *like the dust, which the wind drives from the face of the earth*;[47] *aut annuntiabit veritatem tuam, or declare your truth* such a man, worthily praising or efficaciously admonishing others? Of course not, because *praise is not seemly in the mouth of a sinner*.[48]

29{30}[11] *The Lord has heard, and has had mercy on me: the Lord became my helper.*

Audivit Dominus, et misertus est mei; Dominus factus est adiutor meus.

29{30}[12] *You have turned for me my mourning into joy: you have cut my sackcloth, and have compassed me with gladness.*

Convertisti planctum meum in gaudium mihi; conscidisti saccum meum, et circumdedisti me laetitia.

29{30}[13] *To the end that my glory may sing to you, and I may not regret: O Lord my God, I will give praise to you for ever.*

---

45 E. N. *Sanguis... sedes est animae*: blood is the seat of the soul (or the seat of life). This expression and concept, which comes from Leviticus, is significant theologically in terms of the theology of sacrifice. It also drives many of the Jewish dietary restrictions concerning blood. Lev. 17:11: *anima carnis in sanguine est* (the life of the flesh is in the blood) and Lev. 17:14: *anima enim omnis carnis in sanguine est* (for the life of all flesh is in the blood).
46 E. N. In other words, it is a negative rhetorical question, suggesting a negative answer.
47 Ps. 1:4. See Article VIII (Psalm 1:4) in Volume 1.
48 Ecclus. 15:9.

Ut cantet tibi gloria mea, et non compungar. Domine Deus meus, in aeternum confitebor tibi.

29{30}[11] *Audivit Dominus,* the Lord has heard that, which I said so as to summon and rouse his most visceral mercy,[49] *et misertus est mei, and has had mercy on me,* delivering me from many miseries. *Dominus factus est adiutor meus,* the Lord became my helper, working in me by his grace. **29{30}[12]** *Convertisti, you have turned,* O Lord, *planctum meum in guadium mihi, for me my mourning into joy,* that is, following the pains of sin, from the hope of pardon you poured upon me the grace of consolation. In the manner the Prophet [Habakkuk] said: *when you are angry, you will remember mercy.*[50] And another [prophet Baruch]: *My children, suffer patiently the wrath that is come upon you.*[51] *For he that has brought evils upon you, shall bring you everlasting joy again with your salvation.*[52] *Conscidisti saccum meum, you have cut my sackcloth,* that is, with the labors of penitence — namely, abstinence, vigils, the discipline[53] — you mortified and afflicted my body, *et circumdedisti me laetitia, and have compassed me with gladness,* that is, you have filled my soul after these aforementioned labors with spiritual exultation. For they who afflict themselves worthily with penitential labors are made deserving to be refreshed with all manner of divine consolation, in the manner that the Apostle [Paul] said: *Now all chastisement for the present indeed seems not to bring with it joy, but sorrow: but afterwards it will yield, to them that are exercised by it, the most peaceable fruit of justice.*[54] But also *you have compassed me with gladness* lest I glory in myself; and **29{30}[13]**

---

49 E. N. *viscera misericordiae suae,* literally the viscera, the innards or bowels, of his mercy. By this term, *viscera misericordiae* is understood the "visceral, intimate, and diffusive mercy from the bottom of the heart and depths of the person (*sinu fundo*) of our God, who pitying our most great misery, so as to render aid, gave his viscera, that is, his only-begotten Son, in the Incarnation, and which he pours out upon us." "Understood in an anthropological way (*anthropopathos*), therefore, 'viscera' signifies the intimate and highest mercy of God: because so often in times of great compassion the interior customarily is moved, so also because the viscera of the Father is the Son, God the Father gave to us him whom was begotten as it were his viscera." R. P. Coernelii a Lapide, *Commentaria Scripturam Sacram* (Paris: Bibliopolam Editorem 1891), Vol. 16, No. 78, p. 48 (interpreting Luke 1:78).
50 Hab. 3:2b.
51 Baruch 4:25a.
52 Baruch 4:29. Denis has *laetitiam* instead of the Vulgate's *iucunditatem*. Both words expressive of joy; thus there is no significant change in meaning.
53 E. N. The discipline was a small scourge or whip used by some monastic communities to mortify the flesh.
54 Heb. 12:11.

ut cantet tibi gloria mea, to the end that my glory may sing to you, that is, so that all grace, and all glory, and anything good that is in me, be for me the occasion and the matter for praising you, and rendering thanks to your most high name, *et non compungar*, *and I may not regret*, that is, I may not be troubled with an evil conscience, but may be conscious of nothing [evil] in me, and that nothing may be left in my soul in which a Christian mind might with good cause suffer remorse.

Finally, a holy man and one thankful to the Lord offers himself ready for this, that he might sing to the Lord his glory, and say: *Domine Deus meus, in aeternum confitebor tibi; O Lord my God, I will give praise to you forever*, that is, as long as I can: and this is the word of good hope and the holy undertaking, not one bursting forth from an abundance of presumption, as said above, *I shall never be moved*. But I will praise you forever, because the contemplative life, which attends to the confession of divine praise, begins here, and in the future perseveres, as we know from Revelation: *And they rested not day and night, saying holy, holy, holy, Lord God Almighty.*[55]

ARTICLE LXVI

ANAGOGICAL EXPOSITION OF THE SAME TWENTY-NINTH PSALM.

29{30}[1] *A Psalm of a canticle, at the dedication of David's house.*
Psalmus canti, in dedicatione domus David.

Finally, anagogically, by *David's house* we are to understand any one of the blessed, in whom God dwells in general by consummated grace,[56] perfect charity, and immediate union. And by *dedication* of this house we can understand the assumption of the elect to beatific fruition. According its anagogical meaning, therefore, we understand the sense of the title to be: **29{30}[1]** *Psalmus cantici*, *a Psalm of a canticle*, that is, of an ineffable and celestial joy, *in dedication domus David*, *at the dedication of David's house*, that is, for the assumption of the elect to glory.

29{30}[2] *I will extol you, O Lord, for you have upheld me: and have not made my enemies to rejoice over me.*

---

55   Rev. 4:8b.
56   E. N. Just like grace is inchoate glory, so is glory consummated grace (*gratia consummata*). *Gratia consummata est lumen gloriae.* ST IaIIae, q. III, art. 3, ad 2.

> *Exaltabo te, Domine, quoniam suscepisti me, nec delectasti inimicos meos super me.*

Any person enjoying the beatific vision in heaven (*comprehensor in patria*) says: **29{30}[2]** *Exaltabo te, Domine, I will extol you, O Lord*, who are the object and the cause and the fountain of all heavenly joy, *quoniam suscepisti me, for you have upheld me* an heir and son in eternal joy; *nec delectasti inimicos meos, and have not made my enemies to rejoice*, namely, the demons, *super me, over me*: who rejoiced over me at that time when in the world I lived unjustly, and when I was afflicted in Purgatory; but now they are sorrowful because I am free of fault and punishment[57] and located in heaven. More, the holy angels and the souls of the innocent,[58] and they who never sinned—like Christ and the blessed Virgin—say: *you have not made my enemies to rejoice over me*, for you never permitted me to be stained with vice. For even demons, since they are most envious, sorrow of the permanence and happiness of the holy angels. But these holy angels, as a result of being affixed to the good,[59] give thanks back to God and say: *I will extol you, O Lord, for you have upheld me, and have not made my enemies to rejoice over me.*

29{30}[3] O Lord my God, I have cried to you, and you have healed me.

Domine Deus meus, clamavi ad te, et sanasti me.

29{30}[4] You have brought forth, O Lord, my soul from hell: you have saved me from them that go down into the pit.

Domine, eduxisti ab inferno animam meam; salvasti me a descendentibus in lacum.

29{30}[3] *Domine Deus meus, clamavi ad te; Lord my God, I have cried to you*, while I was in the world or in Purgatory, *et sanasti me, and you have healed me* from all torment. For the souls existing in Purgatory know themselves to be delivered, and they most vehemently desire to be delivered; indeed the delay of glory is to them thus penal in nature, and no sensible punishment in this world is able to equal the punishment

---

57 For the difference between fault (*culpa*) and punishment (*poena*), see footnote 21-146.

58 E. N. By the "souls of the innocent" (*animae innocentium*), Denis appears to be referring to those baptized (and so free of original sin) and who died without committing an actual sin (such as a baptized child who died before he reached the age of reason).

59 E. N. The will of the good angels is confirmed in good; accordingly, they are "affixed to the good." See ST Ia, q.64, art, 2, co.

that they have because of the delay of glory.⁶⁰ For already their wayfaring state is over, and therefore they are not delayed from the heavenly homeland without [suffering] a most bitter pain. And this desire of theirs is called a cry. However, they make no progress in crying, and they are no longer able to merit, nor are they able to help themselves.⁶¹ But when they arrive to the heavenly homeland they will rejoice in the leaving behind of punishment, and they say: *Lord my God, I have cried to you,* by myself, and by those who prayed for me.⁶² Thence the men already saved say: **29{30}[4]** *Domine, eduxisti ab inferno anima meam; You have brought forth, O Lord, my soul from hell,* because you did not allow me to die in mortal sin, for which the blessed in heaven are ineffably thankful to the Lord; *salvasti me a descedentibus in lacum, you have saved me from them that go down into the pit,* that is, you have raised me up from those forsaken and damned, and you have beatified me.

29{30}[5] *Sing to the Lord, O you his saints: and give praise to the memory of his holiness.*

Psallite Domino, sancti eius; et confitemini memoriae sanctitatis eius.

29{30}[6] *For wrath is in his indignation; and life in his good will. In the evening weeping shall have place, and in the morning gladness.*

Quoniam ira in indignatione eius, et vita in voluntate eius ad vesperum demorabitur fletus, et ad matutinum laetitia.

Therefore, the blessed in heaven (*comprehensors*) exhort one another to the giving thanks and divine praise, saying: **29{30}[5]** *Psallite Domine,*

---

60   Those in Purgatory suffer a pain of sense (*poena sensus*) and a pain of loss (*poena damni*), the latter of which is the result of being delayed the beatific vision and of which Denis here speaks. Though both punishments exceed those of this life, the pain of loss exceeds the pain of sense. See ST IIIa Supp. App., q. 1, art. 2, co.
61   "Although the souls in purgation perform supernatural acts, they cannot merit because they are no longer in the state of wayfarers, nor can they increase in supernatural charity. By the same token, they cannot make satisfaction, which is the free acceptance of suffering as compensation for injury, accepted by God on account of the dignity of the one satisfying. The sufferings in purgatory are imposed on the departed, without leaving them the option of 'free acceptance' such as they had in mortal life. They can only make 'satis-passion' for their sins, by patiently suffering the demand of God's justice." See John A. Hardon, S. J. *The Catholic Faith* (San Francisco: Ignatius Press 2001), 5–11.
62   The souls in Purgatory rely on the prayers of others. DS 1398, 1405. The faithful can offer Mass, prayers, alms, and other indulgenced works of piety on their behalf.

sancti eius, et confitemini memoriae sanctitatis eius; Sing to the Lord, O you his saints, and give praise to the memory of his holiness, **29{30}[6]** *quoniam ira,* for wrath, that is, the vengeance of the punishment which we have suffered on account of our faults, was *in indignatione eius,* in his indignation, that is, out of the zeal of divine justice, which does not leave any of the evil unpunished. Or [it can mean], that this word is fittingly said by all the blessed, and so it is explained thus: *for wrath*, that is, the damnation of the reprobate, is *in his indignation*, that is, arises from the offense of God and the contempt with which they were disdainful to God: whence they are not able to be corrected, they will not be penitent, just like Solomon said: *Consider the works of God, that no man can correct whom he has despised.*[63] *Et vita,* and life, that is, our happiness which is eternal life, is *in voluntate eius,* in his good will, that is, it is dispensed at the pleasure of the divine will and out of love. *Ad vesperum,* In the evening, that is, in the external prison house of the infernal darkness, *demorabitur, shall have a place,* that is, will remain forever, *fletus, weeping*: as Christ asserts in the Gospel, At that place *there will be weeping and the gnashing of teeth*;[64] *et ad matutinum,* and in the morning, that is, in the Kingdom of Heaven, where the divine light inaccessible rises, there will stand *gladness,* because there is full and perpetual joy.

29{30}[7] And in my abundance I said: I shall never be moved.

Ego autem dixi in abundantia mea: Non movebor in aeternum.

29{30}[8] O Lord, in your favor, you gave strength to my beauty. You turned away your face from me, and I became troubled.

Domine, in voluntate tua praestitisti decori meo virtutem; avertisti faciem tuam a me, et factus sum conturbatus.

29{30}[9] To you, O Lord, will I cry: and I will make supplication to my God.

Ad te, Domine, clamabo, et ad Deum meum deprecabor.

29{30}[10] What profit is there in my blood, while I go down to corruption? Shall dust confess to you, or declare your truth?

Quae utilitas in sanguine meo, dum descendo in corruptionem? Numquid confitebitur tibi pulvis, aut annuntiabit veritatem tuam?

---

63   Eccl. 7:14.
64   Matt. 8:12; 13:42, 50; 22:13; 24:41; 25:30; Luke 13:28.

29{30}[7] *Ego autem, and I,* who am one of the blessed in heaven, *dixi in abundantia mea, said in my abundance,* that is, in the full joy of my security: *Non movebor in aeternum, I shall never be moved,* that is, never will I depart from God. For all the blessed know they are confirmed in the good, and so they securely affirm, *I shall never be moved.* **29{30}[8]** *Domine, in voluntate tua . . . decori meo; O Lord in your favor, to my beauty,* that is, to my beatitude, which is the highest ornament of the mind, *praestisti . . . virtutem, you gave strength,* that is, the secure stability or confirmation in you. *Avertisti faciem tuam a me, you turned away your face from me,* when I still was wayfaring in the world, *et factus sum conturbatus, and I became troubled* during such a time; but now you have shown your face to me, and therefore I am saved. **29{30}[9]** *Ad te, Domine, clamabo, to you, O Lord, will I cry,* praying for my friends and my family, and those who have implored my prayers; *et ad Deum meum deprecabor, and I will make supplication to my God* for the resuscitation of my body. For the saints in heaven desire the future resurrection. **29{30}[10]** *Quae utilitas in sanguine meo, What profit is there in my blood,* that is, what is it to me, what use to me is the body, which is to cooperate with my soul in the divine service, *dum descendo in corruptionem, when I go down to corruption,* that is, if that body were to remain corrupt, and not rise again? For sometimes something is attributed to the whole by reason of a part, in the manner that Christ is said to have lain in the sepulcher, and Mary Magdalen, believing the body stolen, said: *They have taken away my Lord; and we do not know where they have laid him.*[65] In a similar manner, the blessed [soul] in heaven by reason of the body which he has left on earth, says, *when I go down to corruption.*[66]

---

65 John 20:13b. E. N. Denis has "we do not know" (*nescimus*) of John 20:2, instead of "I do not know" (*nescio*) as indicated in the margins by the Latin editor.

66 E. N. In explaining Ps. 29:10, Denis argues from Scripture's use of synecdoche, where a part is used to refer to the whole. Denis explains this feature in Article IV in Volume 1 as being the fifth rule of Tyconius. The example he gives is that Jesus is said to be in the tomb three days, though it was not three full days, but two partial days and a full day. However, the parts are taken for the whole, and so saying "three days" (synecdochally understood) is accurate. Similarly, Mary Magdalene says to the Apostles Peter and Paul (John 20:2), "we know not (*nescimus*) where they have laid him," but also says to the two angels at the tomb (John 20:13), "I know not (*nescio*) where they have laid him." In John 20:13, Mary has spoken synecdochally, referring to herself for all those with her. *Cf.* Matt. 28:1 (the other Mary); Mark 16:1 (Mary, mother of James, and Salome); Luke 23:55 (women). In a sort of reverse synecdoche, what is happening to a part (the body in corruption) is being referred to the person (the beatified soul).

29{30}[11] *The Lord has heard, and has had mercy on me: the Lord became my helper.*

Audivit Dominus, et misertus est mei; Dominus factus est adiutor meus.

29{30}[12] *You have turned for me my mourning into joy: you have cut my sackcloth, and have compassed me with gladness.*

Convertisti planctum meum in gaudium mihi; conscidisti saccum meum, et circumdedisti me laetitia.

29{30}[13] *To the end that my glory may sing to you, and I may not regret: O Lord my God, I will give praise to you forever.*

Ut cantet tibi gloria mea, et non compungar. Domine Deus meus, in aeternum confitebor tibi.

29{30}[11] *Audivit Dominus*, the Lord has heard these prayers, *et misertus est mei, and has had mercy on me*, not on behalf of myself who am not in a state of misery, but for the misery of those whose salvation I am praying for, and for the resuscitation and glorification of my body. *Dominus factus est adiutor meus, the Lord became my helper*, giving me supernatural virtue by which I will adhere to him invertibly.[67] **29{30}[12]** *Convertisti planctum meum in gaudium mihi, you have turned for me my mourning into joy*, that is, you have changed the tears which I poured out on earth for sins and so as to obtain happiness into a heavenly and eternal joy, in the manner that is written, *Blessed are they that mourn: for they shall be comforted.*[68] Whence in Isaiah Christ says: *The spirit of the Lord is upon me.... to give them a crown for ashes, the oil of joy for mourning, a garment of praise for the spirit of grief.*[69] *Conscidisti saccum meum, you have cut my sackcloth,* that is, you have reduced my body into dust, in the manner that is written, *Dust you are, and into dust you shall return;*[70] *et circumdedisti me laetitia, and you have compassed me with gladness*, that is, you have adorned me with eternal happiness of all kinds; **29{30}[13]** *ut cantet tibi gloria mea, to the end that my glory may*

---

67 *Inavertibiliter*, inavertibly, means so affixed that it cannot be averted, deflected, moved. *The Lexicon Latinatis Nederlandicae Medii Aevi*, IV.F–I (ed. Olga Weijers) (citing Denis) defines this word by the Dutch word *onafwendbaar*, meaning inevitable, ineluctable, unavoidable, inescapable.
68 Matt. 5:5.
69 Is. 1a, 3a.
70 Gen. 3:19.

sing to you, that is, to the end that the blessedness and all the excellence bestowed upon me by you is to me the cause and the reason for praising you with perfect and unceasing praise, *et non compungar, and I may not regret*, that is, at the end of it all I will not be afflicted with any suffering whatsoever, as is stated in Revelation: *God shall wipe away all tears from the eyes of his saints, and death shall be no more, nor mourning, nor crying, nor sorrow shall be any more.*[71] *Domine Deus meus, in aeternum confitebor tibi, O Lord my God, I will give praise to you forever*, that is, I will praise you — the sublime and blessed God — unceasingly, without interruption, fatigue, and tedium.

See how this Psalm — emanating from the treasure of divine wisdom and which is subject to so many expositions — is so succinct, beautiful, and sweet. Let us most devoutly sing it together to the glory of the Creator, in commemoration of his benefits and of the Resurrection and glorification of Christ.

PRAYER

HEAR OUR PRAYERS, O LORD, AND HAVE mercy on us; convert our sorrow into joy and surround us with the happiness of salvation, so that we may sing and give praise to you for all your benefits in the blessed seat of eternity.

Audi, Domine, preces nostras et miserere nobis; converte planctum nostrum in gaudium, et circumda nos laetitia salutis: ut pro universis beneficiis tuis tibi cantemus et confiteamur in beata sede aeternitatis.

---

71 Rev. 7:17; 21:4.

Psalm 30

ARTICLE LXVII

EXPOSITION OF THE THIRTIETH PSALM OF CHRIST: IN TE, DOMINE, SPERAVI, &c. IN YOU, O LORD, HAVE I HOPED, &c.

30{31}[1] *Unto the end, a Psalm for David, in an ecstasy.*

In finem. Psalmus David, pro extasi.

WE HAVE ALREADY WRITTEN ABOUT THE kind of title to this Psalm: **30{31}[1]** *In finem, Psalmus David, pro extasi*; *Unto the end, a Psalm for David, in an ecstasy*: that is, this Psalm is of David, who speaks here in the person of Christ and of the faithful; this Psalm, I say, directing us to our final end, namely, God, is written addressing Christ and his members and in a condition of ecstasy, that is, a going beyond of the mind (*excessu mentis*), which excess occurs either from the fear of great and imminent tribulations, or from the contemplation of sublime trust in divine things. So this Psalm is written about the Passion of Christ and the persecution of the faithful. Whence, it will be expounded first with regard to Christ.

30{31}[2] *In you, O Lord, have I hoped, let me never be confounded: deliver me in your justice.*

In te, Domine, speravi; non confundar in aeternum; in iustitia tua libera me.

Therefore, Christ as man, at the approach of his Passion, said to the Father: **30{31}[2]** *In te Domine, speravi; in you, O Lord, have I hoped*, insofar as man and to a certain degree a wayfarer (*viator*), namely, to the degree the passible nature was not yet glorified. For already it has many times been said how it is fitting for Christ to hope or have hope, that it would give rise to tedium to repeat it again.[1] And so, O Lord Father, not in my created nature, but expectant and confident do I hope in you to redeem the human race cooperating with your power and

---

1 E. N. See for example Articles XIX (Psalm 4:9) and XXXVIII (Psalm 15:9) and footnote 15-31 in Volume 1.

your grace, to rise again, and to defeat all of the evil of the world and of the devil. And so, O Father, *non confundar in aeternum, let me never be confounded*, that is, I will never be confounded with that confusion that arises through some accident that is in him who is confounded, namely from a defect or disorder of nature, fault, or punishment. Or [alternatively]: *Let me never be confounded*: that is, since I was ridiculed and troubled by the Jews during my time in this world before the Passion, during the Passion, and after the Passion, yet let this confusion not last in eternity, but quickly resuscitate me, by miracles also glorify me, and *let them be confounded that persecute me, and let me not be confounded* in the end.² *In iustitia tua, in your justice*, that is, according to the assessment and judgment of your divine justice, *libera me, deliver me* from the passibility of body and the empire of death. Or [we might look at it this way], *in your justice*, that is, according to my justice given to me by you, deliver me.

30{31}[3] *Bow down your ear to me: make haste to deliver me. Be you unto me a God, a protector, and a house of refuge, to save me.*

Inclina ad me aurem tuam; accelera ut eruas me. Esto mihi in Deum protectorem, et in domum refugii, ut salvum me facias.

30{31}[3] *Inclina ad me aurem tuam; bow down your ear to me*, applying to me profusely the effects of your mercy; *accelera ut eruas me, make haste to deliver me*, that is, quickly do that which I ask, and resuscitate me on the third day. *Esto mihi in Deum protectorem; be unto me a God, a protector*: that is, you are to me not only my God in the way that you are the God of all, but be my God as a special object of your care and grace, namely, that you might defend me in all adversity, protecting my body in the sepulcher from corruption, and my name from infamy. This is what the Savior said through Jeremiah: *O Lord, you know, remember me, and visit me, and defend me from them that persecute me.*³ Be unto me also, O Lord, *et in domum refugii, also a house of refuge*, that is, as it were a house of refuge, since in all necessity I seek refuge from you, and I am safe with you. In the way that a man pursued by enemies flees into a fortified house and rests in it in safety, so do I pray also in you to obtain respite, stay steadfast, and remain unafraid. *Ut salvum me facias, to save me* from the passibility of body and bodily death.

---

2 Jer. 17:18a.
3 Jer. 15:15a.

30{31}[4] *For you are my strength and my refuge; and for your name's sake you will lead me and nourish me.*

Quoniam fortitudo mea et refugium meum es tu; et propter nomen tuum deduces me et enutries me.

And this, therefore, I pray, 30{31}[4] *Quoniam firmamentum meum et refugium meum es tu, for you are my strength and my refuge*: that is, other than you I have no other strength, nor [have I any other] refuge; but you are my strength, that is, the cause of all my steadfastness, and the refuge in which—just like the ultimate end—I rest.[4] *Et propter nomen tuum, and for your name's sake*, that is, for you yourself, or for the glorification and the veneration of your name, *deduces me, you lead me* from the Cross into the sepulcher, from the sepulcher to the disciples in the upper room and elsewhere, and from them, even from the Mount of Olives unto the Kingdom of Heaven;[5] *et enutries me, and nourish me*, transferring me from the nutriment (*nutrimento*) of the mortal state, to the subsistence (*alimentum*) of the impassible state, and from earthly food to heavenly food. Or [we can see it in this manner], *you nourish me*, that is, my mystical body, namely the congregation of the faithful, giving them by degrees (*paulatim*) the grace of making progress, and increasing in spiritual virtue.[6] God also nourished

---

4 E. N. Here, Denis makes it clear that the ultimate end of the human nature of Jesus—namely, the beatific vision—he already enjoys even *in statu viae*, as a wayfarer. For Christ is both a wayfarer and a *comprehensor*.

5 E. N. The Mount of Olives is the traditional site of the Lord's Ascension. There is a small chapel or aedicule built there which marks this event. "Christ's Ascension marks the definitive entrance of Jesus' humanity into God's heavenly domain, whence he will come again (*cf.* Acts 1:11); this humanity in the meantime hides him from the eyes of men (*cf.* Col 3:3)." CCC § 665.

6 E. N. Denis realizes that grace perfects and heals nature, but that this process is ordinarily marked by a sort of gradualism. There is then a law of gradualism (*lex gradualitatis*) in the spiritual life. Drawing from various sources, St. Alphonsus describes it thus: "'Not to advance,' says St. Augustine, 'is to go back.' *Non progredi, iam est reverti*. St. Gregory beautifully explains this maxim of spiritual life by comparing a Christian who seeks to remain stationary in the path of virtue to a man who is in a boat on a rapid river, and striving to keep the boat always in the same position. If the boat be not continually propelled against the current, it will be carried away in an opposite direction, and consequently, without continual exertion, its station cannot be maintained." St. Alphonsus Liguori, *The True Spouse of Jesus Christ* (Vol. 1), *The Complete Works: Ascetical Works*, Vol. 10 (New York: Benziger Brothers 1888), 182. (ed. Rev. Eugene Grimm). The law of gradualism (*lex gradualitatis*) should be sharply distinguished from a gradualism of the law (*gradualitas legis*). See Familiaris Consortio, No. 34; *see also* John Paul II, Homily of October 25, 1980 at the Close of the Sixth Synod of Bishops, No. 8: "And so what is known as 'the law of gradualness' or step-by-step advance cannot be identified with 'gradualness of the law,' as if there were different

the early Church, because from day to day he increased the faithful both in merit and in number, as Luke testifies to in the Acts of the Apostles: *The word of the Lord,* he says, *increased,*[7] and comforting them strongly, *the Lord increased daily together such as should be saved.*[8]

> 30{31}[5] *You will bring me out of this snare, which they have hidden for me: for you are my protector.*
>
> *Educes me de laqueo hoc quem absconderunt mihi, quoniam tu es protector meus.*
>
> 30{31}[6] *Into your hands I commend my spirit: you have redeemed me, O Lord, the God of truth.*
>
> *In manus tuas commendo spiritum meum; redemisti me, Domine Deus veritatis.*

30{31}[5] *Educes me de laqueo hoc, you will bring me out of this snare,* that is, from the danger of death, *quem, which* snare *absconderunt mihi, they have hidden from me,* that is, which the Jews considered to contrive secretly amongst themselves for me not to know of their wickedness. For the Jews supposed Christ was ignorant of their endeavors against him. Therefore, you will bring me out of this snare, *quoniam tu es protector meus, for you are my protector,* as I just a short moment ago prayed, saying, *Be you unto me a God, a protector.* And because he absolutely is exactly this [a protecting God], therefore I, Christ, hanging on the Cross say to you,[9] O Father: **30{31}[6]** *In manus tuas, into your hands,* that is, into your power and your charity, *commendo spiritum meum, I commend my spirit,* that is, my soul with the excellence of the action of grace so that you quickly reunify it with the body; *redemisti me, you have redeemed me* from all punishment in this separation of my soul from the body, *Domine, Deus veritatis; O Lord, the God of truth,* that is, the cause, measure, and preserver of all created truth. For the death of Christ was the end of his misery and the beginning of his happiness or glorification in the body. In offering the beginning of this verse, namely, *Into your hands I commend my spirit,* good men, who truly are members of Christ, cheerfully are accustomed to imitate their Head, namely Christ: so that they say when death nears, *Into your hands I commend my spirit.* And

---

degrees or forms of precept in God's law for different individuals and situations."
7   Acts. 6:7a; 12:24.
8   Act. 2:47b. Denis changes the verb *augebat* (imperfect tense) to *auxit* (perfect tense).
9   Luke 23:46.

would, O Lord Jesus, that you would deign to confer such a life to me, so that, at the hour of my death, I may bring forward these most sweet words, worthily, faithfully, and with utmost affection.

30{31}[7] *You have hated them that regard vanities, to no purpose. But I have hoped in the Lord.*

Odisti observantes vanitates supervacue; ego autem in Domino speravi.

30{31}[8] *I will be glad and rejoice in your mercy. For you have regarded my humility, you have saved my soul out of distresses.*

Exsultabo, et laetabor in misericordia tua, quoniam respexisti humilitatem meam; salvasti de necessitatibus animam meam.

30{31}[9] *And you have not shut me up in the hands of the enemy: you have set my feet in a spacious place.*

Nec conclusisti me in manibus inimici; statuisti in loco spatioso pedes meos.

30{31}[7] *Odisti*, you have hated, O Lord, *observantes vanitates*, those that regard vanities, that is, sinners following vain things, *supervacue*, to no purpose, that is, uselessly. But the manner in which God is said to have hate for sinners, though he hates nothing that he has made,[10] is stated in the exposition of the fifth Psalm, in which is said: *You hate all the workers of iniquity*.[11] *Ego autem in Domino speravi*, but I have hoped in the Lord, and not in myself, such as those who observe vanities, of which Micah says, *Woe to you that devise that which is unprofitable, and work evil in your beds*.[12] Therefore, O Lord Father, 30{31}[8] *exultabo*, I will be glad in a public way, *et laetabor*, and I will rejoice in an internal way, *in misericordia tua*, in your mercy, that is, contemplating your mercy, or receiving its effects. Christ was glad and rejoiced in this way in the day of the Resurrection.

Quoniam respexisti, for you have regarded with your eyes of paternal love and of kindly assistance, *humilitatem meam*, my humility, that is me, your Son meek and humble; *salvasti de necessitatibus animam meam*, you have saved my soul out of distresses: that is, you delivered me from the punishments verified by the Scriptures of the Prophets which were necessary for me to suffer by the blessed Resurrection. 30{31}[9] *Nec conclusisti me*

---

10 Wisdom 11:25: *For you love all things that are and hate none of the things which you have made: for you did not appoint, or make anything hating it.*
11 Ps. 5:7. See Article XX (Psalm 5:7) in Volume 1.
12 Micah 2:1a.

in manibus inimici, and you have not shut me up in the hands of the enemy, that is, you have not permitted me to be permanently held or detained in the punishments and reproaches which were brought against me by my adversaries. Or [one can understand it] thus: you have not imprisoned me in the hands of my enemies, that is, you have not permitted me to be overcome and oppressed by my enemies, but I was able to overcome and overwhelm them. Therefore, it continues: *statuisti, you have set,* that is, on the day of the Ascension, *in loco spatioso, in a spacious space,* that is, in the Kingdom of God, *pedes meos, my feet,* that is, placing me at your right in the throne of your majesty. This is what the Savior said in Revelation: *To him that shall overcome, I will give to sit with me in my throne: as I also have overcome, and am set down with my Father in his throne.*[13] Or [alternatively] this: *You have set in a spacious space,* that is, in the entirety of the universe, *my feet,* that is, my operative power (*virtutem operativam*), in the manner that the Gospel of Matthew says, *All power is given to me in heaven and in earth.*[14] Or [also] thus: *You have set me in a spacious space,* that is, breadth of charity, which neither knows how to be narrow or to be short, *my feet,* that is, my deeds and my desires. For Christ unceasingly shows charity toward us, and he charitably *makes intercession for us.*[15] Or [again in this manner]: *You have set me in a spacious space,* that is, you have sent, dispersed, and placed *my feet,* that is, the Apostles and all those devoted preachers who are the columns, the base, and the feet of the Church.

30{31}[10] *Have mercy on me, O Lord, for I am afflicted: my eye is troubled with wrath, my soul, and my belly.*

Miserere mei, Domine, quoniam tribulor; conturbatus est in ira oculus meus, anima mea, et venter meus.

30{31}[11] *For my life is wasted with grief: and my years in sighs. My strength is weakened through poverty and my bones are disturbed.*

Quoniam defecit in dolore vita mea, et anni mei in gemitibus. Infirmata est in paupertate virtus mea; et ossa mea conturbata sunt.

30{31}[10] *Miserere me, Domine;* have mercy on me, O Lord, delivering me in the Resurrection from this misery, by which I was crucified and

---

13 Rev. 3:21.
14 Matt. 28:18. E. N. An operative virtue or operative power (*virtus operativa*) is one relating to the will (dominion) as distinguished from an intellectual or speculative virtue. This power or virtue relates to the rule of justice.
15 Rom. 8:34b.

was killed for men, *quoniam tribulor, for I am afflicted* in the Passion by various punishments; *conturbatus est in ira oculus meus, anima mea et venter meus; my eye is troubled with wrath, my soul, and my belly*. It must be pondered how this fittingly pertains to Christ. For in him there was no inordinate wrath, nor did the Passion in any way impede or becloud his intellect in his acts (which are here designated by the word "eye"). Therefore it is [to be understood] in this sense: *For I am afflicted* with the affliction of those who suffer punishment, not with the affliction of those who suffer fault, *with wrath*, that is, on account of wrath and the effect of wrath, namely the persecution of my enemies, of the Jews, *my eye*, that is, my reason or the consideration of the intellectual virtues (*virtutis cogitativae*). For as has already been made clear, during the time of the Passion the intellect and the will of Christ suffered inasmuch as they were natural powers of the humanity of Christ which endured so great pain. We can also understand by *eye* the bodily eye of Christ because during the Passion, during the most violent punishments of Christ, his bodily eyes were blindfolded, wept, and also turned downward.[16] 30{31}
[11] *Quoniam defecit in dolore vita mea, for my life is wasted with grief*, that is, because of the bitterness of the punishments, my bodily life was ended upon the Cross, *et anni mei in gemitibus, and my years in sighs*: that is, the whole span of my life in the world from the Nativity even unto the Passion was so filled with adversity and compassion toward neighbor, that from the little exultation and prosperity [it enjoyed], it seemed as if wanting. For Christ always chose that which was a greater burden for the flesh, in order that we might imitate his path.[17]

Infirmata est in paupertate virtus mea, my strength is weakened through poverty: that is, my omnipotence or my divine power is weakened, that is, is made apparently alike to, and considered to be similar to the power

---

16   E. N. Upon the Cross, Jesus would have had to look downwards to the Roman soldiers, those mocking him, and to the suffering of his Mother, the Blessed Virgin Mary, and the Apostle John. Similarly, upon his death, his eyes would have been forced shut.
17   E. N. St. John of the Cross quite masterfully expounded upon this sentiment in his *The Ascent of Mount Carmel*: "Endeavor to be inclined always: not to the easiest, but to the most difficult; not to the most delightful, but to the harshest; not to the most gratifying, but to the less pleasant; not to what means rest for you, but to hard work; not to the consoling, but to the unconsoling; not to the most, but to the least; not to the highest and most precious, but to the lowest and most despised; not to wanting something, but to wanting nothing; do not go about looking for the best of temporal things, but for the worst, and desire to enter for [the love of] Christ into complete nudity, emptiness, and poverty in everything in the world." (trans., Kieran Kavanaugh and Otilio Rodriguez, O. C. D.) St. John of the Cross: *The Collected Works of St. John of the Cross* (Washington, D. C.: ICS Publications 2017), 149.

of, one who is weak and frail, because he suspended his action and the nature which he assumed, in the way that he was forsaken in poverty, that is, during the time of my most abject death. Or [we could look at it this way], Christ from the vantage point of the assumed nature thus says: *weakened*, that is, subject to various natural weaknesses and defects that do not detract or derogate from his perfection (*indetrahibilibus*),[18] *my strength*, that is, the person of the Word who is the strength and wisdom of the Father and is also the strength of my supported and preserved assumed nature. This *strength* is *weak* and in a condition of *poverty*, that is, in the assumed humanity, so that those things predicated of [the Word] are fittingly said of it by reason of the assumed nature, even though according to its proper nature it is impassible.[19] For of the person of the Word or the Son of God, indeed of the true and unchanging God,[20] it is truly affirmed that it became incarnate, and thus capable of suffering and dying, and, as a consequence, weakened. But in Christ divine things are fittingly said to the man, and human things to God; and this was necessary to look closely at because of what was said.[21] *Et ossa mea conturbata sunt, and my bones are disturbed*, that is, my flesh and all of my bodily nature are weakened with sorrow on account of the distress of my afflictions. As was said in an earlier Psalm: *I am poured out like*

---

18 E. N. The word *indetrahibilis* means that which does not detract from, or derogate, from perfection. Lexicon Latinatis Nederlandicae Medii Aevi, IV.F–I (ed. Olga Weijers) (s.v. "*indetrabibilis*") defines this word (citing Denis) as *die aan de volmaaktheid geen afbreuk doet*.

19 E. N. Denis is saying that the suffering of the assumed human nature of Christ is fittingly predicated of the person who has assumed that humanity (the Word) even though that person also has a nature that is impassible. This is a reference to the "communication of idioms" (*communicatio idiomatum*) which governs the manner in which the properties of the Divine Word can be ascribed to the man Jesus, and the properties of the man Jesus can be predicated of the person of the Word; that is, it governs how there can be an "exchange of predicates." *See, e.g.*, Paul Gondreau, "St. Thomas Aquinas, the Communication of Idioms, and the Suffering of Christ in the Garden of Gethsemane," *Divine Impassibility and the Mystery of Human Suffering* (Grand Rapids: William B. Eerdmans 2009) 214–45 (eds., James F. Keating and Thomas Joseph White, O. P.). Thus, one can say that "God suffered [in his human nature]" and that "Christ was eternal [in his divine nature]." But it is error to predicate something of one nature to the other nature. Thus it is false to say that God suffered in his divine nature, or that Christ was eternal in his human nature.

20 E. N. In saying that the Word is *de vero et incommutabili Deo*, "from the true and unchanging God," Denis appears to be harkening to the Creed: *Deum verum de Deo vero*, "true God from true God."

21 E. N. Denis is justifying his theological excursus based upon the Psalm (interpreted of Christ) of suggesting weakness in the Word, which required the matter of the communication of idioms to be discussed.

*water; and all my bones are scattered.*²² Finally, that which is said — *my strength is weakened through poverty* — can be explained as relating to the bodily, human, and natural strength and fortitude of Christ according to the understanding of what was said in the earlier Psalm, *My strength is dried up like a potsherd.*²³

30{31}[12] I am become a reproach among all my enemies, and very much to my neighbors; and a fear to my acquaintance. They that saw me without fled from me.

Super omnes inimicos meos factus sum opprobrium, et vicinis meis valde, et timor notis meis; qui videbant me foras fugerunt a me.

30{31}[13] I am forgotten as one dead from the heart. I am become as a vessel that is destroyed.

Oblivioni datus sum, tamquam mortuus a corde. Factus sum tamquam vas perditum.

30{31}[14] For I have heard the blame of many that dwell round about. While they assembled together against me, they consulted to take away my life.

Quoniam audivi vituperationem multorum commorantium in circuitu. In eo dum convenirent simul adversum me, accipere animam meam consiliati sunt.

30{31}[12] *Super omnes inimicos meos*, among all my enemies, that is, among those of my adversaries, *factus sum opprobrium*, I am become a reproach, that is, contemptuous and reviled, *vicinis meis*, to my neighbors, that is, those who at one time followed me and praised my works when they seemed to belong to me. These became *a reproach [valde, strongly]*,²⁴ especially in the Passion, when some of them followed the instructions of the leaders of the priests and cried out before Pilate: Release *not this man, but Barabbas.*²⁵ Also I was made to be *timor notis meis*, *a fear to my acquaintance*, that is, the cause of fear to them who adhered to me familiarly, namely the Apostles and the other disciples, who out of fear fled from me,²⁶ and after the Passion sat in a closed room because of

---

22 Ps. 21:15a.
23 Ps. 21:16a.
24 E. N. This is in brackets in the Latin text, apparently added by the editors.
25 John 13:40.
26 Matt. 26:25.

fear of the Jews. *Qui videbant me foras fugerunt a me, they that saw me without fled from me*: that is, I suffered, was manhandled, and appeared so horribly and miserably that men acted detestably towards me merely by looking at me, and were repelled by me. **30{31}[13]** *Oblivioni datus sum, tanquam mortuus a corde; I am forgotten as one dead from the heart*: that is, the moment I was buried, the unfaithful Jews forgot about me, not strictly speaking (*simpliciter*), because they saw fit to guard the sepulcher, but to this extent: *I am forgotten* since they did not care about me, nor did they regard me as one who might be able to rise again from the dead, but in addition assessed me as being among the damned and the reprobate. In this way even to this day *I am forgotten* in the hearts of the Jews, again I am not strictly speaking forgotten by them, for daily they blaspheme my name and pray for the destruction of the [Holy] Roman Empire and the extinction of the Christian name.[27]

Factus sum tanquam vas perditum, I am become as a vessel that is destroyed: that is, I am held in such contempt by the Jews, as if I had been of absolutely no use, and had contained no good of any kind in me, but had been nothing but full of lies and blasphemies. For the reprobate are called destroyed vessels, because they are empty of grace, and they contain no supernatural merit; but the elect are called vessels of happiness, as Christ said of Paul, *This man*, he said, *is to me a vessel of election*.[28] Therefore, I, Christ, declare myself as having become *a vessel that is* destroyed, **30{31}[14]** *quoniam audivi vituperationem multorum commorantium in circuitu, for I have heard the blame of many that dwell round about*. For during the Days of Unleavened Bread,[29] all the people of the Jews dwelling around Jerusalem flowed into the city of Jerusalem, and nearly all of these, being reproachful of him, consented to the death of Christ. *In eo, in that* time *dum convenirent simul adversum me, while assembled together against me*, namely, in the day of Passover, *accipere animam meam consiliati sunt, they consulted to take away my life*, that is, they consulted to kill my bodily life. For before Pilate they cried out: *Away with him; away with him; crucify him*.[30]

---

27 E. N. This is perhaps a reference to the *birkat haminim* a prayer that allegedly took aim at, and prayed for, the destruction of the Holy Roman Empire and Christians who were labeled as heretic (*minim*). See Ruth Langer, *Cursing the Christians? A History of the Birkat Haminim* (Oxford: Oxford University Press 2012), 104.
28 Acts 9:15a.
29 E. N. Literally *diebus azymorum*, the days of the Azymes, derived from the Ancient Greek word ἄζυμος ἄρτος (*azymos artos*) which means "unleavened," and is a reference to the Passover feast.
30 John 19:15a.

30{31}[15] *But I have put my trust in you, O Lord: I said: You are my God.*

Ego autem in te speravi, Domine; dixi: Deus meus es tu.

30{31}[16] *My lots are in your hands. Deliver me out of the hands of my enemies; and from them that persecute me.*

In manibus tuis sortes meae: eripe me de manu inimicorum meorum, et a persequentibus me.

30{31}[17] *Make your face to shine upon your servant; save me in your mercy.*

Illustra faciem tuam super servum tuum; salvum me fac in misericordia tua.

30{31}[15] *Ego autem in te speravi, Domine; but I have put my trust in you, O Lord*: as it was stated and expounded upon at the beginning of this Psalm. *Dixi: Deus meus est tu; I said: You are my God*, that is, I have confessed you before men, and I have worshiped you in truth, and for that reason I am accused falsely and am unjustly condemned; 30{31}[16] *in manibus tuis, in your hands*, that is, in your strength and at your disposition, are *sortes meae, my lots*, that is my lot [in life] or my portion of time [given me to live]. It is as if he were saying: "Whatever befalls me is in the power of your disposition, and you are able to deliver me from it; for nothing whatsoever befalls me unless it be in accordance under the guidance of your reason. For this reason, I patiently endure all things, knowing that you would not permit it without a great reason."

Eripe me, deliver me, by the blessed and a hastened Resurrection, *de manu inimicorum meorum, out of the hands of my enemies*, that is, from the power of the Jews crucifying me, *et a persequentibus me, and from them that persecute me*, that is, protect my Mystical Body from its persecutors. Whence to Paul still furiously raging, Christ said: *Saul, Saul, why do you persecute me?*[31] Christ therefore prays this for the Church, for that which is inflicted upon their faithful, he testifies, is inflicted upon him.[32] 30{31}[17] *Illustra faciem tuam super servum tuum, make your face to shine upon your servant.* Christ from the beginning was full of wisdom and was a perfect *comprehensor*, and so he does not now pray for the illumination of his mind. And what else then can he mean when he says, *Make your face to shine upon your servant* other than what he said

---

31 Acts 9:4b.
32 Matt. 25:40: *Amen I say to you, as long as you did it to one of these my least brethren, you did it to me.*

elsewhere, *Glorify you me, O Father, with yourself, with the glory which I had, before the world was, with you?*³³ Christ therefore prays that the divine light might adorn his body with glorious brightness, and that he might reveal to men his glory. *Salvum me fac, save me* from bodily death and punishments, *in misericordia tua, in your mercy*, that is, because of you yourself, and the goodness of your name. Although Christ most justly deserved to rise again on the third day, still he is able both to seek to be heard from the Father on account of his divine goodness as well as his human justice. In this he provides to us an example, since however much we have advanced or have been righteous, we must always take confidence principally in the mercy of God.

30{31}[18] *Let me not be confounded, O Lord, for I have called upon you. Let the wicked be ashamed, and be brought down to hell.*

Domine, non confundar, quoniam invocavi te. Erubescant impii, et deducantur in infernum.

30{31}[19] *Let deceitful lips be made dumb. Which speak iniquity against the just, with pride and abuse.*

Muta fiant labia dolosa, quae loquuntur adversus iustum iniquitatem, in superbia, et in abusione.

30{31}[18] *Domine, non confundar; Let me not be confounded, O Lord*, that is, let me not be found to be saying false things in asserting that I would rise against on the third day, *quoniam invocavi te, for I have called upon you*, that is, with internal and affectionate prayers I seek to avoid this thing by pleading to you. And so, I will not be confounded, but better *erubescant impii, let the wicked be ashamed*, that is, the blaspheming Jews, *deducantur in infernum, be brought down to hell*, damned for eternity. This Christ says, either predicting what the future would be, or in conforming himself to the divine justice, or explaining that which the reprobate deserve.³⁴ 30{31}[19] *Muta fiant labia dolos, let deceitful lips be made dumb*: that is, let the mouths of the Jews, who tested me

---

33 John 17:5. E. N. Christ is not praying here for intellectual enlightenment or for the future beatific vision (since he has had the beatific vision from the first moment of his existence as man), but for the accidental glory of his resurrection and the glorification of his body.
34 E. N. In other words, Christ is here praying not willing that the wicked go to hell (optatively), but in a hortatory, predictive, or prophetic sense not inconsistent with his will that all men be saved, though he knows — to his great sorrow — that all men will in fact not be saved. 1 Tim. 2:4. *See* footnote 24-14 in Volume 1.

with such a painful death, be made weak and closed up, and may the shrewd be captured by their own shrewdness; *quae loquuntur adversus iustum iniquitatem, which speak iniquity against the just,* that is, which [by their accusations] heaped sins upon me, the Saint of Saints, and the just Son of God, *in superbia, with pride,* by which they rejected me and vilified me, *et in abusione, and in abuse,* by which they have abused my good works, ascribing all my works and miracles to devils, and labeling my teaching as a sort of seduction: and by this they are abusive to my goods, for where they ought to have become better, there they in effect became worse. This is what Stephen[35] said to the Jews: *You stiffnecked and uncircumcised in heart and ears, you always resist the Holy Spirit: as your fathers did.... Which of the prophets have not your fathers persecuted? And they have slain them who foretold of the coming of the Just One; of whom you have been now the betrayers and murderers.*[36]

30{31}[20] *O how great is the multitude of your sweetness, O Lord, which you have hidden for them that fear you! Which you have wrought for them that hope in you, in the sight of the sons of men.*

Quam magna multitudo dulcedinis tuae, Domine, quam abscondisti timentibus te! Perfecisti eis qui sperant in te, in conspectu filiorum hominum.

30{31}[21] *You shall hide them in the secret of your face, from the disturbance of men. You shall protect them in your tabernacle from the contradiction of tongues.*

Abscondes eos in abscondito faciei tuae, a conturbatione hominum; proteges eos in tabernaculo tuo, a contradictione linguarum.

30{31}[20] *Quam magna multitudo dulcedinis tuae, Domine! O how great is the multitude of your sweetness, O Lord!* Those who have experienced it know this. And because no one experienced it in this life as fully as Christ, so no one is able to say this verse more suitably than Christ. In summary, the *multitude of the sweetness* of God, at its fountainhead, namely in God himself, is truly immeasurable, indeed it is intensively and simply infinite;[37] but also the *multitude of the sweetness* of God,

---

35 E. N. St. Stephen, the deacon and the first martyr (protomartyr). Acts 7:58–59.
36 Acts 7:51, 52.
37 E. N. Denis insists that God is intensively (*intensive infinita*) and simply (*simpliciter*) infinite. The notion of intensive infinity relates to qualities, to essence, to

with which he often fills his beloved attendants, is also exceedingly great, and altogether surpassing of all carnal sweetness: and this sweetness is a certain preamble of the future sweetness of the blessed in heaven.

Quam abscondisti timentibus te; which you have hidden for them that fear you. Fear comes in two forms, namely, filial and servile. Based upon this [distinction], this verse can be explained in two ways. The first is in this way: *which* multitude of your sweetness, *you have hidden,* that is, concealed, you have made it unknown and not something experienced, *for them that fear you* with a servile fear. For such are neither worthy nor have the capacity of the enjoyment of divine sweetness, because they do good, but not out of love of the good, but with the dread of a suppliant. The second is in this way: *you have hidden,* that is, you have shown in a hidden manner, and by an internal relish hidden in the heart, you have disclosed, *for them that fear you* with a filial fear [*the multitude of your sweetness*]. For these persons — because they spurn all disordered joy, all bodily pleasures, and all needless consolations, and because they always are solicitous not to offend God, whom they filially love above all things — are deserving of the experience of how great the *multitude of sweetness* of God is. But on occasion those fearing God with an initial fear, such as the newly converted do at the time they are admitted to the table of the children,[38] taste a little of the sweetness of God and cry out to the Lord: *How great is the multitude of your sweetness, O Lord!* But this Jesus Christ, the Wisdom of God, gives to them to the extent they may be drawn to him, that he may call them from exterior things, and invite him to interior things, making them to be constant in the face of adversity; and he causes them *in the day of evils to be not unmindful of good things.*[39] Whence, let these persons exercise great caution and particular discretion lest they become faint-hearted when they lack these aforementioned consolations for a while, or lest they desire

---

perfection, and not to extension or quantity. God is not extensively infinite as we might propose outer space or a line might be (or as a line might be infinitely divided) since he is not a body and is entirely other than matter. The idea of intensive infinity is meant to transcend our concepts of infinity so that the infinity we hold of God is analogically related to the infinity of bodies or division. By calling God "simply infinite," Denis is saying that God is absolutely, and not relatively, infinite. See ST, Ia, q. 7, arts. 1-4.

38   E. N. The "table of the children," or "table of the sons," *mensa filiorum,* is a reference to the altar, and by implication, the Eucharist. Ernald, Abbot of Rievaulx (1189–99), harkening to the dialogue between the Syrophoenician woman and Jesus (Mark 7:25–29), similarly speaks of the *mensa caelesti,* the heavenly table, the *mensa filiorum Dei,* the table of the sons of God, the table of those who "recline at the table upon the bosom of Jesus." *Comm. In Psal.* CXXXII, PL 189, 1578.

39   Ecclus. 11:27b.

[these consolations] importunately: indeed it must be committed to the Lord when he may deign to give these.

To experience this multitude of divine sweetness is to eat *of the crumbs that fall from the table of their masters,*[40] namely, of those with the vision of God in heaven (*comprehensorum*); and to sit at the table of Christ is when the Wisdom of God the Father invites his elect, when he says: *Eat, O friends, and drink, and be inebriated, my dearly beloved.*[41] And: *Come over to me, all you that desire me, and be filled with my fruits, for my spirit is sweet above honey, and my inheritance above honey and the honeycomb.*[42] And at this table sat the most blessed Jeremiah, who did not desire *the day of man,* that is, the temporal and bodily or human delights,[43] as he openly declared about himself in the book of his visions: *Your word was to me a joy and gladness of my heart.*[44] And in another place: the word of the Lord *came in my heart,* he says, *as a burning fire shut up in my bones, and I was wearied, not being able to bear it.*[45] Hence the Apostle [Paul] said: *As the sufferings of Christ abound in us: so also by Christ does our comfort abound.*[46]

Perfecisti eis qui spirant in te, in conspectu filiorum hominum, which you have wrought for them that hope in you, in the sight of the sons of men: that is, the aforementioned *multitude of your sweetness* you have perfectly manifested, and you have made those who are not embarrassed of your name before men,[47] who, because of the hope that they have in you, patiently put up with adverse things, and in in the face of persecution and contempt they put their trust in you, not ashamed of the way of justice. 30{31}[21] *Abscondes eos in abscondito faciei tuae, a conturbatione hominum; you shall hide them in the secret of your face, from the disturbance of men*: that is, the hearts of them who taste your sweetness, you convert towards you, and you draw back from exterior things to interior things so that they place themselves in the presence of your countenance, and

---

40 Matt. 15:27. (E. N. A reference to the dialogue between the Syrophoenician woman and Jesus).
41 Songs 5:1b.
42 Ecclus. 24:26, 27.
43 Cf. Jer. 17:15a: *And I am not troubled, following you for my pastor, and I have not desired the day of man, you know.*
44 Jer. 15:16a.
45 Jer. 20:9.
46 2 Cor. 1:5.
47 Luke 9:26: *For he that shall be ashamed of me and of my words, of him the Son of man shall be ashamed, when he shall come in his majesty, and that of his Father, and of the holy angels.* 1 Pet. 4:16: *But if as a Christian, let him not be ashamed, but let him glorify God in that name.*

so that they, through genuine contemplation and undisturbed by enemies, may depart with an internal relish and tranquility of mind. For hiding in the face of God is that contemplation of him by which we are secretly turned to God; or it is the very face of God which is hidden from worldly men because *wisdom will not enter into a malicious soul.*[48] In this way God hides those leading a contemplative or solitary life: of which souls that which the Lord says through Hosea is applicable: *Behold I will allure her, and will lead her into the wilderness: and I will speak to her heart. Proteges eos in tabernaculo tuo, you shall protect them in your tabernacle,* that is, in your Church militant, or rather in that chamber of their heart in which they speak within themselves, standing secure before God, *a contradictione linguarum, from the contradiction of tongues,* that is, from the confused din of those adverse to truth, and from all the tumult of those who endeavor to spoil the interior sweetness. From this is shown how necessary it is for him who wishes to experience divine sweetness to flee men, flee disputes, and arguments, and all secular tumult, so that he may remain with the heart tranquil and steadfast.

30{31}[22] Blessed be the Lord, for he has shown his wonderful mercy to me in a fortified city.

Benedictus Dominus, quoniam mirificavit misericordiam suam mihi in civitate munita.

30{31}[22] *Benedictus Dominus, blessed be the Lord,* that is, let God be praised, and blessed, and glorified by all, *quoniam mirificavit misericordiam suam mihi, for he has shown his wonderful mercy to me,* that is, he mercifully dispensed to me his wonderfully great mercy, *in civitate munita, in a fortified city,* that is, in the Church militant and triumphant, both of which are fortified by God the protector. This applies most fully to Christ for—solely by the mercy of God—his humanity was assumed into a personal union with the Word, preserved from all fault, and fully filled with all grace as far as created nature is capable of. God moreover conferred to Christ as man the highest mercy on earth, and thereafter he preserved it and perfected it in heaven. Or [an alternative understanding]: *Blessed be the Lord, for he has shown his wonderful mercy to me,* that is, my praise and my glory, *in a fortified city,* that is, among the Christian people, giving them diverse gifts (*charismata*) of the Holy Spirit, and his ineffable grace, especially in the early Church, and on

---

48 Wis. 1:4. The verse continues: *nor dwell in a body subject to sins.*

the date of Pentecost, when he sent at my instance the Holy Spirit in tongues of fire.[49] Whence Christ said to his disciples: *Behold I will ask the Father, and he shall give you another Paraclete, that he may abide with you forever, the Spirit of truth, whom the world cannot receive.*[50]

30{31}[23] But I said in the excess of my mind: I am cast away from before your eyes. Therefore, you have heard the voice of my prayer, when I cried to you.

Ego autem dixi in excessu mentis meae: Proiectus sum a facie oculorum tuorum: ideo exaudisti vocem orationis meae, dum clamarem ad te.

30{31}[24] O love the Lord, all you his saints: for the Lord will require truth, and will repay them abundantly that act proudly.

Diligite Dominum, omnes sancti eius, quoniam veritatem requiret Dominus, et retribuet abundanter facientibus superbiam.

30{31}[25] Do manfully, and let your heart be strengthened, all you that hope in the Lord.

Viriliter agite, et confortetur cor vestrum, omnes qui speratis in Domino.

30{31}[23] *Ego autem dixi in excess mentis meae*, but I said in the excess of my mind, that is, in the great passion and a certain ecstasy of my heart: *Proiectus sum a facie oculorum tuorum*, I am cast away from before your eyes, that is, forsaken by the sight of your fatherly kindliness. For Christ on the Cross cried out: *My God, my God, why have you forsaken me?*[51] How this is to be understood has been handled in the exposition of the twenty-first Psalm.[52] *Ideo*, therefore, that is, because in such distress I called out to you, *exaudisti vocem orationis meae, dum clamarem ad te;* you have heard the voice of my prayer, when I cried to you, saying on the Cross: *Father, forgive them, for they know not what they do,*[53] and *Father, into your hands I commend my spirit.*[54] And therefore, 30{31}[24] *Diligite Dominum, omnes sancti eius;* O love the Lord, all you his saints, that is, those who have led a spotless life, and have served the Lord without

---

49 Acts 2:3.
50 John 14:16, 17.
51 Matt. 17:46.
52 *See* Article L (Psalm 21:2) in Volume 1.
53 Luke 23:34a.
54 Luke 23:46a.

blame and without complaint, *quoniam veritatem requiret Dominus, for the Lord will require truth,* that is, he demands justice, and for me, who have suffered so much without any personal fault, he will judge, and he will not leave anything uninvestigated; *et retribuet abundanter facientibus superbiam,* and he will repay them abundantly that act proudly: for temporal fault he will inflict upon them eternal punishment, as it is written: *If his pride mount up even to heaven, and his head touch the clouds, in the end he shall be destroyed like a dunghill.*[55] *He shall be punished for all that he did, and yet shall not be consumed: according to the multitude of his devices so also shall he suffer.*[56] Consequently, in Revelation we find this: *As much as she has glorified herself, and lived in delicacies, so much torment and sorrow you give to her.*[57] And the Lord says through Zephaniah: *And I will visit in that day upon every one that enters arrogantly.*[58] 30{31}[25] *Viriliter agite,* do manfully the precepts and the counsels of Christ, *et confortetur cor vestrum,* and let your heart be strengthened, in the grace of God. As the Apostle [Paul] said: *It is best that the heart be established with grace;*[59] *omnes qui speratis in Domino,* all you that hope in the Lord. For he who trusts in himself will be found wanting.

ARTICLE LXVIII

EXPOSITION OF THE SAME THIRTIETH PSALM OF THE CHURCH AND OF ANY ONE MEMBER OF THE FAITHFUL ENCOUNTERING TRIBULATIONS

30{31}[2] *In you, O Lord, have I hoped, let me never be confounded: deliver me in your justice.*

In te, Domine, speravi; non confundar in aeternum; in iustitia tua libera me.

Now the Church and any member of the faithful wearied with persecutions, temptations, and a variety of punishments, and also feeling disheartened, flees to God, and with a most devout heart and says: 30{31}[2] *In te, Domine speravi; in you, O Lord, have I hoped,* not in my own

---

55 Job 20:6-7a.
56 Job 20:18.
57 Rev. 18:7a.
58 Zeph. 1:9a.
59 Heb. 13:9a.

powers: and so *non confundar in aeternum, let me never be confounded*, that is, let me not fall away from my hope, deprive myself of its effect, or be overcome by temptations and fall into eternal confusion after the present life. *In iustitia tua, in your justice*, which is your very essence — in this justice, from which you save those who hope in you, and to which you abandon those who are presumptuous as to themselves and who contrive maliciously — *libera me, deliver me* from temptations and all dangers of interior salvation. Or [we can understand this verse in this manner], *In your justice*, that is, on account of the merits of the just manner of living which you gave to me,[60] so that I might hope in you; deliver me, not permitting me to be tempted, afflicted, and shaken beyond that which I am able to endure, but you will provide together with such temptation a means of overcoming it[61] so that all things work together to my good.[62]

30{31}[3]   Bow down your ear to me: make haste to deliver me. Be you unto me a God, a protector, and a house of refuge, to save me.

Inclina ad me aurem tuam; accelera ut eruas me. Esto mihi in Deum protectorem, et in domum refugii, ut salvum me facias.

30{31}[4]   For you are my strength and my refuge; and for your name's sake you will lead me, and nourish me.

Quoniam fortitudo mea et refugium meum es tu; et propter nomen tuum deduces me et enutries me.

30{31}[3] *Inclina ad me aurem tuam, bow down your ear to me*, that is, pour forth your mercy upon me, and attend to my prayers with kindly favor. I believe enough has been said about how in God there are not bodily ears; but [metaphorically speaking] God's ears are the mercy by which he hears and the wisdom by which he knows all things. *Accelera ut eruas me, make haste to deliver me*, that is, quickly and immediately help me, because I am in momentous need. *Esto mihi in Deum protectorem, be you unto me a God, a protector*, that is, may you be God my protector, *et in domum refugii, and a house of refuge*, that is, a Savior, to whom I

---

60   E. N. This recalls St. Augustine's famous statement: *Ergo coronat te [Deus], quia dona sua coronat, non merita tua.* "Therefore [God] crowns you, because he crowns his own gifts, not your merits." Ennar. In Psalmos (Ps. 102:7), PL 37, 1321.
61   Cf. 1 Cor. 10:13: *Let no temptation take hold on you, but such as is human. And God is faithful, who will not suffer you to be tempted above that which you are able: but will make also with temptation issue, that you may be able to bear it.*
62   Rom. 8:28: *And we know that to them that love God, all things work together unto good, to such as, according to his purpose, are called to be saints.*

might flee always in confidence; *ut salvum me facias*, *to save me*, that is, that you might deliver me from all the sins of the heart, of the mouth, and of deed. **30{31}[4]**[63] *[Quoniam fortitudo mea et refugium meum es tu; for you are my strength and my refuge; and] propter nomen tuum deduces me, for your name's sake you will lead me* in this exile, showing to me the good way through internal illumination, and leading me along the way to the heavenly homeland; *et enutries me, and [you] nourish me*, giving to me daily bread, sacramental bread, the bread of grace, the bread of tears, and conducting me over from every imperfect and beastly state into a spiritual and perfect state.

30{31}[5] *You will bring me out of this snare, which they have hidden for me: for you are my protector.*

Educes me de laqueo hoc quem absconderunt mihi, quoniam tu es protector meus.

30{31}[6] *Into your hands I commend my spirit: you have redeemed me, O Lord, the God of truth.*

In manus tuas commendo spiritum meum; redemisti me, Domine Deus veritatis.

30{31}[7] *You have hated them that regard vanities, to no purpose. But I have hoped in the Lord.*

Odisti observantes vanitates supervacue; ego autem in Domino speravi.

30{31}[8] *I will be glad and rejoice in your mercy. For you have regarded my humility, you have saved my soul out of distresses.*

Exsultabo, et laetabor in misericordia tua, quoniam respexisti humilitatem meam; salvasti de necessitatibus animam meam.

30{31}[9] *And you have not shut me up in the hands of the enemy: you have set my feet in a spacious place.*

Nec conclusisti me in manibus inimici; statuisti in loco spatioso pedes meos.

30{31}[5] *Educes me de laqueo hoc quem absonderunt mihi, you will bring me out of this snare, which they have hidden for me*: that is, you will

---

63 E. N. The beginning of Ps. 30:4 is absent from the text as is any commentary on it. I have included it in brackets.

save me from the traps of all my adversaries, especially of the demons, whose snares are so much more dangerous by being invisible. God leads us away from these snares through the custody of angels, by the prayer of the Saints, by meritorious prayer, and by conferring grace by which we are illuminated, strengthened, and made to struggle against vice. 30{31} [6] *In manus tuas commendo spiritum meum, into your hands, I commend my spirit,* both when existing in the body as well as when leaving from the body, so that in every place, time, and business you may paternally guard it. For you are my faithful Creator, my excellent Lover, my most kind Savior. And so he continues: *Redemisti me, Domine, Deus veritatis; you have redeemed me, O Lord, the God of truth,* O Lord Jesus Christ, by whose precious Blood you have delivered my soul. 30{31}[7][64]. . . *Ego autem in Domino speravi, but I have hoped in the Lord,* that is, in the goodness and the mercy of Christ, and in the virtue and merit of his Passion, hoping to receive however much of his mercy is salvific for me, by the price of his Blood, and the merits of his death, and by the worthiness and holiness of all of his manner of living in this world. 30{31}[8] *Exsultabo et laetabor in misericordia tua, I will be glad and rejoice in your mercy,* that is, in the contemplation of your such great kindliness and beneficence.

Quoniam respexisti humilitatem meam, for you have regarded my humility, that is, you have regarded kindly my poverty, lowness, and littleness, and you have provided aid to me in want and in weakness. For *salvasti de necessitatibus animam meam, you have saved my soul from its necessity,*[65] that is, from the evil I am unable to avoid, which are the evils of venial sins, from which Christ saves us through [temporal] punishment; the evil of our natural passions and of the persecution of enemies, from

---

64 E. N. Denis skips the first part of Psalm 30:7.
65 E. N. The Douay-Rheims translates the Sixto-Clementine Vulgate's *de necessitatibus* as "out of distress." The word *necessitas* denotes unavoidableness, inevitableness, necessity. While the translation of *de necessitatibus* with respect to Christ might be understood as "out of distress," with respect to the faithful in general, the sense of unavoidableness, inevitableness, necessity is more proper, and so I have departed from the Douay-Rheims here. This is because without a special divine privilege or grace — such as that given to the Blessed Virgin Mary — not even a justified person can altogether avoid venial sin. The Council of Trent condemned the proposition that "without a special privilege of God as the Church holds of the Blessed Virgin," "a man once justified can avoid all sins, even venial ones, through his entire life." DS 1573. Pope Innocent XI condemned certain propositions of Miguel de Molinos, which included the proposition that by contemplation one can reach the point in this life "of not committing any more sins, either mortal or venial." DS 2257. Therefore, under our current state *in via* we are to a certain extent confronting the unavoidableness or inevitableness of the venial sin that is the subject of Denis's commentary.

which Christ saves us through patience; and the evil of bodily weakness, from which Christ saves us through temperance.[66] From this necessity we are already saved in hope, and in the future we shall be saved from it in reality, when *this mortal has put on immortality, and this corruptible...incorruption*.[67] Hence the Apostle [Paul]: *We are saved*, he says, *by hope*.[68] And Isaiah: *In silence and in hope shall your strength be*.[69]

30{31}[9] *Nec conclusisti me in manibus inimici*, *and you have not shut me up in the hands of the enemy*, that is, you have not permitted me to be overcome and snatched by my enemies, nor have you damned me while I was worthy of damnation, living in mortal sin; but *statuisti in loco spatioso, you have set...me in a spacious place*, that is, in that Church which has been spread far and wide around the earth's globe, *pedes meos, my feet*, that is, myself and my deeds and my desires, subjecting me to the precepts and the admonitions of Holy Mother Church.

30{31}[10] *Have mercy on me, O Lord, for I am afflicted: my eye is troubled with wrath, my soul, and my belly.*

Miserere mei, Domine, quoniam tribulor; conturbatus est in ira oculus meus, anima mea, et venter meus.

30{31}[11] *For my life is wasted with grief: and my years in sighs. My strength is weakened through poverty and my bones are disturbed.*

Quoniam defecit in dolore vita mea, et anni mei in gemitibus. Infirmata est in paupertate virtus mea; et ossa mea conturbata sunt.

30{31}[10] *Miserere Me, Domine*; *Have mercy on me, O Lord*, mercifully

---

66 E. N. "[L]ighter sins, which are called venial, also require some sort of penance. St. Augustine observes that the kind of penance which is daily performed in the Church for venial sins, would be absolutely useless, if venial sin could be remitted without penance." *Catechism of the Council of Trent*, 271. Denis suggests three forms of this penance: punishments, patience, and temperance or abstinence. Naturally, this presupposes us being in a state of sanctifying grace; otherwise, these acts would have no supernatural merit. Note how it is not our works that save, but Christ that saves through our works: "The merits of our good works are gifts of the divine goodness." CCC § 2009 (citing the Council of Trent, DS 1548: "[A] Christian should never rely on himself or glory in himself instead of in the Lord, whose goodness toward all men is such that he wants his own gifts to be their merits.").
67   1 Cor. 15:54; *cf.* 1 Cor. 15:53.
68   Rom. 8:24a.
69   Is. 30:15b.

exercising forbearance, quickly providing help, and strongly triumphing, *quoniam tribulor, for I am afflicted* with evil disordered desires, with various temptations, and a variety punishments; *conturbatus est in ira oculus meus, my eye is troubled with wrath*, that is, the passion of anger has on occasion been immoderate in me, disturbing the judgment of reason. Or [we can see it] thus: *my eye is troubled with wrath*, that is, I was angered at myself because of my sin, and so I have avenged myself against them, so that *my eye*, both interior as well as exterior, has in some way been troubled, not however in a vicious sense. For there is a wrath that arises through zeal that does not in any manner vex reason; but the wrath that arises from vice, blinds it [reason]. Or [also we can understand it in this way]: *my eye is troubled with wrath*, that is, my eye is troubled because of the wrath of my adversaries who are against me. *Anima mea, my soul*, that is, my sensitive and animal life, *et venter meus, and my belly*, that is, its body. For the passion of anger comes with bodily change, and so being angry disturbs and afflicts all [of one's] nature. Yet by *belly* we are able to understand the memory, which is similar to the belly as a place of forms (*locus specierum*) and of reflection (*cogitationum*).⁷⁰ **30{31}[11]** *Quoniam defecit in dolore vita mea, for my life is wasted with grief*, that is, it has been full with so many miseries, distresses, punishments, and sorrows that it seems to approach towards being a great waste or ruin. Indeed, the passions, especially the penal [passions]⁷¹—such as hate, wrath, sorrow, fear and anguish—seriously weaken, and sometimes entirely extinguish, the life of the body because of the unnatural change that they visit upon the body. *Et anni mei, and my years*, that is, the course of my life, marked out by years, *is wasted in gemitibus, in sighs* and sobbings with which I am afflicted and lament,

---

70   E. N. Denis uses the words *locus specierum*, which is the Latin translation of Aristotle's τόπος εἶδον (*topos eidon*), the "place of forms." The *locus cogitationum*, the "place of thinking," deliberation, meditation, or reflection is a translation of the Greek φροντιστήριον (*phrontistērion*), a phrontistery, a place one goes to think or study. Denis may be harkening back to St. Augustine's *Confessions* (10, 14, 21): *memoria quasi venter est animi*, "the memory is like the belly of the soul." Yet he also says: *Ridiculum est haec illis similia putare, nec tamen sunt omni modo dissimilia*, "it is ridiculous to suppose these two to be similar, but yet they are not in all ways dissimilar." The analogy is that the food—which is sweet or bitter—is no longer tasted when in the belly; it would have to be "regurgitated" into the mouth. So that which is the memory has to be recalled from where it lies unrecalled. PL 32, 788.
71   E. N. As discussed in footnote 17-144 of Volume I, scholastics classified passions as those that were inherently culpable and those that were not, but only became culpable through excess or defect. Some of the culpable or penal passions are listed by Denis here.

because of the evil which I observe the world to be replete of and by which I also am afflicted and in various ways tormented.

Infirmata est in paupertate virtus mea, my strength is weakened through poverty: that is, the perfection of my heart and my efforts at doing good are frequently interrupted and weakened because of the weakness of the flesh and bodily needs; *et ossa mea, and my bones*, that is, the stronger virtues of my soul, *conturbata sunt, are disturbed*, that is, are suspended, impeded, and disturbed from their action: for the interior and exterior passions frequently impede an act of virtue because the soul's attentiveness with the operation of one of its powers is less able to apply itself to the operation of another of its powers.

30{31}[12] *I am become a reproach among all my enemies, and very much to my neighbors; and a fear to my acquaintance. They that saw me without fled from me.*

Super omnes inimicos meos factus sum opprobrium, et vicinis meis valde, et timor notis meis; qui videbant me foras fugerunt a me.

30{31}[13] *I am forgotten as one dead from the heart. I am become as a vessel that is destroyed.*

Oblivioni datus sum, tamquam mortuus a corde. Factus sum tamquam vas perditum.

30{31}[14] *For I have heard the blame of many that dwell round about. While they assembled together against me, they consulted to take away my life.*

Quoniam audivi vituperationem multorum commorantium in circuitu. In eo dum convenirent simul adversum me, accipere animam meam consiliati sunt.

30{31}[12] *Super omnes inimicos meos, among all my enemies*, that is, in preference to all of my enemies: not that I have hatred towards them, but because they hate me; *factus sum opprobrium vicinis meis, I am become a reproach ... to my neighbors*, that is, to my fellow Christians and my next of kin or relatives of the flesh, *valde, very much*, so that many abhor me and spurn me because the adverse and evil things that have befallen me; *et timor notis meis, and a fear to my acquaintance*: that is, I am so full of such misery and affliction that the members of my family fear to see me, and they avoid me, lest they fall into similar evils.

This verse along with the three that follow are highly applicable to the Church furiously oppressed by tyrants, heretics, schismatics, and persecutors, as was the primitive Church, and the Church will be at the time of the Antichrist; and also [they are fitting] to any member of the faithful to whom might befall a succession of evil things, and so gives the appearance of being unfortunate and contemptible before all of those close to him or acquainted with him, in the manner in which the most blessed David, the author of this present Psalm was, when Saul persecuted him.[72] For also this Psalm can easily be explained in reference to him, if it would help bring about devotion. But in a special way, therefore these words are suited to the holy martyrs and just men held in contempt by all the world. For of such Christ in the Gospel says: *And you shall be betrayed by your parents and brethren, and kinsmen and friends . . . and you shall be hated by all men for my name's sake.*[73] And: *Amen, amen I say to you, that you shall lament and weep, but the world shall rejoice; and you shall be made sorrowful, but your sorrow shall be turned into joy.*[74]

All that has been said beforehand applies to that which follows: *Qui videbant me, they that saw me* so afflicted and miserable, *foras fugerunt a me, without fled from me,* lest they happen to share in my punishments, or lest they appear to be in solidarity with me, and from this they might be associated with me in punishment. This is what holy Job said: *My brethren have passed by me, as the torrent that passes swiftly in the valleys,*[75] and *my acquaintance like strangers have departed from me.*[76] 30{31}[13] *Oblilvioni datus sum tanquam mortuus a corde, I am forgotten as one dead from the heart,* that is, the previously-mentioned neighbors and acquaintances are as if dead to me, having no concern for me, nor do they empathize with me, nor render aid to me in my misery. *Factus sum tanquam vas perditum, I am become as a vessel that is destroyed,* that is, in all things reputed to be vile and useless, as being worth nothing to another; 30{31}[14] *Quoniam audivi vituperationem multorum commorantium in circuitu, for I have heard the blame of many that dwell round about:* that is, my neighbors and acquaintances among whom I dwell inveigh against me, detracting, calumniating, and persecuting me. *In eo, in that* occurrence, meeting, business, or time, *dum convenirent simul adversum me, while they assembled together against me,* reaching

---

72 1 Samuel chapters 18–21, 23, 24, 26.
73 Luck 21:16–17.
74 John 16:20.
75 Job 6:15.
76 Job 19:13b.

agreement to harass a blameless man, *accipere animam meam consiliati sunt, they consulted to take away my life*, that is, they have taken counsel among themselves, so that they might extinguish my life, injure it, or subject it to their perverse will, endeavoring to undermine me from the right way, and to conform to their injustices.

30{31}[15] *But I have put my trust in you, O Lord: I said: You are my God.*

Ego autem in te speravi, Domine; dixi: Deus meus es tu.

30{31}[16] *My lots are in your hands. Deliver me out of the hands of my enemies; and from them that persecute me.*

In manibus tuis sortes meae: eripe me de manu inimicorum meorum, et a persequentibus me.

30{31}[17] *Make your face to shine upon your servant; save me in your mercy.*

Illustra faciem tuam super servum tuum; salvum me fac in misericordia tua.

30{31}[18] *Let me not be confounded, O Lord, for I have called upon you. Let the wicked be ashamed, and be brought down to hell.*

Domine, non confundar, quoniam invocavi te. Erubescant impii, et deducantur in infernum.

30{31}[19] *Let deceitful lips be made dumb. Which speak iniquity against the just, with pride and abuse.*

Muta fiant labia dolosa, quae loquuntur adversus justum iniquitatem, in superbia, et in abusione.

30{31}[15] *Ego autem in te speravi, Domine; but I have put my trust in you, O Lord*, placing confidence in your goodness to preserve me and to see me triumph. *Dixi, I said* from the heart and from the mind: *Deus meus es tu, you are my God*, whom alone I worship and I love, and to whom I will eternally adhere to. 30{31}[16][77] *Eripe me de manu inimicorum meorum, deliver me out of the hands of my enemies*, that is, from the powers of my adversaries, lest I consent to their evil, *et a persequentibus me, and from them that persecute me*, that they may not corrupt my life with their evil example, their fraud, or in other similar manner. 30{31}

---

77 Denis skips over the first part of Ps. 30:16, starting mid-verse.

[17] *Illustra faciem tuam, make your face to shine*, that is, may the rays of your knowledge and the light of your wisdom spread out *super, upon* me *servum tuum, your servant*, illuminating faith, directing reason in all things, and filling the understanding with contemplation of heavenly things; *salvum me fac, save me*, in the present from sin by grace, *in misericordia tua, in your mercy*, that is because of the goodness of your mercy. **30{31}[18]** *Domine, non confundar; Lord, let me not be confounded* from confessing my own sins, and obeying your law; let me not be confounded, driven away, or rejected by you, especially when I will be presented before your tribunal, *quoniam invocavi te, for I have called upon you*.

Erubescant impii, let the wicked be ashamed, that is, let them fittingly be shown in confusion, *et deducantur in infernum, and be brought down to hell* after this present life. The Christian faithful says this of the ungodly in the manner that does Christ, namely, foretelling what awaits [the evil if they do not repent], or making known that which the evil deserve, or conforming himself to the divine justice. **30{31}[19]** *Muta fiant labia dolos, let deceitful lips be made dumb*: that is, make it be, either now by repentance or in the future through punishment, that fraudulent words be restrained by you, and that they cease to pull others down; *quae loquuntur adversus iustum, they who speak . . . against the just*, whoever it is they might be, *iniquitatem, iniquity*, incriminating them by their lies, *in superbia, with pride*, that is, from the swelling of their own hearts, *et in abusione, and abuse*, that is, from a perverse display, by which they give the appearance of a just life by simulation or a vain intention; and thus abuse the good example of the just by which they are inflamed with envy when they ought to be edified.

30{31}[22][78] Blessed be the Lord, for he has shown his wonderful mercy to me in a fortified city.

Benedictus Dominus, quoniam mirificavit misericordiam suam mihi in civitate munita.

30{31}[23] But I said in the excess of my mind: I am cast away from before your eyes. Therefore you have heard the voice of my prayer, when I cried to you.

Ego autem dixi in excessu mentis meae: Proiectus sum a facie oculorum tuorum: ideo exaudisti vocem orationis meae, dum clamarem ad te.

---

78 Denis skips verses 20 and 21.

30{31}[22] *Benedictus Dominus, Blessed be the Lord,* that is, I give thanks to God, and I praise him, *quoniam mirificavit, for he has shown wonderfully,* that is, he has done great things by *misericordiam suam mihi, his mercy to me,* giving me great graces, complete pardon, progress in the good, and other gifts given to me who am most unworthy of it: in which he is most consistent, for marvelously great is his mercy. And this mercy he has made marvelous in me *in civitate munita, in a fortified city,* that is, in my soul, which is a city of the heavenly kingdom when it is made beautiful by a conformity with virtue; or [alternatively,] *in a fortified city,* that is, in a devout congregation or cloister; or certainly [it can be understood as referring] in the Church, making me a live and faithful member of it. **30{31}[23]** *Ego autem dixi in excessu mentis meae, but I have said in the excess of my mind,* that is, from the abundance of tribulation and from a certain alienation of my heart from itself, which is cut down by sorrow, fear, or some most bitter affliction: *Proiectus sum, I am cast away,* that is, I am forsaken, *a facie oculorum tuorum, from before your eyes,* that is, from the effect of your most kind regard, namely from your grace and your mercy. In a Psalm above it states that from the abundance of divine consolation and grace: *I shall never be moved;*[79] now, however, it says that from the abundance of tribulations and misery, *I am cast away from before your eyes.* It seems both of these are rash, because whether in prosperity or adversity we ought always to walk forward in the royal way,[80] and we ought not excessively exult or glorify in prosperity nor be dejected in adversity, as it is written: *In the day of good things be not unmindful of evils: and in the day of evils be not unmindful of good things.*[81] And the most wise Paul: *But in all things let us exhibit ourselves as the ministers of God, in much patience ... by the armor of justice on the right hand and on the left.*[82]

---

79 Ps. 29:7b.
80 E. N. Denis talks of the "royal way," the *via regia.* Epiphanius of Salamis (*ca.* 310/20 — 403 AD), wrote of this royal way in his book about heresies called the *Panarion:* "There is a royal way (ὁδὸς βασιλική [*hodos basilikē*)]), which is the Church of God and the road of truth (ἡ ὁδοιπορία τῆς ἀληθείας [*hē hodoiporia tēs alētheias*]). It is a way, he says, from which we ought not to wander either to the right or to the left. PG 41, 1036. St. Augustine in his *City of God* says with respect to the Church: "This is the religion which contains the universal way (*universalem viam*) for the liberation of the soul, because none other than this one is able to liberate in this way. For this is a kind of regal way (*regalis via*), which leads to the kingdom, and which is not uncertain like temporal dignities, but stands secure in eternity." *De Civ. Dei,* X, 32, 1, PL 41, 312.
81 Ecclus. 11:27.
82 2 Cor. 6:4a, 7b.

And that which has not been expounded on at this time can be understood sufficiently from the preceding exposition.[83]

See how clear, full of mystery and affection this Psalm is, in which is contained such ardent prayers, in which there abounds words of good hope, in which the Passion of Christ is explained, in which the abundance of the divine sweetness is recalled, in which the benefits of God are described, in which the fragility of human weakness is disclosed, and in which is set forth why it is we must suffer if we choose to follow the path of Christ. With how much ardent devotion of love, with how much confidence of hope and fervor of prayer is it fitting for us to sing this splendid Psalm, especially at Compline, every time we say that verse, *Into your hands I commend my spirit!*[84] In saying this verse, we ought to entrust ourselves totally to our faithful Creator, with great affection and full confidence against all the troubles of the night.

PRAYER

O GOD, HOPE AND SALVATION OF THE faithful, by placing our hope in you let us not be confounded in eternity: with respect to our lapses, incline your ear of clemency favorably to us who beseech you, and justify us, in mildness relieving us of our debts, and with kindness forgiving our sins, and save us with your ineffable mercy.

Spes et salus fidelium Deus, in te sperantes non confundamur
in aeternum, lapsis nobis te exorantibus aurem clementiae
inclina propitius, et laxando debita mitis nos
iustifica, atque indulta delictorum venia,
salva nos ineffabili misericordia tua.

---

83 Denis thus skips verses 24 and 25.
84 E. N. This verse (Ps. 30:6) — *Into your hands, O Lord, I commit my spirit* — is said daily in the office of Compline in the Short Responsory or Chapter Responsory Verse.

Psalm 31

ARTICLE LXIX

EXPOSITION OF THE THIRTY-FIRST PSALM:
BEATI QUORUM REMISSAE SUNT INIQUITATES, &c.
BLESSED ARE THEY WHOSE INIQUITIES ARE
FORGIVEN, &c.

31{32}[1] *David understanding. Blessed are they whose iniquities are forgiven, and whose sins are covered.*

David intellectus. Beati quorum remissae sunt iniquitates, et quorum tecta sunt peccata.

31{32}[2] *Blessed is the man to whom the Lord has not imputed sin, and in whose spirit there is no guile.*

Beatus vir cui non imputavit Dominus peccatum, nec est in spiritu eius dolus.

HE PSALM WE ARE NOW EXPOUNDING UPON has this title prefixed to it: 31{32}[1] *Intellectus David, David understanding,* that is, the knowledge of a true penitent. For this Psalm teaches that it is necessary to understand a sinner wanting truly to repent, so that one may know that he is cleansed from vices and may judge himself blessed, and may expect to be led to that state. But this cannot be done unless one confesses and bewails his own sins, and totally relies upon the divine goodness and grace; consequently, this Psalm teaches the humble confession of one's own sins, and the confident finding of refuge in the mercy of God.

David, therefore, speaking in the person of a penitent, says: *Beati quorum remissae sunt iniquitates, blessed are they whose iniquities are forgiven,* that is, those whom God has forgiven all sins, through a saving repentance, the grace of baptism, or similar fashion; *et, and* blessed are they *quorum tecta sunt peccata, whose sins are covered,* that is, so blotted out by amendment of life and by grace as if they had never been: it is as if God, even though nothing is hidden from his knowledge, disregards them because he does not remember them or retain the right to issue judgment upon them from that time forwards. But in reality the

106   DENIS THE CARTHUSIAN : *Commentary on the Psalms* : Volume 2

remission of iniquity and the covering of sin is the same thing.¹ **31{32}** [2] *Beatus vir*, blessed is the man, that is, happy the man: happy, I say, in hope and grace, and happy in the future in reality (*in re*) and in glory;² *cui non imputavit Dominus peccatum*, to whom the Lord has not imputed sin, that is, he who by divine judgment is reputed free from, and absolved of, sin. For God does not deceive, but man is able to deceive. Therefore, he of whom man does not impute sin is not to accounted blessed; but most blessed is he of whom God does not impute sin, especially at the time [the soul is] leaving the body.³ *Nec est in spiritu*, and in whose spirit, that is, in the intention or the will, *eius dolus*, there is no guile, that is, simulation, a false confession, a made up excuse; but from the heart of hearts laments, confesses, and makes amendment for his sins.

---

1   *E. N. Realiter vero idem sunt, iniquitatis remissio, peccatique tectio.* By this statement, Denis anticipates Luther's reliance on Ps. 31:1 to justify the theory of forensic justification, which has popularly been described as having justification be analogous to snow covering a dunghill. This forensic theory of justification allows Luther to say we are *simul iustus et peccator*, at once both extrinsically, forensically justified, but ontologically a sinner: at the same time regarded as clean as snow (through imputed justice), though in reality remaining in sin (like dung). However, Denis clearly equates the "covering of sins" of Ps. 31:1 with a full remission (forgiveness) of sin. Denis has a Catholic understanding of this verse. "'Blessed are they whose iniquities are forgiven, and whose sins are covered. Blessed is the man to whom the Lord hath not imputed sin, and in whose spirit there is no guile.' [Ps. 31(32):1-2] The parallelism apparent in this verse allows us to conclude that 'covered' is used in the sense of 'remitted' and that 'he to whom the Lord hath not imputed sin' is identical with the man 'in whose spirit there is no guile.' The text manifestly refers to a real *forgiveness* of sins, for any sin that God "covers" and ceases to "impute," must be blotted out and swept away, because 'all things are naked and open to the eyes' [Heb. 4:13b] of the omniscient Creator." Joseph Pohle & Arthur Preuss, *Grace, Actual and Habitual: A Dogmatic Treatise*, Vol. VII (St. Louis: B. Herder 1917), 306-07.
2   *E. N.* Literally, one might translate "happy, I say, in hope and grace, and happy in the future *in the thing* and in glory." Denis does not use *realiter*, in reality (as if we are not enjoying the reality now) but *in re*. As Cardinal Müller has observed, we must not understand our life of grace as "already, but not yet," a phrase put forth by the Protestant Oscar Cullman (which derives from the Protestant notion of being *simul iustus et peccator*). "[W]hat do we say as Catholics? We affirm that we *already* and *now* have." Gerhard Cardinal Müller with Father Carlos Granados, *The Cardinal Müller Report: An Exclusive Interview on the State of the Church* (Ignatius: San Francisco 2017). Perhaps a crisper formulation of this is the maxim: *gratia est gloria incepta; gloria est gratia perfecta*, "grace [that is, sanctifying, justifying grace] is glory begun; glory is grace perfected." Grace is glory inchoate.
3   *E. N.* Clearly, since he who dies in a state of sanctifying grace is saved, Denis sees the man of whom God does not impute sin as equivalent to a man in sanctifying grace.

31{32}[3] *Because I was silent my bones grew old; while I cried out all the day long.*

Quoniam tacui, inveteraverunt ossa mea, dum clamarem tota die.

These, therefore, are blessed, but I am unhappy and miserable, **31{32} [3]** *Quoniam tacui,* because I was silent, that is, I hid my vices, and so *inveteraverunt ossa mea,* my bones grew old, that is, the virtues of my soul, those infused in Baptism or thereafter,[4] or those acquired, are devoured by longstanding nature of habits of depravity or the duration of sin. For [mortal] sin that is not confessed or of which one is not contrite kills and expels all charity, and grace, and all virtues. And so *my bones grew old, dum clamarem tota die,* while I cried out all the day long, that is, while I incessantly spoke vain things, and I presumed great things about myself, and was disdainful of others. Let us not, therefore, be ignorant of our vices, nor let the sin grow old in our minds; but let us attend to that which Jeremiah said: *How long shall hurtful thoughts abide in you?*[5] And also [let us assure to avoid] that which Job said: *If as a man I have hid my sin, and have concealed my iniquity in my bosom.*[6]

31{32}[4] *For day and night your hand was heavy upon me: I am turned in my anguish, while the thorn is fastened.*

Quoniam die ac nocte gravata est super me manus tua; conversus sum in aerumna mea, dum configitur spina.

31{32}[4] *Quoniam die act nocte,* for day and night, that is, unceasingly, *gravata est super me manus tua,* your hand was heavy upon me: that is, the adversities and punishments which have been inflicted by

---

4 E. N. The "thereafter" must refer to sacramental confession or an act of perfect contrition: "Christ instituted the sacrament of Penance for all sinful members of his Church: above all for those who, since Baptism, have fallen into grave sin, and have thus lost their baptismal grace and wounded ecclesial communion. It is to them that the sacrament of Penance offers a new possibility to convert and to recover the grace of justification. The Fathers of the Church present this sacrament as 'the second plank [of salvation] after the shipwreck which is the loss of grace.'" CCC § 1446. "When it arises from a love by which God is loved above all else, contrition is called 'perfect' (contrition of charity). Such contrition remits venial sins; it also obtains forgiveness of mortal sins if it includes the firm resolution to have recourse to sacramental confession as soon as possible." CCC § 1452. "Contrition is 'sorrow of the soul and detestation for the sin committed, together with the resolution not to sin again.'" CCC § 1451.
5 Jer. 4:14b.
6 Job 31:33.

your justice for sins are multiplied and weigh heavy upon me; so that by chastening you have chastised me with a variety of scourges so that I might return to you: and this I have done. For it continues: *conversus sum in aerumna mea, I am turned in my anguish*: that is, because of the afflictions, the adversities, and the miseries which have come to me under your guidance, I have confronted my sin, and I have examined (*discussi*) my conscience;[7] and I have come to see so much adversity to have befallen me because of my sins by which I have offended you. And so in this distress I have turned back to you, *dum configitur spina, while the thorn is fastened*, that is, while my distress or my misery is affected with various pains and stabs of punishments. This is fitting for those who are compelled to come in,[8] for those who disregard God as long as they are prospering, but when they are vexed by adversity they direct themselves [to God]. And with this aggravation the hand of God reaches out to sinners in the present life with great mercifulness. For God routinely chastises and afflicts the elect in this world, so that they do not perish in eternity. Whence, Jeremiah desiring this chastisement said: *Correct me, O Lord, but yet with judgment: and not in fury, lest you bring me to nothing.*[9] This we also have in Micah: *I will bear the wrath of the Lord, because I have sinned against him.*[10] And the Lord says through Hosea: *Behold I will hedge up your way with thorns, and I will stop it up with a wall.*[11] And in Jeremiah: *I will chastise you in judgment, that you may not seem to yourself innocent.*[12]

31{32}[5]   I have acknowledged my sin to you, and my injustice I have not concealed. I said I will confess against myself my injustice to the Lord: and you have forgiven the wickedness of my sin.

Delictum meum cognitum tibi feci, et iniustitiam meam non abscondi. Dixi: Confitebor adversum me iniustitiam meam Domino; et tu remisisti impietatem peccati mei.

---

7   L. The Latin verb *discussi* suggests that I have had an inner inquisition or scrutiny of conscience, even a shaking of conscience, a struggle where one dashes falsehoods and excuses and presumptions to pieces. In the words of the Council of Trent, the penitent must have "examined himself diligently and explored all the nooks and crannies of his conscience." DS 1682.
8   *Cf.* Luke 14:23: *And the Lord said to the servant: Go out into the highways and hedges, and compel them to come in, that my house may be filled.*
9   Jer. 10:24.
10   Micah 7:9a.
11   Hosea 2:6a.
12   Jer. 30:11b.

31{32}[5] *Delictum meum, my sin,* that is, my sins of omission, *cognitum tibi feci, I have acknowledged to you,* humbly confessing: not as if God does not know something, but speaking in a human fashion to God,[13] in the way that something is told another person to let him know about it even though it has been publicly revealed; *et iniustitiam meam non abscondi, and my injustice I have not concealed,* that is, I have confessed my sins of commission. For we ought not only to examine, judge, condemn, and correct ourselves of the wrong that we have done, but also for the good which we have omitted: because not only is a tree that yields evil fruit cast into the fire, but also that tree which does not yield good fruit is cut down and burnt.[14] Above he said *blessed are they . . . whose sins are covered;* now he asserts that he has made his sin publicly known to the Lord, and not to have hid it from him; by which he intimates that those sins God will cover, and the demon will have no power to accuse him who fully confesses his sins and does not hide them. And so it continues:

Dixi, I said, that is, I have resolved in my mind: *Confitebor adversum me, I will confess against myself,* that is, my own self, and not accusing or blaming others, *iniustitiam meam Domino, my injustice to the Lord,* that is, to the glory of God which I have offended. This is the manner that you ought to confess your sins, attributing all evil to your cowardice, malice, or weakness, not finding excuses for yourself, or accusing others of sin. Doing anything else should make you fear that which the Lord says: *Behold, I will contend with you in judgment, because you have said: I have not sinned.*[15] And again: *Your own wickedness shall reprove you, and your apostasy shall rebuke you.*[16] And so, *I said, I will confess against myself my injustice to the Lord:* not in vain, because of what follows, *et tu, and you,* O Lord, *remisisti impietatem peccati mei, have forgiven the wickedness of my sin,* that is, my impious sin. See how great is the goodness of God, who is naturally good, essentially clement, whose property is always to have mercy and to spare. Indeed, as soon as one is said to confess to the Lord, the Lord yields to it. For the moment that the sinner will have lamented his sin, he will *do judgment and justice,*[17] and God will immediately forgive him. The Christian must nevertheless—when the

---

13   E. N. Compare Rom. 6:19a: *I am speaking in human terms* (ἀνθρώπινον λέγω / *humanum dico*), *because of your natural limitations.* (RSVCE).
14   Matt. 3:10; Matt. 7:19.
15   Jer. 2:35b.
16   Jer. 2:19a.
17   Ez. 18:21b.

opportunity presents itself—confess to the vicar of God: otherwise, he will be found guilty on the grounds of disobedience. A confession before God does not obtain the remission of sins, unless somehow it includes the purpose of confessing to a priest, if it were possible: and so [it must include] the purpose of performing what is commanded.[18] And he ought to proceed to confession not only from servile fear, but also from charity: anything else and the merit is not justly deserving (*de condigno*).[19] However, so long as the sinner does what is possible for him, the Lord immediately infuses grace, and so confession and penance begin to spring forth out of charity.[20]

---

18   E. N. To the argument that perfect contrition may remit all punishment and guilt for sin; and that therefore it is not always necessary for a contrite person to have the purpose of confessing sacramentally and making satisfaction, St. Thomas responds: "Although it is possible that all punishment be remitted by contrition, yet confession and satisfaction still remain necessary. And this because man is not able to be certain of the sufficiency of his contrition to take all [guilt and punishment]. And this also because confession and satisfaction are of precept [that is, commanded by God]. Whence, he becomes a transgressor if he does not confess or make satisfaction." ST Supp. IIIa, q. 1, art. 1, ad 3. Thus, the purpose of confessing sins to a priest and making satisfaction are implicit in any act of contrition, even in an act of perfect contrition. The Council of Trent: "[A]lthough it sometimes happens that this contrition is perfect through charity and reconciles man to God before this sacrament is actually received, this reconciliation, nevertheless, is not to be ascribed to contrition itself without the desire of the sacrament, a desire that is included in it." DS 1677.
19   E. N. Imperfect contrition—known as attrition—"commonly arises either from the consideration of the heinousness of sin or from the fear of hell and of punishment." If this attrition "excludes the will to sin and implies the hope of pardon" it is a "salutary fear," and—though imperfect—still "a gift of God and a prompting of the Holy Spirit." DS 1678. What is considered reprehensible is a sorrow based either *only* on the hope of reward or *only* on the fear of punishment—God being left out of the equation. The first is a mercenary love (*amor mercenarius*), unworthy of a Christian, one "little more than a rude sensual longing for the pleasures of Heaven, similar to that which leads the Turk to people his imaginary paradise with beautiful women," and which seeks eternal happiness without reference to God, but only with reverence to self-advantage." The other sorrow that is a "servilely servile fear," a *timor serviliter servilis*, also an unworthy response to a God who calls us friends, and which is based upon the dread of punishment, but without at the same time loving or even fearing God. This fear is like "the dread a dog feels when he sees the whip in his master's hand." Joseph Pohle and Arthur Preuss, *The Sacraments: A Dogmatic Treatise*, Vol. III (St. Louis: B. Herder 1918), 154–55.
20   Such imperfect sorrow—attrition—is therefore "an impulse by which the penitent is helped to prepare for himself a way unto justice." DS 1678.

31{32}[6] *For this shall every one that is holy pray to you in a seasonable time. And yet in a flood of many waters, they shall not come nigh unto him.*

Pro hac orabit ad te omnis sanctus in tempore opportuno. Verumtamen in diluvio aquarum multarum, ad eum non approximabunt.

31{32}[7] *You are my refuge from the trouble which has encompassed me: my joy, deliver me from them that surround me.*

Tu es refugium meum a tribulatione quae circumdedit me; exsultatio mea, erue me a circumdantibus me.

31{32}[8] *I will give you understanding, and I will instruct you in this way, in which you shall go: I will fix my eyes upon you.*

Intellectum tibi dabo, et instruam te in via hac qua gradieris; firmabo super te oculos meos.

31{32}[9] *Do not become like the horse and the mule, who have no understanding. With bit and bridle bind fast their jaws, who come not near unto you.*

Nolite fieri sicut equus et mulus, quibus non est intellectus. In camo et freno maxillas eorum constringe, qui non approximant ad te.

31{32}[6] *Pro hac, for this* thing, that is, for the remission of sins, *orabit ad te omnis sanctus, shall every one that is holy pray,* that is, every wayfarer (*viator*) howsoever perfect, *in tempore opportuno, in a seasonable time,* that is, not always, but at determinate and fitting times. For as much as *the just is first accuser of himself,*[21] and an implorer of forgiveness, yet the just, perfect, holy, experience, and fervent man ought to occupy himself in yet higher acts, namely in the contemplation of divine things, in the active love of the Godhead, in the mediation of the Lord's Passion, in the study of acquiring greater perfection. But because (Solomon attesting) *there is no just man upon earth, that does good, and sins not,*[22] therefore, every saint needs to pray for the remission of sins at seasonable times. But he who still languishes in passions, and is prone to vice, and does not produce fitting penance to overcome sins, he must pray as it were continually for the remissions of sins: and for such a person, the seasonable

---

21 Prov. 18:17a.
22 Eccl. 7:21.

time for praying for the remission of sins is all the time of his life, until he is led to perfection and is able to busy himself in divine exercises.

Verumtamen in diluvio aquarum multarum, and yet in a flood of many waters, that is, men persevering in the ebb and flow of lust (*luxuriae*), and the superfluity of gluttony, and the other carnal or spiritual vices, *ad eum, unto him,* namely God, *non approximabunt, they shall not come nigh*: because their sins divide between them and God,[23] and as long they endure with the intention of sinning and in vicious acts, they remain in the region of unlikeness, and are far from God—not by place, but by devotion; not by condition, but by love; not by nature, but by grace, not by preservation, but by reverence. It is therefore written: *Now we know that God does not hear sinners: but if a man be a server of God, and does his will, him he hears.*[24] And so if you wish to come close to God, relinquish the intention of sinning; and if you wish to draw even nearer, then keep the commandments; and if you wish to be next to him, fulfill the counsels.[25]

Finally, the penitent after completing confession, with increased trust in attaining God stemming from the remission of sins and the infusion of grace, confidently and lovingly flees to God and says: **31{32}[7]** *Tu es refugium meum, you are my refuge,* that is, him in whom I alone hope to be saved, *a tribulatio, from the trouble,* that is, persecution, temptation, and punishment, *quae circumdedit me, which has encompassed me,* that is, that bestirs and rises up in me in so many ways and from so many places, from the suggestion of demons, from the opinions or the vexatious troubles of the world, and from the law of sin which flourishes in my members; and you, O Lord, are *exsultatio mea, my joy,* that is, the object of my interior joy, the cause of my spiritual happiness, and the entire end of my glorification; therefore, *erue me a circumdantibus me, deliver me from them that surround me,* that is, deliver me from those things that the aforementioned troubles occasion in me, namely, from enemies both visible and invisible.

Moreover, the merciful God showing himself welcoming to the prayers of the penitent, says in a consoling manner to him: **31{32}[8]** *Intellectum tibi dabo, I will give you understanding,* that is, intellectual knowledge; *et instruam te, and I will instruct you,* so that you may know and ponder your misery, your imperfection, your malice, and all things which are useful for you to know about created things; and also, so that you might

---

23 Cf. Is. 59:2: *But your iniquities have divided between you and your God, and your sins have hid his face from you that he should not hear.*
24 John 9:31.
25 E. N. Meaning the evangelical counsels: poverty, chastity, and obedience.

know and contemplate my goodness, perfection, mercy, and grace, and all the benefits which I have given you; *in via hac qua gradieris, in which way you shall go*, that is, in the pilgrimage of this exile. *Firmabo super te oculos meos, I will fix my eyes upon you*: that is, I will provide for you through my wisdom those things necessary for salvation, and through my mercy I will raise you from ruin, and I will always guard you, so that you may be able to say that which is said in a later Psalm: *You are my helper and my protector.*[26] See, most beloved, how fruitful and wholesome and true and humble is the confession of the sinner, how great a plenitude of graces are promised, namely so that the penitent can say to the Lord that which this verse states. How truly blessed and secure is he whom God so enlightens and guards!

But because fraternal charity demands that any graces given to someone by God should be attempted to be shared with others, in accordance with what manner his state permits in this: *As every man has received grace, ministering the same one to another: as good stewards of the manifold grace of God;*[27] therefore, the penitent having received mercy, as if assigned an illumination from God, turns himself to the exhortation of others and says: **31{32}[9]** *Nolite, do not* O sinners, *fieri sicut equus, become like the horse*, that is, do not become proud and rebellious to the light, *et mulus, and the mule*, that is, do not become adverse to divine things, *quibus, who*, namely, the horse and the mule, *non est intellectus, have no understanding*, that is, reason sufficiently powerful to curb the passions of the sensitive appetite. Indeed, since you are a rational creature you ought not to live irrationally, but should curb your passions in accord with reason, and humbly and fervently confess your sins. For (as Aristotle said) a sinful man is ten thousand times worse than a beast.[28] This is true because prayer sometimes profits more than exhortation; therefore, this penitent from the abundance of charity pleads for others, so that his admonishments may be fulfilled, and so he says to God: *In camo et freno, with bit and bridle*, that is, by various adversities and by grace and little afflictions, *maxillas eorum constringe, bind fast their jaws*, that is, silence, close, and restrain their tongue and their mouths, [the mouths] of those, I say, *qui non approximant ad te, who come not near unto you*, that is, of the proud, of the presumptuous, and of those unwilling to confess, in order that instructed by scourges and chastised by sorrows, they might turn back to you.

---

26   Ps. 39:18b.
27   1 Pet. 4:10.
28   E. N. A reference to Aristotle's *Nicomachean Ethics* (1150a7–8) which provides that an evil man can do then thousand times more harm than a beast.

31{32}[10] *Many are the scourges of the sinner, but mercy shall encompass him who hopes in the Lord.*

Multa flagella peccatoris; sperantem autem in Domino misericordia circumdabit.

31{32}[11] *Be glad in the Lord, and rejoice, you just, and glory, all you right of heart.*

Laetamini in Domino, et exsultate, iusti; et gloriamini, omnes recti corde.

31{32}[10] *Multa flagella peccatoris, many are the scourges of the sinner*, that is, various are the punishments of the sinner, especially those who persevere in vice. For in the present they are forsaken by God, and in the future they will be tormented with eternal punishment. *Sperantem autem in Domino misericordia, but hoping in the Lord mercy*, that is, the effects of divine goodness, *circumdabit, will encompass*: because his soul will be filled with grace, virtues, and consolations of the Holy Spirit, and the angel of God will guard him, and he will be unceasingly secure under the shadow of the wings of his Creator.

And finally, already perfected and justified by all the benefits of the most merciful God, the penitent desires all men to praise, and to share in his joy, and to lead them to give back thanks to God, and so he says: 31{32}[11] *Laetamini in Domino, be glad in the Lord*, not in carnal, vain, and transitory things; *et exultate, and rejoice*, that is, show outwardly a sign of your interior joy, praising God out loud, honoring him with religious ceremonies, and joyfully attending to outward acts of worship, O *iusti, you just*, who render back to him all that which is his, as the Apostle [Paul] exhorts: *Owe no man anything, except to love one another*;[29] *et gloriamini omnes recti corde, and glory, all you right of heart*: that is, in God, not in yourselves, in the Cross of Christ, not in the vanities of the world; be joyful all of you whose hearts are right, that is, not turned aside by any vice, not inclined to anything illicit, but subject to the divine law in all things: so that God can say to each one of you, that which he said to the author of this Psalm, *I have found David, the son of Jesse, a man according to my own heart, who shall do all my wills.*[30]

---

29 Rom. 13:8a.
30 Ps. 81:20 (LXX); Acts 13:22b. Acts 13:22 is a Latin translation of the Greek text, which relies upon the Septuagint, the Greek translation of the Old Testament. This reading varies from the Vulgate: *I have found David my servant: with my holy oil I have anointed him.*

Note that this is the second of the Penitential Psalms, small in quantity, but great in power, most instructive and capable of igniting a pious and penitent heart: which is becoming for us to utter with the deepest contrition, humility, and affection of heart, first of all to obtain mercy, then to acquire great hope in the Lord, and third to be directed and guarded by him in all things so we may worthily advance to the heavenly blessedness.

PRAYER

LORD JESUS CHRIST, WISDOM OF GOD the Father, give to us understanding and instruct us with your precepts; affix upon us your eyes in the way wherein we walk, so that, you leading the way, we may arrive without error to you who are the Way, the Truth, and the Life.

Domine Iesu Christe, sapitentia Dei Patris, da nobis intellectum, et instrue nos de praeceptis tuis; firma super nos oculos tuos in via qua gradimur: ut te ductore, ad te qui es via, veritas, et vita, sine errore perveniamus.

Psalm 32

ARTICLE LXX

EXPOSITION OF THE THIRTY-SECOND PSALM:
EXULTATE, IUSTI, IN DOMINO, &c.
REJOICE IN THE LORD, O YOU JUST, &c.

32{33}[1] *A Psalm for David. Rejoice in the Lord, O you just: praise becomes the upright.*

Psalmus David. Exsultate, iusti, in Domino; rectos decet collaudatio.

According to blessed Jerome,[1] in the prologue of his book on the Psalms, many are the Psalms, namely seventeen, which lack titles in the Hebrew, namely the first Psalm, and also the second Psalm, and this one now being expounded, and also others which follow. But commonly in the Latin Bibles and commentaries these are entitled, to which I think fitting to conform. Therefore, its title is: **32{33}[1]** *In finem, Psalmus David*: that is, this Psalm, which directs us towards God, is ascribed to David, who here as a person devoted and fervent with love, praises God over the excellence of his power and mercy, and of the works of creation and restoration.

Therefore, it says: *Exsultate iusti, in Domino; rejoice in the Lord, O you just*, that is, with complete and exuberant affection rejoice in the first principle of all things. Now joy is the expansion of the soul in taking hold of the good, and it arises from the union of power with an appropriate object.[2] For it accompanies certain natural or virtuous operations;

---

1 E. N. St. Jerome (ca. 347–420 AD), translator of the Scriptures into Latin, wrote numerous biblical commentaries, and is a Doctor of the Church.
2 E. N. *Gaudium est diffusio animi in conceptu boni, et oritur ex unione potentiae cum obiecto convenienti*. This definition seems to have Platonic roots. St. Albert the Great attributes the first part of the definition to St. Augustine in his *Summae Theologiae*, tr. 16, q. 63, m. 3, a. 2. St. Augustine describes joy (*laetitia*) as *animi diffusio* (expansion of the spirit) and sadness as *animi* (contraction of the spirit). *Tract. in Ion.*, 46, 8. In the dialog *Cratylus*, Plato has Socrates state that joy (χαρά [*chara*]) is stems from the plenteous expansion or diffusion of the flow of the soul: 'χαρὰ' δὲ τῇ διαχύσει καὶ εὐπορίᾳ τῆς ῥοῆς τῆς ψυχῆς ἔοικε κεκλημένη. *Cratylus* 419c. "Joy," says Réginald Garrigou-Lagrange in his *Life Everlasting*, "does not constitute the possession, but presupposes the possession."

and therefore it is not appropriate to the ungodly, because their operations are unnatural and vicious. For sin is a departure from that which is according to nature and [the moral] order, according to Dionysius [the Areopagite][3] and the Damascene.[4] Whence it is written: *There is no joy to the wicked, says the Lord.*[5] And the Philosopher [Aristotle] said that the sign of virtue is delight in the work.[6] But the operations by which the rational creature is immediately joined to God as object are the operations of the intellect and the will, namely, the contemplation of truth and the delight in the good. And so the rejoicing of the man in God proceeds either from contemplation, or from holy and ordered love, or from other virtuous acts, which are commanded, caused, and directed by the reason and the will. What, therefore, does *rejoice in the Lord, O you just* mean except "Consider God and his works, and love him, and do those things that are pleasing to God"? And in this rejoice with all your heart, not in yourselves, as if the good you do is of your own power, or as if it is something that you possess of yourselves, but [rejoice] in the Lord from whom is *every best gift, and every perfect gift.*[7] But sometimes it is acceptable to rejoice, to be jubilant, to be glad, but more vulgarly and improperly is it to manifest it excessively (*gestire*):[8] and so the divine Scriptures customarily attribute this to the unjust. It is in accordance with this that Solomon said: *they are glad when they have done evil, and rejoice in most wicked things;*[9] and Job: *They take the timbrel, and the harp, and rejoice at the sound of the organ.*[10] *Rectos decet collaudatio,* praise becomes the upright, that is, it is just and becoming that right acting men praise God: first, because they are worthy to praise God; secondly, because they have received greater gifts from God.

---

3   E. N. Pseudo-Dionysius (thought at one time to be biblical Dionysius the Areopagite mentioned in Acts 17:34) now generally believed to be a Christian Neoplatonist of the 5th or 6th century. As an authority, he is highly relied upon by St. Thomas Aquinas and by Denis.

4   E. N. St. John of Damascus (676–749 AD), monk and priest, known for his theological writings in defense of the orthodox faith, in particular his zealous defense of icons. He was declared a Doctor of the Church by Leo XIII in 1890.

5   Is. 57:21. E. N. The Vulgate reads: *Non est pax impiis, dicit Dominus Deus.* "There is no peace to the wicked, says the Lord God." Denis's reading quotation is consistent with the Septuagint which reads: οὐκ ἔστι χαίρειν τοῖς ἀσεβέσιν, εἶπε Κύριος ὁ Θεός. "There is no joy (*charein*) to the ungodly, said the Lord God."

6   E. N. See *Nicomachean Ethics* 1099a10–12.

7   James 1:17a.

8   E. N. Literally, to gesticulate, to be transported by joy in an overly passionate sense.

9   Prov. 2:14.

10   Job 21:12.

32{33}[2] *Give praise to the Lord on the harp; sing to him with the psaltery, the instrument of ten strings.*

Confitemini Domino in cithara; in psalterio decem chordarum psallite illi.

Literally, the holy David exhorted the ministers of the temple to offer to the Lord praise with these musical instruments;[11] but according to a spiritual understanding, by the word harp (*citharam*) we understand works of mercy, and by the word psaltery (*psalterium*) [we understand] the keeping of the commandments. For a harp has a sound box on the bottom, and it returns the sound from the bottom; and it has six strings, or according to some, seven strings, by which we understand the six works of mercy which relate to corporal necessities.[12] But the psalter has ten strings, and its sound box which causes the sound is on the top, by which we understand the divine precepts, which flowed down from the heavens, and which effect a sublime and heavenly melody in the ears of God. And so give praise to the Lord on the harp, that is, praise him by the works of mercy; sing to him with the psaltery, the instrument of ten strings, that is, glorify the Lord by the observance of the divine commandments, not so much by the lips, but by your deeds.

32{33}[3] *Sing to him a new canticle, sing well unto him with a loud noise.*

Cantate ei canticum novum; bene psallite ei in vociferatione.

32{33}[3] *Cantate ei, sing to him,* with a devout and ordered heart, *canticum novum, a new canticle,* that is, praise from recent fervor and from an abiding new affection. For fervent love is unable to tire in the praise of the beloved, but the new always suggests a public expression, and it ignites and breaks out in praise of the beloved in a thousand ways. *Bene psallite ei in vociferatione, sing well unto him with a loud noise*: that is, so praise God with your mouth or with your voice so that your life may conform to what the words declared, and you may observe in your manner of life that which you have stated with your voice, lest what

---

11   1 Chr. 15:16: *And David spoke to the chiefs of the Levites, to appoint some of their brethren to be singers with musical instruments, to wit, on psalteries, and harps, and cymbals, that the joyful noise might resound on high.*

12   E. N. The corporal works of mercy, of which there are traditionally six. "The corporal works of mercy consist especially in feeding the hungry, sheltering the homeless, clothing the naked, visiting the sick and imprisoned, and burying the dead." CCC § 2447.

Isaiah said applies to you: *This people honor me with their lips, but their heart is far from me.*[13]

32{33}[4] *For the word of the Lord is right, and all his works are done with faithfulness.*

Quia rectum est verbum Domini, et omnia opera eius in fide.

Therefore you ought to sing well, **32{33}[4]** *Quia rectum est verbum Domini, for the word of the Lord is right,* that is, sacred Scripture and all divine words are just, true, and holy; *et omnia opera eius in fide, and all his works are done with faithfulness,* that is, they are faithful and irreprehensible, and they have no admixture of deceit. Or [one can think of it this way], *all his works are done with faithfulness,* that is, for anything to be pleasing to God and to be meritorious it is necessary that it be founded in faith and to proceed out of it: because as the Apostle [Paul] attests, *All that is not of faith is sin.*[14] And Habakkuk: *Behold, he that is unbelieving, his soul shall not be right in himself: but the just shall live in his faith.*[15]

32{33}[5] *He loves mercy and judgment; the earth is full of the mercy of the Lord.*

Diligit misericordiam et iudicium; misericordia Domini plena est terra.

The Lord **32{33}[5]** *diligit misericordiam, he loves mercy,* that is, a mutual and fraternal compassion, support, and speedy forgiveness of an offense. This is what the Savior says in the Gospel: *Blessed are the merciful: for they shall obtain mercy.*[16] And so much does the Lord love mercy that in the day of judgment he will especially put forth questions of the performance of works of mercy.[17] Therefore the divine Apostle [Paul] admonishes us: *Put you on therefore, as the elect of God, holy, and beloved, the bowels of mercy, benignity, humility, modesty, patience, bearing*

---

13 Is. 29:13: E. N. The first part is a paraphrase, a foreshortening of the Isaian verse. *Forasmuch as this people draw near me with their mouth, and with their lips glorify me, but their heart is far from me, and they have feared me with the commandment and doctrines of men.*
14 Rom. 14:23b.
15 Hab. 2:4.
16 Matt. 5:7.
17 Matt. 25:35 *et seq.*

with one another, and forgiving one another, if any have a complaint against another: even as Christ *has forgiven you.*[18] This is written about the merciful man elsewhere: *Man to man reserves anger, and does he seek remedy of God? He has no mercy on a man like himself, and does he entreat the Most High for his own sins?... Who shall obtain pardon for his sins?*[19]

And so, the Lord *loves mercy, et iudicium, and judgment,* that is, the act of justice, namely, that man might judge himself and others over whom he has charge with diligent examination and just correction. This in accordance to that which the Apostle [Paul] said: *But if we would judge ourselves, we should not be judged.*[20] And so the Lord issues this advance judgment (*sententiam*) through Zechariah: *Judge,* he says, *true judgment, and show mercy and compassion every man to his brother.*[21] And Micah: *I will show you, O man, what is good, and what the Lord requires of you: Verily, to do judgment, and to love mercy.*[22] And yet there is a kind of temerarious judgment in which man without certainty presumes to judge, either his superior or those who are under his charge. Of which [sort of judgment] Christ [says]: *Judge not, and you shall not be judged.*[23] And the Apostle [Paul]: *Who are you who judges another man's servant? To his own lord he stands or falls.*[24] And: *You, why do you judge your brother?... For we shall all stand before the judgment seat of Christ.*[25] And so the Lord loves the judgment of reward: which [judgment] is twofold, namely, the particular in the death of every single man, and the general in the last day. The Lord loves, renders, and will render both of these judgments.

Misericordia Domini plena est terra, the earth is full of the mercy of the Lord: that is, the Christian men that are wayfaring upon the earth are full with the mercies of God, the grace of Christ, and the various gifts of the Holy Spirit: indeed all men are in a certain way full of the mercy of God because God awaits all with great patience, and offers to all, as much as it is within his power, his grace; and he has disposed it to be that the Gospel of the kingdom be preached everywhere in the world.

---

18 Col. 3:12–13. E. N. Denis replaces "the Lord" with "Christ."
19 Ecclus. 28:3–5.
20 1 Cor. 11:31.
21 Zech. 7:9.
22 Micah 6:8a.
23 Luke 6:37a.
24 Rom. 14:4a.
25 Rom. 14:10.

32{33}[6] *By the word of the Lord the heavens were established; and all the power of them by the spirit of his mouth.*

Verbo Domini caeli firmati sunt; et spiritu oris eius omnis virtus eorum.

32{33}[6] *Verbo Domini, by the word of the Lord,* that is, by the Wisdom of the eternal Father, who is Christ the Lord, *caeli, the heavens,* that is, the heavenly orbs, *firmati sunt, were established,* that is, established and stabilized. For *all things were made by him,*[26] in the manner that the Apostle [Paul] said: Let us give thanks *to God the Father, who . . . has translated us into the kingdom of the Son of his love, . . . who is the image of the invisible God, the firstborn of every creature, . . . for in him were all things created in heaven and on earth, visible and invisible.*[27] And to the Hebrews, speaking of the Son, he said: *Who being the brightness of his glory, and the figure of his substance, and upholding all things by the word of his power, . . . sits on the right hand of the majesty on high.*[28] *Et spiritu oris eius, and by the spirit of his mouth,* that is, from the Holy Spirit, who is the Spirit of the Father, proceeding from the mouth (that is, from the will) of the Father. From this Spirit is *omnis virtus eorum, all the power of them,* that is, all heavenly might and beauty. For the heavenly power is located especially in the stars and planets.[29] Whence it is written elsewhere: *His spirit has adorned the heavens.*[30] Or [another interpretation is] thus: *by the word of the Lord the heavens,* that is, the holy Apostles, *were established.* For Christ said to them: *without me you can do nothing.*[31] *And by the spirit of his mouth,* that is, the Holy Spirit, who also proceeds from the Son, *all the power of them,* that is, all the powers of performing miracles and of speaking efficaciously. Whence it is written: *They began to speak with divers tongues, according as the Holy Spirit gave them to speak.*[32]

---

26 John 1:3a.
27 Coll. 1:12–16.
28 Heb. 1:3.
29 E. N. Denis means that the power and beauty of the stars and the planets provide an ideal analogy of the power and the beauty that are found in the Holy Spirit. He is not equating the created stellar and planetary powers with the uncreated and infinite power of God, as God's power infinitely transcends the physical energies involved in the universe.
30 Job. 26:13a.
31 John 15:5b.
32 Acts 2:4.

32{33}[7] *Gathering together the waters of the sea, as in a vessel; laying up the depths in storehouses.*

Congregans sicut in utre aquas maris; ponens in thesauris abyssos.

Finally, the Lord himself is **32{33}[7]** *congregans sicut in utre aquas maris, gathering together the waters of the sea, as in a vessel*: that is, that element of water or the seas of the Ocean, which circles and girds the earth, the Lord has restrained and kept in one place, as man restrains some water in a vessel, that is, in a leathern water bag. This is what Job concludes: *By his power the seas are suddenly gathered together.*[33] And Solomon: *With a certain law and compass he enclosed the depths (abyssos),*[34] that is, locating and retaining that sea, which is called the depths (*abyssus*), that is, without boundary, because of the unfathomableness of its deepness. For this reason, the Wisdom of God, namely, Christ, the only begotten Son of the eternal Father, says: *I alone have compassed the circuit of heaven, and have penetrated into the bottom of the deep (abyssi).*[35] And so the Lord places and retains depths in treasures, that is, among the secret shores of his hiding places, in the manner he asserts to Job when saying: *Who shut up the sea with doors, when it broke forth as issuing out of the womb, When I made a cloud the garment thereof, and wrapped it in a mist as in swaddling bands? I set my bounds around it, and made it bars and doors: And I said: Hitherto you shall come, and shall go no further, and here you shall break your swelling waves.*[36]

32{33}[8] *Let all the earth fear the Lord, and let all the inhabitants of the world be in awe of him.*

Timeat Dominum omnis terra; ab eo autem commoveantur omnes inhabitantes orbem.

32{33}[9] *For he spoke and they were made: he commanded and they were created.*

Quoniam ipse dixit, et facta sunt; ipse mandavit et creata sunt.

Because the majesty of God is so great, and there is such great excellence and omnipotence of the Creator in his works, therefore,

---

33 Job 26:12a.
34 Prov. 8:27b.
35 Ecclus. 24:8a.
36 Job 38:8–11. E. N. In Job 38:9, Denis uses *involverem* (in + roll) instead of the Vulgate's *obvolverem* (against + roll).

32{33}[8] *Timeat Dominum, fear the Lord*, with a filial and chaste fear, *omnis terra, all the earth*, that is, all its inhabitants. And to those who in considering the greatness of his aforementioned effects do not fear the Creator, he himself says through Jeremiah, *Hear, O foolish people, and without understanding... Will not you... fear me... who have set the sand a bound for the sea, an everlasting ordinance, which it shall not pass over?*[37] *Ab eo autem, and... of him*, that is, from the consideration of the divine power, *commoveantur, let all... be in awe* by penance and saving conversion, *omnes inhabitants orbem, all the inhabitants of the world*, that is, of the sphere or the circular surface of the earth. This is what is written: *There is none like to you, O Lord: you are great and great is your name in might. Who shall [not] fear you, O king of nations?*[38] **32{33}[9]** *Quoniam ipse, for he* almighty God, *dixit, spoke*, that is, within himself through his practical intellect he intellectually produced those things which were produced, *et, and* immediately *facta sunt; ipse mandavit; they were made; he commanded*, that is, by the will he imperially willed that those things which were not might come to be, *et, and* forthwith *creata sunt, they were created*. From which it is known that God is the cause of things by his intellect and will. For "to state" (*dicere*) pertains to the intellect; "to command" (*mandare*) [pertains] to the will. To the intellect belongs [such acts as] to order, to distinguish, to specify; [but it belongs] to the will to follow those things that the intellect determines.

32{33}[10] *The Lord brings to naught the counsels of nations; and he rejects the devices of people, and casts away the counsels of princes.*

Dominus dissipat consilia gentium; reprobat autem cogitationes populorum, et reprobat consilia principum.

32{33}[10] *Dominus dissipat consilia gentium, the Lord brings to naught the counsels of the nations*, that is, he confounds, he destroys, he disperses, and, out of the desired effect, he hinders the searching and devotion of the idolaters, and also the pagan manner of living of Christians. The Lord brings to naught those counsels in the end, although sometimes for a period of time he allows them to reign and to prosper. *Reprobat autem cogitationes populorum, he rejects the devices of people*, not of all, but of the unfaithful and of the evil. Regarding which Isaiah states: *For as the heavens are exalted above the earth, so are my ways exalted above*

---

37 Jer. 5:21–22.
38 Jer. 10:6–7.

your ways, and my thoughts above your thoughts.[39] And the Lord *reprobat consilia principum, casts away the counsels of princes*, who are those of the same kind as the nations and peoples just now described, namely, of the wicked; not, however, of the princes of the good, of which it is said: *But the prince will devise such things as are worthy of a prince.*[40] Whence it says in another scripture: *God does not cast away the mighty, whereas he himself also is mighty.*[41]

32{33}[11] *But the counsel of the Lord stands forever: the thoughts of his heart to all generations.*

Consilium autem Domini in aeternum manet; cogitationes cordis eius in generatione et generationem.

32{33}[11] *Consilium autem Domini in aeternum manet*, but *the counsel of the Lord stands forever*. The term counsel, properly [or strictly] understood, is not fitting to apply to God: for counsel is an inquiry relating to the doing of something; but an inquiry presupposes lack of knowledge, and so the Damascene says that the counsel is [a sign of the] ignorance of nature.[42] Yet, sacred Scripture frequently attributes the act of counsel to God, but when it does this it assumes counsel according to the perfection that is comprehended in his reason. And so it ascribes to God counsel, not so as to suggest any questioning [on the part of God] to remove doubt, but so as to exclude an improvident determination [on the part of God]. For God does nothing fortuitously, but he does all things according to eternal and unchangeable reasons. And so, *the counsel of the Lord stands forever* because nothing is able to resist him, but his power is at hand when he wills,[43] in the manner that he says: *My counsel shall stand, and all my will shall be done.*[44]

---

39 Is. 55:9.
40 Is. 32:8a.
41 Job 36:5.
42 St. John of Damascus. For more on St. John of Damascus, *see* footnote 32-4. The reference is to his *De Fide Orthodoxa: Deus quippe non deliberat: quia ignorantia est consilium inire. Nemo enim de eo deliberaverit, quod exploratum habet.... Quare cum Deus simpliciter omnia norit, in eum non cadit deliberatio.* "Indeed, God does not deliberate, for to enter into council is an indication of ignorance. For nobody deliberates about that which he ascertains.... Wherefore, since God simply knows all things, it does not befall upon him to deliberate." *De Fide Orthodoxa*, II, 22, PG 94, 946.
43 *Cf.* Wis. 12:18: *But you being master of power, judge with tranquility; and with great favor dispose of us: for your power is at hand when you will.*
44 Is. 46:10b.

Cogitationes cordis eius in generatione et generationem, the thoughts of his heart to all generations. For nothing revolving, nothing unstable, nothing changeable is able to be in the eternal God, who also says elsewhere: *For I am the Lord, and I change not.*[45] Therefore, there is not in God any sort of turning or variation of counsel or of thought, especially since whatever is in God, is God himself, sublime and blessed.[46] But this seems to oppose that which Zechariah said: *As I purposed to afflict you, when your fathers had provoked me to wrath, ... so turning again I have thought in these days to do good to the house of Juda, and Jerusalem.*[47] And in another place: *I will suddenly speak against a nation, and against a kingdom, to root out, and to pull it down.... If that nation against which I have spoken, shall repent of their evil, I also will repent of the evil that I have thought to do to them.*[48] But these and similar passages are not to be understood as if there is something that is varying in God; but God is said to convert and to repent, or to hold himself in one way and then another because of the diversity of effects by which is indicated a change in the creature, not in the Creator. For whatever God does with respect to created things, he himself knew and decreed how he would act beforehand from eternity: and so from an invariable and eternal will the supreme artisan is able to proceed temporal and new effects without any kind of change in him. For whatever God does in the world he foresaw himself acting in that moment when it was done, according to all manner and circumstances of its effect; and regarding this some philosophers have greatly erred. Whence [Pope St.] Gregory asserted that God does not change counsel (*consilium*), however much he might change his judgment (*sententia*):[49] [he does not

---

45 Mal. 3:6a.
46 E. N. God's essence is identical to his existence. Moreover, God is identical to the attributes predicated of him—simplicity, perfection, goodness, infinity, omnipresence, immutability, eternity, unity, etc.—since the attributes are not accidental to his substance but are themselves expressive of his substance. So not only is God perfect goodness, God is his own goodness. [C]*um Deus non sit compositus ex materia et forma,... oportet quod Deus sit sua deitas, sua vita, et quidquid aliud sic de Deo praedicatur.* "Since God is not a composite of matter and form, ... it must needs be that God is his own deity, and whatever else is thus predicated of God," including thus his attributes. ST, Ia, q. 3, art. 3, co.
47 Zech. 8:14–15.
48 Jer. 18:7–8.
49 E. N. Pope St. Gregory the Great (*ca.* 540–604 A. D.), in is *Moralia in Iob* stated: *Omnipotens enim Deus etsi plerumque mutat sententiam, consilium nunquam.... Cum ergo exterius mutari videtur sententia, interius consilium non mutatur, quia de unaquaque re immutabiliter intus constituitur, quidquid foris mutabiliter agitur.* "For almighty God though he commonly changes his sentence (judgment), never [does

change] those things which express the eternity of the disposition of divine wisdom, but [he does change] those things which are exhibited in the order of nature and secondary proximate causes. [An example of this is] he foretold Ezechiel's death and the destruction of Nineveh, because the future of both was according to their own causes, namely according to the sickness of Ezechiel and the crimes of Nineveh;[50] but the divine ordination, which embraces and exceeds all secondary causes, foreknew otherwise, and his counsel was unchanged.

32{33}[12] *Blessed is the nation whose God is the Lord: the people whom he has chosen for his inheritance.*

Beata gens cuius est Dominus Deus eius; populus quem elegit in haereditatem sibi.

32{33}[12] *Beata gens,* blessed is the nation now by grace and hope, *cuius est Dominus Deus eius, whose God is the Lord,* that is, the Lord of all is their God in a special way, namely, by faith and in worship. And with merit is it said that such people are blessed, because it is *populus quem elegit, the people whom he has chosen,* that is, whom the Lord has chosen *in hereditatem sibi, for his inheritance:* so that he wills to possess them by a singular providence, and grace brought to highest perfection, that they not perish in eternity, but that they are led to heavenly beatitude. For this reason, it is written: *We are happy... because the things that are pleasing to God, are made known to us.*[51]

32{33}[13] *The Lord has looked from heaven: he has beheld all the sons of men.*

De caelo respexit Dominus; vidit omnes filios hominum.

32{33}[13] *De caelo respexit Dominus, the Lord has looked from heaven:* that is, the Lord, who is in a special way said to be and to dwell in heaven. The Lord looks, therefore, from heaven because he is the provider, ruler, judge, examiner, and witness of all things, in the manner Jeremiah says: *I am the judge and the witness.*[52] *Vidit, he has beheld,* that is, he

---

he change] his counsel.... When, therefore, the exterior sentence (judgment) is seen to change, the interior counsel is unchanged, for, with regard to anything, it [God's interior counsel] is constituted interiorly unchangeable, however much it [the exterior sentence] changes outside." *Mor. In Iob,* XVI, 10, 14; 37, 46, PL 75, 1144.
50   2 King. 20:1; Jonah 3:4.
51   Baruch 4:4.
52   Jer. 29:23b.

has understood, and from eternity known, *omnes filios hominum, all the sons of men,* that is, all the posterity of Adam and Eve. For by using the noun "sons," daughters are not excluded.[53]

32{33}[14] From his habitation which he has prepared, he has looked upon all that dwell on the earth.

De praeparato habitaculo suo respexit super omnes qui habitant terram.

32{33}[15] He who has made the hearts of every one of them: who understands all their works.

Qui finxit sigillatim corda eorum; qui intelligit omnia opera eorum.

32{33}[14] *De praeparato habitaculo suo, from his habitation which he has prepared,* that is, from the highest heaven, since he himself prepares the dwelling of the blessed in heaven, *respexit super omnes, he has looked upon all* men *which habitant terram, that dwell on the earth,* so that he might render to each man that which he deserves, indeed also have mercy on the unworthy. For this reason Ecclesiasticus says: *The eyes of the Lord are far brighter than the sun, beholding round about all the ways of men,... For all things were known to the Lord God before they were created.*[54] And through Jeremiah the same thing is said again: *Am I, think you, a God at hand, says the Lord, and not a God afar off? Shall a man be hid in secret places, and I not see him, says the Lord?*[55] 32{33}[15] *Qui, he who* the Lord *finxit, has made,* that is, created, *sigillatim, every one,* that is, singularly and separately, *corda eorum, hearts... of them,* that is, the souls of men. For the soul is infused when created and is created when infused.[56] The error that proposes that all rational souls were created simultaneously at the beginning of the world with the angels is fully refuted by the fact that the Prophet [David] asserts souls to be produced individually,.[57]

---

53 E. N. In other words, the word sons (*filii*), though of masculine gender, is used generically to refer to sons and daughters both.
54 Ecclus. 23:28–29a.
55 E. N. This saying—*anima creando infunditur, et infundendo creatur,* "the soul when created is infused, and when infused is created"—is commonly attributed to St. Augustine, *e.g.,* St. Thomas in *Super Sent.,* lib. 2 d. 3 q. 1 a. 4 ad 1; however, I have not been able to locate it or anything similar to it in St. Augustine's writings.
56 Jer. 23:23–24.
57 E. N. "Some have proposed that... the souls of men were created at the beginning simultaneously with the angels. But this opinion is false." ST, Ia, q. 118, art. 3, co.

32{33}[16] *The king is not saved by a great army: nor shall the giant be saved by his own great strength.*

Non salvatur rex per multam virtutem, et gigas non salvabitur in multitudine virtutis suae.

32{33}[17] *Vain is the horse for safety: neither shall he be saved by the abundance of his strength.*

Fallax equus ad salutem; in abundantia autem virtutis suae non salvabitur.

32{33}[16] *Non salvatur rex multam virtutem,* **the king is not saved by a great army**: that is, neither bodily welfare (*salutem*), for example, victory [in battle], nor interior salvation (*salutem*), namely beatitude,[58] is obtained by one's own virtue or through the strength of one's effort; but victory is given by divine power according to the ordination of divine providence, just as Solomon says: *The horse is prepared for the day of battle: but the Lord gives safety (salutem).*[59] And without grace one is not able to attain happiness. Whence Jonathan said: *It is easy for the Lord to save either by many, or by few.*[60] And often by divine strength a few have overcome many. *Et gigas non salvabitur in multitudine virtutis suae,* **nor shall the giant be saved by his own great strength**: that is, through his own natural strength, neither with the body will he prevail, nor with the heart will he become blessed except to the extent that God — who is certainly able to defeat a giant through an ordinary man, as he defeated Goliath through David[61] — furnishes it to him.
32{33}[17] *Fallax equus ad salutem,* **vain is the horse for safety**, that is, to arrive at salvation, it is insufficient to ride one's own saddle; indeed, if he places hope in himself, it will elude him; *in abundantia autem virtutis suae,* **neither shall he be saved by the abundance of his strength**, that is,

---

58 L. In Latin, the word *salus* can mean health, wholesomeness, soundness, and safety, but also salvation and the deliverance of sin and its penalties. This divergence can be seen in two maxims, one from Cicero (*De Leg.* III, 3, 8) and one from Canon law (Canon 1752, 1983 Code of Cannon Law). Compare: *Salus populi suprema lex esto,* "the health [welfare or safety] of the people is the highest law" with *salute animarum … in Ecclesia … suprema semper lex,* "the salvation of souls … must always be the supreme law in the Church."
59 Prov. 21:31.
60 1 Sam. 14:6b. E. N. Jonathan was the eldest son of King Saul, and a faithful friend to King David. David's lament following the death of Jonathan is one of the most poignant scenes in the Bible: "Your love to me was wonderful, passing the love of women." 2 Sam. 1:26.
61 1 Sam. 17:49.

in the great strength of the horse, *non salvabitur, he shall not be saved* sitting upon a horse. The Lord for this reason says: *Let not the wise man glory in his wisdom, and let not the strong man glory in his strength, and let not the rich man glory in his riches; but let him that glories glory in this, that he understands and knows me.*[62]

32{33}[18] *Behold the eyes of the Lord are on them that fear him: and on them that hope in his mercy.*

Ecce oculi Domini super metuentes eum: et in eis qui sperant super misericordia eius.

32{33}[19] *To deliver their souls from death; and feed them in famine.*

Ut eruat a morte animas eorum: et alat eos in fame.

32{33}[18] *Ecce oculi Domini*, *behold the eyes of the Lord*, that is, providently caring with wisdom and sparing with mercy, *upon the just; and his ears*, that is, the kindliness and liberality by which he hears and gives, *unto their prayers;*[63] **32{33}[19]** *ut eruat a morte*, *to deliver from death*, that is, from the sin which kills the mind, *animas eorum, their souls*: or also sometimes from bodily death when it is profitable for the common good or the souls of the just. *Et alat eos in fame, and feed them in famine*, their minds thirsting justice, he will fill with grace, and the bodies he will nourish with bread if it may be necessary. Whence, the Savior asserts in the Gospel: *Seek therefore first the kingdom of God, and his justice, and all these things shall be added unto you.*[64]

32{33}[20] *Our soul waits for the Lord: for he is our helper and protector.*

Anima nostra sustinet Dominum, quoniam adiutor et protector noster est.

32{33}[21] *For in him our heart shall rejoice: and in his holy name we have trusted.*

Quia in eo laetabitur cor nostrum, et in nomine sancto eius speravimus.

---

62 Jer.9:23-24a. E. N. Also cited are 1 Cor. 1:31: *As it is written: he that glories, may glory in the Lord*, and 2 Cor. 10:17: *He that glories, let him glory in the Lord.*
63 Ps. 33:16. E. N. It is unclear why Denis skips to 33:16 and does not provide commentary on the remainder of 32:18 — namely, *are on them that fear him: and on them that hope in his mercy.*
64 Matt. 6:33.

32{33}[22] *Let your mercy, O Lord, be upon us, as we have hoped in you. Fiat misericordia tua, Domine, super nos, quemadmodum speravimus in te.*

32{33}[20] *Anima nostra sustinet Dominum,* our soul waits upon the Lord, that is, with calmness and patience it awaits him, hoping grace and mercy from the Lord to be always at hand; in adversity it does not pull away from him, despairing of, or losing confidence in, his goodness; *quoniam adiutor,* for [our] helper in the good, *et protector noster,* and our protector from evil, *est, he is,* the Lord himself. For he works together [with us] and defends [us] with his grace. And a sign to them that he is our helper and protector is that which follows: 32{33}[21] *Quia in eo laetabitur cor nostrum,* for in him our heart shall rejoice: that is, will rejoice, not in ourselves, but in the Lord, in contemplation and love of him and from all his good works and benefits. *Et in nomine sancto eius sperabimus,* and in his holy name we have trusted. But this we can in no manner do unless the Lord himself gives us help. And this is the word of good hope and holy undertaking—not out of presumption or out of trust in our own perfection. For which reason, therefore, O Lord, we place our hope in you, and so 32{33}[22] *Fiat misericordia tua, Domine, super nos;* let your mercy, O Lord, be upon us, that is, the effect of your mercy, namely, help and grace, and fill us with the gifts of the Holy Spirit, *quemadmodum speravimus in te,* as we have hoped in you, that is, so abundantly and speedily, as we have trust in your goodness. And you, therefore, who say this verse, attend to the manner or how much you hope in the Lord, and *before this prayer, prepare your soul: and be not as a man that tempts God.*[65] For you do not actually hope in the Lord if you say this with a wandering mind.

See how there is contained in this Psalm gracious and beautiful praise of the Most High. First of all, it exhorts all generally to the divine praises of all things; thereafter, it leads to the commendation of God; and finally it sets forth the most wholesome doctrine: declaring salvation to be in God alone. And you, therefore, when you say, *Praise becomes the upright,* see to it that your soul is right with God, lest you find yourself to be an unworthy praiser of God. Finally, from the contemplation of the magnificence of God and of his marvelous works, conceive a reverential fear for him; and do that which you sing in this Psalm when you say, *Our soul waits upon the Lord;* and, *In him our heart shall rejoice.* For

---

65   Ecclus. 18:23.

how fruitful it is to find support in the Lord shown by what is written: *You deliver them that wait for you* and *you free them* from all distress, O Lord our God.[66]

Finally to be considered is this: how evidently the most blessed Trinity is mentioned in that verse, *By the word of the Lord the heavens were established and all the power of them by the spirit of his mouth.* For by the noun "Word" is expressive of the Son, of whom in another place it is said, *The word of God on high is the fountain of wisdom;*[67] and again, *In the beginning was the Word.*[68] But by the noun "the Lord" we understand to mean the Father. And by the words "the spirit of his mouth" we take as referring to the Holy Spirit, who proceeds from the Father and the Son, as from one principle, one spiration, and one superlatively most splendid fountain.

PRAYER

O CHRIST, WORD OF THE ETERNAL FATHER, by whom the heavens are made firm, illumine us with the gift of your Spirit, and confirm us in good works, that we might be justified by faith in the Trinity and through works that are pleasing to you, and we may be counted among the people for your inheritance, glorifying you in eternity.

Verbum Patris aeterni, Christe, quo caeli firmati sunt, munere
Spiritus tui nos illustra, et in opere bono confirma: ut fide
Trinitatis et operatione tibi placita iusti simus, et
cum populo in hereditatem tibi deputato, in
aeternum glorificandi.

---

66 Ecclus. 51:12a.
67 Ecclus. 1:5a.
68 John 1:1.

Psalm 33

ARTICLE LXXI

EXPOSITION OF THE THIRTY-THIRD PSALM:
BENEDICAM DOMINUM IN OMNI TEMPORE, &c.
I WILL BLESS THE LORD AT ALL TIMES, &c.

33{34}[1] *For David, when he changed his countenance before Abimelech, who dismissed him, and he went his way.*

David, cum immutavit vultum suum coram Abimelech, et dimisit eum, et abiit.

THE TITLE ASSIGNED TO THIS PSALM IS expounded upon in the title itself: 33{34}[1] *David, cum immutavit vultum suum coram Achimelech, et dimisit eum, et abiit. For David, when he changed his countenance before Achimelech, who dismissed him, and he went his way.* In the first book of Samuel[1] is narrated the story of how the holy David, suffering the persecution of Saul, came to Achis, the king of Geth (who is [also] called by another name, Abimelech) so that he might be saved in his land. But the Philistine servants of Achis recognizing David, told the king, "Isn't this *David the king of the land*, that is, the future king"?[2] [In doing so,] it was as if they were saying: "It is profitable for us to kill him, that he not be promoted to the kingship, lest he make war and oppress our land." Hearing that, the king wanted to kill him. David, sensing this and yet powerless to resist, feigned madness, and struck his hands against the doors, and allowed spittle to run down out of his mouth. Seeing this, Abimelech said to his servants: *You saw the man was mad: why have you brought him to me... to play the madman in my presence?*[3] He therefore caused him to be thrown out [of the city] and David was spared. Whence literally understood this Psalm was made to give thanks to God for this deliverance.

But according to the spiritual and mystical understanding, by David is understood Christ, and by Abimelech, which is understood as meaning

---

1   1 Sam. 21:10–15.
2   1 Sam. 21:11.
3   1 Sam. 21:14–15.

"the reign of my father,"[4] is understood the Jews, of which the Savior in the Gospels said: *The children of the kingdom shall be cast out into the exterior darkness.*[5] For David came to Abimelech, that is, Christ came to the Jews, based upon that which he said: *I was not sent but to the sheep that are lost of the house of Israel.*[6] Whom, when the Jews saw, they said: *This is the heir, let us kill him, that the inheritance may be ours,*[7] lest the Romans come, and take away *our place and nation.*[8] But David feigned madness when they wished to kill him. So also Christ did not respond to Herod: for which reason, they thought him insane, and they made him dress in a white garment and mocked him as if he were a fool.[9] To his servants, Abimelech also said of David, "You have seen an insane man." And the Jews said of Christ: *He is mad.*[10] And Caiaphas said, *You have heard the blasphemy,*[11] which is the greatest insanity. Yet David was freed by the wicked king and his people, gave thanks to God, and authored this present Psalm. Thus also Christ in the Resurrection, freed from the chief priests and the malice of the Jews, returned thanks to the Father, according to that which was said in an earlier Psalm: *I will declare your name to my brethren: in the midst of the Church will I praise you.*[12] And so this Psalm is befitting of Christ, indeed, [it also befits] any Christian who may be delivered from various tribulations, and for this reason giving thanks to the Lord.

> 33{34}[2] *I will bless the Lord at all times, his praise shall be always in my mouth.*
>
> Benedicam Dominum in omni tempore; semper laus eius in ore meo.

The Prophet [David] speaking therefore in the person of these, and desiring to enkindle all men to praise God, says: **33{34}[2]** *Benedicam Dominum, I will bless the Lord,* that is, I will say good things of the Lord, and I will praise him, and I will attribute all good to him, *in omni tempore,*

---

4   E. N. Abimelech is derived from the Hebrew words אב (*ab*), father, and מלך (melech), king.
5   Matt. 8:12a.
6   Matt. 15:24.
7   Luke 20:14. E. N. This comes from the Parable of the Wicked Husbandmen or the Parable of the Bad Tenants.
8   John 11:48b.
9   Luke 23: 9, 11.
10 John 10:20: *He has a devil, and is mad: why hear you him?*
11 Mark 14:64a.
12 Ps. 21:23.

at all times that are opportune and when it is becoming or allotted to me actively to praise. Or simply, *I will bless the Lord at all times*, not with my mouth, but in my deeds, or in the cessation from works, namely when I sleep, because I will ordain all things to the glory of God. *Semper laus eius in ore meo, his praise shall be always in my mouth*. He repeats what he has just said in order to express the fervor of his love which he has for this purpose, that he might be thankful to the Lord. For to bless the Lord is nothing other than to have his praise always in the mouth. For as there is a mental blessing and a vocal blessing, so there is also an interior or mental mouth by which the angels speak, and by which the word of the heart is offered; and there is also an exterior or bodily mouth, by which a word is sounded and transferred. And of both can be understood that which is said: *My soul shall praise the Lord even to death*.[13] And Tobias said: *Bless God at all times: and desire of him to direct your ways, and that all your counsels may abide in him*.[14] And the Apostle [Paul]: *Singing*, he said, *in grace in your hearts to God always*.[15]

Let the praise of God be in your mouth always, therefore, O brother, make it for yourself a good habitual practice, and do not ever give any rest to your lips; become accustomed to repeat the Psalms unceasingly with your mouth, to sing to the Lord, and to rejoice in the praise of God: and however much it may at times be for you a labor to so continue, still, if you constantly labor in doing it, that which before was burdensome and painful will become for you in a brief time light and sweet. For custom or habit is a second nature,[16] and therefore it makes it agreeable. Think about how miserable it is to expend time unfruitfully, and that nothing is a more divine and more excellent and so angelic and heavenly an occupation in this present life than to praise God; and from this consideration, do not become weary in the praise of God, because he says: *whosoever shall glorify me, him will I glorify*.[17]

Additionally, this first verse perfectly agrees with the Lord Savior, since he also enjoyed the beatific vision, so that Christ as man, from the first instant of his conception within his mother, actually blessed the Lord *at*

---

13 Ecclus. 51:8.
14 Tob. 4:20.
15 Col. 3:16: *Let the word of Christ dwell in you abundantly, in all wisdom: teaching and admonishing one another in psalms, hymns, and spiritual canticles, singing in grace in your hearts to God.*
16 E. N. *Consuetudo... seu habitus, est altera natura*, "custom or habit is a second nature," has both Ciceronian (*De finibus*, 5, 25: *Consuetodo quasi altera natura*) and Aristotelian (*Rhetoric*, I, 11, 1370a: ὅμοιον γάρ τι τὸ ἔθος τῇ φύσει) origins.
17 1 Sam. 2:30b. E. N. The verse continues: *but they that despise me, shall be despised.*

all times, and in his mouth revolved his praise, at least in an interior sense. For sleeping, eating, speaking, and such similar things never suspended or hindered the soul of Christ from the active contemplation, love, and praise of the Godhead.

33{34}[3] *In the Lord shall my soul be praised: let the meek hear and rejoice.*
In Domino laudabitur anima mea: audiant mansueti, et laetentur.

33{34}[3] *In Dominio laudabitur anima mea, in the Lord shall my soul be praised*: that is, if anyone might wish to praise me on account of the virtues he sees in me, he may praise me not in myself, but in the Lord, because from him is all my perfection. I have nothing that I have not received from elsewhere:[18] and so I do not wish, nor ought I, praise myself in myself. And so let no one adulate me, let no one applaud me, but rather let him render thanks to the Lord for all virtue and goodness in created things encountered, in the manner that the Apostle [Paul] said, *only to God, be honor and glory.*[19] But to those desirous of praising themselves, the Lord says through Isaiah: *O my people, they that call you blessed, the same deceive you, and destroy the way of your steps.*[20] And as often, therefore, you sense the temptation of caressing yourself with vain praise, or a movement of elation on account of a good you might have, respond: *In the Lord shall my soul be praised.*

---

18 Cf. 1 Cor. 4:7: *For who distinguishes you? Or what have you that you have not received? And if you have received, why do you glory, as if you had not received it?*
19 1 Tim. 1:17. E. N. This expression is the source of the motto of the Society of Jesus. In his *Scintillae Ignatiane* I, 1, the Jesuit Gabriel Hevenesi has some interesting reflections on this: "All for the greater glory of God! St. Ignatius repeats these words and their like 376 times in his Constitutions. In ... life as a whole, happiness consists in this: that at all time and during all our actions we direct ourselves only to the glory of God. This God demands as the supreme law of his dominion; this ought we to have as the essential title of our servitude. He who seeks his own — and not God's — glory is a thief and a robber, for glory is due to God alone, and to [give glory to] ourselves is confusion and scandal. That debt [of giving glory to God] should be our stimulus, even our watchword. No one can be considered worse than he who places his own glory before God's glory; for he experiences loss both in time, and in eternity; he will always be miserable; here because it is true; there, because all is forsaken. This they will acknowledge, but it will be too late. Though we were to work all night, we would achieve nothing. For human glory is nothing at all, for it is as a bloom on top of straw, and it is quickly trampled upon; it is like praising smoke, which perishes. If you esteem glory, seek for the true one."
20 Is. 3:12b.

Audiant mansueti, let the meek hear that which I have said: for that which has been said is very wise. For the irascible, the indignant, and the proud want to praise in themselves, and not in the Lord. But the meek have conquered anger, and, as a consequence indignation and pride (because indignation arises from pride, and from indignation impatience, and from impatience even anger), and so the meek only desire to praise in the Lord; and while their praise by others yields to edification and to the glory of God, freely they then hear his praises. Indeed because of this they sometimes openly speak about their own good, in the manner that Paul frequently did in his epistles: *I have in no way come* short, he says, *of them that are above measure apostles;*[21] and, *I have labored more abundantly than all they;*[22] and, *I know a man in Christ . . . one caught up to the third heaven;*[23] and *I withstood* Cephas, that is the chief of the Apostles Peter, *to the face, because he was to be blamed;*[24] and in many other places. And so *let the meek hear* that which I say, in the Lord my soul ought to praise, *et laetentur, and rejoice,* that is, rejoice with me on the conferred graces, and that they might wish to imitate my desire, seeking to praise the Lord alone: as Zephaniah said, *Seek the Lord, all you meek of the earth, you that have wrought his judgment.*[25]

33{34}[4] O magnify the Lord with me; and let us extol his name together.

Magnificate Dominum mecum, et exaltemus nomen eius in idipsum.

Next, the saintly man, not sufficient in and of himself to praise the Lord sufficiently, incites others to praise God publicly, saying: **33{34} [4]** *Magnificate Dominum mecum, O magnify the Lord with me,* that is, acknowledge, confess, and honor the vastness of God, namely, his boundless perfection, as I do; *et exaltemus, and let us extol,* that is, let us reverently venerate, *nomen eius in idipsum, his name together,* that is, with concordant affection and a like faith, as the Apostle [Paul] admonished, *That you all speak the same thing,*[26] *teaching and admonishing one another in psalms, hymns, and spiritual canticles.*[27]

---

21 2 Cor. 12:11b.
22 1 Cor. 15:10.
23 2 Cor. 12:2.
24 Gal. 2:11.
25 Zeph. 2:3a.
26 1 Cor. 1:10a.
27 Col. 3:16b.

33{34}[5] *I sought the Lord, and he heard me; and he delivered me from all my troubles.*

Exquisivi Dominum, et exaudivit me; et ex omnibus tribulationibus meis eripuit me.

33{34}[5] *Exquisivi Dominum, I sought the Lord*: in the manner that Isaiah exhorts: *Seek the Lord, while he may be found: call upon him, while he is near.*[28] And if you ask when this is, the Apostle [Paul] responds: *Behold, now is the acceptable time; behold, now is the day of salvation.*[29] For *the Lord is nigh* now.[30] And *he who seeks shall find.*[31] And he testifies in Revelation: *Behold, I stand at the gate, and knock.*[32] Therefore, so it is that *I sought the Lord*, faithfully contemplating, ardently loving, rightly living, and devoutly praying, *et exaudivit me, and he heard me*: so I have encountered him, and I am united in him by charity and grace; *et ex omnibus tribulationibus meis eripuit me, and he delivered me from all my troubles*, either entirely removing them from me or giving me the grace patiently to endure them. This also applies to Christ: for through praying he also sought God, and in the day of the Resurrection, God delivered him from all troubles.

33{34}[6] *Come to him and be enlightened: and your faces shall not be confounded.*

Accedite ad eum, et illuminamini; et facies vestrae non confundentur.

33{34}[7] *This poor man cried, and the Lord heard him: and saved him out of all his troubles.*

Iste pauper clamavit, et Dominus exaudivit eum, et de omnibus tribulationibus eius salvavit eum.

And, therefore, also you, O my brothers and my neighbors, acquire that grace, **33{34}[6]** *Accedite ad eum, come to him*, not by movement of the body, but by affection of the heart; not with your feet, but with faith; not only by word, but by deed and in truth. *Et illuminamini, and be enlightened*: that is, if you thus approach him, then certainly he will

---

28 Is. 55:6.
29 2 Cor. 6:2b.
30 Phil. 4:5b.
31 Matt. 7:8b.
32 Rev. 3:20a.

enlighten you interiorly in your soul with the light of grace, and the clarity of wisdom, and the beauty of justice. Whence, blessed James says: *But if any of you want wisdom, let him ask of God, who gives to all men abundantly, . . . and it shall be given him. But let him ask in faith, nothing wavering.*[33] And the Lord speaking through Malachi says: *But unto you that fear my name, the sun of justice shall arise.*[34] *Et facies vestrae non confudentur, and your faces shall not be confounded,* that is, your intellects or hearts will not be defrauded in their hope, nor will they be exposed to contempt, but they will most certainly obtain that which they seek. And this is evident from this: **33{34}[7]** *Iste pauper, this poor man,* namely, Christ, *that being rich he became poor,* for our sakes;[35] or [also], *this poor man,* namely, David, who in the book of Samuel asserts about himself, *I am a poor man, and of small ability;*[36] or [in addition], *this poor man,* that is, anyone humble and little in his own eyes, who is attentive to his imperfection. And so, *this poor man clamavit, cried,* with an ardent affection and devout prayers pleading for the mercy of God; *et Dominus exaudivit eum, et de omnibus tribulationibus; and the Lord heard him: and . . . from out of all his troubles* of mind and body, *salvavit eum, he saved him,* in the present life by alleviation and by hope, and after this present life by all sorts of removal of evil, according to that which is written: *And God shall wipe away all tears from* his *saints' eyes.*[37]

33{34}[8] *The angel of the Lord shall be sent*[38] *round about them that fear him: and shall deliver them.*

Immittet angelus Domini in circuitu timentium eum, et eripiet eos.

33{34}[8] *Immittet angelus Domini,* the angel of the Lord shall be sent, [the angel of the Lord, that is,] his help, *in circuitu timentium eum, round about them that fear him,* namely, [round about them that fear the Lord]: that is, he will protect them from all sides, keeping the attacks of demons and the dangers of the world away from them, and persuading

---

33 James 1:5–6.
34 Mal. 4:2a.
35 2 Cor. 8:9a.
36 1 Sam. 18:23.
37 Rev. 21:4a.
38 *E. N.* The Douay-Rheims has "shall encamp" for *immittet;* however, it might be translated as shall be sent, introduced into, admitted, dispatched. Accordingly, I have changed "shall encamp" to "shall be sent."

and enlightening their interior toward the good. For some angelic spirits, such as archangels, watch over groups of people; and one of these [particular archangels] defends and helps many, namely St. Michael, who now keeps watch over the Church as in the Old Testament he kept watch over the Synagogue.[39] But other angelic spirits have charge over single men, like the angels of the lowest order, and these separately protect individual men.[40] In this place one is to understand where it says, *the angel of the Lord shall be sent*, etc. as a singular being placed for a plural, in the manner that is found written in the book of Exodus, *a grievous fly came into the house of Pharaoh*.[41] *Et eripiet eos*, *and shall deliver them*, namely, the angels [shall deliver] men from many evils. For no man is so ungodly to the point where his holy guardian angel does not still preserve him from many sins.[42]

33{34}[9] *O taste and see that the Lord is sweet: blessed is the man that hopes in him.*

Gustate et videte quoniam suavis est Dominus; beatus vir qui sperat in eo.

33{34}[8] *Gustate et videte*, *O taste and see*, that is, live in such a fashion, adhere to God with such holiness, purity, and integrity, so that he might give you such great grace, by which with certainty and

---

39 Cf. Dan. 12:1.
40 E. N. "From its beginning until death, human life is surrounded by [the angels'] watchful care and intercession. 'Beside each believer stands an angel as protector and shepherd leading him to life.' Already here on earth the Christian life shares by faith in the blessed company of angels and men united in God." CCC § 336 (quoting St. Basil, *Adv. Eunomium* III, I, PG 29, 656). "Each man has an angel guardian appointed to him." ST Ia, q. 133, art. 2, co.
41 Ex. 8:24. E. N. In the Vulgate, the singular term *musca* is used in Exodus 8:24, though clearly the plural "flies" is intended. *Et venit musca gravissima in domos Pharaonis*, "and grievous fly came into the houses of Pharaoh." The Douay-Rheims has already interpreted the singular *musca* as a plural noun ("swarm of flies").
42 E. N. St. Thomas Aquinas explains: "The guardianship of the angels ... is a carrying out of the divine providence over man. But it is manifest that neither man, nor any thing whatsoever, is totally deprived of divine providence: for insofar as a thing participates being it falls, to that extent, under the universal providence over all being. But God is said to forsake man according to the order of his providence, yet this only to the extent he permits men to suffer some defect or punishment or fault. In a similar way, it is also said that the guardian angel never totally forsakes a man, but sometimes he forsakes him in some particular thing, as, for example, he does not prevent him from being placed into some distress, or also does not prevent him from falling into sin, according to the order of the divine judgments." ST Ia, q. 133, art. 6, co.

experientially you will know that which follows in this verse: *quoniam suavis est Dominus, that the Lord is sweet.* For all know God to be sweet by their intellect, but not all taste it through their affections. By natural reason one can recognize the sweetness of God, but it is tasted only by grace. But nothing tastes sweet unless it is loved: and so love is the cause of relish. Therefore, for man to experience divine sweetness, it is necessary that he love God fervidly; and that is not possible unless he excludes from himself those things which diminish charity. For cupidity or an inordinately self-regarding private love is the poison and diminution of charity.[43] But the increase or the progress of charity is the reduction of private love. And the perfection of charity is the total expulsion of private love: when, namely, a man loves himself purely in God, desiring nothing and loving nothing except God because of [God] himself, and himself in relation to God, and all else insofar as by them he may be led to God. He, therefore, who so loves God spurns and flees all bodily delights, all carnal pleasures, all temporal honors, and all fleeting and vain things, because by such things he is kept distant from God. Moreover, he loves mortification of the flesh, the derision and contempt of the world, adversities and difficulties, holy vigils, continual prayers, and such similar things because by such things he is united to God.

And so he who is like this is able to taste *that the Lord is sweet.* For truly sweet is the Lord, and he is the fountain of all sweetness, from which

---

43   E. N. Self-love (*amor sui*), which Denis appears to contrast with private love (*amor privatus*) here, is not necessarily an evil. (After all, we are to love others as ourselves, which necessarily means we must love ourselves. See Mark 12:31. And God necessarily loves himself. DS 3025.) And yet, as St. Thomas states referring to St. Augustine: *omnium peccatorum radix est una, scilicet amor sui,* "the root of all sin is one, namely, love of self." *Super Sent.,* lib. 2, d. 42, q. 2 a. 1, arg. 5. When that self-love becomes disordered, when entirely turned into itself (*ad se recurvus*) and incapable of regarding the beloved for any other reason than self-referent love, that self-love corrupts into what Denis calls the private love which is poisonous to, or privative of, charity. St. Augustine identified the same notion, but he distinguished between an evil, egoistic self-love (*improbus amor sui*, which Denis calls private love) and natural and virtuous self-love (*probus amor sui*). Though an ordered modicum of self-love must be retained by the perfect, the disorder of an excessive self-love, that part Denis calls a private love (because it *deprives* us of charity), must entirely be pared away without excising an ordered, reasonable self-love consistent with charity. "For man must love not only the neighbor out of charity, but also himself out of charity both with respect to the soul and body; and it is in this manner also the Father by the Holy Spirit loves [himself]." *Super Sent.,* lib. 1, d. 32, q. 1, a. 2 ad 3. The notion that perfection is obtained by totally extinguishing self-love — the error of the Quietists such as de Molinos (1627–1696), Madame Guyon (1648–1717), and Fénelon (1651–1715) — has been condemned by the Church. *E.g.,* DS 2256, 2369, 2373.

all sweet things obtain their sweetness: and the most high and blessed God himself is essentially sweetness, and no creature [of its natural powers] has experience with this wholly separate, immense, supersubstantial, and fountainlike sweetness in its fullness. And it is truly entirely most worthy, that he who desires to taste this sweetness of the divine goodness, should abhor all unworthy and vile and transitory delights, so that he might serve God with complete custody of his mind, with charity, and with reverence. For this tasting is a certain and supernatural foretaste of the future beatitude, which none of the philosophers or proud theologians have ever tasted; but those with meek and humble heart, who with all their devotion they affix themselves upon that one who alone is necessary,[44] are deserving to taste it. The most holy Isaiah tasted this sweetness when he said those words sweeter than honey and the honeycomb:[45] *Your name, and your remembrance are the desire of the soul. My soul has desired you in the night: yea, and with my spirit within me in the morning early I will watch for you.*[46] And so also Jeremiah, when he said: *There came in my heart as a burning fire shut up in my bones, and I was wearied, not being able to bear it.*[47] When also in another place it is written: *O how good and sweet is your spirit, O Lord, in all things!*[48]

Beatus vir qui sperat in eo, blessed the man that hopes in him. This verse has already been frequently expounded.[49]

33{34}[10] *Fear the Lord, all you his saints: for there is no want to them that fear him.*

Timete Dominum, omnes sancti eius, quoniam non est inopia timentibus eum.

33{34}[11] *The rich have wanted, and have suffered hunger: but they that seek the Lord shall not be deprived of any good.*

Divites eguerunt, et esurierunt; inquirentes autem Dominum non minuentur omni bono.

---

44   *Cf.* Luke 10:42.
45   E. N. *Cf.* Ps. 18:11: The judgments of the lord are "sweeter than honey and the honeycomb," *dulciora super mel et favum*.
46   Is. 26:8-9a.
47   Jer. 20:9b.
48   Wis. 12:1.
49   E. N. *See* Article LXIX (Psalm 31:2) in this Volume, and especially Article VIII (Psalm 1:1), Article IX (Psalm 1:1), Article X (Psalm 1:1), and Article XI (Psalm 1:1) in Volume 1.

And so that you might be found worthy to taste the sweetness of God, 33{34}[10] *Timete, fear* with a filial,[50] loving, and holy fear, *Dominum, omnes sancti eius; the Lord, all you his saints,* who still are wayfaring upon the earth and are aspiring to the heavenly homeland, *quoniam non est inopia timentibus eum, for there is no want to them that fear him.* For with regard to spiritual and corporal goods, the Lord provides sufficiently to them: indeed also in the interior goods he gives to them daily increase and in great abundance, in the manner that the Savior says in the Gospel: one who has, that is, one who walks before the Lord solicitously and full of thanks, *shall be given, and he shall abound.*[51] 33{34}[11] *Divites eguerunt, the rich have wanted,*[52] that is, glorying in the riches of this world, or desiring them excessively, they have wanted grace and virtues of the soul. For as the Virgin bearer of Christ said: *the rich he has sent empty away,*[53] that is, empty of spiritual graces. *Et esurierunt, and have suffered hunger,* not, of course, for justice and the kingdom of God, but for worldly wealth: because, as it says in Ecclesiastes, *A covetous man shall not be satisfied with money.*[54] For the more they acquire of these riches, the more they desire them. *Inquirentes autem Dominum, but they that seek the Lord,* that is, those hungering and thirsting for justice,[55] *non minuentur omni bono, shall not be deprived of any good.* Indeed, they will make progress incessantly, until rising upwards they come to eternal beatitude.

33{34}[12] *Come, children, hearken to me: I will teach you the fear of the Lord.*
Venite, filii, audite me; timorem Domini docebo vos.

33{34}[13] *Who is the man that desires life: who loves to see good days?*
Quis est homo qui vult vitam, diligit dies videre bonos?

33{34}[12] *Venite, filii, audite me; come, children, hearken to Me,* that is, *gather yourselves together into the house of discipline,*[56] and perceive my instruction with the ears of your heart; *timorem Domini docebo vos, I*

---

50 E. N. On filial, as distinguished from servile or reverential fear, see Article LXVII (Psalm 30:20) in this Volume, and Article XLV (Psalm 18:10) and footnote 18-42 in Volume 1.
51 Luke 19:26; *Cf.* Matt. 25:29.
52 E. N. The word translated here as "have wanted," *ereguerunt,* means to be in want, in need, or lacking, or even poor; in other words, "the rich have needed or lacked."
53 Luke 1:53.
54 Eccl. 5:9a.
55 *Cf.* Matt. 5:6.
56 Ecclus. 51:31b.

will teach you the fear of the Lord, that is, I will show you what pertains to the fear of God, and in what manner it may be acquired, preserved, and perfected. And you ought freely to listen to me, because my instruction avails in obtaining eternal life, which, because you aspire for it, it behooves you to come to me. Therefore, [the verse] follows with: **33{34} [13]** *Quis est homo qui vult vitam, who is the man that desires life*, a religious, spiritual, and holy [life], *diligit dies videre bonos? who loves to see good days?* That is, who is it that desires to acquire eternal life? And he directs his attention to [respond to] that which I ask:

33{34}[14] *Keep your tongue from evil, and your lips from speaking guile.*
Prohibe linguam tuam a malo, et labia tua ne loquantur dolum.

33{34}[15] *Turn away from evil and do good: seek after peace and pursue it.*
Declina a malo, et fac bonum; inquire pacem, et persequere eam.

33{34}[14] *Prohibe linguam tuam a malo, keep your tongue from evil*, that is, contain yourself from any illicit speech; *et labia tua ne loquantur dolum, and your lips from speaking guile*, that is, check yourself so that you do not deceive anyone. **33{34}[15]** *Declina a malo, Turn away from evil*,[57] that is, withdraw from sin, in the manner that is elsewhere written, *Flee from sins as from the face of a serpent*;[58] *et fac bonum, and do good*, that is, keep the commandments and do those things that are pleasing to God. *Inquire pacem, seek after peace*, that is, study and stay busy to have tranquility in mind and to have concord with your neighbor: but most of all do and order all things so that you might merit to be led to the peace of the heavenly homeland; *et persequere eam, and pursue it*, that is, to follow after it perfectly and indefatigably, embracing and doing those things that are conducive to acquiring and conserving peace, and also avoiding those things that destroy peace, namely, quarrels, stubborn defense of your own judgments, stinging and derisive words. For here the Apostle [Paul] said: *If it be possible, as much as is in you, have peace with all men.*[59] And again he says: *Let us follow after the things that are of peace; and keep the things that are of edification one towards another.*[60] And to the Colossians: *And let the peace of Christ rejoice in your hearts.*[61]

---

57 E. N. The Clementine Vulgate has *diverte a malo*, "divert from evil."
58 Ecclus. 21:2a.
59 Rom. 12:18.
60 Rom. 14:19a.
61 Col. 3:15a.

Finally, in that which the Psalmist said, *Turn away from evil and do good*, he touches upon the two parts of justice, the observation of which is in what the height of all perfection consists. And Christ touches upon these two parts of justice in the Gospel, when he says: *Let your loins be girt*, that is, abstain from evil; *and lamps burning in your hands*,[62] that is, do good. It is also clear from this how great a virtue it is to check the tongue from all harmful speech. For this reason, Solomon said: *He that keeps his mouth, keeps his soul: but he that has no guard on his speech shall meet with evils.*[63] And elsewhere: *He that uses many words shall hurt his own soul;*[64] *but he that refrains his lips is most wise.*[65] And James said: *And if any man think himself to be religious, not bridling his tongue, but deceiving his own heart, this man's religion is vain.*[66]

33{34}[16] *The eyes of the Lord are upon the just: and his ears unto their prayers.*

Oculi Domini super iustos, et aures eius in preces eorum.

33{34}[17] *But the countenance of the Lord is against them that do evil things: to cut off the remembrance of them from the earth.*

Vultus autem Domini super facientes mala, ut perdat de terra memoriam eorum.

33{34}[16] *Oculi Domini super iustos*, the eyes of the Lord are upon the just, that is, the sight of divine goodness is wide over them who are obedient to God, so that he might preserve them and direct them; *et aures eius, and his ears*, that is, the mercy and liberality of God, *in preces eorum, unto their prayers*, that he may hear them. *For the prayer of him that humbles himself, shall pierce the clouds.*[67] 33{34}[17] *Vultus autem Domini*, but the countenance of the Lord, that is, the sight of divine justice, *super facientes mala, ut perdat de terra memoriam eorum; is against them that do evil things: to cut off the remembrance of them from the earth*, that is, exclude them from the Kingdom of Heaven, which is the land of the living, the life of the blessed, so that none of the Saints in heaven will be mindful of them in good, namely, feeling condolence for them or interceding for them.

---

62 Luke 12:35.
63 Prov. 13:3.
64 Ecclus. 20:8a.
65 Prov. 10:19b.
66 James 1:26.
67 Ecclus. 25:21a.

33{34}[18] *The just cried, and the Lord heard them: and delivered them out of all their troubles.*

Clamaverunt iusti, et Dominus exaudivit eos; et ex omnibus tribulationibus eorum liberavit eos.

33{34}[19] *The Lord is nigh unto them that are of a contrite heart: and he will save the humble of spirit.*

Iuxta est Dominus iis qui tribulato sunt corde, et humiles spiritu salvabit.

33{34}[18] *Clamaverunt iusti, the just cried,* praying fervently for divine aid; *et Dominus exaudivit eos, et ex omnibus tribulationibus eorum liberavit eos, and the Lord heard them; and delivered them out of all their troubles,* either in the present life, or certainly after this present life, them eternal rest, as it is manifested in the holy martyrs. 33{34}[19] *Iuxta est Dominus, the Lord is nigh,* through grace and his mercy, *his qui tribulato sunt corde, unto them that are of contrite heart,* that is, who suffer on account of justice, or who are afflicted with good sorrow (namely, for sin), or who with equanimity endure adversities for God's sake: indeed he is close to all the distressed, in that—in general and all things being equal—he is more speedily inclined to be merciful, indulgent, and to render aid to them than he is to others. [This is so] because (as the Apostle [Paul] attests) *the weak things of the world has God chosen, that he may confound the strong.*[68] Whence [the prophet] Baruch says: *The soul that is sorrowful for the greatness of evil it has done, and goes bowed down, and feeble, and the eyes that fail...gives glory and justice to you the Lord.*[69] For in them the divine justice shines again, and, therefore, because they have turned around in this life, God bends down to them so that he may have mercy upon them. *Et humiles spiritu salvabit, and he will save the humble of spirit,* in the manner that the Gospels say: *Blessed are the poor in spirit: for theirs is the kingdom of heaven.*[70]

33{34}[20] *Many are the afflictions of the just; but out of them all will the Lord deliver them.*

Multae tribulationes iustorum; et de omnibus his liberabit eos Dominus.

---

68 1 Cor. 1:27b.
69 Baruch 2:18.
70 Matt. 5:3.

33{34}[21] *The Lord keeps all their bones, not one of them shall be broken. Custodit Dominus omnia ossa eorum: unum ex his non conteretur.*

33{34}[20] *Multae tribulations iustorum, many are the afflictions of the just*: for they afflict the heart and body in various ways, and as a result of diverse causes, namely, because of one's own sins, because of the lack of one's perfection, because of our neighbors' errors, and because of the dishonor of God, and other such similar causes; *et de omnibus his liberabit eos Dominos, but out of them all will the Lord deliver them*, in part in this age by the consolation of the Holy Spirit, and perfectly in the future age, when they will possess beatitude in its fullness. For this reason, Scripture says: *The Lord is good and gives strength in the day of trouble: and knows them that hope in him.*[71] 33{34}[21] *Custodit Dominus omnia ossa eorum, the Lord keeps all their bones*, that is, the Lord conserves the virtues of the just, who are strong and fixed and reliant of heart in God;[72] *unum ex his non conteretur, not one of them shall be broken*, that is, no virtue of the just shall perish, but with the Lord's preservative power it will be kept unharmed in temptation, and not overthrown by vice. This is true of the elect and those who persevere [in the grace of God] until the end. Or the sense [of this verse could also be understood] that *their bones* (that is, virtues) are conserved, not by themselves, but by being kept safe by the Lord. This verse can also be explained as referring to the bones of the body, and it may be [thought as referring to the bones] during suffering [in this life], or after death that while, turning to dust or being brought to naught, they may be watched by the Lord, and not finally remain ground to dust; but rather that they might rise again and be joined with the soul, as also with the flesh, in the last day. Christ, in accordance with this manner [of understanding the verse] says in the Gospel: *But a hair of your head shall not perish.*[73]

---

71 Nahum 1:7.
72 E. N. Denis has likened bones to the virtues before. *See* Article LXVIII (Psalm 30:11). This is a common comparison: For example, Pope St. Gregory the Great in his *Moralia in Iob* states: "Bones in Holy Scripture we understand to mean virtues, as it is written 'The Lord keeps all their bones; not one of them shall be broken.' Of course, this is not understood as the bones of the body, but it is said in reference to the powers of the mind. For certainly we know of the many martyrs whose bodily bones were broken." *Mor. In Iob*, XXIII, 48, PL 76, 280.
73 Luke 21:18.

33{34}[22] *The death of the wicked is very evil: and they that hate the just shall be guilty.*

Mors peccatorum pessima; et qui oderunt iustum delinquent.

33{34}[23] *The Lord will redeem the souls of his servants: and none of them that trust in him shall offend.*

Redimet Dominus animas servorum suorum, et non delinquent omnes qui sperant in eo.

33{34}[22] *Mors peccatorum pessima, the death of the wicked is very evil:* because this is the way to eternal death, and after it there is no possible way to make reparation; *et qui oderunt iustum, delinquent; and they that hate the just shall be guilty:* for hatred of the just is a great sin, and it is much greater [a sin] than hatred of the sinner, though both are mortal sins, just as is hatred of the enemy. 33{34}[23] *Redimet Dominus animas servorum suorum, the Lord will redeem the souls of his servants,* forgiving their sins, and transferring them from the way of this exile unto the heavenly homeland; *et non delinquent omnes qui spirant in eo, and none of them that trust in him shall offend:* not that they do not ever sin, but because they do penance, and they do not finally persist in sin. According to this understanding, there is written in another place: *Whosoever is born of God, commits not sin: for his seed abides in him, and he cannot sin,* but the begetting of God preserves him.[74]

See how wonderful the power of this Psalm is, how consoled and happy are those who attentively recite this Psalm. First of all, it contains the praise of the Almighty. Then it excites all men to his praise; it also narrates the various benefits of God, and it invites us to the taste of the divine goodness. It also puts forward most wholesome exhortations and perfect precepts. Finally, it clearly distinguishes between the just and the ungodly; it shows the vanity of the worldly man, and it encourages individuals to look upon the Creator of all things, so that considering all things in the presence of God, men might strive to live in fear. Let us

---

74 1 John 3:9: E. N. Denis has an alternative reading from the Sixto-Clementine Vulgate in the last clause. He states *sed generatio Dei conservat illum,* "but the begetting [generation] of God preserves him." The Vulgate has *quoniam ex Deo natus est,* "because he is born of God." Denis is saying that 1 John 3:9 should be interpreted in the same manner as Psalm 33:23, namely that it does not mean literally we will never sin, but that we do penance and do not finally persist in sin. This, of course, is consistent with 1 John 1:8–9: *If we say that we have no sin, we deceive ourselves, and the truth is not in us. If we confess our sins, he is faithful and just, to forgive us our sins, and to cleanse us from all iniquity.*

therefore be diligent to sing this Psalm with all steadfastness, attention, and fervor: for if we do such a thing, we will experience a marvelous sweetness in him, we will be raised to greater progress, and we will be instructed in the contempt of the world.

PRAYER

GOD, PROPITIATOR OF ALL, MAKE US TO turn away from evil and to do good; give us the desire always to seek after and to follow peace by which, tasting your sweetness, and experiencing your preventing mercy, we who hope in you may be numbered among the blessed in heaven.

Propitiator omnium Deus, fac nos declinare a malo, et facere bonum; da nobis pacem semper inquirere et sectari, per quam, suavitatem tuam gustantes et videntes praeveniente clementia tua, beatificemur in te sperantes.

Psalm 34

ARTICLE LXXII

EXPOSITION OF THE THIRTY-FOURTH PSALM:
IUDICA, DOMINE, NOCENTES ME
JUDGE, O LORD, THEM THAT WRONG ME.

34{35}[1] *For David himself. Judge, O Lord, them that wrong me: overthrow them that fight against me.*

Ipsi David. Iudica, Domine, nocentes me; expugna impugnantes me.

34{35}[2] *Take hold of arms and shield: and rise up to help me.*

Apprehende arma et scutum, et exsurge in adiutorium mihi.

34{35}[3] *Bring out the sword, and shut up the way against them that persecute me: say to my soul: I am your salvation.*

Effunde frameam, et conclude adversus eos qui persequuntur me; dic animae meae: Salus tua ego sum.

THIS PSALM HAS A TITLE ALREADY EXPOUNDED upon: 34{35}[1] *Psalmus ipsi David, a Psalm for David himself*: that is, this Psalm composed by David both befits Christ, who is prefigured by David, and his [Christ's] members. First, therefore, we will see it expounded as to Christ, and then of his members.

Christ, therefore, as man, the Passion already having come upon him, said to the eternal Father, or to the entire superlatively most happy Trinity: *Iudica, Domine, nocentes me; Judge, O Lord, them that wrong me*, that is, carry out the sentence of your judgment against the Jews persecuting me; *expugna impugnantes, overthrow them that fight against me*, that is, vanquish, cast down, and with power, deprive of their ruleship and their country the Jews who are pouncing upon me with words and with lashes. This was fulfilled in the Jews by the leaders of the Romans, who in a most harsh way devastated, battled, expelled, and killed them. 34{35}[2] *Apprehende arma et scutum, take hold of arms and shield*, that is, of the arms and shields of the Roman leaders, namely Vespasian and Titus with their people,[1] against the Jews; *et exsurge in adiutorium mihi, and rise up*

---

1 E. N. For Vespasian and Titus, *see* footnote 27-24.

to help me, that is, through the hands of those battling my adversaries. **34{35}[3]** *Effunde frameam, bring out the sword*, that is, extract the blade, increase the taking of vengeance, and send forth vindication: *et conclude adversus eos qui persequuntur me, and shut up the way against them that persecute me*, that is, bring all this evil punishment upon the Jews, and deliver them over into the hands of their enemies in accordance with the sin which they committed against me.

Or, also in a spiritual sense, [it can be interpreted] thus: *Take hold of arms and shields*, that is, receive your divine and omnipotent virtue by which you yourself are made strong and armed, as it were, and able to defend others. This strength of God is the omnipotent God himself; but so long as God does not use this power, such as, for example, allowing just men to be troubled by evil, then it seems as if his arms and shield have been set aside, according to that which another prophet said: *Why do you not look at the disdainful, O Lord, and are silent, when the ungodly is oppressing the one more just than he?*[2] When God therefore exercises his power, he will deliver the good and will afflict the ungodly; it is then said that he takes up his power, that is, the *arms and shield*. It is in accordance with this sense that we find written: *We give you thanks, O Lord God Almighty, who are, and who were, and who are to come: because you have taken to you yourself great power, and you have reigned.*[3] For as long as he permitted idolatry to grow strong and demons to prevail over men, it was as if he lay down his powers; but since he came incarnate into the world, *he has rejoiced as a giant to run the way,*[4] and in subduing the powers of the air[5] and rescuing men, he has accepted his power, and he reigns over those things where before the devil reigned. Therefore, Christ, as man, says this to God the Father: *Take hold of arms and shield, and rise up to help me*, that is, from my mortality redeem me by the blessed Resurrection; and *say to my soul*, that is, to the life of my body: *I am your salvation*, that is, on the third day I will restore you, and I will make you immortal, uniting your soul with an immortal body. For by this prayer, Christ prays for the resurrection of his body.

---

2   Hab. 1:13. *E. N.* Denis departs from the Sixto-Clementine Vulgate, which reads: *Quare respicis super iniqua agentes, et taces devorante impio iustiorem se? Why do you look upon them that do unjust things, and hold your peace when the wicked devours the man that is more just than himself?* Instead, Denis states: *Quare respicis contemptores, et taces, conculcante impio iustiorem se?*
3   Rev. 11:17.
4   Ps. 18:6b.
5   *E. N. aeries potestates*, aerial powers. *Cf.* Eph. 2:2. A reference to demonic powers.

34{35}[4] *Let them be confounded and afraid that seek after my soul. Let them be turned back and be confounded that devise against me.*

Confundantur et revereantur quaerentes animam meam; avertantur retrorsum et confundantur cogitantes mihi mala.

34{35}[4] *Confundantur*, let them be confounded, that is, let them appear worthy of confusion and incur the punishment of their perversity, *et revereantur*, and afraid,⁶ that is, let them be terrified, inflicting punishment on themselves, *quaerentes animam meam, that seek after my soul*, that is, desiring to extinguish my life. In this way the Jews are confused and afraid in the present life and in the life which follows this one. For now they are disdained and oppressed by all, and after this life they will fall into eternal punishment. Those *cogitantes mihi mala, that devise against me*, that is, who conceive evil things against me, thinking about how they might be able to catch me with speech, to accuse me [of some wrong], and to kill me,⁷ *avertantur retrorsum, let them be turned back*, that is, let them be darkened with a blindness of mind and not be converted to you, but in their obstinacy let them depart from you, *et confundantur*, and [let them] be confounded, that is, by the experience of torment let them be ashamed for their malice during this time or [thereafter] in hell.

34{35}[5] *Let them become as dust before the wind: and let the angel of the Lord straiten them.*

Fiant tamquam pulvis ante faciem venti, et angelus Domini coarctans eos.

34{35}[6] *Let their way become dark and slippery; and let the angel of the Lord pursue them.*

Fiat via illorum tenebrae, et lubricum; et angelus Domini persequens eos.

34{35}[5] *Fiant tanquam pulvis ante faciem venti, let them become as dust before the wind*: that is, let the aforementioned Jews be easily overcome by their enemies, and so dispersed throughout the whole world, deprived of their own land, and driven about as easily as dust by the wind; *et angelus Domini coarctans eos, and let the angel of the Lord straiten them*, that is, let Michael who was at one time prince and protector of

---

6 E. N. The Douay-Rheims has "let them be ashamed"; however, *revereantur* might better translated by "let them be reverent" or even "let them be afraid," or "let them be awed" as Denis appears to understand it.
7 Luke 20:20; John 11:53.

the Synagogue,[8] now abandon them to be destroyed and to be placed in such straitened circumstances by the Roman people in the siege of Jerusalem by Titus. By the term angel one can also understand the evil angel whose collaboration caused the Jews' cruel reduction to straitened circumstances and their being cast aside in vengeance of the Blood of Christ. **34{35}[6]** *Fiat via illorum, let their way become,* that is, namely, let the life and the works of the Jews become, *tenebrae, dark,* that is, blinded and deprived from the light of faith, and the knowledge of Christ, *et lubricum, and slippery,* that is, wandering and inconstant: so that those who negate Christ will be unable to remain in the land of their proper dwelling and will not be supported by another stable foundation. For Christ is the only and true foundation of all the elect, in the manner that the Apostle [Paul] states: *For other foundation no man can lay, but that which is laid, which is Christ Jesus;*[9] *et angelus Domini persequens eos, and let the angel of the Lord pursue them,* that is, let the holy angel be sent down to vex them with persecution. Or [alternatively], the evil angel that he may persecute them, maintaining their hearts in the obstinacy of perfidy and causing them to fall into their temptations.

34{35}[7] *For without cause they have hidden their net for me unto destruction: without cause they have upbraided my soul.*

Quoniam gratis absconderunt mihi interitum laquei sui, supervacue exprobraverunt animam meam.

And this applies to them, **34{35}[7]** *Quoniam gratis absconderunt mihi interitum laquei sui, for without cause they have hidden their net for me unto destruction:* that is, without any fault of mine, they have directed themselves towards laying snares, and they took counsel against me as to how they may bring about my death.[10] For here in this verse death is called falling into a trap, that is, a trap to do away with me. For the Jews most deceitfully, and indeed in a hidden way, discussed among themselves how they would put Christ to death. *Supervacue exprobraverunt animam meam, without cause they have upraided my soul,* that is, they have excessively and uselessly laid upon me many crimes, calling me: a glutton,[11] a seducer of the people,[12] insane,[13] and such similar things.

---

8   Dan. 12:1.
9   1 Cor. 3:11.
10 Matt. 26:4; 27:1.
11 Matt. 11:9.
12 Luke 23:5; John 7:12.
13 John 10:20.

34{35}[8] *Let it come to him, the snare which he knows not; and let the trap which he has hidden catch him: and into that very snare let him fall.*[14]

Veniat illi laqueus quem ignorat, et captio quam abscondit apprehendat eum, et in laqueum cadat in ipsum.

34{35}[8] *Veniat illi,* let it come to him, that is, [let] the people persecuting me [come to it], *laqueus quem ignorat,* the snare which he knows not, that is, the unforeseen tribulation and uncertain death [he thought to entrap me with];[15] *et captio quam abscondit,* and let the trap which he has hidden, that is, the arresting, capturing, and binding up which they proposed to carry out against me, and which they in fact carried out in the night of my Passion, when a cohort and a tribune and the ministers of the Jews, laid their hands on me; *apprehendat eum,* catch him, that is, that his adversaries' capture, binding, and arrest may be for him a cause, reason, and occasion of merit; *et in laqueum cadat in ipsum,* and into that very snare let him fall, that his, this trap which they hid be injurious to them and become a snare of death; but to me let it not be injurious, but let it be the cause of honor and glory. All this we see fulfilled in the Jews and in Christ.[16]

---

14 E. N. I have had to depart significantly from the Douay-Rheims in this verse. The Douay-Rheims has Psalm 34:7 thus: *Let the snare which he knows not come upon him: and let the net which he has hidden catch him: and into that very snare let them fall.* This is problematic from both the underlying Latin and Denis's commentary. First, Denis understands the principal subject of this Psalm as a group of people (those adverse to Christ), and so he refers the personal pronoun, though singular, to this group. Second, the *et in laqueum cadat in ipsum* cannot be translated as "and into that very snare let *them* fall," since *cadat* is third person singular. Putting all these things together, I have translated the Latin as: *Let him [the trapper] come to it [the trap], the snare which he [the trapper] knows not; and let the trap which he [the trapper] has hidden catch him [the trapper]: and into that very snare let him [the trapper] fall.* In short, Ps. 34:7 says, "For 'tis the sport to have the engineer / Hoist with his own petard." Shakespeare, Hamlet, 3.4.230–31. Or, as Peter Lombard in his Commentary on the Psalms quotes St. Augustine saying: *Ipse suus laqueus teneat illos. Ecce digna retributio. Nil enim iustius quam illa evenire quae absconderunt. Inde enim decipiuntur, unde decipere voluerunt; inde nocetur eis, unde nocere voluerunt.* "Let their very own trap catch them. See the wonderful payback. For nothing is more just than that they should encounter that which they sought to hide; and that they be deceived precisely where they sought to deceive; that they are harmed precisely where they wished to harm." *Comm. in Ps.,* 34.9, PL 191, 349.
15 E. N. That is, from the perspective of the people thought to be unforeseen by Christ whom they sought to catch by surprise.
16 E. N. "The significance of the special preparation of the Jewish people *for the rest of pre-Christian* and *all of post-Christian mankind* became all the greater, precisely because this people availed itself so little of the divine commands. For precisely due

Moreover, Christ says all this, not by imprecation or desiring evil upon his adversaries, indeed (as we discuss below) he prays for them; but [he says this] conforming himself to the divine justice, predicting the future, and disclosing what their fault was deserving of. And when it says, *Let them be confounded and ashamed that seek after my soul, etc.* it can be explained in a good way, and by way of [it being] a prayer, so that Christ is understood to be desirous of the conversion of the Jews and their punishment in the present life, lest they be eternally punished, as will be made more clear in the exposition that follows.

34{35}[9] *But my soul shall rejoice in the Lord; and shall be delighted in his salvation.*

Anima autem mea exsultabit in Domino, et delectabitur super salutari suo.

34{35}[10] *All my bones shall say: Lord, who is like to you? Delivering the poor from the hand of them that are stronger than he; the needy and the poor from them that strip him.*

Omnia ossa mea dicent: Domine, quis similis tibi? Eripiens inopem de manu fortiorum eius; egenum et pauperem a diripientibus eum.

34{35}[9] *Anima autem mea exsultabit in Domino, but my soul shall rejoice in the Lord*: for the soul of Christ was always in the actual joy of the beatific enjoyment; *et delectabitur, and shall be delighted* with interior joy, *super salutari suo, in his salvation*, that is, of all the blessedness which the Lord furnished it. **34{35}[10]** *Omnia ossa mea, all my bones*, that is, all my fortitude and all the virtues of my soul, *dicent: Domine, quis similis tui? say Lord, who is like to you?* It is as if they were saying: "No one, because you infinitely exceed all things in all nobility and glory." Or [alternatively, one might understand it] thus: *All my bones say*, that is, the bones of my body declare through devout signs and gestures my interior joy, which I have from my contemplation of you and your benefits. For a great cheerfulness of heart overflows into the body, and it causes in it joyful gestures

---

to its infidelity it was scattered in the last centuries before Christ among the pagan peoples, whereby they became more closely acquainted with it and its fortunes and promises. In the complete dispersion that was caused after the Redeemer's appearance by their denial of Him, this people has become finally a universally visible, public, unassailable witness to the truth of the prophecies and prefigurations of the Redeemer contained in the sacred books." Matthias Scheeben, *Handbook of Catholic Dogmatics*, 5.1, 5 (Steubenville: Erasmus Books 2020), 28–29.

demonstrative of the internal happiness. *O Lord, who is like to you? Eripiens inopem, delivering the poor,* that is, [delivering] me, Christ, insofar as I am poor, so that I do not have a place where I might lay my head,[17] *de manu fortiorum eius, from the hand of them that are stronger than he,* that is, from the power and ire of the Jews, who, with respect to this, appeared to be stronger than I, to the extent that they were allowed to prevail over me, inflicting upon me the death of my body; and delivering in the day of my Resurrection, *egenum, the needy* in temporal goods, since I lived through the means of others, *et pauperem, and the poor,* that is, abject and humble, *a diripientibus, from them that strip,* that is, from them that crucify *eum, him.*

34{35}[11] *Unjust witnesses rising up have asked me things I knew not.*
Surgentes testes iniqui, quae ignorabam interrogabant me.

34{35}[12] *They repaid me evil for good: to the depriving me of my soul.*
Retribuebant mihi mala pro bonis, sterilitatem animae meae.

34{35}[11] *Surgentes testes iniqui, unjust witnesses rising up,* in the night of my Passion in the house of Caiaphas, *quae ignorabam, that I knew not,* by the offer of proof, that is, [accusing me of things] which I did not in fact do, *interrogabant me, they have asked me things,* that is, by the kind of questions that they hurled out at me, seeking a response from me. Whence Matthew says: *And the chief priests [and the elders] and the whole council sought false witness against Jesus, that they might put him to death; and they found not, whereas many false witnesses had come in.*[18] 34{35}[12] *Retribuebant mihi mala pro bonis, they repaid me evil for good:* because they persecuted me even unto death for the preaching, prayers, and miracles by which I sought to convert them to believe. Whence Christ said to the Jews: *Many good works I have showed you from my Father; for which of these works do you stone me?*[19] And elsewhere: *Give heed to me, O Lord, and hear the voice of my adversaries. Shall evil be rendered for good, because they have dug a pit for my soul?*[20] And so, *They repaid me evil for good,* namely, *sterilitatem animae meae, to the depriving me of my soul,* that is, the unfruitfulness of good — or vices which are sterilities of the soul.

17   Luke 9:58: *Jesus said to him: The foxes have holes, and the birds of the air nests; but the Son of man has not where to lay his head.*
18   Matt. 26:59-60. E. N. Denis adds *et seniores,* "and the elders."
19   John 10:32.
20   Jer. 18:19–20a.

34{35}[13] *But as for me, when they were troublesome to me, I was clothed with haircloth. I humbled my soul with fasting; and my prayer shall be turned into my innermost heart.*[21]

Ego autem, cum mihi molesti essent, induebar cilicio; humiliabam in ieiunio animam meam, et oratio mea in sinu meo convertetur.

34{35}[13] *Ego autem, cum mihi molesti essent, But as for me, when they were troublesome to me,* that is, while the Jews were persecuting me, especially during the time of the Passion, *induebar cilicio, I was clothed with haircloth.* We do not literally read [in the Gospels of] Christ using a haircloth, but rather that he fasted. What else therefore is signified by the haircloth other than the infirmity of the flesh and the similarity of sins of the flesh? And so Christ in persecution and in his Passion dressed himself in a haircloth, that is, he hid divinity under the cover of mortal flesh, and so he was able to appear more as a worm than God.[22] For this reason, he says in the Gospel: *Blessed is he that shall not be scandalized in me,*[23] that is, who does not deny to confess in me the nature of God because of the humility and abjectness which I undertook bodily or because of the fact I underwent suffering. And Isaiah says of Christ: *his look was as it were hidden and despised.*[24] *Humiliabam in ieiunio animam meam, I humbled my soul with fasting,* that is, I afflicted myself with corporal fasting, most supremely in the desert, where I lived for forty days and nights without any food.[25] *Et oratio mea, and my prayer,* which I poured out for those unwilling to convert, saying while on the Cross, *Father, forgive them;*[26] as well as in other places often praying for the Jews; *in sinu meo, in my innermost heart,* that is unto myself, [and my prayer] *convertetur, shall be turned into* [my innermost heart], that is, the effect and the merit of the prayer will flow back into me. But these words may appear repugnant to those which have often been mentioned before, namely, that Christ was always heard by the Father, in the manner that he himself attested to: *Father, I give you thanks that you have heard me; and I know that you hear me always.*[27] But I think the satisfactory solution [to this apparent con-

---

21 E. N. I have changed "bosom" into "innermost heart" to translate the Latin *sinu*.
22 Cf. Ps. 21:7.
23 Matt. 11:6.
24 Is. 53:3b.
25 Matt. 4:2.
26 Luke 23:34a. Denis departs from the Sixto-Clementine Vulgate: *Pater, ignosce illis* instead of *Pater, dimitte illis.*
27 John 11:41b–42a. See, e.g., Article XVI (Psalm 3:5), Article XIX (Psalm 4:3),

tradiction] is made clear by those things said during the exposition of the twenty-first Psalm, where we expounded upon the person of Christ with respect to the words, O my God, I shall cry by day, and you will not hear.²⁸

34{35}[14] *As a neighbor and as our brother, so did I find pleasing [to behave]:*²⁹ *as one mourning and sorrowful so was I humbled.*

Quasi proximum et quasi fratrem nostrum sic complacebam; quasi lugens et contristatus sic humiliabar.

34{35}[14] *Quasi proximum, et quasi fratrem nostrum sic complacebam; as a neighbor and as our brother, so did I find pleasing to behave.* This verse can be explained in two ways. The first way is this: You must understand the words *as a neighbor, and as our brother* as including the people of the Jews and any one individual member of them; *so did I find pleasing to behave,* that is, so did I rejoice in their making progress and in their prosperity. Or [we can understand it] thus: *as a neighbor, and as our brother,* that is, just like a neighbor or a brother *did I find pleasing to behave,* that is, within myself I was so pleased with them, and, as a result of that affinity, I rejoiced for them, and I cherished as much as my own soul those who (as was previously mentioned) returned evil for good to me and in the end crucified me.³⁰ *Quasi lugens, as one mourning,* with the eyes of the body, *et contristatus, and sorrowful* with the compassion of kindly affection, *sic humiliabar, so was I humbled,* that is, so did I humiliate and afflict myself for their salvation. Whence it is written: Jesus *seeing the city, he wept over it,*³¹ that is, over its people. And again: Jesus grieved *for the blindness of their hearts.*³² And of course the more those people were closer to him, the more their ingratitude and their hardness more greatly pained him.

34{35}[15] *But they rejoiced against me and came together: scourges were gathered together upon me, and I knew not.*

Et adversum me laetati sunt, et convenerunt; congregata sunt super me flagella, et ignoravi.

Article L (Psalm 21:3) in Volume 1.
28 Ps. 31:3. *See* Article L (Psalm 21:3) in Volume 1.
29 E. N. I have modified the Douay-Rheims from: *As a neighbor and as an own brother, so did I please,* which sounds odd to the modern ear, to *as a neighbor and as our brother, so did I find pleasing [to behave].*
30 *Cf.* John 10:15b: *I lay down my life for my sheep.*
31 Luke 19:41b.
32 Mark 3:5a.

Again, Christ appropriately discloses the ingratitude of the Jews, saying: **34{35}[15]** *Et adversum me laetati sunt*, but they rejoiced against me, that is, out of hatred they were glad as a result of my adversities, in the way that we have it said in Luke: *Judas went, and discoursed with the chief priests . . . how he might betray him to them; and they were glad, and covenanted to give him money.*[33] *Et convenerunt*, and [they] came together, that is they took counsel among themselves against me, as John attests to: *The chief priests and the Pharisees, gathered a council, and said: What do we, for this man does many miracles?*[34] And Matthew: *Then were gathered together the chief priests and ancients of the people [into the court of the high priest, who was called Caiaphas], and they consulted together, that by subtilty they might apprehend Jesus, and put him to death.*[35] *Congregata sunt super me flagella*, scourges were gathered together upon me, that is, persecutions and punishments, especially in the day of Passover, when they were *satisfied with my pains*,[36] *et ignoravi*, and I knew not, that is, I held myself out in the manner of someone ignorant, because I did not take flight. Or [one can understand it thus], *I knew not*, that is, I was not conscious [within myself] of the cause of so much punishment, namely, of fault.[37] Or [yet another way of understanding it is as follows], *I knew not*, according to their estimation and also of the Jews as a whole. It is according to this sense that we find written: *And I was as a meek lamb, that is carried to be a victim: and I knew not that they had devised counsels against me.*[38]

34{35}[16] *They were separated, and repented not: they tempted me, they scoffed at me with scorn: they gnashed upon me with their teeth.*

Dissipati sunt, nec compuncti, tentaverunt me, subsannaverunt me subsannatione; frenduerunt super me dentibus suis.

---

33 Luke 22:4–5.
34 John 11:47.
35 Matt. 26:3-4. E. N. The part in brackets is included where Denis simply has "etc."
36 Job 16:11. The Douay-Rheims has *they are filled (satiati sunt) with my pains* which, in this context, is better rendered *they are satisfied with my pains*.
37 E. N. In other words, Jesus knew himself to be utterly without sin (he had no *malum culpae* in him); since suffering and punishment (*mala poenae*) are caused by the faults of sin (*mala culpae*), Jesus was aware that the suffering and the punishment he was undergoing was entirely unmerited, there being no causal or just connection between the two; by knowing there was no causal or just connection between his punishment and any sin, he was "learnedly ignorant," as it were, of the absence of cause and aware of the lack of justice in an innocent suffering such punishment.
38 Jer. 11:19a.

34{35}[16] *Dissipati sunt, they were separated,* that is, with dissolute hearts, from the fear of the marvelous things which came to pass during the time of the Passion, when clearly they saw the earth move, the sun grow dark, and the temple veil torn in two;[39] *nec compuncti, they repented not,* that is, they did not in any manner repent of their sins, but they remained in disbelief. Or [we can understand it] thus: *They were separated,* that is, they were divided from each other, and were dispersed throughout the whole world;[40] *they repented not,* that is, by such a great punishment arising from their having sinned against me they did not notice themselves as turned away from God. *Tentaverunt me, they tempted me,* saying, *Master, we know that you are a true speaker,*[41] and by other means, so that they might come upon anything worthy of blame in me; *subsannaverunt me subsannatione, they scoffed at me with scorn,* when [while I was] hanging on the Cross they, mocking me, said, *If he be the king of Israel, [let him now come down from the cross, and we will believe him];*[42] or, *If he be Christ, the elect of God,* let him come down from that cross now;[43] *frenduerunt super me dentibus suis, they gnashed upon me with their teeth,* that is, with furious rancor they shrilled loudly at me, while they pierced my head with thorns, struck me with a reed, and before the prefect [Pilate] the Jews cried out: *If you release this man, you are not Caesar's friend.*[44] Whence holy Job said: *They have opened their mouths upon me, and reproaching me they have struck me on the cheek, they are satisfied with my pains.*[45]

34{35}[17] *Lord, when will you look upon me? Restore*[46] *my soul from their malice: my only one from the lions.*

Domine, quando respicies? Restitue animam meam a malignitate eorum, a leonibus unicam meam.

---

39 Matt. 27:45, 51.
40 E. N. This refers, of course, to the Jewish exile or diaspora. The Jews experienced a number of exiles during their history—the Assyrian exile, the Babylonian captivity, both of which were forced, and a voluntary diaspora before the fall of the Second Temple. However, here Denis refers to the forced diaspora after the siege and destruction of Jerusalem and the Second Temple by the Romans.
41 Matt. 22:16a.
42 Matt. 27:42. E. N. I have added the part in brackets for better context.
43 Luke 23:35b.
44 John 19:12a.
45 Job 16:11. On the departure from the Douay-Rheims of this verse, *see* footnote 34-36.
46 E. N. I have changed the Douay-Rheims translation from *rescue* to *restore*, as it is an accurate translation of *restitue*, and it fits better with the argument of Denis.

34{35}[17] *Domine,* Lord, heavenly Father, *quando respicies?* When will you look upon me? That is, when will you show yourself to see with your eye of paternal help? *Restitue animam meam,* restore my soul to the body through the resurrection, *a malignitate eorum,* from their malice, that is, saving it from the persecution of the Jews; *a leonibus, from the lions,* that is, from the proud and cruel Jews, restore or deliver *unicam meam, my only one,* that is, my soul, your most and uniquely beloved;[47] or [alternatively], *my only one,* that is, the only one existing in my body. For in one living body there is but one soul.[48]

34{35}[18] *I will give thanks to you in a great church; I will praise you in a strong people.*

Confitebor tibi in ecclesia magna; in populo gravi laudabo te.

34{35}[18] *Confitebor tibi,* I will give thanks to you God the Father *in ecclesia magna, in a great church,* that is, among the Catholic people by myself and through my ministers, when you make restitution to my soul as a result of their wickedness; then also *in populo gravi, in a strong people,* that is, in the Christian people, with upright, honest, and mature manner of living, *laudabo te,* I will praise you. This is what was said in a Psalm which was explained earlier: *I will declare your name to my brethren: in the midst of the church will I praise you.*[49] It is also another kind of strong people in which Christ does not praise the Father. Of this [people] it is said: *Woe to ... a people laden with iniquity, ... they have forsaken the Lord, they have blasphemed the Holy One of Israel.*[50] Of this people John in Revelation says: *Woe to the sinful nation, a people laden with iniquity, a wicked seed, ungracious children: they say they are Jews and are not, but are the synagogue of Satan.*[51] However even to this [wicked] people Christ in a certain way praises the Father in that he himself and through his disciples preached the word of salvation to them, and thereby made known [to them] the mercy of God and his benefits.

---

47 E. N. Because "something is better the more it is similar to God," it follows that "God loves more the better things." Therefore: "God loves Christ not only more than all the human race, but also more than he loves creation," and "God loves the human nature assumed by the Word of God in the person of Christ more than all the angels." ST, Ia, q. 20, art. 4, s.c., and ad 1, 2.
48 E. N. "It is not possible for there to be plural souls in man. This means, therefore, that all the powers of the soul belong to the same soul." St. Thomas Aquinas, *Compendium theologiae,* lib. 1 cap. 90; *see also* ST Ia, q. 76, art. 4.
49 Ps. 21:23. *See* Article LI (Psalm 21:23) and Article LI (Psalm 21:23) in Volume 1.
50 Is. 1:4.
51 Rev. 2:9b.

34{35}[19] *Let not them that are my enemies wrongfully rejoice over me: who have hated me without cause, and wink with the eyes.*

Non supergaudeant mihi qui adversantur mihi inique, qui oderunt me gratis, et annuunt oculis.

34{35}[19] *Non supergaudeant mihi,* let them not... *rejoice over me:* that is, O Lord Father, although you permit the Jews to rejoice over my punishments even unto the gibbet of the Cross, nevertheless *let them not rejoice over me,* that is, not long after the Passion, let them not rejoice over my death as if I might be entirely extinguished and not rise again; *qui adversantur mihi inique, that are my enemies wrongfully,* that is, the Jews, who without any fault on my part sought to suppress and then to blot out my name and my memory, in that manner that is written about their person: *Let us put wood on his bread,* that is, let us feed him with death of the cross.[52] *Qui, who*—the Jews—*oderunt me gratis, have hated me without cause,* that is, without any fault on my part, because I did nothing to harm them, *et annuunt oculis, and wink with the eyes,* that is, they expressed acts of derision among themselves by which they mutually exhorted themselves to deride me. And also Christ mentions this scripture, saying: *If I had not done among them the works that no other man has done, they would not have sin; but now they have both seen and hated both me and my Father. But that the word may be fulfilled which is written in their law: They hated me without cause.*[53] From it is apparent that this Psalm is literally expounding about Christ, because a [scriptural] assertion or proof is not strong except in its literal sense, according to Augustine.[54] Therefore, the exposition explaining this Psalm literally of David is not as agreeable, although it is possible to apply it literally to David, just as it may be [applied] to other just men, in the way it is handled in the exposition which follows.[55]

---

52 Jer. 11:19b. *E. N.* The verse continues: *and let his name be remembered no more.* The prophecy of Jeremiah that states "let us put wood on his bread," *mittamus lignum in panem eius,* has traditionally been understood as meaning *mittamus crucem in corpus eius,* "let us put the cross on his body." Tertullian, *Adv. Mar.,* Lib. IV, ch. 11, PL 2, 492.
53 John 15:24-25.
54 *E. N.* Denis mentions this rule of construction in Article IV, Article XII (Psalm 2:1), and Article XXVI (Psalm 8:5) in Volume 1. It is found in Letter 93 to Vincentius the Donatist where St. Augustine suggests that it is highly imprudent to argue a point based upon allegorical construction of a verse of scripture in one's favor without any foundation on the literal text (*manifesta testimonia*), by which light the obscurity of the allegorical meaning is made manifest. *Epist.* 93, 8, 24, PG 33, 334. In Article IV of this *Commentary,* Denis insists the literal basis is the foundation for the other senses: allegorical, tropological, and analogical.
55 *E. N.* Article LXXIII.

But some explain this book of Psalms literally to an excessive degree. For they expound not only this Psalm, but also the many other Psalms which manifestly speak of Christ and his Passion and Mysteries—and which Psalms holy and Catholic teachers, namely Jerome, Augustine, Cassiodorus, and Hugh [of St. Cher],[56] explain as applying to Christ—as applying literally to David, not bringing forward any mention of Christ. Especially with respect to the previous Psalm, namely, the thirtieth, whose beginning is *In you, O Lord, have I hoped*, which evidently is concerned with Christ and is not explained in reference to David, from which the defect of their argument [and their over-literalness] is made apparent. For the twenty-first Psalm, whose beginning is, *O God, my God, look upon me*, commends itself from its literal explanation to be of Christ by this fact: that Christ hanging on the Cross recited the beginning of this Psalm just as it was said of his person.[57] If, therefore, from this reason that this [twenty-first] Psalm is explained as relating to Christ, by the same reason also the thirtieth Psalm may be explained as relating to Christ. [This is so] because Christ hanging upon the Cross, uttered forth part of this Psalm, namely, that verse *Into your hands I commend my spirit*,[58] as if said of his person. Similarly, the same thing can be argued about this present Psalm, in which the Prophet [David] says, *they have hated me without cause*, which Christ clearly acknowledged as prophetically applying to him in the Gospel of John.[59] Otherwise, it would not say, *that the word may be fulfilled*, etc., because if this verse were literally said to apply to David, then certainly these words would long ago have been fulfilled before the coming of Christ.

34{35}[20] *For they spoke indeed peaceably to me; and speaking in the anger of the earth they devised guile.*

Quoniam mihi quidem pacifice loquebantur; et in iracundia terrae loquentes, dolos cogitabant.

34{35}[21] *And they opened their mouth wide against me; they said: Well done, well done, our eyes have seen it.*

Et dilataverunt super me os suum; dixerunt: Euge, euge! viderunt oculi nostri.

---

56 All these were renowned for writing Commentaries on the Psalms.
57 Matt. 27:46.
58 Luke 23:46a; Ps. 30:6a.
59 John 15:25: *That the word may be fulfilled (ut adimpleatur sermo) which is written in their law: They hated me without cause.*

Therefore, Christ says: **34{35}[20]** *Quoniam mihi quidem pacifice loquebantur, for they spoke indeed peaceably to me,* that is, the unbelieving Jews spoke words which appeared to be loving and peaceful, as appears in dialog from the Gospel, such as: *Master, which is the greatest commandment in the law?*[60] And of the woman caught in adultery: *Master, this woman was even now taken in adultery,*[61] they asked, what does it appear like to you? And: *Master we would see a sign from you.*[62] *Et iracundiam terrae, in the anger of the earth,* that is, from the ire stirred up from the vicious love of earthly things, *loquentes, speaking,* among themselves and also with me, *dolos cogitabant, they devised guile,* namely, how they might be able to blame me as a transgressor of the law. For the Jews inordinately loved the world, namely, temporal riches, honors, and glory; and because Christ reprimanded them of these things, they conceived ill-will against him, and from the ire of their heart they spoke to him using deceitful words. And so the Savior says in the Gospel: The world hates me, *because I give testimony of it, for the works thereof are evil.*[63] **34{35}[21]** *Et dilataverunt super me os suum, and they opened their mouths wide against me,* that is, with wide mouths they derided, reproached, and blasphemed me — and this most greatly during the time of the Passion — and then *dixerunt, they said: Euge, euge! Well done, well done!* That is, it is excellent now that this has befallen because he has been seized. *Viderunt oculi nostri, our eyes have seen it,* that is, we ourselves have seen the evil which we have imposed upon you clearly because you have seduced the people, you have transgressed the law, and you who have stated yourself to be the Christ.[64] This is what the Jews said before Pilate: *We have a law; and according to the law he ought to die, because he made himself the Son of God.*[65] For often in Scripture the sense of sight is commonly understood as meaning any one of the senses.

34{35}[22] *You have seen, O Lord, be not silent: O Lord, depart not from me.*

Vidisti, Domine, ne sileas; Domine, ne discedas a me.

34{35}[23] *Arise, and be attentive to my judgment: to my cause, my God, and my Lord.*

---

60 Matt. 22:36.
61 John 8:4.
62 Matt. 12:38.
63 John 7:7b.
64 John 7:12.
65 John 19:7.

Exsurge et intende iudicio meo, Deus meus; et Dominus meus, in causam meam.

34{35}[24] *Judge me, O Lord my God according to your justice, and let them not rejoice over me.*

Iudica me secundum iustitiam tuam, Domine Deus meus, et non supergaudeant mihi.

34{35}[22] *Vidisti, Domine, you have seen, O Lord* Father, all the evil unjustly brought against me; *ne sileas, be not silent,* that is, carry out your judgment by approving my justice and reproving their evil. *Domine, ne discedas a me; Lord, depart not from me,* that is, from the human nature which I have assumed, but rather cause it to rise again on the third day, and to ascend on the fortieth day. **34{35}[23]** *Exsurge, arise,* that is, sustain me by means of raising me up, assisting, and rendering aid even to the point of the glorification of the body; *et intende iudicio meo, and be attentive to my judgment,* that is, consider the judgment by which I was so unjustly and ignominiously condemned to death, and by that judgment give to me the power of judging, that it may be manifest that I am the judge of the living and of the dead by its execution.[66] For Christ merited this power and this active judgment because he suffered such an unjust judgment. And so, *be attentive to my judgment,* and adjudge me with the judgment of the aforementioned recompense, *Deus meus, my God; et, and* you who are *Dominus meus, my Lord,* according to the form of the servant I received,[67] direct your attention *in causam meam, to my cause,* that is, be mindful of the reason that I undergo all this, namely, for your honor and the salvation of the world, and not on account of any fault of mine as did the thieves between whom I was led to death and suspended upon the Cross.[68] This is what is written in the book of Job: *Your cause has been judged as that of the wicked, cause and judgment you shall recover.*[69] **34{35}[24]** *Iudica me, judge me* with the judgment of recompense, in regard to accidental reward,[70] *secundum iuistiam tuam, according to your*

---

66 Acts 10:42: *And he commanded us to preach to the people, and to testify that it is he who was appointed by God, to be judge of the living and of the dead.*
67 E. N. In other words, because of the human nature he assumed. For Christ, *being in the form of God, thought it not robbery to be equal with God: But emptied himself, taking the form of a servant, being made in the likeness of men, and in habit [appearance] found as a man.* Phil. 2:6–7.
68 Matt. 27:38.
69 Job. 36:17.
70 E. N. For the distinction between accidental reward or recompense and essential reward or recompense, see Articles XII (Psalm 2:5) and XXIV (Psalm 7:13) and

justice, that is, according to the dictates of your divine justice or according to my justice conferred upon me by you, *Domine Deus meus*, O Lord my God. Christ securely prays this, because he was without any malice, and he knew himself to be the Son of God in whom the Father was supremely pleased.[71] *Et non supergaudeant mihi*, and let them not rejoice over me. This has already expounded upon once in this present Psalm.[72]

34{35}[25] Let them not say in their hearts: It is well, it is well, to our mind: neither let them say: We have swallowed him up.

Non dicant in cordibus suis: Euge, euge, animae nostrae; nec dicant: Devoravimus eum.

34{35}[26] Let them blush: and be afraid together, who rejoice at my evils. Let them be clothed with confusion and fear, who speak great things against me.[73]

Erubescant et revereantur simul qui gratulantur malis meis; induantur confusione et reverentia qui magna loquuntur super me.

34{35}[25] *Non decant in cordibus suis*, let them not say in their hearts, that is, let them not think any more: *Euge, euge, animae nostrae*; It is well, it is well, to our mind: that is, how delightful does it happen to be for us, that we were able to kill him who was *grievous unto us, even to behold*,[74] *to a most shameful death!*[75] *Nec decant: Devorabimus eum;* neither let them say: We have swallowed him up, that is, we will destroy his name and his memory, and all his followers; but manifest me to rise again from the dead by a miracle. Whence Peter, when he cured the man lame from birth, said to the Jews: *You men of Israel, . . . the God of our fathers, has glorified his Son,*[76] that is, he has manifested him alive and glorious through this

---

footnote 1-48 in Volume 1. Denis is here saying that Jesus is asking for the accidental rewards of the resurrection and the glorification of his body, since Jesus, as man, always had the beatific vision from the first instance of existence. For us ordinary mortals, the beatific vision is the essential or fundamental reward of dying in a state of grace of friendship with God.

71 Matt. 3:17; 17:5.
72 See this Article (Psalm 34:19).
73 E. N. I have replaced "let them be ashamed" for *revereantur* in the Douay-Rheims with "let them be afraid," and I have used "fear" for *reverentia* instead of "shame," since this is how Denis plainly understands the Latin.
74 Wis. 2:15a.
75 Wis. 2:20a.
76 Acts 3:12–13.

miracle. Because of the evidence of this miracle, the Jews did not dare to lay a hand upon the Apostles, and ceased in any way to accuse Jesus to be among the iniquitous: for [after this miracle] they desired to appear as being blameless for his death, saying to the Apostles: *Behold, you have filled Jerusalem with your doctrine, and you have a mind to bring the blood of this man upon us.*[77] And so Christ here adds **34{35}[26]** *Erubescant, let them blush,* [that is, let] the Jews heedless of the sin committed against me and the death inflicted upon me by them [blush], *et revereantur simul, and be afraid together,* that is, they will equally fear the vengeance of divine justice, *qui gratulantur malis meis, who rejoice at my evils,* that is, who are joyful of my punishments out of mere ill-will. And the same judgment is included in the next verse using different words. *Induantur confusio et reverentia, let them be clothed with confusion and fear,* that is, confounded and terrified in both soul and body, and let them be totally covered with shame and with fear, in the manner a man is covered with clothing, *qui maligna loquuntur super me, who speak great things against me,* that is, who place upon me [the accusations of] grave crimes.

34{35}[27] Let them rejoice and be glad, who are well pleased with my justice, and let them say always: The Lord be magnified, who delights in the peace of his servant.

Exsultent et laetentur qui volunt iustitiam meam; et dicant semper: Magnificetur Dominus, qui volunt pacem servi eius.

34{35}[27] *Exsultent, let them rejoice* with external joy, *et laetentur, and be glad* with mental delight, *qui volunt iustiam meam, who are well pleased with my justice,* that is, who love, approve, and follow my teaching, my life, and my Passion; *et dicant semper, Magnificetur Dominus; and let them say always, the Lord be magnified,* let them unceasingly praise God, *qui volunt pacem servi eius, who delights in the peace of his servant,* that is, who desire to achieve or who keep with great affection the attained peace of Christ, who is the servant of God in the manner that the Lord said through Zechariah: *Behold, I will bring my servant from the Orient.*[78] And so Christ prays that the children of peace, those who strive after true peace, praise God, because they are worthy to praise God as his children, as Christ himself stated, saying: *Blessed are the peacemakers, for they shall be called children of God.*[79] The peace of Christ is something

---

77 Acts 5:28.
78 Zech. 3:8b.
79 Matt. 5:9.

other than the peace of the world, as he also affirms: *Peace I leave with you, my peace I give unto you: not as the world gives, do I give unto you.*[80] But of the peace of the world he again says: *I came not to send peace, but the sword.*[81] And so the peace of Christ is situated in the interior of man. For it [peace] is a tranquility of the soul or a quiet from the perturbation of sin, consisting in this: that the flesh is perfectly obedient to the spirit, sensuality to reason, and reason to the divine law, so that man is bound fast to God, and of tranquil mind, harboring no bitterness over anyone. Then again, the peace of the world is the quiet enjoyment of temporal goods, rejecting that which frees from or diminishes the carnal pleasures and the transitory delights. This peace is not true peace but is rather a ponderous quiet because the Lord says *there is no peace to the wicked.*[82] Let us seek, therefore, this peace of Christ, let us love and preserve it if we wish to be becoming praisers of the Most High.

34{35}[28] *And my tongue shall meditate your justice, your praise all the day long.*

Et lingua mea meditabitur iustitiam tuam, tota die laudem tuam.

34{35}[28] *Et lingua mea meditabitur*, and my tongue shall meditate, that is, it will speak from the interior mediation, *iustitiam tuam, your justice*, O heavenly Father, teaching the evangelical law, which is the law of perfect justice, *tota die laudem tuam, your praise all the day long*, that is, unceasingly and daily it will praise you.

ARTICLE LXXIII

MORAL EXPOSITION OF THE SAME THIRTY-FOURTH PSALM, OF ANY JUST MAN OR THE CHURCH.

AS A MANNER OF LIVING IS THE WAY THAT any of us can and ought to sing this Psalm in regard to his own person, and to understand it of the Church of Christ, which always desires to conform to its Head and Spouse. Therefore, the faithful man living in a Christ-formed way, and surrounded by various tribulations,

---

80   John 14:27a.
81   Matt. 10:34b.
82   Is. 57:21.

and considering himself unable to prevail with his own strength, cries out to God: *Judge, O Lord, them that wrong me, etc.*

34{35}[1] *For David himself. Judge, O Lord, them that wrong me: overthrow them that fight against me.*

Ipsi David. Iudica, Domine, nocentes me; expugna impugnantes me.

This whole part [of the Psalm], wherein help against enemies is asked for, can be explained in one way as dealing with invisible enemies, in this sense: **34{35}[1]** *Iudica, Domine; judge, O Lord,* that is, justly condemn, *nocentes me, them that wrong me,* that is, the demons tempting me, and frequently impeding me from making progress [in the spiritual life], and introducing to me unprofitable images during the time of divine worship. But since the demons are already judged and are irreparably condemned, why is it necessary to pray that they may be judged? [This we pray], therefore, knowing that the demons do not yet have all the punishment which they will be made to bear: indeed, in great numbers their punishment will be increased all over again. For however they may be at the end [of time], yet—like the holy angels who have custody of men and merit accidental reward [at the end of time]—so demons who tempt godly men are deserving [at the end of time] of an increase of accidental misery, namely, the punishment of sense. But in regard to essential misery, which is the aversion from the sovereign good or the lack of the divine vision, they are entirely at their end; and with respect to that, they can neither merit nor suffer demerit, just like the souls already existing in hell.[83] Since, therefore, he says, *Judge, O Lord, them that wrong me,* namely, the demons, the sense is: censure or afflict them. And in accordance with this sense it is written in Zechariah: *The Lord rebuke you, O Satan: and the Lord rebuke you.*[84] *Expugna impugnantes me, overthrow them that fight against me,* that is, defeat the aerial powers bothering me with various temptations and the others sallying out and pursuing me, granting me grace by which I may effectively resist their suggestions and patiently endure the adversities which befall me as a result of their machinations. Whence the Apostle [Paul] says: *The God of peace crush Satan under your feet speedily.*[85]

---

83 E. N. In other words, the demons, like the souls damned for eternity in hell, are already irreversibly suffering the loss of the vision of God and this punishment remains unchanged at the end of time, and will continue for eternity.
84 Zech. 3:2a.
85 Rom. 16:20a.

34{35}[2] *Take hold of arms and shield: and rise up to help me.*

Apprehende arma et scutum, et exsurge in adiutorium mihi.

34{35}[3] *Bring out the sword, and shut up the way against them that persecute me: say to my soul: I am your salvation.*

Effunde frameam, et conclude adversus eos qui persequuntur me; dic animae meae: Salus tua ego sum.

34{35}[2] *Apprehende arma et scutum*, take hold of arms and shield, that is, take up your power employing it, and by it strengthen and protect me; *et exsurge in adiutorium mihi, and rise up to help me*, that I not succumb to temptation, or follow disordered desires, or fall through weakness. **34{35}[3]** *Effunde frameam, bring out the sword*, that is, the rebuking of, and punishment over, the aforementioned tempters, *et conclude adversus eos qui persequuntur me, and shut up the way against them that persecute me*, that is, draw out a good and triumphant conclusion for me against them, so that their malice may return back upon their head and may not harm me. *Dic animae meae, say to my soul*, by the instinct of the Holy Spirit,[86] or internal revelation, and by the experience of your mercy: *Salus tua ego sum, I am your salvation*, that is, the cause of your salvation, and I will save you from this danger. This is what the Apostle [Paul] said: *For the Spirit himself gives testimony to our spirit, that we are the sons of God.*[87] And so I pray, O Lord, say to my soul, *I am your salvation*: that is, tell me by means of a secret inspiration, those beautiful words, those consoling words, which are written by Micah: *Now, why are you drawn together with grief? Have you no king in you, or is your counsellor perished, because sorrow has taken you as a woman in labor? I will save you*, and *you will be delivered; do not fear.*[88]

---

86 E. N. St. Thomas uses the express "instinct of the Holy Spirit," *Spiritus Sancti instinctus*, as an expression of the prompting of the Holy Spirit which is the effect of the gifts of the Holy Spirit. *[D]ona sunt quaedam hominis perfectiones quibus homo disponitur ad hoc quod bene sequatur instinctum divinum. Unde in his in quibus non sufficit instinctus rationis, sed est necessarius Spiritus Sancti instinctus, per consequens est necessarium donum.* "The gifts [of the Holy Spirit] are certain perfections of man which dispose man to that which is in accord with the divine instinct. Whence, in this the instinct of reason does not suffice, but the instinct of the Holy Spirit is, and as a consequence, the gifts are necessary." ST IaIIae, q. 68, art. 2, co.
87 Rom. 7:16.
88 Micah 4:9, 10b.

34{35}[4] *Let them be confounded and afraid*[89] *that seek after my soul. Let them be turned back and be confounded that devise against me.*

Confundantur et revereantur quaerentes animam meam; avertantur retrorsum et confundantur cogitantes mihi mala.

34{35}[4] *Confundantur, let them be confounded*, that is, let them be driven back from me and overcome in their confusion, and let them be ashamed in their defeat, and let them be confounded eternally by you in the last day,[90] *et revereantur, and afraid*, that is, let them be afraid to fight me in everything else. For demons fear the saints as long as they are defeated by them, and they attack them not without having fear. And so, *let them be afraid*, that is, grant to me such a level of virtue and grace, O Lord, that demons at the sight of my countenance flee as if thoroughly terrified, saying: *These are the camps of God;*[91] *let us flee from Israel: for the Lord fights for them against us.*[92] *Quaerentes animam meam, [they] that seek after my soul*, that is, the devils, who seek it so as to turn it from God, and to associate it with their unhappy company: *avertantur retrorsum, let them be turned back*, that is, may they fall and flee vanquished, *et confundantur, and let them be confounded*, as has already been talked about, those *cogitantes mihi mala, that devise against me*, that is, the demons who take counsel among themselves as to the manner that they may deceive my soul and procure for it eternal punishment.

---

89 E. N. I have departed from the Douay-Rheims translation "ashamed" and replaced it with "afraid," which is in line with Denis's understanding of the Latin word *revereantur*.
90 E. N. The last day, the *die novissimo*, is the day of Final Judgment. *Christus virtute propria, nos virtute Christi resurgemus: Christus die tertio; nos in die novissimo resurgemus*. "Christ by his own power, we by the power of Christ will rise again; Christ on the third day; we in the last day will rise again." Wilhelm Hülsbäumer, *Catechismus Romanus Enucleatus* (Cologne 1771), 207. Satan likewise will be judged. Rev. 20:9-10. "God's triumph over the revolt of evil will take the form of the Last Judgment after the final cosmic upheaval of this passing world." CCC § 677.
91 Gen. 32:2a. E. N. The notion of a soul clothed with sanctifying grace and virtue as a "camp of God," a *castra Dei*, is found, for example, in St. Cyprian of Carthage (*ca.* 200 — 258 A. D.), who speaks about the *castra Dei*, the *castra Christi*, or the *castra Dominica*, the "camp of God," "camp of Christ," or "camp of the Lord," on the one hand, and the *castra diaboli*, the "camp of the devil," on the other. See, *e.g.*, PL 4, 336, 337, 343, 366, 726, 732, 824, 855. The Christian is part of Christ's army, the *militia Christi*. *Armemur, fratres dilectissimi, viribus totis et paremur ad agonem mente incorrupta, fide integra, virtute devota. Ad aciem quae nobis indicitur Dei castra pracedant.* "Let us be armed, most beloved brothers, with our whole strength, and let us be prepared for the struggle with an uncorrupted mind, with an integral faith, with devoted virtue. Let the camp of God sally forth to the battlefield which is indicated for us!" Ep. 56, 8, PL 4, 366.
92 Ex. 14:23b.

34{35}[5] *Let them become as dust before the wind: and let the angel of the Lord straiten them.*

Fiant tamquam pulvis ante faciem venti, et angelus Domini coarctans eos.

34{35}[6] *Let their way become dark and slippery; and let the angel of the Lord pursue them.*

Fiat via illorum tenebrae, et lubricum; et angelus Domini persequens eos.

34{35}[5] *Fiant tanquam pulvis ante faciem venti, let them become as dust before the wind,* that is, may they be driven off and repelled from me as quickly and as easily as the dust is moved and propelled by the wind, so that there is no open gate or door of my heart that has conspired with them: in the manner that the Apostle [Paul] teaches: *Give not place to the devil;*[93] *et angelus Domini coarctans eos, and let the angel of the Lord straiten them,* that is, may the holy angel of God, who is the guardian of my soul,[94] restrain their evil devices and drive them away from me. 34{35}[6] *Fiat via illorum, let their way become,* that is, [let] their contrivance at tempting [become], *tenebrae et lubricum, dark and slippery,* that is, obscure and wavering, so that it may not obtain my consent under the species of good, and it may be recognized by me as a demon's falsehood, for which the gift of discernment of spirits is needed.[95] *For Satan himself transforms himself into an angel of light*[96] and so his way may appear as full of light; but as long as through divine illumination we become aware of his stratagems, then his way appears dark and slippery. *Et angelus Domini persequens eos, and let the angel of*

---

93 Eph. 4:27.
94 *E. N.* On the guardian angel, see footnotes 33-40 and 33-42.
95 The term "discernment of spirits," *discretio spirituum,*" refers to that charism mentioned by St. Paul in 1 Cor. 12:10. In his commentary on First Corinthians, St. Thomas describes the gift or charism of the discernment of spirits as that by which a man is able to distinguish between spirits so we may know *utrum ex Deo sunt,* "whether they are from God." *Super I Cor.,* cap. 12 v. 10. Although there are a variety of "spirits," including the impulses of our weakened and infirm nature (concupiscence), God's grace and the Holy Spirit, good angels, and demons, Denis seems to focus here on the discernment of demonic spirits. *Believe not every spirit, but try the spirits if they be of God.* 1 John 4:1. St. Ignatius Loyola is particularly to be commended as a great teacher in regard to the discernments of spirits. *See, e.g.,* Dan Burke, *Spiritual Warfare and the Discernment of Spirits* (Manchester: Sophia Institute Press 2019) and Timothy Gallaher, O. M. V., *The Discernment of Spirits: An Ignatian Guide for Everyday Living* (New York: Crossroad 2005).
96 2 Cor. 11:14.

the Lord pursue them, that is, let a good angel do battle for us and strike them down. For devils are vehemently distressed while they are overcome by us through the help of holy angels.

34{35}[7] For without cause they have hidden their net for me unto destruction: without cause they have upbraided my soul.

Quoniam gratis absconderunt mihi interitum laquei sui, supervacue exprobraverunt animam meam.

34{35}[7] *Quoniam gratis, for without cause*, that is, without a just and reasonable cause, *absconderunt mihi, they have hidden ... for me*, that is, the devils have hiddenly prepared, *interitum laquei sui, their net ... unto destruction*, that is, the death of their temptations, or their death-dealing temptations which cause the ruin of the soul; *supervacue exprobraverunt animam meam, without cause they have upbraided my soul*, that is, they have fruitlessly assaulted me. For sometimes a demon tempts us by reproaching us with past sins in order that by such means he may drag us to desperation or to lead us back to a secular life.[97] Hence, demons have visibly appeared to some great sinners who have most efficaciously repented, saying, as St. Jerome relates: See, after living for so long a time in all sorts of filth and iniquity, you were subservient to us in all things, and you were content with the pleasure we gave you, and now you wish to convert to Christ and to abandon us![98]

34{35}[8] Let it come to him, the snare which he knows not; and let the trap which he has hidden catch him: and into that very snare let him fall.[99]

Veniat illi laqueus quem ignorat, et captio quam abscondit apprehendat eum, et in laqueum cadat in ipsum.

34{35}[8] *Veniat illi, let him come to him*, that is, to the devil or to the congregation of devils, *laqueus quem ignorat, the snare which he knows not*, that is, the unforeseen and quick restriction by a holy angel; *et captio quam abscondit, and let not the trap which he has hidden*, that is,

---

97 E. N. The devil may use past sins to encourage someone to leave the religious life, abandon the evangelical counsels and monastic vows and return back to a secular manner of life.
98 E. N. I could not find any source for this in St. Jerome.
99 On the departure of the wording of this verse from the Douay-Rheims, *see* footnote 34-14.

the captivity or the harm that he had hiddenly prepared for me, *apprehendat eum*, catch him, that is, harm him and hold him captive, *et in laqueum cadat in ipsum*, and into that very snare let him fall, that is, this trap which he hid from me may become to him a snare of damnation and the cause of torment.[100]

Furthermore, all these passages can also be explained as referring to visible enemies, namely, ungodly men, in this sense:

34{35}[1] ...*Judge, O Lord, them that wrong me: overthrow them that fight against me.*
...*Iudica, Domine, nocentes me; expugna impugnantes me.*

34{35}[1] *Iudica, Domine, nocentes me;* judge, O Lord, them that wrong me: that is, identify, distinguish, and separate from me the men unjustly persecuting me and endeavoring to prevent me from your service: now, indeed, in affection and merit which pertains to the judgment of discretion, and in the future in [in terms of eternal] place and reward, which pertains to the judgment of reward.[101] And the Church or any member of the faithful prays this [verse] and similar [passages] not with an appetite for vindictiveness, but from the zeal of justice, and especially that [the ungodly] may repent; it is rather a foreannouncement of the future and not an imprecation of evil. For this reason, Cassiodorus[102] — in referring to this verse and to similar passages of Scripture in which we see a prayer being said for the damnation or the punishment of enemies — affirms that one ought not to understand them as referring to visible enemies, but to demons, especially since we are commanded

---

100   E. N. As Denis pointed out in the prior Article on this Psalm, although demons have been judged, they will receive increased "accidental" punishments based upon their efforts to tempt man. Article LXXIII (Psalm 34:1).
101   E. N. Denis distinguishes between the judgment of discretion (*iudicium discretionis*) and the judgment of remuneration, reward, or retribution (*iudicium remunerationis*). As he describes these two judgments in Article XXVIII (Psalm 9:1) in Volume 1: "The first is the judgment of discretion, by which someone is called by mercy, but another is relinquished to justice. The second is also the judgment of examination and retribution, which will occur at the end of time, which, although it will be open and visible, yet the day and time are hidden."
102   Flavius Magnus Aurelius Cassiodorus (*ca.* 485–*ca.* 585 A. D.) was a Roman stateman, and a later founder of a monastery school (the *Vivarium*). He wrote a number of historical, philosophical, grammatical, and theological works, perhaps his most famous being his Exposition of the Psalms (*Expositio psalmorum*) to which Denis here refers.

to love our enemies and to do good to our adversaries.[103] But however that may be, it is generally thought that these sorts of passages can be understood as applying also to visible enemies as far as temporal punishments are concerned, namely, so that they may amend their life in the present, lest they perish eternally.

Thus, that which is stated—*Judge, O Lord, them that wrong me*—can be understood as referring to the judgment of retribution, in which God frequently in the present avenges and punishes those who do wrong so that they may cease from doing evil. Also, we can desire the casting down and affliction—as far as temporal evils, namely, losses and punishments in the present life—of those who oppose themselves to the common good, and the Christian faith, and the unity of the Church, so that they may be restrained from their evil. For which reason the following is added: *expugna impugnantes me, overthrow them that fight against me*, that is, fight for me, and vanquish my adversaries. The Church particularly prays this against infidels and tyrants, heretics and schismatics, of whom it sometimes licitly desires their bodily death, because there is no other way to provide for their salvation.

34{35}[2] *Take hold of arms and shield: and rise up to help me.*

Apprehende arma et scutum, et exsurge in adiutorium mihi.

34{35}[3] *Bring out the sword, and shut up the way against them that persecute me: say to my soul: I am your salvation.*

Effunde frameam, et conclude adversus eos qui persequuntur me; dic animae meae: Salus tua ego sum.

34{35}[2] *Apprehende arma et scutum*, take hold of arms and shield. This has already been satisfactorily explained. *Et exsurge in adiutorium mihi*, and rise up to help me, that is, be ready and quick to render me aid, so that no bad example of an impious man, or false blandishment, threats on the part of enemies, erroneous doctrines, or tyrannical prosecutions may lead me away from your will and law, scandalize me, or overcome me. 34{35}[3] *Effunde frameam*, bring out the sword, that is, show forth your chastisements and apply the scourge of paternal correction, *et conclude adversus eos qui persequuntur me*, and shut up the way against them that persecute me, that is, impose [such chastisements and scourges] upon those evil men who are afflicting me, and by this restrict and confine

---

103 Matt. 5:44; Rom. 12:20.

their evil so that they do not henceforth become powerful and do evil, but that punished through bodily infirmity or suffering of the soul they may learn to do well.[104]

34{35}[4] Let them be confounded and afraid[105] that seek after my soul. Let them be turned back and be confounded that devise against me.

Confundantur et revereantur quaerentes animam meam; avertantur retrorsum et confundantur cogitantes mihi mala.

34{35}[5] Let them become as dust before the wind: and let the angel of the Lord straiten them.

Fiant tamquam pulvis ante faciem venti, et angelus Domini coarctans eos.

34{35}[6] Let their way become dark and slippery; and let the angel of the Lord pursue them.

Fiat via illorum tenebrae, et lubricum; et angelus Domini persequens eos.

34{35}[4] *Confundantur, let them be confounded,* of their irrational endeavor and unjust life, *et revereantur, and [let them be] afraid,* that is, let them be terrified of their imminent punishment, *quaerentes animam meam, that seek after my soul* to undermine it, or to destroy my life entirely. *Avertantur retrorsum, let them be turned back,* that is, may they cease from their evil purpose, and draw back from commencing [any evil] deed, *et confundantur, and [let them] be confounded,* since they have

---

104   E. N. One must distinguish between moral evil (which God never wills), and physical evil which operates under different principles. With respect to physical evil and its relationship to the divine will (and therefore whether it can be prayed for in certain circumstances and with a proper motive), we might look toward the words of Dr. Ludwig Ott: "God does not (*per se*) desire physical evil, for example, suffering illness, death, that is not for the sake of the evil or as an aim. Wis. 1:13 *et seq.*: "For God has not made death: neither hath He made pleasure in the destruction of the living. For He created all things that they might be." However, God wills physical evil, natural evil as well as punitive evil, *per accidens*, that is, as a means to a higher end of the physical order (for example, for punishment or for moral enlightenment). Ecclus. 11:14: "Good things and evil, life and death, poverty and riches are from God." *Cf.* Ecclus. 39:35 *et seq.* Am. 3, 6. Ludwig Ott, *Fundamentals of Catholic Dogma* (Fort Collins: Roman Catholic Books (no date)), 45-65.
105   E. N. I have departed from the Douay-Rheims translation "ashamed" and replaced it with "afraid," which is in line with Denis's understanding of the Latin word *revereantur*.

performed such dishonest things, [that is, those] *cogitantes mihi mala, that devise against me.* **34{35}[5]** *Fiant tanquam pulvis ante faciem venti, let them become as dust before the wind,* that is, let them move easily into repentance, and not harden as rock; but as dust follows the impetus of wind, so let these follow the internal direction of holy angels. Therefore, it continues: *et angelus Domini sit coarctans eos, and let the angel of the Lord straiten them,* that is, divert them from evil, and if it pertains to a deed, to constrain it by tribulation. **34{35}[6]** *Fiat via illorum tenebrae et lubricum, let their way become dark and slippery,* that is, let their works be similar to dark and slippery paths so that just as men in such paths often stumble, fall, and become weary and are not easily able to attain towards the end, but return [to their point of origin]; thus, in their unjust works, let them be impeded, tire, and not be permitted to attain their object, but let them be converted and live; *et angelus Domini persequens eos, and let the angel of the Lord pursue them,* that is, let the holy angel punish their sins, or allow [their sins] to be punished during this time, never ceasing to check them in following their evil desires. For this is very desirable as we find in the book of Maccabees: *For it is a token of great goodness when sinners are not suffered to go on in their ways for a long time but are presently punished.*[106]

34{35}[7] *For without cause they have hidden their net for me unto destruction: without cause they have upbraided my soul.*

Quoniam gratis absconderunt mihi interitum laquei sui, supervacue exprobraverunt animam meam.

34{35}[8] *Let it come to him, the snare which he knows not; and let the trap which he has hidden catch him: and into that very snare let him fall.*[107]

Veniat illi laqueus quem ignorat, et captio quam abscondit apprehendat eum, et in laqueum cadat in ipsum.

But this evil comes to them in the present life **34{35}[7]** *Quoniam gratis, without cause,* that is, without an apparent reason, *absconderunt mihi interitum laquei sui, they have hidden their net for me,* that is, they have prepared against me deceptions and traps; *supervacue exprobraverunt animam meam, without cause they have upbraided by soul,* that is, they

---

106   2 Macc. 6:13.
107   On the departure of the wording of this verse from the Douay-Rheims, see footnote 34-14.

have uselessly attacked me with invective, abuse, and insults. This verse, like the preceding ones, especially speaks to the Church about heretics, schismatics, the unfaithful, and tyrants. **34{35}[8]** *Veniat illi, let it come,* that is to anyone of them, *laqueus quem ignorat, the snare which he knows not,* that is, an unforeseen tribulation that is corrective; *et captio quam abscondit, and let that trap which he has hidden,* that is, the evil which he hiddenly attempted to occasion in me, *apprehendat eum, catch him,* that is, return back to him, so that he himself punishes himself for his sin; *et in laqueum cadat in ipsum, and into that very snare let him fall,* that is, let it turn him around to carry upon himself the yoke of Christ, namely, so that he may more ardently do so from the consideration of his sins, and more perfectly take upon himself the yoke of Christ, for *where sin abounded, grace did more abound.*[108]

Moreover, if those things which have been said of that verse, *bring out the sword,* are referred to eternal damnation, or referred to the just vengeance of divine justice upon sinners (which greatly agrees with a literal exposition, as was explained in the preceding exposition), then they are to be understood not as being wished for, but as foreannouncing, in the manner that has often been explained.[109]

34{35}[9] *But my soul shall rejoice in the Lord; and shall be delighted in his salvation.*

Anima autem mea exsultabit in Domino, et delectabitur super salutari suo.

34{35}[10] *All my bones shall say: Lord, who is like to you? Delivering the poor from the hand of them that are stronger than he; the needy and the poor from them that strip him.*

Omnia ossa mea dicent: Domine, quis similis tibi? Eripiens inopem de manu fortiorum eius; egenum et pauperem a diripientibus eum.

34{35}[9] *Anima autem mea exsultabit in Domino, but my soul shall rejoice in the Lord,* that is, it will breathe in his mercy, and it will receive consolation from the reflection of the Passion of Christ: indeed it will endure all things even cheerfully, so as to conform with its Lord; *et delectabitur, and it shall be delighted,* with a mental and intellectual delight,

---

108 Rom. 5:20.
109 See, e.g., Article LXI (Psalm 27:4) and footnote 27-16, Article LXXIII (Psalm 34:1) in this Volume, and Article LVI (Psalm 24:4) and footnote 24-14 in Volume 1.

super salutari suo, in his salvation, that is, of the salvation by which he redeems me, and of the beatitude which he promised: as the Apostle [Paul] says, *we glory in the hope [of the glory] of the sons of God*.[110] And Isaiah: *Lo, this is our God, . . . we shall rejoice and be joyful in his salvation*.[111] And you, O Lord, are 34{35}[10][112] *eripiens inopem, delivering the poor*, that is, me, a poor and afflicted man, *de manu fortiorum eius, from the hand of them that are stronger*, that is, from the power and the persecution of visible and invisible enemies against whom I have no power of my own to resist. For who by his own industry is able to resist the subtlety of demons? And you are delivering *egenum et pauperum, the needy and the poor*, that is, anybody disdaining temporal things, and he who is poor of spirit, *a diripientibus, from them that strip*, that is, from those that infest, plunder, or kill *eum, him*: in the manner that we find in Isaiah: *O Lord, . . . my God, I will exalt you, . . . because you have been a strength to the poor, a strength to the needy*.[113]

34{35}[11] *Unjust witnesses rising up have asked me things I knew not.*
Surgentes testes iniqui, quae ignorabam interrogabant me.

34{35}[12] *They repaid me evil for good: to the depriving me of my soul.*
Retribuebant mihi mala pro bonis, sterilitatem animae meae.

34{35}[11] *Surgentes testes iniqui, quae ignorabam interrogabant me, unjust witnesses rising up have asked me things I knew not*, that is, they have reproached me with things I have not done. Any Christian burdened with the accusations or testimony of false witnesses can say this, such as Naboth the Jezreelite—whom Ambrose in his book *On the Duties of the Clergy* calls a saint and martyr—was able.[114] 34{35}[12] *Retribuebant*

---

110 Rom. 5:2. E. N. The text does not have that portion in brackets; however, the margin notes of the editor suggest it should be included.
111 Is. 25:9.
112 E. N. Denis skips over the first part of the verse, *All my bones shall say: Lord, who is like to you?*
113 Is. 25:1a, 4a.
114 1 Kings 21:13: *And bringing two men, sons of the devil, they made them sit against him: and they, like men of the devil, bore witness against him before the people, saying: Naboth hath blasphemed God and the king: wherefore they brought him forth without the city, and stoned him to death*. Naboth was a citizen of Jezreel who was executed by Queen Jezebel so that Ahab, her husband, could possess his vineyard to use it for an herb or vegetable garden. Denis's reference is to St. Ambrose (ca. 340–397 A. D.) and his *De Officii Ministrorum*, III, 9, 63, PL 16, 163: *Quid vero sancto Nabuthe, quae fuit causa mortis, nisi honestatis contemplatio?* "But what of the holy

mihi mala pro bonis, they repaid me evil for good. This is fitting of the Church and all of the faithful and good of heart, who pray for those who are adversaries, and who receive hate from the ingrate in response to love and evil in response to kindness. *Sterilitatem animae mea, to the depriving me of my soul*. To understand this verse we have to supply what is implied, namely that they returned this in response to fruitfulness, so that it is as if he were saying: "I, with regard to them, was fruitfully doing good; but they, with respect to me, were unfruitful, returning nothing good, desiring not to enrich me either spiritually or temporally."

34{35}[13] But as for me, when they were troublesome to me, I was clothed with haircloth. I humbled my soul with fasting; and my prayer shall be turned into my inner part.

Ego autem, cum mihi molesti essent, induebar cilicio; humiliabam in ieiunio animam meam, et oratio mea in sinu meo convertetur.

34{35}[13] *Ego autem, quum mihi molesti essent*, but as for me, when they were troublesome to me, [that is, when] ungodly and ungrateful men [were troublesome to me], *induebar cilicio*, I was clothed with a haircloth, that is, with a penitential robe. *Humiliabam in ieiunio animam meam, I humbled my soul with fasting*, that is, by abstinence I afflicted myself, so that I might attain pardon for them and protection for myself. The Church frequently does this when heretics or schismatics arise, or when serious wars menace: just as we read Josaphat, the king of Juda, and all his people did.[115] It is written that most holy Esther[116] and the venerable Judith[117] did similarly. And therefore let us also follow their example: let us maintain patience while troublesome and ungrateful men seek to destroy, [and let us remain] glorying in this, that we are worthy

---

Naboth, what was the cause of his death, unless it be in contemplation of virtue?" St. Ambrose also wrote a whole monograph on Naboth, *De Nabuth Jezraelita*, PL 14, 765. It famously begins: *Nabuthe historia tempore vetus est, usu quotidiana*. "The story of Naboth in time is old; yet of daily use."

115 1 Chr. 20:3: *And Josaphat being seized with fear betook himself wholly to pray to the Lord, and he proclaimed a fast for all Juda.*

116 Esther 4:16: *Go and gather together all the Jews whom you shall find in Susanna, and pray for me. Neither eat nor drink for three days and three nights: and I with my handmaids will fast in like manner, and then I will go in to the king, against the law, not being called, and expose myself to death and to danger.*

117 Judith 8:6: *And she wore haircloth upon her loins, and fasted all the days of her life, except the sabbaths, and new moons, and the feasts of the house of Israel.*

to conform to the Lord and Savior. For to suffer in this manner is a gift of God, in the way that the Apostle [Paul] says: *For unto you it is given for Christ, not only to believe in him, but also to suffer for him.*[118] *Et oratio mea in sinu meo convertetur*, and *my prayer shall be turned into my inner part*, that is, the prayers which I pour out for adversaries, and false men, or the guilty, or undeserving, will be meritorious for me and will provide satisfaction for my own faults.[119] For however much this is not profitable to them because of their unworthiness or their incapacity, it does not for all that remain without fruit: indeed, any act proceeding from charity is meritorious of eternal life.

34{35}[14] *As a neighbor and as our brother, so did I find pleasing:*[120] *as one mourning and sorrowful so was I humbled.*

Quasi proximum et quasi fratrem nostrum sic complacebam; quasi lugens et contristatus sic humiliabar.

34{35}[14] *Quasi proximum, et quasi fratrem nostrum*, as a neighbor and as our brother which encompasses every single one of the faithful and also of the enemy, *sic complacebam*, so did I find pleasing, that is, so did I rejoice in their progress and prosperity; *quasi lugens et contristatus sic humiliabar*, as one mourning and sorrowful so was I humbled, that is, so am I afflicted by their adversity. This is what the Apostle [Paul] says: *Rejoice with them that rejoice; weep with them that weep.*[121] In this manner the holy evangelist John is pleased with his children, of whom he says: *I have no greater grace than this, to hear that my children walk in*

---

118   Phil. 1:29.
119   "Absolution takes away sin, but it does not remedy all the disorders sin has caused. Raised up from sin, the sinner must still recover his full spiritual health by doing something more to make amends for the sin: he must 'make satisfaction for' or 'expiate' his sins. This satisfaction is also called 'penance.'" CCC § 1459. "The satisfaction that we make for our sins, however, is not so much ours as though it were not done through Jesus Christ. We who can do nothing ourselves, as if just by ourselves, can do all things with the cooperation of 'him who strengthens' us. Thus man has nothing of which to boast, but all our boasting is in Christ ... in whom we make satisfaction by bringing forth 'fruits that befit repentance.' These fruits have their efficacy from him, by him they are offered to the Father, and through him they are accepted by the Father." CCC § 1460 (quoting the Council of Trent, DS 1691, which itself quotes Phil. 4:13, Luke 3:8, and Matt. 3:8, but refers also to 1 Cor. 1:31; 2 Cor. 10:17; Gal. 6:14).
120   E. N. I have modified the Douay-Rheims from: *As a neighbor and as an own brother, so did I please* (which sounds odd to the modern ear) to *as a neighbor and as our brother, so did I find pleasing*.
121   Rom. 12:15.

truth.[122] We ought not rejoice therefore in the adversity of our enemies, but we should rejoice in their progress, so that we might be worthy to say with holy Job: *If I have been glad at the downfall of him that hated me, and have rejoiced that evil had found him*.[123] And again: *I wept heretofore for him that was afflicted, and my soul had compassion on the poor*.[124] This perfection extends most especially to prelates.[125]

34{35}[15] *But they rejoiced against me, and came together: scourges were gathered together upon me, and I knew not.*

Et adversum me laetati sunt, et convenerunt; congregata sunt super me flagella, et ignoravi.

34{35}[16] *They were separated, and repented not: they tempted me, they scoffed at me with scorn: they gnashed upon me with their teeth.*

Dissipati sunt, nec compuncti, tentaverunt me, subsannaverunt me subsannatione; frenduerunt super me dentibus suis.

Therefore, I do for them such good; but what about them? It continues: 34{35}[15] *Et adversum me laetati sunt*, but they rejoiced against me, that is, they rejoiced in my misfortune and punishments and evil, *et convenerunt*, and came together, so that not able to overcome me by reason, they might defeat me by their numbers; *congregata sunt super me flagella, et ignoravi*; scourges were gathered together upon me, and I knew not, that is, unforeseen persecutions of men and temptations of demons befell me. 34{35}[16] *Dissipati sunt*, they were separated, that is, my adversaries just spoken of were fractured by true constancy and were divided by charity, *nec compuncti*, and repented not, that is, they did not repent of their evil; *tentaverunt me*, they tempted me, frightening, coaxing, tormenting, and pressing upon me, *subsannaverunt me subsannatione*, they scoffed at me with scorn. To express such a replication or repetition of the same thing is a custom of Hebrew idiom, as [for example] the manner in which Zechariah says: *Angry is the Lord with your fathers with anger!*[126] The

---

122 3 John 4.
123 Job 31:29. E. N. To contextualize Job 31:29, one must turn to Job 31:14: *For what shall I do when God shall rise to judge? and when he shall examine, what shall I answer him?.... If I have been glad at the downfall of him that hated me, and have rejoiced that evil had found him?* In other words, Job was not glad at the downfall of his enemies in a vindictive sense.
124 Job 30:25.
125 E. N. Prelates are churchmen with a superior rank such as bishops or abbots.
126 Zech. 1:2. E. N. The Douay-Rheims already considers the Hebraicism when

Church or each just man says: *they scoffed at me with scorn,* that is, my enemies which I have not harmed, but have benefited, have insulted and mocked me. This is what the Apostle [Paul] says: *We are reviled, and we bless; . . . we are blasphemed, and we entreat.*[127] *Frenduerunt super me dentibus suis, they gnashed upon me with their teeth,* as if they might wish to devour me from the fervor of their rancor or the impulse of passion.

34{35}[17] *Lord, when will you look upon me? Restore*[128] *my soul from their malice: my only one from the lions.*

Domine, quando respicies? Restitue animam meam a malignitate eorum, a leonibus unicam meam.

34{35}[17] *Domine, quando respicies? Lord, when will you look upon me?* That is, How long have you disregarded and abandoned me to afflict me? But now, look upon me, *restitue anima meam, restore my soul* to its former peace and your grace, *a malignitate eorum, from their malice* I was delivered; *a leonibus unicam meam, my only one from the lions,* that is, from the demons, who like roaring lions go about seeking,[129] and proud men, who oppress the innocent, in the manner that lions do sheep, restore my only one, that is my soul, which I so singularly need to protect, as it would be of no profit to me if I were to gain the whole world and yet to lose it.[130]

34{35}[18] *I will give thanks to you in a great church; I will praise you in a strong people.*

Confitebor tibi in ecclesia magna; in populo gravi laudabo te.

34{35}[19] *Let not them that are my enemies wrongfully rejoice over me: who have hated me without cause, and wink with the eyes.*

Non supergaudeant mihi qui adversantur mihi inique, qui oderunt me gratis, et annuunt oculis.

---

it translates this verse: *The Lord has been exceeding angry with your fathers.* The Vulgate (and Denis) have *Iratus est Dominus super patres vestros iracundia,* which I have translated literally so the reader can see what Denis is speaking of as: "Angry is the Lord with your fathers, with anger!"
127 1 Cor. 4:12b-13a.
128 E. N. I have changed the Douay-Rheims translation from *rescue* to *restore,* as it is also an accurate translation of *restitue,* and it fits better with the argument of Denis.
129 *Cf.* 1 Pet. 5:8.
130 *Cf.* Matt. 16:26.

34{35}[20] *For they spoke indeed peaceably to me; and speaking in the anger of the earth they devised guile.*

Quoniam mihi quidem pacifice loquebantur; et in iracundia terrae loquentes, dolos cogitabant.

34{35}[21] *And they opened their mouth wide against me; they said: Well done, well done, our eyes have seen it.*

Et dilataverunt super me os suum; dixerunt: Euge, euge! viderunt oculi nostri.

Consequently the faithful say: 34{35}[18] *Confitebor tibi, I will give thanks to you,* that is, to your glory, with confessions of your praise, and also confessions of my sinfulness,[131] *in Ecclesia Magna, in a great Church,* Christian, Apostolic, and Catholic.

34{35}[19] *Non supergaudeant mihi, let them not . . rejoice over me,* that is, let them not overly rejoice over the ruin of my soul from its seduction, *qui adversantur mihi inique, who are my enemies wrongfully,* that is, the demons and perfidious and pestilential men who strive to cause me spiritual injury: of whom it is said in an earlier Psalm, *They that trouble me will rejoice when I am moved;*[132] *qui oderunt me gratis, who have hated me without cause,* that is, without any wrongdoing on my part, *et annuunt oculis,* that is, they mutually show themselves disposed towards persecuting and assaulting me. 34{35}[20] *Quoniam mihi quidem pacifice loquebantur, for they spoke indeed peaceably to me:* that is, the demons suggested evil to me under the guise of good, and fraudulent men spoke words of concord to me in deceit, as Joab did with Abner and Amasa;[133] *et in iracundia terrae loquentes, dolos cogitabant; and speaking in the anger of the earth, they devised guile.* Demons speak to us interiorly *in the anger of the earth,* that is, out of the anger that they have against us, because we are possessed by the land of the living *(terram viventium),*[134] which

---

131 E. N. On the two types of confession, see footnote 27-49.
132 Ps. 12:5b.
133 2 Sam. 3:27: *And when Abner was returned to Hebron, Joab took him aside to the middle of the gate, to speak to him treacherously: and he stabbed him there in the groin, and he died, in revenge of the blood of Asael his brother.* 2 Sam. 20:9-10: *And Joab said to Amasa: God save you, my brother. And he took Amasa by the chin with his right hand to kiss him. But Amasa did not take notice of the sword, which Joab had, and he struck him in the side, and shed out his bowels to the ground, and gave him not a second wound, and he died.*
134 E. N. The phrase "land of the living," *terra viventium,* commonly a reference to the life of the blessed in heaven, or the Church, *see, e.g.,* Article LXI (Psalm 26:13), Article LX (Psalm 26:13), and Article LXXI (Psalm 33:17). *Credo videre bona Domini*

they, through their pride, lost; and they think up deceits, namely, so that they might lead us to sensible loves and carnal things, and so by them we might be lost to the kingdom of heaven. But evil men speak to the just *in the anger of the earth*, that is, out of anger conceived against them because of the love of earthly goods: such as when worldly men are envious and angry at the religious, because they possess temporal goods. **34{35}[21]** *Et dilitaverunt super me os suum*, *and they opened their mouth wide against me*, that is, with a wide mouth they spoke against me that which follows. *Dixerunt: Euge, euge*; *they said: Well done, well done*, that is, it is well, it is well, *viderunt oculi nostri*, *our eyes have seen it*, [that is,] the evil which befell you and therefore we rejoice.

34{35}[22] *You have seen, O Lord, be not silent: O Lord, depart not from me.*

Vidisti, Domine, ne sileas; Domine, ne discedas a me.

34{35}[23] *Arise, and be attentive to my judgment: to my cause, my God, and my Lord.*

Exsurge et intende iudicio meo, Deus meus; et Dominus meus, in causam meam.

34{35}[24] *Judge me, O Lord my God according to your justice, and let them not rejoice over me.*

Iudica me secundum iustitiam tuam, Domine Deus meus, et non supergaudeant mihi.

34{35}[25] *Let them not say in their hearts: It is well, it is well, to our mind: neither let them say: We have swallowed him up.*

Non dicant in cordibus suis : Euge, euge, animae nostrae; nec dicant: Devoravimus eum.

34{35}[26] *Let them blush: and be afraid together, who rejoice at my evils. Let them be clothed with confusion and fear, who speak great things against me.*[135]

Erubescant et revereantur simul qui gratulantur malis meis; induantur confusione et reverentia qui magna loquuntur super me.

---

in terra viventium, I believe to see the good things of the Lord in the land of the living. Ps. 26:13. It is used here to refer to the life of grace.

135 E. N. I have replaced the Douay-Rheims's "let them be ashamed" for *revereantur* with "let them be afraid," and its "shame" for *reverentia* with "fear," since this is how Denis plainly understands the Latin in this manner.

34{35}[22] *Vidisti, Domine; You have seen, O Lord,* this, you who know all things; *ne sileas, be not silent* by the delay in judgment, but judge for me and speak to me by hidden inspiration. *Domine, ne discedas a me, O Lord, depart not from me,* withdrawing from me consolation and grace. 34{35}[23] *Exsurge et intende iudicio meo, Deus meus; arise, and be attentive to my judgment,* . . . *my God,* that is, diligently consider what judgment I — who endure so much evil for justice's sake — deserve. This I pray with security, because I know the Scripture: *Blessed are they that suffer persecution for justice's sake: for theirs is the kingdom of heaven.*[136] *Et, and* you who are *Dominus meus, my Lord,* be attentive *in causam meam, to my cause,* that is, see my justice for which I am judged by the ungodly as if unjust: for they hate me for the good that I do. 34{35}[24] *Iudica me secundum iustitiam tuam, Domine Deus meus; Judge me, O Lord my God, according to your justice,* that is, render to me according to the justice which I have worked by your grace.[137] But always mix in your mercy with your judgment. *Et non supergaudeant mihi, and let them not rejoice over me:* as it now is stated. 34{35}[25] *Non dicant, let them not say* finally *in cordibus suis, in their hearts: Euge, euge, anima nostrae; it is well, it is well, to our mind:* that is, how happily it has befallen us, that we have seduced this one, and we have afflicted him with punishment! *Nec decant: Devorabis eum; neither let them say: We have swallowed him up,* killing in him the charity of God and neighbor and in addition the gifts of the Holy Spirit. 34{35}[26] *Erubescant et revereantur simul [qui gratulantur malis meis; inducantur confusione et reverentia qui magna loquuntur super me]; Let them blush: and be afraid together, [who rejoice at my evils. Let them be clothed with confusion and fear, who speak great things against me].*[138] This is [the same thing as] what was said at the beginning of this Psalm: *Let them be confounded and afraid that seek after my soul.*

34{35}[27] *Let them rejoice and be glad, who are well pleased with my justice, and let them say always: The Lord be magnified, who delights in the peace of his servant.*

Exsultent et laetentur qui volunt iustitiam meam; et dicant semper: Magnificetur Dominus, qui volunt pacem servi eius.

---

136   Matt. 5:10.
137   E. N. "Filial adoption, in making us partakers by grace in the divine nature, can bestow true merit on us as a result of God's gratuitous justice." CCC § 2009.
138   E. N. The parts in brackets have been added where Denis simply placed "*etc.*"

34{35}[28] *And my tongue shall meditate your justice, your praise all the day long.*

Et lingua mea meditabitur iustitiam tuam, tota die laudem tuam.

34{35}[27] *Exsultent et laetentur,* let them rejoice and be glad in you, O Lord God, and let them give you thanks, *qui volunt iustitiam meam,* who are well pleased with my justice, that is, to whom my progress in spiritual things is pleasing and who cooperate with me in good; *et dicant semper, Magnificetur Dominus, quo volunt pacem servi eius;* and let them say always: the Lord be magnified, who delights in the peace of his servant, that is, who desire me, a servant of Christ, to have true and stable peace. 34{35}[28] *Et lingua mea meditabitur iustitiam tuam,* and my tongue shall mediate *your justice,* that is, I will speak about your law and mention it to others, *tota die laudem tuam, your praise all the day long,* that is, I will always ascribe all good to you. The rest is clear from the preceding exposition.

See how full of meaning and how in so many diverse ways this Psalm, which hiddenly describes the mysteries of Christ, which so evidently instructs charity, teaches patience, and informs the faithful of all perfection. And so with all attention let us read it and live in such a manner so that those things which are written in it might truly apply to us.

PRAYER

GOD, POWERFUL AND STRONG, TAKE hold of arms and shield, and rise up in our aid against those that fight against us, and everywhere defend our weakness from those with ill-will so that exulting and rejoicing in you, we so defended may always magnify you, and may all the days of eternity sing praises to you.

Deus potens et fortis, apprehende arma et scutum, et contra nos impugnantes exsurge nobis in adiutorium, et ab eorum malignitate fragilitatem nostram ubique defende: ut in te exsultantes et laetantes, te semper tuti magnificemus, et tota die perennitatis laudes tibi decantemus.

Psalm 35

ARTICLE LXXIV
EXPOSITION OF THE THIRTY-FIFTH PSALM:
DIXIT INIUSTUS UT DELINQUAT
THE UNJUST HAS SAID THAT HE WOULD NOT SIN.

35{36}[1] *Unto the end. For the servant of the Lord, a Psalm of David.*

In finem. Servo Domini Psalmus David.

SCRIBED TO THIS PSALM, IS AGAIN THIS title: 35{36}[1] *In finem, servo Domini Psalmus David; Unto the end, for the servant of the Lord, a Psalm of David*: that is, this Psalm directs us *unto the end*, that is, unto God, to whom we ascend by humility; this Psalm is of holy David, *for the servant of the Lord*, that is, for the instruction of any one of the servants of God. Or [we could see it in this way], it is a Psalm of David *for the servant of the Lord*, that is, it applies to David himself as a *servant of the Lord*, understanding by David [a figure of] any one of the true faithful. For this Psalm teaches us to abhor pride, to increase humility, to affix all hope in the Lord, and to ascribe all good to him.

35{36}[2] *The unjust has said within himself, that he would sin: there is no fear of God before his eyes.*

Dixit iniustus ut delinquat in semetipso: non est timor Dei ante oculos eius.

35{36}[3] *For in his sight he has done deceitfully, so that his iniquity may be found to be hatred.*[1]

Quoniam dolose egit in conspectu eius, ut inveniatur iniquitas eius ad odium.

And so it says: 35{36}[2] *Dixit iniustus*, the unjust has said, that is, he has set himself, and has firmly proposed, *ut delinquat in semetipso*, within

---

1 E. N. In light of Denis's *Commentary*, I have rendered "that his iniquity may be found unto hatred" in the Douay-Rheims translation to "so that his iniquity be found to be hatred."

himself that he would sin, that is, that he might do evil from deliberate reason and with full consent. For as the Philosopher [Aristotle] says, man sins in a twofold manner, namely out of passion and out of evil habit:[2] and theologians say that is so because man sins in one fashion through weakness, and in the other way out of a certain malice, from deliberate reason, and from a full consent to sin. But he who sins from passion or weakness quickly feels sorry and makes amends. [This is so] because when the passion (which is nothing other than the actual motion of the sensitive appetite from an apprehension of the sensible good or evil) ceases so does the sin cease, as is apparent in the incontinent; but he who sins out of bad habit is corrected only with difficulty, and he does not stop easily: indeed, according to the Philosopher he is as though incorrigible, because the reason of sinning, namely, the vicious habit, has taken root in him, as is apparent in the intemperate man.[3] Nevertheless, by the grace of God such men frequently quickly convert and become most virtuous: for grace has dominion over nature.[4] And so in this manner the unjust man, that is, he who is habituated in evil, proposes to sin and customarily violates the divine law. But the good do not sin in such a manner, but rather from weakness and passion. Also, the virtuous do not all at once

---

2 *E. N.* For example, in his *Rhetoric*, Aristotle states that crimes are either done ignorantly or against a person's will or voluntarily and with knowledge. If done voluntarily and with knowledge, then they either arise deliberately (habit) or from passion. *Arist. Rh.* I, 13, 1373b. St. Maximus the Confessor (*ca.* 580–662 A. D.) applies this principle this way: "[I]t is one thing to sin through habit and another to sin through being carried away. In this [latter] case, the sinner did not fully reflect either before or after the sin but rather was deeply grieved over the incident. The one who sins from habit is quite the reverse, for first he does not cease sinning in thought and after the act he maintains the same disposition." *Maximus Confessor: Selected Writings,* "Four Hundred Chapters on Love: Third Century," No. 74 (Paulist Press: 1985), 71 (George Charles Berthold, trans.)
3 This distinction between incontinence and intemperance is derived from Aristotle's *Nicomachean Ethics, Nich. Ethic.* II, 1104b.9–13. See St. Thomas's commentary on this Aristotle's Ethics, *Sententia Ethic.*, lib. 7 l. 1.
4 *E. N.* Denis says *gratia dominatur naturae*, grace has dominion over nature, or grace dominates nature. This is a strong phrase that perhaps is a reference to Romans 6:14: *For sin shall not have dominion over you; for you are not under the law, but under grace.* "As grace makes our soul a spouse of God, the King of Heaven and earth, so it elevates the same to be queen over all things, because, as God says to His Son, so He says to the spouse of His Son: 'All I have is thine.'... If God by grace makes us partakers of His Divine nature, and gives us His own Divine being for our possession and enjoyment, will He not also present and subject all other things to us? Certainly, for this precisely follows from all the properties of grace that we have hitherto considered." Matthias Joseph Scheeben, *The Glories of Divine Grace* (New York: Benziger Brothers 1886), 184-85.

slide into such a great sinkhole where they might sin out of choice or out of habit. Whence Origen in *On First Principles* said: None of those who abide at the highest and perfect level are quickly overcome; but it is necessary to overcome them gradually and bit by bit.[5]

Consequently, touching upon this issue—why the unjust man sins in this manner—[the Psalm states]: because *non est timor Dei ante oculos eius, there is no fear of God before his eyes,* that is, he does not have the fear of the Lord, nor do his heart's eyes consider those things which the fear of God leads to, for example, that God the Judge will discern all things, will leave no evil unavenged, and will abandon those who do not fear eternal punishments. For *the fear of the Lord* (as Scripture says) *drives out sin.*[6] And again, it is written: *He that fears God, neglects nothing.*[7] But since the fear of God is not before the sight of the unjust, hence this follows: **35{36}[3]** *Quoniam dolose egit in conspectu eius, for in his sight he has done deceitfully,* that is, it is audacious to do things deceitfully and to deceive one's neighbor with God present, seeing, and prohibiting, *ut inveniatur iniquitas eius ad odium, so that his iniquity may be found to be hatred.* This is said, not causally, but consecutively. For one does not undertake deceit so that his iniquity might be found to be hateful, that is, so that his malice is hateful to God and all saints; but this follows from [such deceit], that is, not having the fear of God, yet doing deceitful things before him.[8]

---

5   E. N. The reference is to Origen's *Peri Archon, On First Principles,* I, 3, 8, 11 PG 135. In his *Disputed Questions on the Virtues,* St. Thomas Aquinas refers to this text in discussing whether the virtue of charity can exist with mortal sin, which Origen's text could be construed as implying (similar to the notion of "fundamental option" rejected explicitly by St. John Paul II in his encyclical *Veritatis Splendor,* 65–70): "Origen says in 1 *Periarchon*: 'I do not believe that anyone persisting in the highest and perfect state would suddenly collapse and fall, but necessarily he must ebb away little by little and gradually.'" Thomas, however, responds: "The words of Origen are not to be so understood that a man, however perfect, sinning mortally, does not quickly lose charity, but because it does not easily happen that a perfect man would at that point commit a mortal sin, but through negligence a number of venial sins, he might be disposed finally to slip into mortal sin." *De virtutibus,* q. 2 a. 6 arg. 1, and ad 1. St. Thomas rejected a notion of "fundamental option" centuries before Pope St. John Paul II did in his encyclical *Veritatis splendor,* Nos. 65–70.
6   Ecclus. 1:27.
7   Eccl. 7:19b.
8   E. N. Denis is saying here that the hatred of sin by God and his saints is not caused by the sinner (*i.e.,* the sinner's sin is not an efficient cause of that hatred); nor is it the sinner's intent to cause that hate. Instead, such hatred to sin follows naturally, ontologically as it were, from the fact of the audacity of the sin by the sinner who does not fear God. "God hates sin, to the degree he is able to hate. He hates sin, as

35{36}[4] *The words of his mouth are iniquity and guile: he would not understand that he might do well.*

Verba oris eius iniquitas, et dolus; noluit intelligere ut bene ageret.

35{36}[4] *Verba oris eius iniquitas et dolus*, the words of his mouth are iniquity and guile, that is, iniquitous and fraudulent; *noluit intelligere ut bene ageret*, he would not understand that he might do well, that is, he was not satisfied with holy doctrine, and he did not wish to know the testimony of the Scriptures which teach how many torments threaten evil men. For many there are who sin greatly unconcerned, and do so with great delight, not wanting to advert to, understand, or discover the truth of Scripture. Of these, holy Job said: *They have said to God: Depart from us, we desire not the knowledge of your ways.*[9] These sorts of men sin out of vicious habit, and, as has been said before, they amend their ways only with the greatest difficulty, as we read about such in Jeremiah: *If the Ethiopian can change his skin, or the leopard his spots: you may also do well, when you have learned evil.*[10] If, therefore, you wish to turn away from evil and to do good, learn the Scriptures, listen to the word of salvation, love and understand the truth. For these things the divine word exhorts us to do: *Be instructed*, says the Lord, *lest my soul depart from you.*[11] At again: *Ask for... which is the good way, and walk in it, and you shall find refreshment for your souls.*[12] And the Apostle [Paul]: *Attend unto reading, to exhortation, and to doctrine.*[13] *For all scripture, inspired of God* (as the same divine Apostle attests), *is profitable to teach, to reprove, to correct, to instruct in justice, that the man of God may be perfect, furnished to every good work.*[14] It is true that there are many who desire to know, not so that they might do good, but so that they might appear wise: they want to know not for reasons of virtue, but for reasons of vanity. Of such persons Isaiah says: *Your wisdom, and your knowledge, this has deceived you;*[15] and again: *Woe to you that*

---

much as he loves his Son. He hates sin as much as he loves himself. He hates sin alone. He hates it infinitely. He hates it necessarily. He hates it essentially. He perseveres in that hate eternally." Johannes Grasset, S. J., *Nova Forma Meditationum* (1739), 22.
9   Job. 21:14.
10 Jer. 13:23.
11 Jer. 6:8a.
12 Jer. 6:16a.
13 1 Tim. 4:13.
14 2 Tim. 3:16-17a.
15 Is. 47:10a.

are wise in your own eyes, and prudent in your own conceits.[16] These are unhappy men, and most worthy of all condemnation: because as Peter said, *For it had been better for them not to have known the way of justice, than after they have known it, to turn back.*[17]

35{36}[5] *He has devised iniquity on his bed, he has set himself on every way that is not good: but evil he has not hated.*

Iniquitatem meditatus est in cubili suo; astitit omni viae non bonae, malitiam autem non odivit.

35{36}[5] *Iniquitatem meditatus est,* he has devised iniquity unjustly *in cubili suo,* on his bed, that is, in his heart, and this deliberation has led to an effect, because *adstitit omni viae non bonae,* he has set himself on every way that is not good, that is, he has adhered to all works of evil; *malitiam autem,* but evil, that is, sin, *non odivit,* he has not hated, but has loved. He has not loved evil under the aspect of evil, but by reason of it being an apparent good, insofar as it is delightful to the sinner.[18] Whence, according to Dionysius [the Areopagite],[19] none undertake an act with the end of doing evil (as evil).[20]

35{36}[6] *O Lord, your mercy is in heaven, and your truth reaches even to the clouds.*

Domine, in caelo misericordia tua, et veritas tua usque ad nubes.

---

16 Is. 5:21.
17 2 Pet. 2:21a.
18 E. N. St. Thomas Aquinas teaches that just as the intellect tends towards the true, so also the human will "can tend to nothing except under the aspect of the good *(sub ratione boni).*" This tendency is general, however, and "because good is of many kinds *(bonum est multiplex),*" "the will is not of necessity determined" to any particular good. For this reason, something evil may be chosen as an apparent good or as something evil under the aspect of good. ST Ia, q. 82, art. 2, ad 1. "All thought is displayed on a substratum of truth, all will upon a substratum of good. In all error there is a truth misapprehended, misapplied, or perverted; in all evil there is a good misapprehended, misrepresented, misapplied, or abused." Orestes A. Brownson, *The Works of Orestes A. Brownson* (Detroit: Thorndike Nourse 1884), Vol. VII, 524.
19 E. N. As to Dionysius the Areopagite (Pseudo-Dionysius), *see* footnote 32-3.
20 The maxim is: *nemo intendens ad malum operatur,* "no man intends to do evil [as evil]." It may be found in chapter IV, section 19 of Dionysius the Areopagite's *On the Divine Names.* PG 3, 715 *ff.* This is consistent with St. Thomas Aquinas's insistence that the will always chooses, even an evil, under the guise of it being a good.

35{36}[6] *Domine, in caelo misericordia tua; O Lord, your mercy is in heaven*: that is, your mercy appears and is resplendent particularly in the elect, namely in the holy angels and good men who are in the heavenly city, just as your justice is with the reprobate. For the elect are *the vessels of mercy* in honor, and the reprobate are the *vessels of wrath* in ruin.[21] *Et veritas tua usque ad nubes, and your truth reaches even to the clouds*: that is, your illumination of truth extends to those holy preachers and enlightens them. Of these Isaiah in admiration says about them: *Who are these that fly as clouds?*[22] Dionysius [the Areopagite] also says that by clouds in sacred Scripture we are to understand the holy angels, because just like material clouds they are first and foremost illuminated by the sun rather than the earth; so, compared to men, angels are first and fully illuminated by God. Therefore, one can expound the verse that says, *and your truth reaches even to the clouds*, in this sense: Your truth, that is Christ, who is Wisdom,[23] the Word, and your Son, even unto the clouds, that is, his rays of illumination continuously expand and flow into the angelic minds. For Christ (even as man as such) enlightens all angels much more excellently than some superior angels do the inferior angels.[24]

35{36}[7] *Your justice is as the mountains of God, your judgments are a great deep. Men and beasts you will preserve, O Lord.*

Iustitia tua sicut montes Dei; iudicia tua abyssus multa. Homines et iumenta salvabis, Domine.

35{36}[8] *O how have you multiplied your mercy, O God! But the children of men shall put their trust under the covert of your wings.*

Quemadmodum multiplicasti misericordiam tuam, Deus. Filii autem hominum in tegmine alarum tuarum sperabunt.

35{36}[9] *They shall be inebriated with the plenty of your house; and you shall make them drink of the torrent of your pleasure.*

---

21 Rom. 9:22, 23: *What if God, willing to show his wrath, and to make his power known, endured with much patience vessels of wrath, fitted for destruction, that he might show the riches of his glory on the vessels of mercy, which he has prepared unto glory?*
22 Is. 60:8a.
23 Cf. 1 Cor. 1:24b: *Christ the power of God, and the wisdom of God.*
24 E. N. Denis cites to chapter 15 of Dionysius's *On the Celestial Hierarchy* (*De Caelisti Hierarchia*). Denis mentions this notion in Article XLV (Psalm 18:3) in the first Volume.

Inebriabuntur ab ubertate domus tuae, et torrente voluptatis tuae potabis eos.

35{36}[7] *Iustitia tua sicut montes Dei, iudicia tua abyssus multa; your justice is as the mountains of God, your judgments are a great deep.* Just as the justice of God is compared to a great deep, that is, as a sea which to us is infinite, so the divine justice is compared to the mountains of God. For just as from our vantage point the most high mountains seem as of infinite altitude, so that our sight is unable to make out their peak or to measure their height, so does the divine justice exceed the sight of our interior eyes and cannot be comprehended by us.[25] In a similar manner, like a great deep [an abyss], that is, a great sea, because of its expanse and its depth is neither able to be seen nor measured, so the divine judgments are incomprehensible to us because of their profundity. As the Apostle [Paul] exclaims: *O the depth of the riches of the wisdom and of the knowledge of God! How incomprehensible are his judgments, and how unsearchable his ways!*[26] A judgment is an act of justice. Whence by judgments we are able to understand the election of the good and the reprobation of the evil, seen actively, as they are in God, according to that which the Lord says: *I have loved Jacob, but I have hated Esau.*[27] Or by judgments are understood the hidden effects of divine justice, namely predestination, election, and obstinacy, passively understood.[28] Since, therefore, the judgments of God are a great deep, we do not presume to discuss them, for as Solomon said: *As it is not good for a man to eat much honey, so he that is a searcher of majesty, shall be overwhelmed by glory.*[29] For which reason the Apostle [Paul] also says: *O man, who are you that replies against God?*[30]

Homines et iumenta, men and beasts, that is, the Jews and the Gentiles, or spiritual men or beastly men, *salvabis, Domine, you will preserve, O Lord.* For *Christ died for all,*[31] and all are preserved (*salvavit*) by his

---

25 With God's justice as with anything else pertaining to God, we might recall St. Augustine's statement: *Si enim comprehendis, non est Deus.* "If you comprehend it, it is not God." *Sermo,* 117, 3, 5.
26 Rom. 11:33.
27 Mal. 1:2b–3a.
28 E. N. These mysteries understood passively (*passive acceptae*), that is, as something suffered or received by the creature. Such passive reception includes not only the order of creation (being created), but also the order of grace (of being chosen, called, and justified).
29 Prov. 25:27.
30 Rom. 9:20a.
31 2 Cor. 5:15a.

death, and by his grace sinners are converted,[32] and he makes spiritual men from beastly ones. **35{36}[8]** *Quemadmodum multiplicasti misericordiam tuam, Deus; O how have you multiplied your mercy, O God*, that is, just as you copiously and marvelously poured out over the human race your kindness and your grace, reconciling all to yourself, and, as it were, compelling them to come in.[33] One may also understand the words *and beasts* as referring to the brute animals, which God preserves (*salvat*) with regard to their bodily life, giving them the necessary things of life, as it says in a later Psalm: [it is God] *who gives*, it says, *to beasts their food*.[34] And in the book of Job: [when it describes God as he] *who provides food for the raven, when her young ones cry to God, wandering about, because they have no meat?*[35] And in the Gospel the Savior says: *Behold the birds of the air, for they neither sow, nor do they reap, nor gather into barns: and your heavenly Father feeds them*.[36]

Filii autem hominum, *but the children of men*, that is, the posterity of the first parents, or the Church militant, and especially men who are not beastly but are living humanely, and piously, and reasonably, *in tegmine alarum tuarum, under the covert of your wings*, that is, under the protection of your mercy and your power, *sperabunt, they shall put their trust*, and not in their own merits and virtues. Therefore, **35{36}[9]** *Inebriabuntur ab ubertate domus tuae, they shall be inebriated with the plenty of your house*. The house of God can be understood as the Church militant or triumphant. But the plenteousness of the Church militant is the affluence of the grace of the Holy Spirit, with which God fills the elect in the present life, in the manner that the Apostle [Paul] states: *God has sent the Spirit of his Son into your hearts*.[37] And the plenteousness of the

---

32   E. N. This is not to be understood as suggesting universal salvation; Denis is merely observing that Christ's death redeemed all mankind, that those men who are saved (in a strict sense) and justified are saved and justified by Christ's death (and no other way), and that by God's grace they are converted to repent, to believe, and to become baptized, so as to make the redemption effective for their salvation, bringing the potentiality of salvation present in the Redemption into an active salvation or justification. Denis is well-aware that some men for whom Christ died and who were redeemed by his death will die with mortal sin on their souls and therefore will be damned. The underlying verb *salvare* can mean both to save and to conserve or preserve.
33   *Cf.* Luke 14:23: *And the Lord said to the servant: Go out into the highways and hedges, and compel them to come in, that my house may be filled.*
34   Ps. 146:9a.
35   Job 38:41.
36   Matt. 6:26.
37   Gal. 4:6.

Church triumphant is the beatitude of the Saints. And so, the *children of men* trusting *under the cover of the wings* of God are inebriated, that is, so copiously filled by the affluence of the grace of the Holy Spirit that they withdraw and alienate themselves from themselves, and they are absorbed by God through the fervor of charity while in the wayfaring state. But in the heavenly homeland they will be filled with such beatitude that they will be most perfectly transformed in God by a deiform assimilation without interruption and without end,[38] in accordance to this: *we shall be like to him: because we shall see him as he is.*[39]

Et torrente voluptatis tuae, *and of the torrent of your pleasure*, that is, of you yourself, who are the fountainlike torrent and first origin of pure and internal delight, *potabis eos, you shall make them drink*, that is, you will flood and make fruitful the heart of these men [the elect], manifesting yourself to them: in which manifestation consists the happiness of created minds, whose certain happiness is the river of your uncreated pleasure, and the drink which you give to refresh and by which you inebriate all the blessed in heaven. This is what the Lord says through Isaiah: *Behold I will bring upon her as it were a river of peace, and as an overflowing torrent the glory.*[40] Whence also the Apostle [Paul] says: *Eye has not seen, nor ear heard, neither has it entered into the heart of man, what things God has prepared for them that love him.*[41] For what else has the most bountiful and supremely most sweet God prepared for those who love him other than his very self? For he is the immediate object and the proximate cause of the universal glory of the elect, as Moses asserts: *He, the Lord, is your life, and the length of your days.*[42] He is also food and drink, and he himself invites the elect to spiritual relish and sober intoxication, saying: *Eat, O friends, and drink, and be inebriated, my dearly beloved.*[43] See how great is the joy of the elect. But how immaculate and holy must the intellectual creature be, who is so singularly and so intimately coupled with the

---

38 E. N. Denis draws directly from Dionysius the Areopagite and perhaps also Thomas Gallus (*ca.* 1200–1246 AD) (also known as Thomas of St. Victor or Thomas Vercellensis), the famous medieval commentator on Pseudo-Dionysius and the Songs of Songs, whom Denis cites in other works. The words deiform assimilation (*assimilationem deiformem*) are used by Thomas Gallus to describe the union of the blessed in heaven in God.
39 1 John 3:2b.
40 Is. 66:12a.
41 1 Cor. 2:9.
42 Deut. 30:20a.
43 Songs 5:1b.

immense fountain of beauty and infinite holiness and most pure torrent of delight, God most high and blessed! Certainly it is necessary for him to be so stainless and so pure of all guilt or vice if he is to be worthy to hear from the Lord: *You are all fair, O my love, and there is not a spot in you.*[44] If, therefore, you desire to see God, strive to have a clean heart: because the more you cleanse your affections the more clearly you will see him. For which reason he himself said through the prophet [Jeremiah]: *Wash your heart from wickedness,... that you may be saved.*[45]

35{36}[10] *For with you is the fountain of life; and in your light we shall see light.*

Quoniam apud te est fons vitae, et in lumine tuo videbimus lumen.

And in this way, O Lord, you will give drink and intoxicate men in the wayfaring state in an inchoate way, and in the heavenly homeland in a consummate manner. **35{36}[10]** *Quoniam apud te est fons vitae, for with you is the fountain of life*, that is, in you yourself is the fountain-like and unfailing origin of all life, namely, of the life of nature, of the life of grace, and of the life of glory: indeed, you yourself are the first, superessential, and unchangeable life, and the created beatitude, which is a certain participation in your most blessed life,[46] because you, O Lord, are in essence life, and are the fountain of life by communion, therefore you are able to intoxicate the elect, as we have shown. *Et in lumine tuo videbimus lumen, and in your light we shall see light.* This [verse] can be explained in three ways. The first way is in this manner: O God, Father, *in your light*, that is in the Incarnate Word, who is *the true light enlightening* every *man*,[47] *we shall see*, in the heavenly homeland *light*, that is the supermostglorious Trinity,[48] which is the one infinite and

---

44 Songs 4:7.
45 Jer. 4:14a.
46 E. N. Denis distinguishes between the essential beatitude of God and the created beatitude. The latter is the participation in God's beatitude by the creature. *See* ST Ia, q. 26, arts. 1-4.
47 John 1:9.
48 E. N. On Denis's use of super-superlatives, here *supergloriosissima*, and whether they are intended to connote something *most eminently within the genus* or to connote *beyond but analogous to the genus see* footnote 17-128 in Volume 1. Thus, we might translate this as meaning "eminently most glorious," or "beyond the most glorious," or "*more than* most glorious." But rather than choosing between apophatic or cataphatic

most simple light, in whose vision consists all happiness. For the blessed in heaven are said to see all things in the Word, because wisdom is appropriated to the Word.[49] The second way is this: *In your light*, that is, by the divine essence united by way of intelligible form,[50] *we shall see, O God three and simple, light*, that is, you yourself who are pure and perfect light. For the created intellect is not able to see God by image (*per speciem*) and *as he is*,[51] or, as the Apostle [Paul] says, *face to face*,[52] but only by some created form: because any created form is infinitely distant from the divine perfection.[53] Therefore it [the created form] is not able to represent him as he is. It is necessary, therefore, that the divine essence itself be united to the minds of the blessed by

---

senses, I have translated *supergloriossima* supermostglorious so that the reader can be aware of both senses.

49   E. N. "The Church is accustomed most fittingly to attribute (*tribuere*) to the Father those works of the Divinity in which power excels, to the Son those in which wisdom excels, and those in which love excels to the Holy Spirit. Not that all perfections and external operations are not common to the Divine Persons; for 'the operations of the Trinity are indivisible, even as the essence of the Trinity is indivisible,' because as the three Divine Persons 'are inseparable, so do they act inseparably.' But by a certain comparison and a kind of affinity between the operations and the properties of the Persons, these operations are attributed (*addicuntur*) or, as it is said, 'appropriated' (*appropriantur*) to one Person rather than to the others 'Just as we make use of the traces or similarity or likeness that we find in creatures for the manifestation of the Divine Persons, so do we use their essential attributes; and this manifestation of the Persons by their essential attributes is called appropriation (*appropriatio*)." DS 3326 (Leo XIII, *Divinum illud munus* (quotes are to St. Augustine's *De Trinitate* and St. Thomas Aquinas's *Summa Theologiae*)).

50   E. N. The issue here is whether the blessed in heaven see God directly and immediately or mediately, that is, through some intermediate image. St. Thomas (like Denis) insists that the blessed in heaven see God without mediation. *[V]identes Deum per essentiam, ea quae in ipsa essentia Dei vident, non vident per aliquas species, sed per ipsam essentiam divinam intellectui eorum unitam.* "Those seeing God by essence [*i.e.*, the blessed in heaven], see that which they see in the essence of God, they do not see by another species (intellectual image), but by the divine essence itself united to their intellect." ST, Ia, q. 12, art. 9, co.

51   1 John 3:2b.

52   1 Cor. 13:12a.

53   E. N. Our knowledge of God while in the wayfaring state is analogical. As Pope Benedict XVI stated in his famous Regensburg Lecture: "[T]he faith of the Church has always insisted that between God and us, between his eternal Creator Spirit and our created reason there exists a real analogy, in which—as the Fourth Lateran Council in 1215 stated—unlikeness remains infinitely greater than likeness, yet not to the point of abolishing analogy and its language." Yet the mental images by which we intellectually "grasp" God as wayfarers are themselves an "image" (*specie*) in a created intellect, and therefore, "some created [intellectual] form" that is "infinitely distant from the divine perfection," as Denis concludes.

way of an intelligible species or form, not that it is an inhering form (*forma inhaerens*), but an illuminating (*illustrans*) one.[54] But since it is in this way that we will see God, *we shall be* truly *like to him*, and we will know him as we are known,[55] as the Apostle [Paul] says. Because in God that which is seen and that by which he sees is the same thing (for God sees himself by himself), so, at that time [in heaven], that which we shall see and that by which we see will be the same for us, because we shall see God by God himself. And because this union of the created mind with the divine essence is in all regards supernatural, therefore the created mind needs some supernatural disposition by which it might be elevated and made apt for such divine union: and this disposition is called the light of glory, of which light, in a wayfaring state, grace, is the beginning.[56] Whence the third way to expound [on this verse] is on the light of glory: *In your light*, that is, by means of the light of glory infused into the mind, *we shall see light*, the divine light, which is the object of all felicity.

35{36}[11] *Extend your mercy to them that know you, and your justice to them that are right in heart.*

Praetende misericordiam tuam scientibus te, et iustitiam tuam his qui recto sunt corde.

35{36}[12] *Let not the foot of pride come to me, and let not the hand of the sinner move me.*

Non veniat mihi pes superbiae, et manus peccatoris non moveat me.

35{36}[13] *There they who are workers of iniquity are fallen, they are cast out, and could not stand.*

Ibi ceciderunt qui operantur iniquitatem; expulsi sunt, nec potuerunt stare.

---

54 An inhering form (*forma inhaerens*) is equivalent to a substantial form; our union with God is not substantial—we do not become God himself and our substance does not disappear; hence, the form is one that enlightens, illuminates, divinizes, an illustrating or illuminating form (*forma illustrans*).
55 1 John 3:2b; cf. 1 Cor. 13:12b.
56 The Scholastic adage is *grace is the beginning of glory, gratia inchoatio gloriae*. See, e.g., ST IIaIIae, q. 24, art. 3, ad 2. [G]*ratia et gloria ad idem genus referentur, quia gratia nihil est aliud quam quedam inchoatio gloriae in nobis.* "Grace and glory are referred to the same genus, because grace is nothing other than a certain beginning of glory in us."

35{36}[11] *Praetende, extend, O Lord, misericordiam tuam scientibus te, your mercy to them that know you,* that is, those who diligently search for you with their whole heart by faith, hoping only in you, of whom we have spoken previously, *And let them trust in you who know your name;*[57] *et iustitiam tuam his qui recto sunt corde, and your justice to them that are right in heart,* that is, increase the justice of the just, giving them an increase in grace for their good works done in their wayfaring state, and eternal life in the heavenly homeland.[58] 35{36}[12] *Non veniat mihi pes superbiae, let not the foot of pride come to me,* that is, let not the state of self-exaltation arise in my heart, which state is called a foot, because by it man struts towards hell. Or [we might understand it] thus: *Let not the foot of pride come to me,* that is, let not the proudful man and the persecuting tyrant come upon me or oppress me. *Et manus peccatoris, and the hand of the sinner,* that is, the power of a demon or the deeds of an evil man, *non moveat me, let [it] not . . . move me* from the observation of the divine law; but may I remain fixed and right in you, O Lord, my God. 35{36}[13] *Ibi, there,* that is, in the state of pride, *ceciderunt, they are fallen* from the state of salvation and of grace, in the state of damnation or eternal death, all *qui operantur iniquitaem, who are workers of iniquity,* that is, who are not repentant of their sin. For pride is to be found in every sin because in every sin God is disdained since his precepts are violated and little cared for. *Expulsi sunt, they are cast out,* those aforementioned iniquitous men [are cast out] from God, from charity, from the society of the humble. For by pride they are averse to God; and having lost charity they do not belong to the society of the good. *Nec potuerunt stare, they could not stand* in the way of salvation: not that they could not repent, but because they subjected their will to sin, and they became servants of sin.[59]

See how this Psalm, so brief with words, is so marvelously powerful, so full of meaning, and so inspiring. For first it describes the wicked

---

57 Ps. 9:11a. See Article XXVIII (Psalm 9:11) in Volume 1.
58 E. N. The Church in the Council of Trent teaches that when "'faith is active along with works,' the Christian faithful can "increase in the very justice they have received through the grace of Christ and are further justified, as it is written 'Let he who is just be still more justified' [Rev. 22:11]; and again: 'Fear not to be justified until you die' [Sir. 18:22, *Vulg.*]; and again: 'You see that a man is justified by works and not by faith alone' [Jas 2:24]." DS 1535. "If anyone says that justice received . . . is not increased before God through good works, but that such works are merely the fruits and the signs of the justification obtained, and not also the cause of its increase, let him be anathema." DS 1574; see also DS 1582,
59 John 8:34b. *Jesus answered them: Amen, amen I say unto you: that whosoever commits sin, is the servant of sin.*

man so that one might avoid his maliciousness. Second, it commends to God by reason of his mercy made evident by the heavens, by reason of this truth extending up to the clouds, by reason of his justice similar to the mountains, by reason of his inscrutable judgments similar to a great deep. Third, it recalls to the faithful the benefits of God and the good promises so that it might ignite our heart divine with love. Finally, it prays most devoutly and in a most brief way that nothing might impede the attainment of such great goods. Let us therefore always sing this Psalm with reverence, affection, and a steadfast mind.

PRAYER

LORD, HOLD FORTH MERCY TO US WHO seek refuge from you, that anointed and sanctified by the spirit of humility, the foot of pride might be removed from us, and, led by that same spirit, with humble foot we might make our steps right.

Confugientibus ad te, Domine, misericordiam nobis praetende:
ut spiritu humilitatis uncti et sanctificati, pedem superbiae
a nobis removeamus; et eodem spiritu ducti, humili
pede gressus nostros rectos faciamus.

Psalm 36

ARTICLE LXXV

EXPOSITION OF THE THIRTY-SIXTH PSALM:
NOLI AEMULARI IN MALIGNANTIBUS
BE NOT EMULOUS OF EVILDOERS.

36{37}[1] *A Psalm for David himself. Be not emulous of evildoers; nor envy them that work iniquity.*

Psalmus ipsi David. Noli aemulari in malignantibus, neque zelaveris facientes iniquitatem.

BRIEF AND PLAIN IS THE TITLE OF THIS Psalm, namely: 36{37}[1] *Psalmus ipsi David*, a *Psalm for David himself*: that is, this Psalm relates to the holy David insofar as authorship. He speaks here in the person of Christ or of the Church, most beautifully inveighing against the temporal prosperity of evil men, showing the happiness of the worldly man to be vain and false and not to be strived for. No one ought to be scandalized or weakened [in resolve] either from the consideration of the prosperity of the ungodly or from the consideration of the adversity of the good. For it is to be expected that the little ones and the weak ones, *who have the zeal of God, but not according to knowledge*,[1] may wonder, be afflicted, sorrow, and be scandalized when they see the ungodly prosper and the innocent oppressed. And in Jeremiah such persons are written about: *You indeed, O Lord, are just, if I plead with you, but yet I will speak what is just to you: Why does the way of the wicked prosper: why is it well with all them that transgress?*[2] But the perfect are not moved by this, because they understand that the Apostle [Paul] says: *All that will live godly in Christ Jesus, shall suffer persecution.*[3] And God himself: *Such as I love, I rebuke and chastise.*[4]

Instructing, therefore, the little ones, that they might not be scandalized with such events, the Prophet [David] says: *Noli aemulari in malignantibus,*

---

1 Cf. Rom. 10:2b. E. N. Denis quotes the verse as *qui zelum Dei habent*, "who have the zeal of God"; however, the Sixto-Clementine Vulgate has *aemulationem Dei habent*, "who have the emulation [or the desire to attain] of God."
2 Jer. 12:1.
3 2 Tim. 3:12.
4 Rev. 3:19a.

be not emulous of evildoers. On occasion, the word to emulate means to love, as when the Apostle [Paul] said: *For I am emulous (aemulor) of you with the emulousness (aemulatione) of God.*[5] Sometimes [the word to emulate] signifies to imitate, as when the same Apostle says: *But be emulous for the better gifts.*[6] But sometimes it signifies to have envy, and in turn [meaning] to be haughty. Now here [in this Psalm] it can be taken as to have envy and to imitate, as in this sense: Do not be tormented with envy because of the prosperity of the evildoers, lest you imitate them.[7] *Neque zelaveris facientes iniquitatem, nor envy them that work iniquity,* that is, do not be lovingly attached to those doing evil things. Zeal is caused by love. And just as love is of two kinds, namely divine and private,[8] so zeal is of two kinds. [One kind is] good and spiritual, of which Elijah says, *With zeal have I been zealous for the Lord God of hosts;*[9] and in a later Psalm Christ says, *For the zeal of your house has eaten me up.*[10] The other [kind of zeal] is an inordinate zeal, private and carnal, by which men are jealous of their wives, and proud men [jealous] of the proud, for one does not hinder the excellence which another loves: and of this [bad] envy that this Psalm now speaks.

---

5   2 Cor. 11:2.
6   1 Cor. 12:31a.
7   E. N. There are two problems confronting us in Denis's discussion of Psalm 36:1. The first has to do with the Latin word *aemulari*. The second has to do with the English word *jealousy*, which the Douay-Rheims uses in this verse. The Latin *aemulari* has both a positive and negative connotation. Peter Berchorius (*ca.* 1290–1362 A. D.) also known as Pierre Bersuire was a Benedictine monk and encyclopedist. In his *Dictionarium*, Berchorius addresses this issue: "Observe that *aemulari* is sometimes used for the malignity of envy (*invidiae*), sometimes for the immensity of love (*amoris*), and sometimes for the bitterness of jealousy (*zelotypiae*)." This view is consistent with Denis's argument. Now, the translators of the Douay-Rheims use the word jealousy. While the good sense of jealousy has largely been lost to us, it was not so to the translators who used the word *jealousy*. For example, in a sermon of John Donne (1572–1631 A. D.): "Where there is ... a spirit of uncleannesse, there will necessarily be ... a spirit of jealousie...[but when] jealousie is a care and not a suspition, God is not ashamed to protest of himself that he is a jealous God. ... Jealousie that implies care, and honour, and counsel, and tendernesse, is rooted in God." Charles R. Smith, *Jealousy: Chaucer's Miller and the Tradition*, The Chaucer Review, Vol. 43, No. 1 (2008), 16, 27. So in 2 Cor. 11:2, the word *jealous* must be understood as meaning the healthy and ordered solicitude for the beloved arising from love. To resolve this problem in this translation of Denis's *Commentary*, however, I have modified 2 Cor. 11:2. Since a similar problem occurs in 1 Cor. 12:31, where *be zealous* is used to translate the word *aemulamini*, I have had to modify that verse as well.
8   E. N. For the meaning of "private love," *see* footnote 33-43.
9   1 Kings 19:10a. E. N. This, of course, is the motto of the Discalced Carmelites.
10 Ps. 68:10a. E. N. The reason why Denis puts this in the mouth of Christ is because the Gospel writers recognize this as Christ's thoughts when he cleansed the Temple in Jerusalem of the money changers. John 2:17.

36{37}[2] *For they shall shortly wither away as grass, and as the green herbs shall quickly fall.*

Quoniam tamquam foenum velociter arescent, et quemadmodum olera herbarum cito decident.

After saying this, the reason behind his teaching is given: 36{37}[2] *Quoniam tanquam foenum velociter arescent, for they shall shortly wither away as grass*: that is, the wicked who prosper during time quickly lose their prosperity *the way the grass ... which is today, and [which] tomorrow is cast into the oven.*[11] Whence, Isaiah says: *Indeed, the people is grass.*[12] *Et tanquam olera herbarum cito decident, and as the green herbs shall quickly fall:*[13] that is, like green herbs, which now flourish on the earth and soon become uprooted or decay, so do the ungodly now appearing to flourish and prosper quickly tumble down and perish. But because the ungodly often reign for a long time, and they prevail over the good, as even Saul for a long time persecuted David, the appearance is the contrary.[14] In response to this [situation, one must keep in mind that] the temporal prosperity of the ungodly that is allowed and occasionally appears prolonged is as if but momentary in comparison with the misery which they obtain by it. And in this same way the Apostle [Paul] says that the tribulations of the just are in this age: they will exist momentarily, even those that frequently last even unto death. Whence, he says: *That which is at present momentary and light of our tribulation, works for us above measure exceedingly an eternal weight of glory.*[15] Secondly, we can say that the prosperity of the ungodly quickly is cut short, because its lastingness will be cut short when its limit is reached. For this is what Mattathias[16] said: *Fear not the words of a sinful man, for his glory is dung, and worms. Today he is lifted up, and tomorrow he shall not be found, because he is returned into his earth; and his thought is come to nothing.*[17]

---

11 Matt. 6:30a.
12 Is. 40:7b.
13 E. N. Denis has *tanquam*, "like," in lieu of *quemadmodum*, "in the manner of," without significant change in meaning.
14 1 Sam. chps. 18–27.
15 2 Cor. 4:17.
16 E. N. Mattathias ben Johanan (or Mathathias) (died ca. 166 B. C.), the father of Judas Maccabeus and his brothers, was a Jewish priest involved in the Maccabean Revolt who resisted Hellenization and sought Jewish independence against the Seleucid Empire.
17 1 Mach. 2:62–63.

36{37}[3] *Trust in the Lord, and do good, and dwell in the land, and you shall be fed with its riches.*

Spera in Domino, et fac bonitatem; et inhabita terram, et pasceris in divitiis eius.

36{37}[3] *Spera in Domino, trust in the Lord:* according to that which we read elsewhere, *Have confidence in the Lord with all your heart;*[18] *et fac bonitatem, and do good,* that is, live in a praiseworthy way. It is as if he were saying, "Do not so hope in God that you neglect to do that which is in you, in the manner of false men who presume on the mercy of God, as if there is no justice in him." Hope in God, therefore, not with an unformed hope, but with a formed hope,[19] that is, do good works while hoping in accordance with that which Solomon said, *Whatever your hand is able [to do], do it earnestly.*[20] For not the slothful, but the fervid, not the one asleep, but the vigilant comes to the Kingdom of Heaven. For this reason, Joshua says: *Now therefore fear the Lord, and serve him with a perfect and most sincere heart.*[21] *Et inhabita terram, and dwell in the land:* that is, by obedience and purity of faith remain in the unity of the Church. Or [we might understand it in this manner], *dwell in the land,* that is, possess and hold subject your own body lest the flesh dominate the soul, and sensuality [dominate] reason. Or [alternatively], *dwell in the land,* that is, await the Kingdom of Heaven, which is the land of the living, by desire and hope.[22] And in both these senses one can understand that which the Savior said: *Blessed are the meek, for they shall possess the land.*[23] *Et pasceris in divitiis eius, and you shall be fed with its riches:* that is, your soul will be fed and will be fattened with the grace of Christ, the consolations of the Holy Spirit, the Sacraments of the Church, and especially the most precious Body and most sacred Blood of the Son of God. These are the riches of holy mother Church, of which it is written: *What is the good thing of the Lord, and what is his beautiful thing, but the corn of the elect, and wine springing forth virgins?*[24]

---

18 Prov. 3:5a.
19 E. N. By a "formed hope," a *spes formata*, Denis is analogizing with the notion of a *fides formata*, a formed faith, that is one active in charity and in good works. Just like St. Paul in Gal. 5:6 speaks of a faith that works by charity," a *fides quae per caritatem operatur*, so does Denis state hope must be, a *spes quae per caritatem operatur*. Anything else is presumption.
20 Eccl. 9:10a.
21 Joshua 24:14a.
22 E. N. For the expression "land of the living" as meaning heaven, *see* footnote 34-134.
23 Matt. 5:4.
24 Zech. 9:17.

36{37}[4] *Delight in the Lord, and he will give you the requests of your heart.*
Delectare in Domino, et dabit tibi petitiones cordis tui.

36{37}[5] *Reveal your way to the Lord, and trust in him, and he will do it.*[25]
Revela Domino viam tuam, et spera in eo, et ipse faciet.

36{37}[4] *Delectare in Domino, delight in the Lord*: that is, with open and joyful spirit serve him, and in consideration of, and with delight in, the divine goodness and bountifulness exult him. This is as we read with Tobias, *And I and my soul will rejoice in him.*[26] We should not therefore rejoice in things of the sense and in fleeting things, nor in any creature, except to the extent that by them we are led to and are helped in the way leading to God. If you will do this, you will experience what follows: *et dabit tibi petitiones cordis tui, and he will give you the requests of your heart,* that is, he will hear your prayers. Now prayer, according to the Damascene,[27] is not the petition to God for any sort of thing, but for what is fitting, namely, spiritual goods for themselves, and bodily things ordered by spiritual things, [the bodily things being] not more than are necessary for the things of the spirit, as the Apostle [Paul] says: *having food, and wherewith to be covered, with these we are content, for they that will become rich, fall into temptation, and into the snare of the devil.*[28] 36{37}[5] *Revela Domino, reveal . . . to the Lord,* who knows all things, *viam tuam, your way*: that is, as before a most faithful friend pour out your heart faithfully before God: account for your sins, expose your weaknesses, lament of your imperfections, and survey and explore the entirety of your life; *et spera in eo, and trust in him*: that is, [revealing yourself in such a manner] so trust most certainly that whatever your desire you will obtain, so long as you constantly seek it. And so is appended [to this verse]: *et ipse faciet, and he will do it,* that which you desire, forbearing faults, conferring grace, and granting consolations.

---

25   E. N. I have departed from the Douay-Rheims which translated *revela* as "commit," rather than "reveal." Since Denis's understanding involves our intimate revealing, disclosure, or unveiling to God, I felt the need to conform the Douay-Rheims to Denis's Commentary.
26   To. 13:9a.
27   E. N. For St. John of Damascus, known as the Damascene, see footnote 32-4. The definition of prayer is found in St. John of Damascus's *De Fide Orthodoxa,* 3, 24: *Oratio est ascensus mentis in Deum: aut eorum quae consentanea sunt postulatio a Deo.* "Prayer is the ascent of the mind in God: or the petitioning to God for those things which are fitting." PG 94, 1089-90.
28   1 Tim. 6:8-9a.

36{37}[6] *And he will bring forth your justice as the light, and your judgment as the noonday.*
Et educet quasi lumen iustitiam tuam, et iudicium tuum tamquam meridiem.

36{37}[6] *Et educet quasi lumen iustitiam tuam,* and he will bring forth your justice as the light: that is, your life will be manifested to others with the purpose of their edification, so that which is written might be fulfilled in you: *So let your light shine before men;*[29] and again: *A city seated on a mountain cannot be hid;*[30] *et iudicium tuum tanquam meridiem, and your judgment as the noonday*: that is, the Lord in the aforementioned manner will lead the judgment of your discretion, by which you judge yourself and elect to follow Christ, *as the noonday*, that is, as a brilliant light. For it extends to the divine order that a just and humble man who always desires to be forgotten or spurned by others,[31] will be recognized as being just, and will be honored and will be made leader over others, when finally the Lord will summon him to his judgment as the noonday. For he will summon him for his hiding place out to the public, according to that which Christ in the Gospels mystically stated: *Neither do men light a candle and put it under a bushel, but upon a candlestick, that it may shine to all that are in the house.*[32] The light is a just man, in the manner that Christ attested about John [the Baptist]: *He was a burning and a shining light.*[33] Christ ignites this light with divine love and illuminates it with the light of his grace, not so that it might hide itself, but so that it might shine upon others with life, favor, or example; and while such a man remains constant in truth and in judgment, then the Lord will summon him to his judgment as the noonday, placing him upon a candlestick,

---

29 Matt. 5:16a. E. N. The verse continues: *that they may see your good works, and glorify your Father who is in heaven.*
30 Matt. 5:14b.
31 E. N. We might here profitably recall some of Raphael Cardinal Merry Del Val y Zulueta's lovely Litany of Humility: *Iesu, mitis e humilis corde, Exaudi me ... A cupiditate, ut amer, libera me Domine ...A cupiditate, ut lauder, libera me Domine ... A timore, ne humilier, libera me Domine, A timore, ne spernar, libera me Domine ... Ut alii extollantur in mundi existimatione, ego autem minuar, Iesu, da mihi gratiam desiderandi.* "Jesus, meek and humble of heart, hear me ... From the desire of being loved, deliver me, O Lord ... From the desire of being praised, deliver me, O Lord ... From the fear of being humiliated, deliver me, O Lord ... From the fear of being spurned, deliver me, O Lord ... That others may be extolled in the estimation of the world, but I might decrease, Jesus grant me the grace of desiring it."
32 Matt. 5:15.
33 John 5:35a.

that is, in the seat of a prelate,[34] or high in the opinion of others: and so that which is said through Isaiah might be fulfilled: *All that shall see them, shall know them, that these are the seed which the Lord has blessed.*[35]

36{37}[7] Be subject to the Lord and pray to him. Envy not the man who prospers in his way; the man who does unjust things.

Subditus esto Domino, et ora eum. Noli aemulari in eo qui prosperatur in via sua, in homine faciente iniustitias.

36{37}[8] Cease from anger, and leave rage; have no emulation to do evil.

Desine ab ira, et derelinque furorem; noli aemulari ut maligneris.

36{37}[9] For the evildoers shall be cut off: but they that wait upon the Lord shall inherit the land.

Quoniam qui malignantur exterminabuntur; sustinentes autem Dominum, ipsi haereditabunt terram.

36{37}[7] *Subditus esto Domino, be subject to the Lord*, that is, observe the commandments, *et ora eum, and pray to him*: because that prayer pleases God where the life conforms to the prayer, as asserted in Ecclesiasticus: *The prayer of him that humbles himself, shall pierce the clouds.*[36] *Noli aemulari, envy not*, that is, do not be tormented with envy, or imitate that which you see, *in eo qui prosperatur in via sua, the man who prospers in his way*, and not in the way of God, namely, he who temporally does well, *in homine faciente iniustitias, as the man who does unjust things*, the man who follows and fulfills his own will and not the divine law. 36{37}[8] *Desine ab ira, cease from anger* through vice, not from anger through zeal, which is a fellow worker of justice, and of which was spoken about above, *be angry, and sin not.*[37] And so *cease from anger*, that is, cease from an appetite of vengeance, and pardon your neighbor, and suffer with your erring brother; *et derelinque furorem, and leave rage*, that is, a raging anger which fully disrupts the judgment of reason. *Noli aemulari, have no emulation*, that is, [do not] imitate or allow it to influence you, *ut maligneris, to do evil*, that is, that you might accomplish something bad, and do something wretched either in yourself or to your neighbor.

---

34   E. N. As used by Denis, a prelate is a bishop or other cleric with ecclesiastical authority or jurisdiction.
35   Is. 61:9b.
36   Ecclus. 35:21.
37   Ps. 4:5a. E. N. See Article XVIII (Psalm 4:5) and Article XIX (Psalm 4:5) in Volume 1.

36{37}[9] *Quoniam qui malignantur, for the evildoers*, that is, those who do evil deeds and harm others, *exterminabuntur, shall be cut off* from Christ's sheepfold and from the Kingdom of Heaven, in the manner that is written, *Let the ungodly man be removed so that he does not see the glory of God*.[38] *Sustinentes autem Dominum, but they that wait upon the Lord*, that is, who await him patiently and faithfully in adversity, *ipsi hereditabunt terram, they shall inherit the land*, that is, they will possess the inheritance of the Kingdom of Heaven, and also their own body in the resurrection of the saints, when that said by the Apostle [Paul] will be fulfilled: *Christ will reform the body of our lowness, made like to the body of his glory*.[39] For from that time our soul will have the body united to itself in a perpetual union, glorious and blessed: and so then truly it will inherit the land, that is, its own body.

36{37}[10] *For yet a little while, and the wicked shall not be: and you shall seek his place, and shalt not find it.*

Et adhuc pusillum, et non erit peccator; et quaeres locum eius, et non invenies.

36{37}[10] *Et adhuc pusillum, for yet a little while*, that is, wait for a little while and with a little patience anticipate, *et non erit peccator, and the wicked shall not be*, that is, he will not remain in the present life. For it has already been stated that the evildoers quickly dry up as if grass. *Et quaeres locum eius, et non invenies; and you shall seek his place, and shall not find it*. For one's own place, of which is spoken of here, and one's space, are the same, according to the Philosopher:[40] because place is the outmost surface of the containing body. Removed, therefore, from that space, its place does not remain. And so, *you shall seek his place, and you shall not find it*, that is, if you seek it, you will not discover it. Or [it can also be understood], *you shall seek its place*, that is, that use that it has in the nature of things, which use is [sought], that it might

---

38 E. N. Denis departs from the Sixto-Clementine Vulgate and quotes the Latin translation of the Greek Septuagint: *Tollatur impius ne videat gloriam Dei*. The Vulgate has *non videbit gloriam Domini*, "he shall not see the glory of the Lord."
39 Phil. 3:21.
40 E. N. The reference is to Aristotle's *Physics: locus et locatum sunt simul. Phys.* IV, 1, 209a5–209a7. The point being made is that place and space cannot be a body, for, if it were, there would be two bodies occupying the same place or space which is impossible; consequently, it can be inferred that neither place or space are bodies. Moreover, the life of the wicked is ephemeral like a body passing through space or place, which leaves nothing behind when it departs.

be employed harmlessly.⁴¹ For this reason, therefore, the sinner and his place and work are quickly found wanting. That is why it is written: *The praise of the wicked is short, and the joy of the hypocrite but for a moment. As a dream that flees away, he shall not be found, he shall pass as a vision of the night.*⁴² Whence also the ungodly overcome by their punishment say: *What has pride profited us? Or what advantage has the boasting of riches brought us? All those things are passed away like a shadow, and like a messenger that runs on. So we also being born, forthwith ceased to be ... but are consumed in our wickedness.*⁴³

36{37}[11] *But the meek shall inherit the land, and shall delight in abundance of peace.*

Mansueti autem haereditabunt terram, et delectabuntur in multitudine pacis.

36{37}[11] *Mansueti autem*, but the meek, that is, men who have learned to overcome the impulse of anger, *haereditabunt terram, shall inherit the land*: as has already been stated and expounded upon of those who wait upon the Lord; *et delectabuntur in multitudine pacis*, and shall delight in abundance of peace, that is, with the peace of Christ, which surpasses all understanding, most abundantly bringing delight: now surely for a time by grace, but in the future unceasingly by glory. For the meek of heart have the highest level of peace already, and are composed within themselves, because it is said that peace is the tranquility of order.⁴⁴ But nothing impedes this tranquility except disorder. Now anger and the vices that are born from it generate the greatest amount of disorder in spirit, and cause a man to be like the irrational beasts, as Ecclesiastes

---

41 "For the Fathers of the Church, the command to *sequi naturam* [follow nature] and the *sequela Christi* [following of Christ] are not in opposition to each other. On the contrary, the Fathers generally adopt the idea from Stoicism that nature and reason indicate what our moral duties are. To follow nature and reason is to follow the personal Logos, the Word of God. The doctrine of the natural law, in fact, supplies a basis for completing biblical morality." International Theological Commission, *In Search of a Universal Ethics; A New Look at the Natural Law* (2009), No. 26. http://www.vatican.va/roman_curia/congregations/cfaith/cti_documents/rc_con_cfaith_doc_20090520_legge-naturale_en.html#*.
42 Job 20:5, 8.
43 Wis. 5:8, 9, 13. E. N. I have changed "post" in the Douay-Rheims to "messenger" to translate *nuntius* in Wis. 5:9.
44 E. N. The definition of peace as the "tranquility of order," *tranquilitas ordinis*, is Augustinian. It comes from his book *On the City of God. Pax omnium rerum tranquilitas ordinis. De Civ. Dei*, XIX, 13, 1, PL 41, 640.

says: *Anger rests in the bosom of a fool.*[45] Thus the meek or the gentle obtain a more ample, more sweet, and more stable peace because they have overcome anger. And it is meekness, the great and lovable virtue, that restores man not only to God, but also is most amiable to all men, as it says in Scripture: *My son, do your works in meekness, and you shall be beloved above the glory of men.*[46] And also Dionysius [the Areopagite] in his letter to the monk Demophilus[47] strongly commends meekness, affirming with respect to Moses, Joseph, David, and some others, that they found the greatest grace with the Lord because they were so meek. If, therefore, we desire to enjoy the peace of Christ, let us hear and let us fulfill the exhortation, indeed his precept, which says: *Learn of me, because I am meek, and humble of heart.*[48] Whence in the *Lives of the Fathers* it is written that even were an angry man to raise the dead, yet he would not be pleasing to God.[49] And again: as smoke expels a guest, so anger expels the Holy Spirit from the heart.

36{37}[12] *The sinner shall watch the just man: and shall gnash upon him with his teeth.*

Observabit peccator iustum, et stridebit super eum dentibus suis.

36{37}[13] *But the Lord shall laugh at him: for he foresees that his day shall come.*

Dominus autem irridebit eum, quoniam prospicit quod veniet dies eius.

36{37}[12] *Observabit peccator iustum,* the sinner shall watch the just man, that is, he will test his works with the intention of doing him injury, *et stridebit super eum dentibus suis,* and shall gnash upon him with his teeth, from the cruelty and furor of his soul. 36{37}[13] *Dominus autem irridebit eum,* but the Lord shall laugh at him, that is, he will expose him as worthy of confusion: as we see in the second Psalm, *He that dwells in heaven shall laugh at them:*[50] because he will be thoroughly examined. *Quoniam prospicit quod veniet dies eius,* for he foresees that his day shall

---

45 Eccl. 7:10b.
46 Ecclus. 3:19.
47 *Epist.* VIII, *ad Demophilo Monacho,* PG 3, 1083 ff.
48 Matt. 11:29.
49 E. N. *Dixit abbas Agatho: Iracundus si mortuos suscitet, no placet Deo propter iracundiam suam,*"Abba Agathon said: if an angry man were to raise the dead it would not be pleasing to God because of his anger." *De Vitis Patrum,* V, 10, 13, PL 73, 914.
50 Ps. 2:4a.

come: that is, the Lord himself knows the day of final vengeance and judgment, in which the sinner will receive what he deserves: in which he will be filled with what he himself testified through Isaiah, *Ah! I will comfort myself over my adversaries: and I will be revenged of my enemies.*[51]

36{37}[14] *The wicked have drawn out the sword: they have bent their bow. To cast down the poor and needy, to kill the upright of heart.*

Gladium evaginaverunt peccatores, intenderunt arcum suum, ut deiiciant pauperem et inopem, ut trucident rectos corde.

36{37}[15] *Let their sword enter into their own hearts, and let their bow be broken.*

Gladius eorum intret in corda ipsorum, et arcus eorum confringatur.

36{37}[14] *Gladium evaginaverunt peccatores*, the wicked have drawn out their sword. This is the sword of the tongue, of which a later Psalm says: *their tongue [is] a sharp sword.*[52] To unsheathe this sword is to throw out menacing, injurious, false, or defamatory words. Of a different sort is the sword of which Christ speaks to Peter: *Put up again your sword into the scabbard.*[53] Here, to draw out the sword is to attack another with arms. And sinners unsheathe both kinds of swords. *Intenderunt arcum suum, they have been their bow*, that is, their snares or their material bows, *ut decipiant pauperem, to cast down the poor*, that is, the humble and those wanting in temporal things, *et inopem, and the needy*, that is, others who do not have help, *ut trucident rectos corde, to kill the upright of heart*, that is, so that the just might bodily or spiritually die. They wish to deceive with the sword of the mouth or with insidious schemes, and they want to kill with the sword of the hand the bodily bow. 36{37}[15] *Gladis eorum intret, let their sword enter*, that is it will enter, *in corda ipsorum, into their hearts*: for he who takes the sword shall perish with the sword.[54] It is not that a material sword is able to enter into the mind or the soul, or that all who take the sword die [literally] by the sword, since neither

---

51 Is. 1:24b.
52 Ps. 56:5b. *And he has delivered my soul from the midst of the young lions. I slept troubled. The sons of men, whose teeth are weapons and arrows, and their tongue a sharp sword.*
53 Matt. 26:52; John 18:11. Denis blends the two verses, the first part taken from Matthew, the last half from John.
54 *Cf.* Matt. 26:52. Denis changes the person of the verbs from third person plural to third person singular.

the thief that hung by Christ, nor Peter [died by the sword]; but this is said in reference to entering the sheath of the heart, which means to kill those who harm others because their malice first harms them and spiritually kills their soul. Whence that which the Savior says, *He who takes the sword shall perish by the sword*,[55] is simply saying that any malignity flows back unto one's own head, and more greatly harms the doer that the recipient.[56] In this way, a sword enters into the heart of tyrants and it kills them eternally. But it enters into the bodies of martyrs, and it crowns them in heaven. *Et arcus eorum confringatur, and let their bow be broken*, that is, their schemes be frustrated in their desired effect.

36{37}[16] *Better is a little to the just, than the great riches of the wicked.*
Melius est modicum iusto, super divitias peccatorum multas.

36{37}[17] *For the arms of the wicked shall be broken in pieces; but the Lord strengthens the just.*
Quoniam brachia peccatorum conterentur, confirmat autem iustos Dominus.

36{37}[16] *Melius, better*, that is, more useful, happy, and more sufficient, *est modicum, is a little*, that is, that amount that is necessary to sustain life, *iusto, to the just*, who ordain the temporal to the spiritual, *super divitias peccatorum multas, than the great riches of the wicked*, that is, than the many temporal personal and real properties of the avaricious and ungodly. For the just man, since he has what is necessary, gives thanks to the Lord, is at peace, is content, and spiritually advances; but avaricious sinners are not satisfied with riches, nor are they thankful to the liberal-giving God of all, and by these their riches are submerged into the depths of hell. For this reason it is written: *Nothing is more wicked than the covetous man.*[57] And again: *There is not a more wicked thing than to love money: for such a one sets even his own soul to sale.*[58] And again: *Woe to you that join house to house and lay field to field, even to the end of the place: shall you alone dwell in the midst of the earth?*[59]

---

55 Matt. 26:52b.
56 E. N. As St. Augustine, echoing Socrates in Plato's Dialogue *Gorgias* (475e) and St. Peter (1 Pet. 3:17), says in his *On Christian Doctrine*: "it is better to suffer injustice than to commit it," *pati melius est iniquitatem quam facere*. *De Doctr. Christ.*, I, 36, PL 34, 34.
57 Ecclus. 10:9a.
58 Ecclus. 10:10a.
59 Is. 5:8.

36{37}[17] *Quoniam brachia peccatorum conterentur, for the arms of the wicked shall be broken in pieces*: that is the fortitude and strength and riches of the ungodly will be reduced to nothing, so that they will serve them nothing towards salvation, nor will they deliver them from eternal death; *confirmat autem iustos Dominus, but the Lord strengthens the just* by the grace of the Holy Spirit, as the Apostle [Paul] says, *For it is best that the heart be established with grace.*[60]

36{37}[18] The Lord knows the days of undefiled; and their inheritance shall be forever.

Novit Dominus dies immaculatorum, et haereditas eorum in aeternum erit.

36{37}[19] They shall not be confounded in the evil time; and in the days of famine they shall be filled.

Non confundentur in tempore malo, et in diebus famis saturabuntur.

36{37}[20] Because the wicked shall perish. And the enemies of the Lord, presently after they shall be honored and exalted, shall come to nothing and vanish like smoke.

Quia peccatores peribunt. Inimici vero Domini mox ut honorificati fuerint et exaltati, deficientes quemadmodum fumus deficient.

36{37}[18] *Novit Dominus dies immaculatorum, the Lord knows the days of the undefiled*: that is, he approves the manner of living of those who attend themselves to be without mortal sin, as the Apostle [Paul] says: *The sure foundation of God stands firm, having this seal: the Lord knows who are his.*[61] *Et hereditas eorum in aeternum erit; and their inheritance shall be forever*: that is, the reward of the saints or their beatitude which they receive from God as the good of inheritance is without end. For since the just are sons of God, it follows that they are heirs: *heirs indeed of God, and joint heirs with Christ.*[62] 36{37}[19] *Non confundentur in tempore malo, they shall not be confounded in the evil time*, that is, in this age, of which the Apostle [Paul] says, *Redeeming the time, because the days are evil.*[63] Or [we can understand it thus], *in the evil time*, that is, in days of adversities

---

60 Heb. 13:9a. For Denis's belief in St. Paul being the author of the Epistle to the Hebrews, *see* footnote 8-34 in Volume 1.
61 2 Tim. 2:19a.
62 Rom. 8:17a.
63 Eph. 5:16.

and tribulations; but then they will hope in the Lord, and he will protect them, so that they will rejoice in adversity, in the manner that James in his epistle admonishes: *My brethren, count it all joy, when you shall fall into diverse temptations.*[64] *Et in diebus famis saturabuntur, and in the days of famine they shall be filled.* Famine is of two kinds. One is bodily, which desires food and drink: and in this famine, or in times of scarcity, the just will be filled, because the Lord will provide to them what is necessary, in the manner that Christ promised in the Gospel.[65] The other [famine] is famine of the mind, of which the Lord says through the prophet Amos: *Behold ... I will send forth a famine into the land: not a famine of bread, nor a thirst of water, but of hearing the word of God.*[66] And in this sort of days of famine the just shall be filled by God with spiritual fatness and multiple graces of the Holy Spirit, as it has been stated in a previous Psalm: *They that seek the Lord shall not be deprived of any good.*[67] And in the Gospel, Christ says: *Blessed are they that hunger and thirst after justice: for they shall have their fill.*[68] 36{37}[20] *Quia peccatores peribunt, because the wicked shall perish*: that is, a sign of that which we have spoken of, namely, that the just shall not be confounded in the evil time, [and in the days of famine they shall be filled], is that *the wicked shall perish*, that is, because of their ingratitude they will be confounded, especially when they will hear: *Depart from me, you cursed, into everlasting fire.*[69]

Inimici vero Domini mox ut honorificati fuerint et exaltati, and the enemies of the Lord, presently after they shall be honored and exalted: that is, up to now the rebellious and ungodly in the present life have achieved honor, fame and dignity, or supremacy; [yet] *deficientes quemadmodum fumus deficient, they shall come to nothing and vanish like smoke*, that is, they will suddenly begin to weaken, and they will incessantly dissipate in the manner that smoke dissipates, which is a quickly occurring vaporization. This is what it says in another place in Scripture: *What is your life? It is a vapor which appears for a little while, and afterwards shall vanish away.*[70]

---

64 James 1:2.
65 Matt. 6:31-33: *Be not solicitous therefore, saying, What shall we eat: or what shall we drink: or wherewith shall we be clothed? For after all these things do the heathens seek. For your Father knows that you have need of all these things. Seek therefore first the kingdom of God, and his justice, and all these things shall be added unto you.*
66 Amos 8:11. E. N. Denis replaces the "the word of the Lord," *verbum Domini*, in the Vulgate with "the word of God."
67 Ps. 33:11.
68 Matt. 5:6.
69 Mat. 25:41b.
70 Jams 4:15a.

36{37}[21] *The sinner shall borrow, and not pay again; but the just shows mercy and shall give.*

Mutuabitur peccator, et non solvet, iustus autem miseretur et tribuet.

36{37}[22] *For such as bless him shall inherit the land: but such as curse him shall perish.*

Quia benedicentes ei haereditabunt terram: maledicentes autem ei disperibunt.

36{37}[21] Mutabitur peccator, *the sinner shall borrow*, that is, he will receive many talents from the Lord, namely natural and gratuitous gifts: and whatever it is that he has in the manner of talents he has received from the Lord, so he must render an account of their use during that time and whether during that time he has used it well to the glory of God and his own salvation. This is in the manner that Christ orders in the Gospel: *Trade till I come*;[71] et non solvet, *and not pay again*, that is, he will not be thankful to God, and he will not be able to render an account, because he misused the gifts of God. Iustus autem miseretur et tribuet, *but the just shows mercy and shall give*: that is, he will feel compassion from his soul to the needy, and he will render to him in accordance his ability, as our Savior exhorts: *Give to everyone who asks you.*[72] *The bowels of the wicked are cruel.*[73] And you, O brother, assume your deiform property, as it is proper to God to be merciful,[74] and as *he gives to all men abundantly*,[75] so also you must have compassion on the needy, and you must render help within the bounds of what is possible for you. For this is written: *According to your ability be merciful. If you have much, give abundantly; if you have little, take care even so to bestow willingly a little.*[76] But all of this the just man does to the praise and glory of God. 36{37}[22] Quia benedicentes ei, *for such as bless him*, that is, they who with mouth and works give thanks to the Lord and offer him praise, hereditabunt terram, *shall inherit the land*: as it has by now often been expounded;[77] maledicentes autem ei, *but such as curse*

---

71 Luke 19:13. E. N. This is taken from the Parable of the Talents or Parable of the Minas, Luke 19:11-27; see also Matt. 25:14-30.
72 Luke 6:30a.
73 Prov. 12:10b.
74 E. N. "But mercy... is an attribute to God Himself." Shakespeare, *The Merchant of Venice*, Act 4, sc. 1.199, 201.
75 James 1:5a.
76 Tob. 4:8-9.
77 E. N. See Article LXXV (Psalm 36:9); see also Article LVI (Psalm 24:25) in Volume 1.

him, namely the unbeliever, the obstinate, the blasphemers, *disperibunt, shall perish*: because they will be eternally damned in the manner that is set forth in Revelation: *But the fearful, and unbelieving, and the abominable . . . and all liars, they shall have their portion in the pool burning with fire and brimstone, which is the second death.*[78]

36{37}[23] With the Lord shall the steps of a man be directed, and he shall like well his way.

Apud Dominum gressus hominis dirigentur; et viam eius volet.

36{37}[24] When he shall fall, he shall not be bruised; for the Lord puts his hand under him.

Cum ceciderit, non collidetur, quia Dominus supponit manum suam.

36{37}[23] *Apud Dominum, with the Lord*, that is, before the Lord, and in his sight and with his good pleasure, *gressus hominis, the steps of a man* by a reasonable manner of living, that is, a life or an action that is just, *dirigentur, shall be directed*. For the reason of man, illumined by faith and the grace of the Holy Spirit, directs his works according to the tenor of the divine law or according to the precepts and the counsels of Christ. In this way Elijah and Elisha directed their steps, and they said: *As the Lord lives, in whose sight I stand today.*[79] Whence the Lord said to Abraham: *I am the Almighty God: walk before me, and be perfect.*[80] *Et viam eius, and his way*, that is, the deeds of the just man, *volet, he shall like*, that is, the Lord will approve and will reward, in the manner that God told Abraham: *I am your protector, and your reward exceeding great.*[81] 36{37}[24] *Cum ceciderit, non collidetur; when he shall fall, he shall not be bruised*: that is, when a just man sins out of human weakness and departs from the grace of God, he will not be bruised, that is, he will not completely perish in his soul and will not persevere in evil; *quia Dominus supponit manum suam, for the Lord puts his hand under him*, that is, through his mercy he sustains and raises him up, furnishing to him some occasion by which he may be fitted again with grace, which when done, the Lord will fill him with grace, in the manner shown clearly by [the examples of] Peter and David.[82]

---

78 Rev. 218.
79 1 Kings 17:1a (Elijah): *As the Lord lives the God of Israel, in whose sight I stand*; 2 Kings 5:16: (Elisha) *As the Lord lives, before whom I stand.*
80 Gen. 17:1b.
81 Gen. 15:1.
82 E. N. The reference being to David's multiple sins arising out of his lust for

36{37}[25] *I have been younger,*[83] *and now am old; and I have not seen the just forsaken, nor his seed seeking bread.*

Iunior fui, etenim senui; et non vidi iustum derelictum, nec semen eius quaerens panem.

36{37}[26] *He shows mercy, and lends all the day long; and his seed shall be in blessing.*

Tota die miseretur et commodat; et semen illius in benedictione erit.

36{37}[25] Iunior fui, I have been younger, than I am now, *etenim senui,* and now I am old, as is now obvious about me; *et non vidi iustum derelictum,* and I have not seen the just forsaken by God in the end — which, by the just is to be understood the predestined — *nec semen eius quaerens panem,* nor his seed seeking bread. This literally cannot refer to children of the flesh or the bread of the stomach, because as we read in Genesis, the sons of Jacob twice descended into Egypt so that they might purchase food so that they would not die.[84] And the Apostle [Paul] among the number of his discomforts lists hunger and thirst.[85] What, therefore, is to be understood by the word seed other than the imitators of the just? [For those who imitate the just] are spiritually generated by them, following their doctrine, life, and morals, as the Apostle [Paul] says: *My little children, of whom I am in labor again, until Christ be formed in you.*[86] This sort of seed [of which Paul speaks], therefore, does not seek bread,

---

Bathsheba, repentance of which led to one of the most beautiful Psalms of repentance: the *Miserere,* and of St. Peter's denial, which led to one the most poignant and heart rending events in the Gospel, where, "the Lord turning looked on Peter," pricked his conscience, resulting in "Peter going out," where he "wept bitterly." Here, we might pause and reflect on portions of St. Ambrose's morning hymn, *Aeterne Rerum Conditor,* on how ready God is to take us back when we fall through our weakness: *Surgamus ergo strenue: / Gallus iacentes excitat, / Et somnolentos increpat, / Gallus negantes arguit. // Gallo canente spes redit, / Aegris salus refunditur, / Mucro latronis conditur, / Lapsis fides revertitur. // Iesu labantes respice, / Et nos videndo corrige: / Si respicis, labes cadunt, / Fletuque culpa solvitur.* "Let us strenuously arise / The rooster rousing those rising / And those sleeping chiding / The rooster censuring those refusing // The chanting rooster returns hope / Restores health to the sick / The robber's sword is sheathed / The fallen returns to faith // Jesus attend to the tottering / And seeing us fall, [Lord] restore / If you attend, our sins are shed / And our tears the guilt dissolve."
83 E. N. I have changed the Douay-Rheims from "young" to "younger," which is closer to the Vulgate and Denis's argument.
84 Gen. 42:2, 3; 43:2, 15.
85 *Cf.* 2 Cor. 11:27.
86 Gal. 4:19.

that is, the grace and justice of God, as if it were outside of them, and as if it lacks that bread, since it is said, *he who fears him wants nothing*;[87] for they seek so that they may have it more abundantly. Or [we can understand it] thus: *nor his seed seeking bread*, that is, I did not see the works of the just to be deprived of reward. 36{37}[26] *Tota die, all the day long*, that is, at every convenient and opportune time, the just man *miseretur et commodat, shows mercy and lends*, that is, he has compassion and he renders aid to his neighbor; *et semen illius in benedictione erit, and his seed shall be in blessing*, that is, his works will be blessed by God. For the imitators [of the just] are blessed by God, in the present by grace and by increase [in perfection], but in the future by glory and rest, according to that which is written: *The blessing of the Lord is upon the head of the just*;[88] therefore, *he gave him an inheritance*.[89]

36{37}[27] Decline from evil and do good, and dwell for ever and ever.

Declina a malo, et fac bonum, et inhabita in saeculum saeculi.

36{37}[28] For the Lord loves judgment, and will not forsake his saints: they shall be preserved for ever. The unjust shall be punished, and the seed of the wicked shall perish.

Quia Dominus amat iudicium, et non derelinquet sanctos suos; in aeternum conservabuntur. Iniusti punientur, et semen impiorum peribit.

36{37}[29] But the just shall inherit the land, and shall dwell therein for evermore.

Iusti autem haereditabunt terram, et inhabitabunt in saeculum saeculi super eam.

36{37}[27] *Declina a malo, decline from evil*, that is, withdraw from sin through repentance, *et fac bonum, and do good*, that is, work the virtues. For it is not sufficient to withdraw from evil, but it is necessary also to do good works: because *every tree that does not yield good fruit, shall be cut down, and cast into the fire*.[90] *Et inhabita in saeculum saeculi*,

---

87 E. N. Curiously, Denis quotes Psalm 33:10 as *nihil deest timentibus eum*, "those who fear him want nothing," which differs from the Sixto-Clementine Vulgate's *non est inopia timentibus eum*, "because there is no want to them that fear him," which he quoted earlier in this Commentary.
88 Prov. 10:6a.
89 Ecclus. 44:26b.
90 Matt. 3:10; 7:19.

and dwell for ever and ever, that is, even until the end persevere in the faith, and in unity and obedience with holy Mother Church. **36{37}[28]** *Quia Dominus amat iudicium, for the Lord loves judgment* of discretion,[91] by which any man scrutinizes and judges himself, *et non derelinquet sanctos suos, and will not forsake his saints*, that is, his elect; *in aeternum conservabuntur, they shall be preserved for ever* in the love and grace of God. For here they are temporarily preserved until they end their life in the good, and in doing this they will be confirmed in the good; for he who dies in grace, will be confirmed in the state of good; and the soul will eternally remain in that state in which it left its body, in the manner that Solomon says: in whatever place *the tree fall, . . . there shall it be*.[92] **36{37}[29]** *Iusti autem, but the just,* who persevere in good, *haereditabunt terram, inherit the land* of the living, as the Lord says in Revelation: *Be faithful until death: and I will give you the crown of life;*[93] *et inhabitabunt in saeculum saeculi super eam, and shall dwell therein for evermore,* that is, without end they will remain in the Kingdom of Heaven, accord to that which the Savior again promises: *To him that shall overcome, I will give to sit with me in my throne: as I also have overcome, and am set down with my Father in his throne.*[94]

36{37}[30] *The mouth of the just shall meditate wisdom: and his tongue shall speak judgment.*

Os iusti meditabitur sapientiam, et lingua eius loquetur iudicium.

36{37}[31] *The law of his God is in his heart, and his steps shall not be supplanted.*

Lex Dei eius in corde ipsius, et non supplantabuntur gressus eius.

36{37}[30] *Os iusti, the mouth of the just,* that is, the intellect of him who interiorly causes the word to grow, *meditabitur sapientiam, shall meditate wisdom,* that is, he will sweetly ponder contemplation of divine things with delightful affection, examining heavenly things, as the Apostle [Paul] says: *We all beholding the glory of the Lord with open face.*[95] Or [it can be interpreted] thus: *the mouth of the just shall meditate wisdom,* that is, it will

---

91 E. N. For judgment of discretion (*iudicium discretionis*) and the judgment of retribution, *see* footnote 34-101.
92 Eccl. 11:3b.
93 Rev. 2:10b.
94 Rev. 3:21.
95 2 Cor. 3:18a.

speak out of interior meditation. Or [it could be understood this way], *shall meditate*, not thinking, but doing: [in other words, not] as is written about some people by the Apostle [Paul]: *They profess that they know God: but in their works they deny him.*[96] *Et lingua eius loquetur iudicium*, and *his tongue shall speak judgment*, that is, [he will practice] discretion or the distinguishing between the true and the false, good and evil: teaching and affirming the good to be that which pleases God but evil to be that which displeases him. This is what Solomon says: *My mouth shall meditate truth, and my lips shall hate wickedness.*[97] **36{37}[31]** *Lex Dei eius in corde ipsius, the law of his God is in his heart*, that is, the divine law is in the memory of the just man so that he may fulfill it, as it stated in an earlier Psalm: *And on his law he shall meditate day and night;*[98] *et non supplantabuntur gressus eius*, *and his steps shall not be supplanted*, that is, the operations of the just will not be overthrown, they will not be deprived of their reward: indeed, if perchance for a time the just elect were to stray [from the truth or the good], and his good works were killed by sin, the Lord will quickly convert him toward himself so that he will be restored to grace; and so the works for a time dead, will be made to live; and they will neither be supplanted nor disregarded; and they will not be finally extinguished by anything.[99]

36{37}[32] *The wicked watches the just man, and seeks to put him to death.*

Considerat peccator iustum, et quaerit mortificare eum.

36{37}[33] *But the Lord will not leave him in his hands; nor condemn him when he shall be judged.*

Dominus autem non derelinquet eum in manibus eius, nec damnabit eum cum iudicabitur illi.

36{37}[32] *Considerat peccator iustum*, *the wicked watches the just man*, not so that he might imitate him, but so that he may oppose him. Therefore, there is appended to this, *et quaerit mortificare eum*, *and seeks to put him to*

---

96 Tit. 1:16a.
97 Prov. 8:7.
98 Ps. 1:2b.
99 E. N. Denis is referring to a very consoling, merciful fact. "All merit is lost when mortal sin is committed. When grace is recovered, it is the consentient opinion of theologians that the former merit is restored. They infer this from the text 'For God is not unjust, that He should forget your work and the love which you have shown in His name' (Hebr. VI, 10). If merit were not restored, the loss would not be wholly repaired, yet the sin is certainly wholly forgiven; which seems to be inconsistent." Charles Coppens, S. J., *A Systematic Study of the Catholic Religion* (St. Louis: B. Herder Book Company 1917), 215.

death, either by killing his body or by drawing his soul to sin, or by affecting the just man with various tribulations, so that he sometimes becomes wearied of his life, in the way the Apostle [Paul] says: *We were pressed out of measure... so that we were weary even of life.*[100] **36{37}[33]** *Dominus autem non derelinquet eum in manibus eius*, but *the Lord will not leave him in his hands*, that is, he will not permit the just man finally to be oppressed by the violent power of the iniquitous, however much he permits him to be afflicted during this age. For after this temporal life, he will eternally free him from all distress. Nor in the present life does he completely leave him always in the hands of the ungodly: because while he may allow the impious to violently vex his body, he will not however be able to compel his soul to vice, or to deflect him from the way of justice, as is said by St. Gregory: *They can be killed, but they cannot be bent;*[101] consequently, they are adjudged hardier and by their death stronger. *Nec damnabit eum cum iudicabitur illi*, nor *condemn him when he shall be judged*: that is, in the day which the Lord will carry out the judgment of remuneration, *he*, namely the just man to his glory; or, *he*, that is the sinner to his punishment: then the just man will not be condemned, but he will save him. For Christ in the day of judgment will say to the just: *Come, you blessed of my Father, possess you the kingdom prepared for you from the foundation of the world.*[102] Whence also Abraham said the Lord: *Will you destroy the just with the wicked? This is not beseeming to you: you who judge all the earth.*[103]

36{37}[34] *Expect the Lord and keep his way: and he will exalt you to inherit the land: when the sinners shall perish you shall see.*

Exspecta Dominum, et custodi viam eius; et exaltabit te ut haereditate capias terram; cum perierint peccatores, videbis.

Because it is so, therefore, **36{37}[34]** *Exspecta Dominum, et custodi via eius; expect the Lord and keep his way.* This [has the same meaning as] what was said and expounded upon around the beginning of this Psalm, *Trust in the Lord, and do good.* For to expect God is nothing other than

---

100 2 Cor. 1:8b. E. N. St. Paul is here speaking of his tribulations in Asia (Minor). What sort of trial he was referring to is uncertain, though perhaps it refers to the riot raised by the silversmith Demetrius and the worshippers of Diana which is documented in Acts 19:29 *ff.*
101 E. N. The reference is to Pope St. Gregory the Great, who in his Homily 27(4) on the Gospels says famously regarding the martyrs: *Occidi possunt et flecti nequeunt.* PL 76, 1207.
102 Matt. 25:34b.
103 Gen. 18:23b, 25b.

to trust [or hope] in him, because hope is the expectation of future happiness. *Et exaltabit te, and he will exalt you*, God, who exalts the humble [will exalt you],[104] *ut hereditate capias terram, to inherit the land*, that is, that you might possess in eternity the Kingdom of Heaven; *cum perierint peccatores, videbis, when the sinners shall perish, you shall see*: because in the present life you will see them to languish [spiritually], and in the last judgment you will see them descend into hell covered over by earth.[105]

36{37}[35] *I have seen the wicked highly exalted, and lifted up like the cedars of Lebanon.*

Vidi impium superexaltatum, et elevatum sicut cedros Libani.

36{37}[36] *And I passed by, and lo, he was not: and I sought him and his place was not found.*

Et transivi, et ecce non erat; et quaesivi eum, et non est inventus locus eius.

36{37}[35] *Vidi impium superexaltatum, I have seen the wicked highly exalted*, that is, with dignity, honor power, glory, and riches lifted up on high beyond any measure, *et elevatum, and lifted up* with these things *sicut cedros Libani, like the cedars of Lebanon*, that is, so eminently excelling others in temporal things, in the splendor and height of prosperity, as the cedars of Lebanon, that is, trees growing in the mountains that are called Lebanon, which excel other trees in beauty and in locality. For Lebanon is interpreted as whiteness.[106] For this reason, the ungodly who temporally

---

104 Luke 18:14b.
105 E. N. Though there is no reference in the Latin text, the image as the descent into hell as being akin to the horrors of vivisepulture is clearly taken from Num. 16:33, where the punishment meted out by God at the request of Moses against the leaders of a rebellion against Moses and Aaron—Dathan, and Abiron—is narrated. God caused the ground beneath their feet to split open and then close, covering them—burying them alive. "'But if the Lord do a new thing,' said Moses, 'and the earth opening her mouth swallow them down, and all things that belong to them, and they go down alive into hell, you shall know that they have blasphemed the Lord.' And immediately as he had made an end of speaking, the earth broke asunder under their feet: And opening her mouth, devoured them with their tents and all their substance. And they went down alive into hell the ground closing upon them, and they perished from among the people." Num. 16:30–33.
106 E. N. Lebanon refers to a mountain range between lower Syria and upper Galilee, running north/south. The word Lebanon is derived from the Semitic triconsonantal root lbn, which yields *laban* (לבן) in Hebrew, meaning "white," a reference probably to the snow-capped nature of these mountains. See Scott Hahn, ed. *The Catholic Bible Dictionary* (New York: Doubleday 2009), 534. (s.v. "Lebanon").

prosper and flourish are compared to the cedars of Lebanon; because such persons are buffeted and razed by the winds like cedars, so that all the haughtiness of vanity and the ardor of passion of the ungodly are scattered about them and fall to ruin. 36{37}[36] *Et transivi, and I passed by,* that is, I have laid bare my life, with resolve I scrutinized all things, I lifted up my mind from earthly things to heavenly things, *et ecce non erat; and lo, he was not,* that is, the ungodly has already fallen: because his glory does not last long, in the manner that the book of Wisdom says in the person of the impious: *For our time is as the passing of a shadow.*[107] *Et quaesivi eum, and I sought him,* that is, I inquired where he might be; or, *I sought him,* that is, I have scrutinized his condition and quality, considering within me how much his vanity was; *et non est inventus locus eius, and his place was not found.* This is that which a short time ago was asserted — *and you shall seek his place, and shall not find it*[108] — and upon which we have already expounded. And this is what Wisdom recalls: *For the hope of the wicked is as dust, which is blown away with the wind, and as a thin froth which is dispersed by foam, ... and as the memory of a guest of one day.*[109]

36{37}[37] *Keep innocence, and behold justice: for there are remnants for the peaceable man.*

Custodi innocentiam, et vide aequitatem, quoniam sunt reliquiae homini pacifico.

36{37}[37] *Custodi innocentiam,* keep innocence, that is, turn away from all evil, *et vide aequitatem, and behold justice,* that is, consider, and — so considering — do justice. This is what in the Acts of the Apostles is written, for Paul taught them about continence and justice.[110] *Quoniam sunt reliquiae homini pacifico, for there are remnants for the peaceable man:* that is, they await great goods in the future, and they are ready for peace in heaven with those who love or those who practice it — whether in their own heart, or among others — in the manner that Christ attests to: *Blessed are the peacemakers: for they shall be called children of God.*[111] Or

---

107 Wis. 2:5a.
108 Ps. 36:10.
109 Wis. 5:15.
110 Acts 24:25. E. N. St. Paul was teaching Governor Felix and his Jewish wife and the youngest of Herod Agrippa's daughter, Drusilla: *And as he [St. Paul] treated of justice, and chastity, and of the judgment to come, Felix being terrified, answered: For this time, go your way: but when I have a convenient time, I will send for you.* There is no evidence of either of their conversions.
111 Matt. 5:9.

[we can expound it] thus: *For there are remnants for the peaceable man,* that is, they who spurn all transitory things, peaceably make their own innocence and justice, and are bound to it, and preserve it, since they adhere to God in true peace. For as long as they part with all exterior and transient things, then innocence and justice will remain in them. For since they have wholeheartedly desired peace, they have not occasioned any harm, and they have not withheld and kept for themselves the goods of anyone; but they have totally emptied themselves in the service of peace. Indeed, innocence disposes to peace; but justice keeps the peace because it removes the obstacles of peace. Hence it is written in Isaiah: *The work of justice shall be peace, and the service of justice quietness, and security for ever. And my people shall sit in the beauty of peace, and in the tabernacles of confidence, and in wealthy rest.*[112] And yet, peace is the direct and proper effect of charity: which is why we find it said in a later Psalm, *Much peace have they that love your law.*[113] Also, peace is called the work of justice (*opus iustitiae*) inasmuch as justice removes impediments to peace.[114]

36{37}[38] *But the unjust shall be destroyed; together the remnants of the wicked shall perish.*

Iniusti autem disperibunt; simul reliquiae impiorum interibunt.

36{37}[38] *Iniusti autem disperibunt,* but *the unjust shall be destroyed*: because they will be eternally in distress. For this is written in the book of Job: *Remember, I pray you, who ever perished being innocent? ... On the contrary I have seen ...* the *wicked perishing by the blast of* the *Lord.*[115] *Simul reliquae impiorum interibunt, together the remnants of the wicked shall perish:* that is, their seed, their words, their imitators, and their glory and memory will be condemned by the Lord, they will be forsaken by the saints, and they will be lost to any happiness, as it is written: *As a cloud is consumed, and passes away: so he that shall go down to hell shall not come up.*[116] And this is what is said in a subsequent Psalm, *For when he shall die he shall take nothing away.*[117]

---

112 Is. 32:17–18.
113 Ps. 118:165a.
114 E. N. This is an implied reference to Isaiah 32:17: *And the work of justice shall be peace (opus iustitiae pax), and the service of justice quietness, and security forever. Opus iustitiae pax* was the motto of Eugenio Pacelli (1876–1958 AD), who reigned as Pope Pius XII between 1939 and 1958.
115 Job 4:7–9a.
116 Job 7:9.
117 Ps. 48:18a.

36{37}[39] *But the salvation of the just is from the Lord, and he is their protector in the time of trouble.*

Salus autem iustorum a Domino; et protector eorum in tempore tribulationis.

36{37}[40] *And the Lord will help them and deliver them: and he will rescue them from the wicked, and save them, because they have hoped in him.*

Et adiuvabit eos Dominus, et liberabit eos; et eruet eos a peccatoribus, et salvabit eos, quia speraverunt in eo.

36{37}[39] *Salus autem iustorum a Domino*, but the salvation of the just is from the Lord: that is, whatever perfection and grace they have in mind and body flows from and is given by God. For *what have you that you have not received?*[118] *Et protector eorum*, and he is their protector, that is, the Lord [is the protector] of the just, *in tempore tribulationis*, in the time of trouble, temptation, infirmity, and death. 36{37}[40] *Et adiuvabit eos Dominus*, and the Lord will help them, strengthening natural virtue with the help of grace, *et liberabit eos*, and he will rescue them from the chains of vice; *et eruet eos a peccatoribus*, and he will rescue them from the wicked, that is, from the temptations and the distresses of impious men and demons, *et salvabit eos*, and he will rescue them in the Reign of Heaven, after the course of this age and time of exile. But by whose merit? It states: *quia speraverunt in eo*, because they have hoped in him, that is, they have expected all good from his mercy, they have ascribed nothing to their own strength, but with all attention they have placed their confidence in God, doing nothing less than what was in them: because true, saving, and perfect hope is the certain expectation of future beatitude[119] [which comes] from the mercy of God and being born (*nascens*) with one's own merit:[120] therefore, [it comes from] an

---

118 Cf. 1 Cor. 4:7: *For who distinguishes you? Or what have you that you have not received? And if you have received, why do you glory, as if you had not received it?*

119 E. N. St. Thomas defines hope as the *expectatio futurae beatitudinis*, "the expectation of future beatitude," in ST IaIIae, q. 17, art. 6, arg. 2; q. 18, art. 4, s.c., IIIa, q. 7, art. 4, arg. 2.

120 E. N. The principle of any human merit, as it is the "permanent principle of the supernatural life," DS 3714, is sanctifying or habitual grace; there is no merit without it. And yet being "reborn" in a state of grace, we are given the grace "with fear and trembling" to "work out" our salvation. Phil. 2:12. There is no question of earning the first grace. "Human merit does not precede the grace of God, but grace itself merits increase, so that the increase merits perfection, the will accompanying not leading, walking right behind, not before." *[N]on gratiam Dei aliquid meriti*

act of formed hope, proceeding from charity.[121] Also, this definition can be given of an act as from the habit of hope: because in itself hope is an infused habit[122] and not one obtained by [human] effort and not caused by one's own merits. But because no one knows without a special revelation whether one is worthy with love,[123] how is a man able to have certain knowledge of the expectation of future happiness? By knowing that hope principally is founded upon the mercy of God rather than one's own merits. Certitude, therefore, is fitting of hope, insofar as those things which are founded upon the divine mercy. For it is certain that a falling away from salvation is not on the part of the mercy of God [failing or being insufficient]. Nor is the certitude of hope properly founded on the part of one's own merit, unless perchance one is able to know himself confirmed in grace as were the Apostles after the coming of the Paraclete.[124] And so, the Lord saves the just because they have hoped in him, in the manner that he himself said attesting through Jeremiah: *Delivering, I will deliver you, and ... your life shall be saved for you, because you have put your trust in me, says the Lord.*[125]

---

praecedit humani, sed ipsa gratia meretur augeri, ut aucta mereatur perfici, comitante, non ducente, pedissequa, non praevia voluntate. St. Augustine, *Epist.* 186, 3, 10, PL 33, 819. Thus, Denis is saying that the principle of merit is born the same time that a formed hope proceeding from charity is possessed, both of which are equivalent to saying the soul is in sanctifying or habitual grace as a result of the mercy of God.

121   E. N. On "formed hope," *spes formatae*, see footnote 36-19.

122   E. N. As used here, a "habit," like clothing worn by a monk, is a relatively fixed disposition that inclines one's nature, faculty, or powers to either good or evil. They can be natural and acquired, or supernatural and infused.

123   Eccl. 9:1b: *Man knows not whether he be worthy of love, or hatred*. E. N. One cannot be certain of being in a state of sanctifying grace (possessed of informed charity or "worthy with love" in Denis's words) or having the grace of final perseverance without a special revelation. DS 1534, 1540, 1565–66.

124   E. N. As St. Thomas Aquinas says (*De Veritate*, q. 24, art. 9, ad 2), the Blessed Virgin Mary, "because she was the mother of divine wisdom," as well as the Apostles, "because they were as the foundation and basis of the whole ecclesiastical structure," were confirmed in the good, meaning that that their state of sanctifying grace was assured and their salvation was certain. As St. Alfonso Rodriguez succinctly states this: "The apostles could not sin mortally, after they were confirmed in grace, yet this grace did not destroy their liberty, but, on the contrary, perfected it; because it helped to confirm their will in the good, for which they were created." Alfonso Rodriguez, *The Practice of Christian and Religious Perfection* (Dublin: James Duffy 1914), Vol. 3, 112. With respect to the Blessed Virgin Mary, this confirmation went further in that, redeemed in a most perfect manner through the merits of Christ her Son, DS 3909, 4173, she was preserved not only from original sin from the first moment of her conception, DS 2803-04, but also from that moment of all future mortal and venial sin, DS 1573, 2800, 3908, 3915.

125   Jer. 39:18.

See how moral and consolatory this Psalm is. It behooves us diligently to pay heed to it, so that we might learn to esteem little all transitory things and always fervently to opt for lasting heavenly things.

PRAYER

GRANT, WE BESEECH YOU, O MERCIFUL GOD, that placing our hope in you, we might continually do good, by which, brought to completion, we might dwell in the land of the living, in which, lavishly bestowing your grace, we might delight in eternal riches.

Concede, quaesumus, misericors Deus, ut in te sperantes, bonitatem iugiter faciamus: in qua consummati, habitationem terrae viventium obtineamus; in qua, tua gratia largiente, aeternis divitiis pascamur.

Psalm 37

ARTICLE LXXVI

EXPOSITION OF THE THIRTY-SEVENTH PSALM:
DOMINE, NE IN FURORE.
REBUKE ME NOT, O LORD.

37{38}[1] *A Psalm for David, for a remembrance of the Sabbath.*
Psalmus David, in rememorationem de sabbato.

NOW THE TITLE OF THIS PSALM IS: 37{38}[1] *Psalmus David, in rememoratione sabbati, a Psalm for David, for a remembrance of the Sabbath.* The Sabbath signifies the rest of eternity: which by sinning we lose, and which we recover by recalling in a penitent way the sins we have committed. Therefore, the sense of this title is: *a Psalm for David*, that is, this Psalm is written by David as author, and speaking in the person of a penitent; *for a remembrance of the Sabbath*, that is, for the recollection and forgiveness of sins, which recollection is occupied with the desire of coming to the rest of the blessed [in heaven], and is ordained towards it as its end.

37{38}[2] *Rebuke me not, O Lord, in your indignation; nor chastise me in your wrath.*

Domine, ne in furore tuo arguas me, neque in ira tua corripias me.

37{38}[3] *For your arrows are fastened in me: and your hand has been strong upon me.*

Quoniam sagittae tuae infixae sunt mihi, et confirmasti super me manum tuam.

Speaking therefore in the person of any great sinner that is wholeheartedly penitent, he says: 37{38}[2] *Domine, ne in furore tuo arguas me, neque in ira tua corripias me; rebuke me not, O Lord, in your indignation; nor chastise me in your wrath.* This verse has been diligently explained in the beginning of the explanation of the sixth Psalm;[1] therefore, I refer

---

1 Psalm 6:2 is identical to Psalm 36:2. *See* Article XXII (Psalm 6:2) in Volume 1.

the reader to that place. 37{38}[3] *Quoniam sagittae tuae infixae sunt mihi, for your arrows are fastened in me*: that is, I pray on that account that I be not rebuked in your indignation, because *your arrows*, that is, the vindications or punishments you inflict for sins, *are fastened in me*, that is, penetrate me deeply. For in the manner that original justice provided a certain restraint of the soul by which in all things the flesh was subordinated to the spirit, the sensitive part to reason, and reason to God,[2] so the punishments inflicted for this loss of justice are applicable to all men. [This is so] because the body by its weakness and by necessity is subjected to death, the sensitive part of the soul is filled with most disorderly passions and a most vicious concupiscence, and also the intellective part of the soul is vulnerable to ignorance, instability, and malice. For there is ignorance in reason, instability in memory, but malice in the will. But all these evils are arrows inflicted upon the human race because of original sin: and this is *a heavy yoke* that (Scripture attests) has been placed *upon the children of Adam, from the day of their* birth even until the day of their death.[3] But there are also other arrows which are inflicted on account of individual actual sins,[4] such as the threat of God (*comminatio Dei*),[5] the fear of judgment, the remorse of conscience,

---

2 "The first man was not only created good, but was also established in friendship with his Creator and in harmony with himself and with the creation around him, in a state that would be surpassed only by the glory of the new creation in Christ. The Church, interpreting the symbolism of biblical language in an authentic way, in the light of the New Testament and Tradition, teaches that our first parents, Adam and Eve, were constituted in an original 'state of holiness and justice.' ... By the radiance of this grace all dimensions of man's life were confirmed.... The inner harmony of the human person ... comprised the state called 'original justice.' The 'mastery' over the world that God offered man from the beginning was realized above all within man himself: *mastery of self*. The first man was unimpaired and ordered in his whole being because he was free from the triple concupiscence that subjugates him to the pleasures of the senses, covetousness for earthly goods, and self-assertion, contrary to the dictates of reason.... This entire harmony of original justice, foreseen for man in God's plan, will be lost by the sin of our first parents." CCC §§ 374–77, 379 (citations omitted).
3 Ecclus. 40:1.
4 *E. N.* The Baltimore Catechism succinctly distinguishes between original sin and actual sin: "51. Q. Is original sin the only kind of sin? A. Original sin is not the only kind of sin; there is another kind of sin, which we commit ourselves, called actual sin. 52. Q. What is actual sin? A. Actual sin is any willful thought, word, deed, or omission contrary to the law of God. 53. Q. How many kinds of actual sin are there? A. There are two kinds of actual sin—mortal and venial."
5 *E. N.* The notion of the *comminatio Dei*, or the commination, or threat, or menace of God under which we live, is virtually forgotten today. "Perhaps the greatest sin in the world today is that men have begun to lose the sense of sin." (Pius XII,

the sorrow for past faults, adversities, misfortunes, the suspension of the consolations and the grace of God, and many other scourges of the present life. Of which things holy Job says: *For the arrows of the Lord are in me, the rage whereof drinks up my spirit, and the terrors of the Lord war against me.*⁶ And Ecclesiastes: *All his days are full of sorrows and miseries, even in the night he does not rest in mind.*⁷ And again: *To the sinner,* he says, God *has given vexation, and superfluous care.*⁸ *Et confirmasti, and strong upon me,* O Lord, *super me manum tuam, your hand has been,* that is, the very arrows and punishments strongly put pressure upon me and are continually pressing upon me even until death: as is particularly clear in the punishments of the body, such as are hunger, thirst, and certain other inevitable evils.

37{38}[4]   *There is no health in my flesh, because of your wrath: there is no peace for my bones, because of my sins.*

Non est sanitas in carne mea, a facie irae tuae; non est pax ossibus meis, a facie peccatorum meorum.

37{38}[4] *Non est sanitas in carne mea a facie irae tuae, there is no health in my flesh, because of your wrath*: that is, there is not a stable, integral, and perfect health in my body because the animadversion⁹ or the gaze

---

Radio Message, October 26, 1946). Along with the loss of a sense of sin is a loss of the menace (or commination) of God. We might turn to St. Thomas More for a recapitulation of this notion: "If God was so wroth with pride that he spared not to drive down into hell for pride the noble high excellent angels of heaven, what state can there be so great in this wretched world that hath not high cause to tremble and quake every joint in his body as soon as he feeleth a high proud thought enter once into his heart? Remembering the terrible commination and threat of God in holy scripture, *Potentes potenter tormenta patientur,* The mighty men shall mightily suffer torments. [Wisdom 6:7] And then if it be so sore a thing and so far unfitting in the sight of God, to see the sin of pride in the person of a great estate, that hath yet many occasions of inclination thereunto; how much more abominable is that peevish pride in a lewd, unthrifty javell, that hath a purse as penniless as any poor pedlar, and hath yet a heart as high as many a mighty prince?" St. Thomas More, "A Treatise upon the Passion of Christ," *Selections from His English Works and from the Lives of Erasmus & Roper* (Oxford: Clarendon 1924), 151–52.
6   Job. 6:4.
7   Eccl. 2:23.
8   Eccl. 2:26a.
9   L. *animadversionem.* There is not one English word that adequately comprehends and so adequately translates this, so I have elected to use the English animadversion, though it is not a common word. The Latin *animadversionem* encompasses notions of observation, inquiry, reproach, chastisement, censure, and punishment: it is akin,

of your justice, which considers my sins, and avenges them with the aforementioned arrows, filling the flesh with maladies and other diverse punishments. But these torments we should suffer patiently, since they serve to cleanse our vices, in the manner that Micah states: *I will bear the wrath of the Lord, because I have sinned against him; until he judge my cause.*[10] And Jeremiah says: *Truly this is my own evil, and I will bear it.*[11] *Non est pax ossibus meis, there is no peace for my bones*: that is, the previously mentioned vindications of divine justice touch even to furthest parts of my flesh, and disturb and afflict its bones: for flesh and bones are tormented by maladies and punishments, and thus the whole body is afflicted with punishment; *a facie peccatorum meorum, because of my sins,* that is, on account of the sins which pound against me, and of which I am conscious. Or [we can see it] thus: *There is no health in my flesh*: that is, I have so afflicted my flesh in the works of penance *because of your wrath*, that is, in consideration of your justice, which I have regarded as terribly imminent, since *there is no health in my flesh*; but attenuated and emptied through abstinence, prayer, the discipline, or blows and vigils. *There is no peace for my bones*: that is, the bones and the skin and flesh of my body are as it were made naked because of the labor that I have assumed *because of my sins*, that is from the consideration of my offenses against you. And with merit do I afflict myself so harshly:[12]

37{38}[5] *For my iniquities are gone over my head: and as a heavy burden are become heavy upon me.*

Quoniam iniquitates meae supergressae sunt caput meum, et sicut onus grave gravatae sunt super me.

37{38}[5] *Quoniam iniquitates meae supergressae sunt caput meum, for my iniquities are gone over my head*: that is, my vices and disordered desires have blinded, overcome, and oppressed the light of my reason, and I have been led captive in the law of sin, as Daniel says: *Beauty has deceived you, and lust has perverted your heart.*[13] Against which Paul says:

---

or analogous to, to the entirety of a legal or judicial process.
10 Micah 7:9a.
11 Jer. 10:19b.
12 "[H]e who has practiced the greatest mortifications during life shall enjoy the greatest glory. St. Peter says the saints are the living stones of which the celestial Jerusalem is built. But before they are translated to the city which is above, they must be polished by the salutary chisel of penance." St. Alphonsus Liguori, "The True Spouse of Jesus Christ," *The Complete Works* (New York: Benziger Bros. 1929), 213.
13 Dan. 13:56b.

Be not overcome by evil, but overcome evil by good.[14] *Let no sin reign in your mortal body, so as to obey the lusts thereof; neither yield your members as instruments of iniquity unto sin.*[15] *Et sicut onus grave gravatae super me, and as a heavy burden are become heavy upon me*: that is, through evil practices or negligence or obstinacy my iniquities are made many and great, and so gravely have they dragged away my affection unto inferior and vile strivings, as a weight drags a light body so that it does not ascend. Our sins, therefore, impede us from contemplation of heavenly things, press against the judgment of reason, as also other vices bend us down by their weight, and finally they submerge the impenitent soul in hell. For which reason Jeremiah says: *Your sins have withheld good things from you.*[16]

37{38}[6] *My sores are putrefied and corrupted, because of my foolishness.*
Putruerunt et corruptae sunt cicatrices meae, a facie insipientiae meae.

37{38}[6] *Putruerunt et corruptae sunt cicatrices meae, my sores are putrefied and corrupted*: that is, [my sores which are] the remnants or healings of my guilt have gone back to the original languor of sin, because I have returned to the vices forgiven by my penance and have incurred the earlier malady of the soul. Putrefaction disposes one to corruption; and thinking or consent [disposes] one to the deed. Therefore, when we consent again in past sins, the sores of our soul are putrefied; but they are completely corrupted when we proceed to the [evil] deed.[17] *A facie insipientiae meae, because of my foolishness*: that is, this relapse of this sin comes to me out of my foolishness, namely, because I did not reflect on how dangerous, deadly, or ungrateful it is to heap evil upon evil, and to be ensnared again in the former fetters: as is written in Ecclesiasticus: *The sinner will add sin to sin.*[18] Against which in the same book we find written: Children, *add not sin upon sin, and say not, the mercy of the Lord is great.*[19] For his ire is just as great as his mercy is great.

---

14 Rom. 12:21.
15 Rom. 6:12–13a.
16 Jer. 5:25b.
17 E. N. *Sed nisi ad nos oleant et mala nostra, numquam istis gemitibus confitemur: Computruerunt et putuerunt livores mei.* "But unless also our evil stinks to us, we will never confess with these lamentations: 'My sores are putrefied and corrupted.'" St. Augustine, *Enarr. in Ps.* 37, 9, PL 36, 401.
18 Ecclus. 3:29b.
19 Ecclus. 5:5b, 6a.

37{38}[7] *I am become miserable, and am bowed down even to the end: I walked sorrowful all the day long.*

Miser factus sum et curvatus sum usque in finem; tota die contristatus ingrediebar.

37{38}[7] *Miser factus sum, I am become miserable,* that is, by sinning I have lost grace, and I am deprived of all spiritual goods, and I have let slip by me the eight Evangelical beatitudes, *et curvatus sum, and am bowed down,* that is, I have turned aside from the rectitude of justice, and I have abandoned the way of truth, *usque in finem, even to the end,* that is, even up to consenting in mortal sin, which is the death of the soul and the end of the spiritual life it previously possessed. Or [we might understand it] thus: *I am become miserable,* that is, I know myself to be miserable, and I have humbled my spirit, which considered itself happy in evil; and *I am bowed down even to the end,* that is, I have placed the yoke of God upon my shoulders, and began to carry the burden of Christ and his Cross even unto the end, that is, perseveringly, or to this end: that I might acquire God, who is the sovereign end of all things. This sort of bowing down is good. For of it is written: *The soul which... goes bowed down... gives glory... to you, the Lord.*[20] *Tota die contristatus ingrediebar, I walked sorrowful all the day long,* that is, because of my sin I was unceasingly sorrowful with good sorrow. Of which the Apostle [Paul] says: *The sorrow that is according to God works penance, steadfast unto salvation.*[21] And Ecclesiastes: *The heart of the wise is where there is mourning, and the heart of fools where there is mirth.*[22] And the sorrow for sin in the beginning ought to be more frequent and nearly continuous; but in going forward, when penitent and advanced to higher things, it is proper that it not be so frequent and continuous: indeed, by then such a person ought to be occupied with works of divine charity and more sublime exercises, contemplating the divine goodness and his benefits and promises. But, on the other hand, most especially at the beginning of one's acts, he ought both to humble himself and to recollect his sins, and by this means most humbly approach God. Therefore, Scripture says: *The just is in the beginning the accuser of himself.*[23]

---

20 Baruch 2:18.
21 2 Cor. 7:10a.
22 Eccl. 7:5.
23 Prov. 18:17. E. N. Denis's reading of this verse differs slightly from the Vulgate: *Iustus in principio acusator est sui* instead of the Vulgate's reading: *Iustus prior est accusator sui,* "The just is first accuser of himself."

37{38}[8] *For my loins are filled with illusions; and there is no health in my flesh.*

Quoniam lumbi mei impleti sunt illusionibus, et non est sanitas in carne mea.

37{38}[8] *Quoniam lumbi mei impleti sunt illusionibus, for my loins are filled with illusions*: that is, I, in whose loins[24] thrives the motions of lust, am befouled with carnal desire and am seduced by lustful pleasures. And pleasures and acts of lust are called illusions because they so greatly overwhelm the intellect and completely deceive men. But this, by the grace of God, does not apply to all men. For it does not apply to them who are virgins both in heart and body: but [it did apply] to David, who sinned so greatly with the wife of Uriah;[25] and also to Solomon[26] of whom we read, *You did bow yourself to women, . . . you have stained your glory.*[27] He to whom this does not apply, therefore, should not vainly take glory or swell with pride; rather he should give thanks to the Lord, and all the more ardently the greater this gift. *Et non est sanitas in carne mea*, *and there is no health in my flesh*: for, as the Apostle [Paul] says, *He that commits fornication, sins against his own body.*[28]

37{38}[9] *I am afflicted and humbled exceedingly: I roared with the groaning of my heart.*

Afflictus sum, et humiliatus sum nimis; rugiebam a gemitu cordis mei.

37{38}[10] *Lord, all my desire is before you, and my groaning is not hidden from you.*

Domine, ante te omne desiderium meum, et gemitus meus a te non est absconditus.

37{38}[9] *Afflictus sum, I am afflicted* with the divine chastisement and salutary punishments for my sins; *et humiliatus sum nimis*, and am

---

24 E. N. The Douay-Rheims translates the Latin *lumbi* as "loins." St. Jerome notes: *Omnis igitur adversus viros diaboli virtus in lumbis est: omnis in umbilico contra feminas fortitudo. Epistulae*, 22, 11. Every power of the devil against men, therefore, is in the loins, all his force against women is the navel." St. Jerome is here explaining Job 2:3: "His strength is in the loins, and his force is in the navel." These terms, St. Jerome says, are "respectably" used to refer to the reproductive organs of men and women, respectively (*viri mulierisque genitalia immutatis sunt appellate nominibus*). PL, 22, 401.
25 2 Sam. 11:4
26 1 Kings 11:4–8.
27 Ecclus. 47:21–22a.
28 1 Cor. 6:18b.

humbled exceedingly: that is, I have humbly endured these afflictions placed upon me because of my sins; indeed, I have regarded myself as the most vile of irrational creatures. *Rugiebam a gemitu cordis mei, I roared with the groaning of my heart*: that is, out of the greatness of my interior sorrow for sin, I have burst forth in great exterior sobbing and groaning, in the manner that Job says: *Before I eat I sigh: and as overflowing waters, so is my roaring.*[29] And from this we are taught how true repentance ought to be, namely, that we express the most heartfelt compunction, and that we might entirely express sorrow, and chastise and humiliate ourselves. **37{38}[10]** *Domine, ante te omne desiderium meum; Lord, all my desire is before you*: that is, O Lord, you see the heart of your servant, and you know all of its affections, and you perceive that I seek nothing else but you; *et gemitus meus a te non est absconditus, and my groaning is not hidden from you*: that is, you see that I am not sorrowful in a worldly way, nor do I groan because of temporal things, but because I have offended you.

37{38}[11] *My heart is troubled, my strength has left me, and the light of my eyes itself is not with me.*

Cor meum conturbatum est, dereliquit me virtus mea, et lumen oculorum meorum, et ipsum non est mecum.

37{38}[11] *Cor meum conturbatum est, my heart is troubled*: that is, my reason is disordered by vice, and it has departed from true tranquility. Or [another way of looking at it is], *my heart is troubled*, with a healthy and good trouble, namely, one ordered towards penance, and tears, and the fear of future judgment; and by a certain dismay at my ingratitude, so that in considering myself I am discontented with myself and am astounded by the greatness of my perversity. *Dereliquit me virtus mea, my strength has left me*: that is, my natural power was insufficient to obtain for me salvation. Or [in an alternative understanding], *my strength has left me*, that is, by sinning I have departed from the spiritual progress to which I had arrived. Also, I have left *et lumen oculorum meorum, and the light of my eyes*, that is, habitual grace and the actual illumination of the Holy Spirit have departed from when I sinned; *et ipsum non est mecum, and itself is not with me*, that is, the light of grace is not in me so long as I remain in sin. Or [an alternative explanation might be] thus: *My strength has left me*, that is, I am not able to undertake a penance that is equivalent

---

29 Job 3:24.

(*condignam penitentiam*) to my sins;[30] *et lumen oculorum meorum, and the light of my eyes,* that is, I am not able fully to comprehend the gravity of my sins because of their enormity. For the more fully a man is illuminated by the Holy Spirit the more amply he is able to weigh, assess the gravity of, and abhor his own sins, so that that which to others might appear small and nearly nothing, he will consider to be most grave. And such a man—and no other—is able to understand the sense of this Psalm. *Et ipsum non est mecum, and [the light of my eyes] itself is not with me,* that is, I am still deficient in the consideration of my malice, and I am not able to grasp fully how wretched and miserable I have become, especially in that I have repeated past evil. For this reason it is written: *How exceeding base have you become, going the same ways over again!*[31]

37{38}[12] *My friends and my neighbors have drawn near, and stood against me. And they that were near me stood afar off. And they that sought my soul used violence.*

Amici mei et proximi mei adversum me appropinquaverunt, et steterunt; et qui iuxta me erant, de longe steterunt, et vim faciebant qui quaerebant animam meam.

37{38}[13] *And they that sought evils to me spoke vain things, and studied deceits all the day long.*

Et qui inquirebant mala mihi, locuti sunt vanitates, et dolos tota die meditabantur.

Furthermore, that which follows pertains to the perfection of the penitent, and relates to that which is fitting to him after conversion and beginning [the life of] penance. **37{38}[12]** *Amici mei et proximi*

---

30 A condign repentance or penance is one that—of itself—would be sufficient, in strict justice, to make satisfaction for the guilt of sin and the punishment associated with it. Given the infinite chasm between creature and Creator, and given the infinite affront and injustice to God by a creature's sins, such is simply not possible. Thus: "Condign satisfaction requires a satisfaction made in accord with the demands of strict equivalence.... Thus condign satisfaction must have something of the infinite in it, but no creature is capable of effecting that kind of satisfaction since no creature can do anything that is infinite.... '[E]ven the whole human race lacks the necessary resources to make a condign satisfaction." Romanus Cessario, O. P., *The Godly Image: Christian Satisfaction in Aquinas* (Washington, D. C.: CUA Press 2020). 99, 163. "'Thus, for condign satisfaction the act of the one atoning should be infinite in worth—an act, that is, of one who is both God and man.'" *Ibid.*, 163 (quoting ST, IIIa, q. 1, art. 2, ad 2).

31 Jer. 2:36a.

mei, my friends and my neighbors, that is, they who at one time were collaborators with me, when, namely, I was in agreement with their will, living a worldly way, and loving worldly delights and honors, *adversum me appropinquaverunt et steterunt; have drawn near and stood against me,* that is, after my conversion they were adversarial against me, and they persevered in malice against me because my life was dissimilar to their lives, and I abandoned and condemned those things which they seek and approve. And this is what Christ said to such persons in the Gospel: *And you shall be betrayed by your parents, and family, and friends, and some of you they will put to death.*[32] *Et qui iuxta me errant, and they that were near me,* during the time of my prosperity, *de longe steterunt, stood afar off,* that is, with their minds they are adverse to me when I employ the scourges of penance and when I endure with patience the various adversities with which I am afflicted. This is most evidently apparent with holy Job.[33] Whence, in Ecclesiasticus we have: *If you would get a friend, try him before you take him, and do not credit him easily. For there is a friend for his own occasion, and he will not abide in the day of your trouble.*[34] *Et vim faciebant, and they... used violence,* that is, they have inflicted violence upon me, *qui quaerebant animam meam, they that sought my soul,* that is, who endeavor to separate me from God, and lure me back again to a worldly manner of living; or [an alternative construction], they who venture to extinguish my life, because I am unwilling to acquiesce to them. **37{38}[13]** *Et qui inquirebant mala, and they that sought evils,* that is, they who love the world and those things that are of the world; or [alternatively], they who devise deceptive counsels; *mihi locuti sunt vanitates, to me spoke vain things,* that is, have proposed inane reasons and useless opinions to me, since they would like to call me back from my seizing upon a path of penance, and entangle me in my former life of vanity; *et dolos tota die meditabantur, and studied deceits all the day long,* that is, with adulations, threats, and various deceits they have strived to trip my soul, namely, that it might long for temporal prosperity and mundane happiness.

But the penitent can also say this against the demons, from this place forward: *and they... used violence, etc.* For also they tempt us frequently with a certain violent attack, and they express the joys of the world under a magnificent appearance, so that they might incline us to them.

---

32 Luke 21:16.
33 E. N. We might recall that Job was a figure or type of Christ. *See* footnote 21-95 in Volume 1.
34 Ecclus. 6:7–8.

37{38}[14] *But I, as a deaf man, heard not: and as a dumb man not opening his mouth.*
Ego autem, tamquam surdus, non audiebam; et sicut mutus non aperiens os suum.

37{38}[15] *And I became as a man that hears not: and that has no reproofs in his mouth.*
Et factus sum sicut homo non audiens, et non habens in ore suo redargutiones.

But let us now hear how the penitent encounters so much persecution and trouble. 37{38}[14] *Ego autem tanquam surdus non audiebam, and I became as a man that hears not*: that is, I did not give consent, or I feigned myself to hear, or I did not hear anything at all because I averted my ears, and I departed; *et sicut mutus non aperiens os suum, and as a dumb man not opening his mouth*, that is, I responded with nothing, I did want to contend with words, I endured invective patiently and with silence, and I have disregarded and abhorred the vain counsels and temptations of the devil since I had reputed them as not worthy of a response. But this way of thinking is related more clearly in the following verse. 37{38}[15] *Et factus sum sicut homo non audiens, and I became as a man that hears not*: that is, I have suffered with such equanimity the words of evildoers, and they were to me as if they had not been said, in the manner that a deaf man is not able to be irritated by words that he does not hear; *et non habens in ore suo redargutiones, and that has no reproofs in his mouth*: that is, I have become as a man who knows not how to confute someone arguing something, who does not return an evil word to one speaking evil, and who does not respond to the fool according to his foolishness.[35] Whence the Scripture exhorts: *Hedge in your ears with thorns, hear not a wicked tongue, and make doors to your mouth, and bars for your ears.*[36]

Moreover, the optimal remedy to overcome the temptations of blasphemy of the Spirit is handled in these two verses.[37] For there is no better

---

35 E. N. Denis cites to Prov. 26:5: *Answer a fool according to his folly, lest he imagine himself to be wise.* But it would appear that the proper cite is to Prov. 26:4: *Answer not a fool according to his folly, lest thou be made like him.*
36 Ecclus. 28:28. E. N. Denis departs from the Sixto-Clementine Vulgate, which reads: *Sepi aures tuas spinis: linguam nequam noli audire: et ori tuo facito ostia et seras. Hedge in your ears with thorns, hear not a wicked tongue, and make doors and bars to your mouth.*
37 E. N. Blasphemy of the Holy Spirit (*see* Matt. 3:29) is a particularly significant thing to avoid given the warning issued with its identification: *But he that shall blaspheme against the Holy Ghost, shall never have forgiveness, but shall be guilty of an everlasting sin.*

way to defeat the demon of blasphemy, unless it be in this manner: that a man completely turns himself away from consideration of the suggestions with which he is being met, neither disputing nor discussing with this pestiferous temptation, nor being sorrowful with himself because of these kinds of attacks, but rather turning to other fruitful exercises, and disclosing clearly to spiritual men his temptation. For this especially weakens the power of the devil. But if someone because of an evil shame of, and inexperience with, such a temptation dares not to reveal that which he is enduring: that is very dangerous. Nevertheless, it is not expedient to reveal indifferently to anyone such a temptation, but to a learned man or to an expert, one who knows immediately the consolation that is to be applied. If, therefore, you feel such a temptation, say with your heart the previous verses, and soon you will feel relief. For since the demon is proudful, he is unable to bear that he is so disregarded, and therefore he will depart. Nevertheless (as Cassian[38] teaches) there is a certain evil taciturnity which may sometimes disturb and excite his brothers and neighbor more than if he had resisted them openly: for such taciturnity is not from humility, but it arises from pride or from contempt of another person, and it is nourished by hardness of heart. While, therefore, you are able to heal and piously instruct a neighbor with a sweet word, do not keep silent (*noli tacere*); but if in responding you would more inflame than mitigate matters, then keep silent (*tace*). For this is written: *There is one that holds his peace (tacens), because he knows not what to say: and there is another that holds his peace, knowing the proper time.*[39]

37{38}[16] *For in you, O Lord, have I hoped: you will hear me, O Lord my God.*

Quoniam in te, Domine, speravi; tu exaudies me, Domine Deus meus.

†[40] 37{38}[16] *Quoniam*, for in all evil *in te*, in you alone, *Domine*, O Lord, who mutes sorrow in joy, *speravi*, have I hoped, because of you

---

38 E. N. John Cassian (*ca*.360–*ca*.435 AD), also known as John the Ascetic or John the Hermit, was a Christian monk whose fame stems from his role in bringing monasticism to the West from the Middle East. He is best known for this work *Institutes* and *Conferences*. Denis seems to be referring to John Cassian's *Conferences* (chapter 18 of Conference 16).
39 Ecclus. 20:6. E. N. Denis's text departs from the Sixto-Clementine, but not in any significant sense.
40 The editor of the Latin text states that the text between the two crosses is not in the archetype.

furnishing all that has been said and expecting relief from you. For to keep trust while exposed to evil and never to give up is the medicine of wellbeing. Therefore, by the merit of hope, *tu exaudies me, Domine Deus; you will hear me, O Lord my God.* † If, therefore you desire to be heard, hope in God; and to the degree you hope, to that degree you will obtain [what you hope for] — at least if you immediately and worthily pray for those things which pertain to true beatitude and do so in the name of Jesus. Since beatitude is our final end, therefore, it also is to be desired, hoped for, and sought in itself (*per se*); but other things [are to be sought] in accordance to their [proper] order, and neither more nor less than are useful to arrive at beatitude. See how full of trust this word is, *You will hear me, O Lord, my God.*

37{38}[17] *For I said: Lest at any time my enemies rejoice over me: and while my feet are moved, they speak great things against me.*

Quia dixi: Nequando supergaudeant mihi inimici mei; et dum commoventur pedes mei, super me magna locuti sunt.

What it is that he desires to be heard follows: 37{38}[17] *Quia dixi, for I said,* in prayer which has been directed to you: *Nequando supergaudeant mihi inimici mei, lest at any time my enemies rejoice over me,* that is, never let evil men or demons who begrudge my spiritual progress unnecessarily rejoice in the ruin of my soul or of their victory over me. And this is what Scripture says: *O Lord, father, and sovereign ruler of my life, leave me not to their counsel.... and my enemy rejoice over me.*[41] *Et dum commoventur pedes mei, and while my feet are moved,* that is, while my desires and my works — by which I advance either toward hell or toward heaven — may be deflected and deviated from the right way, *super me magna locuti sunt, they speak great things against me,* that is, they magnificently vaunted themselves, for they had overcome me, and with boldness rejoiced in it. This is what is said in an earlier Psalm: *They that trouble me will rejoice when I am moved.*[42]

37{38}[18] *For I am ready for scourges: and my sorrow is continually before me.*

Quoniam ego in flagella paratus sum, et dolor meus in conspectu meo semper.

---

41 Ecclus 1, 3b.
42 Ps. 12:5b.

37{38}[19] *For I will declare my iniquity: and I will think for my sin.*
Quoniam iniquitatem meam annuntiabo, et cogitabo pro peccato meo.

Therefore, O Lord, you will hear me, 37{38}[18] *Quoniam ego in flagella paratus sum, for I am ready for scourges,* that is, I have readily undergone the rod of your reproach and punishment for fault; indeed whatever adversities might befall me, I reckon that they happened because of my fault or for the obtaining of grace: for which reason I will bear all things most willingly. *Et dolor meus in conspectu meo semper, and my sorrow is continually before me:* that is, I ought to accept the sorrow, which I deserve by reason of my sins, and it is at all times suitable in consideration of my soul, so that I consider that I have so awfully offended my God as much as the sorrows are to me. And that this is so is clear from this, 37{38}[19] *Quoniam iniquitatem meam annuntiabo, for I will declare my iniquity,* accusing myself before you, and undertaking confession to your vicar, a priest; *et cogitabo pro peccato meo, and I will think for my sin,* that is, I will consider diligently so that I might recall all my sins, confess them, and obtain forgiveness for them.[43] Whence we read in the book of Job: *I will reprove my ways in his sight, and he shall be my savior.*[44] And elsewhere: *He that hides his sins, shall not prosper: but he that shall confess, and forsake them, shall obtain mercy.*[45]

37{38}[20] *But my enemies live, and are stronger than I: and they that hate me wrongfully are multiplied.*
Inimici autem mei vivunt, et confirmati sunt super me: et multiplicati sunt qui oderunt me inique.

---

43 "Confession to a priest is an essential part of the sacrament of Penance: 'All mortal sins of which penitents after a diligent self-examination are conscious must be recounted by them in confession, even if they are most secret and have been committed against the last two precepts of the Decalogue; for these sins sometimes wound the soul more grievously and are more dangerous than those which are committed openly.' When Christ's faithful strive to confess all the sins that they can remember, they undoubtedly place all of them before the divine mercy for pardon. But those who fail to do so and knowingly withhold some, place nothing before the divine goodness for remission through the mediation of the priest, 'for if the sick person is too ashamed to show his wound to the doctor, the medicine cannot heal what it does not know.'" CCC § 1456 (quoting DS 1680).
44 Job 13:15b–16a.
45 Prov. 28:13.

37{38}[21] *They that render evil for good, have detracted me, because I followed goodness.*
Qui retribuunt mala pro bonis detrahebant mihi, quoniam sequebar bonitatem.

37{38}[20] *Inimici autem mei vivunt,* but my enemies live, not the life of grace, but of nature, and they temporarily flourish; *et confirmati sunt super me,* and are stronger than I, that is, they have been made stronger than I, so that I am not able through natural power to prevail over them, overcome all their vexations, temptations, and suggestions, but I stand in need of the help of your grace: as Job describes: *Behold there is no help for me in myself.*[46] *Et multiplicati sunt, qui oderunt me inique;* and they that hate me wrongfully are multiplied, that is, my visible and invisible enemies, who from a destructive hatred seek to ruin my soul, are many. 37{38}[21] *Qui retribuunt mala pro bonis,* they that render evil for good, that is, the ungrateful, *detrahebant mihi,* have detracted me, wrongfully interpreting my words, and placing upon me crimes that I have not committed, so that I do not edify others by my penance, lest they follow my path. Whence follows, *quoniam sequebar bonitatem,* because *I followed goodness:* that is, from the fact that I have withdrawn from evil, and have followed it with virtuous works, they have been moved by ill-will, and have sought to detract me.

37{38}[22] *Forsake me not, O Lord my God: do not depart from me.*
Ne derelinquas me, Domine Deus meus; ne discesseris a me.

37{38}[23] *Attend unto my help, O Lord, the God of my salvation.*
Intende in adiutorium meum, Domine, Deus salutis meae.

37{38}[22] *Ne derelinquas me, Domine Deus meus;* forsake me not, O Lord my God, that is, do not altogether desert me, withdrawing grace; *ne discesseris a me,* do not depart from me, that is, do not increase your distance from me, as if beginning to forsake me, or reducing grace; but 37{38}[23] *Intende in adiutorium meum,* attend to my help, that is, consider that which I am in need of, and with kindness fill, preserve, and perfect that, *Domine, Deus, salutis meae;* O Lord, the God of my salvation, that is, God in whose power is all my happiness, and who is the object and cause of all my beatitude.

---

46 Job 6:13a.

A BRIEF EXCURSUS ON PARTS OF THIS PSALM THAT BEFIT CHRIST

37{38}[12] *My friends and my neighbors have drawn near, and stood against me. And they that were near me stood afar off. And they that sought my soul used violence.*

Amici mei et proximi mei adversum me appropinquaverunt, et steterunt; et qui iuxta me erant, de longe steterunt, et vim faciebant qui quaerebant animam meam.

37{38}[13] *And they that sought evils to me spoke vain things, and studied deceits all the day long.*

Et qui inquirebant mala mihi, locuti sunt vanitates, et dolos tota die meditabantur.

Now briefly in this place, that which pertains to the praise of the penitent can be expounded fittingly of Christ, as in this sense: 37{38}[12] *Amici mei et proximi mei, my friends and my neighbors*, that is, the Jews, who appeared to be my friends, declaring themselves to love God and to expect his Son, Christ: who were my neighbors, because they were born from the seed of Abraham, as also I was; *adversum me appropinquaverunt et steterunt, have drawn near and stood against me*, when, namely, they gathered together in counsel to discuss how to kill me,[47] and when they cried out before Pilate: *Away with him, away with him; crucify him.*[48] *Et qui iuxta me errant, and they that were near me*, that is, those who at one time were disciples of mine, but turned departing, saying, *This saying is hard,*[49] *de longe steterunt, stood far off*, that is, they entirely alienated themselves from me: indeed the Apostles also who before the Passion were near me, as if ready to die with me, fled from me.[50] *Et vim faciebant qui quaerebant animam meam, and they that sought my soul used violence*: that is, the Jews and the ministers of Pilate, who desired to kill me, placed violent hands upon me, seizing me, tying me, striking me, piercing me, and crucifying me. 37{38}[13] *Et qui inquirebant mala, and they that sought evils*, that is, the Jews seeking any occasion to use against me, *mihi locuti sunt vanitates, to me spoke vain things*, that is, words full of praise, saying, *Master we know that you are a true speaker, and teach the way of God in*

---

47 John 11:47.
48 John 19:15a.
49 John 6:61. E. N. This of course relates to Christ's teaching on the Eucharist: *After this many of his disciples went back; and walked no more with him.* John 6:67.
50 Mat. 26:35, 56.

truth, neither care you for any man.[51] *Et dolos tota die meditabantur, and studied deceits all the day long*, thinking about and inquiring what manner they might be able to ensnare me in my words, and flattering me so as to lead me to it, that I might do something more agreeable to them rather than [something that would be] consonant with justice.

37{38}[14]   But I, as a deaf man, heard not: and as a dumb man not opening his mouth.

   Ego autem, tamquam surdus, non audiebam; et sicut mutus non aperiens os suum.

37{38}[15]   And I became as a man that hears not: and that has no reproofs in his mouth.

   Et factus sum sicut homo non audiens, et non habens in ore suo redargutiones.

37{38}[14] *Ego autem tanquam surdus non audiebam*; but I, as a deaf man, heard not. Christ as man, did not hear all which was said against him with bodily ears: he heard, however, many that were present, but he did not hear so as to defend against the vain and evil things that the Jews said about him, because he most patiently endured all things, but like a deaf man, he disregarded all these things. *Et sicut mutus non aperiens os suum, and as a dumb man not opening his mouth.* For Christ during his Passion responded neither to Pilate nor Herod, so that Pilate was astonished at it and he emphatically said: *Speak you not to me?*[52] 37{38}[15] *Et factus sum sicut homo non audiens*, and I became as a man that hears not. For as Luke attests, Herod questioned Jesus with many words; but Jesus did not respond to him with one word.[53] *Et non habens in ore suo redargutiones, and that has no reproofs in his mouth*: that is, during the Passion I so carried myself as they who do not excuse themselves, nor accuse others, but are completely silent. For this reason, Pilate said: *Do you not hear how great testimonies they allege against you?*[54] This is what is said about Christ by Isaiah: *He shall be led as a sheep to the slaughter, and shall be dumb as a lamb before his shearer.*[55] And Peter, speaking of Christ: *When he suffered*, he said, *he threatened not; when he was reviled, he did not revile.*[56]

---

51   Matt. 22:16.
52   John 19:10.
53   Luke 23:9.
54   Matt. 27:13.
55   Is. 53:7b.
56   1 Pet. 2:23. E. N. There is some transposition or internal editing of this verse by Denis.

37{38}[16] *For in you, O Lord, have I hoped: you will hear me, O Lord my God.*

Quoniam in te, Domine, speravi; tu exaudies me, Domine Deus meus.

37{38}[17] *For I said: Lest at any time my enemies rejoice over me: and while my feet are moved, they speak great things against me.*

Quia dixi: Nequando supergaudeant mihi inimici mei; et dum commoventur pedes mei, super me magna locuti sunt.

37{38}[18] *For I am ready for scourges: and my sorrow is continually before me.*

Quoniam ego in flagella paratus sum, et dolor meus in conspectu meo semper.

37{38}[19] *For I will declare my iniquity: and I will think for my sin.*

Quoniam iniquitatem meam annuntiabo, et cogitabo pro peccato meo.

37{38}[16] *Quoniam in te, Domine; for in you, O Lord* Father, *speravi, have I hoped*, according that as man he was in a certain sense a wayfarer (*viator*),[57] *tu exaudies, you will hear me*, whatever from deliberate reason I absolutely pray for.[58] 37{38}[17] *Quia dixi, for I said* in prayer: *Nequando supergaudeant mihi inimici mei, lest at any time my enemies rejoice over me,* that is, the Jews who until the day of Pentecost rejoiced in my death, as if I was entirely extinguished and detained in hell; beyond this time let them not rejoice so about me, but then, by the sending of the Paraclete, through the preaching of the Apostles, by signs and great prodigies, let my name be glorified in their sight. And you may then show me risen, glorified, and raised above the heavenly heights, in order that they might be confounded and made sorrowful by those who rejoice over me. *Et dum commoventur pedes mei, and while my feet are moved,* that is, while I am pierced with nails and am affixed upon the Cross, *super me magna*

---

57 E. N. In various places, Denis expounds on the very limited scope of Christ's virtue of hope given that he, as man, enjoyed the beatific vision from the first moment of his conception. See, e.g., Article XIX (Psalm 4:9), Article XXXVIII (Psalm 15:9) and footnote 1-46 in Volume 1. Christ's hope was limited to the accidental rewards of the Resurrection of the body and its glorification.
58 E. N. "Jesus' filial prayer is the perfect model of prayer in the New Testament. Often done in solitude and in secret, the prayer of Jesus involves a loving adherence to the will of the Father even to the Cross and an absolute confidence in being heard." CCC § 2620.

locuti sunt, they speak great things against me, insulting, deriding, and blaspheming, and saying: Well done, well done, how the king of Israel is crowned! 37{38}[18] *Quoniam ego in flagella paratus sum, for I am ready for scourges.* For Christ was more prepared to suffer all things which had been prophesized of him. For which reason, he told the Father: *Your will be done.*[59] And through the prophet Isaiah he attested: *I have given my body to the strikers, and my cheeks to them that plucked them: I have not turned away my face from them that rebuked me, and spit upon me.*[60] *Et dolor meus in conspectu meo semper, and my sorrow is continually before me*, that is, the Passion which I endured for the world is unceasingly contained in my memory, so that I offer it to the Father, and by its merit I always save men. Whence the Apostle [Paul]: *It behooved him in all things to be made like unto his brethren, that he might become merciful.*[61] Now, the verse which follows Christ does not say in his own person, but in the person of his members or of his Mystical Body,[62] namely, 37{38}[19] *Quoniam iniquitatem meam anuntiabo [et cogitabo pro peccato meo]; for I will declare my iniquity: [and I will think for my sin].*[63]

37{38}[20] But my enemies live, and are stronger than I: and they that hate me wrongfully are multiplied.

Inimici autem mei vivunt, et confirmati sunt super me: et multiplicati sunt qui oderunt me inique.

37{38}[21] They that render evil for good, have detracted me, because I followed goodness.

Qui retribuunt mala pro bonis detrahebant mihi, quoniam sequebar bonitatem.

37{38}[22] Forsake me not, O Lord my God: do not depart from me.

Ne derelinquas me, Domine Deus meus; ne discesseris a me.

---

59 Matt. 26:42.
60 Is. 50:6.
61 Heb. 2:17: E. N. The verse continues: *that he might become a merciful and faithful priest before God, that he might be a propitiation for the sins of the people.*
62 E. N. This is an excellent example of the application of Tyconius's first rule where language referring to the person of Christ *qua* Christ will transition into Christ *qua* Mystical Body. See Article IV, Volume 1. There is therefore a modulation as the Psalm moves from the *vox Christi*, the voice of Christ, to the *vox Ecclesiae*, the voice of the Church (also known as the *vox totius Christi*, the voice of the whole Christ, or the *vox Corporis Mystici*, the voice of the Mystical Body of Christ).
63 E. N. The words in brackets replace Denis's "etc."

37{38}[23] *Attend unto my help, O Lord, the God of my salvation.*
Intende in adiutorium meum, Domine, Deus salutis meae.

37{38}[20] *Inimici autem mei vivunt*, but my enemies live, that is, the Jews then for a time were vigorous, *et confirmati sunt super me*, and are stronger than I, as far as this: that they were able to put me to death; *et multiplicati sunt, and they . . . are multiplied*, by both number and malice, not in virtue and grace, *qui oderunt me inique, that hate me wrongfully*, namely, the Jews who willingly hated both me and my Father,[64] saying: *This is the heir: come, let us kill him.*[65] 37{38}[21] *Qui retribuunt mala pro bonis, they that render evil for good*, that is, the ungrateful Jews, to whom I gave many excellent benefits teaching, doing miracles, *detrahebant mihi, have detracted me*, saying among themselves: He seduces the people, he is mad, he is a glutton;[66] *quoniam sequebar bonitatem, because I have followed goodness*, that is, because I lived in a just manner regarding all things, and I was not silent regarding their vices. Whence Christ said of the ungrateful Jews through the prophet Micah: O my people, what have I done to you, or in what have I molested you? Answer me.[67] 37{38}[22] *Ne derelinquas me, Domine Deus meus; forsake me not, O Lord my God*, that is, do not forsake my body in the sepulcher, but vivify it on the third day; *ne discesseris a me, do not depart from me*, that is, do not abandon my soul in hell beyond the third day.[68] 37{38}[23] *Intende in adiutorium meum, attend unto my help*, that is, assist and work with me, so that I might lead out of the limbo of hell all saints, and with them climb up into heaven, *Domine, Deus salutis meae, O Lord, the God of my salvation*, that is, O God three-in-one, who is the cause of the salvation of all that is created in me.

See how this Psalm is so full of affection, and how admirably it instructs what it is that befits a true penitent, namely, that he vigorously magnify and humbly set forth his sins, and be ready to suffer any penalty. But because this Psalm is one of the Penitential Psalms,[69] we

---

64 John 15:24b.
65 Mat. 21:38b. E. N. This is derived from Jesus's Parable of the Wicked Husbandmen, Matt. 21:33–46; see also Luke 20:9–19 and Mark 12:1–12.
66 John 23:12b, John 10:20b, Matt. 21:38a. Luke 23:2 (perverting our nation).
67 Micah 6:3.
68 E. N. This is not the hell of the damned, but Sheol or the *limbus partum*, the "hell" of the Creed that Christ descended to during the "harrowing" of hell. For the limbo of the Fathers (*limbus patrum*) see Article LXI (Psalm 27:1) and see footnote 23-14 of Volume 1.
69 E. N. Traditionally, there are seven such Penitential Psalms: Psalms 6, 30, 37, 50, 101, 129, and 142.

ought especially to labor that we may understand it clearly (for in some ways it is obscure), and we may recite it devoutly. For some expound it as literally being of David: which exposition seems to be less fruitful, because it does not show how it can be read by anyone as applying to his own person. But Cassiodorus expounded it in the person of Job.[70]

PRAYER

SEEKING THE EAR OF YOUR KINDNESS, we suppliantly beg, O Lord our God, that you do not forsake us, and that you do not withdraw from us: grant that what it is not possible for us to have in the nature of our weakness, we might perceive to be given to us by your grace.

Aurem pietatis tuae quaerentes, supplices deprecamur, ne nos, Domine Deus noster, derelinquas, ne a nobis discedas: praesta, ut quod in natura fragilitatis nostrae possibile non habemus, per tuam gratiam nobis subministrari sentiamus.

---

70 See Cassiodorus, *Explanations of the Psalms* (Mahwah, NJ: Paulist 1990), Vol. 1, 337 *ff*. (P. G. Walsh, trans.)

Psalm 38

ARTICLE LXXVII
EXPOSITION OF THE THIRTY-EIGHT PSALM:
DIXI, CUSTODIAM VIAS MEAS, &c.
I SAID: I WILL TAKE HEED OF MY WAYS, &c.

38{39}[1] *Unto the end, for Jedithun himself, a canticle of David.*
In finem, ipsi Idithun. Canticum David.

THIS PSALM IS INTRODUCED WITH THIS title: **38{39}[1]** *In finem, canticum David, pro Idithun; unto the end, for Jedithun himself, a canticle of David.* As we see written in the first book of Chronicles, the holy David installed two hundred and eighty-eight singers so that they might sing divine praises in the house of the Lord in alternation.[1] And he set in authority three principle cantors, namely Asaph, Heman, and Jeduthun. And David wrote Psalms which would be sung by his cantors. Therefore, this Psalm was sung by Jedithun and those under him.[2] But Jedithun is interpreted as meaning "jumping across others":[3] by which is designated a faithful and true Israelite, not by word, but in spirit, not by descent of the flesh, but by firmness of the faith, who forsakes earthly things, and flies to the heavenly things through contemplation. Therefore, the sense of this title is: *In the end, a canticle of David*, that is, this Psalm, which is called a canticle because it contains spiritual joy[4] and which has to do with eternal beatitude, is ascribed to David as author: the canticle, I say, directs us towards Christ, who is the *Alpha and Omega, the beginning and the end;*[5] and *for Jedithun himself,* that is it is fitting to a perfect man leaping across time, who with the Apostle [Paul] is able to say: *Unhappy man that I*

---

1 1. Chr. chps. 16, 25. E. N. This number of singers was divided into twenty-four orders, each to serve on a particular day.
2 E. N. There are three Psalms which bear Jeduthun's name: Psalm 38(39), 62(63), and 76(77).
3 E. N. This interpretation of the Jedithun (or Jedithun) was a commonplace in medieval commentators, but not accurate. The root of the name comes from the Hebrew ידי (*yada*), which means to praise or to confess.
4 For the various kinds of Psalms, including canticle, *see* footnote 29-1.
5 Rev. 1:8, 22:13.

am! *Who shall deliver me from the body of this death?*[6] And again: *But our conversation is in heaven.*[7]

38{39}[2] *I said: I will take heed to my ways: that I sin not with my tongue. I have set guard to my mouth, when the sinner stood against me.*

Dixi: Custodiam vias meas; ut non delinquam in lingua mea: posui ori meo custodiam cum consisteret peccator adversum me.

38{39}[3] *I was dumb, and was humbled, and kept silence from good things: and my sorrow was renewed.*

Obmutui, et humiliatus sum, et silui a bonis; et dolor meus renovatus est.

Therefore, speaking in the person of the Church or a virtuous man, desiring with an ardent desire to make progress, the Prophet [David] says: **38{39}[2]** *Dixi, I said,* that is, I have constantly proposed, and asserted with my heart and mouth: *custodiam vias meas: I will take heed of my ways,* that is, I will guard my thoughts, my affections, and my deeds from disorder and fault, which are here called "ways," because by them I tend to a certain end, namely, to heavenly felicity or to infernal misery. *Ut non delinquam in lingua mea, that I sin not with my tongue:* that is, to this end I will remain steadfast in guarding my ways, so that I do not offend in word, but in every way I might temper my lips. See how notable, full of meaning, and instructive this verse is. For it touches upon three most useful things. First it touches upon the resolution of doing good when it says, *I said.* Second, it touches upon that which a good resolution ought to strive for when it adds, *I will take heed of my ways.* Third, it touches upon that in which his perfection constitutes, at least in exterior matters, since it adds, *that I sin not with my tongue.*

Therefore, if you desire to strive the moderation of the tongue and true perfection: First, in your heart make a firm resolution to yourself fervently to advance, and never to pull away from the divine law. This was the resolution of holy Job, saying, *Until I die I will not depart from my innocence;*[8] and Peter, who said to Christ, *Yea, though I should die with you, I will not deny you.*[9] But pay attention that this is not resolving to lean upon your own

---

6   Rom. 7:24.
7   Phil 3:20a.
8   Job. 27:5b.
9   Matt. 26:35.

strength, but humbly leaning upon the graces of the most merciful Creator, considering that which Jeremiah said, *I know, O Lord, that the way of a man is not his: neither is it in a man to walk, and to direct his steps;*[10] and that of the Apostle [Paul], *It is not of him that wills, nor of him that runs, but of God that shows mercy.*[11] Second, busy yourself with keeping guard in all your ways, wisely considering the testimony of Scripture and the example of the Saints, as to what pleases God, what is good, what is better, what is the best. For this the Apostle [Paul] admonished: *See ... how you walk circumspectly;*[12] and again, *with fear*, he says, *and trembling work out your salvation.*[13] Whence, Solomon asserts: *Blessed is the man that is always fearful.*[14] In this way, Job kept guard of his ways, as he attests: *I feared all my works, knowing that you did not spare the offender.*[15] And finally, third, fulfill that which is perfect, namely, that you not sin with your tongue. In this [control of the tongue] a kind of beatitude exists, as it states in Ecclesiasticus: *Blessed is the man that has not slipped by a word out of his mouth.*[16] And James says: *If any man offend not in word, the same is a perfect man.*[17] But in order that one not sin with his tongue, there are many things that must be observed. First, he must not speak about something illicit, because as the Apostle [Paul] attests: *Evil communications corrupt good manners.*[18] And to Timothy: *And their speech spreads like a cancer.*[19] Second, we need to be mindful that we speak of good things and licit things, as the Apostle [Paul] says: *Speak the things that become sound doctrine.*[20] For the most important thing in having command of the tongue is to desist from evil, and then to undertake the good.

But because a good work ought to be done well, namely, in accord with the circumstances that are required by an act of virtue, so in speaking about good things [we ought keep the following in mind]: First, taking care to whom we speak, so that we might also proportion our speech according to the exigency, the condition, and the quality of him with whom we speak, not perchance presuming to teach the more wise, to chide those more

---

10 Jer. 10:23.
11 Rom. 9:16.
12 Eph. 5:15.
13 Phil. 2:12b.
14 Prov. 28:14a.
15 Job 9:28.
16 Ecclus. 14:1a.
17 James 3:2a.
18 1 Cor. 15:33b.
19 2 Tim. 2:17a.
20 Titus 2:1.

old, to praise the vain, to counsel inexpertly, to reproach the obstinate, to instruct the unheeding, to propose something lofty to the more simple, or to pour out words among the foolish. For this is well stated: *Young man, scarcely speak in your own cause. If you are asked twice, let your answer be short.*[21] And again: *In the company of great men do not presume to speak: and when the ancients are present, speak not much;*[22] and *Where there is no hearing, pour not out words.*[23] Solomon also: *Speak not in the ears of fools: because they will despise the instruction of your speech.*[24] The second thing to keep in mind is when the proper time is for speaking: for there is *a time to keep silence, and a time to speak.*[25] For it is time to be quiet when nothing useful is expected to be born from words or nothing useful is hoped for; however, it is time to speak when one has probable hope of obtaining salubrious fruit. Whence elsewhere it is written: *A wise man will hold his peace till he see opportunity: but a babbler, and a fool, will regard no time.*[26] Third, we ought to think where the speaking takes place, for example, not in the church, nor in prohibited places. Fourth, how much [we speak], that is to say, not more than is fitting or expedient. For this reason, Solomon says: *In the multitude of words there shall not want sin: but he that refrains his lips is most wise.*[27] And again: *A fool utters all his mind: a wise man defers, and keeps it till afterwards.*[28] Whence, elsewhere we have: *The words of the wise shall be weighed in a balance.*[29] Therefore, our speech should be dressed with the seasoning of discretion, in the way the Apostle [Paul] says: *Let your speech be always in grace seasoned with salt: that you may know how you ought to answer every man.*[30] Fifth, we ought to think how something should be spoken, namely, modestly, gently, and sweetly. Whence, Solomon says: *A mild answer breaks wrath: but a harsh word stirs up fury.*[31] And Ecclesiasticus: *A sweet word multiplies friends, and appeases enemies, and a gracious tongue in a good man abounds.*[32] And therefore the Apostle [Paul] admonishes: *Contend not*

---

21 Ecclus. 32:10–11.
22 Ecclus. 32:13.
23 Ecclus. 32:6a.
24 Prov. 23:9.
25 Eccl. 3:7b.
26 Ecclus. 20:7.
27 Prov. 10:19.
28 Prov. 29:11.
29 Ecclus 21:28b.
30 Col. 4:6.
31 Prov. 15:1.
32 Ecclus. 6:5.

in words, for it is to no profit, but to the subverting of the hearers.[33] And sixth and lastly and most especially, we ought to consider, why — that is, with what intention — we speak. Now without question the general, final, and highest intention [in our speech] should be the honor of God. Yet there can be many and various secondary and proximate intentions, for example, to instruct another, or that we might be instructed by another, or for recreation, or similar reason. And, in accordance with the measure of the final intention [which is the honor of God], we ought to consider, keeping in mind all that we have said, whether we may achieve that final intention through that which we wish to speak.

For if we think and observe these things then we will not sin with our tongue; yet no one is strong enough to fulfill this through natural virtue, according to that which was said by James: *But the tongue no man can tame.*[34] But by grace it can be done, as we read: *It is the part of man to prepare the soul: and of the Lord to govern the tongue.*[35] Let us invoke, therefore, the grace of Christ, and let us say that which we find in a later Psalm: *Set a watch, O Lord, before my mouth: and a door round about my lips.*[36] Moreover, that which is now said — *I will take heed of my ways* — is most clearly expressed in a later Psalm, where the Psalmist says: *I have sworn and am determined to keep the judgments of your justice.*[37]

Posui ori meo custodiam, I have set guard to my mouth, lest I speak incautiously or maliciously to someone, *dum consisteret peccator adversum me, when the sinner stood against me,* intending to provoke me or to deceive me with his words. Let us not return, therefore, an evil word for an evil word, in the manner that Solomon commands: *Say not: I will return evil: wait for the Lord and he will deliver you.*[38] **38{39}[3]** *Obmitui, I was dumb* not with disdain, but from patience and prudence, seeing I would profit nothing by speaking; *et humiliatus sum, and was humbled,* that is, in my heart I thought myself deserving of being attacked with defamatory and evil words; *et silui a bonis, and kept silence from good things,* [from good] words: because they speaking evil about me were unwilling to receive an excusing, satisfactory, or reasonable response. Therefore, I considered it better to be silent in all things than to offer good words of truth to those who held me in contempt.

---

33 2 Tim. 2:14.
34 James 3:8a.
35 Prov. 16:1.
36 Ps. 140:3.
37 Ps. 118:106.
38 Prov. 20:22.

Et dolor meus renovatus est, and my sorrow was renewed: because while I suffered punishment and injuries from others, I recalled anew my sins, for which I deserved being the subject of anger, and so I sorrow as if I had recently sinned. For punishment and adversities inflicted upon sinners bring back to their memories the evil which they have done, according to this: *I will chastise you in judgment, that you may not seem to yourself innocent.*[39] Or [we might think of it this way]: *My sorrow was renewed*, that is, as before I sorrowed as a result of my own fault, so in a way I am saddened by the sins of my neighbors and by the various errors of the world. For such sorrow proceeds from charity and is very meritorious and pleasing to God. Which [sorrow] Jeremiah expressed he was familiar with, since he said: *Who will give water to my head, and a fountain of tears to my eyes, and I will weep day and night for the slain... of my people?*[40] And if it is pious to lament those killed in body, how much more benevolent is it to lament the dead in soul? And so this sorrow the Apostle [Paul] also confessed himself to have, since he said: *I have great sadness, and continual sorrow in my heart, for I wished myself to be an anathema from Christ, for my brethren, the Jews.*[41] Whence also the holy Micah, the prophet of God, with regard to Israel, whose future punishments he predicted, felt compassion for them, so that he said: *Would God I were not a man that has the spirit, and that I rather spoke a lie.*[42] You see, therefore, how ineffably lively is the brotherly love of the saints, even for the ungrateful and the ungodly. For here, Moses said to the Lord: *Either forgive them this trespass, or if you do not, strike me out of the book that you have written.*[43] Undoubtedly this sort of compassion especially belongs to prelates.[44]

---

39 Jer. 30:11b.
40 Jer. 9:1. E. N. The verse reads "weep day and night for the slain of the daughter (*filiae*) of my people." Denis leaves out the "of the daughter" (*filiae*).
41 Rom. 9:2–3.
42 Micah 2:11a. E. N. In his Commentary on this verse, Denis explains that Micah, in saying that he wishes he were not a prophet or was able to say something other than the truth, speaks hyperbolically, and not literally, the way that St. Paul does in Romans 9: 2–3, because he sorrowed greatly at having to prophesy that so many of his fellow Jews would reject Christ, the Son of God. Doctoris Estatici D. Dionysii Cartusiani, *Opera Omnia*, Vol. 10 (Montreuil: 1900), 480–81.
43 Ex. 32:31b–32. E. N. The context is Moses interceding for the Hebrew people who had sinned by worshipping the golden calf.
44 E. N. Those with the cure of souls, the *cura animarum*, namely, bishops, abbots, even priests.

38{39}[4] My heart grew hot within me: and in my meditation a fire shall flame out.

Concaluit cor meum intra me; et in meditatione mea exardescet ignis.

38{39}[4] *Concaluit cor meum intra me,* my heart grew hot within me: that is, while I was so dumb, and recently afflicted with sorrow, my soul was kindled with ardent desire, in order that it might acquire in the present for itself the perfection of grace, and it might be more stirred to be led to the light of glory, and that it might save neighbors from error and provide aid to those in need. Did not the heart within Paul grow hot like this when he said, *My dearly beloved brethren, and most desired, my joy and my crown; so stand fast in the Lord?*[45] *Et in meditatione mea exardescet ignis,* and in my meditation a fire shall flame out: that is, in consideration of the goodness and the benefits of God, and in consideration of the dangers and of the vices which entangle men, the love of God and neighbor will be inflamed in me, so that I by rebuking, instructing, and exhorting might impede injuries to God and might assist brothers unto salvation. It is necessary that preachers and teachers of the word of God fulfill this from the fervor of charity, with all constancy and strength of mind, in the manner that Micah attests as to himself: *I,* he says, *am filled with the strength of the spirit of the Lord, with judgment, and power: to declare unto ... Israel his sin.*[46] For which reason the Apostle [Paul] says: *Preach the word: be instant in season, out of season: reprove, entreat, rebuke in all patience.*[47]

38{39}[5] I spoke with my tongue: O Lord, make me know my end. And what is the number of my days: that I may know what is wanting to me.

Locutus sum in lingua mea: Notum fac mihi, Domine, finem meum, et numerum dierum meorum quis est, ut sciam quid desit mihi.

38{39}[5] *Locutus sum in lingua mea,* I spoke with my tongue, that is, with my mouth, namely, secretly praying, in the manner that the mother of Samuel was led to: *Now Hannah spoke in her heart, and only her lips moved, but her voice was not heard at all.*[48] But what is spoken in prayer

---

45   Phil 4:1.
46   Micah 3:8.
47   2 Tim. 4:2.
48   1 Sam. 1:13. E. N. Hannah was praying to the Lord for a son, which prayer was answered when she conceived the great prophet Samuel, the birth of whom resulted

is indicated by what follows: *Notum fac mihi, Domine, finem meum; O Lord, make me know my end.* Our consuming end (*finis consumens*), is death; but the consummating end (*finis consummans*) is God or eternal life.[49] For God is the extrinsic objective end (*finis obiectalis extrinsecus*); but beatitude or eternal life is our intrinsic end (*finis noster intrinsecus*). Therefore, when it says, *make me know my end*, one can expound every one of these ends. With respect to the consuming end, we can understand it in this sense: *O Lord, make me know my end*, that is, grant to me to consider my approaching death daily, so that assiduous mediation on death might make me strongly separate from, and diligently vigilant against, sin: in the way Ecclesiasticus says, *In all your works remember your last end, and you shall never sin.*[50] And in the Gospel, Christ says: *Watch therefore, because you know not the day nor the hour.*[51] The second [exposition, based upon understanding the end as referring to the consummating end] is thus: *O Lord, make me know my end*, that is, you yourself, that I might consider myself created because of you; and so restless is my heart until it comes to you and holds fast to nothing else but you.[52] The third [exposition, based upon the understanding of end as the objective end is] thus: *O Lord, make me know my end*, that is, grant me to attend to that heavenly beatitude, for which you have created my soul, and not in any other fleeting created good, but let my soul order itself to you alone as its end. For this reason the Apostle [Paul] says: *May the Father of glory give unto you the spirit of wisdom ... that you may know what the hope is to which you have been called,*[53] that is, that you may know what hope is awaiting, to that which he calls us. But the thing that is hoped for is eternal beatitude, which is our end. It is this, therefore, that we pray to him to reveal, when we say: *O Lord, make me know my end.*

Also make me to know *et numerum dierum meorum, quis est; and what is the number of my days.* This can be understood in two ways. First, of

---

in her the beautiful hymn or poem of thanks known as the Song of Hannah (1 Sam. 2:1–10).
49 E. N. Denis has a play on words between the word *consumens*, a consuming of something, and *consummans*, the consummating of something.
50 Ecclus. 7:40.
51 Matt. 25:13.
52 E. N. Here, of course, is a reference to the *cor inquietum*, the "restless heart," of St. Augustine which we find in his famous plaint about how too late in life he recognized the end, the *finis consummans*, for which he was created: *Tu excitas ut laudare te delectet quia fecisti nos ad te et inquietum est cor nostrum donec requiescat in te*, "You rouse [man] that he might delight to praise you, for you have made us for yourself, and our heart is restless until it rests in you." *Conf.* I, 1, 1, PL 32, 657.
53 Eph. 1:17b–18a.

the days of the present life, so that it reads in this sense: give to me the grace actually to heed and diligently to think about how brief and how evil and full of misery are the days in which I live in this world, so that by regarding lightly this present life I might with all my heart aspire to the future. This asks to be as [those people the] Apostle [Paul] [refers to when he] says, *They that use this world, as if they used it not: for the fashion of this world passes away;*[54] and again, *We have not here a lasting city, but we seek one that is to come.*[55] Secondly, we can understand this as referring to the days of the future age, which are called days of eternity. And so this is its sense: give to me to contemplate by faith, so that I might always desire it, that duration, that embracing length of innumerable days, namely, that aeviternity (*aevum*) in which the blessed in the heavenly homeland reign without end. This duration of the blessed (*duratio beatorum*) is called *the number of* our *days*, which is, that is to say, that they do not have succession, adulteration, or end, but it truly exists, because it fixedly remains. But it is not like the number of days of this life, because these days do not stand still, and we have nothing of time except for a *Now*: which also is not time, nor a part of time, but by its flow causes time. Whence this duration of aeviternity can be called many days or a number of days because it includes all time, and [also] one day, for in reality it is unable to be multiplied. Therefore, it is written of it: *And there shall be one day, which is known to the Lord, not day nor night... and in that day... the Lord shall be king over all the earth.*[56] And in designation the unending permanence of this duration or this day, Isaiah says of it: *And there shall be month after month, and sabbath after sabbath.*[57]

---

54 1 Cor. 7:31.
55 Heb. 13:14.
56 Zech. 14:7–9.
57 The term *aevum* was used by Scholastic theologians to refer to the time that has a beginning (as creation does) but not an end. Thus, it is distinguishable from eternity which has neither beginning nor end, and utterly different from time because it is outside order of matter. St. Thomas makes clear that eviternity is different from time and from eternity both, and he refers to it as "the mean existing between them": *aevum differt a tempore et ab aeternitate, sicut medium existens inter illa.* ST Ia, q. 10, art. 5, co. Clearly, Denis's point is that human language is inadequate to express this concept, and he points to the various ways the prophets stutter about it. Frank Sheed tackled this intermediate state between the eternity of God (and his changelessness or immutability) and the constant flux of time (we experience while living within matter). "Time is the duration of that which changes, as eternity is the duration of that which changes not. But what of spirit? Because it knows change at all, even if only accidental change, it is not in eternity; but because the changes it knows are not continuous, it is not exactly in time either.... For this duration

And so, O Lord, *make me know what is the number of my days, ut sciam quid desit mihi, that I may know what is wanting in me,* that is, so that I might diligently know how much is wanting in me of perfection and of grace in my forward march to those eternal days; or that I may solicitously think, from the consideration of the brevity of days which I will live in this life, what is wanting in me of the spiritual advance and the interior improvement, and, in the little time that here remains for me, I might quickly direct myself towards the heavenly homeland, and exclude all torpor, fervently devoting myself to you. For thus the Apostle [Paul] says: *Let us hasten therefore to enter into that rest.*[58]

38{39}[6] *Behold you have made my days measurable: and my substance is as nothing before you. And indeed all things are vanity: every man living.*

Ecce mensurabiles posuisti dies meos, et substantia mea tamquam nihilum ante te. Verumtamen universa vanitas, omnis homo vivens.

38{39}[6] *Ecce mensurabiles, behold . . . measurable,* that is, brief and easily numbered, *posuisti dies meo, you have made my days:* which I will live according to your ordering of this world. Whence, it is written clearly in a later Psalm: *The days of our years in them are threescore and ten years.*[59] And Job: *The days of man are short, and the number of his months is with you: you have appointed his bounds which cannot be passed.*[60] *Et substantia mea tanquam nihilum ante te, and my substance is as nothing before you:* that is, my own subsisting, which I see as something else in comparison to your immensity, and that I am more nothing than something: because between the finite and the infinite there exists no proportion.[61] For which reason we read in Isaiah: *Behold the Gentiles*

---

too there is a word—the word *aevum* or aeviternity, the duration of that which is its essence of substance that knows no change: though by its accidents it can know change, and to that extent is in time, too, but a sort of discontinuous time, not the ever-flowing time of matter. Aeviternity is the proper sphere of every created spirit, and therefore of the human soul [following its death]." Frank Sheed, *Theology and Sanity* (New York: Sheed & Ward 1946), 115–16.
58 Heb. 4:11a.
59 Ps. 89:10a. The Psalm continues in part: *But if in the strong they be fourscore years: and what is more of them is labor and sorrow.*
60 Job 14:5.
61 *E. N. In IV Sent.* 49, 2, 1, ad 6, St. Thomas specifically says *quod quamvis finiti ad infinitum non possit esse proportio,* there is no proportion between finite and

are as a drop of a bucket, and are counted as the smallest grain of a balance. All nations are before him as if they had no being at all, and are counted to him as nothing, and vanity[62] Here also Nebuchadnezzar experiencing the majesty of God, humbly uttered: *I, Nebuchadnezzar, lifted up my eyes to heaven, and my sense was restored to me: and I blessed the most High, and I praised and glorified him that lives forever, for his power is an everlasting power... and all inhabitants of the earth are reputed as nothing before him.*[63]

Verumtamen universa vanitas, and indeed all things are vanity: that is, not only is my substance as nothing before God, but also all things, greatly inferior and corruptible, are vanity, that is, are trifling, unstable, unhappy, and fleeting: in the manner that Ecclesiastes says, *Vanity of vanities, and all is vanity*;[64] and the Apostle [Paul], *For the creature*, he says, *was made subject to vanity.*[65] *Omnis homo vivens*, every man living: that is, not only irrational things, but also every man in the wayfaring state and every sinner, is vanity, that is, subject to change and to many miseries. Or thus [it can be interpreted]: *And indeed all things are vanity, every man living*, that is, so great is this misery and imperfection of man because of the evil of fault (*mala culpae*), the evil of punishment (*mala poenae*), and the evil of nature (*mala naturae*) which is in him,[66] that all men according to common law are able to be said to be universally vanity, that is, totally vain and fully of vanity. For which reason, Paul speaking of the Apostles said: *We*, he said, *groan within ourselves, who have accepted the first fruits of the spirit, waiting for* the revelation of the glory of God.[67]

---

infinite. Denis's reflections on our nothingness brings to mind a prayer by his fellow Carthusian, Dom Jean-Baptiste Porion: *Mon Dieu, je crois que vous êtes ici présent en moi, moi pauvre néant. Si je n'étais que néant! mais je Vous ai offensé, je me suis révolté contre Vous. Je suis donc au-dessous du néant.* Jean-Baptiste Porion, O. Cart., *Écrits Spirituels* (Casalibus 1992), 11. "My God, I believe that you are present in me, even though I am nothing. Indeed, I am less than nothing since I have offended you and rebelled against you! I am therefore below nothing."
62 Is. 40:15a, 17.
63 Dan. 4:31–32a.
64 Eccl. 1:2b.
65 Rom. 8:20a.
66 E. N. For the difference between evil of fault (*mala culpae*) and evil of punishment (*mala poena*), see footnote 21-146 in Volume 1. In speaking of the evil of nature (*mala naturae*), Denis is not suggesting that human nature is evil or depraved absolutely; rather, he is referring to the evil arising from the Fall, from original sin, which is a lack of an order that should be there. It could also include natural evils (disease and natural defects or natural dangers).
67 Rom. 8:23. Denis departs significantly from the text, almost paraphrasing it.

38{39}[7] *Surely man passes as an image: yea, and he is disquieted in vain. He stores up: and he knows not for whom he shall gather these things.*

Verumtamen in imagine pertransit homo; sed et frustra conturbatur: thesaurizat, et ignorat cui congregabit ea.

38{39}[7] *Verumtamen in imagine pertransit homo*, surely man passes as an image: that is, since man is so much vanity, so also is he passing in image, that is, the image of the holy Trinity by which his soul is signed, lives in time and runs towards the end. Or [we can understand it] thus: *surely man passes as an image*, that is, so quickly does his life flow and run out, as an image appearing in a mirror, and a shadow which appears on earth,[68] in the manner that is said in Job: *Our days upon earth are but a shadow;*[69] and elsewhere, *We all die, and like waters...we fall down into the earth.*[70] *Sed et frustra conturbatur, and he is disquieted in vain*: that is, beyond this fact—that the present life is so brief—man himself is troubled and anxious where he ought not to be anxious or troubled, namely, in the amassing or the loss of temporal things: and so he is entangled with the solicitude of worldly things, as if he would never be called from this world. And so it follows: *Thesaurizat, he stores up*, that is, he gathers together temporal wealth, *et ignorat cui congregabit ea, and he knows not for whom he shall gather these things*. For since death is uncertain, he is unable to know whether he will long use his riches. And in a similar way, he does not know whether his sons or another, to whom he proposes to leave his goods, will long possess them. This storing up of riches is therefore vain. Whence, to this method—of storing up, and proposing to take delight in riches, and saying to oneself: *Soul, you have much goods laid up for many years, take your rest; eat, drink, make good cheer*—God says: *You fool, this night do they require your soul of you: and whose shall those things be which you have provided?*[71] Other Scripture also says this: *Where are the princes of the nations, and they that rule over the beasts that are upon the earth, that take their diversion with the birds of the air, that hoard up silver and gold, wherein men trust,*

---

68 E. N. "Tomorrow, and tomorrow, and tomorrow, / Creeps in this petty pace from day to day / To the last syllable of recorded time, / And all our yesterdays have lighted fools / The way to dusty death. Out, out, brief candle! / Life's but a walking shadow, a poor player / That struts and frets his hour upon the stage / And then is heard no more." Shakespeare, *Macbeth*, 5.5.19–27.
69 Job 8:9b.
70 2 Sam. 14:14a.
71 Luke 12:9–20.

and there is no end of their getting?[72] They have been exterminated, and they have descended into hell, and others have risen into their place. But there is also another kind of storing up which is good, of which the Savior says: *Make to yourselves bags which grow not old, a treasure in heaven which fails not.*[73] Of the possession of, and taking delight in, this sort of storing up, it is written in Isaiah: *The riches of salvation, wisdom and knowledge: the fear of the Lord is his treasure.*[74]

38{39}[8] *And now what is my hope? Is it not the Lord? And my substance is with you.*

Et nunc quae est exspectatio mea: nonne Dominus? Et substantia mea apud te est.

38{39}[8] *Et nunc quae est exspectatio mea? Nonne Dominus? And what is now my hope? Is it not the Lord?* See, here is expressed that the prayer, which above this was poured out to the Lord, has been heard, [that is, the prayer] saying *O Lord make me know my end,* that is, the final and ultimate and highest good for which I ought to strive. And therefore it says: *Et nunc, and now,* that is, while others store things up on earth, *where the rust, and moth consume, and where thieves break through and steal,*[75] *quae est exspectatio mea? what is my hope?* that is, what is the thing that I finally await and which is most supremely to be chosen? And he responds: *Nonne Dominus? Is it not the Lord?* It is as if he were saying, "Surely it is God, glorious and holy, whom I finally expect, and toward whom I order all things." For God is the entirety of our good, and he is our all, and *one thing* (that is he) *is necessary.*[76] Therefore, by Isaiah is said: *For the Lord is our judge, the Lord is our lawgiver, the Lord is our king: he will save us.*[77]

Et substantia mea apud te est, and my substance is with you. Sometimes the word substance is accepted as meaning riches or possessions, in the way we find written of the father of the prodigal son: *And he divided unto them his substance.*[78] But the riches of the saints are virtuous works, and charity and grace, and the other gifts of the Holy Spirit. And these are

---

72 Baruch 3:16–19a.
73 Luke 12:33.
74 Is. 33:6.
75 Matt. 6:19.
76 Luke 10:42a.
77 Is. 33:22.
78 Luke 15:12b.

riches before God, for they please him, and they receive a reward from him, as that said in Jeremiah: *Let your voice cease from weeping,... for there is a reward for your work.*[79] Of these riches, therefore, he says: *my substance*, that is, my interior riches, namely merits and rewards, are with you, that is, in the good pleasure of your memory. But while it says earlier [in verse six of this Psalm], *My substance is as nothing before you*, this assumed the word substance as meaning one's essence or exterior goods. Yet it is also possible now to accept it [*i.e.*, the word substance as used in this verse eight] as meaning essence. For those who are said to be in God are said to be with God, as is said of the Son, *The Word was with God*,[80] that is, in God, according to that which the Son speaking to the Father attested to: *You, Father, in me, and I in you.*[81] And understood in this fashion our substances — as indeed, all creation — are with God, because all things are in him. That which *was made*, that is, all that is not God, namely all creation, *in him was life.*[82] For all live unto God, and all are alive in him. For which reason, the Apostle [Paul] says: *of him, and by him, and in him, are all things.*[83]

---

79 Jer. 31:16a.
80 John 1:1b.
81 John 17:21a.
82 John 1:3b, 4a. E. N. "[T]he divine nature is not only *being* but also *life*; the divine existence is a *living existence....* Life is one of God's products, consequently it must be in Him. However, it is not in God as it is in the universe." Charles R. Baschab, *A Manual of Neo-Scholastic Philosophy* (St. Louis: B. Herder Book Co. 1923), 422.
83 Rom. 11:36. Denis is here referring *not* to the supernatural life, the life of grace, but to the natural life, not to God as Redeemer, but rather to God as Creator, as First Cause. "'Not only does God watch over and administer every thing that exists: the things that are moved and that act He also impels by intrinsic power to motion and action in such a way that, without hindering the operation of secondary causes, He (as it were) goes before it (*præveniat*), since His hidden might belongs to each thing, and, as the Wise Man testifies, 'He reacheth from end to end mightily, and ordereth all things sweetly.' Wherefore it was said by the Apostle, when preaching to the Athenians the God Whom they worshipped unwittingly: 'He is not far from every one of us, for in Him we live and move and be" (Catechism of the Council of Trent, pt. i., ch. ii., n. 22). Holy Scripture refers to the Divine Concurrence in the texts which ascribe to God the operations of creatures, or which directly attribute to Him the effects of created activity. 'There are diversities of operations, but the same God Who worketh all in all' (ὁ ἐνεργῶν τὰ πάντα ἐν πᾶσιν, 1 Cor. 12:6); 'My Father worketh until now, and I work' (John 5:17); 'It is He Who giveth to all life, and breath, and all things.... Although He be not far from every one of us; for in Him we live and move and be' (Acts 17:25, 28); 'Of Him, and by Him, and in Him are all things' (ἐξ αὐτοῖ καὶ δι' αὐτοῦ καὶ εἰς αὐτὸν τὰ πάντα, Rom. 11:36)." Joseph Wilhelm & Thomas Scannell, *A Manual of Catholic Theology* (London: Kegan Pau. Trench, Trübner & Co. 1906), Vol. I, 366.

38{39}[9] *Deliver me from all my iniquities: you have made me a reproach to the fool.*

Ab omnibus iniquitatibus meis erue me: opprobrium insipienti dedisti me.

38{39}[10] *I was dumb, and I opened not my mouth, because you have done it.*

Obmutui, et non aperui os meum, quoniam tu fecisti.

38{39}[9] *Ab omnibus iniquitatibus meis erue me, deliver me from all my iniquities*, granting indulgence, and pouring out grace. *Opprobrium insipienti dedisti me, you have made me a reproach to the fool*: that is, you have allowed me, when I have clung only to you, to be derided by the unlearned, by those not regarding divine and eternal things, in accordance with justice. *For the simplicity of the just man is laughed to scorn.*[84] And Solomon says: *He that walks in the right way, and fears God, is despised by him that goes by an infamous way.*[85] Whence it is written in another place: *Ezekiel shall be unto you for a sign of things to come.*[86] **38{39}[10]** *Obmutui, et; I was dumb, and*, that is to say, *non aperui os meum, I opened not my mouth*, since I had to bear adversities, *quoniam tu fecisti, because you have done it*, that is, you have allowed or directed adversities to befall me punishing my fault through temporal punishments. So similarly ought we to do while we suffer reproaches, ascribing them to our own departures [from God's will], and submitting ourselves to the divine judgment. For the salubriousness of [doing] this is expressed in Ecclesiasticus, where we read: *Who will set a guard before my mouth, and a sure seal upon my lips, that I fall not by them, and that my tongue destroy me not?*[87]

---

84 Job 12:4b.
85 Prov. 14:2.
86 Ez. 24:24. E. N. By referring to Ezechiel as being a sign or portent, Denis is pointing to the Lord's earlier command to Ezechiel not to mourn the death of his wife: *Son of man, behold I take from thee the desire of your eyes with a stroke: and you shall not lament, nor weep: neither shall your tears run down.* Ez. 24:15 Ezechiel's stoicism is to be a sign, *so when the Israelites face adversity, you shall not lament nor weep [for your wife], but you shall pine away for your iniquities.* (Ez. 24:23). This same message is involved in Psalm 38:9-10: that reproach that we encounter from scoffers when walking in the ways of God ought to be ascribed to our sins, and we ought not lament or complain of the adversities or the reproaches we suffer.
87 Ecclus. 22:33.

38{39}[11] *Remove your scourges from me. From the strength of your hand I was made faint in rebukes.*

Amove a me plagas tuas. A fortitudine manus tuae ego defeci in increpationibus.

38{39}[12] *You have corrected man for iniquity. And you have made his soul to waste away like a spider: surely in vain is any man disquieted.*

Propter iniquitatem corripuisti hominem: et tabescere fecisti sicut araneam animam eius: verumtamen vane conturbatur omnis homo.

38{39}[11] *Amove a me plagas tuas, remove your scourges from me,* that is, mitigate, remove, and excuse the rigor of your punishment by which you chastise me, and do not do to me what might be demanded by my vices, nor hand me over to the power of my enemies. Whence also Paul three times prayed to the Lord that he might remove from him a *sting of the flesh,* which, of course, he had in him by reason of affliction or punishment, but not [because of any] fault.[88] And Daniel prayed: *O Lord, hear: O Lord, be appeased,*[89] *let your wrath...be turned away.*[90] And holy Job says: *Withdraw your hand far from me, and let not your dread terrify me.*[91] And so, O Lord, remove from me your afflictions: therefore, I pray that *a fortitudine manus tuae ego defeci in increpationibus, from the strength of your hand I was made faint in rebukes,* that is, by the power of your vengeance by which you have scourged me, I yielded, not being powerful enough to withstand such heavy chastisements, for I am being tried and afflicted beyond my strength. But you, O Lord, I do not blame, for justly I have suffered these because of my sins. Therefore, it continues: 38{39}[12] *Propter iniquitatem corripuisti hominem, you have corrected man for iniquity,* that is [man as] sinner. But this seems to be in opposition to what the Apostle [Paul] says: *God is faithful, who will not suffer you to be tempted above that which you are able.*[92] In response, [one must recall] that God does not allow us to be tempted above that

---

88 2 Cor. 12:8. Presumably, since St. Paul—like the other apostles—was confirmed in the good (*see* footnote 36-124), he would not have been subject to suffering as a result of the evil of fault, so the "sting of the flesh" which he mentions would have been either for merit or for temporal punishment of sins before being called to be an apostle.
89 Dan. 9:19a.
90 Dan. 9:16a.
91 Job. 13:21.
92 1 Cor. 10:13b.

which we are, by grace, able to suffer. And therefore they who do not seek refuge in his grace by invoking the divine aid are vanquished; but they who seek refuge in him saying, *And lead us not into temptation*,[93] are not defeated.

Therefore, upon encountering affliction and temptation where it appears that one is tempted beyond one's power and one must surely succumb, if one cries out to the Lord, *Remove your scourges from me*, then the Lord will help him. [The Lord] will not allow him to be afflicted beyond his power, for he inspires him with the desire to pray. *For we know not what we should pray for as we ought; but the Spirit himself asks for us*,[94] that is, he makes us requesters. But this inspiration of the Holy Spirit is the first help of God which is followed by another help, which is the effect or the merit of the prayer. And so it follows from this that on occasion a devout man can pray for mitigation or the removal of adversity or affliction which he is suffering, whether these are from natural or from divine disposition. And with respect to this he knows that, so long as he does everything that he can, he will be able to bear it. But the imperfect are unable to bear as much as the perfect, to which Paul says, *Power is made perfect in infirmity*.[95]

Et tabescere fecisti sicut araneam animam eius, *and you have made his soul to waste away like a spider*. A spider is a rapacious and harmful animal; yet it can easily be injured or killed. Therefore, [the verse] is [to be understood] in this sense: As a spider is easily impaired or injured, so by the scourges of your justice you have caused a weakening, that is, you have humiliated and afflicted and cast down the soul of man or man himself. Whence also holy Job, enduring scourges and weighed down with their rigor, said: *I that was formerly so wealthy, am all on a sudden broken to pieces*.[96] And Jeremiah subdued the same way, cried out: *Woe is me, wretch that I am, for the Lord has added sorrow to my sorrow: I am wearied with my groans, and I find no rest*.[97] And also elsewhere he exclaims: *O you sword of the Lord, how long will you not be quiet?*[98] *Verumtamen vane conturbatur omnis homo*: *surely in vain is any man disquieted*: that is, however much are the instabilities and the miseries of the present life which have been discussed, still also any man, that is, nearly everyone (or, every, that is, some of all conditions or kinds of

---

93 Matt. 6:13.
94 Rom. 8:26a.
95 2 Cor. 12:9a.
96 Job 16:13a.
97 Jer. 45:3.
98 Jer. 47:6a.

men), is disturbed with concerns over temporal things and the care of worldly matters, with vain things, that is, with unnecessary things. It is according to this sense that we have in Isaiah: *They all love bribes, they run after rewards.*[99] And elsewhere: *From the least of them even to the greatest, all are given to covetousness.*[100]

38{39}[13] *Hear my prayer, O Lord, and my supplication: give ear to my tears. Be not silent: for I am a stranger with you, and a sojourner as all my fathers were.*

Exaudi orationem meam, Domine, et deprecationem meam; auribus percipe lacrimas meas. Ne sileas, quoniam advena ego sum apud te, et peregrinus sicut omnes patres mei.

But I ought not to be troubled with vain things, 38{39}[13] *Exaudi orationem meam, Domine; Hear my prayer, O Lord,* by which I seek forgiveness, *et deprecationem meam, and my supplication,* by which I plea for grace; *auribus percipe lacrimas meas, give ear to my tears*: that is, mercifully and diligently avert the affections of my soul, from which flow tears; but also look upon those tears because of the fountain from which they pour forth: because tears are the sign of the affections, and they share in the strength of the prayer. This is so even if the desire of the heart or the prayer of the mouth is not directed directly and immediately to God, but a man speaks with himself, and laments to himself out of the remorse of conscience, or out of the desire of the heavenly homeland, as is written: *I will speak in the affliction of my spirit: I will talk with the bitterness of my soul.*[101]

Ne sileas, be not silent, that is, do not keep still from the affections of my prayers, nor keep quiet from the pious inspirations and internal responses; but say to my soul, *I am your salvation*;[102] *quoniam advena*

---

99 Is. 1:23a.
100 Jer. 6:11b.
101 Job 7:11b. E. N. Denis here appears to be distinguishing between contrition and attrition (also called imperfect contrition). "The contrition called 'imperfect' (or 'attrition') is also a gift of God, a prompting of the Holy Spirit. It is born of the consideration of sin's ugliness or the fear of eternal damnation and the other penalties threatening the sinner (contrition of fear). Such a stirring of conscience can initiate an interior process which, under the prompting of grace, will be brought to completion by sacramental absolution. By itself however, imperfect contrition cannot obtain the forgiveness of grave sins, but it disposes one to obtain forgiveness in the sacrament of Penance." CCC § 1453. *Cf.* Council of Trent (1551): DS 1678; 1705.
102 Ps. 34:3b.

ego sum apud te, for I am a stranger with you, that is, a wayfarer and exiled from the heavenly homeland to come. Other versions [of the Scriptures] have here: *for I am an inhabitant*,[103] that is, from the power of the enemy translated over to the Kingdom of God, and from the state of damnation placed in the state of salvation; and so I have become an inhabitant of the Church, when I was at one time a servant of the devil, and a slave to sin. Whence also the Apostle [Paul] said: *We give thanks to God, and the Father of our Lord Jesus Christ*,[104] *who has translated us into the kingdom of the Son of his love.*[105] *Et peregrinus sicut omnes patres mei, and a sojourner as all my fathers were*: that is, just as all saints departed from this life were in this world sojourners, not having here a permanent place,[106] but rather a desired heavenly homeland, so similarly I also am a sojourner before you, because I believe in, I hope for—indeed, I seek—another life and another country. For this reason, the Apostle [Paul] said: Abraham *looked for a city that has foundations; whose builder and maker is God.*[107] And the same Apostle speaking of all the ancient saints sad: *All these died according to faith, not having received the promises, but beholding them afar off, and saluting them, and confessing that they are pilgrims and strangers on the earth. For they that say these things, do signify that they seek a country.*[108] Hence also the most holy patriarch Jacob, questioned by Pharaoh, *How many are the days of the years of thy life?* responded with: *The days of my pilgrimage are a hundred and thirty years, few, and evil, and they are not come up to the days of the pilgrimage of my fathers* on earth.[109] See the way that all the old saints acknowledged themselves to be pilgrims. And, therefore, we value little this world and all those things that pertain to it, and, like prudent travelers, we hasten towards that heavenly homeland, casting off all the baubles of this world.

And yet that which the Apostle says—*you are no more strangers and foreigners; but you are fellow citizens with the saints*[110]—appears to oppose this. In response, that which the Apostle says here relates to distinguishing the faithful from the unbelieving who are like complete

---

103   *E. N.* Other versions say *quoniam incola ego sum* instead of *quoniam advena ego sum apud te.*
104   Col. 1:3b.
105   Col. 1:13b.
106   *Cf.* Heb. 13:14: For we have not here a lasting city, but we seek one that is to come.
107   Heb. 11:10.
108   Heb. 10:13–14.
109   Gen. 47:6, 9.
110   Eph. 2:19.

foreigners to God. Someone may be called a foreigner (*advena*) and a pilgrim (*peregrinus*) or stranger (*hospes*) in two ways. First, because he dwells in hope and faith, and not yet in reality and by sight: and in this way all travelers (*viatores*) are pilgrims and foreigners, according to that Apostle [Paul], *While we are in the body, we are absent (perigrinamur) from the Lord. For we walk by faith, and not by sight*.[111] Second, someone may be called to be a pilgrim and a foreigner, in the sense that he does not belong to the place wherein he is, and where by just deserts he is traveling. And it is in this way that unbelievers and the wicked, whose manner of living is not in heaven, are pilgrims (*peregrini*).

38{39}[14] *O forgive me, that I may be refreshed, before I go hence, and be no more.*

Remitte mihi, ut refrigerer priusquam abeam et amplius non ero.

38{39}[14] *Remitte mihi*, O forgive me, O Lord, of all sin and owed punishment, *ut refrigerer*, that I may be refreshed, that is, so that I may breathe again in your mercy, I may soothe the anxiety of my conscience, and that by the consolation of the Holy Spirit, I might drive away those sorrows that arise in me; *priusquam abeam*, before I go hence, that is, before I may die, *et amplius non ero, and be no more*, that is, after death, I will no longer remain in the state of obtaining merit,[112] nor will I return to the state of this world.[113] If, therefore, O man, you have some particular friend living in a way that is dangerous, pray for him before death. Indeed, as much as is in your power, come to the aid of all those whom you are under a special obligation in justice before they depart [in death]. For you can procure grace for them before death, but not after death.[114] Consequently, just as it is a greater thing to rescue a soul

---

111   2 Cor. 5:6b–7.
112   E. N. "At the moment of his death every man is judged according to his deserts. The time for merit is over; a man is either a friend or an enemy of God and so he remains for eternity." George Brantl, *Catholicism* (New York: George Braziller, Inc. 1961), 232.
113   E. N. "Death is the end of man's earthly pilgrimage, of the time of grace and mercy which God offers him so as to work out his earthly life in keeping with the divine plan, and to decide his ultimate destiny. When 'the single course of our earthly life' is completed, we shall not return to other earthly lives: 'It is appointed for men to die once.' There is no 'reincarnation' after death." CCC § 1013 (quoting the Roman Missal, Preface of Christian Death, VII *Lumen Gentium*, 48 § 3, and Heb. 9:27).
114   E. N. "It is clear that no one is able to merit the first grace for another with condign merit except only Christ.... But one is able through congruous merit to merit the first grace of another. Because a man in grace fulfils the will of God, it

from the punishments of Hell than from the punishments of Purgatory, so it is greater to obtain the grace of conversion for a sinner in this life than it is to procure the remission of the penalty of a departed soul abiding in Purgatory.

See how admirable and excellent the power of this Psalm is. Let us therefore apply ourselves to implement its example, to pass over fleeting things, to hunger ardently for heavenly things, and to sing this Psalm with all manner of devotion.

PRAYER

O LORD, EXPECTATION OF THOSE WHO love you, deliver us from all iniquity, and make us to praise you in continuous quiet, so that strengthened with your protection, we may be always strong enough immovably to adhere to you.

Exspectatio te diligentium, Domine, ab omnibus iniquitatibus nos erue, et continua quiete in te fac exsultare: ut tua muniti protectione, immobile tibi semper valeamus adhaerere.

---

is congruent, and in agreement with friendship, that God should fulfill the will of man in regard to the salvation of another, though it may be that sometimes there exists an impediment on the part of the other whose salvation the saint [i.e., the man living in a state of grace] desires.... The impetration of prayer relies on mercy, but condign merit relies on justice. And so a man praying may impetrate (*orando impetrat*) many things from the Divine mercy in prayer which he does not merit according to justice." ST IaIIae, q. 114, art. 6, co. & ad 2.

Psalm 39

ARTICLE LXXVIII

EXPOSITION OF THE THIRTY-NINTH PSALM OF CHRIST:
EXSPECTANS EXSPECTAVI, &c.
WITH EXSPECTATION, I HAVE WAITED, *&c.*

39{40}[1] *Unto the end, as Psalm for David himself.*

In finem. Psalmus ipsi David.

THIS PSALM AGAIN HAS THIS TITLE: 39{40}
[1] *In finem. Psalmus ipsi David*: that is, this Psalm, which is a Psalm of David as author, directs us to the end, that is, unto Christ, of whom this Psalm literally speaks, for the Apostle [in his letter to] the Hebrews in large part asserts that this Psalm prophecies of Christ, and is fulfilled in Christ, as will be made clear.[1] The Catholic teachers, therefore, expound upon this Psalm as applying to the whole Christ, namely of his head and his members: so that sometimes it applies to Christ and sometimes to the Church. We will busy ourselves, to the extent it can be done, to explain the whole Psalm with respect to Christ, and the whole Psalm with respect to the Church.

39{40}[2] *With expectation I have expected the Lord, and he was attentive to me.*[2]

Exspectans exspectavi Dominum, et intendit mihi.

39{40}[3] *And he heard my prayers, and brought me out of the pit of misery and the mire of dregs. And he set my feet upon a rock, and directed my steps.*

---

1 Heb. 10:5-9.
2 L. This is not apparent in the English, but the Latin *exspectavi* (which is translated as "I have waited" in the Douay-Rheims is derived from *ex* (=out) and *spectare* (=to see, behold, gaze). It might also be translated as "keep a look out for," but to match the parallelism in the Latin text, I have translated it as "I have expected." To get a full grasp of Denis's commentary of this Psalm one should keep in mind that Christ had the beatific vision, and so he "looked upon" or "expected" God in a manner we will only enjoy in heaven.

Et exaudivit preces meas, et eduxit me de lacu miseriae et de luto faecis. Et statuit super petram pedes meos, et direxit gressus meo.

39{40}[4] *And he put a new canticle into my mouth, a song to our God. Many shall see, and shall fear: and they shall hope in the Lord.*

Et immisit in os meum canticum novum, carmen Deo nostro. Videbunt multi, et timebunt, et sperabunt in Domino.

39{40}[5] *Blessed is the man whose trust is in the name of the Lord; and who has not had regard to vanities, and lying follies.*

Beatus vir cuius est nomen Domini spes eius, et non respexit in vanitates et insanias falsas.

Christ as man, therefore, at the foundation of the Church says: **39{40} [2]** *Expectans exspectavi Dominum,* with expectation I have expected the Lord, that is, with hope I have hoped in the Lord God, living and true. For since hope is defined as being a certain expectation (*exspectatio*) of future blessedness, it follows that it is the same thing to expect (*exspectare*) the Lord as it is to hope (*sperare*) in him.[3] But in what way can hope be spoken of in reference to Christ has been often explained.[4] So Christ expected the Lord while suffering, while hanging on the wood [of the Cross], while praying, seeing that he would be raising him again from the dead and would be glorifying him in body. For this reason he said: *Now is my soul troubled. And what shall I say? Father, save me from this hour.*[5] *Et intendit mihi, and he was attentive to me,* that is, he regarded and diligently paid heed to the desire of my hope and my long-suffering longing. **39{40}[3]** *Et exaudivit preces meas, and he heard my prayers.* For whatever Christ absolutely and with deliberate reason prayed for, he obtained. *Et eduxit me de lacu miseriae, and he brought me out of the pit of misery,* that is, he led my soul out of the limbo of hell.[6] Or [an alternate explanation is], *out of the pit of misery,* that is, he led me out of the vale of tears or the world full of misery on the day of the Resurrection and Ascension. *Et de luto faecis, and the mire of*

---

3   E. N. There is a play on words not apparent in the English *exspectare* (to expect) and *sperare* (to hope) sharing a common *spe*.
4   E. N. See footnote 27-11 on Christ's hope being limited to the accidental rewards of the Resurrection of the body and its glorification since he enjoyed the vision of God—the hope of the blessed—even while wayfaring on the earth.
5   John 12:27.
6   E. N. This is the limbo of the Fathers, not the hell of the damned. For the limbo of the Fathers (*limbus patrum*) see Article LXI (Psalm 27:1).

dregs, that is, he led out my body from the grave, and delivered it from putrefaction, lest it see corruption.

Et statuit supra petram pedes meos, and he set my feet upon a rock, that is, he placed me upon his omnipotent and divine powers, defending me from all adversity, granting me an impassible body in the Resurrection, and affirming me immovably in himself;[7] *et direxit gressus meo, and directed my steps*, that is, he ordained all my doings, and he rightly directed the departure of the soul from my body, its return from limbo, and its Ascension to heaven. **39{40}[4]** *Et immisit in os meum canticum novum, and he put a new canticle into my mouth*. For Christ taught the evangelical law, founded the New Testament, and after his Resurrection possessed within himself an unheard of and newly-received joy, and he made it known to others: as when he said, *I ascend to my Father and to your Father*;[8] and, *whose sins you shall forgive, they are forgiven them*;[9] and, *I send the promise of my Father upon you*.[10] *Carmen Deo nostro, a song to our God*: that is, the new canticle that the Lord placed in my mouth is a song, that is, praise to our God that is to the honor and glory of God. Whence Christ says: *If I glorify myself, my glory is nothing*.[11] For Christ as man referred all his honor ultimately back to God.

Videbunt multi, many shall see: that is, all those that convert to the faith will discern with the eyes of faith the mystery of my Incarnation, Passion, and Resurrection; *et timebunt, and shall fear* me, they will not be ungrateful to me, nor will they be condemned by me. They will not fear men, because it is written, *He that fears man shall quickly fall*;[12] but [they will fear] him who has the power to destroy in hell both the body and the soul.[13] *Et sperabunt in Domino, and they shall hope in the Lord*, in God the eternal Father, who *spared not his only Son, but delivered him up for us all*.[14] Believing this, the faithful hope in the Lord. For if we consider what the Father wished the Son to assume, to do, and to suffer,

---

7 E. N. For the notion of being rendered immobile or immovable in God see footnote 20-8 in Volume 1. Obviously, this ought not to be thought of as a way of life that is rigid, static, for the best analogy for the beatific vision is not being buried in concrete, but—paradoxically—the beatific vision should be viewed as a dynamic immobility or an immobile dynamism.
8 John 20:17b.
9 John 20:23a.
10 Luke 24:49a.
11 John 8:54a.
12 Prov. 29:25a.
13 *Cf.* Matt. 10:28.
14 Rom. 8:32a.

and [we consider] their nature and amount, we are not able to despair; but we can be most certainly confident, *for he has care* of us,[15] and he does not want to lose the sinner, but rather that he be converted and live,[16] as Scripture asserts: *God will not have a soul to perish, but recalls, meaning that he that is cast off should not altogether perish.*[17] They shall hope, therefore, in the Lord: and this is strongly salubrious, because **39{40}[5]** *Beatus vir cuius est nomen Domini spes eius, blessed is the man whose trust is in the name of the Lord*: that is, happy is the man to whom the Lord himself is the object and cause of hope, so that he has trust in the Lord and not in vain things, and he does not place his ultimate hope in anyone but the Lord; *et non respexit in vanitates, and who has no regard to vanities*, that is, he does not direct himself toward, nor cling to, fleeting, transitory, and carnal things, *et insanias falsas, and lying follies*, that is, he does not follow after, or give consideration to, fallacious doctrines, irrational movements, and false gods, but all of his affection is ultimately affixed upon God, and he discovers, holds, and possesses all good in him, knowing what Truth asserted to be true: *But one thing is necessary*,[18] and also considering that which the Lord says through Jeremiah: *What iniquity have your fathers found in me, that they are gone far from me, and have walked after vanity, and are become vain?*[19]

39{40}[6] *You have multiplied your wonderful works, O Lord my God: and in your thoughts there is no one like to you. I have declared and I have spoken they are multiplied above number.*

Multa fecisti tu, Domine Deus meus, mirabilia tua; et cogitationibus tuis non est qui similis sit tibi. Annuntiavi et locutus sum, multiplicati sunt super numerum.

Then Christ as man says: **39{40}[6]** *Multa fecisti tu, Domine Deus meus, mirabilia tua; you have multiplied your wonderful works, O Lord my God*, in me and by me. For God performed all miracles through Christ the man, and he performed the greatest of marvels in him, uniting human nature with the person of the Word, and gracing the soul of Christ with the beatific enjoyment from the first instant of its creation;

---

15 1 Pet. 5:7b.
16 *Cf.* Ez. 18:23: *Is it my will that a sinner should die, says the Lord God, and not that he should be converted from his ways, and live?*
17 2 Sam. 14:b.
18 Luke 10:42a.
19 Jer. 2:5.

and many other supernatural things he did in him.[20] For the human nature of Christ was a conjoined, animated, and proper instrument of the divinity to which it was united. But the action of the instrument is correctly ascribed to the principal agent of which it is the instrument; and so Christ as man attributes to God the miracles which he effected through divine power. Whence Dionysius [the Areopagite] calls the works of Christ theandric (*theandricam*), that is, divinemanly (*deivirilem*).[21] For this reason Christ said: *The Father who abides in me, he does the works.*[22] And again: *The Son cannot do anything of himself, but what he sees the Father doing.... For the Father loves the Son, and shows him all things which he himself does.*[23] *Et cogitationibus tuis non est qui similis sit tibi, and in your thoughts there is no one like you*: that is, no created mind can be compared to the divine mind in the depth of thinking, in the foreknowledge of the future, or in the immensity of wisdom. What are the thoughts of God, which no one except for the inscrutable height of divine counsel is able to assimilate, whereby God in himself finds the means of saving the human race so that justice was not derogated and mercy was satisfied? For of this thinking the Lord said through Jeremiah: I think *thoughts of peace, and not of affliction.*[24] And elsewhere: *My thoughts are not your thoughts: nor your ways my ways, says the Lord: for as the heavens are exalted above the earth, so are ... my thoughts above your*

---

20 The graces of Christ stem from three general sources as St. Thomas summarizes in Chapter 214 of his *Compendium Theologiae*: "A threefold grace is usually pointed out in Christ. The first is the grace of union (*gratia unionis*), whereby the human nature, with no merits preceding (*nullis meritis praecedentibus*), received the gift of being united in person to the Son of God. The second is the singular grace (*gratia singularis*) whereby the soul of Christ was filled with [sanctifying or habitual] grace and truth beyond all other souls. The third is the grace of being head (*gratia capitis*), in virtue of which grace flows from Him to others. The Evangelist presents these three kinds of grace in due order (John 1:14, 16). Regarding the grace of union he says: 'The Word was made flesh.' Regarding Christ's singular grace he says: 'We saw [Him as it were] the only begotten of the Father, full of grace and truth.' Regarding the grace of head he adds:'And of His fullness we all have received.' St. Thomas Aquinas, *Compendium of Theology* (St. Louis: B. Herder Book Co. 1947). 244–45 (Cyril Vollert, S. J., trans.).
21 E. N. The Latin word *theandrica* is derived through transliteration from the Greek θεανδρικός (*theandrikos*) which is a compound of the Greek words for God (θεός/*theos*) and man (ανήρ/*anēr*), whereas the Latin word *deivirilem* is a direct translation of the Greek through the use of two Latin words, God (*Deus*) and man (*vir*). The word stems from Pseudo-Dionysius. See *Epistle* 4, PG 3, 1072, 1073–74 (*dei-virilem operationem* / θεανδρικὴν ἐνέργειαν).
22 John 14:10b.
23 John 5:19–20a.
24 Jer. 29:11b.

thoughts.[25] And in the book of Wisdom: *For who among men is he that can know the counsel of God? Or who can think what the will of God is?*[26] Now that which follows all [commentators] expound as being about Christ. *Annuntiavi et locutus sum, I have declared and I have spoken*. For Christ is first among the Prophets and Patriarchs, and so by himself he taught men the marvels of God, and by himself and his Apostles he set forth the evangelical law. Whence after his Resurrection Christ told the Apostles: *You shall be witnesses unto me in Jerusalem, and in all Judea, and Samaria, and even to the uttermost part of the earth.*[27] That therefore Christ now says, *I have declared and I have spoken*, Isaiah foretold: *He will teach us his ways, and we will walk in his paths.*[28] *Multiplicati sunt super numerum, they are multiplied above number*, those who through the announcement and the preaching of my ministers have been converted. Although *for all men have not faith,*[29] and few are declared elect in comparison to those who are called,[30] nevertheless, speaking absolutely, very many are the elect, as we read in a later Psalm: *I will number them, and they shall be multiplied above the sand.*[31] And it is read in Revelation about the elect: *I saw a great multitude, which no man could number.*[32]

39{40}[7] *Sacrifice and oblation you did not desire; but you have pierced ears for me. Burnt offering and sin offering you did not require.*

Sacrificium et oblationem noluisti; aures autem perfecisti mihi. Holocaustum et pro peccato non postulasti.

39{40}[8] *Then said I, Behold I come. In the head of the book it is written of me.*

Tunc dixi: Ecce venio. In capite libri scriptum est de me.

39{40}[9] *That I should do your will: O my God, I have desired it, and your law in the midst of my heart.*

Ut facerem voluntatem tuam. Deus meus, volui, et legem tuam in medio cordis mei.

---

25 Is. 55:8-9.
26 Wis. 9:13.
27 Acts 1:8b.
28 Is. 2:3b.
29 2 Thess. 3:2b.
30 *Cf.* Matt. 20:16.
31 Ps. 138:18a.
32 Rev. 7:9a.

39{40}[7] *Sacrificium et oblationem noluisti, sacrifice and oblation you did not desire.* Here Christ expresses the cessation of the Old Law and its sacrifices, and the institution, promulgation, and the permanent continuation of the New Law and its sacrifice. For the sacrifices of the Old Law were for a time good and licit; but because they were figurative of Christ and his immolation on the Cross, as the Paschal lamb especially makes clear, they needed to cease, therefore, with the truth made manifest, that is, when Christ was announced by the Apostles to men. And so, Christ wanting to signify the insufficiency of the sacrifices of the Old Law and the necessity of his immolation said: *Sacrifice and oblation* of the Old Testament *you did not desire*, because in themselves they contained no grace, nor did they have the power to remove sins, nor were they by themselves acceptable and meritorious, but only from the devotion of the person offering.[33] Although, therefore, God regarded as pleasing for a time the sacrifices of the Old Law, finally, however, and in perpetuity, they did not please him, because Christ having come and being known, they began to cease. And the Apostle [Paul] of Christ asserts this very scripture to the Hebrews, saying: *It is impossible that with the blood of oxen and goats sin should be taken away.* Therefore, the Only-Begotten of God, coming into the world in the flesh he assumed, said: *Sacrifice and oblation you did not desire: but a body you have fitted to me.*[34] And the Apostle [Paul] shows how a great portion of the following words were fulfilled in Christ, although in the words there is somewhat of a difference: because Christ and the Apostles sometimes bring forward the meaning of the Prophets, rather than the words themselves. Further according to this sense the words of the Prophets are understood in passing to disapprove the sacrifices of the Old Law, as is the case here: *I desire not holocausts of rams, and fat of fatlings.*[35] And again: *He that sacrifices an ox, is as if he slew a man: he that kills a sheep in sacrifice, as if he should brain a dog.*[36] And elsewhere: *Shall I offer holocausts unto him? ... May the*

---

33 E. N. As St. Thomas states: "The sacrifice of the New Law, that is, the Eucharist, contains Christ himself, who is the author of sanctification, for he sanctified the people by his blood, as it says in Hebrews [Hebrews 13:12]. And so this sacrifice is also a sacrament. But the sacrifices of the Old Law did not contain Christ, but they prefigured him; hence they are not called sacraments." ST IaIIae, q. 101, art. 4, ad 2. In short, the sacrifices of the Old Law were not intrinsically efficacious, they were not *objectively* valid *ex opera operato*, by the very action performed. Rather, they had value as figures and based upon the subjective intention or faith of the person offering, that is *ex opera operantis*, from the subjective disposition of the one performing the act.
34 Heb. 10:4, 5a.
35 Is. 1:11b.
36 Is. 66:3a.

Lord be appeased with thousands of rams, or with many thousands of fat he goats?[37] For which reason we read in Jeremiah: *What is the meaning that my beloved has wrought much wickedness in my house? Shall the holy flesh take away from you your crimes, in which you have boasted?*[38]

And so Christ as man says to God the Father, or to the whole superlatively most blessed Trinity: *Sacrifice*, that was done of brute animals and birds, *and oblation*, that were done of inanimate things, *you did not desire*, that is, in themselves you did not accept them, nor did they have the power to take away the sins of the world; *aures autem perfecisti mihi, but you have pierced my ears*, that is, you have given me obedient ears, for I was *obedient even unto death*.[39] And this is the same thing that the Apostle [Paul] says: *a body you have fitted to me*,[40] that is, you gave to me a body fitted for suffering and that which was necessary for the redemption of the human race.

Holocaustum, burnt offering, that is, the sacrifice that is entirely consumed, as it is set fire to in its entirety, for it is offered to God out of reverence of his majesty and his goodness, *et pro peccato, and sin offering*, that is, the offered victim for the fault of sin which is in part consumed by fire and in part eaten by the priest, *non postulasti, you did not require*, as if it was to be sufficient to continue in perpetuity: for God commanded them to immolate in such a manner at and for a particular time. We know that one reason behind the sacrifices under the Law was that the Jews, by presenting such sacrifices to God, were turned away from the sacrifices to idols; and therefore God did not give the precepts relating to sacrifices except after they turned aside to idolatry. Whence the Lord says through Jeremiah: *For I spoke not to your fathers, and I commanded them not, in the day that I brought them out of the land of Egypt*.[41] And elsewhere: *Did you offer victims and sacrifices to me in the desert for forty years, O house of Israel?*[42] **39{40}[8]** *Tunc dixi: Ecce venio; then said I, Behold I come*: that is, because I knew the sacrifices of the Law are not received [by God in an objective sense] nor able to blot out the sins of the world, then I, the incarnate Son of God said to God the Father: *Behold I come* to my Passion and the immolation of myself upon the Cross, as the Apostle [Paul] says, *Walk in love, as*

---

37 Micah 6:6b.
38 Jer. 11:15.
39 Phil 2:8: *He humbled himself, becoming obedient unto death, even to the death of the cross.*
40 Heb. 10:5a.
41 Jer. 7:22.
42 Amos 5:25.

Christ also has loved us, and has delivered himself for us, an oblation and a sacrifice to God for an odor of sweetness.[43]

In capite libri scriptum est de me, [39]{40}[9] *ut facerem voluntatem tuam; in the head of the book it is written of me that I should do your will.* This can be explained in three ways. The first, in this way: *In the head of the book,* that is, in the first Psalm, which is the head of this book [of Psalms], *it is written of me that I should do your will,* that is, that I will be obedient to you. For that scripture is: *His will is in the law of the Lord.*[44] And according to this, the first Psalm needs to be literally explained as referring to Christ. Yet at the time that David wrote this Psalm the first Psalm was not yet so designated, since it is believed that Esdras is the one who did so; therefore, it is necessary in advancing this explanation to assert that David in the spirit foresaw that this Psalm would be gathered together with the others, and that it would be placed as a sort of prologue to this book. The second explanation is this: *In the head of the book,* that is, in the beginning of Genesis, *it is written of me.* For there we have: *In the beginning,* that is, in the Word, God created the heaven and earth.[45] For *all things were created by him*; and so the Apostle [Paul] says, *in him were all things created in heaven and on earth.*[46] The third is this: *In the head of the book,* that is, utmost in the book of divine predestination, *it is written of me.* For in the divine predestination is contained all that pertains to the salvation of the elect; and to the extent that something pertains more to that salvation, to that extent is it said to be more principally written in the divine predestination. Because, therefore, before all other things the mystery of the Incarnation and the Passion of Christ pertains to human liberation, therefore it is said to be written at the head of the book, that is, at the topmost part of its beginning. *That I should do your will,* that is, your precepts which are a sign of your uncreated will, which no one is able to do. For Christ said this: *As the Father has given me commandment, so do I.*[47] And elsewhere: *I came down from heaven, not to do my own will, but the will of him that sent me.*[48] *Deus meus volui;* O *my God, I have desired it,* as you will; *et legem tuam in medio cordis mei, and your law in the midst of my heart,* that is, I have maintained the evangelical law

---

43 Eph. 5:2.
44 Ps. 1:2a.
45 Gen. 1:1.
46 Col. 1:16.
47 John 14:31.
48 John 6:38.

in the intimate recesses of my heart, as was said in a Psalm just above, *In his law he shall meditate day and night.*[49]

39{40}[10] *I have declared your justice in a great church, lo, I will not restrain my lips: O Lord, you know it.*

Annuntiavi iustitiam tuam in ecclesia magna, ecce labia mea non prohibebo; Domine, tu scisti.

39{40}[11] *I have not hid your justice within my heart: I have declared your truth and your salvation. I have not concealed your mercy and your truth from a great council.*

Iustitiam tuam non abscondi in corde meo; veritatem tuam et salutare tuum dixi; non abscondi misericordiam tuam et veritatem tuam a concilio multo.

39{40}[10] *Annuntiavi iustitiam tuam, I have declared your justice,* that is, the precepts and counsels of the New Law by which one remains firm in the fullness of justice, *in ecclesia magna, in a great church,* that is, in the temple that was in Jerusalem, in which I frequently preached, in the manner that Malachi attested to: *And presently the Lord, whom you seek ... shall come to his temple.*[50] Or [we can understand it in this way], *in a great church,* that is, in the Christian people, which I have instructed by myself or through my disciples. *Ecce labia mea non prohibebo; lo, I will not restrain my lips,* I will not suffer to be restrained, but I will announce the truth. This is what Christ asserts: *For this was I born, and for this came I into the world; that I should give testimony to the truth.*[51] *Domine, O Lord* Father, *tu scisti, you know it,* that is from eternity you foreknew that I would so be made. 39{40}[11] *Iustitiam tuam non abscondi in corde meo, I have not hid your justice within my heart,* but (as has been already stated) I have declared it *in a great church. Veritatem tuam, your truth,* that is, the fulfillment or verification of the Scriptures of the Old Testament in me, *et salutare tuum, and your salvation,* that is, salvation and grace which you confer through me upon those believing in me, *dixi, I have declared* to all willing to hear. Whence we read in the Gospel: *Grace and truth came by Jesus Christ.*[52] And Zechariah says: *He shall speak peace to the Gentiles.*[53]

---

49 Ps. 1:2b.
50 Mal. 3:1.
51 John 18:37b.
52 John 1:17b.
53 Zech. 9:10b.

Non abscondi misericordiam tuam, I have not concealed your mercy, which by me you worthily confer upon the whole world, *et veritatem tuam,* and your truth, that is, the righteousness of your justice by which you did not wish the sin of the world to remain unavenged, *a concilio multo, from a great council,* that is, from the great church; but I announced to all publicly the mercy of the Father, which he willed by me to redeem the world, and his justice, which so greatly abhors sin, so that he might not spare me, his beloved Son, but might hand me over to death for all.[54] Or [we can look at it] this way: *I have not concealed your mercy and your truth from a great council,* that is, from Annas, Caiaphas, and the other Scribes and Pharisees, magistrates, and priests, who early in the morning on the day of preparation before Passover (*Parasceves*) questioned me, saying: *Tell us if you be the Christ.*[55] For I confessed myself to them to be the Christ and the judge of the world, and that they would see me come again on the clouds of the heavens to judge the world. Whence in John we read Christ responded to Annas: *I have always taught in the synagogue, and in the temple, where all the Jews resort; and in secret I have spoken nothing.*[56] Yet this which is now said about Christ appears to be repugnant to that brought up by Isaiah of him: *He shall not cry, ... neither shall his voice be heard abroad.*[57] How then, therefore, did he publicly announce the justice of God? The response to this question is that the Prophet [Isaiah] did not intend to refer to the open preaching by Christ: for just a short time before he stated, *He shall bring forth judgment to the Gentiles;*[58] but [Isaiah was referring to] an inordinate clamor, and so he follows up with, *He shall not be sad, nor troublesome.*[59]

39{40}[12] Withhold not you, O Lord, your tender mercies from me: your mercy and your truth have always upheld me.

Tu autem, Domine, ne longe facias miserationes tuas a me; misericordia tua et veritas tua semper susceperunt me.

39{40}[12] *Tu autem, Domine, ne longe facias miserationes tuas;* withhold not you, O Lord, your tender mercies, that is, the effects of your mercy,

---

54 Cf. Rom. 8:32: *He that spared not even his own Son, but delivered him up for us all, how has he not also, with him, given us all things?*
55 Matt. 26:63; Luke 22:66.
56 John 18:20.
57 Is. 42:2.
58 Is. 42:1b.
59 Is. 42:4a.

a me, from me; but immediately on the third day resurrect and glorify me. *Misericordia tua et veritas tua, your mercy and your truth,* that is, you yourself who are merciful and true, indeed eternal mercy and uncreated truth, *semper susceperunt me, have always upheld me,* that is, my prayers have always been heard. For in all the works of God his mercy and truth are joined and combined, as it said in an earlier Psalm: *All the ways of the Lord are mercy and truth.*[60] And therefore I pray, *withhold not your tender mercies* from me.

39{40}[13] *For evils without number have surrounded me; my iniquities have overtaken me, and I was not able to see. They are multiplied above the hairs of my head: and my heart has forsaken me.*

Quoniam circumdederunt me mala quorum non est numerus; comprehenderunt me iniquitates meae, et non potui ut viderem. Multiplicatae sunt super capillos capitis mei, et cor meum dereliquit me.

39{40}[13] *Quoniam circumdederunt me mala, quorum non est numerus; for evils without number have surrounded me,* that is, innumerable punishments of the soul and the body, most especially during the time of the Passion, when from the sole of the foot unto the top of the head there did not remain soundness in me and every one of the powers of the soul was afflicted with its own pain. *Comprehenderunt me iniquitates meae, my iniquities have overtaken me*: that is, the sins of my Mystical Body, namely, the Church, which I received upon me, made it that I be overtaken and bound fast by the fetters of torture, as the Lord said about me through Isaiah: *For the wickedness of my people have I struck him;*[61] *et non potui ut viderem, and I was not able to see* the punishments that were at hand, that is, not in the sense that I did not have foresight or knowledge, but because I did not flee, as was explained in the thirty-fourth Psalm where it is written, *Scourges were gathered together upon me, and I knew not,*[62]

---

60 Ps. 24:10.
61 Is. 53:8b.
62 E. N. Article LXXII (Psalm 34:15). There is no question of any ignorance in Christ; accordingly, three explanations are given. The first is that this is said in the sense that Christ behaved as someone that had no foresight or knowledge because he made no effort to flee. An alternative explanation is that Christ was not conscious of any personal fault that would give rise to such punishment. The third explanation is that it was the estimation of his captors and the Jews that Christ did not foresee or know.

and where it is more fully explained. *Multiplicati sunt super capillos capitis mei, they are multiplied above the hairs of my head*, the Jews and Gentiles rising up against me in the day of preparation before the Passover [are so multiplied]. This manner of expressing and designating the multitude of the adversaries of Christ is hyperbolic[63] *Et cor meum dereliquit me, and my heart has forsaken me*, that is, the bodily heart itself, which is the first in living and the last in dying,[64] gave up its natural vigor in the Passion, and is separated from my soul.[65]

39{40}[14]   Be pleased, O Lord, to deliver me, look down, O Lord, to help me.

Complaceat tibi, Domine, ut eruas me; Domine, ad adiuvandum me respice.

39{40}[15]   Let them be confounded and ashamed together, that seek after my soul to take it away. Let them be turned backward and be ashamed that desire evils to me.

Confundantur et revereantur simul, qui quaerunt animam meam, ut auferant eam; convertantur retrorsum et revereantur, qui volunt mihi mala.

39{40}[16]   Let them immediately bear their confusion, that say to me: 'Tis well, 'tis well.

Ferant confestim confusionem suam, qui dicunt mihi: Euge, euge!

39{40}[17]   Let all that seek you rejoice and be glad in you: and let such as love your salvation say always: the Lord be magnified.

Exsultent et laetentur super te omnes quaerentes te, et dicant semper: Magnificetur Dominus, qui diligunt salutare tuum.

---

63   E. N. Hyperbole (from Greek ὑπερβολή, *hyperbolē* derived from ὑπέρ (*hyper* = above) and βάλλω (*ballō* = throw) is a rhetorical device or manner of expression which makes its point by an exaggeration.

64   The notion of the heart being the *primum vivens* and *ultimum moriens*, the first thing to live and the last thing to die, is from Aristotle. See footnote 21-83 in Volume 1.

65   E. N. Even after the soul of Jesus left his body, the lifeless heart of our Lord (like all other parts of his body, and his body as a whole) remained hypostatically united to God the Son, and thus remained an object of adoration. "If, then, it had been true that during those three days, the Sacred Heart had been really separated from the rest of the adorable Humanity, it would nevertheless be itself an object of adoration, because that separation would not have caused it to be deserted by the Person of the Everlasting Word." John Bernard Dalgairns, C. O., *Devotion to the Heart of Jesus* (London: Thomas Richardson & Son 1853), 117.

39{40}[14] *Complaceat tibi, Domine, ut eruas me;* be pleased, O Lord, to deliver me from the hands of the Jews, and my soul from the limbo of hell and my body from the sepulcher, and, the soul thus reunited to the body, deliver me from all passibility *(passibilitate).*[66] *Domine, ad adiuvandum me respice;* O Lord, to deliver me, look down, that is, by your divine power and grace, cooperate in all things with the humanity assumed by me, so that I might destroy the work of the devil, and that I might lead the saints out of limbo, and ascend with them to heaven. **39{40}[15]** *Confundantur et revereantur simul, etc.;* Let them be confounded and ashamed together, etc. This verse with the two which follow we find in the thirty-fourth Psalm almost under the same form of words;[67] and there the way that such speaking can be understood in three different ways has been abundantly and diligently explained: and so to avoid tedium, I refer the reader to the exposition of that Psalm.[68] **39{40}[17]** *Exsultent et laetentur super te omnes quaerentes te,* let all that seek you rejoice and be glad in you: that is, let those who search for you by faith, and adhere to you through charity, and sincerely trust in you, rejoice with both heart and body in you and not in illicit things; *et decant semper: Magnificetur Dominus;* and let them ... say always: the Lord be magnified, that is, let them always magnify the Lord and let them desire that he be magnified by others, *qui diligent salutare tuum,* as love your salvation, that is, eternal life, which is the beatitude and salvation of the created mind, or me Christ your Son, who am your salvation,[69] that is, the Savior by whom and in whom the human race is worthy to be saved.

39{40}[18] But I am a beggar and poor: the Lord is careful for me. You are my helper and my protector: O my God, be not slack.

Ego autem mendicus sum et pauper; Dominus sollicitus est mei. Adiutor meus et protector meus tu es; Deus meus, ne tardaveris.

39{40}[18] *Ego autem mendicus sum;* but I am a beggar. For the Evangelist attesting, Susanna and other certain women that had been healed

---

66 E. N. Passibility is the capacity for suffering. "Understanding passion in its proper sense, there will not be in the risen body of the saints potentiality with regards to passion. And so they are said to be impassible." ST, III (Supp.), q. 82, art. 1, co.
67 Ps. 34:4.
68 E. N. Article LXXII (Psalm 34:4–5).
69 Luke 2:30: *Because my eyes have seen your salvation* (Song of Zechariah).

by Christ and were following him, ministered to him of their substance.⁷⁰ *Et pauper,* and poor. For Christ indeed was poor, as he said: *The Son of Man has nowhere to lay his head.*⁷¹ Whence Jeremiah, admiring with vehemence the poverty of the Christ to come, spoke thus of him: *Why will you be a stranger in the land, and as a wayfaring man turning in to lodge? Why will you be as a wandering man?*⁷² *Dominus sollicitus est mei, the Lord is careful for me.* God had a most singular providence over Christ as man. Hence he says in the Gospel: *I am not alone, but I and the Father that sent me.*⁷³ *Adiutor meus, my helper,* that is, the cooperator in my humanity, *et protector meus, and my protector,* that is, the defender of the same from evil, *tu es, you are,* O Lord God. For in the [doing of] good the divine power always cooperated with Christ the man, for which reason he himself attested, *I cannot of myself do anything.*⁷⁴ But God also preserved the soul of Christ from all evil of fault, and so he protected him: indeed, for a while he defended him from the evil of punishment, as when the Jews wanted to throw him off a cliff and stone him.⁷⁵ *Deus meus, ne tardaveris; O my God, be not slack* to hear these prayers.

But from all that has been said, I wish most diligently to consider something. For you see, this Psalm, in which is contained some things that are not fittingly applied to Christ — namely, *My iniquities have overtaken me* — is by apostolic authority⁷⁶ to be literally expounded as probative of Christ, at least in greater part. But much more ample are those Psalms in which nothing is contained that is not fittingly applied to Christ, that are expounded as referring to him, even though none of the Apostles or Evangelists assert them as applying to Christ. And so some are satisfied with a superficial expounding of the Psalms, explaining many Psalms as literally referring to David or some certain person when they are also most properly and most truly appropriate to Christ.

---

70 Luke 8:2, 3. E. N. Luke mentions Mary, Joanna, the wife of Chusa, Herod's steward, and Susanna "and many other who ministered unto him of their substance."
71 Matt. 8:20; Luke 9:58.
72 Jer. 14:8b, 9a.
73 John 8:16b.
74 John 5:30a.
75 Luke 4:29; John 8:49; 10:31.
76 E. N. This apostolic authority the result of its mention in Hebrews 10:5-10, where Psalm 39 is given a Messianic interpretation. Denis's argument points out that some Psalms, not all of which are appropriate to Christ, are specifically identified in the New Testament as Messianic. The implication is that those Psalms which are clearly all appropriate to Christ may also be said to be Messianic, despite there being no confirmation in the New Testament of their Messianic nature.

ARTICLE LXXIX

EXPOSITION OF THE SAME THIRTY-NINTH PSALM OF
THE CHURCH AND ANY MEMBER OF THE FAITHFUL:

39{40}[2] *With expectation I have expected the Lord, and he was attentive to me.*[77]

Exspectans exspectavi Dominum, et intendit mihi.

39{40}[3] *And he heard my prayers, and brought me out of the pit of misery and the mire of dregs. And he set my feet upon a rock, and directed my steps.*

Et exaudivit preces meas, et eduxit me de lacu miseriae et de luto faecis. Et statuit super petram pedes meos, et direxit gressus meo.

39{40}[4] *And he put a new canticle into my mouth, a song to our God. Many shall see, and shall fear: and they shall hope in the Lord.*

Et immisit in os meum canticum novum, carmen Deo nostro. Videbunt multi, et timebunt, et sperabunt in Domino.

ANY MEMBER OF THE FAITHFUL DESIRING the spiritual advent of Christ,[78] who daily comes through grace into the souls of the faithful, can say: 39{40}[2] *Exspectans exspectavi Dominum, with expectation I have expected the Lord,* that is, I am ready, with an interior and heartfelt sense of God's presence, so that he might build a mansion in my heart; *et intendit mihi, and he was attentive to me,* that is, he turned the eyes of his kindness toward me awaiting in such

---

77 See footnote 39-2.
78 *E. N. Christi adventum spiritualem.* The notion of the "spiritual advent of Christ" is perhaps best known from the Advent sermons of St. Bernard of Clairvaux (1090–1153 AD), who speaks of the "three advents" of Christ, *ad homines, in homines, contra homines*: to men during his Incarnation and pilgrimage on earth, *in men* who are justified, who love God, and who keep the law, and *against* men in the Second Coming and Final Judgment. It is the second advent, which is "spiritual and hidden," where God lives in the justified soul by grace, and of whom Christ said: "If any one love me, he will keep my word, and my Father will love him, and we will come to him, and will make our abode with him." (John 14:23). "Blessed is he within whom you build a mansion, Lord Jesus," said St. Bernard. "Blessed is he in whom Wisdom builds himself a house, carving seven columns. Blessed is the soul which is a throne of Wisdom. And who is he? Certainly, the soul of the just man." *In Adventu Domini Sermo III*, 4. PL, 183, 45.

a manner. **39{40}[3]** *Et exaudivit preces meas*, and *he heard my prayers*, coming to me in the loving manner he promised in the Gospel to the one expecting, saying: *my Father will love him, and we will come to him, and will make our abode with him.*[79] *Et eduxit me de lacu miseriae*, and *brought me out of the pit of misery*, that is, from this body in which I dwell, which is full of misery, he led me through contemplation and the hope of future goods: so that my *conversation* begins to be *in heaven even while living in the flesh*,[80] not that I might walk according to the flesh, but according to the spirit, and so that I might be found worthy to hear that Apostle: *But you are not in the flesh, but in the spirit.*[81] *For they who are in the flesh*, he says, *cannot please God.*[82] Or [alternatively], *from the pit of misery*, that is, from evil habits (which is a deep and miserable cavity, of which Solomon says, *The wicked man when he is come into the depth of sins, despises*[83]) he leads me by the grace of conversion to saving repentance. Or [another sense might be], *from the pit of misery*, that is, from hell, in which I might have fallen into, and still remained fallen into, had not the mercy of God rendered aid. Or [yet another interpretation], *from the pit of misery*, that is, from this world, from which you lead me, deflecting my affection from worldly loves, in the manner that John in his epistle warns, *Love not the world, nor the things which are in the world.*[84] Whence also it is written elsewhere: *Know you not that the friendship of this world is the enemy of God? Whosoever will be a friend of this world, will become an enemy of God* [85] *Et de luto faecis*, and *the mire of dregs*, that is, he led me out from carnal concupiscence or the stench of lust most repulsively deforming the soul, and he conferred grace so as to fulfill that [command of the] Apostle [Paul]: *We should live soberly, and justly, and godly in this world.*[86]

And we can especially expound this part as referring to the synagogue of the ancient fathers freed by Christ from the limbo of hell,[87] Of these, therefore, all of them giving thanks to God for the advent of the reign

---

79 John 14:23.
80 Phil 3:20a.
81 Rom. 8:9a.
82 Rom. 8:8.
83 Prov. 18:3.
84 1 John 2:15a. The verse continues: *If any man love the world, the charity of the Father is not in him.*
85 James 4:4.
86 Tit. 2:12b.
87 E. N. This is not the hell of the damned, but the *limbus patrum*, the limbo of the fathers.

of the Messiah and their own liberation, said: *With expectation I have expected the Lord*. For with greatest affection the ancient saints awaited the advent of Christ. Whence Jacob said: *I will look for your salvation, O Lord*.[88] And Micah: *I will look towards the Lord*, he said, *I will wait for God my Savior: my God will hear me*.[89] And this is what is written in Isaiah: *Would that you would rend the heavens, and would come down*.[90] For which reason Moses said: *I beseech you, Lord send whom you will send*.[91] *He was attentive to me*, that is, Christ the Son of God descended into the world by his Incarnation, as he desired. *And he heard my prayers*, doing and suffering all things which were written about him and which were necessary for the redemption of humans; *and he brought me out of the pit of misery, and the mire of dregs*, that is, from the limbo of hell, in the way Zechariah, speaking of Christ, prophesied: *You also by the blood of your testament have sent forth your prisoners out of the pit, wherein is no water*.[92]

Et statuit supra petram pedes meo, *and he set my feet upon a rock*: that is, the Lord stabilized and confirmed my desires in the love of Christ, so that I might be able to say that which the Apostle said: *Who then shall separate us from the love of Christ?*[93] *Et direxit gressus meos, and he directed my steps*, that is, he disposed my works by his law: the way that Solomon attests to, *The heart of man disposes his way: but the Lord must direct his steps*.[94] **39{40}[4]** *Et immisit in os meum canticum novum, and he put a new canticle into my mouth*, that is, new praise and the giving of thanks for all his aforementioned benefits that were given to me: in the manner that the Apostle [Paul] says, *I am filled with comfort: I exceedingly abound with joy in all our tribulation;*[95] and elsewhere, *The old things are passed away*.[96] For the ancients in the Old Testament sang of the future with anxious desire and affliction of soul because of the delay. But those of the evangelical law or New Testament, the Christians, sing with joy and with a thankful mind for it has already been done. And so in Revelation John says of Christ: *And he that sat on the throne, said: Behold, I make all things new*.[97] *Carmen Deo nostro, a song*

---

88   Gen. 49:18.
89   Micah 7:7.
90   Is. 64:1a.
91   Ex. 4:13.
92   Zech. 9:11.
93   Rom. 8:35a.
94   Prov. 16:9.
95   2 Cor. 7:4b.
96   2 Cor. 5:17b.
97   Rev. 21:5a.

to our God, that is, this canticle is a song sung to the honor and glory of God. *Videbunt multi, many shall see*, that is, they will be illuminated by faith and grace, and they will consider his miracles, as was predicted by Isaiah: *The people that walked in darkness, have seen a great light;*[98] *et timebunt, and shall fear* God, from the contemplation of those things they know by faith; also, they will fear the pains of hell; *et sperabunt in Domino, and they shall hope in the Lord*, that by grace they might avoid the torments of hell, and arrive at the joys of heaven.

39{40}[6][99] *You have multiplied your wonderful works, O Lord my God: and in your thoughts there is no one like to you. I have declared and I have spoken they are multiplied above number.*

Multa fecisti tu, Domine Deus meus, mirabilia tua; et cogitationibus tuis non est qui similis sit tibi. Annuntiavi et locutus sum, multiplicati sunt super numerum.

Now the Church or any one Christian says to Christ or to the whole Trinity: **39{40}[6]** *Multa fecisti tu, Domine Deus meus, mirabilia tua; you have multiplied your wonderful works, O Lord my God.* For many and great were the miracles of Christ. Whence in the Gospel is written: *Virtue went out from him and he healed all;*[100] and again, *Whoever touched the hem of his garment* was healed.[101] And Christ said to his disciples of John [the Baptist]: *Go and relate to John what you have heard and seen. The blind see, the lame walk, the lepers are cleansed, the deaf hear, the dead rise again.*[102] And that these miracles were to be accomplished in the advent of Christ was predicted by Isaiah in prophesying of the coming of Christ: *Then shall the eyes of the blind be opened, and the ears of the deaf shall be unstopped; then shall the lame man leap as a hart,*[103] *and the tongue of the stammerers shall speak readily.*[104] The Church recounts these miracles of Christ in the way that we see in Ecclesiasticus: *Has not the Lord made the saints to declare all his wonderful works, which the Lord Almighty has firmly settled to be established for his glory? O how desirable are all his works! And who shall be filled with beholding his glory?*[105]

---

98 Is. 9:2a.
99 Denis skips over Ps. 39:5.
100 Luke 6:19b.
101 Mark 6:56b.
102 Matt. 11:4–5.
103 Is. 25:5-6a; 32:4.
104 Is. 32:4b.
105 Ecclus. 42:17, 23a

Further, the Church in the person of the Apostles and preachers and doctors, says: *Annuntiavi, I have declared* first to the Jews, and thereafter to the Gentiles, and daily I preach to all the faithful, O Lord Jesus Christ, your life and your marvels; *et locutus sum, and I have spoken*, putting forth before them your evangelical doctrine; *multiplicati sunt super numerum, they are multiplied above number*, who by my preaching and faith have converted: because it is not possible to number these, although they are not infinite in a strict sense.[106] Whence the Lord said through Malachi: *For from the rising of the sun even to the going down, my name is great*,[107] *for I am a great King, says the Lord, and my name is dreadful among the Gentiles*.[108] God the Father speaking to Christ his Son through Isaiah evidently predicted this announcement of the Apostles and the multiplication of the faithful: *It is a small thing that you should be my servant to raise up the tribes of Jacob, and to convert the dregs of Israel. Behold, I have given you to be the light of the Gentiles, that you may be my salvation even to the farthest part of the earth.*[109]

39{40}[7] *Sacrifice and oblation you did not desire; but you have pierced ears for me. Burnt offering and sin offering you did not require.*

Sacrificium et oblationem noluisti; aures autem perfecisti mihi. Holocaustum et pro peccato non postulasti.

39{40}[7] *Sacrificium et oblationem, sacrifice and oblation*, that is, legal sacrifice,[110] *noluisti, you did not desire*, during the time of the New Law.

---

106   E. N. The number of the elect is finite. As St. Augustine states in his *De Correptione et Gratia* (*On Rebuke and Grace*), 13, 39: *Qui praedestinati sunt in regnum Dei, quorum ita certus est numerus, ut nec addatur eis quisquam, nec minuatur ex eis.* "They who are predestined to the kingdom of God, of whose number is so certain that none can be either added to them or removed from them." PL 44, 940. It is unknown to all but God what that number is. In the Third Secret of the First Sunday of Lent, we pray: *Deus, cui soli cognitus est numerus electorum in superna felicitate locandus: tribue quæsumus, ut intercedentibus omnibus sanctis tuis, universorum quos in oratione commendatos suscepimus, et omnium fidelium nomina, beatæ prædestinationis liber adscripta retineat.* "O God, to whom alone is known the number of your elect to be placed in eternal bliss: grant, we beseech you, by the intercession of all your saints, that the book of predestination may contain the names of all those whom we have undertaken to pray for, as well as those of all the faithful."
107   Mal. 1:11a.
108   Mal. 1:14b.
109   Is. 49:6.
110   E. N. In other words, sacrifice under the old dispensation, sacrifice under the Law.

Aures autem, but ears of the heart, of which the Gospel says, *He that has ears to hear, let him hear;*[111] *perfecisti mihi, you have pierced...for me*, that is, you brought it about in me so that I might promptly obey you in all things, as in an earlier Psalm you said of me: *A people, which I knew not, has served me: at the hearing of the ear they have obeyed me.*[112] These ears the Jewish people did not have. Of which the Lord says through the Prophet [Isaiah]: *Who is blind, but my servant? Or who is deaf, but he to whom I have sent my messengers?*[113] *Holocaustum*, burnt offering of the law, *et pro peccato*, and sin offering, that is, a victim immolated for sin, *non postulasti, you did not require*, during the time of the evangelical law.

For it should be considered that three-fold were the precepts of the Old Testament, namely, moral, judicial, and ceremonial. And the moral precepts remained during the time of the New Law, since they are of the natural law, and they have been perfected by the counsels given by Christ in the Gospels: and to these precepts belong the Ten Commandments. Now the judicial precepts could be observed in the New Law without danger if they were instituted by someone with the power to promulgate law. But the ceremonial precepts, to which pertains the precepts having to do with sacrifice, are [spiritually] deadly at the time of the New Law, since they were only figurative in nature (*figuralia*). And so to keep them would be in reality to say that Christ had not yet come. That which the Lord asserted through Ezechiel is understood to apply to these [ceremonial] precepts: *I also gave them statutes that were not good, and judgments, in which they shall not live;*[114] And that which the Apostle maintained in Hebrews, *The law having a shadow of the good things to come, not the very image of the things...can never make the comers thereunto perfect.*[115] And elsewhere, *The law brought nothing to perfection.*[116] But the cessation of these legal sacrifices and the institution of the one true sacrifice and one of perpetual duration was predicted by the Holy Spirit through Micah: *I have no pleasure in you...and I will not receive a gift of your hand.... In every place there is sacrifice, and there is offered to my name a clean oblation,*[117] namely the Body and Blood of Christ, which is precisely intended to be the final sacrifice and to succeed all the sacrifices of the Law. The

---

111 Luke 8:8b.
112 Ps. 17:45.
113 Is. 42:19a.
114 Ez. 20:25.
115 Heb. 10:1.
116 Heb. 7:19a.
117 Mal. 1:10b, 11b.

three-fold nature of the precepts of the Old Law is most elegantly and beautifully addressed by the glorious and holy doctor, blessed Thomas in the first part of the second part [of his *Summa Theologiae*].[118]

39{40}[8] *Then said I, Behold I come. In the head of the book it is written of me.*

Tunc dixi: Ecce venio. In capite libri scriptum est de me.

39{40}[9] *That I should do your will: O my God, I have desired it, and your law in the midst of my heart.*

Ut facerem voluntatem tuam. Deus meus, volui, et legem tuam in medio cordis mei.

39{40}[8] *Tunc*, then, that is, now during the time of grace when the sacrifices of the law cease, *dixi, said I*, I following in the footsteps of Christ, or I the Church, the spouse of Christ: *Ecce, behold*, O Lord Jesus, *venio, I come* to your faith and grace, and hoping in you I hope to be saved; I do not place salvation in the law. I come also that I might offer to you myself, surrendering myself entirely to the divine service, and dying to myself every day on account of you. What I therefore do, because *in capite libri, in the head of the book*, that is, in the second verse of the first Psalm, *scriptum est de me*, 39{40}[9] *ut facerem voluntatem tuam; it is written of me*, 39{40}[9] *that I should do your will*, O God. For there is said: *His will is in the law of the Lord.*[119] *Deus meus, volui; O my God, I have desired* to obey you in all things; *et legem tuam, and your law*, namely, the evangelical law, *in medio cordis mei, in the midst of my heart* I have infixed, hidden, and fully maintained. And this is a sacrifice pleasing to you, and supremely honoring you, in the manner that is beautifully presented in Isaiah: *The Lord will give you rest continually, and will fill your soul with brightness.*[120] *If you ... glorify him, while you do not your own ways, and your own will is not found: to speak a word: Then shall you be delighted in the Lord, and I will lift you up above the high places of the earth,*[121] says the Lord. And this is what Christ says in the Gospel to those who want to imitate him in a cruciform way (*cruciformiter*), and who want to sacrifice themselves daily: *If any man*

---

118 E. N. ST, IaIIae, qq. 98–103. This is part of St. Thomas Aquinas's so-called "Treatise on Law."
119 Ps. 1:2a.
120 Is. 58:11a.
121 Is. 58:13b–14a.

will come after me, he said, *let him deny himself, and take up his cross daily, and follow me.*[122]

39{40}[10]   *I have declared your justice in a great church, lo, I will not restrain my lips: O Lord, you know it.*

Annuntiavi iustitiam tuam in ecclesia magna, ecce labia mea non prohibebo; Domine, tu scisti.

39{40}[11]   *I have not hid your justice within my heart: I have declared your truth and your salvation. I have not concealed your mercy and your truth from a great council.*

Iustitiam tuam non abscondi in corde meo; veritatem tuam et salutare tuum dixi; non abscondi misericordiam tuam et veritatem tuam a concilio multo.

39{40}[12]   *Withhold not you, O Lord, your tender mercies from me: your mercy and your truth have always upheld me.*

Tu autem, Domine, ne longe facias miserationes tuas a me; misericordia tua et veritas tua semper susceperunt me.

39{40}[10] *Annuntiavi iustitiam tuam in ecclesia magna*, I have declared your justice in a great church, that is, in all the Christian people, for the sound of the Apostles went forth to all the earth, and their words to the ends of the world's sphere.[123] 39{40}[11] *Iustitiam tuam non abscondi in corde meo*, I have not hid your justice within my heart, but I have preached it publicly, because I heard, O Lord, your terrible menace in the Gospel: *For he that shall be ashamed of me and of my words, of him the Son of man shall be ashamed* when he comes into his kingdom.[124] And so Peter said to the chief of the priests: *If it be just in the sight of God, to hear you rather than God, judge you. For we cannot but speak the things which we have seen and heard.*[125] The justice of God—that is the doctrine of Christ—is not therefore to be hidden, but the neighbor is to be instructed. For *wisdom that is hid, and treasure that is not seen: what profit is there in them both?*[126] Whence of the indolent and the hiding of the justice of God, it is written in Isaiah: *His watchmen are all*

---

122   Luke 9:23.
123   E. N. Denis skips the rest of Ps. 39:10.
124   Luke 9:26a.
125   Acts 4:19-20.
126   Ecclus. 20:32.

blind, they are all ignorant: dumb dogs not able to bark, seeing vain things, sleeping:[127] this is especially said against negligent and unlearned prelates. *Veritatem tuam, your truth* contained in Sacred Scripture, *et salutare tuum, and your salvation,* that is, the happiness prepared for the faithful in heaven, *dixi, I have declared* to my neighbor. But how does it now say, *I have not hid your justice in my heart,* where in a later Psalm it says, *Your words have I hidden in my heart, that I may not sin against you?*[128] And the response to this [apparent dilemma] is that sacred doctrine is both hidden in the heart and not hidden. For it is hidden, not so that it may be consigned to oblivion, but that it not be set forth or announced for reasons of arrogance or ostentation; but it is not hidden [in the sense that] it not be communicated to one's neighbor and remain unfruitful: For this reason was the slothful servant rebuked by the Lord because he hid the talent committed to him in the earth.[129]

Non abscondi misericordiam tuam, I have not concealed your mercy, that is, your benefits so mercifully shown us, or the goodness and liberality of your goodness, *et veritatem tuam a concilio multo, and your truth from a great council,* that is, to the Christian people requiring counsel so as to how they may attain true beatitude. **39{40}[12]** *Tu autem, Domine ne longe facias miserationes tuas a me; withhold not you, O Lord, your tender mercies from me,* but take away my sins, grant me grace, preserve my virtues, concede to me a happy consummation. *Misericordia tua et veritas tua semper susceperunt me; your mercy and your truth have always upheld me,* when I have perseveringly prayed. For as you have promised your truth in the Gospel, saying, *Ask, and it shall be given you;*[130] so in your mercy hear and grant whatever is prayed for salubriously and constantly. And therefore trustingly to be believed is an Ecumenical Council directed by the Holy Spirit, because of that which the Savior said: *If two of you shall consent upon earth, concerning anything whatsoever they shall ask, it shall be done to them by my Father.... For where there are two or three gathered together in my name, there am I in the midst of them.*[131] How much more if all agree and come together so that they might be heard, and have Christ in their midst? Hence it is also reasonable for a General Council to be of more authority than any of the four Doctors.[132]

---

127 Is. 56:10.
128 Ps. 118:11.
129 Matt. 25:24–30 (a reference to the Parable of the Talents).
130 Matt. 7:7a.
131 Matt. 18:19–20.
132 The "Four Doctors" of the Church are those four doctors that were particularly authoritative, namely Sts. Ambrose (*ca.* 340–397 AD), Jerome (347–420 AD),

39{40}[13] *For evils without number have surrounded me; my iniquities have overtaken me, and I was not able to see. They are multiplied above the hairs of my head: and my heart has forsaken me.*

Quoniam circumdederunt me mala quorum non est numerus; comprehenderunt me iniquitates meae, et non potui ut viderem. Multiplicatae sunt super capillos capitis mei, et cor meum dereliquit me.

39{40}[13] *Quoniam circumdederunt me mala, for evils... have surrounded me,* evils of punishment and fault, *quorum non est numerus, without number* certainly to me. For *many are the afflictions of the just,*[133] because in the midst of snares we have been placed,[134] and *a just man shall fall seven times;*[135] and the venial sins which we commit by thinking, speaking, or doing, or that we incur by omission, are moreover so many, that they appear to exceed all number. *Comprehenderunt me iniquitates mea; my iniquities have overtaken me,* that is, they have led me captive through the law of sin, and they have made me subject to the yoke of sin and the servitude of the devil, and they have bound me with the fetters of malice. Whence the Savior says: *Whosoever commits sin, is the servant of sin.*[136] *Et non potui ut viderem, and I was not able to see,* that is, I am unable to know with specificity or singly all the previous evil with which I am surrounded. See how great our misery is, and how much it behooves us to fear the divine judgment. For in the day of judgment how much will those vices already forgotten surge up against us, [vices] that will rise up against us as if in ambush? Let us humble ourselves therefore *under the mighty hand of God,*[137] saying that which is said in an earlier Psalm: *From my secret ones cleanse me, O Lord.*[138] Let us weep

---

Augustine (354–430 AD), and Pope Gregory the Great (540–604 AD). So authoritative were they that they were analogized to the four Evangelist. For example, in a painting found in the Louvre in Paris entitled "The Four Doctors of the Church," Pier Francesco Sacchi (1485–1528 AD) painted the Four Doctors with the insignia of the Evangelists: St. Ambrose with the winged lion of Mark, St. Augustine with the eagle of St. John, St. Jerome with the angel of Luke, and Pope St. Gregory the Great with the bull of St. Matthew.
133 Ps. 33:20a.
134 E. N. These are the opening words of what was thought to be Augustine's work *Manuale: Quoniam in medio laqueorum posit sumus,* "Because we have been placed in the midst of snares." PL 40, 951.
135 Prov. 24:16a.
136 John 8:34b.
137 1 Pet. 5:6a.
138 Ps. 18:13b.

and let us make amends at least in general where we are unable to weep specifically [because we cannot recall them or are unaware of them]; and let us apply ourselves—beyond our debt (*debita nostra*)—some (indeed, even much) good works against these unknown sins, lest a demon introduce them against us in the day of our judgment.[139]

Multiplicati sunt super capillos capitis mei, they are multiplied above the hairs of my head the aberrations of my sins, especially with regard to venial evils; *et cor meum dereliquit me*, and my heart has forsaken me, that is, the intellect is deficient in the consideration of the great number of my sins. For because their number far exceeds the hairs of my head, it is certain that my heart is not able to think about them singly. Let us say, therefore, with complete sincerity and with great humility that which Manassas, that king of Judah, said: *I have sinned beyond the number of the sands of the sea, and my sins have been multiplied, and I am bowed down with fetters of iron, and there is no breath in me: for I have provoked your wrath, setting up abominations and multiplying offenses. And now I bend the knee of my heart, beseeching you, O Lord, to forgive me, do not destroy me together with my iniquities, nor reserve evil for me in eternity.*[140] This also Ezra said: *My God I am confounded and ashamed to lift up my face to you: for our iniquities are multiplied over our heads, and our sins are grown up even unto heaven.*[141] For our heart forsakes us when it is taken from us. And it is taken from us when the use of reason is impeded, darkened, or deceived by the fog of vices. For this reason, Hosea said: *Fornication, and wine, and drunkenness take away the heart (understanding).*[142] As often, therefore, we are led away from the midst of reason by the force of passion, as often as permit ourselves to consent to sin, as often as we act against the sovereign God, and turn to

---

[139] This is the theme of the penitential responsory *Emendemus in Melius*—rendered so beautifully by William Byrd and Cristobal de Morales: *Emendemus in Melius / Quae ignoranter peccavimus, / Ne subito praeoccupati die mortis / Quaeramus spatium poenitentiae / Et invenire non possumus. / Attende, Domine, et miserere, / Quia peccavimus tibi. / Adiuva nos, Deus salutaris noster, / Et propter honorem nominis tui / Libera nos*. Let us amend unto good / Those things in which we have ignorantly sinned / Lest, the day of death suddenly overtake us / And seeking a time for repentance / And be unable to find it / Hear, O Lord, and have mercy, / For we have sinned against you. / Help us, O God of our salvation, / And, for the glory of your name, / Deliver us.
[140] Prayer of Manasseh (partial).
[141] Ezra 9:6.
[142] Hosea 4:11. The Douay-Rheims translates the Latin *cor*—heart—with understanding. Denis likewise associates the heart with understanding in his commentary on Psalm 39:13.

unfruitful and vain things, and leave behind the one thing necessary[143] and wander off to something else, that often does our heart forsake us. And these are fornications of the human heart, which is a fornication against God, and for which it will be condemned by God, as the Lord said through Ezechiel: *I have broken their heart fornicating and revolting from me.*[144] Also, with respect to men having such a heart, elsewhere the divine word says: *Rejoice not, O Israel... for you have committed fornication against your God.*[145] With all watchfulness, therefore, we ought to keep our hearts, most especially in divine things, for life proceeds out of it, if we keep it well;[146] but without [such safekeeping] then surely death proceeds out of it, as Christ said in the Gospel: *From the heart come forth evil thoughts,... thefts...* and other evils.[147]

39{40}[14] Be pleased, O Lord, to deliver me, look down, O Lord, to help me.

Complaceat tibi, Domine, ut eruas me; Domine, ad adiuvandum me respice.

39{40}[18][148] But I am a beggar and poor: the Lord is careful for me. You are my helper and my protector: O my God, be not slack.

Ego autem mendicus sum et pauper; Dominus sollicitus est mei. Adiutor meus et protector meus tu es; Deus meus, ne tardaveris.

39{40}[14] Complaceat tibi, Domine, ut eruas me; be pleased, O Lord, to deliver me from all evil. See how pleasant, sweet, full of affection prayer is. *May it be pleasing,* he says, *to you, O Lord:* it is as if he is saying, *Not as I will, but as you will.*[149] And this is what in the Lord's prayer

---

143 *Cf.* Luke 10:42a.
144 Ez. 6:9a. The Douay-Rheims translates the Latin *fornicans* as "faithless." I have rendered it literally into "fornicating" so that it fits better with the Commentary.
145 Hosea 9:1a.
146 *Cf.* Prov. 4:23.
147 Matt. 15:19. E. N. This brings to mind the famous passage of St. Augustine in his *Confessions* (XIII, 21): "I did not love you [my God], and I committed fornication against you, and amid my fornications from all sides there sounded the words, 'Well done! Well done!' Love of this world is fornication against you, but 'Well done! Well done!' is said, so that it will be shameful for a man to be otherwise." *The Confessions of St. Augustine* (New York: Image Books 1960), 14–15. (John Kenneth Ryan, trans.).
148 Denis skips over verses 15–17.
149 Matt. 26:39b.

we say daily: *Thy will be done.*[150] *Domine, ad adiuvandum me respice; O Lord, to help me,* that is, intend that for me, so that in your kindness you might save me because of your clemency, so that you do not justly cast me aside because of my malice. **39{40}[14]** *Ego autem mendicus sum, but I am a beggar:* for daily and unceasingly I cry out in the Lord's prayer, *Give us this day our daily bread.*[151] I do not seek as much bodily bread day by day, but spiritual bread, namely, the bread of tears, the bread of salvation and grace (of which Christ affirms, *My meat is to do the will of my Father*),[152] and I also unceasingly beg for the bread of the Eucharist: *et pauper, and poor* I am, that is, spiritually imperfect, and lacking in all things. For which reason David said: *I am a poor man, and of small ability.*[153] *Dominus sollicitus est mei, the Lord is careful for me.* For he is the caretaker of all things: how much more [then will he take care] of the rational creature?[154] For this reason it is written: *You, O Lord, are our father, our redeemer,*[155] *and we are clay: and you are our maker, and we all are the works of your hands.*[156]

Let us contemplate how determined this prayer is. For he calls himself a beggar and poor so that he may summon mercy; not justice, as did the Pharisee who said, *I am not as the rest of men.*[157] And you, therefore, if you desire to summon the mercy of God, if you want to receive from God his copious bounty and rich bread, if you wish to be spiritually enriched and satisfied, place yourself before God as the beggar does before the worldly rich man from whom he begs alms. They who are wounded of body—ulcerous, dropsical, paralytic, or similarly weak with disease—remove their garment from the spot of their infirmity, they proclaim their indigence, they openly profess themselves to be poor. Let us therefore show to God the wounds of our souls, let us humbly disclose our poverty, and let us with great feeling invoke the aid of the mercy of God: and the more we profess our misery with more heartfeltness and more profound humility, the greater grace we will acquire from God.

Finally, let us reflect on how this splendid and noble Psalm is excellent and beautiful. First, it shows thanks to God for all his benefits,

---

150 Matt. 6:10.
151 Matt. 6:11.
152 John 4:34a.
153 1 Sam. 18:23b.
154 *Cf.* 1 Pet. 5:7: *Casting all your care upon him, for he has care of you.*
155 Is. 63:16b.
156 Is. 64:8.
157 Luke 18:11.

especially for the Incarnation of his Son. Second, Christ speaks to the Father, declares the abrogation of the legal sacrifices and the necessity of the true sacrifice, which is the Passion of Christ. And it teaches that Christ most greatly pleased God, that he obeyed his will, in the manner that Samuel bore witness: *Does the Lord desire holocausts and victims, and not rather that the voice of the Lord should be obeyed? For obedience is better than sacrifices: and to hearken rather than to offer the fat of rams. Because it is like the sin of witchcraft, to rebel: and like the crime of idolatry, to refuse to obey.*[158] Also in this Psalm is declared the institution of the Church through the preaching of Christ. Finally, it shows the most efficacious prayer to God and a most humble confession of sin. So let us apply ourselves always to say this Psalm with becoming and due devotion. And that [part of the Psalm] not expounded upon [here], may be made clear in the preceding article.

PRAYER

GOD OF INFINITE MERCY, HOLD OUT your hands to those who have fallen, and guide us from the pit of misery and the mud of impurity, so that our paths being directed by you, we might render to you with unceasing voice a hymn of praise and conciliation.

Deus infinitae misericordiae, manum tuam porrige lapsis, et educ nos de lacu miseriae et de luto faecis: ut per te directis gressibus nostris, hymnum tibi laudis et placationis incessabili voce persolvamus.

---

158   1 Sam. 15:22–23a.

Psalm 40

ARTICLE LXXX
LITERAL EXPOSITION OF THE FORTIETH PSALM:
BEATUS QUI INTELLIGIT.
BLESSED IS HE THAT UNDERSTANDS.

40{41}[1] *Unto the end, understanding for the sons of Korah.*[1]
In finem, intellectus filiis Core.

PLACED BEFORE THIS PSALM IS THE FOLLOWing title: **40{41}[1]** *In finem, intellectus filiis Core; Unto the end, understanding for the sons of Korah.* Korah, who we read in the book of Numbers perished as a result of his ambition,[2] is interpreted as Calvary (*Calvaria*),[3] which is the name of the place where Christ was crucified.[4] But the sons of Korah are in a spiritual sense understood to mean "sons of the Cross," or the imitators of Christ crucified. And because of this interpretation there is mention of the sons of Korah often in title of the Psalms. For these did not follow their father in his sin; for this reason they deserved to assume a temple ministry.[5] The sense of the title, therefore, is this: *Intellectus*, understanding of this Psalm tending *in finem, unto the end*, that is, directing us to Christ, is assigned *filiis Core, for the sons of Korah*, that is, it coincides to the imitators of the Passion of Christ, since the prediction and the sense of this Psalm is that they

---

1 E. N. So reads Denis's version. Commentators such as Peter Lombard claimed that St. Jerome changed the title from *In finem psalmus David* to *In finem intellectus filiis Core*. Marcia L. Colish, *Peter Lombard* (New York: E. J. Brill 1994), Vol. 1, 178–79. The Sixto-Clementine Vulgate does not follow Denis's text, but has *In finem. Psalmus ipsi David. Unto the end, a Psalm for David himself.*
2 The sons of Korah (קֹרַח), also known as the sons of Core, were the sons of Moses's rebellious nephew whose name was Korah. "[W]hen Core [Korah] perished, his sons did not perish." Num. 26:11. Various of the Psalms are identified as being by the "sons of Korah": Psalms 41(42), 43(44)–48(49), 83(84), 84(85), 86(87), and 87(88).
3 As St. Augustine explains in his exposition of Psalm 83:2 and 84:2, the name Korah is interpreted as "bald," which in turn suggests a "skull," which in turn suggests Golgotha, the "place of the skull," or, in Latin, *Calvariae locus*, or "Calvary." See Luke 23:33, Matt. 27:33, Mark 15:22, and John 19:17. See St. Augustine, *Expositions of the Psalms* (Hyde Park, NY: New City Press 2000) (240, n. 6) (Maria Boulding, O. S. B., trans.)
4 Matt. 27:33.
5 Cf. 1 Chr. 15:5. E. N. See also 1 Chr. 9:19.

more perfectly turn to Christ and conform to his Passion. Finally, that this Psalm literally speaks of Christ is clear from the fact that Christ asserts that the words of this Psalm are prophetic of him, saying in the Last Supper: *But that the scripture may be fulfilled: He that eats bread with me, shall lift up his heel against me.*[6] According to all Catholic expositors [this is a reference to] words written in this Psalm: *For even the man of peace, in whom I trusted, who ate my bread.* For Christ sometimes refers more to the sense than the [literal] words of the Prophets. The doctors therefore universally explain part of this Psalm as referring to Christ, and part as referring to the Church, as will be apparent; but as much as is possible, it is to be endeavored to be explained as referring entirely to Christ. For it is becoming to the Christian to hear and to speak of Christ with ready pleasure, and not ever to be wearied with doing this.

40{41}[2] *Blessed is he that understands concerning the needy and the poor: the Lord will deliver him in the evil day.*

Beatus qui intelligit super egenum et pauperem: in die mala liberabit eum Dominus.

Therefore the Prophet [David] says: **40{41}[2]** *Beatus qui intelligit super egenum et pauperem*, blessed is he that understands concerning the needy and the poor: that is, Christ himself—who with kindly understanding looked upon, and mercifully regarded, the human race liable to the punishment of damnation because of original sin—is blessed. For as God, he is essentially blessed; but as man, he was blessed in the soul from the first moment of his conception in the Virgin Mother.[7] For Christ lovingly regarded needy and poor mankind when he predicted through Jeremiah: *I think ... thoughts of peace, and not of affliction*;[8] and through Zechariah: *Behold I come, and I will dwell in the midst of you*;[9] and through Micah: *Your salvation is close, I will save you, do not fear*;[10] and Isaiah, *I myself that spoke, behold I am*

---

6 John 13:18b (referring to Ps. 40:10).
7 E. N. In reference to the human nature of Christ, Denis here uses the word "blessed" as meaning including the beatific vision, by which the blessed in heaven see God as he is—face to face, and not through a glass darkly. *Cf.* 1 Cor. 13:12. During his entirely earthly life, Jesus, as man, had the beatific vision—that is, he "saw" God, and thus did not have or need the virtue of faith, which is the "evidence of things *not seen.*" (Heb. 11:1).
8 Jer. 29:11a.
9 Zech. 2:10b.
10 E. N. These words do not appear to be in Micah. The words are redolent of the hymn *Rorate Caeli* and the Antiphons in Advent.

here.[11] All of these [prophecies] we know are fulfilled in Christ, as is also written elsewhere: *He who made the stars, this is our God; and afterwards he was seen upon earth, and conversed with men.*[12] And so Christ kindly regarded the human race needy and poor when he himself in the Gospel said: *For God sent not his Son into the world, to judge the world, but that the world may be saved by him.*[13] And again: *For the Son of man is come to seek and to save that which was lost.*[14] And yet again: *I lay down my life for my sheep.*[15] But most kindly did the Lord Jesus regard [the human race] needy and poor when, at the beginning of the Passion, he said: *Father, if this chalice may not pass away, but I must drink it, your will be done;*[16] and when, suspended on the Cross, he cried out: *I thirst:*[17] for what else [did he thirst], surely, except for the salvation of the world? But superlatively most kindly (*superpiissime*) did he regard the needy and the poor when, praying for transgressors and those who were crucifying him, he said *Father, forgive them*. And so that his prayer would be better received, he added an excuse for the impious, saying: *For they know not what they do.*[18]

In die mala, in the evil day, that is, during all the time that Christ suffered persecution, and most particularly on the day of his crucifixion, *Dominus,* the Lord God, *liberabit eum*, will deliver him, and already delivered him. For he was delivered when the Jews wanted to throw him off a cliff and to stone him:[19] and although he sometimes permitted him to suffer contumely and finally to suffer death, he nevertheless always delivered him; for Christ overcame through patience, and he merited for himself the crown of accidental reward for himself, and the essential crown of reward for the whole world.[20] In the Passion he also delivered him, in this respect, that his Passion was the end of all his suffering and persecutions.

---

11 Is. 52:6b.
12 Baruch 3:35b, 36a, 38.
13 John 3:17.
14 Luke 19:10.
15 John 10:15b.
16 Matt. 26:42b.
17 John 10:28b.
18 Luke 23:34a.
19 Luke 4:29; John 8:59; 10:31.
20 E. N. For the distinction between accidental reward or recompense and essential reward or recompense, see the treatment of that issue in footnote 1-48 in Volume 1. Since Jesus had the beatific vision (here called by Denis the crown of essential reward) from the first moment of his conception in the womb of the Blessed Virgin Mary, he did not merit that reward, but he merited the crown of accidental reward (namely, his rising again from the dead and the glorification of his human body). On the other hand, Jesus merited all the supernatural graces for all mankind, suffering

40{41}[3] *The Lord preserve him and give him life, and make him blessed upon the earth: and deliver him not up to the will of his enemies.*

Dominus conservet eum, et vivificet eum, et beatum faciat eum in terra, et non tradat eum in animam inimicorum eius.

That which follows is to be called more a prophesying and a rejoicing rather than praying. 40{41}[3] *Dominus conservet eum, the Lord preserve him.* For God the Father preserved Christ the man from all evil of fault, for *he prevented him with blessings of sweetness;*[21] and he confirmed his soul in all good from the beginning of its creation; but he also preserved him from evil of punishment, but in this respect: that these punishments were not harmful to him spiritually, but were useful. *Et vivificet eum, and give him life,* that is, raise him up from the dead on the third day, *et beatum faciat eum in terra, and make him blessed upon the earth,* that is, make his blessedness manifest to men through the preaching and the miracles of the Apostles and of other Saints, in the manner that God speaks of Christ through Isaiah: *Behold my servant shall understand, he shall be exalted, and extolled, and shall be exceeding high.*[22] *Kings shall shut their mouth at him.*[23] Whence also elsewhere this is brought out: *His power shall be from sea to sea, and from the rivers even to*

---

and redeeming all men. "The Church, following the apostles, teaches that Christ died for all men without exception. 'There is not, never has been, and never will be a single human being for whom Christ did not suffer.'" CCC § 605. At the same time, as St. Thomas makes clear, mankind participates in that redemption in a range of ways. There are those united to Christ in glory (the saints in heaven), those united to him by charity, those united to him by faith without charity, those united to him in potentiality which is not yet reduced to act, but will be reduced to act before their death, and those united to him in potentiality which will never be reduced to act. These latter, the damned or reprobate, on "on their departure from the world, wholly cease to be members of Christ, as being no longer in potentiality to be united to Christ." ST, IIIa, q. 8, art. 3, co. (English Dominican Province translation).
21 Ps. 20:4. The English word prevent (from Latin *prae-venire*, to come before) means to go before someone, to be in front, to anticipate. Such a sense is still found, for example, in the notion of prevenient grace, or a preventative remedy. As Denis himself explains Ps. 20:4 in reference to Christ: "For with all grace you most excellently adorned the soul of Christ from the instant of its creation, preserving it immune from all original and actual sin, filling it with all the most sweet gifts of the Holy Spirit, and—that [gift to his humanity outside of the grace of union] which is above all these—you graced it with your beatific vision; and all this you did without his antecedent [or foreseen] merits. Truly, the blessing of God is called the collective bestowal of his grace. Therefore, the soul of Christ was prevented with the blessings of delight, with the gratuitous gifts of the divine collective bestowal [of graces] without foreseen merits (*sine praeviis meritis*)."
22 Is. 52:13.
23 Is. 52:15a.

the end of the earth.[24] And Daniel says: *I beheld ... and lo ... the Son of Man come, and he came even to the Ancient of days, ... and he gave him power, and glory, and a kingdom: and all peoples, tribes, and tongues shall serve him.*[25] And knowing this, the most blessed Virgin and Mother blessing Christ on earth and herself blessed by those who would believe in her Son, broke out into prophetic song: *All generations,* she said, *shall call me blessed.*[26] Or [we can understand it] thus: *make him blessed upon the earth,* that is, make Christ glorious in body, and elevate him above the heavens; and then beatify him in the land of the living with accidental beatitude,[27] which consists in created things relating to God, namely in their good use by which one creature has power over another, or is made joyful by it, or uses it.[28]

Et non tradat eum in animam inimicorum eius, and deliver him not up to the will of his enemies: that is, God the Father will not finally abandon Christ into the power of the Jews, nor will he subject him to their will. This Christ showed as fulfilled within himself when he said: *I have power to lay my life down: and I have power to take it up again.* And again: *No man,* he said, *takes my life away from me: but I lay it down and again to take it up.*[29] For which reason Isaiah said this about it: *He was offered because it was his own will.*[30] And this is most clearly apparent from that which is said in John: *Jesus therefore, knowing all things that should come upon him, went forth, and said to them: Whom do you seek? They answered him: Jesus of Nazareth. Jesus said to them: I am he.... As soon therefore as he had said to them: I am he; they went backward, and fell to the ground.*[31]

24 Zech. 9:10b.
25 Dan. 13–14a.
26 Luke 1:48b.
27 E. N. For the expression "land of the living" as meaning heaven, see footnote 34-134. For the notion of accidental beatitude as involving only the "accidental" blessings of his Resurrection, glorification, and Ascension, and not including any "essential" beatitude since Jesus had the beatific vision from the first instance of his conception in the Blessed Virgin Mary, see footnotes 1-46 and 1-48 in Volume 1.
28 "All theologians ... hold as certain that, besides essential beatitude in beatified souls, there are some accidental rewards which are designated by the name of *accidental beatitude*.... As it is a joy about created things, by reason of its various objects, it can be distinguished into accidental beatitude arising from the goods of the soul, from the goods or perfections of the body, and from external goods, or, in other words, the pleasure arising to the soul from the knowledge of creatures, from the beauty and perfection of the glorified bodies, and from the social joys of heaven." Arthur Devine, *A Manual of Ascetical Theology: Or, The Supernatural Life of the Soul ono Earth and in Heaven* (London: R & T Washbourne 1902), 522-23.
29 John 10:18.
30 Is. 53:7a.
31 John 18:4–6.

How then is it that the Apostle [Paul] says, God *spared not even his own Son, but delivered him up for us all?*[32] In response to this, God the Father delivered him over so as to permit him to be killed by the evildoers: but not that those evildoers would be able to bring about torments against his will; for Christ willingly handed himself over to death, in the manner that Isaiah said: *He has delivered his soul unto death.*[33] And in Galatians, the Apostle asserted: *I live in the faith of the Son of God, who loved me, and delivered himself for me.*[34] In one way, therefore, Judas delivered Christ over, and, in another way, the Father did.

40{41}[4] *The Lord help him on his bed of sorrow: you have turned all his couch in his sickness.*

Dominus opem ferat illi super lectum doloris eius; universum stratum eius versasti in infirmitate eius.

40{41}[4] *Dominus opem ferat illi super lectum doloris eius*, the Lord help him on his bed of sorrow. Christ's bed of sorrow was the gibbet of the Cross, upon which he had no cushion to rest even briefly his tired, spine-pierced head.[35] Upon this small bed God gave aid to Christ as man, for he preserved him in good and worked together with him for the redemption of the human race and in the conquering of death and the devil. For all the efficacy of the merits of Christ were from the divine union.[36] For although Christ said: *My God, my God, why have you forsaken me?*[37] (evidencing the withdrawing from the inferior powers the customary overflowing of beatitude which he had in his soul and the suffering of nature), nevertheless,

---

32   Rom. 8:32a.
33   Is. 53:12a.
34   Gal. 2:20b.
35   *Cf.* Luke 9:58: *Jesus said to him: The foxes have holes, and the birds of the air nests; but the Son of man hath not where to lay his head.* This brief, yet poignant reflection by Denis brings to mind part of the Passion hymn attributed to St. Bernard so beautifully rendered into music by Bach (BWV 244) and which we know as "O Sacred Head, Sore Wounded": *Salve, caput cruentatum, / Totum spinis coronatum, / Conquassatum, vulneratum, / Arundine sic verberatum. / Facie sputis illita.* Hail, head covered in blood, / Fully crowned with thorns, / Battered, wounded, / Beaten so with a reed, / With your face besmeared with spit.
36   "The ultimate foundation of Christ's universal social merit is to be placed... in the hypostatic union." W. Lynn, *Christ's Redemptive Merit: The Nature of its Causality according to St. Thomas* (Rome: Gregorian University Press 1962), 167; "[T]he Incarnation is the principle of the whole of Christ's merit...." Reginald Garrigou-Lagrange, O. P., *Christ the Savior* (St. Louis, MO: B. Herder Book Co. 1950), 190-91 (Dom Bede Rose, O. S. B., trans.).
37   Matt. 27:46; Mark 15:34.

he was not entirely abandoned, but *God was in* him *reconciling the world to himself*, according to the Apostle.³⁸ *Universum stratum eius, all his couch*, that is, the entire gibbet of the Cross of Christ, or, better said, the whole Christ suspended on the Cross, since the container is being placed for the contained,³⁹ *versasti, you have turned*, that is, you have frequently and variously directed yourself, *in infirmitate eius, in his sickness*, that is, precisely in the Passion of Christ. For Christ turned to the Cross not in terms of place, but in terms of devotion, namely, with diverse affections: at one time because of the bitterness of the Passion crying out, *Why have you forsaken me?*⁴⁰ as if he was suffering against his will (not, however, that he suffered against his will, since [he suffered] most willingly, like the most ardent lover of men and one zealous for paternal honor); at another time as he freely suffered because of the desire of human salvation, saying, *I thirst*;⁴¹ at yet another time in neglect of his own sufferings, when he was concerned over his mother, telling John, *Behold your mother*.⁴²

40{41}[5] *I said: O Lord, be merciful to me: heal my soul, for I have sinned against you.*

Ego dixi: Domine, miserere mei; sana animam meam, quia peccavi tibi.

40{41}[5] *Ego dixi: Domine, miserere mei*, etc. *I said: O Lord, be merciful to me*, etc. This prayer does not pertain to Christ, but to his Mystical Body; and this verse will be treated in the following exposition.

40{41}[6] *My enemies have spoken evils against me: when shall he die and his name perish?*

Inimici mei dixerunt mala mihi: Quando morietur, et peribit nomen eius?

40{41}[6] *Inimici mei, my enemies*, namely the Jews persecuting me, *dixerunt mala mihi, have spoken evils against me*, that is, toward my ignominy and defamation. They continually repeated what they said, *Quando morietur? When shall he die?* That is, when will he be killed by

---

38 2 Cor. 5:19a.
39 E. N. Denis is saying here that the container is being used to describe that which it contains (*continens pro contento*), which is a form of synecdoche, so that the Cross (the "container") is used to describe the crucified Lord (the "contained").
40 Matt. 27:46.
41 John 19:28.
42 John 19:27.

us? *Et peribit nomen eius? And his name perish?* That is, when will his fame and his memory be entirely extinguished? This is what John states the priests and the Pharisees declare: *Do you see that we prevail nothing? Behold, the whole world is gone after him.*[43] And again the Scriptures say in Matthew: *Then were gathered together the chief priests and ancients of the people into the court of the high priest... and they consulted together, that... they might apprehend Jesus, and put him to death.*[44]

40{41}[7] *And if he came in to see me, he spoke vain things: his heart gathered together iniquity to itself. He went out and spoke to the same purpose.*

Et si ingrediebatur ut videret, vana loquebatur; cor eius congregavit iniquitatem sibi. Egrediebatur foras et loquebatur.

40{41}[8] *All my enemies whispered together against me: they devised evils to me.*

In idipsum adversum me susurrabant omnes inimici mei; adversum me cogitabant mala mihi.

40{41}[9] *They determined against me an unjust word: shall he that sleeps rise again no more?*

Verbum iniquum constituerunt adversum me: Numquid qui dormit non adiiciet ut resurgat?

40{41}[7] *Et si ingrediebatur, and if he came.* Frequently in this Psalm, as in others, the Prophet [David] changes person and number: sometimes speaking in singular, other times in plural, sometimes in third person, sometimes in second. Therefore, now he says speaking in the singular: *And if he*—meaning my enemy, namely the traitor Judas—*came*, with the other Apostles with me in the upper room and in the house of Martha, *ut videret, to see*, that is, so that he might observe and investigate what would have to be done; *vana loquiebatur cor eius; he spoke vain things: his heart*: because he thought within himself that I did not know his purpose. In both his heart and mouth he said vain and false and dissimulating words when he was indignant with Mary Magdalen because she poured out upon my head the precious ointment from the alabaster box, and said: *To what purpose is this waste?*[45] For this ointment

---

43 John 12:19b.
44 Matt. 26:3-4.
45 Matt. 26:7-9.

could have been sold for more than three hundred denarii and given to the poor. He said this, *not because he cared for the poor; but because he was a thief, and having the purse, carried the things that were put therein*: as John stated.⁴⁶ *Congregavit iniquitatem sibi, it gathered together iniquity to itself*, that is, Judas accumulated a diversity of sins to himself. For out of avarice he was envious and indignant of Mary Magdalen, and he harbored [within himself] the purpose to sell Christ and to deliver him over to this enemies in death. *Egrediabatur foras, and he went out,* Judas himself [departed] from me, four days before my Passion, entering into the house in which he knew that the council of the Jews would be meeting against me; *et loquebatur* 40{41}[8] *in id ipsum, and he spoke to the same purpose*, that is, he said before that whole council: *What will you give me, and I will deliver him unto you?*⁴⁷ This the Evangelists clearly attest to. Or [we can interpret it in this way], he went out in the hour of the Supper, in the manner that John attests to, saying: *That which you do, do quickly. He therefore having received the morsel, went out immediately.*⁴⁸

Adversum me susurrabant omnes inimici mei, against me all my enemies whispered together, namely, the chief priests and the teachers of the temple with the entire council, which in a stealthy manner and in a disparaging way took counsel among themselves regarding how they might crucify me; *adversum me cogitabant mala mihi; they devised evils to me*, that is, many and great torments they proposed to heap upon me, as is stated in the book of Wisdom, *Let us condemn him to a most shameful death.*⁴⁹ Jeremiah, who by his prophecies and his sufferings most openly prefigured the Passion of Christ, frequently foreannounced this: *You, O Lord, have shown me, and I have known.... Let us put wood on his bread.*⁵⁰ And elsewhere: *They have dug a pit for my soul.*⁵¹ 40{41}[9] *Verbum iniquum constituerunt adversum me, they determined against me an unjust word*, that is, the Jews firmly conceived evil words against me. But what does the expression that follows mean: *Numquid qui dormit, non adiiciet ut resurgat? Shall he that*

---

46 John 12:3–6.
47 Matt. 26:15.
48 John 13:27, 30.
49 Wis. 2:20a.
50 Jer. 18:19b. Denis does not explain this verse, probably because its meaning would have been familiar to his audience. It was commonplace to understand this as referring to the crucifixion. For example, Lactantius, the "Christian Cicero," (*ca.* 250–*ca.* 325 AD) in his *Divine Institutes* (4.18) states with respect to Jer. 11:18: "But the wood signifies the Cross, and the bread his Body, for he is food, and he is life to all who believe in the Flesh that he carried, and the Cross upon which he hung." PL 6, 568.
51 Jer. 18:20a. E. N. A reference to the scheming devices of the chief priests and the Pharisees and the other enemies of our Lord as they sought to ensnare or entrap him.

sleeps rise again no more? That is, shall he who said that he would rise again from the dead truly be able to rise again, when he will have slept in death, and he will be thrown into a closed sepulcher? It is as if they were saying, "No."[52] And this is what is said in Matthew: *The chief priests said to Pilate: Sir, we have remembered, that that seducer said, while he was yet alive: After three days I will rise again. Command therefore the sepulcher to be guarded [until the third day: lest perhaps his disciples come and steal him away, and say to the people: He is risen from the dead; and the last error shall be worse than the first.]*[53] The Jews supposed, of course, that were Christ to die, he would neither rise again nor his memory remain. This was in the manner that was foretold by Jeremiah saying, *Let us cut him off from the land of the living, and let his name be remembered no more.*[54]

40{41}[10] *For even the man of peace, in whom I trusted, who ate my bread, has greatly overthrown me.*[55]

Etenim homo pacis meae, in quo speravi, qui edebat panes meos magnificavit super me supplantationem.

And what marvel is that if the Jews did these things? 40{41}[10] *Etenim homo pacis meae, in quo speravi; for even the man of peace, in whom I trusted,* that is, my disciple Judas, with whom I was at peace, and to whom I extended a sign of peace, and to whom I so charitably held myself out to, and of whom I had expected much service: for I myself appointed him treasurer, and he stole from the burse; *qui edebat panes meo, who ate my bread,* because he often ate with me, and he lived partly from the alms that were given me, and at the Last Supper he received twice bread from my hand, namely, the dipped bread by which I showed him to be the traitor to John,[56] and the morsel under which was my Body, of which John says, *And after the morsel, Satan entered into him.*[57] *Magnificavit super me supplantationem, he has greatly overthrown me,* that is, he haughtily led my adversaries upon me, who overthrew and killed me. When also holy Job in the figure of Christ said: *He whom I love most is turned against me.*[58]

---

52   E. N. In other words, it was a rhetorical question that implied a negative answer.
53   Matt. 27:62–64. The part in brackets replaces Denis's "etc."
54   Jer. 11:19.
55   I have replaced the Douay-Rheims "supplanted" with "overthrown."
56   John 13:26.
57   John 13:27a. E. N. In other words, the Eucharist proper, the transubstantiated bread
58   Job 19:19b.

40{41}[11] *But you, O Lord, have mercy on me, and raise me up again: and I will requite them.*

Tu autem, Domine, miserere mei, et resuscita me; et retribuam eis.

40{41}[11] *Tu autem, Domine, miserere mei;* but you, O Lord have mercy on me, delivering from the punishments of the body, *et resuscita me, and raise me up again* on the third day; *et retribuam eis, and I will requite them,* that is, I will show just vengeance upon the Jews, blinding their hearts, and delivering them over to the hand of the Romans, and condemning eternally those who do not believe. Whence Christ said through Isaiah: *I have trampled on them in my indignation, and have trodden them down in my wrath.... For the day of vengeance is in my heart, the year of my retribution has come.*[59] And Jeremiah writes something similar, saying: *But you, O Lord of Sabaoth, who judges justly, and tries the reins and hearts, let me see your revenge on them: for to you I have revealed my cause.*[60]

40{41}[12] *By this I know, that you have had a good will for me: because my enemy shall not rejoice over me.*

In hoc cognovi quoniam voluisti me, quoniam non gaudebit inimicus meus super me.

40{41}[13] *But you have upheld me by reason of my innocence: and have established me in your sight for ever.*

Me autem propter innocentiam suscepisti; et confirmasti me in conspectu tuo in aeternum.

40{41}[12] *In hoc cognovi,* by this I know, O Lord Father, that is, I will learn experimentally,[61] *quoniam voluisti me,* that you have had a good

---

59 Is. 63:3b–4. E. N. In lieu of the Sixto-Clementine Vulgate's *annus redemptionis meae venit,* "the year of my redemption is come," Denis has a variant reading: *annus retributionis meae venit,* "the year of my retribution has come."
60 Jer. 11:20. On the meaning of "reins," kidneys, as being one's innermost self, see footnote 7-10 in Volume 1.
61 E. N. Christ, as man, had knowledge in three modes. First, the knowledge arising from the beatific vision, where he saw all things in God. Second, he had infused knowledge. These two were perfect and therefore not subject to increase. However, Christ as man, also gained knowledge—like all men—through acquired or empirical knowledge, *i.e.,* experientially. This acquired or empiric knowledge could grow, and so what Christ, as man, would have known in God through the beatific vision, or known as a result of infused knowledge, he might also learn through the means of acquired or empirical knowledge. See ST IIIa, q. 12, arts. 1-3.

will for me, that is, that you have loved me, and that I am pleasing to you, *quoniam non gaudebit inimicus meus super me, because my enemy shall not rejoice over me*, that is, because the Jewish people opposing me and my members[62] will not long or finally rejoice concerning me by seeing my name entirely extinguished or by me not rising from the grave. Rather, they will be confounded and they will sorrow when they will see miracles being done in my name, and when many thousands convert to the faith by the preaching of the Apostles, as we have already seen fulfilled. **40{41} [13]** *Me autem, but . . . me*, Christ your beloved Son, *propter innocentiam suscepisti, have upheld . . . by reason of my innocence*, that is, because of my immaculate and just life you have heard the prayers which I have just brought before you, and in the day of Resurrection you raised me up to an impassible state; and also in the day of the Ascension, you have raised me up to your right hand, *et confirmasti me in conspectu tuo in aeternum, and you have established in your sight forever*, that is, you have placed me without end upon the throne of glory and in the empyreal heaven, as the Apostle [Paul] said to the Hebrews: Christ *for that he continues forever, has an everlasting priesthood, whereby he is able also to save forever them that come to God by him; always living to make intercession for us.*[63]

40{41}[14] *Blessed be the Lord the God of Israel from eternity to eternity. So be it. So be it.*

Benedictus Dominus, Deus Israel, a saeculo, et usque in saeculum. Fiat, fiat.

Finally, Christ as man praises the three-and-one God for all of this, and says: **40{41}[14]** *Benedictus Dominus Deus Israel, blessed be the Lord the God of Israel*: that is, from all may God the Trinity, who is the God of Israel, that is, of Jacob who is named Israel, be blessed, praised, and honored; or, Israel, that is the people contemplating heavenly things by faith; *a saeculo et in saeculum, from the age and in the age,*[64] that is, through all ages, and from the first age, namely from the beginning of the world even unto that future age, which will never have an end. *Fiat,*

---

62 E. N. The members of his Mystical Body, namely, the faithful.
63 Heb. 7:24–25.
64 E. N. Denis departs by saying *a saeculo et in saeculum*, "from age and in age," whereas the Sixto-Clementine Vulgate has *a saeculo et usque in saeculum*, which the Douay-Rheims renders "from eternity and even unto eternity." Denis's departure is indicated by the editor in the margins. I have kept the verse in the Commentary as Denis has it, and have departed from the Douay-Rheims because Denis founds an argument upon it.

fiat; so be it, so be it, that is, may it be so, may it be so. The replication of words is an indication of greater desire.

See how most evidently and fully this Psalm speaks of the Passion of Christ, and how much the mystery of Christ David knew, and how beautiful and glittering is the agreement of these prophetic foretellings with the history of the Gospels. Finally, according to those who divide the book of Psalms into five partial books, this is the place that the first book is considered at an end.[65]

ARICLE LXXXI

TROPOLOGICAL EXPOSITION OF THE SAME FORTIETH PSALM:

40{41}[2] *Blessed is he that understands concerning the needy and the poor: the Lord will deliver him in the evil day.*

Beatus qui intelligit super egenum et pauperem: in die mala liberabit eum Dominus.

TROPOLOGICALLY UNDERSTOOD, THIS PSALM is expounded as relating to the members of Christ, or each individual faithful. Therefore, it says: **40{41}[2]** *Beatus qui intelligit super egenum et pauperem,* blessed is he that understands concerning the needy and the poor, which can be explained in two ways. The first is this: *Blessed is he that understands [concerning the needy and poor],*[66] that is, by hope happy is the man who wisely recognizes that Christ in the mortal flesh was once subject to suffering and poor, so that in him he considers two natures, namely, a divine and a human. He neither negates true humanity in him because of the signs of divinity, nor does he negate true divinity in him because of the humbleness and abjectness of humanity. And this is what the Savior said. For after he had explained his divine miracles, he added: *Blessed is he that shall not be scandalized in me.*[67] It is as if he were saying: "Blessed is he who because of the human weakness and suffering that he sees in me does not deny me being divine." Certainly, many heretics considering the humility and indignity that they read about Christ abhor

---

65   E. N. The "five books" Denis refers to are enumerated as follows: 1-40, 41-71, 72-88, 89-105, and 106-150 [1-41, 42-73, 73-89, 90-106, 107-150].
66   E. N. I have replaced the "etc." with the part in brackets.
67   Matt. 11:6.

the acknowledgement of true divinity in him. But others, considering the sublime things that are written of him, reject the assertion that true humanity exists in him. But we understand both to exist in him, and we ascribe both divine and human [natures] to Christ; but the reason why it [the dual nature] applies to him is to be prudently considered.

The second explanation is thus: *Blessed is he that understands concerning the needy and poor*, that is, he who shows a merciful eye, provides aid, and shares spiritual and corporal alms to the members of Christ, namely, the needy. For as Christ attested, he who does something to one of his own, does it to him.[68] And also in the day of judgment, it will be asked of them how they perceived the needy: *I was hungry, and you gave me to eat; I was thirsty, and you gave me to drink; ... naked, and you covered me.*[69] Whence it is written elsewhere: *Deal your bread to the hungry, and bring the needy and the vagrant into your house.... Then shall your light break forth as the morning*[70] And elsewhere: *Cast your bread upon the running waters: for after a long time you shall find it again.*[71] And Christ in the Gospel: *That which remains, give alms; and behold, all things are clean unto you.*[72] Here also Job speaks of himself, saying: *I was an eye to the blind, and a foot to the lame. I was the father of the poor: and the cause which I knew not, I searched out most diligently.*[73] And again, he says: *If I have eaten my morsel alone, and the fatherless has not eaten thereof: For from my infancy mercy grew up with me: and it came out with me from my mother's womb.*[74] *The stranger did not stay without, my door was open to the traveler.*[75] And if exercising oneself in bodily alms and exterior works of mercy is so salubrious, how much more salubrious and sublime is it to engage in spiritual almsgiving: teaching the ignorant, censuring the errant, counseling the uncertain, praying for the impious, teaching the sinner, consoling the sorrowful. Therefore, someone in whom more greatly abounds these almsgivings does as Tobias told his son to do: *Turn not away your face from any poor person: for so it shall come to pass that the face of the Lord shall not be turned from you. According to your ability be merciful.*[76]

---

68 Matt. 25:40: *Amen I say to you, as long as you did it to one of these my least brethren, you did it to me.*
69 Matt. 25:35–36a.
70 Is. 58:7a, 8a.
71 Eccl. 11:1.
72 Luke 11:41.
73 Job 29:15–16.
74 Job 31:17–18.
75 Job 31:32.
76 Tob. 4:7–8.

And so, *blessed is he who understands concerning the needy and the poor*: and this is so because *in die mala*, *in the evil day*, that is, in the day of temptation and persecution and adversity, *liberabit eum Dominus, the Lord will deliver him*, not allowing him to be defeated by temptation, nor to be overcome with impatience in persecution, nor to be disheartened in adversity. He will also deliver him from past sins, and from the guilt of sins: because as *water quenches a flaming fire, so alms extinguish sins*.[77] For this reason Daniel told king Nebuchadnezzar: *Redeem your sins with alms, and your iniquities with works of mercy to the poor*.[78] If, therefore, you wish to preserve yourself from evil, be merciful, console your neighbor, and render aid to the needy. For Christ said: *Blessed are the merciful: for they shall obtain mercy*.[79] And Solomon is exhorted: *Let not mercy and truth leave you, . . . and you shall find grace and good understanding before God and men*.[80] But as far as the spiritually needy and poor, let us wisely comprehend, let us be attentive to fulfil, that [exhortation] of the Apostle [Paul]: *Rebuke the unquiet, comfort the feeble minded, support the weak, be patient towards all men*.[81]

40{41}[3] *The Lord preserve him and give him life, and make him blessed upon the earth: and deliver him not up to the will of his enemies.*

Dominus conservet eum, et vivificet eum, et beatum faciat eum in terra, et non tradat eum in animam inimicorum eius.

40{41}[4] *The Lord help him on his bed of sorrow: you have turned all his couch in his sickness.*

Dominus opem ferat illi super lectum doloris eius; universum stratum eius versasti in infirmitate eius.

40{41}[3] *Dominus conservet eum*, the Lord preserve him in good, and may he make him stand firm in the good; *et vivificet eum*, *and give him life* in the present by grace, and in the future by glory; *et beatum faciat eum in terra*, *and make him blessed upon the earth*, that is, in the pilgrimage of this life, in mortal flesh, in the Church militant he makes him

---

77 Ecclus. 3:33. E. N. Denis's version says *eleemosyna exstinguit peccatum*, "alms extinguish sins," but the Sixto-Clementine Vulgate has *eleemonsyna resistit peccatis*, "alms resist sins."
78 Dan. 4:24b.
79 Matt. 5:7.
80 Prov. 3:3–4.
81 1 Thess. 5:14.

blessed in hope and with the sufficiency of temporal things, and in the heart of his neighbor, so that all men might bless him as a pious man pleasing to God. For all these things accompany the merciful man in the present life, in the manner that is written: *A merciful man does good to his own soul*;[82] and again, *He that is inclined to mercy shall be blessed.*[83] In the land of the living and in the Church triumphant, the Lord will make him blessed in reality, and in the most full possession of all good. *Et non tradat eum in animam inimicorum eius*, *and deliver him not to the will of his enemies*, that is, he will not permit him to be spiritually wounded, overcome, or oppressed by his adversaries, so that the snares of his enemies do not harm his soul. **40{41}[4]** *Dominus opem ferat illi super lectum doloris eius, the Lord help him on his bed of sorrow*, that is, in the place and the time of his weakness or indigence and especially in the hour of death, in order that during that time he may obtain mercy when he most stands in need of mercy. *Universum stratum eius versasti in infirmitate eius, you have turned all his couch in his sickness*: that is, his body, in which his soul as it were cast into a couch, you have in multiple ways changed from annoyance to alleviation, from suffering to intermission, and sometimes from sickness to health. Or [it can be understood in this way], *you have turned all his couch*, that is, casting him upon the couch, you comforted him with your internal consolations. For during this time [on earth] God is inclined frequently and with great kindness to palliate and give comfort to men who are merciful.

40{41}[5] *I said: O Lord, be merciful to me: heal my soul, for I have sinned against you.*

Ego dixi: Domine, miserere mei; sana animam meam, quia peccavi tibi.

40{41}[5] *Ego dixi, I said*, with my heart and my mouth, considering myself: *Domine, miserere mei, O Lord, be merciful to me*, that is, fill me with the effects of your mercy, and assist me as if you were suffering with me; *sana animam meam, heal my soul* from the lesion of sin, and the lack of grace. Therefore, this I pray, *quia peccavi tibi, for I have sinned against you*, that is, to your suffering injustice. O how affectionately and pithily and effective is the prayer of this verse! O would that we would say it not so much with the mouth, but with the innermost heart and with a humble repentance.

---

82 Prov. 11:17a.
83 Prov. 22:9a.

40{41}[6] *My enemies have spoken evils against me: when shall he die and his name perish?*

Inimici mei dixerunt mala mihi: Quando morietur, et peribit nomen eius?

40{41}[7] *And if he came in to see me, he spoke vain things: his heart gathered together iniquity to himself. He went out and spoke to the same purpose.*

Et si ingrediebatur ut videret, vana loquebatur; cor eius congregavit iniquitatem sibi. Egrediebatur foras et loquebatur.

40{41}[8] *All my enemies whispered together against me: they devised evils to me.*

In idipsum adversum me susurrabant omnes inimici mei; adversum me cogitabant mala mihi.

40{41}[9] *They determined against me an unjust word: shall he that sleeps rise again no more?*

Verbum iniquum constituerunt adversum me: Numquid qui dormit non adiiciet ut resurgat?

40{41}[6] *Inimici mei dixerunt mala mihi,* my enemies have spoken evils against me, those, namely, who [are described in the words that] follow: *Quando morietur, et peribit nomen eius?* When shall he die and his name perish? This the early Church was particularly able to say when all those who killed Christians thought themselves as rendering a service to God.[84] For both Diocletian and various other tyrants intended to wipe away entirely the name of Christian from the earth, and to eradicate totally the faith of Christ. Also, any Christian suffering persecution or death for justice's sake is able to say this verse. But of the invisible enemies any one of us can say it. For demons daily say among themselves: *When shall he die?* That is, when might we induce him to mortal sin, which is the death of the soul? *And his name perish* from the Book of Life,[85] and the memory of the blessed and the mercy of God, namely that they may be eternally condemned with us? **40{41}[7]** *Et si ingrediebatur, and if he came in* to me, the ambusher—a heretic, a schismatic, or one

---

84 *Cf.* John 16:2.
85 E. N. The Book of Life, the *Librum Vitae*, repeatedly referred to in Revelation (*e.g.*, 3:5, 13:8, 17:8, 20:12, 21:27, 22:19). It contains the names of the elect of God, "And whosoever was not found written in the book of life, was cast into the pool of fire." Rev. 20:15.

corrupt — to the Church of Christ or the just man, *ut videret, to see* what I might believe, hope, love, and do, *vana loquebatur cor eius, he spoke vain things [to] his heart,* that is, he thought about deceits, proposing to oppose the orthodox faith or the virtuous and just life; *congregavit iniquitatem sibi, he gathered together iniquity to himself,* that is, reflecting upon various ways of causing injury, he multiplied his sins to his own damnation. *Egrediebat foras, he went out,* to the patrons and partners of his malice, *et loquebatur* 40{41}[8] *in id ipsum, and spoke to the same purpose... together,* that is, he set forth to them that which he conceived against me. This the Church or any just man can say of false brethren and prying persons and hypocrites and other perverse men. Of which John in his epistle writes: *They went out from us, but they were not of us. For if they had been of us, they would no doubt have remained with us.*[86]

Then the Church says of this: *Adversum me susurrabant, [they] whispered against me,* that is they spoke in a hidden and malicious way, *omnes inimici mei; adversum me cogitabant mala mihi; all my enemies, they devised evils to me,* namely, in what way they might be able to afflict me. Whence John says: *Wonder not, brethren, if the world hate you. We know that we have passed from death to life, because we love the brethren.*[87] 40{41}[9] *Verbum iniquum constituerunt, they determined... an unjust word,* that is, they stated [an unjust word], *adversum me,* against me, saying: *Numquid qui dormit, non adiiciet ut resurgat? Shall he that sleeps rise again no more?* That is, whether the next life and beatitude in which they will live and reign after this life is as the Christians — whom we have in all sorts of ways killed — say? Or shall there be in the future the resurrection of the dead? This the infidels said against the Christians, particularly in the early Church.

40{41}[10] *For even the man of peace, in whom I trusted, who ate my bread, has greatly overthrown me.*[88]

Etenim homo pacis meae, in quo speravi, qui edebat panes meos magnificavit super me supplantationem.

40{41}[10] *Etenim homo pacis meae, in quo speravi, qui edebat panes meos; for even the man of peace, in whom I trusted, who ate my bread,* that is, those who appeared to be of the household of faith[89] and the sons of the

---

86 1 John 2:19a.
87 1 John 3:13–14a.
88 E. N. I have replaced the Douay-Rheims "supplanted" with "overthrown."
89 E. N. The *domesticos fidei,* the "domestics of the faith," or "those of the household of faith," is a synonym for the Christian faithful. *Domo fidei,* a synonym for

Church, and my kinsmen and neighbors, when they received with others the Sacrament of the Body of Christ, *magnificavit super me supplantationem, has greatly overthrown me*, that is, such men incited great persecution and adversities against me. The Church says this in a particular way against heretics, who for a time were in the Church, but then departed, introducing sects of perdition. And this verse may also be said by whoever has had a special and familiar friend, if that friend has become distant from him and has opposed himself against him in words and deeds, and also in revealing that which during the time of familiarity and friendship he received in confidence. But such a person who so becomes distant from a friend, and opposes him and detracts him, most gravely and more than mortally sins: because he acts directly not only against charity, but also greatly against both charity and justice. And still more grave would be that sin if it occurred within those bound by a pact or treaty of friendship which cannot be dissolved without mortal sin, according to St. Thomas Aquinas in the fourth book of his *Commentary on the Sentences*. Whence it is written: *Shall he escape that has broken the covenant?*[90] Therefore, most gravely do they sin who are so troublesome or unfaithful to their former friends, and make public things that had been told in secret. For this reason it is stated in Ecclesiasticus: *He that discloses the secret of a friend loses his faith.*[91] *For to disclose the secrets of a friend, leaves no hope to an unhappy soul.*[92] Solomon also says: *He that walks deceitfully, reveals secrets: but he that is faithful, conceals the thing committed to him by his friend.*[93]

40{41}[11] *But you, O Lord, have mercy on me, and raise me up again: and I will requite them.*

Tu autem, Domine, miserere mei, et resuscita me; et retribuam eis.

Thereafter the Church prays: 40{41}[11] *Tu autem, Domine, miserere mei; but you, O Lord, have mercy on me* so afflicted *et resuscita me, and raise me up again*, that is, through the increase of believers, repair the death of

---

the Church, which expression is taken from St. Paul's letter to the Galatians: Gal. 6:10: *Therefore, while we have time, let us work good to all men, but especially to those who are of the household of the faith* (*domesticus fidei* / οἰκείους τῆς πίστεως-*oikeious tēs pisteōs*).
90   Ez. 17:15b.
91   Ecclus. 27:17a. E. N. I have replaced the Douay-Rheims translation of *fidem* from "credit," to "faith."
92   Ecclus. 27:24.
93   Prov. 11:13.

the faithful dead. Or [alternatively], *raise me up* from the sleep of sin,[94] as the Apostle [Paul] exhorts: *Rise you that sleep*;[95] and again, *It is now the hour for us to rise from sleep.*[96] Or [yet another understanding], *raise me up* in the blessed resurrection of the last day, *we all shall rise again, but we shall not all be changed.*[97] *Et tribuam eis*, *and I will requite them*, that is, I will visit just vengeance upon my enemies either in the present by excommunicating them or the day of judgment by judging them with you: in the manner that is written in another place, *The saints shall judge nations*;[98] and as the Apostle [Paul] affirms, *Know you not that the saints shall judge this world?*[99]

40{41}[12] *By this I know, that you have had a good will for me: because my enemy shall not rejoice over me.*

In hoc cognovi quoniam voluisti me, quoniam non gaudebit inimicus meus super me.

40{41}[13] *But you have upheld me by reason of my innocence: and have established me in your sight forever.*

Me autem propter innocentiam suscepisti; et confirmasti me in conspectu tuo in aeternum.

40{41}[12] *In hoc cognovit*, *by this I know*, O Lord, *quoniam voluisti me*, *that you have good will for me*, that is, that I am chosen by you, and I have pleased you, *quoniam non gaudebit inimicus meus super me*, *because my enemy shall not rejoice over me*, that is, neither my visible or invisible enemies will exult eternally because of my adversities, however much you permit me to be afflicted by them during time. For at least after this life their joy will cease, and it will be converted into eternal grief, just as also my temporary sadness, this finite life, will be converted into eternal joy. Also in that day of judgment, when I shall stand *with great constancy against those that have afflicted* me, and these *seeing* me, *shall be troubled*

---

94 The expression "sleep of sin," *somno peccati*, appears to be derived from 1 Thess. 5:6 and Eph. 5:14 and Rom. 13:11, where the state of a sinner is compared to a sleeper, and the believer as one awake. In his epistle to Pammachius, St. Jerome says drawing from the Pauline source: "For there is a sleep of sin, which leads to death." *Ep.* 119, PL 22, 972. "Preserve me from the black sleep of sin," wrote St. John Henry Newman, translating the Greek Devotion of Bishop Lancelot Andrews, Διαφύλαξον ἐμὲ ἀπὸ τοῦ ζοφεροῦ ὕπνου τῆς ἁμαρτίας.
95 Eph. 5:14a.
96 Rom. 13:11a.
97 1 Cor. 15:51b.
98 Wis. 3:8a.
99 1 Cor. 6:2a.

with terrible fear... groaning for anguish of spirit.[100] For here the Lord says to the Church through Isaiah: *For a small moment have I forsaken you, but with great mercies will I gather you. In a moment of indignation have I hid my face a little while from you, but with everlasting kindness have I had mercy on you.*[101] **40{41}[13]** *Me autem propter innocentiam suscepisti*, but you have upheld me by reason of my innocence, that is, you have heard me and have approved me. For Christ has chosen for himself *a glorious Church, not having spot or wrinkle*,[102] according to the Apostle [Paul]. And the Church also has been granted this innocence by Christ. She is therefore chosen, not because innocent and immaculate, but she is innocent and immaculate because she is chosen. *Et confirmasti me in conspectu tuo in aeternum*, and [you have] established me in your sight for ever, that is, you have strengthened me in faith even up until the end of this world, as you have promised: *Behold I am with you all days, even to the consummation of the world.*[103] And elsewhere: *I will espouse you to me forever... and I will espouse you to me in faith.*[104] For the Church of God will not be found entirely to fail so long as the generations of man last.[105]

40{41}[14] *Blessed be the Lord the God of Israel from eternity to eternity. So be it. So be it.*

Benedictus Dominus, Deus Israel, a saeculo, et usque in saeculum. Fiat, fiat.

Finally, the Church gives thanks to God and says: **40{41}[14]** *Benedictus Dominus, Deus Israel*; Blessed be the Lord the God of Israel. This verse is explained in the previous exposition.[106]

---

100 Wis. 5:1, 2a, 3a.
101 Is. 54:7-8.
102 Eph. 5:27a.
103 Matt. 28:20b.
104 Hosea 2:19a, 20a.
105 E. N. "The Church is indefectible, that is, she remains and will remain the Institution of Salvation, founded by Christ, until the end of the world." Ludwig Ott, *Fundamentals of Catholic Dogma* (North Carolina: TAN Books 1974), p. 296 (trans., Patrick Lynch, ed. James Canon Bastible)."Now, what Christ, the Lord ... established in the blessed apostle Peter for the perpetual safety and everlasting good of the Church must, by the will of the same, endure without interruption in the Church, which was founded on the rock and which remains firm until the end of the world." DS 3056. "In saying that the Church is indefectible we assert both her imperishableness, that is, her constant duration to the end of the world, and the essential immutability of her teaching, her constitution and her liturgy. This does not exclude the decay of individual "churches" (*i.e.*, parts of the Church) and accidental changes." Ott, p. 296.
106 *See* Article LXXX (Psalm 40:14).

This most beautiful Psalm strongly recommends works of mercy; and it clearly demonstrates how many are the persecutions of the just, recognizing that the ungodly will whisper against the blameless. For this reason it is useful to consider what it is to whisper, and of the gravity of that sin.[107] We know, therefore, that a whisperer (*susurrator*) and detractor (*detractor*) are alike in the matter and form of speaking: for both speak of another, and this in a hidden way. But they differ in their end, for the detractor intends to denigrate the reputation of another; but the whisperer intends to disseminate discord among friends, and to extinguish mutual love. Whence Scripture provides: *when the whisperer is taken away, contentions shall cease.*[108] And so in whispering one does not always intend to say something evil of another, but [rather he intends to say] whatever he supposes can destroy the concord of friends. For he [the whisperer] speaks to each of them that which he figures each of them will find displeasing in the other: and so whispering (*susurro*) and being double-tongued (*bilinguis*) are the same. But he who engages in contumely (*contumeliosus*) intends to derogate another of honor.[109] From which it can clearly be seen which of these vices is the most grievous. For to say something to hurt another is to sin, especially since it is committed against one's neighbor: the more the sin produces damage, therefore, the more grievous it is. But friendship is a greater good than honor or good repute according to this, *Nothing can be compared to a faithful friend.*[110] Honor appears to be a greater good than a good name: therefore whispering (*susurratio*) is a greater sin than contumely (*contumelia*) or detraction (*detractio*). Also, contumely is worse than detraction, and detraction is more grievous than theft, because it robs a greater good than theft, namely, a good reputation, which is greater and more desirable than an exterior thing according to this, *Take care of a good name.*[111] For this will be more lamentable to you than a thousand great and precious treasures. Theft also is of its nature (*ex genere suo*) a mortal sin because it

---

107 E. N. The discussion which follows generously draws from St. Thomas's *Summa Theologiae*, where the sins of relating to "injuries inflicted by words uttered extrajudicially," *de iniuriis verborum quae inferuntur extra iudicium*, are treated. The sins of whispering (*susurratio*), and detraction (*detractio*), and contumely (*contumelia*) are treated in ST IIaIIae, qq. 72–74.
108 Prov. 26:20. E. N. I have departed from the Douay-Rheims by replacing "talebearer" with "whisperer" for the Latin *susurrator*.
109 E. N. "For who would bear the whips and scorns of time, / Th'oppressor's wrong, the proud man's contumely." Shakespeare, Hamlet, 3.1.70–71.
110 Ecclus. 6:15a.
111 Ecclus. 41:15a.

is contrary to justice. If, therefore, theft is a mortal sin, and if detraction is more grievous than theft, and detraction more than contumely, and whispering worse than contumely, it follows that whispering is a mortal and pestiferous sin. For which we reason we find in Ecclesiasticus: *The whisperer and the double tongued is accursed: for he has troubled many that were at peace.*[112] And again: *The whisperer shall defile his own soul, and shall be hated by all;*[113] *and an evil mark of disgrace upon the double tongued (bilinguem).*[114] Yet frequently whispering and detraction are assumed to be the same, as also in this present Psalm. Let us flee, therefore, dear ones, this vice which is so venomous and deadly as if it were a poisonous lizard or snake; and let us take away from this Psalm true mercy and a steadfast patience.

PRAYER

WE BESEECH YOU, O GOD OF CLEMENCY, O Father of indulgence, who alone are powerful to loose the sins of men, have mercy on us, we plead of you, and deign to heal the souls which sinned against you: raise us from the sepulchral mound of vice, and, in that evil day, deliver us for your name's sake.

Quaesumus, Deus clementiae, Pater indulgentiae, qui solus
hominum potens es peccata relaxare, nostri, deprecamur,
miserere, et animas tibi peccantium sanare dignare :
resuscita nos de tumulis vitiorum, et in die
mala libera nos propter nomen tuum.

---

112 Ecclus. 28:15.
113 Ecclus. 21:31. E. N. I have replaced the Douay-Rheims's "talebearer" to translate *susurro* with "whisperer" so that there is consistency in Denis's *Commentary*.
114 Ecclus. 5:17a.

Psalm 41

ARTICLE LXXXII
EXPOSITION OF THE FORTY-FIRST PSALM:
QUEMADMODUM DESIDERAT CERVUS.
AS THE HART PANTS.

41{42}[1] *Unto the end, understanding for the sons of Korah.*
In finem, intellectus filiis Core.

PLACED ABOVE THIS PSALM THAT WE ARE now explaining is this title: 41{42}[1] *In finem, intellectus filiis Core; unto the end, understanding for the sons of Korah*: that is, this understanding directing us to the end or to eternal life coincides with the sons of Korah, that is, imitators of Christ crucified, who despise the world, and desire *to be dissolved and to be with Christ*.[1] And Jerome affirms this Psalm to be from the sons of Korah, or [perhaps] better [said], most excellently composed by one of them. Whence, in its translation according to the Hebrew, he put this title on it: *In finem, intellectus doctissimi filiorum Core, unto the end, most learned of the sons of Korah*. But Augustine, who asserts that David composed all the Psalms attributed to David, says this Psalm is ascribed to the sons of Korah because of its spiritual interpretation, as the title of the prior Psalm was shown to be in the explanation [of that Psalm], or because it was sung by them in the temple.[2]

41{42}[2] *As the hart pants after the fountains of water, so my soul pants after you, O God.*
Quemadmodum desiderat cervus ad fontes aquarum, ita desiderat anima mea ad te, Deus.

Therefore, the author of this Psalm speaks in the person of an ardent lover, one who is able to say this, *Stay me up with flowers, compass me about with apples: because I languish with love*,[3] and says: 41{42}[2] *Quemadmodum desiderat cervus ad fontes aquarum, ita desiderat anima*

---

1 Phil 1:23b.
2 E. N. The reference, of course, is to St. Augustine's *Enarrationes in Psalmos*.
3 Songs 2:5.

mea ad te, Deus; As the hart pants after the fountains of water, so my soul pants after you, O God. O most sweet word, O burning speech, O spark sent from the divine fire! For in fact our God is a fire.[4] And how can I say this [verse] unhappy or being lukewarm and by this be worthy to be vomited?[5] For the very utterance of the word just recited is in need of exhortation, not explanation. O truly blessed is the man who is able to say this word truly and of himself, whose soul is wounded with charity, whose complete affection is purely and immovably affixed upon the Godhead, so that he can say with the Apostle [Paul]: *And I live, now not I, but Christ lives in me.*[6] But no man is or has the power to be such a man unless he thoroughly uproots his own self-love, and has all of his soul's affections quieted and ordered, and he spurns all the world as if it were nothing in order to adhere, plunge, and inviscerate himself, as much as he is able, and with pure and greatest desire, only in the most sweet God,[7] counting all things *as dung* so that he might gain Christ and possess God.[8] For the more perfectly one's affection attaches to any particular good, the less he is divided among many [goods].

And therefore it says: *As the hart pants after fountains of water, so my soul pants after you, O God,* that is, as a hart fatigued after being pursued or being hunted most ardently desires a stream of water, and with

---

4 *Cf.* Deut. 4:24: *The Lord your God is a consuming fire, a jealous God.*
5 *Cf.* Rev. 3:16: *Because your lukewarm, and neither cold, nor hot, I will begin to vomit you out of my mouth.*
6 Gal. 2:20a.
7 L. Denis uses an unusual and starkly visual, word *inviscerari*—to inviscerate, that is, to make oneself a part of another's viscera, his insides, to incorporate oneself within another's body—as an analogy of the desire to immerse oneself in the *Being* of God, "in whom we live, and move, and have our being." Acts 17:28 (RSVCE). Curiously, the notion seems to have had a direct influence on the Puritan divines. It is found, for example, in the Puritan Thomas Watson's (*ca.* 1620–1686) reflections on the Lord's Prayer, "A saint would have more knowledge, more sanctity, more of Christ's presence.... *Dulcissimo Deo totus immergi cupit et inviscerari.* We would be swallowed up in God, and be ever bathing ourselves in those perfumed waters of pleasure which run at his right hand forever." *A Body of Practical Divinity in a Series of Sermons on the Shorter Catechism* (Aberdeen: 1838), 568. The Oxonian theologian Nathaniel Culverwell (*ca.* 1619–1651) likewise: "The thirsty hart pants על אפיקי מים [after springs of water] and the Christian after fullness of communion with his God: *Dulcissimo Deo totus immergi cupit et inviscerari,* as the *Carthusian* speaks." *An Elegant and Learned Discourse of the Light of* Nature, (Oxford: Henry Dymock Bookseller 1669), 70. Cotton Mather (1663–1728), in his *The Life of Mr. Nathanael Rogers,*" speaks of his subject's religious exercises, observing that "at length he so abounded, that as *Carthusian* speaks, *Dulcissimo Deo totus immergi cupit & inviscerari.*" *Magnalia Christi Americana* (Hartford: Silas Andrus and Son 1855), 415.
8 Phil. 3:8.

greatest speed runs toward it; *so, O my Creator, my God, and my Lord, my soul* wearied by the miseries of this life, bothered by temptations, and often hindered by the various impediments of human weakness from contemplation and loving you, *pants after you*, that is, its desire strains out to you, the sovereign and immutable Good, desiring to the utmost and singularly and finally to come to you, desiring to embrace you, to enjoy your sweetness, to gaze upon your beauty, desiring to unite with you inavertibly,[9] and blessedly, intimately, and closely. For you, O holy Lord, O blessed God, O glorious Creator, are my treasure: and so where you are, there is my heart.[10] You are the entirety of my good, and you alone are my all; I desire to be dissolved,[11] I desire to enter into the joy of my Lord, I desire to know and to be known.[12] And because I am not able, in this mortal life, to seek perfectly to love, incessantly to praise, clearly to know, and totally to honor you, therefore, *as a hart pants after fountains of water, so my soul pants after you*, God: not indeed principally looking towards my own reward and happiness, but with divine love of honor and goodness so that I may perfectly love, that I may unceasingly praise, that I may see you face to face,[13] and I may worship you in all integrity. For you are the eternal and infinite Good, in which is found the perfect possession of all goodness and beauty and all that is desirable.

And so three are those things that ought to induce us to love God. The first is the very goodness and love (*caritas*) of God, which, since it exceeds infinitely all goods and created love, so it follows that he is infinitely more desirable and more loveable than all created goods: and so, we ought to love God infinitely more than ourselves, more than any created good, or more than all things put together. The second is the consideration of the benefits of God, namely, of the natural and gratuitous gifts. And in support of either of these reasons we might refer to that which John said: *Let us love God, because he first has loved us.*[14] The third is the consideration of the promises of God, namely of the beatitude which he promises and prepares for us in heaven, as the Savior himself says: *I go to prepare a place for you; and I will take you up unto myself, so that where I am, you also may be.*[15]

---

9   E. N. This word *inavertibiliter* is frequently used by Denis to describe the fixity with which our union with God enjoys. For further commentary, see footnote 29-67.
10 *Cf.* Matt. 6:21.
11 Phil. 1:23b.
12 *Cf.* 1 Cor. 12b: *Now I know in part; but then I shall know even as I am known.*
13 *Cf.* 1 Cor. 12a: *We see now through a glass in a dark manner; but then face to face.*
14 1 John 4:19.
15 John 14:2b, 3b.

Finally, desire proceeds from love: for no one desires that which he does not love.[16] But love is both absent and present; for both wayfarers (*viatores*) and the blessed in heaven (*comprehensores*) are said to love God. Now, properly speaking, desire is increased to the extent [the object desired] is absent: and so, properly speaking, this [sort of desire] never applies to Christ, for his soul from its very beginning always enjoyed God's presence; nor is it applicable to the blessed in heaven, unless [the concept of] desire is employed for the purpose of excluding a sense of surfeit (*fastidium*),[17] in the way that Peter in his epistle says, that upon Christ *the angels desire to look*.[18] Since Christ was in a certain sense also a wayfarer (*viator*), and he prayed for the glorification of his body and its ascension into heaven, thus this verse along with the following one can fittingly be applied to him.[19] Whence also he in the Gospel said: *O incredulous generation, how long shall I be with you? How long shall I suffer you?*[20] By this he plainly declares himself to desire to return to the Father by means of his bodily glorification. This he also showed to his disciples saying: *If you loved me, you would indeed be glad, because I*

---

16 E. N. *Contemplationis desiderium procedit ex amore obiecti: quia ubi amor, ibi oculos.* "The desire of contemplation proceeds from the love of its object, for where there is love, there are the eyes." St. Thomas Aquinas, *In Sent.*, III, 35, 1, 2.

17 E. N. On the notion of *fastidium*, and the sense of surfeit, *ennui*, boredom, and even disgust and hatred that often results in the satisfaction of earthly, worldly loves, and the theological efforts to address this and negate even the possibility of that sort of occurrence with respect to the blessed in heaven's attainment of God and the fulfillment of their desire, *see* footnote 20-35 in Volume 1. The traditional formula is that, in heaven, "there is desire with satisfaction, and satisfaction with desire," *desiderium cum satietate, et satietas cum desiderio*. This lack of full accord between the "three loves" we know and experience in nature—whether it be *storgē* (στοργή), *philia* (φιλία), *erōs* (ἔρως)—and the fulfillment of charity or agape (ἀγάπη/*caritas*) in heaven shows the *analogous* relationship between human love and the divine love, so while human love and divine love are not entirely *equivocal* concepts, they are manifestly not *univocal*. For the "four loves," *see* C. S. Lewis, *The Four Loves* (New York: Harcourt Brace 1991). On the relationship between *eros* and *agape*, *see* Benedict XVI, *Deus caritas est*, Nos. 3–12 and Martin Cyril D'Arcy, S. J., *The Mind and Heart of Love: Lion and Unicorn, A Study in Eros and Agape* (Providence, RI: Cluny Media 2019).

18 1 Pet. 1:12b.

19 E. N. God was never absent from the human nature of the Lord Jesus, as in his humanity he enjoyed the vision of God, the face-to-face encounter in the very presence of the Holy Trinity, throughout his whole life; thus, Jesus could not *desire* to see God in the way we, who are fully wayfarers, must. Yet Jesus did have a limited desire consistent with being a wayfarer, namely, the desire that his body be raised from the dead, be glorified, and ascend to heaven to be seated at the right hand of the Father.

20 Mark 9:18.

*go to the Father.*²¹ *Glorify* (he said) *you me, O Father, with yourself, with the glory which I had, before the world was made.*²² And he desired most ardently to go to the Father, when hanging and dying on the Cross, he said: *Father, into your hands I commend my spirit.*²³

But love is the end, the summit, and the mistress of all virtues.²⁴ For this reason, Moses writes: *And now, Israel, what does the Lord your God require of you, but that you ... love him, and serve ... him, with all your heart, and with all your soul?*²⁵ Therefore to love corresponds the essential reward in the heavenly homeland, namely, the vision of God. For we will see God more clearly and with more delight the more we now desire more ardently to see him, because love of the way causes desire. But desire lays bare and opens the affection of the lover to the receiving of the beloved: indeed, what else is desire but for the opening up of the appetite disposing one to the receiving of the beloved? How gloriously, clearly, and intimately will he, who so desires him now, see God in the heavenly homeland as a hart drinking from the stream! Let us therefore love and with the greatest devotion desire God, sublime and holy, the Father of lights, the fount of sweetness, the principle of all decorum, in whom is immeasurable beauty, infinite felicity, most superlatively sweet peace, the most full life, interminable wisdom, and the abundance of all desire without measure: and all these things are not in him anything other except the most simple Being, pure Unity, and substance above all substances, and subsistence wholly unknown.

41{42}[3] *My soul has thirsted after the strong living God; when shall I come and appear before the face of God?*

Sitivit anima mea ad Deum fortem, vivum; quando veniam, et apparebo ante faciem Dei?

---

21 John 14:28b.
22 John 17:5.
23 Luke 23:46 (*see also* Ps. 30:5 [(31):6]).
24 E. N. [C]*aritas est virtus dignissima, omniumque virtutum forma, vita, vertex, finis, regina, ac motrix. Nec aliqua virtus tam efficaciter et valenter movet ac incitat ad omnem actum virtutum, nec ita celeriter et potenter retrahit a peccatis, ut amor Dei.* "For charity is the most worthy virtue, and the form, life, summit, end, queen, and engine of all virtues. No other virtue so efficaciously and powerfully moves and incites to every act of virtue, nor so swiftly and powerfully holds one back from sin, as the love of God." Denis the Carthusian, *Inflammatorium Divini Amoris sive Tractatus Dialogicus inter Salvatorem & Hominem* (Cologne: 1605), 9.
25 Deut. 10:12.

Therefore, the Prophet [David] modulates his speech to us,[26] since he wants to excite us to love God by his example, adding: **41{42}[3]** *Sitivit anima mea, my soul has thirsted*, that is, ardently and with fiery affection it desires *ad Deum fortem, after the strong* and omnipotent *Deum vivum, the living God* and fountainlike principle of all life, from whom comes the life of nature, the life of grace, and the life of glory. Of whose strength, king Darius who knew by experience said: *It is decreed by me, that in all my empire and my kingdom all men dread and fear the God of Daniel, for he is the living... God for ever.*[27] And he is called the living God to differentiate him from the imagined gods and immortal men whose bodies are putrefied, and their souls damned, namely Jove, Saturn, Mars, Mercury.[28] Also, it is better that *strong living God* is written than "living fountain" (*fontem vivum*)."[29] For in Hebrew we have "strong living" (*fortem vimum*). *Quando veniam, when shall I come* from this body of death to the impassible state, from this exile unto the kingdom, and from the pilgrimage of this life to the heavenly homeland? *Et apparebo ante faciem Dei, and* [when shall I] *appear before the face of God*, so that he appears to me, and manifests himself to me by sight? For then *I shall be satisfied, when* in this way his *glory shall appear*.[30] For by the face of God is understood God himself, as present and known. In this way the soul of Paul thirsted for God, who cried out: *Unhappy man that I am, who shall deliver me from the body of this*

---

26   E. N. The Psalm shifts or modulates from addressing God to addressing the reader or hearer of the Psalm.
27   Dan. 6:26. E. N. King Darius experienced Daniel being unharmed by the lions in the lion's den, and those conspiring against him being devoured by the lions.
28   E. N. Denis supports the theory of Euhemerism, named after the 4th century BC Greek mythographer, Euhemerus, who held that the Greek gods were historical men, generally kings, who through historical accretions and cultivation came to be apotheosized or regarded as gods. This was a commonly held opinion by the Fathers of the Church and later Scholastics. St. Isidore, for example, in his *Origins* or *Etymologies* (VIII, 11, 1) states: *Quos pagani deos asserunt, homines olim fuisse produntur, et pro uniuscuisque vita vel meritis coli apud suos post mortem coeperunt ut apud Aegyptum Isis apud Creatam Iovis, apud Mauros Iuga, apud Latinos Faunus, apud Romanos Quirinus.* "Those the pagans regarded as gods are known to have been at one time, and in accordance with each one of their life and merits they began to be worshiped after their death among their own people, as with Egypt, Isis; with Crete, Jove; with the Moors, Juba; with the Latins, Faunus; with the Romans, Quirinus." The Latin text from http://www.thelatinlibrary.com/isidore/8.shtml.
29   E. N. Some versions of the Latin Vulgate had *fontem vivum*, "living fountain," instead of *Deum fortem, vivum*, "strong living God," which the Sixto-Clementine Vulgate has.
30   Ps. 16:15b.

*death?*³¹ So also Moses, who said to the Lord: *If therefore I have found favor in your sight, show me your face, that I may know you.*³²

41{42}[4] *My tears have been my loaves day and night, while it is said to me daily: Where is your God?*³³

Fuerunt mihi lacrimae meae panes die ac nocte, dum dicitur mihi quotidie: Ubi est Deus tuus?

41{42}[4] *Fuerunt mihi lacrimae meae panes die ac nocte,* my tears have been my loaves day and night: that is, this alone was to me consolation, restoration, and refreshment of the mind thirsting for God, which on account of the desire of God during this life is able to shed tears and sigh day and night, that is, at certain times of the day or night. *For hope that is deferred afflicts the soul:* similarly, desire ardently torments the lover until he is united with the beloved. Whence, he who truly and fervently loves God and the heavenly homeland is in no little way afflicted by the lengthening out of the delay: for which reason paleness and leanness are signs of love. But interior sorrow is mitigated by exterior tears, for, through weeping, the affliction of the mind, which before was enclosed upon itself, breaks forth: and so it [sorrow] is diminished, especially because the interior of the heart is diffused by many things, and in this manner interior sorrow is lessened. And therefore the loaves of tears represent the sighing and loving souls, and they are sweetly consoled, abundantly filled, and made fat with the grace of God. Whence in a later Psalm it is written: *you will feed us with the bread of tears.*³⁴ But then my tears were bread to me, *dum dicitur mihi quotidie,* while it is said to be daily, by the unfaithful and the perverse: *Ubi est Deus tuus,* where is your God, in whom you hope, and whom you so desire? It is as if they were saying: "Your faith is foolish, and your hope has become vain." This the early Church was able to say when the persecutors killed and derided the faithful and blasphemed the name of Christ, saying: Where is your Christ? Let him help you and free you now, if his is able.

---

31 Rom. 7:24b.
32 Ex. 33:13a.
33 E. N. The Douay-Rheims translates *panes* as "bread," even though *panes* is plural. Because Denis's argument assumes the plural, I have modified the Douay-Rheims to read "loaves." The Hebrew has לחם (*lechem*) and the Septagint ἄρτος (*artos*), both singular.
34 Ps. 79:6a.

41{42}[5] *These things I remembered, and poured out my soul in me: for I shall go over into the place of the wonderful tabernacle, even to the house of God: With the voice of joy and confession; the noise of one feasting.*[35]

Haec recordatus sum, et effudi in me animam meam, quoniam transibo in locum tabernaculi admirabilis, usque ad donum Dei, in voce exsultationis et confessionis, sonus epulantis.

41{42}[5] *Haec, these things,* namely, the delay of the presence of God and the derision of evil men, *recordatus sum; et effudi in me animam meam; I remembered, and poured out my soul in me,* that is, I have detached myself from exterior things and things of the senses, turning my reflection to my interior, and thinking of matters of salvation: as Jeremiah said, *It is good to wait with silence for the salvation of God;*[36] and again, *He shall sit solitary, and hold his peace: because he has taken it up upon himself.*[37] And so, *I poured out my soul in me,* in order that, set free from exterior and useless things, I might have the leisure for divine things with a free mind, which he who is entangled in the hustle and bustle of things is unable to do. And this is what the Lord says through another Prophet: *If you return and be quiet, you shall be saved: in silence and in hope shall your strength be.*[38]

Therefore *I have poured out my soul in me, quoniam transibo in locum tabernaculi admirabilis usque ad domum Dei; for I shall go over into the place of the wonderful tabernacle, even to the house of God,* that is, because I have hope that—once this pilgrimage completed—I will enter the eternal house not made by human hands in heaven, namely the Kingdom of Heaven, the empyreal heaven, which is the tabernacle of the Blessed and the triumphant Church, which is the house of God. Whence the Apostle [Paul] says: *we know, if our earthly house of this habitation be dissolved, that we have a building of God, a house not made with hands, eternal in heaven.*[39] And to the Hebrews: *Having confidence,* he says, *in the entering into the holies by the blood of Christ, let us approach with a*

---

35 E. N. The Douay-Rheims translates the Latin *confessionis* as "with the voice of praise." The Latin *confessio* can be understood as denoting confession of praise, but also as denoting confession of sin. See footnote 27-49. Denis understands *confessionis* as "with the voice of confession" of sins. Accordingly, I have adapted the Douay-Rheims to accord with his *Commentary*.
36 Lam. 3:26.
37 Lam. 3:28.
38 Is. 30:15.
39 2 Cor. 5:1.

sincere heart in the fullness of faith, the hearts cleansed from an evil conscience. But that which now is said in this Psalm — *wonderful tabernacle* — can be construed jointly and severally. For heaven is the place of the tabernacle, which is wonderful in itself; and this same tabernacle is wonderful, that is, of God, who is the height of all wonders, of which we see in a later Psalm, *God is wonderful in his saints*.[40] But in the interim, while namely I am compelled to remain in this body, I will *go over* daily *into the place of* this *tabernacle*, by contemplation and by hope: as the Apostle [Paul] says, but *We... beholding the glory of the Lord with open face;*[41] and the heavenly promises, or the goods of this *wonderful tabernacle*, I behold and greet from afar, and I confess that I am a pilgrim and stranger on the earth;[42] and by this I will fulfill that which the divine and holy Apostle exhorted, *Let us hasten therefore,* he says, *to enter into that rest*, so that we might not find something to be lacking in us. In this manner the heavenly Spouse proceeded forward daily toward this tabernacle, who says to the virgin Bridegroom: *Draw me and we will run after you to the odor of your ointments.*[43]

In voce exsultationis et confessionis, sonus epulantis; with the voice of joy and confession, the noise of one feasting. This can be explained in two ways. First of wayfarers, so that it is understood in this sense: *the noise of one feasting,* that is, his word or speech wherein in the present he relishes and experiences how sweet the Lord is, and eats the bread of children at Christ's sacrificial table, is *with the voice of joy,* that is, in delightful remembrance of the goodness and benefits of God, *and confession,* that is, in mournful remembrance of one's own ingratitude and sinfulness. For, according to the exhortation of the Apostle [Paul], provided we feast *not with the old leaven,* that is, in the observance of the ceremonies of

---

40 Ps. 67:36a.
41 2 Cor. 3:18a. E. N. Denis is a bit cryptic here. The full passage in 2 Cor. 3:18 is: *But we all beholding the glory of the Lord with open face, are transformed into the same image from glory to glory, as by the Spirit of the Lord.* What does St. Paul mean by this? Perhaps we can turn to Walter Hilton (1340/1345–1396) who says with respect to this verse: "It is the same, as if... he said this: 'We first being reformed in virtues, having the face of our soul uncovered by opening our spiritual eyes, behold as in a mirror the heavenly joy. Additionally, we being encompassed and fully shaped are one with the image of our Lord, from the clarity of faith into clarity of understanding, or from a clear desire into that of blessed love; and all this is brought in a man's soul by the spirit of Our Lord.' This part of contemplation, God gives it where and to whom He will." Walter Hilton, *Ladder of Perfection* (USA: Revelation Insight Publishing) 26. It appears to be a reference to *infused* contemplation.
42 *Cf.* Heb. 11:13.
43 Songs 1:3.

the law, *nor with the leaven of malice and wickedness,*[44] glorying in evil, and exulting *in most wicked things,*[45] but *with the unleavened bread of sincerity and truth.*[46] Together ought we to remember then the divine goodness and liberality and also our own depravity and perversity. And so contemplating the mercy of God, let the sound of our voices burst forth in exultation, saying that which Jeremiah said: *There is none like to you, O Lord: you are great and great is your name in might. Who shall fear you, O king of nations?*[47] Contemplating also our misery, let the sound of our voices burst forth in confession, saying that which Job said: *I will reprove my ways in his sight, and he shall be my Savior.*[48] The Second exposition is this: *the noise of one feasting,* that is, the one tasting the divine sweetness in his fountain, and the one happily enjoying God in the heavenly homeland, is *with the voice of joy,* that is, in most exuberant joy arising from the contemplation of the Godhead, *and confession,* that is, of the divine praises, in the manner that is stated in Isaiah: *The giving of thanks shall be found in it and the voice of praise.*[49]

41{42}[6]   *Why are you sad, O my soul? And why do you trouble me? Hope in God, for I will still give praise to him: the salvation of my countenance,*

Quare tristis es, anima mea? Et quare conturbas me? Spera in Deo, quoniam adhuc confitebor illi, salutare vultus mei,

41{42}[7]   *and my God. My soul is troubled within myself: therefore I will remember you from the land of Jordan and the Hermonites, from the little hill.*

et Deus meus. Ad meipsum anima mea conturbata est; propterea memor ero tui de terra Iordanis, et Hermoniim a monte modico.

Since, therefore, so great are the promised good and the things prepared for you, **41{42}[6]** *Quare tristis es anima mea, Why are you sad, O my soul,* with earthly and evil and disordered sorrows on account of temporal adversities and evils? *Et quare conturbas me, and why do you trouble me* with troubles that impede the act of reason, and give disquieting birth

---

44   1 Cor. 5:8a.
45   Prov. 2:14b.
46   1 Cor. 5:8b.
47   Jer. 10:6-7a.
48   Job. 13:15b–16a.
49   *Cf.* Is. 51:3. E. N. Denis liberally rearranges this verse which reads: *Joy and gladness shall be found therein, thanksgiving, and the voice of praise.*

of superfluous thoughts? For there is a certain disordered sorrow which is not found in a just man, according to that which Solomon asserts: *Whatsoever shall befall the just man, it shall not make him sad.*[50] And Ecclesiasticus: *The joyfulness of the heart, is the life of a man . . .* But *drive away sadness far from you, because sadness has killed many, and there is no profit in it.*[51] And this kind sorrow is understood to be that which Christ has indicated through Isaiah: *He shall not be sad, nor troublesome.*[52] Patience is ordered against this sorrow, just like meekness is to anger: of which the Apostle [Paul] says, *Patience is necessary for you; that, doing the will of God, you may receive the promise.*[53] This sorrow, therefore, with contemplation and the hope of future goods will be stopped completely, and of this [sorrow] this Psalm now most capably speaks. There is, however, a certain good sorrow which is an act of virtue proceeding out of the consideration of one's own imperfections and fault, or of the delay of glory, or from the contemplation of the errors and vices by which men are entangled. Of this sorrow it is written: *The heart of the wise is where there is mourning, and the heart of fools where there is mirth.*[54] And again: *By the sadness of the countenance the mind of the offender is corrected.*[55] And this sadness was in Christ, in the way that is said by the Evangelist: Jesus was grieved *by the blindness of their hearts.*[56] And he himself: *My soul is sorrowful even unto death.*[57] Yet this sorrow is restrained, lest he who has overmuch sorrow be absorbed by it.[58] For this sort of sorrow although good in itself, yet also accidently is able to be harmful because of the weakness of bodily nature, according to that which Solomon professes: *A joyful mind makes age flourishing: a sorrowful spirit dries up the bones.*[59] Whence that which has now been said — *Why are you sad, O my soul?* — of this sort [good] sorrow [which is accidentally harmful] it may in some way also be said.

Thence is given the best counsel against sadness. *Spera in Deo, quoniam adhuc confitebor illi; hope in God, for I will still give praise to him*: that is, trust that by the grace of God you may overcome ultimately such causes of sorrow, and you will confess to the Lord with the perfect and perpetual

---

50   Prov. 12:21a.
51   Ecclus. 30:23–25.
52   Is. 42:4a.
53   Heb. 10:36.
54   Eccl. 7:5.
55   Eccl. 7:4b.
56   Mark 3:5a.
57   Matt. 26:38a.
58   *Cf.* 2 Cor. 2:7.
59   Prov. 17:22.

confession of praise. For hope expels sorrow, as is clear from that which is said in Scripture: *You that fear the Lord, hope in him: and mercy shall come to you for your delight.*[60] And so I will give praise to the Lord, who is *salutare vultus mei, the salvation of my countenance,* that is, the object and the cause of the beatitude of my soul, both in the present as well as the future: as it is written, I am the Savior of the people, says the Lord.[61] And by Hosea, outside of me *there is no Savior.*[62] [He is that Savior] who also is 41{42}[7] *Deus meus, my God,* from whose causality I depend, and under whose providence I am subject.

Ad me ipsum anima mea turbata est, my soul is troubled within myself: that is, within myself, my soul has incurred trouble from my disordered manner of living and from inferior and sensible goods. For sins hinder true tranquility and peace, and lead to confusion and disturbances. But so long as we turn to God we obtain peace. For which reason it is said by Hosea: *Return ... to the Lord your God, for you have fallen down by your iniquity.*[63]

Propterea memor ero tui de terra Iordanis et Hermoniim, therefore I will remember you from the land of Jordan and the Hermonites. In the book of Joshua we find written the manner in which the waters of the Jordan turned back upon themselves, and the sons of Israel passed through the dried up channel. And this walk through the Jordan is a figure of the immersion of the faithful in Baptism, especially since Christ chose to be baptized in the Jordan.[64] And so it is [to be understood] in this sense: *I will remember you from the land of the Jordan and the Hermonites,* that is, of marvels, or because of the marvels which you did in the land or in the river bottom of the Jordan, and in the land of Hermon, which is situated alongside the Jordan, and whose name is obtained from Hermon, the small mountain located next to the Jordan. *I will remember,* I say, namely recalling the miracles which during the time of the sons of Israel you performed in this land. And most of all it is fitting for us to be mindful of the Lord Jesus in the land of Jordan, that is, because of his works in the Jordan; so that we might recall his ineffable dignity and his incomprehensible humility by which he, the King of glory, the Saint of Saints, and the Incarnate God, came to John in the Jordan, in order to be baptized by him, amidst others who were sinners.[65] [And we might also recall] how there his touch of his most pure flesh gave to all water regenerative

---

60 Ecclus. 2:9.
61 *Cf.* Is. 43:11: *I am, I am the Lord: and there is no Savior besides me.*
62 Hosea 13:4b.
63 Hos. 14:2.
64 Matt. 3:13, 16; Luke 3:21.
65 Matt. 3:13.

power, and besides how the mystery of the superlatively holy Trinity was revealed there, when the Son appeared in the flesh, the Spirit in the form of a dove, and the Father by voice.[66] [And we might further recall] the manner that, upon Jesus being baptized, the heavens were opened as a sign that in Baptism all sins are remitted. Or [we can think of it] thus: *I will remember you from the land of the Jordan*, that is, from the fount of Baptism, and *the Hermonites*, that is, from the renunciation of the devil or the anathematization of sin.[67] Indeed, by Jordan is interpreted their descent, and by Hermonites, anathema.[68] *A monte modico, from the little hill*, that is, from the knowledge of myself, which you have given me by grace and by which I recognize my own littleness and humility. It is [to be understood] in this sense: *I will remember*, O Lord, how great a mercy I was given in Baptism, how I there put on Christ, received the virtues, renounced the works of the devil, and gave up the high mount of pride, recognizing myself to be a little hill. And so of the land of Jordan explained in this way, namely as Baptism which we ought always to be mindful of, so that we might keep watch of that received garment of innocence or repair its loss, is written: *That day there shall be a fountain open to the house of David, and to the inhabitants of Jerusalem: for the washing of the sinner, and of the unclean woman.*[69]

41{42}[8] *Deep calls on deep, at the noise of your floodgates. All your heights and your billows have passed over me.*

Abyssus abyssum invocat, in voce cataractarum tuarum; omnia excelsa tua, et fluctus tui super me transierunt.

41{42}[8] *Abyssus abyssum invocat*, Deep calls upon deep. By the word deep is meant as if something were without end. Whence also the sea on account of its depth is called deep. But what in the things of creation are without end in such a manner as is our ignorance, as is our misery, as is our malice? And what in God is so without end as is his wisdom which is without measure, as is his mercy which is without boundary, as is his goodness which has utterly no end? Therefore, the verse has this sense: The *deep* of our blindness and ignorance *calls*, O Lord God, *upon the deep* of

---

66 Luke 3:21.
67 E. N. "Baptism signifies," and effects, "liberation from sin and from its instigator the devil." CCC § 1237,
68 E. N. *Iordanis pro baptismo accipitur: Hermon, anathema interpretatur*, "By Jordan baptism is accpeted; Hermon is understood as anathema." *Breviarum in Psalmos*, PL 26, 950 (attributed to St. Jerome).
69 Zech. 13:1.

your mercy and your sufficiency. In short, the *deep* of our depravity prevails *upon the deep* of your goodness. And this, *in voce cataractarum tuarum, at the noise of your floodgates*, that is, in the words and the examples of sacred Scripture, which is the voice of your floodgates, that is, the teacher and herald of your goodness, mercy, and charity. For in sacred Scripture we learn how kindly the Lord is, how favorably disposed towards indulgence, and how loving he is by the works of his hands, especially to the rational creature. And from this knowledge we should be incited to beseech the mercy of God; and so *deep* prays to *deep* saying that which Daniel did: *For your own sake, incline, O my God, your ear, and hear; . . . for it is not for our justifications that we present our prayers before your face, but for the multitude of your tender mercies.*[70] Now, aqueducts of water, or the mouths of rivers, or the window or clouds from which rain is born may properly be called floodgates. Whence in Genesis we read when the flood covered things: *The fountains of the great deep were broken up, and the flood gates of heaven were opened.*[71] And with Malachi, the Lord says: *Bring all the tithes into the storehouse, that there may be meat in my house, and try me in this, . . . if I open not unto you the flood-gates of heaven* and *I will give you rain.*[72] Now the wisdom and mercy, or the kindness and power of God, are the highest principles of all the emanations of God in his relations outside of himself (*ad extra*). (For, according to Plato, in knowing, being able, and willing, each person is perfected by operation.) For this reason wisdom, goodness, and the power of God are able to be called his floodgates, for from these are produced and flow the divine gifts, as water from the mouth of an aqueduct.

Omnia excelsa tua, all your heights, that is, your high and inscrutable judgments, *et fluctus tui*, and your billows, that is, the punishments and tribulations prepared for the reprobate, or those cleansing the just during this age, *super me transierunt*, *have passed over me*, that is, were in consideration of my soul, and they pushed against and surmounted its defense, for I am discouraged in consideration of your judgment and have not the means satisfactorily to fear the punishments of hell. Also, of the present punishments, I do not know whether they are preambles of future punishments, or whether rather they are as remedies for my vices, because of what is written: *All things are kept uncertain for the time to come, because all things equally happen to the just and to the wicked, . . . to the clean and to the unclean.*[73]

---

70   Dan. 17b–18.
71   Gen. 7:11b.
72   Mal. 3:10.
73   Eccl. 9:2a.

41{42}[9] *In the daytime the Lord has commanded his mercy; and a canticle to him in the night. With me is prayer to the God of my life.*

In die mandavit Dominus misericordiam suam, et nocte canticum eius; apud me oratio Deo vitae meae.

41{42}[10] *I will say to God: You are my support. Why have you forgotten me? And why go I mourning, while my enemy afflicts me?*

Dicam Deo: Susceptor meus es; Quare oblitus es mei? Et quare contristatus incedo, dum affligit me inimicus?

41{42}[11] *While my bones are broken, my enemies who trouble me have reproached me; While they say to me day by day: Where is your God?*

Dum confringuntur ossa mea, exprobraverunt mihi qui tribulant me inimici mei, dum dicunt mihi per singulos dies: Ubi est Deus tuus?

41{42}[9] *In die mandavit Dominus misericordiam suam, in the daytime the Lord has commanded his mercy*: that is, in the time of prosperity, of grace and of joy, God directs that all of his goods be ascribed to his kindness: since *he that glories, let him glory in the Lord*;[74] and let him who has made progress attribute to God his progress, because all *our sufficiency is from God*;[75] and let him who receives forgiveness of sins give thanks not to his works, but to God, according to that which the Lord said through Isaiah, *I am he that blots out your iniquities for my own sake*.[76] *Et nocte canticum eius, and a canticle to him in the night*: that is, in times of adversity and affliction, and of the suspension of grace and divine consolation, God commands his song, that is, the humble giving of thanks, and patience, and the blessing of the divine name: since neither in prosperity nor in adversity ought our heart to recede from God, but let it fulfill that which Hosea says, *Keep mercy and judgment, and hope in your God always*.[77] Job sang this song to the Lord in that darkest of nights of his incomparable tribulations, when he said: *The Lord gave, and the Lord has taken away: as it has pleased the Lord so is it done: blessed be the name of the Lord*.[78] And elsewhere: *Although he should kill me, I will trust in him*.[79] Tobias also, of whom it is written:

---

74 2 Cor. 10:17.
75 2 Cor. 3:5b.
76 Is. 43:25a.
77 Hos. 12:6b.
78 Job 1:21b.
79 Job. 13:15a.

Tobias *repined not against God because the evil of blindness had befallen him, but continued immoveable in the fear of God, giving thanks to God all the days of his life.*[80] For this reason, he himself said: *I bless you, O Lord God of Israel, because you have chastised me.*[81] Let us therefore use diligence to follow the paths of the saints and glory in afflictions, accounting like the Apostle [Paul]: *For as the sufferings of Christ abound in us: so also by Christ does our comfort abound. Know, therefore, that as you are partakers of the sufferings, so shall you be also of the consolation.*[82]

Apud me oratio Deo vitae meae, with me is *prayer to the God of my life*: that is, in my not inconstant heart that is recollected within itself is the prayer that I offer to God, who is the principle of all my life, both natural and meritorious.[83] For God is to be entreated, not with a heart divided within itself and inconstant, but with an internal and stable disposition. **41{42}[10]** *Dicam Deo*, *I will say to God*, with great trust: *Susceptor meus es*, *you are my support*, who props me up in my failures, who lifts me up when I fall, who hears me when I pray, who keeps me standing, and who, when I am seeking refuge, embraces me with the paternal and sweet kindness out of the intimacy of your mercy,[84] as you attest to doing in the Gospel: *Him that comes to me, I will not cast out.*[85] And with Jeremiah: *Return, you rebellious children, and I will heal your rebellions.*[86] Since therefore it is so, *Quare*, *why, O Lord, oblitus es mei*, *have you forgotten me?* That is, why do you delay in helping me, and why do you hold yourself back from me as if you have forgotten my need? *Et quare tristis incedo*, *and why go I mourning*,[87]

---

80 Tob. 2:13b–14.
81 Tob. 11:17a.
82 2 Cor. 1:5, 7.
83 E. N. When Denis speaks of the meritorious life, he is referring to the *vita merendi* or *status merendi*, in other words, the supernatural life of grace, a life lived in a state of being able to gain merit, which means that we are *in a state of grace in this life*. For the opportunity for merit ceases with death, see footnote 38-12, and the opportunity for merit is impossible outside of a state of sanctifying grace, see footnote 36-120.
84 L. *viscera misericordiae*, literally, the "bowels of mercy." It is the same expression as found in the Song of Zechariah (Luke 1:78) (*per viscera misericordiae Dei*), which has been translated as "the bowels of the mercy of our God" in the Douay-Rheims, but other translators, less literally inclined, have proffered: "tender mercy of our God." The Greek word is σπλάγχνων (*splagchnōn*), which means the inward parts (the heart, liver, lungs—the *viscera*).
85 John 6:37b.
86 Jer. 3:22.
87 E. N. Denis has the variant reading: *et quare tristis incedo*, which departs from the Sixto-Clementine Vulgate.

that is, sorrowing and without consolation, *dum affligit me inimicus, while my enemy afflicts me*, that is, while the world persecutes, the flesh goads, and the devil tempts me? **41{42}[11]** *Dum confringuntur ossa mea, while my bones are broken*, that is, while bodily I am consumed, burdened, struck down, or spiritually overcome, and I lose the grace and the virtues which are the bones of the soul,[88] *exprobraverunt mihi, they have reproached me*, and insulted and derided me, *qui tribulant me inimici mei, my enemies who trouble me*, namely, the tyrants, or demons, heretics, and perverse men. For out of their hate these rejoice over the adversities of the just. We say this verse to the Lord when grave temptations and great sorrow rush in against us, in the manner that Jonah said: *When my soul was in distress within me, I remembered the Lord. You will bring up my life from corruption, O Lord my God.*[89] *Dum dicunt mihi per singulos dies, Ubi est Deus tuus? While they say to me day by day: Where is your God?* This restates what was said and expounded upon above: *My tears have been my breads day and night, while it is said to me daily: Where is your God?*[90]

41{42}[12] Why are you cast down, O my soul? And why do you disquiet me? Hope in God, for I will still give praise to him: the salvation of my countenance, and my God.

Quare tristis es, anima mea? Et quare conturbas me? Spera in Deo, quoniam adhuc confitebor illi, salutare vultus mei, et Deus meus.

41{42}[12] *Quare tristis es, anima mea? Et quare conturbas me? Why are you cast down, O my soul? And why do you disquiet me?* It is as if it said: You ought not to be sorrowful or disturbed on account of those reproaching or persecuting or deriding, but you ought to bear it patiently and with equanimity, and you ought to rejoice in adversity weighing carefully that which Isaiah said: *Fear not the reproach of men, and be not afraid of their blasphemies.* Who are you, that you should be

---

88 E. N. Likening the virtues (and the supernatural grace by which they come) as the "bones of the soul" is a standard understanding. In his discussion of Psalm 140(141):7, Evagrius Ponticus (345–399 A. D.) states: "The powers of the soul (δυνάμεις τῆς ψυχῆς) are called bones of the soul (ὀστᾶ τῆς ψυχῆς ὀνομάζει), because when held firm, they scatter vices and ignorance." http://www.ldysinger.com/Evagrius/08_Psalms/04_ps101-150.htm. See also footnote 33-72.
89 Jonah 2:8a, 7b.
90 E. N. Psalm 40:4.

afraid of a mortal man, and of the son of man, who shall wither away like grass? [91] And also that by the Apostle [Paul]: *In all things we suffer tribulation, but are not distressed; always bearing about in our body the mortification of Jesus, that the life also of Jesus may be made manifest in our mortal flesh.*[92] *Spera in Deo, [quoniam adhuc confitebor illi, salutare vultus mei, et Deus meus.] Hope in God, [for I will still give praise to him: the salvation of my countenance, and my God].*[93] This verse it seems has already been satisfactorily elucidated.

See how glorious and most sacred is this Psalm we have heard. Surely would not a man who would utter this most sweet Psalm without emotion be harder than iron or stone? I beseech you, O Lord God, eternal lover and nonconsumingly burning fire,[94] may your flame of love furiously ignite my soul whenever I utter the first verse of this Psalm so that I may sing this entire Psalm with greatest affection.[95]

APPLICATION TO PRIESTS

Finally, this Psalm can be particularly applied to a priest celebrating [Mass], indeed to anyone participating in Communion. For the priest of Christ ought to pant, to thirst, and to hasten to the most superlatively worthy Sacrament of the Altar consecrating, handling, offering, and consuming it with great fervor of heart. Let the most devout priest of Christ, therefore, when about to celebrate [Mass] say: **41{42}[2]** *As*

---

91 Is. 51:7b.
92 2 Cor. 4:8a, 10a, 11b.
93 E. N. The part in brackets replaces Denis's "etc."
94 E. N. Denis describes God as *ignis innocue ardens*, an innocuously or harmlessly burning fire, that is, a fire that is not destructive, but—quite the opposite—constructive. It is a fire that does not consume (*non combureretur*). Ex. 3:2. This particular expression of God as *ignis innocue ardens* may be derived from St. Anselm (1033–1109), who in his *Meditatio XIII* refers to God as follows: *Tu Dominus noster, ignis es innocue ardens, et tuae Divinitatis immediate approximatio totus charitate ignitur*, "You, our Lord, are a fire burning without harm, and all charity is ignited by the immediate coming close to your Godhead." PL 158, 774. Because of the reference to the burning bush, I have translated *innocue* as nonconsumingly, rather than "harmlessly" or "innocuously," because these latter really do not seem fitting to be applied to God.
95 *¡Oh cuántas veces me acuerdo, cuando ansí estoy, de aquel verso de David: Quemadmodum desiderat cervus ad fontes aquarum, que me parece lo veo al pie de la letra en mí.* "Oh, how often do I remember, when I am in this state [her heart spiritually transverberated or pierced], that verse of David: *Quemadmodum desiderat cervus ad fontes aquarum*, that they seem to apply literally of me." Santa Teresa de Jesús, *Libro de la Vida* (Madrid: Verbum 2015), 184.

the hart pants after the fountains of water, so my soul pants after you, O God: to you, O Lord Jesus Christ, who are the true God and eternal life, whose *Flesh is food indeed*, and whose *Blood is drink indeed*,[96] who are contained, adored, and consumed truly and essentially, God and man, in the sacred Host. **41{42}[3]** *My soul has thirsted after the strong living God*, that is, after Christ, who is the power and wisdom of the Father. *When shall I come* to the altar *and appear* there *before the face of God*, that is, before the eternal Father, that in the office of Mass I offer to him his most beloved Son, and I stand there as a mediator of God and of the people? **41{42}[4]** *My tears have been my loaves day and night*. For the priest ought, if the Lord provides, to shed abundant and warm tears before the celebration [of the Mass] out of the longing of Christ and out of sorrow of his sins.

41{42}[5] *These things*, namely that Christ is consumed in the altar, *I remembered, and poured out my soul in me*, considering such an inestimable benefit of God, and the unworthiness and ingratitude and the sins of my soul; considering also what I offer, to whom I offer, and the reason for which I offer. For all these things should be considered by the priest, not cursorily, but with great diligence and with the greatest effort. *For I shall go into the place of the wonderful tabernacle*, that is, in the Church of Christ, which is the house of God. *With the voice of joy and confession, the noise of one feasting*: that is, the words and all pronunciations of the priest at Mass, sweetly and faithfully consuming the Body and Blood of Christ, ought to be in a voice of exultation, that is, in most joyous commemoration of the benefits and mystery of Christ and [in a voice] of divine praise; and in a voice of confession, so that he might pray for his and the people's ignorance. For these two things particularly ought to be frequently done in the office of Mass. Since, therefore, such a good thing is consumed in the celebration, something to which the worth of the whole world cannot be compared, **41{42}[6]** *Why are you sad, O my soul? And why do you trouble me?* For with good cause ought you to rejoice greatly of such great benefits of Christ that no temporal affliction ought to be able to make you sorrow. *Hope in God*, and not in your own merits; do not suppose yourself worthy of a ministry that is so divine, but hope in the divine goodness, in the merits of Christ, and so proceed. From this the rest [of the meaning Psalm in reference to the priestly celebrant] is easily apparent.

---

96 John 6:56.

GENERAL CONCLUSION

And last of all, ponder a hart burdened with age, desiring to refresh itself, draws out a snake with the breath of its nose, and extracts it out of a cavern. And when the serpent is killed and devoured, he burns with its venom, and so most ardently runs toward water. When the water once drunk, it sets aside fur and horns.[97] So the sinner, and especially the priest infected with the poison of vice, ought with fervent appetite to approach Christ the eternal fountain, since he shall draw the waters of grace, the streams of mercy, and the rains of wisdom *out of the Savior's fountains*,[98] and by this he will be inwardly renewed, in the manner that the Apostle [Paul] says: *Though our outward man is corrupted, yet the inward man is renewed day by day*.[99]

PRAYER

MAY YOUR POWER, O LORD, SHOW ITSELF in us, lest our soul, despairing on account of its offenses, become exceedingly engulfed by its sorrow; but seized by the tranquility of your indulgence, let us daily desire you God, as a hart does fountains of water.

Appareat in nobis, Domine, virtus tua, ne desperando pro offensis anima nostra nimia absorbeatur tristitia; sed tranquilitate indulgentiae tuae percepta, desideremus quotidie te Deum, sicut cervus ad fontes aquarum.

---

97 E. N. It is difficult to trace precisely the source of Denis's notions about stags, but some of them are detectable in Pliny the Elder's *Natural History*, VIII, 50; XII, 115 and St. Isidore's *Etymologies*, XII, 1:18–22. For this reason, stags are frequently shown devouring or battling snakes with their nostrils in medieval art. This exposition, however, is not peculiar to Denis, and in fact was common. It is found, for example, in Cassiodorus's exposition of this Psalm, *Explanation of the Psalms* (New York Paulist Press 1990). Vol 1, 416. (P. G. Walsh, trans.) and St. Augustine's *Expositions of the Psalms (33-50)* (Hyde Park, NY: New City Press 200), 241 (Maria Boulding, trans.).
98 Is. 12:3.
99 2 Cor. 4:16.

Psalm 42

ARTICLE LXXXIII
EXPOSITION OF THE FORTY-SECOND PSALM:
IUDICA ME, DEUS, ET DISCERNE.
JUDGE ME, O GOD, AND DISTINGUISH.

42{43}[1] *A psalm for David. Judge me, O God, and distinguish my cause from the nation that is not holy: deliver me from the unjust and deceitful man.*

Psalmus David. Iudica me, Deus, et discerne causam meam de gente non sancta, ab homine iniquo et doloso erue me.

THIS PSALM HAS A BRIEF AND PLAIN TITLE, namely: 42{43}[1] *In finem, psalmus David; in the end, a Psalm for David:*[1] that is, this Psalm directs us unto Christ, and it is fittingly applied to a faithful man choosing to separate himself from evil men and to number himself among the just.

Therefore, he says: *Iudica me, Deus; Judge me, O God,* in the present age with the judgment of discretion,[2] that you might pour out upon me grace; and in the future, judge me with the judgment of blessed remuneration, that you might give glory. And so, *Judge me*, that is, do to me in accordance with your justice, giving salvific effect to my desire, so that you see the affection and the diligence of my heart, how I seek you, and how I desire only to please you, doing all that is in me. You, therefore, *judge me*, that is do what I am unable to do: and as you promised to those seeking you, that you would immediately come to their aid, so long as they have done all that was in them, as much as possible applying their minds, in the manner that Samuel admonished, *Prepare your hearts unto the Lord, and serve him only, and he will deliver you;*[3] such, I ask, O Lord, that you do to me. For I do not so ask to be judged as if I considered myself to be without sin, or I desired my vices to be examined by you, because Scripture says: *What is man that he should be without spot, and he that is born of a woman that he should appear just?*

---

1 E. N. The Sixto-Clementine varies from Denis's version in this regard and simply states *Psalmus David.*
2 E. N. On the "judgment of discretion," *iudicio discretionis*, see footnote 34-101.
3 1 Sam. 7:3b.

Behold among his saints none is unchangeable, and the heavens are not pure in his sight.[4] And Solomon said: *Who can say: My heart is clean, I am pure from sin?*[5] Whence that which is said—*Judge me, O God*—is explained by what follows: *et discerne causam meam de gente non sancta*, *and distinguish my cause from the nation that is not holy*, that is distinguish and separate my life from the life of evil men, that I may not displease you along with them and be condemned; *ab homine iniquo, from the unjust man*, manifestly harmful, *et doloso*, *deceitful*, hiddenly harmful, *erue me*, *deliver me*: indeed deliver me from my own self, who was unjust and deceitful, lest I be now no different than what I was, but let me be removed from other men, and let me be called by you another name, so that you might say to me this, *You are mine*; and *I have loved you*.[6]

42{43}[2] *For you are God my strength: why do you cast me off? And why do I go sorrowful while the enemy afflicts me?*

Quia tu es, Deus, fortitudo mea, quare me repulisti? Et quare tristis incedo, dum affligit me inimicus?

Therefore I pray to be delivered by you, **42{43}[2]** *Quia tu es, Deus, fortitudo mea; for you are God my strength*, that is the cause of all my fortitude; *quare me repulisti, why do you cast me off*, delaying the help of your grace, and permitting me to be repulsed and to be separated from you by the temptations of the devil or in some other way? This is what we have said in Isaiah: *Behold, O Lord, you are angry, and we have sinned . . . and we are all become as one unclean.*[7] *Et quare tristi incedo, dum affligit inimicus? And why do I go sorrowful while the enemy afflicts me?* That is, why do you deprive me of your consolation while the devil and the world tempt me and aggravate me? Yet a holy man says this, not that he figures it will be done or allowed to take place without reasonable cause, but so that by a loving and trusting complaint he might summon the mercy of divine goodness.

42{43}[3] *Send forth your light and your truth: they have conducted me, and brought me unto your holy hill, and into your tabernacles.*

Emitte lucem tuam et veritatem tuam; ipsa me deduxerunt, et adduxerunt in montem sanctum tuum, et in tabernacula tua.

---

4 Job 15:14–15.
5 Prov. 20:9.
6 Is. 43, 1b, 4b.
7 Is. 64:5b–6a.

42{43}[3] *Emitte lucem tuam, send forth your light,* that is, flood my soul with the rays of your eternal and uncreated light. Now this ray is the grace of God which is the supernatural participation in the divine essence. And also send forth *et veritatem tuam, and your truth*: that is, fill those who beseech you with your mercy promised in the testimony of the Scriptures, and make it truly manifest in me so that the Apostles and Prophets, who say that those who invoke you cannot possibly perish, may be found faithful.[8] And so, *send forth your light,* that is, fill me with grace and the clarity of wisdom; and *your truth,* that is, make me experience your mercy, and so recognize Scripture—which pronounces you to be merciful—to be true. *Ipsa, they,* namely, the light of grace and the truth of Scripture, *me deduxerunt, have conducted me* by right paths, *et adduxerunt in montem sanctum tuum, and brought me unto your holy hill,* that is, in the Church militant, for by faith and grace I have become a true son of the Church; *et in tabernacula tua, and into your tabernacles,* that is, into celestial mansions, of which you say, *In my Father's house there are many mansions;*[9] and again, *Make unto you friends of the mammon of iniquity; that when you shall fail, they may receive you into everlasting dwellings (tabernacula).*[10] Now these tabernacles are distinct congregations of saints, in the manner that the Apostle [Paul] professes: *For you are the temple of the living God,* as the Lord says: *I will dwell in them, and walk among them.*[11] By grace and truth and faith we are already introduced actually or in reality into the Church militant, that is, in the society of the faithful; but we are not yet in reality introduced into the future and eternal tabernacle other than through contemplation and hope.[12] So the sense of

---

8 *Cf.* Ecclus. 36:18: *Reward them that patiently wait for you, that your prophets may be found faithful: and hear the prayers of your servants.*
9 John 14:2a.
10 Luke 16:9.
11 2 Cor. 16:16. *For you are the temple of the living God; as God says: I will dwell in them, and walk among them; and I will be their God, and they shall be my people Cf.* Lev. 26:12: *I will walk among you, and will be your God, and you shall be my people.*
12 E. N. This tension between the life of grace and faith lived now, and the life of glory and vision of the future has a "now, but not yet" quality. See Heb. 2:8 ("now, but not yet," *nunc autem necdum,* νῦν δὲ οὔπω). In speaking of the heavenly Jerusalem and its relationship to the Church in pilgrimage, Pope Benedict XVI observed: "This magnificent icon [of the heavenly Jerusalem towards which we strive] has an *eschatological* value: it expresses the mystery of the beauty that is *already* the essential form of the Church, even if it has *not yet* arrived at its fullness. It is the goal of our pilgrimage, the homeland which awaits us and for which we long. Seeing that beauty with the eyes of faith, contemplating it and yearning for it, must not serve as an excuse for avoiding the historical reality in which the Church lives as she shares the joys and hopes, the grief and anguish of the people of our time, especially those who are poor or afflicted. If the beauty of the heavenly Jerusalem is the glory of

this versicle is stated by the author of the book of Wisdom but by means of other words: *Send, he says, her out of your holy heaven . . . that she may be with me, and may labor with me, that I may know what is acceptable with you: for she knows . . . all things, and shall lead me soberly.*[13]

42{43}[4] *And I will go in to the altar of God: to God who gives joy to my youth.*

Et introibo ad altare Dei, ad Deum qui laetificat iuventutem meam.

42{43}[4] *Et introibo ad altare Dei,* and *I will go in to the altar of God,* that is, to Christ, the mediator of God and man, by whom and in whom we ought to offer all our sacrifices, since they will be accepted by his merits. We ought also to build and place upon him all that which we do. Whence the Apostle [Paul] exhorted the Hebrews: *Let us go therefore with confidence to the throne of grace: that we may obtain mercy, and find grace in seasonable aid.*[14] Or [we might understand it in this way], *I will enter in to the altar of God,* which is made of matter and made with human hands in the church, since I will receive the Sacrament of Christ, or I will offer the oblation [of the Mass]; I will not halt at that altar, but I will enter with the affection of the mind and with the care that is due *ad Deum qui laetificat iuventutem meam, to God who gives joy to my youth,* not bodily or exterior, but spiritual and interior, which does not grow old with the body, but unceasingly grows by grace, until the holy soul is carried over to the heavenly homeland. For which reason the Apostle [Paul] commands: *Strip yourselves of the old man with his deeds,* and put on *the new, who is renewed unto knowledge of God, according to the image of him that created him.*[15] This youth and spiritual growth is, therefore, in the grace of God. This God gives joy to, since the soul serves the Lord with a happy and fervent heart, saying that which is contained in a later Psalm:

God—his love in other words—then it is in charity, and in charity alone, that we can approach it and to a certain degree dwell within it even now. Whoever loves the Lord Jesus and keeps his word, already experiences in this world the mysterious presence of the Triune God. We heard this in the Gospel: 'we will come to him and make our home with him' (Jn 14:23). Every Christian is therefore called to become a living stone of this splendid 'dwelling place of God with men.' What a magnificent vocation!" http://www.vatican.va/content/benedict-xvi/en/homilies/2007/documents/hf_ben-xvi_hom_20070513_conference-brazil.html

13 Wis. 9:10–11.
14 Heb. 4:16.
15 Col. 3:9b–10.

I have run the way of your commandments, when you did enlarge my heart.[16]

42{43}[5] To you, O God my God, I will confess upon the harp: why are you sad, O my soul? And why do you disquiet me?[17]

Confitebor tibi in cithara, Deus, Deus meus. Quare tristis es, anima mea? Et quare conturbas me?

42{43}[5] *Confitebor tibi,* I will confess to you, that is, I will praise you, *in cithara,* upon the harp, that is in the observance of the heavenly commandments, which observance, when mixed with tribulations, are designated by the harm, in the manner that we have fully stated in the explanation of the thirty-second Psalm, where we read thus: *Give praise to the Lord on the harp.*[18] Therefore in adversity I will praise you so, *Deus, Deus meus. Quare tristis es anima mea? Et quare conturbas me? O God, my God. Why are you sad, O my soul? And why do you disquiet me?* This, along with the following verse, I consider to have sufficiently explained before.[19]

APPLICATION TO PRIESTS

Finally, this Psalm like the preceding one is particularly applicable to priests, whose life ought to be much more excellent than the lives of the people as he approaches that much closer to God and he stands at a higher level.[20] Therefore, the celebrating priest, must undertake to give thanks to Christ in a singular way, says: *Judge me, O God, and distinguish my cause from the nation that is not holy* (according to the sense already discussed), lest there be fulfilled in me that which is foretold in Isaiah and Hosea: *And it shall be as with the people, so with the priest.*[21]

---

16 Ps. 118:32.
17 E. N. I have translated *confitebor* with "I will confess," though the confession of praise is clearly intended, since it is demanded by the subsequent commentary.
18 Ps. 32:2a. See Article LXX (Psalm 32:2).
19 Article LXXXII (Psalm 41:6, 12).
20 "Most sublime... is the dignity of the priesthood.... [S]o holy an office demands holiness in him who holds it. A priest should have a loftiness of spirit, a purity of heart, and a sanctity of life befitting the solemnity and holiness of the office he holds.... 'They who are the intermediaries between God and His people,' says St. Thomas, 'must bear a good conscience before God, and a good name among men.' On the contrary, whosoever handles and administers holy things, while blameworthy in his life, profanes them and is guilty of sacrilege: 'They that are not holy ought not to handle holy things.'" Pope Pius XI, *Ad Catholici Sacerdotii,* Nos. 31–33.
21 Is. 24:2a; Hosea 4:9.

ARTICLE LXXXIV

ALLEGORICAL EXPOSITION OF THE SAME FORTY-SECOND PSALM OF CHRIST.

42{43}[1] *A psalm for David. Judge me, O God, and distinguish my cause from the nation that is not holy: deliver me from the unjust and deceitful man.*

Psalmus David. Iudica me, Deus, et discerne causam meam de gente non sancta, ab homine iniquo et doloso erue me.

42{43}[2] *For you are God my strength: why do you cast me off? And why do I go sorrowful while the enemy afflicts me?*

Quia tu es, Deus, fortitudo mea, quare me repulisti? Et quare tristis incedo, dum affligit me inimicus?

ONLY CHRIST, LACKING ALL STAIN, AND FULL of all grace, can most safely say, the Passion already before him, and consistently while suffering it: 42{43}[1] *Iudica me, Deus; judge me, O God,* the Trinity, that is, according to your justice and the merits of my life requite me, not forsaking my soul in hell, nor my body in the sepulcher; and now set free the holy fathers, for whom I suffered death, from their lengthy stay in limbo; *et discerne causam me, and distinguish my cause,* that is, the justice of my manner of living for which the envy of the Jews put me to death, divide and distinguish in place and reward, *de gente non sancta, from the nation that is not holy* crucifying me, giving to me in accordance with my justice, and showing the false [justice] being imposed upon me. *Ab homine iniquo et doloso, from the unjust and deceitful man,* that is, from the Jews who for a while hiddenly, and now publicly are persecuting me, *erue me, deliver me,* by the blessed Resurrection. 42{43}[2] *Quia tu es, Deus, fortitudo mea; for you are God my strength,* insofar as I am man, for I am unable to do anything of myself.[22] For insofar as I am a man, I differ from other men only by grace. *Quare me repulisti? Why do you cast me off?* That is, why did you so forsake me on the Cross, so that I would cry out *my God, my God, why have you forsaken me?*[23] In what manner this is to be understood is made clear in the exposition of

---

[22] John 5:19: *Amen, amen, I say unto you, the Son cannot do anything of himself, but what he sees the Father doing: for whatsoever thing he does, these the Son also does in like manner.*

[23] Matt. 27:46.

the twenty-first Psalm.²⁴ *Et quare tristis incedo, dum affligit me inimicus? And why do I go sorrowful while the enemy afflicts me?* For Christ, in the night of the Last Supper, leaving Jerusalem crossed the brook Cedron²⁵ with the disciples saying to them: *My soul is sorrowful even unto death.*²⁶ For it was then that the enemy, that is, Judas, afflicted him for he led with him the ministers of the Jews.

42{43}[3] *Send forth your light and your truth: they have conducted me, and brought me unto your holy hill, and into your tabernacles.*

Emitte lucem tuam et veritatem tuam; ipsa me deduxerunt, et adduxerunt in montem sanctum tuum, et in tabernacula tua.

42{43}[4] *And I will go in to the altar of God: to God who gives joy to my youth.*

Et introibo ad altare Dei, ad Deum qui laetificat iuventutem meam.

42{43}[3] *Emitte lucem tuam, send forth your light*, that is, *glorify me, as I have glorified you* … *and have manifested your name to men;*²⁷ *et veritatem tuam, and your truth*: that is, so do as you said you would do through the Prophets, raising me up on the third day, and fulfill all that was prophesized about me, sending the Holy Spirit to the Apostles as Joel had predicted,²⁸ also converting the world to the faith. *Ipsa me deduxerunt et adduxerunt in montem sanctum tuum, they have conducted me and brought me unto your holy hill*, that is, to the throne of grace, so that I might sit with you at your right hand,²⁹ *et in tabernacula tua, and into your tabernacles*, that is, in the congregations of the celestial citizens,

---

24 Article L (Psalm 21:2) in Volume 1.
25 E. N. Cedron (also called Kidron) was a stream or brook and valley (wadi) that ran southwards under the eastern wall of Jerusalem. *When Jesus had said these things, he went forth with his disciples over the brook Cedron, where there was a garden, into which he entered with his disciples.* John 18:1.
26 Matt. 26:38.
27 John 17: 5, 4, 6.
28 Joel 2:28-29: *And it shall come to pass after this, that I will pour out my spirit upon all flesh: and your sons and your daughters shall prophesy: your old men shall dream dreams, and your young men shall see visions. Moreover upon my servants and handmaids in those days I will pour forth my spirit.* Peter refers to this in his Pentecost sermon. See Acts 2:14-18.
29 Ps. 101:1: *The Lord said to my Lord: Sit at my right hand: Until I make your enemies your footstool.*

so that as I *was seen upon earth, and conversed with men,*[30] so I will be seen by the blessed *comprehensors* in heaven,[31] and I will recline at the table with them full of joy. For the humanity of Christ, or Christ as man, was assumed to the throne of glory above all heavens by the grace of God, so that the truth of Scripture might be fulfilled. 42{43}[4] *Et introibo ad altare Dei, and I will go in to the altar of God,* that is, I will ascend to the altar of the Cross in which I will offer myself to the Father; and then I will go *ad Deum qui laetificat iuventutem meam, to God who gives joy to my youth,* ascending to the heavens. For it *was right for Christ to have suffered these things, and so to enter into his glory.*[32] Or [we can see it] thus: *And I will go in to the altar of God,* etc. That is, I will enter into heaven itself, which is the altar of God, in which the holy angels offer to God the prayers and the devotions of the wayfarers, and in which I appeal to the Father for the world: as the Apostle [Paul] says, *For Jesus is not entered into the holies made with hands, ... but into heaven itself, that he may appear now in the presence of God for us.*[33]

42{43}[5] *To you, O God my God, I will confess upon the harp: why are you sad, O my soul? And why do you disquiet me?*[34]

Confitebor tibi in cithara, Deus, Deus meus. Quare tristis es, anima mea? Et quare conturbas me?

42{43}[6] *Hope in God, for I will still confess to him: the salvation of my countenance, and my God.*[35]

Spera in Deo, quoniam adhuc confitebor illi, salutare vultus mei, et Deus meus.

42{43}[5] *Confitebor tibi, in cithara; I will confess upon the harp to you,* that is in obedience and patience, doing always and suffering that which is pleasing to you, *Deus, Deus meus, O God, my God.* In this way, Christ confessed to the Father the confession of praise, not of fault, when he said: *Your will be done;*[36] and again, *Father, into your hands I*

---

30 Baruch 3:38.
31 E. N. A *comprehensor* is one who has obtained the full apprehension of God, the beatific vision of God, in heaven.
32 Luke 24:26.
33 Heb. 9:24.
34 E. N. I have translated *confitebor* with "I will confess," though the confession of praise is clearly intended, since it is demanded by the subsequent commentary.
35 *See* footnote above.
36 Matt. 26:42.

*commend my spirit.*³⁷ *Quare tristis es, anima mea; why are you sad, O my soul,* with a natural, not disordered, sorrow, in accordance with the natural horror towards punishment and death? *Et quare conturbas me, and why do you disquiet me,* so that I might be in agony? How there was [emotional] disturbance in Christ has often been discussed.³⁸ 42{43} [6] *Spera in Deo, hope in God,* to the degree you are a wayfarer and are passible, *confitebor illi, I will confess to him,* praising him before those to whom I appeared after the Resurrection. Whence it is said in an earlier Psalm, *I will declare your name to my breathren; in the midst of the church will I praise you.*³⁹ And so I will confess to you, who are *salutare vultus mei, the salvation of my countenance,* that is the beatitude of my created intellect, and the cause of its soundness, *et Deus meus, and my God.* For God, who is the God of all, in a most singular way is the God of Christ as man, according to which he was incomparably forechosen, assumed, and glorified. I have quickly passed through this exposition because it can be easily known from what was abundantly stated beforehand.

PRAYER

O GOD, OUR STRENGTH, SEND FORTH YOUR light and your truth in our hearts: by which, contemplating the sweetness of your majesty, we may with full intention of mind quickly arrive at the infinite joy of your vision.

Fortitudo nostra, Deus, emitte lucem et veritatem tuam in cordibus nostris: quibus, contemplata dulcedine maiestatis tuae, ad infinita visionis tuae, tota mentis intentione festinemus pervenire.

---

37 Luke 23:46.
38 E. N. For example in Article L (Psalm 21:2); *see also* footnote 29-18.
39 Ps. 21:23.

Psalm 43

ARTICLE LXXXV
LITERAL EXPOSITION OF THE FORTY-THIRD PSALM:
DEUS, AURIBUS NOSTRIS AUDIVIMUS.
WE HAVE HEARD, O GOD, WITH OUR EARS.

43{44}[1] *Unto the end, for the sons of Korah, to give understanding.*
In finem. Filiis Core ad intellectum.

THE TITLE TO THIS PSALM IS: 43{44}[1] *IN finem, filiis Core, ad intellectum; unto the end, for the sons of Korah, to give understanding,* a Psalm for David. The words in the title to this Psalm have the same sense as the similar title of the forty-first Psalm: and so the reader should refer back to that place. But generally the commentators explain this Psalm as partly referring to the people of the Synagogue, and partly to the people of the Church, that is to say, it is a mixture of both. But of both people we must take good care to explain separately and totally. For literally, [this Psalm] is written of the people of the Old Law; but [understood] morally [or tropologically] it can be understood of the Christian people.

43{44}[2] *We have heard, O God, with our ears: our fathers have declared to us, the work you have wrought in their days, and in the days of old.*

Deus, auribus nostris audivimus, patres nostri annuntiaverunt nobis, opus quod operatus es in diebus eorum, et in diebus antiquis.

Speaking, therefore, in the person of the Synagogue, the Prophet [David] or any member of the faithful under the Old Testament, says: 43{44}[2] *Deus,* O God of our fathers, who through Moses says: *Thus shall you say to the children of Israel: The Lord God of our fathers, the God of Abraham, the God of Isaac, and the God of Jacob, has sent me to you: This is my name forever, and this is my memorial unto all generations.*[1] And so, O God, *auribus nostris audivimus,* we have heard ... with our ears. The use of such

---

1   Ex. 3:15.

replication of the same thing, whether of name or things, is a mannerism of the Hebrew language, as when in Isaiah it is said: *Hearing, hear,*[2] and you do not understand. And again: *With desolation shall the earth be made desolate, with trembling shall the earth tremble.*[3] One should not assess this manner of speaking as superfluous, because by it something is insinuated as being more serious or more worthy of attention. Therefore, it is in this sense: *O God, with our ears,* not only of the body, but also of the heart, we diligently have we heard and given heed. And with merit, because *patres nostri annuntiaverunt nobis, for our fathers have declared to us,* namely, Moses, Joshua, and the other Prophets. For it is fitting diligently to give heed to that which goes back to the fathers. For this reason we find in Ecclesiasticus: *The wise men will seek out the wisdom of all the ancients, and will be occupied in the prophets.*[4] And in Ecclesiastes: *that which by the counsel of masters are given from one shepherd, more than these, my son, require not.*[5]

And what is heard and narrated follows: *Opus quod operatus es in diebus eorum; the work you have wrought in their days,* that is, the marvels that you did in the land of Egypt, in the Red Sea, in the desert, and in the land of promise;[6] *et in diebus antiquis, and in the days of old,* that is, the marvels which you have done from the beginning of the world even unto the time of Abraham or Moses: how, namely, you brought upon the world of the ungodly a flood, you confounded the lips of all flesh, and you overthrew Pentapolis,[7] namely, Sodom, Gomorrah, Adamah, Zeboim, and Zoar with fire and sulfur.[8]

43{44}[3] *Your hand destroyed the Gentiles, and you planted them: you did afflict the people and cast them out.*

Manus tua gentes disperdidit, et plantasti eos; afflixisti populos et expulisti eos.

43{44}[3] *Manus tua gentes disperdidit, your hand destroyed the Gentiles:* that is, your omnipotent power in various ways — that is to say, by

---

2 Is. 6:9b.
3 Is. 24:3a, 19b. E. N. I have modified the Douay-Rheims translations so that the reduplication or replication of words is rendered clearer.
4 Ecclus. 39:1.
5 Eccl. 12:11b–12a.
6 Ex. 7, *et seq.*
7 A reference to the five Sodomite cities, which are called Pentapolis (Greek = Πεντάπολις, meaning a group of five cities), so-called expressly in Wis. 10:6: *She delivered the just man who fled from the wicked that were perishing, when the fire came down upon Pentapolis.*
8 Gen. chps. 7, 11, 19.

hailstones and the hands of the sons of Israel—brought to ruin and put to death the inhabitants of the land of promise, namely, the Canaanites, the Jebusites, etc.; *et plantasti eos, and you planted them*, that is, you firmly rooted our fathers in, and caused them to inhabit, the land of promise. *Aflixisti populos, you did afflict the people* of the Canaanites with fear and desperation: because as it is written in the book of Joshua, *there remained no spirit in them* by reason of the fear [in them] when they had heard the sons of Israel had crossed the Jordan; *et expulisti eos, and you cast them out* from their land, through death or flight.

43{44}[4] *For they got not the possession of the land by their own sword: neither did their own arm save them. But your right hand and your arm, and the light of your countenance: because you were pleased with them.*

Nec enim in gladio suo possederunt terram, et brachium eorum non salvavit eos; sed dextera tua et brachium tuum, et illuminatio vultus tui, quoniam complacuisti in eis.

43{44}[4] *Nec enim in gladio suo possederunt terram, for they got not the possession of the land by their own sword*, that is, our fathers did not acquire the aforesaid land by the power of their arms, *et brachium eorum non salvavit eos, neither did their own arm save them*, that is, their natural power did not deliver them from the hands of their enemies, for—looking at things from the standpoint of human power—they were much weaker than them. Whence Moses said to the Hebrew people: Do not say in your heart: My own might, and the strength of my own hand have achieved all these things for me; but remember the Lord your God, that he has given you strength.[9] The verse continues: *Sed dextera tua, but your right hand*, O Lord, that is, your prosperous and pleasing help, *et brachium tuum, and your arm*, that is, your power, *et illuminatio vultus tui, and the light of your countenance*, that is, the righteous way in which you filled them with good and right counsel by grace: this, I say, saved them, *quoniam complacuisti in eis, because you were pleased with them*: that is, because of your special goodness, by which you chose them, and by which you made them pleasing to you, and not because of their own justice, you furnished them with these good things. And this is what Moses said: Do not say in your heart, Because of my justice the Lord led us to this land, for you are a very stiff-necked people.[10]

---

9   Deut. 8:17–18a.
10 Cf. Deut. 9:4, 6.

43{44}[5] *You are yourself my king and my God, who commands the saving of Jacob.*

Tu es ipse rex meus et Deus meus, qui mandas salutes Iacob.

43{44}[6] *Through you we will blow down our enemies with the horn: and through your name we will despise them that rise up against us.*[11]

In te inimicos nostros ventilabimus cornu, et in nomine tuo spernemus insurgentes in nobis.

43{44}[5] *Tu,* you, God of our fathers, *es ipse rex meus,* are yourself my king, who governed the sons of Israel with a singular providence, as if they were your own people, *et Deus meus,* and my God, attend to me in a special way by extirpating vice and pour forth thanks: whom also I in a special way worship: believing, hoping, loving, and serving;[12] *qui mandas salutes Iacob, who commands the saving of Jacob,* that is, who through the Prophets announced good things, and promised victory to the seed of Jacob. Whence Moses openly professed: *The Lord your God has chosen you, to be his peculiar people of all peoples that are upon the earth: not because you surpass all nations in number... for you are the fewest of any people; but because the Lord has loved you.*[13] **43{44}[6]** *In te,* through you hoping, and trusting in your power, *inimicos nostros ventilabimus, we will blow down our enemies,* that is, in all wind and earth we will disperse, *cornu,* with the horn, that is, with the cry of devout prayer and of humble confession; *et in nomine tuo,* and through your name hoping, *spernemus, we will despise,* that is, we will neither give great regard to nor fear, *insurgentes in nobis, them that rise up against us*: because we will believe that which Moses said to be true: One of yours will persecute one hundred, and ten of yours a thousand, and none of yours will it be possible to resist.[14] That is why

---

11 E. N. I have replaced the Douay-Rheims' "push down" with "blow down."
12 E. N. A little jarringly, Denis shifts from second person to first person. Presumably, Denis is observing that he also worships the "God of Abraham, Isaac, and Jacob." This is redolent of Blaise Pascal's "Night of Fire" conversion in 1654 described in his *Mémorial*: "FIRE: God of Abraham, God of Isaac, God of Jacob not of the philosophers and of the learned. Certitude. Certitude. Feeling. Joy. Peace. God of Jesus Christ. My God and your God. Your God will be my God." David Wetsel, *Pascal and Disbelief: Catechesis and Conversion in the Pensées* (Washington, DC: Catholic University of America Press, 1994), 344–45.
13 Deut. 7:6–8.
14 *Cf.* Lev. 26:7–8: *You shall pursue your enemies, and they shall fall before you. Five of yours shall pursue a hundred others, and a hundred of you ten thousand: your enemies shall fall before you by the sword.*

it states in the second book of Chronicles: *O Lord, there is no difference with you, whether you help with few, or with many.*[15]

43{44}[7] *For I will not trust in my bow: neither shall my sword save me.*

Non enim in arcu meo sperabo, et gladius meus non salvabit me.

43{44}[8] *But you have saved us from them that afflict us: and have put them to shame that hate us.*

Salvasti enim nos de affligentibus nos, et odientes nos confudisti.

43{44}[9] *In God shall we glory all the day long: and in your name we will give praise forever.*

In Deo laudabimur tota die; et in nomine tuo confitebimur in saeculum.

43{44}[7] *Non enim in arcu meo sperabo, et gladius meus non salvabit me; for I will not trust in my bow, neither shall my sword save me:* that is, I will not put my hope in any kind of arms or human help, nor will any of them defend me from my enemies. For here it is written: *Help us, O Lord our God: for with confidence in you, and in your name, we are come against this multitude.*[16] 43{44}[8] *Salvasti enim nos de affligentibus nos,* but *you have saved us from them that afflict us:* as is most frequently written in the book of Judges: that is, those who have presumed that they would vanquish or kill us, you caused to be vanquished or killed by us, or you have turned them around in flight, or you have shown them suitable for another form of confusion. For which reason it is written in the book of Judges: the Lord *was moved to mercy, and heard the groanings of the afflicted, and delivered them from the slaughter of the oppressors.*[17] 43{44}[9] *In Deo laudabimur tota die, in God shall we glory all the day:* that is, victory, salvation, and our excellence is assiduously ascribed to God, and we will praise God from the goods given to us: not in ourselves, lest we be found vain, proud, or ungrateful and [our praise] not be accepted, but in God; *et in nomine tuo,* and *in your name,* O Lord, *confitebimur in saeculum, we will give praise forever,* that is, we will unceasingly confess your good and your renown, and our evil and our misery, to the honor and glory of your name, in the manner that Jeremiah says: *Be not proud....*

---

15 2 Chr. 14:11a.
16 2 Chr. 14:11b.
17 Judges 2:18.

Give glory to the Lord your God, before it be dark, and before your feet stumble upon the dark mountains.[18]

43{44}[10] *But now you have cast us off, and put us to shame: and you, O God, will not go out with our armies.*

Nunc autem repulisti et confudisti nos; et non egredieris, Deus, in virtutibus nostris.

43{44}[11] *You have made us turn our back to our enemies: and they that hated us plundered for themselves.*

Avertisti nos retrorsum post inimicos nostros; et qui oderunt nos diripiebant sibi.

43{44}[10] *Nunc autem,* but now, O Lord, namely, in the time of the Babylonian captivity, and in the time of the Maccabees, and often after the death of a Judge,[19] *repulisti nos, you have cast us off,* that is, you have deprived us of your help, *et confudisti nos, and put us to shame,* delivering us over into the hands of our enemies. For which reason Baruch says: *To the Lord our God belongs justice, but to us confusion of our face: as it is come to pass at this day.*[20] *Et non egredieris, Deus, in virtutibus nostris; and you, O God, will not go out with our armies,* that is, you will not be the leader of our armies, neither fighting for us nor showing your power in us, letting us fall into the hands of our adversaries. [You will not be for us] as you were the leader, the vanguard, and the warrior of our fathers, in the manner that is written: *God is the leader in our army.*[21] And Moses said to the Lord: *If you yourself do not go before, bring us not out of this place. For how shall we be able to know... that we have found grace in your sight, unless you walk with us?*[22] **43{44}[11]** *Avertisti nos retrorsum, you have made us turn,* that is, you have allowed us to turn in flight, *post inimicos nostros, our back to our*

---

18 Jer. 13:15b–16a.
19 E. N. The Babylonian captivity or exile refers to the destruction of the temple in Jerusalem and the forced exile of the Jews to Babylon by the Persian empire (approximately between 568 and 538 BC). Reference to the Maccabees refers to the Jewish rebellion against the Seleucid Empire and the foundation of the Hasmonean dynasty (between 167 to 37 BC). In the Book of Judges (referring roughly to a four-hundred year period between 1400-1020 BC), the cycle is repeated where the people are unfaithful to the Lord and are delivered into the hands of their enemies, whereupon they repent, ask for mercy, and are delivered by a leader or judge (*shophet*). Thereupon they enjoy prosperity which leads again to their infidelity, and the cycle is repeated.
20 Baruch 1:15.
21 2 Chr. 13:12a.
22 Ex. 33:15-16.

enemies, so that we would turn our back to our enemies in the manner that Joshua said: *My Lord God what shall I say, seeing Israel turning their backs to their enemies?*[23] Baruch also: *We are brought under*, he said, *and are not uppermost: because we have sinned against the Lord our God.*[24] *Et qui oderunt nos, diripiebant sibi; and they that hated us plundered for themselves*, that is, ourselves and our possessions have become the prizes of our enemies.

43{44}[12] *You have given us up like sheep to be eaten: you have scattered us among the nations.*

Dedisti nos tamquam oves escarum; et in gentibus dispersisti nos.

43{44}[13] *You have sold your people for no price: and there was no reckoning in the exchange of them.*

Vendidisti populum tuum sine pretio; et non fuit multitudo in commutationibus eorum.

43{44}[12] *Dedisti nos tanquam oves escarum, you have given us like sheep to be eaten*: that is, you have permitted us to be devoured and oppressed by our enemies, in the manner that sheep, which are food, are devoured by the wolf and are eaten by men: as Isaiah foresaw, *They shall devour Israel*, he said, *with open mouth.*[25] This was often fulfilled in the Jews, most especially during the time of the siege of Jerusalem by the king of Babylon, when they were in such dire straits that Jeremiah attests to: *The hands of the pitiful women have sodden their own children: they were their meat.*[26] *Et in gentibus dispersisti nos, and you have scattered us among the nations*, namely, permitting us to be expelled from our own lands. 43{44}[13] *Vendidisti populum tuum sine pretio, you have sold your people for no price*, that is, you have allowed them to be sold in such a buyer's market that their prices could be reckoned as to be almost nothing; *et non fuit multitudo, and there was no reckoning* of money or of a buyer *in commutationibus, in the exchange*, that is, in the sale, *eorum, of them*, but few were the buyers, and small was the price in regard to them at which they were sold. For this reason, we read in the second book of Maccabees: *And there were slain in the space of three whole days fourscore thousand, forty thousand were made prisoners, and as many sold.*[27]

---

23 Joshua 7:8.
24 Baruch 2:5.
25 Is. 9:12a.
26 Lam. 4:10.
27 2 Macc. 5:14.

43{44}[14] *You have made us a reproach to our neighbors, a scoff and derision to them that are round about us.*

Posuisti nos opprobrium vicinis nostris, subsannationem et derisum his qui sunt in circuitu nostro.

43{44}[15] *You have made us a byword among the Gentiles: a shaking of the head among the people.*

Posuisti nos in similitudinem gentibus, commotionem capitis in populis.

43{44}[14] *Posuisti nos opprobrium vicinis nostris,* you have made us a reproach to our neighbors, that is, contemptible and abject before the people who are against us or around us. You have made us *subsannationem et derisum,* a scoff and derision, that is, you have allowed us to be mocked with wrinkled nose and derided with mouth open wide[28] to *his qui sunt in circuitu nostro,* them that are round about us, namely, from the Samaritans and the Moabites and the Ammonites. Whence Nehemiah said: *Hear us, our God, for we are despised.*[29] 43{44}[15] *Posuisti nos in similitudinem gentibus,* you have made us a byword among the Gentiles, that is, an example of malediction: for you have brought upon us such affliction that when one wants to say something evil to another, he says: "So may it befall you what has befallen on that people"; *commotionem capitis in populis,* a shaking of the head among the people; that is, you have so allowed us to suffer devastation that all who hear of it, move their head, either out of astonishment, or congratulation, or compassion, as was foretold by Jeremiah: *I will forsake you, and the city which I gave to you, and to your fathers... and I will bring upon you reproach... and shame.*[30]

---

28 E. N. These expressions refer to the two kinds of mockery, by gestures (*subsannatio*) and by word (*derisio* or *irrisio*). Mockery by gesture (*subsannatio*) was known as mockery "with wrinkled nose," *naso rugato,* whereas mockery with words (*derisio* or *irrisio*) was known as mockery "with mouth open wide," *ore lato.* An instance of this usage can be found in St. Thomas's *Summa Theologiae: subsannatio et irrisio conveniunt in fine, sed differunt in modo, quia irrisio fit ore, idest verbo et cachinnis; subsannatio autem naso rugato, ut dicit Glossa.* "Mockery [by gesture] and derision agree as to their end, but differ in manner, for derision is done with the mouth, that is, with word and cackling; but mockery [by gesture] with wrinkled nose, as the Gloss states." ST IIaIIae, q. 75, art. 1, ad 1.
29 Neh. 4a.
30 Jer. 33:39–40.

43{44}[16] *All the day long my shame is before me: and the confusion of my face has covered me.*

Tota die verecundia mea contra me est, et confusio faciei meae cooperuit me.

43{44}[17] *At the voice of him that reproaches and detracts me: at the face of the enemy and persecutor.*

A voce exprobrantis et obloquentis, a facie inimici et persequentis.

43{44}[16] *Tota die verecundia mea contra me est, all the day long my shame is before me:* that is, the shame or shamefacedness with which I am ashamed because of the sins I have committed and the punishments I suffer incessantly afflicts me; *et confusio faciei meae, and the confusion of my face,* by which I confuse myself, *cooperuit me, has covered me,* that is, was so great and so wide that it covered me up like a garment and covered up every part of me. As is said about sinners by Ezechiel: *Be confounded, and ashamed at your own ways.*[31] Whence it is written, *All the house of Jacob was covered with confusion,*[32] as we see in the time of king Antioch afflicting the people of Israel.[33] 43{44}[17] *A voce exprobrantis et obloquentis, a facie inimici et persequentis; at the voice of him that reproaches and detracts me: at the face of the enemy and persecutor:* that is, my shame and confusion brought upon me from them who reproached and detracted me, and from them who pursued me, namely, from the Gentiles spurning and rejecting the law of Moses and the observances of Judaism.

43{44}[18] *All these things have come upon us, yet we have not forgotten you: and we have not done wickedly in your covenant.*

Haec omnia venerunt super nos; nec obliti sumus te, et inique non egimus in testamento tuo.

43{44}[19] *And our heart has not turned back: and you have turned aside our steps from your way.*

Et non recessit retro cor nostrum; et declinasti semitas nostras a via tua.

---

31 Ez. 36:32b.
32 1 Macc. 1:29b.
33 E. N. King Antiochus refers to the Seleucid King Antiochus IV Epiphanes (*ca.*215–164 BC) who laid siege to Jerusalem, and commanded his soldiers "to kill, and not to spare any that came in their way, and to go up into the houses to slay. Thus there was a slaughter of young and old, a destruction of women and children, and killing of virgins and infants. And there were slain in the space of three whole days fourscore thousand, forty thousand were made prisoners, and as many sold." 2 Macc. 5:12–14.

43{44}[18] *Haec omnia,* all these things, these bad things already mentioned, *venerunt super nos, nec obliti sumus te; have come upon us, yet we have not forgotten you,* that is, withdrawing from the faith, *et inique non egimus in testamento tuo, and we have not done wickedly in your covenant,* that is, we have not transgressed the commandments of the divine law. 43{44}[19] *Et non recessit retro cor nostrum, and our heart has not turned back,* forsaking you, the sovereign and immutable good, and pursuing fleeting and vain things. But since God does not render punishment without fault, and [since he] especially promised through Moses and the Prophets to defend the sons of Israel against the assaults of all enemies, it seems astonishing why such great punishments befell them if they were so innocent and so just. To respond to this [apparent quandary], this Psalm speaks in diverse persons. For at one time it takes up that which is fitting to the good; but at another time that which is fitting for the evil. So, therefore, some of the sons of Israel sinned and deserved the meted punishments; others, however, remained firm in the faith and the worship of the Creator, and in those persons is the Prophet [David] now speaking. Whence God says to Elijah: *I will leave me seven thousand men in Israel, whose knees have not been bowed before Baal.*[34]

Et declinasti semitas nostras a via tua, and you have turned aside our steps from your way. This can be explained in two ways. First, as if said in the person of the good man; and it will be in this sense: *and you have turned aside our steps,* that is, by grace you have made it so that we turn away and avoid our carnal and evil thoughts and vices *from your way,* that is, from your precepts by which we travel towards you. And so it is that we reject and relinquish our own wide and spacious ways, and we enter in your way and the gate of salvation, which is strait and narrow.[35] And so we fulfill that in Ecclesiasticus, *Go not after your lusts, but turn away from your own will;*[36] and that of Jonah, *Let them turn away every one from his evil way, and from the iniquity that is in their hands.*[37] Whence about these ways or paths of human invention is written of in Isaiah: *All we like sheep have gone astray; every one has turned aside into his own way.*[38] The second, and (as will be seen) more literal exposition, is as if said in the person of the evil man; and this is its sense: *You have turned*

---

[34] 1 Kings 19:18a. Rom. 11:4–5: *But what saith the divine answer to him? "I have left me seven thousand men, that have not bowed their knees to Baal." Even so then at this present time also, there is a remnant saved according to the election of grace.*
[35] Matt. 7:13, 14.
[36] Ecclus. 18:30.
[37] Jonah 3:8b.
[38] Is. 53:6a.

aside our steps, that is, you have permitted our works to be erroneous and *departing from your way*, that is, from the divine law, not applying grace, and so leaving our hearts in their errors. According to this sense, we find written: *Why have you made us to err, O Lord, from your ways: why have you hardened our heart, that we should not fear you?*[39]

43{44}[20] *For you have humbled us in the place of affliction: and the shadow of death has covered us.*

Quoniam humiliasti nos in loco afflictionis, et cooperuit nos umbra mortis.

43{44}[20] *Quoniam humiliasti nos in loco afflictionis, for you have humbled us in the place of affliction*: that is, in the land of captivity or of our persecution you have subjected us to the powers of our enemies, who regard us in contempt; *et cooperuit nos umbra mortis, and the shadow of death has covered us*: that is, so much tribulation [has come upon us] that because of its vehemence we can call it an image of death; and, similar to those on the verge of death, it can come to us from anywhere. Whence David in great tribulation said: *There is but one step between me and death.*[40] And at times such were the tribulations of the Jews, as is clearly manifest in the books of Judges, and Kings, and Maccabees.

43{44}[21] *If we have forgotten the name of our God, and if we have spread forth our hands to a strange god.*

Si obliti sumus nomen Dei nostri, et si expandimus manus nostras ad deum alienum.

43{44}[22] *Shall not God search out these things? For he knows the secrets of the heart. Because for your sake we are killed all the day long: we are counted as sheep for the slaughter.*

Nonne Deus requiret ista? Ipse enim novit abscondita cordis. Quoniam propter te mortificamur tota die; aestimati sumus sicut oves occisionis.

43{44}[21] *Si obliti sumus nomen Dei nostri, if we have forgotten the name of our God*, that is, if we have neglected to observe the divine precepts, and we have discarded the contemplation of the divine law. For the name of God is neglected, indeed also forgotten, by him who does not fulfill

---

39 Is. 63:17a.
40 1 Sam. 20:3b.

his precepts, in the manner that we find in the epistle of John: *By this we know that we have known him, if we keep his commandments. He who says that he knows him, and keeps not his commandments, is a liar.*[41] And of disobedience to God, Paul attests: *They profess that they know God: but in their works they deny him.*[42] And therefore another scripture says: *Wisdom will not enter into a malicious soul.*[43] *Et si expandimus manus nostras ad Deum alienum, and if we have spread our hands to a strange God*, that is, if we have adored or worshipped something other than the true God, we have more served creatures than Creator; if our belly is our God,[44] if we hope in gold, or if we say to fine gold, *My confidence:*[45] it is as if saying, "No" [to God]. For anyone who more serves and loves creatures more than the Creator makes for himself that creature to be a god, and his hands (that is his desires) are extended unto an alien god. 43{44}[22] *Nonne Deus requiret ista? Shall not God search out these things?* Indeed, certainly. For he is the just judge, examining all things, disposing all things justly, according to that which the holy Job asserts: *Does he not consider my ways, and number all my steps?*[46] And again, *I feared all my works*, he said, *knowing that you did not spare the offender.*[47] *Ipse enim novit abscondita cordis, for he knows the secrets of the heart. For all things are naked and open to his eyes,*[48] according to the Apostle [Paul]. For this reason, elsewhere it is written: *Shall a man be hid in secret places and I not see him? says the Lord.*[49]

Quoniam propter te mortificamur tota die, because for your sake we are killed all the day long: that is, we suffer continual persecutions for justice's sake, and we are worn down by many scourges because we are unwilling to relinquish the faith and your law; *aestimati sumus sicut oves occisionis, and we are counted as sheep for the slaughter:* that is, as sheep which are killed and are valued as nothing useful other than to be killed and to be eaten, so the unbelievers and evildoers regard us as unworthy of life. But this was seen fulfilled especially during the time of the Maccabees, when Antiochus ordered that all those who observed the law of Moses should be massacred.[50] Whence it is written: *We are*

---

41 1 John 2:3–4.
42 Titus 1:16.
43 Wis. 1:4.
44 Cf. Phil. 3:19.
45 Job. 31:24b.
46 Job 31:4.
47 Job 9:28.
48 Heb. 4:13b.
49 Jer. 23:24a.
50 1 Macc. 1:52.

ready to die rather than to transgress the laws of God received from our fathers.[51] And again: *The King of the world will raise us up, who die for his laws, in the resurrection of eternal life.*[52]

43{44}[23] Arise, why do you sleep, O Lord? Arise, and cast us not off to the end.

Exsurge; quare obdormis, Domine? Exsurge, et ne repellas in finem.

43{44}[24] Why do you turn your face away? And forget our want and our trouble?

Quare faciem tuam avertis? Obliviseris inopiae nostrae et tribulationis nostrae?

Finally the Prophet [David] prays for the deliverance from the mentioned evils: **43{44}[23]** *Exsurge, arise,* that is, hold yourself out in the manner of someone rising from sitting, and help us; *quare obdormis, Domine? Why do you sleep, O Lord?* That is, why stop from rendering assistance, and disregard the prayers of your servants? *Exsurge, arise,* from this point forwards favoring us, *et ne repellas in finem, and cast us not off to the end,* that is, do not will to forsake us for a long while or altogether, since you defer to render aid for a time. **43{44}[24]** *Quare faciem tuam, why . . . your face,* that is, the aspect of your kindness and the grace of your aid, *avertis, do you turn,* not immediately providing us help who are so afflicted, *obliviseris inopiae nostrae et tribulationis nostrae, and forget our want and our trouble*: that is, why you so hold yourself out to us as if you do not pay attention to the poverty which we incur for your sake, and the tribulation which for we suffer for your sake? This is said not as an absolute assertion[53]—for as an earlier Psalm says, *The Lord is nigh unto them that are of a contrite heart*[54]—but it is said expressing the affection of a hurting soul calling upon the ears of kindliness. It is the same kind of way that holy Job spoke to the Lord: *I cry to you, and you hear me not: I stand up, and you do not regard me. You are changed to be cruel toward me, and in the hardness of your hand you are against me.*[55] Whence also

---

51   2 Macc. 7:2b.
52   2 Macc. 7:9b.
53   E. N. Denis says this is not asserted *simpliciter*, that is absolutely and without qualification. It is a qualified (*secundum quid*) statement; namely, it is asserted in a plaintive sense. Therefore, Psalm 43:24 does not contradict Psalm 33:19.
54   Ps. 33:19a.
55   Job 30:20-21.

Habakkuk, as if impatient because of the delay of the divine hearkening, so commenced [his prayer]: *How long, O Lord, shall I cry, and you will not hear? Shall I cry out to you suffering violence, and you will not save?*[56] Also the prophet Isaiah: *[Where is] the multitude of your bowels, and of your mercies they have held back themselves from me?*[57] Therefore, in such cases, we must not give up, nor ought we to cease from prayer, but we ought unalterably to believe it more possible that heaven and earth should perish than that one who trusts in the Lord and perseveringly knocks will be forsaken. And so the Savior says: *He that shall persevere unto the end, he shall be saved;*[58] and *we ought always to pray, and not to faint.*[59] For God delays for a time so that he might prove our constancy, and so that our desires may grow with the delay, and by such grace bring about greater exuberance. For which reason Moses said: *You shall remember all the way through which the Lord your God has brought you . . . to afflict you and to prove you, and that the things that were in your heart might be made known, whether you would keep his commandments or not.*[60]

43{44}[25] *For our soul is humbled down to the dust: our belly cleaves to the earth.*

Quoniam humiliata est in pulvere anima nostra; conglutinatus est in terra venter noster.

43{44}[25] *Quoniam humiliata est in pulvere anima nostra,* for our soul is humbled down to the dust: that is, we have humbled ourselves before you, tossing dust and ashes upon our head; *conglutinatus est in terra venter noster,* our belly cleaves to the earth: that is, we fall down prone upon the earth, and our whole body lies prostrate before your honor and majesty, so that we might obtain mercy. For to do this during times of necessity was a Jewish custom. Whence it is said: *Joshua fell flat on the ground before . . . the Lord until the evening.*[61]

43{44}[26] *Arise, O Lord, help us and redeem us for your name's sake.*

Exsurge, Domine, adiuva nos, et redime nos propter nomen tuum.

---

56   Hab. 1:2.
57   Is. 63:15b.
58   Matt. 10:22b; 24:13.
59   Luke 18:1b.
60   Deut. 8:2.
61   Joshua 7:6a.

The prayer that follows is very devout, and efficacious, and ignitive: 43{44}[26] *Exsurge, Domine, adiuva nos; Arise, O Lord, help us,* for no one but you is our helper, *et redime nos, and redeem us* from the evil of punishment and of fault, and of all danger, *propter nomen tuum, for your name's sake,* that is, for you yourself and your goodness and to the honor of your name, as you said through Ezechiel: *It is not for your sake that I will do this, be it known to you, but for my holy name's sake.*[62]

ARTICLE LXXXVI

MORAL ELUCIDATION OF THE SAME FORTY-THIRD PSALM.

43{44}[2] *We have heard, O God, with our ears: our fathers have declared to us, the work you have wrought in their days, and in the days of old.*

Deus, auribus nostris audivimus, patres nostri annuntiaverunt nobis, opus quod operatus es in diebus eorum, et in diebus antiquis.

NOW, VIEWED FROM A MORAL POINT OF VIEW, fitting is this Psalm in addressing the manifold tribulations of the Church of Christ, or of any one Christian full of afflictions of body or mind, and most of all of the holy martyrs. Any one of these, therefore, recalling the pristine benefits of God, and placing before God his own persecution, and desiring to be delivered from it, says 43{44}[2] *Deus, O God,* Only-begotten of God, *auribus nostris audivimus, we have heard with our ears*: especially with the ears of our heart, of which the Gospel says, *He that has ears to hear, let him hear.*[63] These the Jews, of whom Moses spoke, did not have, when he said: *You have seen all these* marvelous things *that the Lord did before you; and the Lord has not given you a heart to understand, and eyes to see, and ears that may hear, unto this present day.*[64] Of this also Isaiah attested: *For the heart of this people is grown gross, and with their ears have they heard heavily.*[65] *Patres nostri, our fathers,* namely the holy Apostles

---

62 Ez. 36:22a; Ez, 36:32a. This is a patchwork quote, drawing from Ez. 36:22, 35:32, and again from 36:22.
63 Luke 8:8b.
64 Deut. 29:2a, 4.
65 Is. 6:10. E. N. Denis quotes Isaiah from the Septuagint version, not from the

and Evangelists, *annuntiaverunt nobis, have declared to us*, in their sermons and in their writings, *opus quod operatus es in diebus eorum, the work you have wrought in their days*, that is, the miracles that you performed before them before the Passion and after the Passion, *et in diebus antiquis, and in the days of old*, that is, the marvels which you did in the time of Moses. Whence the Apostle Jude says: *Jesus, having saved the people out of the land of Egypt, did afterwards destroy them that believed not.*[66]

43{44}[3] *Your hand destroyed the Gentiles, and you planted them: you did afflict the people and cast them out.*

Manus tua gentes disperdidit, et plantasti eos; afflixisti populos et expulisti eos.

43{44}[3] *Manus tua, your hand*, that is, your power, O Lord Jesus almighty, *gentes, the Gentiles*, that is, the tyrants and the persecutors of the Church, and the people of the Jews who purposed to extinguish completely the early Church, as it is related in Acts that the chiefs of the priests ordered the Apostles *not to speak at all, nor teach in the name of Jesus*.[67] And so these people your hand *disperdidit, destroyed*, because many of them in the present life were overcome by an unfavorable death and others perished eternally. Also often the sword of the Christian princes destroyed the Gentiles, namely Theodosius, Charlemagne, and Godfrey of Bouillon.[68] Whence in Micah it is foretold regarding Christ: *His going forth is from the beginning, from the days of eternity, and he shall*

Vulgate translation of Is. 6:10. This verse is found in Matt. 13:15 and in Acts 28:27, where the Septuagint is quoted in the Greek text and translated into Latin in the Vulgate.
66   Jude 5.
67   Acts 4:18b.
68   E. N. Theodosius (*ca.* 346–395 AD) "the Great" was emperor of Byzantium and played an important role in stamping out paganism and Arianism and in Christianising the law. When his zeal overstepped Christian boundaries (as during the massacre of Thessalonica), St. Ambrose chastised and excommunicated the emperor until he repented of his crime. St. Ambrose famously stated in his Sermon against the Arian Auxentius: *Imperator enim intra Ecclesiam, non supra Ecclesiam est*, "the Emperor is within the Church, not over the Church." *Sermo contra Auxentium*, 36, PL 16, 1018. Charlemagne (748–814 AD) was, of course, the famous King of the Franks and later Emperor of the Romans from 800 until his death. Known as the "Father of Europe," Charlemagne cooperated with the papacy and clerics such as St. Alcuin to establish the Christian faith throughout his lands, and he fought against the Muslims in Spain and the pagan Saxons. Godfrey of Bouillon (1060–1100 AD) was a French nobleman notable for being one of the leaders of the First Crusade to regain the Holy Land and battle against militant Islam. He was also the first ruler of the Kingdom of Jerusalem (1099–1100) and was succeeded after his death by his brother Baldwin.

be magnified even to the ends of the earth.[69] And through Isaiah, the eternal Father says of Christ: *I will distribute to him very many, and he shall divide the spoils of the strong.*[70] And Zechariah speaking of Christ: *The Lord shall go forth, and shall fight against* the nations, *and his feet shall stand in that day upon the mount of Olives.*[71] *Et plantasti eos, and you planted them,* namely, our fathers the Apostles, making them *princes over all the earth,*[72] as it says in the Psalm which follows this one. *Afflixisti populos, you did afflict the people* that were unfaithful, in the manner that was foretold, *et expulisti eos, and cast them out.* For you cast out the Jews from the land of promise, and you caused Christians to dwell in it; and also you gave to Christians many regions once subject to the Gentiles.

43{44}[4] *For they got not the possession of the land by their own sword: neither did their own arm save them. But your right hand and your arm, and the light of your countenance: because you were pleased with them.*

Nec enim in gladio suo possederunt terram, et brachium eorum non salvavit eos; sed dextera tua et brachium tuum, et illuminatio vultus tui, quoniam complacuisti in eis.

43{44}[4] *Nec enim in gladio suo possederunt, for they got not the possession . . . by their own sword,* our faithful fathers in Christ [did not obtain possession], *terram, of the land,* that is, of the orb of the world, which they brought to the faith and filled with Christians. For the Apostles were few and they were commoners; they were not gifted with human eloquence. When the Apostle [Paul] said: *My speech and my preaching was not in the persuasive words of human wisdom, but in showing of the Spirit and power.*[73] *Et brachium eorum, and their arm,* that is, their natural power, *non salvavit eos, neither . . . did it save them,* from the dangers from which they were frequently saved. For when the Apostles were placed in prison, an angel led them out.[74] Christ also delivered Paul from three shipwrecks at sea;[75] and John was spared from a boiling vat of oil.[76]

---

69 Micah 5:2b, 4b.
70 Is. 53:12a.
71 Zech. 14:3b–4a.
72 Ps. 44:17b.
73 2 Cor. 2:4.
74 Acts 5:18–19.
75 2 Cor. 11:25; Acts 27:44.
76 E. N. This is related in non-biblical (apocryphal) sources, and found in other sources such as, for example, in Tertullian's (*ca.* 155–240 A. D.) *Prescription against*

Sed dextera tua, but *your right hand*, that is, your kindly custody, *et brachium tuum*, and *your arm*, that is, by the operation of miracles, *et illuminatio vultus tui*, and *the light of your countenance*, that is, the wisdom that you gave them, especially in the day of Pentecost, sending them the Holy Spirit, which taught them all truth, and conferred upon them foreknowledge of the future. For by this, the Church of Christ was instituted, augmented, and stabilized, so that Christians who are the seed and sons of the Apostles might possess the earth and be saved from invisible and visible enemies. Here the Apostle [Paul] says: *The signs of my apostleship have been wrought on you, in all patience, in signs, and wonders, and mighty deeds.*[77] And to the Hebrews he openly said: *How shall we escape if we neglect so great a salvation which ... was confirmed unto us, God also bearing witness by signs, and wonders, and diverse miracles, and distributions of the Holy Spirit?*[78] And Christ also foretold the light of his countenance over the Apostles: *For I will give you a mouth and wisdom, which all your adversaries shall not be able to resist and gainsay.*[79] And finally, from his right hand, that is, with the grace of his presence and his kindly protection, he says: *Behold I am with you all days, even to the consummation of the world.*[80]

And so by this salvation of mind and body Christians are chosen, *quoniam*, because, O Christ, *complacuisti in eis*, you were pleased with them, as you bear witness to in the Gospel: *You have not chosen me: but I have chosen you.*[81] Whence Peter writes to the believers: *You are a chosen generation, a kingly priesthood, a holy nation, a purchased people: that you may declare his virtues, who has called you out of darkness into his marvelous light.*[82] And so Christians were led to the faith of Christ and interior salvation by the undertaking of preaching by the Apostles, for they were chosen by Christ. For in this regard Paul told the Athenians: God who overlooked the prior time of ignorance, *now declares unto men, that all should everywhere do penance, because he has appointed a day wherein he will judged the world in equity, by the man whom he has appointed.*[83] And

---

Heretics, who says that sometime after the death of Sts. Peter and Paul, St. John *in oleum igneum demersus, nihil passus est, in insulam relgatur,* "was submerged in fiery oil, and suffered nothing, and was exiled to the island [of Patmos]." *De Praesc. Adv. Haer.*, 36, PL 2, 49.

77 2 Cor. 12:12.
78 Heb. 2:3b-4. For Denis's belief that St. Paul was the author of Hebrews, see footnote 8-34 in Volume 1.
79 Luke 21:15.
80 Matt. 28:20.
81 John 15:16a.
82 1 Pet. 2:9.
83 Acts 17:30b-31a.

also the Ephesians: *According to revelation, the mystery has been made known to me,*[84] *which in other generations was not known to the sons of men, as it is now revealed to his holy apostles and those in the Spirit,*[85] *to be fellow heirs, and of the same body, and co-partners of the promises of God in Jesus Christ.*[86] Indeed all the faithful and the predestined are chosen from eternity in Christ, in the manner that the Apostle again confessed: *He chose us in him before the foundation of the world, that we should be holy and unspotted in his sight.*[87] Whence, according to Augustine in the book *On the Predestination of the Saints*, Christ is the most brilliant exemplar and cause of predestination of all the elect.[88]

Reflecting upon this, with respect to predestination two things are to be considered, namely, [first of all,] the very act of predestination: in this neither Christ, nor anyone else, is the cause of predestination, because predestination thus understood is God predestinating just as active creation[89] is God creating. Secondly, we must consider in predestination the grace of predestination, which is the effect of predestination. For predestination is the preparation of grace in the present, and of glory in the future: and in this manner Christ's predestination is the exemplar and cause of the predestination of the Saints. For God foreordained the world to be saved by Christ, and through his merits to confer upon man grace. And so the Apostle [Paul] says: God *has predestined us into the adoption of children through Jesus Christ, ... according to the purpose of his will unto the praise of the glory of his grace, in which he has graced us in his beloved*

---

84 Eph. 3:3a.
85 Eph. 3:5.
86 Eph. 3:6.
87 Eph. 1:4.
88 E. N. ST, IIIa, q. 24, art. 3, co. (Christ's predestination is our exemplar) & art. 4 co. (Christ's predestination is the cause of ours) In his *sed contra* to article 3, St. Thomas quotes St. Augustine's statement in his *On the Predestination of the Saints* that Christ is the *praeclarissimum lumen praedestinationis et gratiae,* "the most brilliant light of predestination and grace." De Praedest Sanct., 15, 30, PL 44, 981.
89 E. N. Denis speaks of *creatio activa*, active creation. Theologians distinguished between *creatio activa*, active creation, which is the exclusive and nondelegable act of creation from nothing (*ex nihilo*), and *creatio passiva*, passive creation, which is the actual coming to be of the world, the product, as it were, of the *creatio activa*. A similar distinction was made with respect to predestination. As the Franciscan *Francesc Eiximenis* (ca. 1330–1409) put it, "Predestination is two-fold, namely, active and passive. Active predestination is the eternal and merciful God determining to give someone eternal glory.... Passive predestination is the rational nature ordained to glory by the eternal and merciful God." *Quaedam Notiones Philosophico-Theologiae*, Archivum Franciscanum historicum (Rome: Collegio S. Bonaventura, 1978), Vols. 71–72, 41.

Son.⁹⁰ And elsewhere: *For whom he foreknew, he says, he predestinated to be made conformable to the image of his Son, that he might be the first born among many brethren.*⁹¹ And so Christ, appointed to be cause of the light of the lowly, for that cause he was led to conformity with the divine will, saying *I confess to you, O Father, Lord of heaven and earth, because you have hidden these things from the wise and prudent, and have revealed them to little ones. Yea, Father, for so it has seemed good in your sight.*⁹² Whence also God most candidly said to Moses: *I will have mercy on whom I will, and I will be merciful to whom it shall please me.*⁹³ From which the most sacred of our philosophers concludes: *Therefore he has mercy on whom he will; and whom he will, he hardens.*⁹⁴ But these things are brought forth against the enemies of the grace of God, namely, against Pelagians, and also so that no one ever presumes to glory in himself, but that he might know that all our good, that is, merit and reward, is a gift of God, and it is only grace that saves us. And so the Apostle states: *God, who is rich in mercy, for his exceeding charity wherewith he loved us, since even when we were dead in sins, he has quickened us together in Christ, by whose grace you are saved. For by grace you are saved by faith: and that not of yourselves, for it is a gift of God; not of works, that no man may glory.*⁹⁵

43{44}[5] *You are yourself my king and my God, who commands the saving of Jacob.*

Tu es ipse rex meus et Deus meus, qui mandas salutes Iacob.

Then the Church or any one of the faithful says: **43{44}[5]** *Tu, you,* O Lord Jesus, *es ipse rex meus, are yourself my king and God.* Of whom is written: *The Lord is our judge, the Lord is our lawgiver, the Lord is our king: he will save us.*⁹⁶ And: *I will raise up to David a just branch: and a king shall reign, and shall be wise.*⁹⁷ And: *Behold your king will come to you, the just, and Savior: he is poor, and riding upon an ass.*⁹⁸ For Christ rules, cares for, cleanses, and perfects the Church and leads it to eternal life. Whence in another place is written regarding Christ: *He shall stand, and feed in the*

---

90 Eph. 1:5–6.
91 Rom 8:29.
92 Luke 10:21.
93 Ex. 33:19b.
94 Rom. 9:18.
95 Eph. 2:4–5, 8–9.
96 Is. 33:22.
97 Jer. 33:5.
98 Zech. 9:9b.

strength of the Lord, ... and they shall be converted to him.[99] And the Lord through Ezechiel said: *I will save my flock ... and I will set up on shepherd over them, and he shall feed them, even my servant David.... And I the Lord will be their God, and my servant David their prince.*[100] But by David, according to all teachers—even those of the Hebrews[101]—understand the king to be the Messiah or Christ. And you, O Lord Jesus Christ, are *et Deus meus*, also my God. For you are the only begotten of God, consubstantial, coequal, and coeternal with God the Father. Whence John says: *May we be in his true Son. This is the true God and life eternal.*[102] *Qui mandas salutes Iacob*, who commands the saving of Jacob, that is, you who confer and offer freely your grace and mercy to the Church and the supplanters of vices,[103] of which in the Gospel you say: *Come to me, all you that labor, and are burdened, and I will refresh you.*[104] And again: *Ask, and it shall be given you: seek, and you shall find: knock, and it shall be opened to you.*[105]

43{44}[6] *Through you we will blow down our enemies with the horn: and through your name we will despise them that rise up against us.*[106]

In te inimicos nostros ventilabimus cornu, et in nomine tuo spernemus insurgentes in nobis.

43{44}[6] *In te inimicos nosotros, through you ... our enemies*, namely, the demons, *ventilabimus cornu, we will blow down ... with the horn*, overcoming their temptations by your grace. For [thus] the Apostle [Paul]: *I can do all these things*, he says, *in him who strengthens me.*[107] Also, Christ said to his disciples: *Behold, I have given you power ... over all demons.*[108] And frequently the princes of the Christians overcome enemies with

---

99   Micah 5:4a.
100 Ez. 34:22-24.
101 E. N. Meaning Jewish Biblical exegetes or commentators of the Old Testament.
102 1 John 5:20b.
103 E. N. This is a reference to Jacob as the "supplanter," and Israel as "man seeing God." Earlier in this *Commentary* Denis states: "The faithful, therefore, who supplants sin, is Jacob; and this is the same as Israel, to the extent he is contemplating God." Article XXXV (Psalm 13:7) in Volume 1. The "supplanters of vices" are, therefore, the individual Christian faithful. See also Article XXVI (Psalm 13:7) in Volume 1.
104 Matt. 11:28.
105 Matt. 7:7.
106 E. N. I have replaced the Douay-Rheims' "push down" with "blow down."
107 Phil 4:13.
108 Luke 10:19: *Behold, I have given you power to tread upon serpents and scorpions, and upon all the power of the enemy: and nothing shall hurt you.*

visible power. *Et in nomine tuo spernemus insurgentes in nobis, and through your name we will despise them that rise up against us*, not fearing those who can kill the body, but implementing that which you yourself say: *Be not afraid of them who kill the body, ... but fear him who has power to destroy both the body and the soul in hell.*[109] And again: *Let not your heart be troubled, nor let it be afraid.*[110] This the most blessed martyrs, who derided and spurned tyrants, most excellently fulfilled. And of the first of our princes, namely of the holy Apostles, it is written: *They went from the presence of the council, rejoicing that they were accounted worthy to suffer reproach for the name of Jesus.*[111]

43{44}[7] For I will not trust in my bow: neither shall my sword save me.

Non enim in arcu meo sperabo, et gladius meus non salvabit me.

43{44}[8] But you have saved us from them that afflict us: and have put them to shame that hate us.

Salvasti enim nos de affligentibus nos, et odientes nos confudisti.

43{44}[9] In God shall we glory all the day long: and in your name we will give praise forever.

In Deo laudabimur tota die; et in nomine tuo confitebimur in saeculum.

43{44}[7] *Non enim in arcu meo, for ... not ... in my bow*, that is, in natural industry or subtle counsel, or fraudulent inventions, *sperabo, will I trust*. 43{44}[8] *Salvasti enim nos de affligentibus nos, but you have saved us from them that afflict us*, that is, from the persecutors and tyrants, because through the bodily death that they have directed against us, we have obtained eternal life; *et odientes nos confudisti, and have put them to shame that hate us*, because you have outwardly condemned the aforementioned adversaries of the faith and the Church. This verse can also be explained as referring to the demons that tempt us, and the evil desires that attack us—against which holy men constantly battle, but who prevail over all their enemies in the name of Christ. 43{44}[9] *In Deo laudabimur tota die; et in nomine tuo confitebimur in saeculum; In God shall we glory all the day long; and in your name we give praise forever*. This verse is satisfactorily explained in the previous exposition.

---

109 Luke 12:4–5.
110 John 14:27b.
111 Acts 5:41.

But that it especially applies to the Church of Christ is obvious from that which Scripture says: *All they that believed, were together, and had all things common;* and *they took their meat with gladness and simplicity of heart, and praising God, and having favor with all the people.*[112]

43{44}[10] *But now you have cast us off, and put us to shame: and you, O God, will not go out with our armies.*

Nunc autem repulisti et confudisti nos; et non egredieris, Deus, in virtutibus nostris.

43{44}[11] *You have made us turn our back to our enemies: and they that hated us plundered for themselves.*

Avertisti nos retrorsum post inimicos nostros; et qui oderunt nos diripiebant sibi.

43{44}[12] *You have given us up like sheep to be eaten: you have scattered us among the nations.*

Dedisti nos tamquam oves escarum; et in gentibus dispersisti nos.

43{44}[13] *You have sold your people for no price: and there was no reckoning in the exchange of them.*

Vendidisti populum tuum sine pretio; et non fuit multitudo in commutationibus eorum.

43{44}[10] *Nunc autem,* but now: namely, when heretics, schismatics, pagans, tyrants, and the ungodly devastate the orthodox Church and kill martyrs; *repulisti, you have cast us off,* O Lord Jesus, that is, you have permitted your people to be afflicted; *et confudisti nos, and you have put us to shame,* permitting us to be mocked and despised by the ungodly: just as the Apostle [Paul] says, *We are made a spectacle to the world, and to angels, and to men;*[113] *et non egredieris, Deus, in virtutibus nostris; and you, God, will not go out with our armies,* that is, you will not deliver us from the tribulations and punishments of death in the present age. **43{44}[11]** *Avertisti nos retrorsum post inimicos nostros, you have made us turn our back to our enemies.* For frequently, the faithful not yet ready for martyrdom, fled, and abandoned their own dwelling place for fear of the persecutors, and were taken captive, and afterwards were dragged back to the enemy all bound up. *Et qui oderunt nos, diripiebant sibi, and they that hated us plundered for themselves* the lands, cities, and all our goods

---

112 Acts 2:44, 46b, 47a.
113 1 Cor. 4:9b.

which we abandoned by fleeing or being captured. Indeed, in the time of martyrs the tyrants plundered the goods of all those who were martyrs. **43{44}[12]** *Dedisti nos tanquam oves escarum, you have given us like sheep to be eaten*: that is, you have allowed us to be killed abundantly, even as we were worth nothing, as sheep are slaughtered and eaten. For you have fulfilled in us, O Lord Jesus, that which you predicted in the Gospel: *The hour comes, that whosoever kills you, will think that he does a service to God.*[114] And again: *And you shall be betrayed by your parents and brethren, and kinsmen and friends; and some of you they will put to death.*[115] *Et in gentibus dispersisti nos, you have scattered us among the nations*. Even today many faithful remain among infidels under serious tribute and suppressed in the manner that the Jews dwell among us. **43{44}[13]** *Vendidisti populum tuum sine pretio, you have sold your people for no price*. In the way that befell the people of the Old Testament, in that manner and even more greatly, Christians were frequently afflicted with evils or punishments which are recited in this verse and the two following verses. And so their explanation is apparent from the preceding exposition.

43{44}[16] *All the day long my shame is before me: and the confusion of my face has covered me.*

Tota die verecundia mea contra me est, et confusio faciei meae cooperuit me.

43{44}[16] *Tota die verecundia mea contra me est, all the day long my shame is before me.* For the Church of Christ is shamed—either because its members are weak, who sometimes from the horrors of punishments of martyrdom forsook [the faith], or fled, or hid themselves; or because it saw the law of God condemned or held in contempt by its own [members]. Or [we can understand this verse in this manner]: because Christians are disdained by all as irrational or dabbling in magic or with imaginary things, as will be said of them by the unbelievers in the day of judgment: *These are they, whom we had some time in derision, and for a parable of reproach; we fools esteemed their life madness, and their end without honor. How they are numbered among the children of God, and their lot is among the saints?*[116] Whence also holy Job said: *The simplicity of the just man is laughed to scorn.*[117]

---

114 John 16:2b.
115 Luke 21:16.
116 Wis. 5:3b–5.
117 Job 12:4b.

43{44}[18] *All these things have come upon us, yet we have not forgotten you: and we have not done wickedly in your covenant.*

Haec omnia venerunt super nos; nec obliti sumus te, et inique non egimus in testamento tuo.

43{44}[19] *And our heart has not turned back: and you have turned aside our steps from your way.*

Et non recessit retro cor nostrum; et declinasti semitas nostras a via tua.

43{44}[18][118] *Haec omnia, all these things,* torments and hard things, *venerunt super nos, have come upon us,* your martyrs and servants, O Lord Jesus Christ; *nec obliti sumus te, yet we have not forgotten you,* negating your faith; *et inique non egimus in testamento tuo, and we have not done wickedly in your covenant,* that is, we have not abandoned in any manner the way of justice on account of persecutions; 43{44}[19] *Et non recessit retro cor nostrum, and our heart has not turned back,* forsaking you and holding on to transitory things.

43{44}[22] ... *Because for your sake we are killed all the day long: we are counted as sheep for the slaughter.*

... *Quoniam propter te mortificamur tota die; aestimati sumus sicut oves occisionis.*

43{44}[22][119] *Quoniam propter te, because for your sake,* that is, from your love, and because of hope in eternal life, *mortificamur tota die, we are killed all the day long,* in the work of penance, in fasting, and tears and lamentation, in vigils and corrections of mind and body, and all manner of denials of our own will, carrying daily the Cross of Christ,[120] and following in his footsteps, in the manner that the Apostle [Paul] admonished: *Laying aside every weight and sin which surrounds us, let us run by patience to the fight proposed to us: Looking on Jesus, the author and finisher of faith* lest our souls become weary.[121] *Aestimatis sumus sicut oves occisionis, we are counted as sheep for the slaughter.* This [verse] and the others now omitted are seen to be sufficiently elucidated in the preceding exposition. But the Apostle asserts this verse as applying as

---

118 Denis skips over verse 17.
119 Denis skips over the latter part of verse 19, and all of verses 20 and 21.
120 *Cf.* Luke 9:23.
121 Heb. 12:1–2.

much to himself as to his disciples to show that no adversity is able to deter us from the love of God. For he introduces it thus: *Who then shall separate us from the love of Christ? Shall tribulation? or distress? or famine? or nakedness? or danger? or persecution? or the sword? As it is written: For your sake we are put to death all the day long. We are accounted as sheep for the slaughter.*[122] And elsewhere he says: *I die daily, I protest by your glory, brethren, which I have in Christ Jesus our Lord.*[123]

PRAYER

WE BESEECH, O ALMIGHTY ONE, MERCY: do not turn away our paths from your way on account of our sins, but let us hold fast to your paths living justly and piously, so that we may obtain from you the saving commands of Jacob in eternity.

Quaesumus, Omnipotens misericordia, propter delicta nostra ne declines semitas nostras de via tua; sed sic eas iuste et pie vivendo teneamus, ut a te mandatas salutes Iacob in aeternum obtineamus.

---

122   Rom. 8:35–36 (quoting Ps. 43:22b).
123   1 Cor. 15:31.

Psalm 44

ARTICLE LXXXVII

EXPOSITION OF THE FORTY-FOURTH PSALM: ERUCTAVIT COR MEUM. MY HEART HAS UTTERED.

44{45}[1] *Unto the end, for them that shall be changed, for the sons of Korah, for understanding. A canticle for the beloved.*

In finem, pro his qui commutabuntur. Filiis Core, ad intellectum. Canticum pro dilecto.

THIS TITLE HAS ALREADY BEEN NOTED IN A Psalm already explained: 44{45}[1] *In finem, pro iis qui commutabuntur. Filiis Core, ad intellectum. Canticum pro dilecto; unto the end, for them that shall be changed, for the sons of Korah, for understanding. A canticle for the beloved.* This glorious and noble Psalm most excellently and clearly treats of the dual nature of Christ, and of his divine generation, and of the unity of his person, and also of the connection between Christ the Bridegroom and the Church, his Bride, or the glorious Virgin, or faithful souls. And so it is called an epithalamium, that is, a marriage poem, highly praising the nuptials of the Bridegroom and the Bride. The sense of this title is this: *Canticum, in finem; a canticle, unto the end,* that is, this Psalm which is called a canticle, relates to Christ, who is the principle of our creation, and the end of our re-creation: *a canticle* written, I say, *pro his qui commutabuntur, for them that shall be changed,* that is, for the elect, who not only rise again, but will be changed, that is, they will obtain blessed immortality, namely for *filiis Core, the sons of Korah,* that is, the imitators of Christ crucified in the place of Calvary. For Korah is interpreted as Calvary.[1] *Pro dilecto, for the beloved:* that is, this canticle is also written for Christ, to whom the Father said: *You are my beloved Son.*[2] And so, therefore, this canticle speaks for Christ and his faithful, that is, of the Bridegroom of the Church and of that Church. *Ad intellectum, for understanding,* that is, so that

---

1 E. N. See Article LXXX (Psalm 40:1) and *see also* footnote 40-2 for an explanation of the relationship between Korah and Calvary.
2 Matt. 3:17; 17:5; Luke 3:22; 9:35.

Christ's faithful wisely understand Christ, and faithfully contemplate his mysteries, namely, the Incarnation and his connection with the Church. Yet in his translation from the Hebrew, Jerome puts this title on the Psalm: *To the victor, for the lilies of the sons of Korah, a canticle of the most beloved*: and concludes with the same as the first-mentioned title. For by lilies is understood the faithful member of Christ, which are children of the Bride.[3]

44{45}[2] *My heart has uttered a good word: I speak my works to the king; my tongue is the pen of a scrivener that writes swiftly.*

Eructavit cor meum verbum bonum; dico ego opera mea regi. Lingua mea calamus scribae velociter scribentis.

Following the opening of this Psalm, we come upon the first two verses which can be explained in two ways. The first is that they are the word of God the Father, in whose person the Prophet [David] is speaking, saying: **44{45}[2]** *Eructavit cor meum verbum bonum, my heart has uttered a good word*: that is, my paternal Mind, or I myself who am nothing except the most simple and pure paternal Mind, or my eternal Intellect, or my fruitful Memory, of its plenitude of its infinite fruitfulness and goodness and of that fountain of my essence full with infinite divinity, I intellectually brought forth, I eternally said, and truly begot my only Son consubstantial to me, who is the good Word. Of whom it is written: *The word of God on high is the fountain of wisdom*;[4] and, *In the beginning was the Word, and the Word was with God, and the Word was God.*[5] And of whom was said in an earlier Psalm: *By the word of the Lord the heavens were established.*[6] And Wisdom also: *For while all things were in quiet silence, and the night was in the midst of her course, your almighty Word, O Lord, leapt down from heaven from your royal throne and came.*[7] *Dico ego*, I speak, I, the eternal Father, *opera mea*, my works, that is, whatever I do, *regi, to the king*, that is to Christ my most beloved Son, who is *King of kings and Lord of lords.*[8] This is what Christ says:

---

3   E. N. The change is explained by St. Jerome in his epistle to the virgin Principa. *Epist.* 65, 3, PL 22, 624–25. Denis is saying that the difference in translation arrives to the same conclusion since the "sons of Korah" and the "lilies of the sons of Korah" are essentially the same thing, both meaning faithful members of Christ or his Church.
4   Ecclus. 1:5a.
5   John 1:1.
6   Ps. 32:6a.
7   Wis. 18:14–15.
8   Rev. 19:16b.

The Father loves the Son, and shows him all things which he himself does.[9] For whatever the Father knows in himself, this he expresses in the Son. For he, the Only-begotten, is the eternal Word of the paternal Mind, the Speech of Intelligence, and the full Expression of his Wisdom. And so whatever the Father in the order of things created in the beginning, this he said eternally in his Word, and, in time, he did it together with him.[10] For which reason, John states: *All things were made by him;*[11] and again, *[without him was made nothing] that was made, and in him was life.*[12]

Thereafter the eternal Father says: *Lingua mea calamus scribae velociter scribentis, my tongue is the pen of a scrivener that writes swiftly*: that is, my intellect is similar to the pen of a man writing quickly. And this is so for two reasons. First, because as the word that is written by a pen does not make a sound and is not transient, but is rather silent, firm, and permanent, so the Word of God the Father is not transient, does not make a sound, and is not unstable, but is hidden, firm, immoveable, and eternal. Second, because as the pen of a quickly-writing scrivener makes its mark without labor and notable delay, so the divine Intellect speaking within itself (*ad intra*), or God the Father, without movement, labor, and delay produces his Word in himself in the moment of eternity, in the manner that eternal Wisdom, which is the Word or the Son of God, says: *The Lord possessed me in the beginning of his ways, before he made anything from the beginning; I was set up from eternity, the depths were not as yet, and I was already conceived.*[13]

Secondly, this part can be explained as if they were the words of the Prophet [David]; and it would be in this sense: *My heart has uttered a good word*: that is, my intellect brings forth from the fulness of divine illumination and from the abundance of prophetic knowledge, saying within itself and with the mouth expresses this present Psalm, which is a good and saving word, and an optimum speech. *I speak my works to the king*: that is, this scripture and all other [scriptures] that I do, say, sing, and I will write to the glory of the Messiah king, of whose nuptials I will address in this Psalm. *My tongue is the pen of a scrivener that writes*

---

9   John 5:20a.
10 E. N. All the works of the Trinity *ad extra* (as distinguished from the subsistent relations between the Father, Son, and Holy Spirit "within" or *ad intra* the Trinity) are indivisible. DS 254, 281, 284, 421, 428. When it comes to God's interaction with creation, therefore, it is the Trinity that indivisibly creates, redeems, sanctifies, and glorifies.
11 John 1:3a.
12 John 1:3b, 4a. I have included the section in brackets, for otherwise the quote does not appear to make full sense.
13 Prov. 8:22, 23a, 24a.

swiftly: that is, the tongue of my mouth in writing this Psalm was a pen, a stylus, a quill, or a writing style of a scrivener quickly writing; that is, I write this Psalm without my own exertion and without labor, according to that which the Holy Spirit tells me. For the tongue of the Prophet was an instrument of his soul, in the manner that a quill is an instrument in the hand of a scrivener. And the Prophet wrote this Psalm quickly, as Jeremiah has related: *Baruch said to the princes of Juda: With his mouth Jeremiah pronounced all these words as if he were reading to me: and I wrote in a volume with ink.*[14] Or [is another way of looking at it is] thus: *My tongue is the pen of a scrivener that writes quickly*, that is, the Holy Spirit, who inspires what to write, makes the writing to be quick."For the grace of the Holy Spirit does not know delayed efforts," as Ambrose attests.[15] And this sense agrees with what David acknowledges in another place: *The spirit of the Lord has spoken by me and his word by my tongue.*[16]

But the first explanation of this verse is better and more profound, and it agrees with that which God the Father says through Isaiah: *The word of justice shall go out of my mouth, and shall not return;*[17] also that in Ecclesiasticus: *I came out of the mouth of the most High, the firstborn before all creatures.*[18] But not only does he say *my heart has uttered a word*, but [he says] *a good Word*, so as to make known that this Word is true God. For Christ testified, *None is good but one, that is God.*[19] For God himself is naturally and in every which way good; and according to Dionysius [the Areopagite] his nature is goodness; and the first name of God is good.[20]

44{45}[3] *You are beautiful above the sons of men: grace is poured abroad in your lips; therefore has God blessed you forever.*

Speciosus forma prae filiis hominum, diffusa est gratia in labiis tuis; propterea benedixit te Deus in aeternum.

Consequently, the Prophet [David] breaks forth in praise of this king, and he first commends him because of beauty, saying: 44{45}[3] *Speciosus*

---

14   Jer. 36:18.
15   E. N. *Nescit tarda molimina Spiritus sancti gratia*. A direct quotation from St. Ambrose, Exposition of the Gospel of Luke, II, 19 (*vers.* 39, 40), PL 15, 1560.
16   2 Sam. 23:2.
17   Is. 45:23.
18   Ecclus. 24:5.
19   Mark 10:18b.
20   E. N. This is a reference to Pseudo-Dionysius's *De divinis nominibus* (*On the Divine Names*), and the discussion of God and "goodness" as his first name can be found particularly in chapters 2, 4, and 13 of that work.

forma prae filiis hominum, you are beautiful above the sons of men. There were three kinds of beauty in Christ. One eternal, divine, and infinite, which comes to him by reason of his divine nature, and it is essentially the same with the divine essence, and in the three Persons one and indivisible.[21] And of this beauty of Christ, which is the Wisdom of the Father, is written: Wisdom is *a certain pure emanation of the glory of the almighty God.... For she is the brightness of eternal light, and the unspotted mirror of God's majesty, and the image of his goodness.*[22] And the Apostle [Paul]: *He who being the brightness of his glory, and the figure of his substance,... sits on the right hand of the majesty on high.*[23] Whence Saint Hilary pointing out that which is appropriated (*appropriata*) of the divine persons: "Eternity," he says, "is in the Father, form in the image, use in the gift."[24] But what else can "form in the image" mean except that Beauty is as proper to the Son since he is in all things similar to God the Father? Of which the Son gave witness: *He that sees me sees the Father also.*[25] For he says this not because of the identity of persons, as that enemy of the Holy Trinity Sabellius asserted,[26] but because they

---

21   E. N. "God is absolute beauty.... His beauty is a substantial beauty which encompasses and infinitely transcends all the beauty of the created world." Ludwig Ott, *Fundamentals of Catholic Dogma* (North Carolina: TAN Books 1974), 35 (trans., Patrick Lynch, ed. James Canon Bastible). "I invoke you.... O God, the Good and Beautiful, in whom and from whom and through whom all things are good and beautiful, which anywhere are good and beautiful." St. Augustine, *Soliloquies*, I, 3.
22   Wis. 7:25–26.
23   Heb. 1:3.
24   E. N. The reference is to St. Hilary of Poitier's (*ca.* 310–*ca.* 367 AD) *De Trinitate*, 2.1, PL 10, 51. However, Denis is actually quoting St. Augustine's paraphrase of this text: *Aeternitas, inquit, in patre, species in imagine, usus in munere. De Trinitate*, X, 11, PL 42, 931. St. Hilary actually says *Nec deesse quidquam consummationi tantae reperietur, intra quam sit, in Patre et Filio et Spiritu sancto, infinitas in aeterno, species in imagine, usus in munere.* "Nor can anything be found lacking in such a great consummation within which is the Father, and the Son, and the Holy Spirit, infinity in eternity, the species in the image, and the use in the gift." "Eternity is in the Father; beauty is in the Image (Word); and use (happiness) is in the Gift (Paraclete) [*infinitas in aeterno* (= *Patre*), *species in imagine* (= *Filio*), *usus in munere* (= *Spirit Sancto*).]" Ott, *op. cit.*, 73.
25   John 14:9b.
26   E. N. Sabellius (*fl. ca.* 215 AD) was a priest whose teaching on the Trinity was heretical. His Trinitarian theology was modal, and so the Father, Son, and Holy Spirit were different modes, aspects, masks, or faces (*prosopa*) of the one person (*hypostasis*) in God, so that, like the one sun has warmth, light, and circular form, or a clover three leaves, so God has three modes of existence or appearance. Thus, Sabellius did not distinguish between the three persons (*hypostases*) of the Trinity. Eventually, he was excommunicated by Pope Calixtus I (r. 217–222 AD) and Sabellianism condemned by Pope Dionysius I (r. 259–268 AD). DS 112.

are in every way similar to each other, according to what the Apostle [Paul] said: *Who is the image of the invisible God, the firstborn of every creature.*[27] Of this uncreated beauty of God, Dionysius [the Areopagite] spoke most beautifully.[28] Because of this beauty, Peter the Apostle also says of Christ: *On whom the angels desired to look.*[29]

Another [beauty] is the created and spiritual beauty of Christ, which consists in the perfection of his wisdom, in the excellence of his grace, and the eminence of his charity and virtues. And this beauty of Christ was total and incomparable; indeed, it was greater than [the beauty of] all of the elect put together, for it is written, *God does not give the spirit by measure*, by which must be understood, Christ as man.

And the third beauty of Christ was created and corporal, and this consists in due proportion, placement, and extent of his members and in the harmonious superfusion of lively color. And this beauty of Christ was great and vigorous. First, because there was no lack of natural perfection in him. Second, because it was becoming that his most holy and most beautiful soul receive a proportionate, that is, beautiful and magnificent, body. Third, because the body of Christ was assumed from most pure matter, namely from the most clean blood of the most worthy Virgin. Fourth, because it was formed and joined by that infallible, unerring agent, namely, the Holy Spirit. True, whether or not this bodily beauty of Christ was simply greater than the beauty of any other man may be discussed in various ways. But I piously believe, for the reasons already given, that my Lord Jesus Christ even with respect to his bodily beauty exceeded all other men, indeed it exceeded even [the beauty] of Absalom.[30] Not however always (as I believe) did he appear equally beautiful

---

27 Col. 1:15.
28 "Throughout the *Corpus Dionysiacum*, beauty performs an important and indispensable role in almost every primary theme treated but with a degree of subtlety that makes it difficult to comprehend. Its most obvious role is found in the sequence of divine names where it is articulated in progression with the Good, Light, and Love. Throughout the remainder of *On the Divine Names*, beauty is present in the constitutions and dynamisms of a number of other names. Beauty is also instrumental in other treatises of the *Corpus Dionysiacum*. It is a fundamental feature of hierarchical activity in both the Ecclesial and the Celestial orders. It enters into Dionysius's Christological teachings, plays a role in the mystical way of unknowing, and is associated directly with the hiddenness of God." Brendan Thomas Sammon, *The God Who is Beauty: Beauty as a Divine Name in Thomas Aquinas and Dionysius the Areopagite* (Cambridge: James Clark & Co. 2014), 123–24.
29 1 Pet. 1:12b.
30 2 Sam. 14:25: *But in all Israel there was not a man so comely, and so exceedingly beautiful as Absalom: from the sole of the foot to the crown of his head there was no blemish in him.*

in visage, because he was not solicitous [toward his appearance], but he spurned those who adorned and maintained their bodily beauty. But his spiritual beauty was always consistent, for he did not advance in grace.[31] But during the time of his Passion his bodily beauty so greatly vanished that of him Isaiah could say: *There is no beauty in him, nor comeliness: and we have seen him, and there was no sightliness*.[32] But of this varied beauty of the heavenly Bridegroom and Messiah king, the Bride says: *My beloved is white and ruddy, chosen out of thousands;*[33] and, *Behold you are fair, my beloved, and comely*.[34] So, therefore, O Christ, *you are beautiful above the sons of men*. For that this literally applies to Christ is declared clearly from the Chaldaic translation, considered authentic with the Hebrews, which states thus: *Your beauty, Messiah king, is greater than the sons of men.*

Finally, in the books of annals of the Romans[35] we read that Christ was of moderately tall and respectable stature, having a venerable appearance which those looking upon it could like and fear; having hair the color of an unripe hazel nut, falling plainly to about the ears, from the ears curled ringlets somewhat bluish and more fulsome, flowing freely upon the shoulders; having it parted in the middle of the head as is the custom of the Nazarenes; his forehead smooth and most serene, without blemish or wrinkle, made lovely with a moderate ruddiness; nose and ears are altogether faultless; having a full beard the same color as the hair, not long, but parted slightly into two at the chin, his appearance is ingenuous and mature, eyes sparkling, appearing diversely colored and bright; terrible in rebuking, pleasant and loving in admonition, joyful with reserved gravity; on some occasions he would shed tears, but he never laughed; the stature of his body forward and straight, but the arms and

---

31 *E. N.* Christ did not advance in grace because he had the absolute perfection of grace. "He who from the very beginning possessed the fulness of created grace could not advance in interior holiness. Christ was equally holy as a babe and as an adult man.... The Fathers and theologians explain His advance in wisdom and grace [as stated in Luke 2:52] not as an increase in, but merely as an outward manifestation of, sanctifying grace." Joseph Pohle and Arthur Preuss, *Christology* (St. Louis: B. Herder 1913), 237; see also ST, IIIa, q. 7, art. 12, ad 3.
32 Is. 53:2b.
33 Songs 5:10.
34 Songs 1:15.
35 *E. N.* Denis draws from the apocryphal letter of Publius Lentulus which purports to be a letter written by a procurator of Judea prior to the procuratorship of Pontius Pilate and is in the form of a letter to the Roman Senate. See Cora E. Lutz, "The Letter of Lentulus Describing Christ," The Yale University Library Gazette, Vol. 50, No. 2 (October 1975), 91–97.

hands agreeable to the sight, grave, sparse, and modest in speech: certainly in all things such as one can befittingly say, *beautiful above the sons of men*. Thereafter Christ is praised because of his eloquence. *Diffusa est gratia in labiis tuis, grace is poured abroad in your lips*: that is, a fruitful and efficacious eloquence has been given to you. Whence Christ said through Isaiah: *He has made my mouth like a sharp sword*.[36] And also the adversaries of Christ themselves were compelled to say: *Never did man speak like this man*.[37] And also with respect to this we read in Luke: *They wondered at the words of grace that proceeded from his mouth*.[38] But the efficacy of Christ in speaking is related by the Evangelist when he says: *He was teaching them as one having power, and not as the scribes and Pharisees*.[39] Also, knowing that Christ had the gift of tongues, as he did other gratuitous graces *(gratias gratis datas)*,[40] yet we do not read that he used this gift, because he did not preach except in Hebrew. Whence he said: *I was not sent but to the sheep that are lost of the house of Israel*.[41] Now as the hand is the organ of the practical intellect, so the tongue is the organ or instrument of the speculative intellect. In the manner, therefore, that Christ has the highest wisdom, so was it becoming to have the highest eloquence. Hence, of the grace of the lips of Christ her Bridegroom, the Bride says: *My soul melted when he spoke*.[42] *Propterea benedixit te Deus in aeternum, therefore, has God blessed you forever*. The blessing of God is the aggregation or infusion of grace and the divine gifts and the increasing of the same. Yet Christ did not advance in grace, nor did he merit for himself any essential reward, as he had these from inception in abundance. In what manner, therefore, is the blessing from

---

36 Is. 49:2a.
37 John 7:46b.
38 Luke 4:22a.
39 Matt. 7:29.
40 E. N. Denis asserts that Christ enjoyed all so-called gratuitous graces or graces gratuitously given *(gratiae gratis datae)*, including the charism of the gift of tongues (though Christ was not known to use it). These graces are independent of the graces relating to the holiness of the recipient (the *gratia gratum faciens*, i.e., sanctifying or habitual grace). See 1 Cor. 12:4–11. "Unlike the *gratia gratum faciens* (habitual grace) a *gratia gratis data* has as its immediate purpose, not the sanctification for the one who receives it, but the spiritual benefit of others. It is called *gratis data* not only because it is above the natural power of man but because it is something outside the realm of personal merit." Antonio Royo Marín, O. P., *The Theology of Christian Perfection* (Eugene: Wipf & Stock 2011), 640 (Jordan Aumann, O. P., trans.); see also ST IaIIae, q. 111, art. 1.
41 Mat. 15:24.
42 Songs 5:6.

God because of the grace of his lips meant? In response, this blessing is understood as referring to the accidental rewards of Christ. For by his most holy preaching he merited for himself the glorification of his body and his Ascension.[43] The blessing can also refer to the fruit of the eloquence of Christ, and to the mystery of his Body [meaning the Church]. For we say that the earth or tree is blessed when it bears copious fruit. Similarly, Christ is said to be blessed by reason of his eloquence because many obtained salvation through the teaching of Christ.

44{45}[4] *Gird your sword upon your loin,*[44] *O you most mighty.*
Accingere gladio tuo super femur tuum, potentissime.

44{45}[4] *Accingere gladio tuo super femur tuum, potentissime; gird your sword upon your loin, O you most mighty:* that is, O Christ the King, you who are the almighty Savior and the most powerful conqueror of the powers of the air,[45] gird, that is gird yourself, that you may be girt by the total Trinity, with your sword, that is, the divine preaching, the word of God, the speech of justice so that you dispense the grace of your lips all about, and you might use it to inform the world: gird, I say, *upon your loin,* that is, upon your intellect, so that you might speak wisely, and teach efficaciously.[46] Well indeed by the word "sword" is understood the word of God or the preaching of the Gospel, according to that divine

---

43   E. N. On the distinction between accidental and essential rewards in Christ, see footnote 1-48.
44   E. N. I have departed from the Douay-Rheims "thighs," which translates *femur,* and opted for the equally legitimate "loins." Given the *Commentary,* it is clear that Denis is speaking not of the thigh (upper leg), but of the region of the man's body that deals with procreation as an analogy to what occurs with the intellect.
45   E. N. See footnote 34-5.
46   E. N. This linkage of the intellect with one's loin may, to modern sensibilities, seem far-fetched. However, we might keep in mind the gentle reproof of Edward Ingram Watkin: "Symbolism, the reader may object — surely a *jeu démodé* [an old-fashioned game] — a quaint conceit of fancy, worked to death by the Fathers and medieval exegetes — moreover quite arbitrary and fantastic in the extreme. No doubt symbolism may be, and has been, abused, as literal exegesis of Scripture or as supplying the premises of a demonstration. But to go to the other extreme, and reject all symbolism in our interpretation of God's written or unwritten Scripture, is to deny the analogy which everywhere obtains between the various levels of being, in virtue of which the lower is always representative of the higher.... 'All things' are thus 'double one against the other' — outer corresponding with inner, material with spiritual. To be blind to this inner significance is to refuse credit to the vision of the poet or artist. It is what Blake condemned as 'single vision.'" E. I. Watkin, "The Bow in the Clouds," *The Persistence of Order* (Providence: Cluny Media 2019), Vol. III, 84.

Apostle [Paul]: *In all things taking the shield of faith ... and the sword of the Spirit, which is the word of God.*⁴⁷ And again: *For the word of God is living,* he says, *and effectual, and more piercing than any two edged sword.*⁴⁸ For the word of God is called a sword by reason of its effects, because it penetrates the interior of the mind, it kills sin, and it overcomes demons. Whence the Lord said to Jeremiah: *Are not my words as a fire, ... and as a hammer that breaks the rock in pieces?*⁴⁹ And Ecclesiastes says: *The words of the wise are as goads, and as nails deeply fastened in.*⁵⁰

Also, by the word "loin" is fittingly understood the intellect. For in the way that the body's loin is the seed-plot of generation, according to this — *The scepter shall not be taken away from Juda, nor a ruler from his loin, till he come that is to be sent*⁵¹ — so the intellect is the seed-plot of spiritual procreation. For as Christ asserted in the Gospel, *the seed is the word of God.*⁵² Now, the word proceeds from the intellect, as the Philosopher [Aristotle] says. There are [in those words] that are in the voice, those notes [or signs] which are in the affections in the soul.⁵³ So the intellect by the word of the mouth generates spiritually, as the Apostle said to the Galatians: *My little children, of whom I am in labor again, until Christ be formed in you.*⁵⁴ Of this intellectual loin, to which the sword of the word is girded, Jeremiah says: *Convert me, O Lord, and I shall be converted. For after you did convert me, I did penance; and after you did show unto me, I struck my loin.*⁵⁵ But of the power of Christ, in the elucidation of the preceding Psalm has been greatly described, to which that which Micah says of it may be added: *Your hand shall be lifted up over your enemies, and all your enemies shall be cut*

---

47   Eph. 6:16–17.
48   Heb. 4:12a.
49   Jer. 23:29.
50   Eccl. 12:11a.
51   Gen. 49:10a. E. N. Again, as with Ps. 44:4, I have rendered *de femore eius* in Gen. 49:10 as "from his loin," and departed from the Douay-Rheims's translation of "from his thigh."
52   Luke 8:11b.
53   E. N. Denis is quoting Aristotle's *On Interpretation* (16a3) as translated by Boethius: *sunt ergo ea quae sunt in voce, earum quae sunt in animo passionum notae.* St. Thomas draws on this in his Commentary on the Gospel of John: *Ad intellectum autem huius nominis verbum, sciendum est quod, secundum philosophum ea quae sunt in voce, sunt signa earum, quae sunt in anima, passionum.* "Now to understand the name 'word,' we should note that according to the Philosopher those [words] that are in sound are signs of those [words] which are of the affections in the soul." *Super Io.*, cap. 1 l. 1.
54   Gal. 4:19.
55   Jer. 31:18b–19a.

off.[56] And the Apostle [Paul] speaking of Christ: *Being the brightness of his glory,* he says, *and upholding all things by the word of his power.*[57] When Christ says of the wisdom of God: *By my power I have trodden under my feet the hearts of all the high and low.*[58]

44{45}[5] *With your comeliness and your beauty set out, proceed prosperously, and reign. Because of truth and meekness and justice: and your right hand shall conduct you wonderfully.*

Specie tua et pulchritudine tua intende, prospere procede, et regna, propter veritatem, et mansuetudinem, et iustitiam; et deducet te mirabiliter dextera tua.

44{45}[5] *Specie tua,* your comeliness that is created, *et pulchritudine tua,* and your beauty that is uncreated, *intende prospere,* set out... prosperously, that is, look upon happily and regard with kindliness the human race with respect to its eternal prosperity so that you might save them; *procede,* proceed from the bosom of the Father in the womb of the Virgin, from the highest heaven to the inferior parts of the earth, from the womb of the Mother to the stable, from the stable to the public, and thence to the Cross, and at length to heaven. Therefore, proceed in this way as the Bride says: *Behold he comes leaping upon the mountains, skipping over the hills.*[59] *Et regna,* and reign in the Church militant by faith and grace and in the Church triumphant by the blessed vision. And so, O Christ, reign so that this might be fulfilled, *In that day... the Lord shall be king over all the earth;*[60] as well as this, *The kingdom shall be for the Lord.*[61] Regarding this reign of Christ, the Apostle [Paul] also says: *God has exalted him, and has given him a name which is above all names, that at the name of Jesus every knee should bow, of those that are in heaven, on earth, and under the earth.*[62] And again: *God,* he says, *set him on his right hand in the heavenly places, above all principality, and power, and virtue, and dominion.*[63] For this reason Christ also in the Gospel affirms: *All power is given to me in heaven and in earth.*[64] But keeping in mind

---

56 Micah 5:9.
57 Heb. 1:3a.
58 Ecclus. 24:11.
59 Songs 2:8.
60 Zech. 8a, 9a.
61 Obad. 21.
62 Phil. 2:9–10.
63 Eph. 1:20b, 21a.
64 Matt. 28:18b.

that Christ said this after his Resurrection, this assertion is not to be so understood as if it was then that Christ as man was first given that power; indeed, from the first instant of his human conception all power in heaven and on earth was given him. For by the very fact that in Christ the human nature is united in a personal union with God, all creation is subject to him. And so the Baptist said to Christ before his Passion: *The Father loves the Son, and he has given all things into his hand.*[65] And Christ said: *Whatever things the Father does these the Son also does in like manner.*[66] And by saying this Christ insinuates one and the same essence and power between him and the Father, for numerically the same operation cannot emanate from diverse or distinct persons unless they are the same in nature and power; indeed, by these words Christ discloses himself to be true God. For unless he were true God, he could not do that which the Father does, similarly to the Father, or similar just as the Father. For if he were pure creature, as the Arians falsely assert,[67] the Father would do something principally, and the Son instrumentally.

Propter veritatem et mansuetudinem et iustitiam, because of truth and meekness and justice: that is, because you were confirmed in truth and meekness and justice, O Christ, from the womb of your mother; therefore *et deducet te mirabiliter [dextera tua], and your right hand shall conduct you wonderfully*, that is, your divine nature — which is of greater dignity and more powerful than your human nature (as the right hand is more noble and powerful than the left) — will direct your entire manner of life entirely blamelessly, without any fault. For Christ lived among men without any sin, which is indeed something above men and is exceedingly marvelous, especially since *a just man falls seven times a day.*[68] Or [we can understand it] thus: *Because of your truth and meekness and justice*, that is, because of those acts of virtue and their merits, namely, because you were right in life and in doctrine, and in adversity meek and patient, and in all things just, not for your own, but for your Father's glory, seeking the salvation of men; for these reasons *your right hand shall conduct you wonderfully*, namely, elevating you from the earth to the heavens, and establishing you as judge of all. For Christ merited the Ascension

---

65 John 3:35.
66 John 5:19b.
67 E. N. The Arians, led by the priest Arius (*ca.* 250–336 AD), rejected the idea that the Son of God, the Word, was the same substance as the Father (ὁμοούσιον τῷ Πατρί / *homoousion tō Patri*); rather, they maintained that the Son or the Word was a creature, had a beginning in time, and thus only of a similar substance as the Father ὁμοιούσιον τῷ Πατρί / *homoiousion tō Patri*).
68 Prov. 24:16a.

and the judicial power [to judge all mankind] by his emptying out self (*exinanitione*) and his holy manner of living.[69] For in all things Christ told and observed the truth, according to that which he testified before Pilate: *For this was I born, and for this came I into the world; that I should give testimony to the truth.*[70] He also was meek, in the manner that he expressed: *Learn of me, because I am meek, and humble of heart.*[71] He was just, as Stephen said to the Jews: *Which of the prophets have not your fathers persecuted? And they have slain them who foretold of the coming of the Just One; of whom you have been now the betrayers and murderers.*[72]

44{45}[6] *Your arrows are sharp: under you shall people fall, into the heart of the king's enemies.*[73]

Sagittae tuae acutae, populi sub te cadent, in corde inimicorum regis.

44{45}[6] *Sagittae tuae acutae, your arrows are sharp*: that is, the words of your preaching, O Christ, penetrate the heart, and are interiorly cleansing of the soul, and instill a healthy fear; *populi sub te cadent, under you shall people fall*: that is, the unfaithful, who before your coming were disobedient and rebellious, will hear your preaching and that of your disciples, will be converted to the faith, and will be obedient to you. But they will fall under you *in corde, in the heart*, that is, in the middle, *inimicorum regis, of the king's enemies*, that is, the Gentiles who were your enemies, you who are the sovereign and true king. For throughout the whole world those that had spiritually fallen, that is, who during the time of disbelief existed as enemies, through faith became subject to Christ. Whence the Apostle [Paul] said: *God commends his charity towards us, because while we were still his enemies, he died for us.*[74] And: *Christ is*

---

69 E. N. The word *exinanitione* (exinanition, emptying out, humiliation, abasement) stems from Phil. 2:7 — *he emptied himself (exinanivit/ ἐκένωσεν), taking the form of a servant, being made in the likeness of men, and habit found as a man.*
70 John 18:37b.
71 Matt. 11:29a.
72 Acts 7:52.
73 E. N. Denis's Latin departs slightly from the Sixto-Clementine Vulgate having *in corde*, "in the heart," and not *in corda*, "into the hearts." I have departed from the Douay-Rheims accordingly.
74 Rom. 5:8a, 9a. Denis replaces "while we were yet sinners," with "while we were yet his enemies." The equating of sinners with enemies is consistent with Rom. 5:10, where St. Paul states, *For if, when we were enemies [=sinners], we were reconciled to God by the death of his Son.*

our peace, who has made both one,[75] by the Cross killing the enmities in himself.[76] All this is consistent with what was predicted of Christ: *And this man shall be our peace, when the Assyrian shall come into our land, and when he shall set his foot in our houses.*[77] And this explanation agrees with that which a subsequent Psalm says of Christ: *Rule in the midst of your enemies;*[78] also [it is consistent] with that which Micah says, *They shall be converted* (to him), for *now shall he be magnified even to the ends of the earth.*[79] But of this falling of the people under Christ and the reign over their enemies is beautifully foretold by Daniel: *The God of heaven*, he says, *will set up a kingdom that shall never be destroyed... according as you saw that the stone was cut out of the mountain without hands, and broken in pieces, and the clay, the iron, and the brass, and the silver, and the gold.*[80] For the stone cut out of the mountain without hands is Christ, born of the Virgin without the seed of man: and this stone broke the metals that are listed, by which are designated the kingdoms of the world since the Apostles, by the power of Christ, converted to the faith and to his service the entire world. And this is what is brought forth by Zephaniah: *The Lord shall be terrible upon them, and shall consume all the gods of the earth: and they shall adore him every man from his own place, all the islands of the Gentiles.*[81] For this reason the Prophet [Isaiah] says: *Idols shall be utterly destroyed.*[82] Or [we can understand it] thus:

---

75 Eph. 2:14a.
76 Eph. 2:16b.
77 Micah 5:5. E. N. Denis does not explain the pertinence of Micah 5:5 in this context. His *Commentary on Micah* helps supply the explanation: "When the Assyrian shall come into our land, and when he shall set his foot in our houses. This ... can be explained in various ways. For Jerome, Bede, and the Gloss explain it thus: *When the Assyrian*, that is, the devil accusing us and directing us to perdition (for an Assyrian is interpreted as one directing or accusing), *comes into our land*, that is, unto our flesh, tempting, inflaming, or troubling it, in the manner that Paul was given a thorn in the flesh, an angel of Satan, who also struck Job *with a very grievous ulcer, from the sole of the foot even to the top of his head* (Job 2:7); *and when he shall set his foot in our houses*, that is, in our bodies, which are the homes or dwellings of our souls, subjecting them to the evils of punishment or fault, when, namely, we deliver the instruments or our members to the sin of iniquity. Or *our houses* refers to the congregations of our faithful, which are agitated by devils, but protected by Christ, and will obtain peace and victory." Doctoris Ecstatici D. Dionysii Cartusiani, *Opera Omnia*, Vol. 10 (Montreuil: 1900), 497.
78 Ps. 109:2b. The verb "rule," *dominare*, is in the imperative case.
79 Micah 5:4b.
80 Dan. 2:44–45.
81 Zeph. 2:11.
82 Is. 2:18.

under you shall people fall, into the heart, that is, this fall will be spiritual by the obedience of the mind, and not bodily.

44{45}[7] *Your throne, O God, is for ever and ever: the scepter of your kingdom is a scepter of uprightness.*

Sedes tua, Deus, in saeculum saeculi; virga directionis virga regni tui.

44{45}[7] *Sedes tua, Deus, in saeculum saeculi;* your throne, O God, is for ever and ever: that is, the throne of your glory and your judicial power, O Christ, who are true God, will eternally stand firm and will never in the least way fail, in the way that it is said by another, *His power is an everlasting power that shall not be taken away: and his kingdom that shall not be destroyed;*[83] and by another, *He shall bear the glory, and shall sit, and rule upon his throne.*[84] *Virga directionis virga regni tui, the scepter of your kingdom is a scepter of righteousness*: that is, your law or your doctrine, which is the scepter of your kingdom, that is, the Church, and by which you rule and judge the faithful, is the scepter of righteousness, that is, the just direction and the right judgment, which flatters no one and is no respecter of persons. For Christ set up at the inception of his Church the rules of justice by which he would govern Christians. Of this scepter of Christ, Isaiah says: *He shall strike the earth with the rod of his mouth, and with the breath of his lips he shall slay the wicked.*[85] Or [we can understand it] thus: *The scepter of your kingdom,* that is, that rule of yours, by which you rule and adjudge the Church which is your kingdom, is the *scepter of righteousness,* that is, the just correction, the right retribution, and the directive governance of all. For Christ in himself is a just judge, and he directs each person one by one most rightly and justly. Whence of this judicial scepter of Christ we read in Isaiah: *He shall not judge according to the sight of the eyes, nor reprove according to the hearing of the ears; but he shall judge the poor with justice, and shall reprove with equity for the meek of the earth.*[86] Whence also Christ in the Gospel says: *Judge not according to the appearance.*[87] But also of this scepter of the rule of Christ is stated in Jeremiah: *A king shall reign, and shall be wise, and shall execute judgment and justice in the earth.*[88]

---

83 Dan. 7:14b.
84 Zech. 6:13a.
85 Is. 11:4b.
86 Is. 11:3b–4.
87 John 7:24a.
88 Jer. 23:5b.

And the Apostle [Paul] asserts to the Hebrews that this verse along with the one following is prophetic of Christ.[89] Whence it is clear that this Psalm literally is written of Christ. Finally, we should most diligently direct our attention to the fact that the holy Prophet [David] in this verse openly insinuates Christ to be God. For what has been said of those words already stated— *You are beautiful above the sons of men*, etc. applies uninterruptedly up to this verse now, and to that verse which is now added, *your throne, O God, is forever and ever*. And the fact that it is said of Christ is most evidently apparent because it is in continuity with that of which has been spoken.

44{45}[8]   *You have loved justice, and hated iniquity: therefore God, your God, has anointed you with the oil of gladness above your fellows.*

Dilexisti iustitiam, et odisti iniquitatem; propterea unxit te Deus, Deus tuus, oleo laetitiae, prae consortibus tuis.

44{45}[8] *Dilexisti iustitiam, et odisti iniquitatem; propterea unxit te Deus; you have loved justice, and hated iniquity: therefore God . . . has anointed you*. For this [regarding the anointment] is not said of God according to his divine nature, for he is not anointed with respect to it [his divine nature]: this is said with respect to the incarnate God. For since it was fitting to both natures to love justice and to bear hatred toward sin, so also in the present place they are said of Christ according to his assumed humanity, because of what follows, *therefore God has anointed you*. In the preceding verse it calls Christ God, now it calls him anointed by God. This intimates there to be a personal distinction in God;[90] and it is in this sense [that it should be understood]: Because, O Christ, you have loved justice, and hated iniquity, therefore the God of all things has anointed you, *Deus tuus, your God* in a most singular way, *oleo laetitiae, with the oil of gladness*, that is, the glory of the Resurrection and Ascension and the accidental rewards,[91] *prae consortibus tuis, above your fellows*, that is, above and more fully than all men, because you are *the first born from the dead*.[92] Others explain this [verse] in different ways, saying: *therefore God, your God, has anointed you, with*

---

89 Heb. 1:8–9.
90 E. N. Because one person of God (the Father) is anointing the other person of God (the Son) in his human nature.
91 E. N. On the "accidental rewards" as distinguished from the "essential rewards," see for example footnote 1-48 in Volume 1.
92 Col. 1:18.

the oil of gladness, that is, with the sweetness and fullness of grace and the preservation from all sin. But this appears to oppose the fact that Christ from the first moment of his human conception was full of all virtue and grace, and that he did not in any way merit by preceding acts the infusion of grace.[93] But about this it can be said, if I do not err, that the word *"therefore"* is not said as indicative of cause, but as a sign. For that Christ loved justice is a sign that God anointed him with the oil of grace, according to that which has been introduced [in a prior Psalm]: *For you have prevented him with blessings of sweetness*.[94] And Christ himself says through Isaiah: *The spirit of the Lord is upon me*, he said, *because the Lord has anointed me*.[95]

44{45}[9] *Myrrh and stacte and cassia perfume your garments, from the ivory houses: out of which . . .*

Myrrha, et gutta, et casia a vestimentis tuis, a domibus eburneis; ex quibus delectaverunt te . . .

44{45}[10] *. . . the daughters of kings have delighted you in your glory. The queen stood on your right hand, in gilded clothing; surrounded with variety.*

. . . filiae regum in honore tuo. Astitit regina a dextris tuis in vestitu deaurato, circumdata varietate.

44{45}[9] *Myrrha, et gutta, et casia a vestimentis tuis, a domibus eburneis; myrrh and stacte and cassia perfume your garments, from the ivory houses.* By myrrh — which is bitter, and also from the fact that it preserves from putrefaction a cadaver, and averts worms — is understood the mortification of the flesh which expels, according to what the Apostle says, the stenches of concupiscence and the squalors of vices: *There is now therefore no condemnation to them that are in Christ Jesus, who walk*

---

93 E. N. On Christ's human nature not meriting the grace of union, *see* footnotes 39-20 and 40-21.
94 Ps. 20:4. E. N. For more elaboration on Ps. 20:4, *see* Article XLVIII (Psalm 20:4) and Article XLIX (Psalm 20:4) in Volume 1.
95 Is. 61:11a; Luke 4:18a. E. N. What Denis is trying to avoid is the implication that *because* Christ's human nature loved justice and hated iniquity *therefore* he was anointed since that would run afoul of the notions that the human nature of Christ did not merit any of the graces given to him at the time of the Incarnation and that Christ had them from the first instant of that Incarnation. By saying that Christ's anointment is *a sign* of his loving justice and hating iniquity there is no implication that it he did not have it at one time, and so was caused by (or merited by) his prior loving justice and hating iniquity.

*not according to the flesh.*⁹⁶ And again: *For if you live according to the flesh, you shall die: but if by the Spirit you mortify the deeds of the flesh, you shall live.*⁹⁷ By stacte (*gutta*),⁹⁸ which is aromatic, and takes away swelling and hardness, is indicated humility. Whence Solomon says: *He that is hardened in mind, shall fall into evil;*⁹⁹ but *glory shall uphold the humble of spirit.*¹⁰⁰ But by cassia,¹⁰¹ which grows in humid places and which grows very high, is understood baptism or faith.

And so the sense is this: *myrrh and stacte and cassia*, that is, the virtues signified by these aromatic spices, *perfume your garments*, that is, go forth and are given to your Church from your human nature, O Christ, which was like a garment of your divine nature, go forth and are given to your Church: for all our sufficiency is from you.¹⁰² And these virtues, to the extent that they are in act, not only *perfume your garments*, but also are *a domibus eburneis, from the ivory houses*, that is, from a chaste and constant sincerity of mind. For it is necessary for us to cooperate with the grace of God, and therefore the acts of virtue are at the same time from you and from virtuous men, of which the Apostle [Paul] says, *We exhort you, that you receive not the grace of God in vain.*¹⁰³ And to Timothy: *Neglect not the grace that is in you.*¹⁰⁴ *Ex quibus, out of which* virtues **44{45}[10]** *filiae regum delectaverunt te, the daughters of the king delighted you*, that is, religious souls prevailing over the world, and the flesh, and the devils pleased you *in honore tuo, in your glory*, that is, doing good works to the glory of your name. For the virtues alone make the intellectual creature acceptable and pleasing to God. And also [this may apply] literally to many daughters of kings, such as Catharine, Barbara, and the most holy Ursula with her most happy and beloved companions;¹⁰⁵ they delightfully pleased Christ because of

---

96 Rom. 8:1.
97 Rom. 8:13.
98 E. N. Stacte (from Greek στακτή, *staktē*), which translates the Latin *gutta* and the Hebrew אהלים (*ahalim*) is a component of the incense used in Temple ceremonies.
99 Prov. 28:14b.
100 Prov. 29:23b.
101 E. N. Cassia, which translates the Latin *cassia* and the Hebrew קציעה (*qetsiah*) is a spice, not clearly identified, that was used to prepare incense for Temple ceremonies.
102 *Cf.* 2 Cor. 3:5: *Not that we are sufficient to think anything of ourselves, as of ourselves: but our sufficiency is from God.*
103 2 Cor. 6:1.
104 1 Tim. 4:14a.
105 Denis is referring to three virgin martyrs who were of noble birth, Sts. Catherine (or Katherine), Barbara, and Ursula. St. Catherine (*fl.* 4th century), reputed to be a daughter of Constus, the governor of Alexandria during the reign of the emperor

the aforementioned virtues, so that his delights were to be with such daughters of kings.[106]

Adstitit, stood, O Christ, *regina, the queen,* that is, your spouse, the holy Church, *a dextris tuis, on your right hand,* that is, in the most preferable gifts of your grace, and in your prosperous good favor, *in vestitu deaurato, in gilded clothing,* that is, adorned in divine charity with holy works, *circumdata varietate, surrounded with variety,* that is, everywhere adorned with the diverse gifts of the grace of the Holy Spirit, and from diverse kinds of people, states, offices, and walks of life. Indeed, the holy Church stands, as it were, ready to obey his command, and, cooperating with the grace of her Bridegroom, she teaches, corrects, and perfects her sons. She stands also at his right hand, and not at his left, as the most beloved stands by her Bridegroom in the manner that the Apostle states: *Christ loved the Church, and delivered himself up for her, that he might sanctify her, cleansing her by the laver of water in the word…, that he might present her to himself a glorious Church, not having spot or wrinkle.*[107] Of this Bride of Christ, mother Church, and queen, is written about in Revelation: *And a great sign appeared in heaven: A woman clothed with the sun, and the moon under her feet, and on her head a crown of twelve stars: And being with child, she cried travailing in birth that she might be delivered.*[108] For this woman is clothed with the sun, that is, Christ, as the Apostle [Paul] says, Let us put on *the Lord Jesus Christ;*[109] and the moon, which is waning and inconstant, is beneath her feet. And so John says in Revelation: *The marriage of the Lamb is come, and his wife has prepared herself.*[110] And

---

Maximian, and therefore a princess; St. Barbara (*fl.* 3rd century), also a martyr, was said to be the daughter of Dioscorus, a rich pagan. St. Ursula (*fl.* 4th century) was the daughter of King Dionotus, king of a small kingdom in South West England known as Dumonia. The "companions" of Ursula that Denis refers to are the 11,000 or so virgins who fled with Barbara and travelled to the continental Europe to avoid being ravished by the marauding pagan Saxons, only to be martyred for their purity and faith in Cologne. *See, e.g.,* St. Ursula and her companions in the frescoes of the Church of St. Ursula in Vigo di Cadore, Veneto, Italy. These three are part (at least in some formulations) of the "Four Capital Virgins." *See, e.g.,* the painting by the Master of the *Virgo inter Virgines* (*fl. ca.* 1480–1495), which depicts Sts. Catherine, Barbara, Ursula, and Cecilia surrounding the Blessed Virgin Mary. These regal virgin martyrs were extremely popular saintly patrons during the middle ages. See Jacobus de Voragine's *Golden Legend* (*Aurea Legenda*), https://sourcebooks.fordham.edu/basis/goldenlegend/index.asp, under the names of these saints.

106 *Cf.* Prov. 8:31: *My delights were to be with the children of men.*
107 Eph. 5:25–27.
108 Rev. 12:1–2.
109 Rom. 13:14a.
110 Rev. 19:17b.

this queen is bedecked and dressed with gold. For by gold is understood charity, as it is here: *I counsel you to buy of me gold fire tried.*[111] For this is said of the lukewarm.[112]

44{45}[11] Hearken, O daughter, and see, and incline your ear: and forget your people and your father's house.

Audi, filia, et vide, et inclina aurem tuam; et obliviscere populum tuum, et domum patris tui.

44{45}[12] And the king shall greatly desire your beauty; for he is the Lord your God, and him they shall adore.

Et concupiscet rex decorem tuum, quoniam ipse est Dominus Deus tuus, et adorabunt eum.

Then this is said to the queen and bride of Christ: **44{45}[11]** *Audi, hearken* to the word of God: For *blessed are they who hear the word of God and keep it;*[113] *O filia, daughter* in Christ, regenerated through water and the Holy Spirit; *et vide, and see,* consider by faith all those things that are pleasing to Christ your Bridegroom, *et inclina aurem tuam, and incline your ear,* so that you might obey him; *et obliviscere populum tuum, and forget your people,* that is, set aside the inordinate affection toward men known to you, *et domum patris tui, and your father's house,* that is, flee the society of the perverse, and cease to love carnally neighbors in order that you might adhere totally to God. Which, if you are able to achieve, then **44{45}[12]** *concupiscent rex decorum tuum, the king shall greatly desire our beauty,* that is, Christ will love the beauty of your soul, *quoniam ipse est Dominus Deus tuus, for he is the Lord your God,* to whom alone you ought to want to please, and not to prefer over him any other bridegroom; *et adorabunt eum, and him they shall adore,* [that is,] all of them believing in him [shall adore him]: as is written in Daniel, *All peoples, tribes and tongues shall serve him.*[114] See here again the writer of the Psalm attests the king of whom we now speak, namely Christ, to be God, indeed the true God, in that which he says, [namely,] *and they shall adore him.* For adoration properly understood is appropriate only to the true God.[115] And on account of this loving desire

---

111   Rev. 3:18a.
112   *E. N.* In other words it is the lukewarm that are counseled to increase in charity, that is, buy gold fire tried.
113   Luke 11:28.
114   Dan. 7:14a.
115   *E. N.* Strictly speaking, the adoration due God alone is known as *latria,* and this is distinguished from a lesser veneration, or *dulia,* of which saints, their relics,

by which Christ loves the beauty of his Bride, he says in the Song of Solomon: *You have wounded my heart, my sister, my spouse, you have wounded my heart;*[116] and, *Open to me, my sister, my love, my dove;*[117] and, *Put me as a seal upon your heart, as a seal upon your arm, for love is strong as death.*[118]

44{45}[13] *And the daughters of Tyre with gifts; all the rich among the people, shall entreat your countenance.*

Et filiae Tyri in muneribus vultum tuum deprecabuntur; omnes divites plebis.

44{45}[13] *Et filiae Tyri in muneribus,* and *the daughters of Tyre with gifts.* The city of Tyre, neighboring Judea yet pagan, was famous and noble: and so by Tyre is designated the Gentiles. And it is in this sense [the verse should be understood]: Not only converts from the Jews would adore Christ, but also the *daughters of Tyre with gifts,* that is, the Gentiles converted to the faith would adore Christ, offering gifts, that is, themselves and the sacrifice of the New Law, and other offerings that are customary and licit in the time of the New Law. And this is what Isaiah said: *The Lord shall be known by Egypt, and the Egyptians shall know the Lord in that day, and shall worship him with sacrifices and offerings.*[119] For by this and in similar places is insinuated the conversion of all the Gentiles to Christ, according as we read: *In that day the root of Jesse, who stands for an ensign of the people, him the Gentiles shall beseech, and his sepulcher shall be glorious.*[120] These things were most truly fulfilled in Jesus of Nazareth. For Tyre itself for a long time also was dedicated to Christian worship.[121]

---

or icons may be due. "On account of his excellence, reverence is due to God, which is communicated to certain creatures not according to equality, but according to a certain proportion. Therefore, of one kind is the reverence by which we venerate God, which pertains to *latria,* and of other kind is the reverence pertaining to certain excellent creatures, which pertains to *dulia.*" ST, IIaIIae, q. 84, art. 1, co.

116 Songs 4:9.
117 Songs 5:2.
118 Songs 8:6a.
119 Is. 19:21.
120 Is. 11:10.
121 E. N. Soon after the deacon St. Stephen was killed, a church was established in the Phoenician town of Tyre, which, in fact was visited by St. Paul. As Christianity grew, the pagan Roman emperors battled it and persecuted the young Tyrean church. Eusebius observes that Origen died in Tyre, succumbing to the injuries he received during torture. The city was eventually incorporated into the Byzantine empire until finally taken over by Muslims forces in 650 AD, and, except for a short period during the time of the Crusades (1124–1291), remained under Muslim rule up until the time Denis penned these words and beyond.

Vultum tuum deprecabuntur omnes divites plebis, all the rich among the people shall entreat your countenance: that is, through yourself, O Church of Christ, or through your participation or presence, all men converted to the faith (who are spiritually rich in charity and grace) prayed. For as we have already seen, all the faithful—both great and small—entreat the pastors and priests of the Church so that they might pray for them, and they might communicate to them the word of God and the Sacraments, as we read in Malachi: *The lips of the priest shall keep knowledge, and they shall seek the law at his mouth.*[122] Or [we can look at this verse] this way: *Your countenance,* O Church, *all the rich among the people shall entreat,* so that your countenance may be that which they go towards, not that from which they go away. That is [it is to be understood] in this sense: They shall entreat from God your countenance in order that they may belong to the flock of believers, because outside of the Church there is no salvation,[123] just like outside the ark of Noah no one was saved from the flood.[124]

44{45}[14] *All the glory of the king's daughter is within in golden borders,*

Omnis gloria eius filiae regis ab intus, in fimbriis aureis,

44{45}[15] *Clothed round about with varieties. After her shall virgins be brought to the king: her neighbors shall be brought to you.*

Circumamicta varietatibus. Adducentur regi virgines post eam, proximae eius afferentur tibi.

44{45}[16] *They shall be brought with gladness and rejoicing: they shall be brought into the temple of the king.*

Afferentur in laetitia et exsultatione; adducentur in templum regis.

---

122   Ma. 2:7.
123   "Above all else, it must be firmly believed that 'the Church, a pilgrim now on earth, is necessary for salvation: the one Christ is the mediator and the way of salvation; he is present to us in his body which is the Church. He himself explicitly asserted the necessity of faith and baptism (*cf.* Mk 16:16; Jn 3:5), and thereby affirmed at the same time the necessity of the Church which men enter through baptism as through a door.'" Declaration *Dominus Iesus*, 20 (quoting VII, LG, 14). See DS 575, 792, 802, 879, 1191, 1351, 2720, 2730f., 2785, 2865, 2867, 2917, 2997-2999, 3304, 3821f., 3866-3873, 4136. The comparison of the Church to the ark of Noah is commonplace: "The Fathers, for example, St. Cyprian, St. Jerome, St. Augustine, St. Fulgentius, regard, as types of the necessity of the Church for salvation, the saving Ark of Noah." Ott, *Fundamentals*, 313.
124   Gen. 7:23.

44{45}[14] *Omnis gloria eius, all her glory,* namely, *filia regis, or the king's daughter,* who now is called a queen, and the Bride of Christ and the Church, *ab intus, is within:* that is, all the perfection of the faithful consists in adornments in the interior of the soul, not in fleeting and vain exterior things. For *the Lord beholds the heart,*[125] and scrutinizes the soul; but man [scrutinizes] those things that are seen on the outside. But because interior virtue ought to show itself in exterior holy deeds — in the manner that Christ said, *And why call you me, Lord, Lord; and do not the things which I say?*[126] — therefore there is added, *in fimbriis aureis,* 44{45}[15] *circumamicta varietatibus, in golden borders, clothed round about with varieties:* that is, the glory or the excellence of life consists in works of charity. And this glory or perfection is *clothed round about with varieties,* that is, adorned with diverse acts of virtue: for as the Apostle [Paul] said, *Charity is patient, is kind: charity envies not, deals not perversely; is not puffed up, . . . seeks not her own.*[127] The perfection of the Christian's soul, therefore, is most especially interiorly situated. For which reason, the Apostle [Paul] warns: *Be renewed in the spirit of your mind, and put on the new man, who is created according to God.*[128] And again he exhorts: *Let us cleanse ourselves from all defilement of the flesh and of the spirit, perfecting sanctification in the fear of God.*[129]

Adducentur regi virgines post eam; after her shall virgins be brought to the king: that is, after the early Church of Christ shall be brought to Christ through holy preachers, men with continent and pure minds and bodies;[130] *proximae eius, her neighbors,* that is, the married folk and others who approach the virgins inasmuch as they do not attach themselves in any final sense to the desires of the flesh,[131] *afferentur tibi, shall be brought to you,* O Christ, by faith and devoted worship. For in that Church will be congregated virgins and married; and all will be united to Christ by faith and grace. For of these virgins Christ in the Gospel says: *There are eunuchs, who have made themselves eunuchs for the kingdom of heaven.*[132] Of these it is written: *Behold I am a dry tree, for these says*

125   1 Sam. 16:7b.
126   Luke 6:46.
127   1 Cor. 13:4–5a.
128   Eph. 4:23–24a.
129   2 Cor. 7:1.
130   "Morally, virginity signifies the reverence for bodily integrity which is suggested by a virtuous motive. Thus understood, it is common to both sexes." Catholic Encyclopedia (New York: Robert Appleton Co. 1912), Vol 15 (s.v. "virginity").
131   It seems that Denis is here referring to so-called Josephite marriages, where spouses take vows of celibacy within the marriage.
132   Matt. 19:12b.

the Lord to the eunuchs, they that shall keep my sabbaths, and shall choose the things that please me, and shall hold fast my covenant, I will give them in my house, and within my walls, a place and a name better than sons and daughters.[133] 44{45}[16] *Afferentur in laetitia et exsultatione, they shall be brought with gladness and rejoicing,* that is, they will come near to Christ with joy of mind and body, and they will be devoted to him; *adducentur in templum regis, they shall be brought unto the temple of the king,* that is, unto the Church triumphant or the Kingdom of Heaven after dwelling in this place of exile.

44{45}[17] *Instead of your fathers, sons are born to you: you shall make them princes over all the earth.*

Pro patribus tuis nati sunt tibi filii; constitues eos principes super omnem terram.

44{45}[17] *Pro patribus tuis nati sunt tibi filii, instead of your fathers, sons are born to you*: that is, in place of the Patriarchs and the Prophets there will be raised for you, O Church of God, apostles and other disciples of Christ, who shall succeed the fathers, and are born from their seed;[134] *constitues eos, you shall make them,* O Christ, *principes super omnem terram, princes over all the earth*: for this earth, which the Apostles converted unto the faith, was divided among them as princedoms, as John in Asia, Andrew in Achaia, Peter and Paul in Italy, Thomas and Bartholomew in India.[135] For of this mission and principate of the Apostles, Christ said through Isaiah: *I will send of them that shall be saved, to the Gentiles into the sea, into Africa, and Lydia them that draw the bow: into Italy, and Greece, to the islands afar off, to them that have not heard of me, and have not seen my glory. And they shall declare my glory to the Gentiles.*[136]

---

133   Is. 56:3–5.
134   E. N. Gal. 3:29: *If you are Christ's, then are you Abraham's seed, heirs according to promise.* In his Commentary on the Gospel of John, Origen suggests that those who have believed in Christ—although they are not physically of the "seed of the patriarchs" (*semen patriarcharum* / σπέρμα τῶν πατριαρχῶν)—are yet collected from the tribes of Israel in a spiritual sense. *Comm. in Ev. Ioann.*, I, 1, PG 14, 23-24. And there is always the succinct: "Spiritually, we are Semites," attributed to Pope Pius XI, Allocution to the Belgian Pilgrims, Sept. 16, 1938, in an informal comment. See http://www.vatican.va/content/benedict-xvi/en/speeches/2008/september/documents/hf_ben-xvi_spe_20080912_parigi-juive.html
135   E. N. This refers to the tradition that the Apostles divided the world among them by lot (*sortes apostolorum* or *divisio apostolorum*) so as to fulfill Christ's injunction to preach the Gospel to all nations.
136   Is. 66:19.

44{45}[18] *I shall remember your name throughout all generations. Therefore shall people confess you forever; and, forever and ever.*[137]
Memor ero nominis tui in omni generatione et generationem: propterea populi confitebuntur tibi in aeternum, et in saeculum saeculi.

44{45}[18] *Memor ero,* I shall remember, I the Prophet, the author of this Psalm, or I the Church, *nominis tui,* your name, O Lord, Christ the King, *in omni generatione et generationem,* throughout all generations. For the Prophet of the Lord has in mind the length of time this Psalm will be recited by the faithful, for this induces others to bring God to mind. The Church also, through its incessant preaching, announces the name of Christ. *Propterea populi,* therefore ... the people, the Christians, *confitebuntur tibi,* shall confess you, that is, they shall praise you, and they will lay bare before you their sins to the honor of your name, *in aeternum, forever,* that is, even until the end of the world, as long as the Christian faith will have lasted, *et in saeculum saeculi, and forever and ever*: that is, this praise will begin in the present life, and it will continue in the age to come without end.

BRIEF EXPOSITION ON CERTAIN OTHER THINGS

Finally, let us reflect that the Bride of Christ is three-fold, namely, universal, which is the Church; particular, namely the faithful soul; and singular, that is to say the divine Virgin. Therefore, in the way the Song of Songs can be explained as involving these three brides of Christ, so that which is now said of the universal bride of Christ can be said of his particular and singular bride. For any one particular pious and faithful soul united by faith to Christ, espoused by charity, and made fruitful in good works by Christ can be called queen as well as the daughter of the most high king, the bride and coheir of Christ, and impregnated by the light of grace from the Holy Spirit. And this queen stands at the right hand of Christ in a golden vestment, according to the explained understanding. The other matters also can easily be applied to any particular holy soul.[138]

---

137 Denis has *memor ero*, "I shall remember," which departs from the Sixto-Clementine *memores erunt*, "they shall remember." I have gone with Denis's reading. I have also rendered *confitebuntur* into "shall confess" instead of "shall praise."
138 E. N. Wearing the beautiful garment of perfect virtues and the gifts of the Holy Spirit renders the soul to "appear worthily before the King and deserve that he make her his equal and place her at his side like a queen; this she merits through

AGAIN ANOTHER EXPOSITION

Also, in a most proper way this [Psalm] can be fittingly applied to the blessed Virgin. For she is the unique and most high Queen always standing at the right hand of her Son, who ineffably delights the eternal Father, and pleases incomparably the Bridegroom and her Son, for see the manner that the heavenly Bridegroom says to her: *You are beautiful, O my love, sweet and comely;*[139] and again, *One is my dove, my perfect one.*[140] But this Queen stands by this King of glory in a most gold, most splendid, and most red dress: because she so ineffably and most excellently burned and burns with the charity of God and neighbor, with most ardent desire praying that the grace of the death and the Blood of Christ her Son would bear fruit in us, and she was superlatively and entirely full with these holy works. For this reason, the Song of Songs proclaims: *Stay me up with flowers, compass me about with apples: because I languish with love.*[141] Whence also we find in Proverbs about her: *Strength and beauty are her clothing.*[142] She also was surrounded with a variety of all the virtues, as is spoken of her by Solomon: *An inestimable odor is upon her garments,*[143] that is, a wonderful fragrance of spiritual sweetness in her virtues and her works. For of such odor also Paul attests: *we are the good odor of Christ unto God.*[144] And Moses said: *The Lord smelled a sweet savor,*[145] that is, of pious devotion.

And so of this Daughter he says:[146] *Hearken, O daughter,* whatever things are written in the Law and the Prophets, and that which the

---

the beauty of such variety. Hence David speaks to Christ on this subject: *Astitit regina a dextris tuis in vestitu deaurato, circumdata varietate* (the queen stood at your right hand, clothed in a garment of gold, surrounded with variety) [Ps. 44(45):9]. This would be similar to saying: She stood at your right clothed in perfect love and surrounded with a variety of perfect gifts and virtues." St. John of the Cross, *The Spiritual Canticle* in *The Collected Works of St. John of the Cross* (Washington, DC: ICS Publications 2017), 593 (trans., Kieran Kavanaugh and Otilio Rodriguez).
139 Songs 6:3a.
140 Songs 6:8a.
141 Songs 2:5.
142 Prov. 31:25a.
143 *Cf.* Songs 4:11: *Your lips, my spouse, are as a dropping honeycomb, honey and milk are under your tongue; and the smell of your garments, as the smell of frankincense.*
144 2 Cor. 2:14–15: *Now thanks be to God, who always makes us to triumph in Christ Jesus, and manifests the odor of his knowledge by us in every place. For we are the good odor of Christ unto God, in them that are saved, and in them that perish.*
145 Gen. 8:21a.
146 This exposition relies upon portions of Ps. 44:11–13, 15.

Lord God has spoken in you;[147] hear also the angel's greeting;[148] *and see, what and how often God promised men through the Prophets; and incline your ear so that you might find rest in all things through divine inspiration, and you might believe the angelic announcement, and might show consent; and forget your people,* that is, Israel according to the flesh and the letter, not according to the spirit and spiritually understood, *and your father's house,* of which you were born in the flesh, so that you might in all things adhere to the spiritual Father. For then *the king,* the Messiah, the Only-begotten of God, *shall greatly desire your beauty,* [your] interior [beauty], namely, humility, chastity, and charity. For the Son of God so vehemently desires the beauty of Mary, that he might rejoice as *a giant to run the way,*[149] and he might descend into her most pure and sweet womb, and assume to himself from her a human body, and he might unite with his divinity a part of her virginal substance. For this is what the Songs of Songs says about her: *Show me your face, let your voice sound in my ears: for your voice is sweet, and your face comely.*[150] And how much does God love you, O most worthy Virgin! How blessed you are, my Lady, to have merited to conceive, to nourish, to give birth to, to handle, to nurse, to kiss, to embrace, and even to guide him as he grew! Well will you say those words of Solomon, *I to my beloved, and his turning is toward me;*[151] and this also, *A bundle of myrrh is my beloved to me, he shall abide between my breasts.*[152] For certainly Jesus, that young and most beautiful Son, frequently found rest and slept with you in a bed of flowers and nursed upon your virginal breasts, looking caressingly, kissing sweetly, and embracing you most reverently.

Your countenance, O Lord, all the rich among the people shall entreat. For all generations shall call you blessed,[153] shall implore your mercy, and shall flee to you as a most kind advocate in all their necessities. *After her shall virgins be brought to the king.* For all virgins approaching Christ in the way by faith, and in heaven through hope, follow Mary as first and foremost and they submit to Christ her exemplar.[154]

---

147 *Cf.* Ps. 84:9a: *I will hear what the Lord God will speak in me.*
148 Luke 1:28-33: *Hail, full of grace, the Lord is with you: blessed art you among women.*
149 Ps. 18:6b.
150 Songs 2:14b.
151 Songs 7:10.
152 Songs 1:12.
153 Luke 1:48.
154 *E. N.* "The Saviour to come is not only the reason for Mary's existence, He is also her exemplar in all things." Abbot Prosper Guéranger, O. S. B., The Liturgical

See how very brilliant and most glorious this Psalm is. And with what kind of worthy language it unfurls its proclamation? But because it is difficult to do so in a satisfactory manner, let us apply ourselves so as to understand it clearly, and so also to sing it with suitable devotion.

PRAYER

MAKE US, WE BESEECH YOU, O GOD, eternal Father, to love the beauty and splendor of your only-begotten Son, and dispose us to desire with all our heart his beauty before all the sons of men; and that, anointed with the oil of the Holy Spirit, we might through his grace always be pleasing in your eyes.

Fac nos, quaesumus, Deus Pater aeterne, speciem et pulchritudinem unigeniti Filii tui diligere, ipsumque speciosum forma prae filiis hominum toto corde desiderare; et uncti oleo Sancti Spiritus, ipsius gratia semper tuis in oculis placeamus.

Year (London: Burns & Oates 1910), vol. V, 208.

Psalm 45

ARTICLE LXXXVIII

EXPOSITION OF THE FORTY-FIFTH PSALM:
DEUS NOSTER REFUGIUM ET VIRTUS.
OUR GOD IS OUR REFUGE AND STRENGTH.

45{46}[1] *Unto the end, for the sons of Korah, for the hidden.*

In finem, filiis Core, pro arcanis. Psalmus.

THIS PSALM HAS THIS TITLE WHICH HAS been previously treated: 44{45}[1] *In finem, filiis Core, pro arcanis; unto the end, for the sons of Korah, for the hidden*: that is, this Psalm directs us to Christ our end, which is appropriate to the sons of Korah, that is, the faithful of Christ crucified worthy of following in his footsteps; *for the hidden*, that is, this Psalm touches upon of the secret mysteries of Christ, namely of his advent and Incarnation.

45{46}[2] *Our God is our refuge and strength: a helper in troubles, which have found us exceedingly.*

Deus noster refugium et virtus; adiutor in tribulationibus quae invenerunt nos nimis.

In such a person [that is, one faithful to Christ crucified,] the Prophet [David] speaks: 45{46}[2] *Deus noster, our God*: of whom Moses said: *You shall adore the Lord your God, and shall serve him alone.*[1] Which also elsewhere is attested: *See you that I alone am, and there is no other God besides me.*[2] And so this God is our *refugium, refuge*, and he is whom we ought faithfully approach in all our necessities and dangers so that we might be protected by him. For he alone, and no one else, is able to save us from all peril: and so there follows, *et virtus, and strength*, that is, our God is our strength, or there is strong and omnipotent refuge for those who seek refuge in him, in the manner we are told: *Behold the hand of the Lord is not shortened that it cannot save.*[3] For the name of the Lord is

---

1 Deut. 6:13b. E. N. In lieu of the Sixto-Clementine's *timebis*, "you shall fear," Denis's version states *adorabis*, "you shall adore." I have followed Denis.
2 Deut. 32:39a.
3 Is. 59:1.

a strong tower: the just run to it, and shall be saved.[4] But some seek refuge in themselves, and these do not have the power to save either themselves or those fleeing to them. Of these is written: *The eyes of the wicked shall decay, and the way to escape shall fail them, and their hope the abomination of the soul.*[5] You, therefore, reflecting upon your own insufficiency, affix all your hope in the Lord, recalling what the Lord said: *Destruction is your own, O Israel: your help is only in me.*[6] And so also Job: *Behold, he says, there is no help for me in myself.*[7] Moreover, our God is *adiutor in tribulationibus*, a helper in troubles, as is expressed here: *The Lord is good and gives strength in the day of trouble.*[8] Whence in a subsequent Psalm we have: *Call upon me in the day of trouble: I will deliver you.*[9] God therefore is our helper in troubles, *quae invenerunt nos nimis*, which have found us exceedingly, that is, which have abundantly come upon us. *For all that will live godly in Christ Jesus, shall suffer persecution.*[10] And: *Man born of a woman, living for a short time, is filled with many miseries.*[11] And so in troubles God is most prone to provide help.

45{46}[3] *Therefore we will not fear, when the earth shall be troubled; and the mountains shall be removed into the heart of the sea.*

Propterea non timebimus dum turbabitur terra, et transferentur montes in cor maris.

Now that which follows can be understood in many ways. We can expound it literally in this way: 45{46}[3] *Propterea non timebimus dum turbabitur terra, et transferentur montes in cor maris; therefore we will not fear when the earth shall be troubled, and the mountains shall be removed into the heart of the sea*: that is, because our God is our refuge, our strength, and our helper, we will not fear, even if the earth should furiously quake, and the mountains be violently removed and cast into the deepest abysses or in the middle of the sea; for (as the Apostle [Paul] says): *If God be for us, who is against us?*[12] And it is written: *He that*

---

4 Prov. 18:10. Denis's version has *salvabitur*, "they shall be saved," instead of the Sixto-Clementine Vulgate's *exaltabitur*, "they shall be exalted." Given the Commentary's subsequent point (that we cannot save ourselves), I have followed Denis's version.
5 Job 11:20.
6 Hosea 13:9.
7 Job 6:13a.
8 Nahum 1:7a.
9 Ps. 49:15.
10 2 Tim. 3:12.
11 Job 14:1.
12 Rom. 8:31b.

fears the Lord shall tremble at nothing.[13] See how great is the security of the mind that hopes in God, how stable is the heart that believes in God. For in no situation will he whose soul is truly fixed upon God be struck with fear. The second [way of expounding this verse is] this: *We will not fear,* we who have believed in God, *when the earth shall be troubled,* that is, earthly men, who fear temporal damages and bodily torments: who in the day of judgment will be *troubled with a terrible fear, when the just shall stand with great constancy:*[14] according to that which is written, *The wicked man is reserved to the day of destruction, and he shall be brought to the day of wrath,*[15] *and he shall drink of the wrath of the Almighty.*[16] *And the mountains shall be removed into the heart of the sea:* that is, we will not fear that time when the proud will be thrown into the pit of hell, when the Judge will tell them, *Depart from me, you cursed, into everlasting fire.*[17] For then the just with security and joy will hear, *Come, you blessed of my Father.*[18]

The third way [of expounding this verse is] this way: that these are the words of the early Church which placed complete faith in the Lord, and said: *Therefore we will not fear* with a carnal, human, and disordered fear, *when the earth shall be troubled,* that is, Judah or the Jewish people who out of irrational perturbation of the passions sought to obliterate and extirpate all the disciples of Christ. Whence we read of the early Church that they so prayed, since the chief of the priests prohibited them to preach the name of the Lord Jesus: *Grant unto your servants, O Lord, that with all confidence they may speak your word.*[19] *And when they had prayed, the place wherein they were moved; and they were all filled with the Holy Spirit, and they spoke the word of God with confidence.*[20] *And the mountains shall be removed into the heart of the sea:* that is, like the Apostles — who because of the height of [their] life and wisdom are called mountains, and who left Judea and traveled over to the Gentiles so as to convert them — we will not now fear. For the Gentiles dwelled in the heart of the sea, that is, in the middle of the world: of which we see in a subsequent Psalm, *So is this a great sea, which stretches wide its arms;*[21]

---

13 Ecclus. 34:16a.
14 Wis. 5:2a, 1a.
15 Job. 21:30.
16 Job. 21:20b.
17 Matt. 25:41b.
18 Matt. 25:34a.
19 Acts 4:29b.
20 Acts 4:31a.
21 Ps. 103:25a.

and again, *I am come into the depth of the sea.*[22] And it is clear that at the time of the division of the Apostles, the Christians remaining with James [the Lesser] in Jerusalem remained secure and unfearful, certain that Christ would be their protector. Whence James, the blessed brother of the Lord,[23] weighing lightly worldly men and the servants of Christ esteeming little all things said: *Go now, you rich men, weep and howl in your miseries, which shall come upon you.*[24] *You have stored up to yourselves wrath against the last days.*[25] Thereupon, speaking to the faithful: *Be patient,* he says, *until the coming of the Lord ... and strengthen your hearts, for the coming of the Lord is at hand.*[26]

45{46}[4] *Their waters roared and were troubled: the mountains were troubled with his strength.*

Sonuerunt, et turbatae sunt aquae eorum; conturbati sunt montes in fortitudine eius.

45{46}[4] *Sonuerunt,* they roared, the previously-mentioned mountains, that is, the holy Apostles preached the Gospel of Christ, *et turbatae sunt aquae eorum, and their waters ... were troubled*: that is, the peoples to whom the Apostles were sent heard their preaching and they were troubled: some from impatience and persecution, some from penitence and imitation, as it is frequently related in the Acts of the Apostles. *Conturbati sunt montes, the mountains were troubled,* that is, the rulers among men, *in fortitudine eius, with his strength,* namely, [the strength] of Christ, that is, from the power preaching and the miraculous works

---

22 Ps. 68:3b. E. N. The link between the Gentile nations and the sea (or other waters) is not as farfetched as one may think. *See, e.g.,* Dan. 7:3 (beasts arising from the sea representing Gentile nations: Babylon, Medo-Persia, Greece, and Rome); see also Ps. 64:8; 143:7; Is. 8:7–8; 17:12; 60:5; Jer. 46:7–8; 47:2; 51:55; Ez. 26:3; Rev. 17:15.

23 E. N. The precise relationship of James the Less to our Lord is not established with certainty (there is evidence for various possible relationships explaining his kinship to the Lord); but we know as a matter of dogmatic and certain fact (and hence also historically certain fact) that James, the "brother of the Lord," was not a son of the Blessed Virgin Mary, since it is *de fide* that Mary was "ever-virgin" (*virgo ante partum, virgo in partu, virgo post partum,* virgin before birth, during birth, and after birth) and only Christ, who was virginally conceived, was born of her, and she conceived no other child. *E.g.,* DS 44, 485 ("he [Jesus] alone was born of her," *et natus ex ipsa solus*), 503, 571, 1400, 1880.

24 James 5:1.

25 James 5:3b.

26 James 5:7-8.

of the Apostles and the other disciples of Christ. This trouble can also be understood in good and in bad ways. For some of the powerful and the great, both from the Jews as well as the pagans, converted to the faith, in the manner that is written: *A great multitude also of the priests obeyed the Gospel.*[27] But some were troubled with fear of the great disorder, as Luke attests: *Many, he says, wonders and signs were done by the Apostles in Jerusalem, and there was great fear in all.*[28] Some, even a great number of the former were troubled with an evil trouble, namely the corrupt princes of the Jews and the tyrants of the people. Truly, for the most part, the mountains of the world, that is, the potentates and the nobles, remained in their malice. For which reason, the Apostle [Paul] said: *See your vocation, brethren, that there are not many wise according to the flesh, not many mighty, not many noble among you.*[29] And James: *Has not God, he says, chosen the poor in this world, [to be] rich in faith?*[30] And all mountains, that is, the proud and rebellious against God are troubled either in the present or in the future, indeed also both times: because nowhere will they who resist God have true peace, according to this: *He is wise in heart, and mighty in strength. Who has resisted him, and has had peace?*[31] And by Isaiah, the Lord says: *I will take vengeance, and no man shall resist me.*[32] And elsewhere: *Who is like to me? And who shall abide me? And who is that shepherd that can withstand my countenance?*[33]

But if someone desires to take this literal exposition in a grammatical [non-metaphorical] sense, then it is plain that by the divine power the mountains of the earth are troubled, and are transferred from their place and shattered to pieces, according to that which we read in the book of Job: *Who has removed the mountains, ... and who shakes the earth out of its place, and the pillars thereof tremble.*[34] And the Savior said: *Have the faith of God. Amen I say to you, that whosoever shall say to this mountain, Be you removed and be cast into the sea, and shall not be irresolute in his heart, but believe, that whatsoever he says shall be done; it shall be done unto him.*[35] For *all things* (as Mark writes) *are possible to him who believes.*[36]

---

27 Acts 6:7b.
28 Acts 2:43.
29 1 Cor. 1:26.
30 James 2:5.
31 Job 9:4.
32 Is. 47:3b.
33 Jer. 49:19b.
34 Job 9:5–6.
35 Mark 11:22–23. I have replaced the Douay-Rheims "stagger" with "be irresolute," for the Latin *haesitaverit*.
36 Mark 9:22b.

45{46}[5] *The stream of the river makes the city of God joyful: the most High has sanctified his own tabernacle.*

Fluminis impetus laetificat civitatem Dei: sanctificavit tabernaculum suum Altissimus.

45{46}[6] *God [is] in the midst thereof, [it] shall not be moved: God will help it in the morning early.*

Deus in medio eius, non commovebitur; adiuvabit eam Deus mane diluculo.

45{46}[5] *Fluminis impetus, the stream of the river*, that is, the fountain of sacred Baptism, *laetificat, makes joyful*, with spiritual joy, *civitatem Dei, the city of God*, that is, the Church militant of Christ. For the faithful rejoice in this Sacrament because of its great benefits, in which all sin is remitted, grace is infused, and man is spiritually reborn. Of this *stream of the river* is written: *Behold waters issued out from under the threshold of the house toward the east*;[37] and *every living creature that creeps whithersoever the torrent shall come, shall live.*[38] *Sanctificavit tabernaculum suum, he has sanctified his own tabernacle*, that is, the Church of the elect, or his elect, *Altissimus, the most High* God, who alone is able to make clean from the unclean.[39] Of this tabernacle the Apostle [Paul] says: *You are the temple of the living God*, as the Lord says: *I will dwell in them.*[40] And again he says: *The temple of God is holy, which you are.* 45{46}[6] *Deus in medio eius non commovebitur, God is in the midst thereof, it shall not be moved.* This may be read in two ways. The first in this manner: *God is in the midst thereof,* the unspoken reference is this: in the same city or the militant Church; [and this is] in accordance with this: *Where there are two or three gathered together in my name, there am I in the midst of them*;[41] *it shall not be moved,* that is, the Church will not fall from the faith[42] because Christ is in the midst of it, nor will it be overcome by trials [to the faith] according to that which Christ told Peter in the name of the Church: *Behold, Satan has desired to have you, that he may sift you as wheat; but I have prayed for*

---

37 Ez. 47:1a.
38 Ez. 47:9a.
39 *Cf.* Job 14:4: *Who can make him clean that is conceived of unclean seed? is it not you who only are?*
40 2 Cor. 6:16a. Lev. 26:12: *I will walk among you, and will be your God, and you shall be my people.*
41 Matt. 18:20.
42 E. N. A reference to the indefectibility of the Church. For more on this, see footnote 40-105.

you, that your faith fail not.[43] *Deus mane, God... in the morning,* that is, immediately when we cry out to him, *adiuvabit eam,* will help it, namely, the Church, *diluculo,* early *[at daybreak],* that is, at the spiritual dawn, namely, at the infusion of grace, or the illumination of the Holy Spirit.[44]

And this part can also be explained in an anagogical sense, so that it reads in this sense: *Fluminis impetus, the stream of the river,* that is, the fountain of wisdom, or the overflowing of the Holy Spirit, or God himself, who (as it is written) is a glorious river (*fluvius gloriosus*) springing forth in the thirsting land,[45] *laetificat, makes joyful,* with the joy of beatific enjoyment, *civitatem Dei, the city of God,* that is, the Church triumphant. *Sanctificavit tabernaculum suum, has sanctified his own tabernacle,* that is, the hearts of the blessed [in heaven], *Altissimus, the most High*: for there can be no impurity in the heavenly homeland. *Deus in medio eius est, God is in the midst thereof*: for God is seen face to face in the Church triumphant, in the way that Isaiah says, *The Lord shall be for you an everlasting light*:[46] and so *non commovebitur, it shall not be moved,* the Church triumphant [shall not be moved] from its blessed state, but it will enjoy God eternally. *Deus mane, God... in the morning,* that is, [God,] the moment when one will have called out to him, *adviuvabit eam,* will help it, that is, the heavenly city, *diluculo,* early, that is, right away when any one of the Saints will be received into heaven, he will be confirmed in the good, so that he will be unable to sin any more.

Finally, we can expound this passage as referring to the glorious Virgin in this way: *Fluminis impetus laetificat civitatem Dei, the stream of the*

---

43 Luke 22:31–32.
44 E. N. I have had to rearrange this sentence because of the syntactic differences between Latin and English.
45 *Cf.* Amos 8:8. Amos 8:8 states *fluvius universus,* "universal river," or "total river," or (as the Douay-Rheims has it "altogether as a river," and not *fluvius gloriosus,* which is what Denis has in the text. However, the notion of God as a glorious river, a glorious torrent, a *fluvius gloriosus* appears to come from an alternative rendition of Is. 32:2, based upon a Latin translation of the Septuagint: *Et erit vir abscondens sermones suos, et apparebit in terra Sion, sicut fluvius gloriosus in terra sitienti.* "And you will be a man hidden in your words, and you will appear in the land of Sion, as a glorious river in the land of the thirsty." We find it beautifully used by St. Bernard: *Fluvius iste est Dominus meus Iesus, qui de duobus locis voluptatis egreditur, ex utero Patris, et ex utero Virginis. Unde propheta: Dominus Deus noster fluvius gloriosus, exiliens in terram sitientem.* "This river is my Lord Jesus, who flows forth from two places of delight, from the womb of the Father, and from the womb of the Virgin. Whence the prophet: The Lord our God is a glorious river, springing forth in the thirsting land." Sancti Bernardi, *Opera Omnia* (Milan: Edente Iacobo Gnocchi Bibliopola 1852), III, 894.
46 Is. 60:19b.

river makes joyful the city of God: that is, the Word of God, in whom is the fountain of all holy delights and boundless affluence,⁴⁷ made holy Mary exult, especially when he descended into her womb in all his fullness, and truly assumed human nature from her. *Sanctificavit tabernaculum suum Altissimus, the most High has sanctified his own tabernacle.* For Christ, preserved his most pure Mother from all stain of fault when he created and chose her,⁴⁸ and he sanctified her while in the womb of his mother, and filled her with the Holy Spirit much more sublimely than he did Jeremiah or John the Baptist.⁴⁹ *Deus in medio eius, God in their midst*: for Christ, both God and man, reposed for nine months in the womb of the most holy Virgin. And so the Christ-bearing Virgin *non commovebitur, shall not be moved* from good into evil, but she will be firm and remain firm in God.⁵⁰ *Adiuvabit eam Deus mane diluculo, God will help her in the morning*, that is, from the womb of his Mother, he stabilized her in all perfection and grace according to both act and habit or immediate disposition.

But according to the second way of reading it, that which is stated — *God in their midst shall not be moved* — [can be understood]

---

47   E. N. This should be understood in terms both of spiritual affluence (riches) and spiritual flowing.
48   E. N. This beautiful truth is *de fide*, that is "revealed by God," and therefore must be "firmly and constantly believed by all the faithful": "[T]he Most Blessed Virgin Mary, at the first instant of her conception, by the singular grace and privilege of almighty God and in view of the merits of Jesus Christ, the Savior of the human race, was preserved from all stain of original sin." DS 2803.
49   Jer. 1:5: *Before I formed you in the womb of your mother, I knew you: and before you came forth out of the womb, I sanctified you, and made you a prophet unto the nations.* Luke 1:15: *For he shall be great before the Lord; and shall drink no wine nor strong drink: and he shall be filled with the Holy Ghost, even from his mother's womb.* Based upon these verses, it is commonly believed that both Jeremiah and St. John the Baptist were sanctified (in essence "baptized") in their mothers' wombs so that they were *conceived* in original sin, but were not *born in original sin*. Based upon these cites, St. Thomas Aquinas states (ST IIIa, q. 27, art. 1, co.): "We find also that others have been granted, by way of privilege, the concession of being sanctified in the womb, such as Jeremias . . . and such as John the Baptist." Jeremiah and St. John the Baptist were, it is believed by special privilege, also preserved from mortal sin during their lives. ST IIa, q. 27, art. 6, ad 1.
50   E. N. Not only was the Blessed Virgin preserved from original sin by the grace of God, she, also by the grace of God, was preserved, "with a most singular benevolence," from sin, both mortal and venial, throughout her whole life, so that "she, being always and absolutely free from every stain of sin, completely beautiful and perfect, would possess such a plenitude of innocence and sanctity that, under God, none greater could be known and, apart from God, no mind could ever succeed in comprehending." DS 2000.

as having no reference,[51] so that it would be understood in this sense: *God in the midst thereof shall not be moved* in the middle of the Church militant, triumphant, or the virgin Mary. For although God in himself exists as entirely impassible and unalterable, it is also customary to ascribe to him the appearance of passions and movements: for the rational creature sees such things this way, as if such expressions were truly becoming for him. For this we read with Malachi: *You have wearied the Lord with your words.*[52] And also in the following chapter: *You afflict me, even the whole nation of you.*[53] *Your words have been unsufferable to me.*[54] And the Apostle [Paul] is very free with [this kind of expression]: *And grieve not the holy Spirit of God.*[55] In a similar way, God is said to move when he condemns and recedes from the sinner; but he said not to move when he remains unceasingly in a person by grace.

45{46}[7] *Nations were troubled, and kingdoms were bowed down: he uttered his voice, the earth trembled.*

Conturbatae sunt gentes, et inclinata sunt regna: dedit vocem suam, mota est terra.

45{46}[7] *Conturbate sunt gentes,* nations were troubled from the preaching and the miracles of the disciples of the Savior, towards saving repentance and wonder; but certain men towards obstinacy and resistance. *Et inclinata sunt regna,* and kingdoms were bowed down, that is, that inhabitants of kingdoms were humbled toward the faith and a holy manner of living, learning from Christ because he was meek and humble of heart.[56] This is what the most blessed Isaiah predicted of Christ: *For he shall bring down them that dwell on high, the high city he*

---

51 E. N. Previously, Denis interpreted this passage under the assumption that *God in their midst* referred implicitly or *subaudi* to the Church militant. Here he does not suppose such a thing.
52 Mal. 2:17a.
53 Mal. 3:9b.
54 Mal. 3:13.
55 E. N. Denis concedes that any cataphatic (affirmative) expressions of God suggesting internal or external movements on the part of God are fully inaccurate *quoad se* (in and of themselves) since God is impassible and unchanging, but are customary *quoad nos* (with respect to us) because of the limitations of our created reason. Thus anthropomorphisms (language suggesting human form to God) or anthropopathisms (language suggesting emotions or passions in God) are part of the cataphatic expressions of God, and are analogically (or "improperly" or not strictly) predicated of God, although they contain truths about God in some fashion.
56 *Cf.* Matt. 11:29.

*shall lay low.*⁵⁷ By the high city is understood the city of Rome, which at that time was the empress of the world. Of which the same prophet added: *The feet of the poor, the steps of the needy shall tread it down.*⁵⁸ By the feet of the poor we understand Peter the fisherman; by the steps of the needy, [we understand] the preaching of Peter and Paul wishing to possess nothing in this world. For out of this preaching the unbelieving glory and pompous heights of the Romans were led to the lowness of Christian humility. *Dedit vocem suam,* he uttered his voice, Christ by himself or by the preaching of his servants; *mota est terra, the earth trembled* to faith and wonder, or also to perturbation and hardening, especially with respect to the Jews: of which Christ states through Isaiah: *Israel has not known me, and my people have not understood.*⁵⁹ And that which it says — *the earth trembled* — conveniently is referred to the following verse, which says:

45{46}[8] *The Lord of armies is with us: the God of Jacob is our protector.*

Dominus virtutum nobiscum; susceptor noster Deus Iacob.

45{46}[8] *Dominus virtutum nobiscum,* the Lord *of armies is with us:* that is, Christ, the King of Glory, *the power and wisdom* of the Father,⁶⁰ comes to us, and dwelt among us through the assumption of flesh and rational soul. And thus is added, *susceptor noster,* and *our protector,* that is, he who assumes our nature and redeems us is *Deus Iacob, the God of Jacob* the patriarch, that is, the true God, not a mere creature, as the heretics claim.⁶¹ And this exposition agrees with that which the Lord asserts: *Yet one little while, and I will move the heaven and the earth, and the sea, and the dry land ... and the desire of all nations shall come.*⁶² For around the coming and during the coming of Christ the heavens moved when the angel,

---

57 Is. 26:5a.
58 Is. 26:6.
59 Is. 1:3b.
60 1 Cor. 1:24b.
61 E. N. This is likely a reference to the heresiarch Arius, but it certainly would include anyone "who denies that Jesus is the Christ," (1 John 2:22) that is, who denies the divinity of Jesus. "It was the doctrine of Arius that our Lord was a pure creature, made out of nothing, liable to fall, the Son of God by adoption not by nature, and called God in Scripture, not as being really such, but only in name. At the same time he would not have denied that the Son and the Holy Ghost were creatures transcendentally near to God, and immeasurably distant from the rest of creation." John Henry Cardinal Newman, *Tracts: Theological and Ecclesiastical* (New York: Longmans, Green & Co. 1913), 149.
62 Hag. 2:7-8.

announcing to the shepherds the birth of Christ, there came with him a multitude from the heavenly army, praising God and saying, *Glory to God in the highest*;[63] when also the star more radiant than the others appeared to the Magi, and it led them to the Creator of the heavens become man.[64] But the earth moved when all marveled because of what they said to the shepherds.[65] Yet the sea and the dry land were moved before the coming of Christ when by divine dispensation the kingdoms of the world and the islands of the sea were subject to the power of the Romans.[66] Then, therefore, the *Desire of all nations*, that is, Christ, came: of which Jacob predicted: *He shall be the expectation of nations*;[67] and of whom now is also said, *the Lord of armies is with us*; of whom elsewhere is written, *His name shall be called Emmanuel*,[68] *which being interpreted is God with us*.[69]

Finally, [expounded] morally, *the Lord of armies*, that is, God the Trinity, is *with us*, when by charity and grace he abides in our hearts; and *our protector*, that is, the hearer of our prayers is *the God of Jacob*, that is, the supplanter of vices.[70] For they who struggle against vices deserve to be heard, and not those who purpose to remain in vice. For which reason the blind man said: *Now we know that God does not hear sinners: but if a man be a server of God, and does his will, him he hears*.[71] Which agrees with that which Scripture says elsewhere: *God will not cast away the simple, nor reach out his hand to the evildoer*.[72]

45{46}[9] *Come and behold the works of the Lord: what wonders he has done upon earth.*

Venite, et videte opera Domini, quae posuit prodigia super terram.

45{46}[10] *Making wars to cease even to the end of the earth. He shall destroy the bow, and break the weapons: and the shield he shall burn in the fire.*

---

63 Luke 11:13–14.
64 Matt. 2:2, 9, 11.
65 Luke 2:18.
66 E. N. The Mediterranean Sea was called *Mare Nostrum*, "Our Sea," and *Mare Internum*, "Internal Sea," by the Romans.
67 Gen. 49:10b.
68 Is. 7:14b.
69 Matt. 1:23b.
70 On Jacob as the "supplanter" of vices, see footnote 43-103.
71 John 9:31.
72 Job 8:20.

Auferens bella usque ad finem terrae. Arcum conteret, et confringet arma, et scuta comburet igni.

45{46}[9] *Venite, come,* not with the steps of feet, but with faith and affections of the heart; *et videte, and behold* with the eyes of the mind, O all of you who wish to be saved, *opera Domini, quae posuit prodigia super terram; the works of the Lord, what wonders he has done upon earth,* that is, the marvelous works of the Creator done on earth. Of which it adds: **45{46}[10]** *auferens bella usque ad finem terrae, making wars to cease even to the end of the earth.* For in the coming of Christ an unheard-of peace was in the world with all people subject to the Roman empire:[73] although, of course, it was not the result of human, but divine ordinance and power that it came to be, and not because of the merits of the Romans then existing, but on account of the future elect. *Arcum conteret, et confringet arma, et scuta comburet igni; he shall destroy the bow, and break the weapons: and the shield he shall burn in the fire:* that is, this uncommon peace lasted as long as the use of arms remained ceased for a more than usual period of time; and so, God so disposing, men converted the instruments of war into other uses, as happens every day in lands in which wars have subsided for a long time. And this is what is said elsewhere: *The law shall come forth from Sion, and the word of the Lord from Jerusalem . . . and they shall turn their swords into ploughshares, and their spears into sickles; nation shall not lift up sword against nation, neither shall they be exercised any more to war.*[74] This is stated in that manner in other situations when something lasts longer than usual and wherein we say, "This will never come to an end," when, nevertheless, we would regard it as normally ending within a day, or a month, or an hour.

One can also spiritually interpret this section so that it reads in this sense: *Come and behold the works of the Lord: what wonders he has done on earth,* that is, the Incarnation of the Son, the birth of the Virgin, the Passion and the Resurrection of the Savior: which is *making wars to cease even to the end of the earth,* that is, who removes us from temptation, and reconciles men to God. *For he is our peace, who has made us both one,*[75] that is, he has gathered together the Gentiles and the Jews in the unity

---

73 E. N. A reference to the so-called *Pax Romana*, a period of relative peace that is commonly measured to have been shortly after the Octavian's defeat of Mark Antony and Cleopatra at the Battle of Actium (31 BC), which led to his becoming Roman emperor in 27 BC and the death of emperor Marcus Aurelius in 180 AD. The expression has been traced to Seneca the Younger in his *de Clementia* 1.4.2.
74 Is. 2:3b–4a; Micah 4:2-3.
75 Eph. 2:14a.

of faith, in the manner that we read, Peace *shall be between them both*;[76] and according to the Apostle [Paul], *God was in Christ, reconciling the world to himself.*[77] *He shall destroy the bow,* that is, Christ will condemn and destroy the hidden snares of evil, *and break the weapons,* that is, the open persecutions and the diabolical attacks; *and the shield,* that is, the deceitful defenses, by which the perverse undertake to defend their errors, *he shall burn in the fire,* infernal [fire], damning the perverse, or with the fire of the Holy Spirit illuminating the faithful so as to resist those who are in error.

45{46}[11] *Be still and see that I am God; I will be exalted among the nations, and I will be exalted in the earth.*

Vacate, et videte quoniam ego sum Deus; exaltabor in gentibus, et exaltabor in terra.

45{46}[11] *Vacate, et videte quoniam ego sum Deus; be still and see that I am God.* See how kindly and sweetly the Lord our God exhorts us. *Be still,* he says, that is, withdraw your hearts from vain and evil and useless things, and with your whole mind adhere to me, reach out to me, fasten your desires in me, simplify and recollect all your occupations in me; and *see,* by an affectionate contemplation and the taste of experience, that *I am God,* your Creator, your Provider, your Savior, your Teacher, who incessantly has care of you, and provides help to you always, and am ready to pour out consolation, so that you might know me experientially to be your God. For he who sincerely desires to taste and reach out toward God needs with all watchfulness to take custody of his heart,[78] to flee from disordered desires, to esteem lightly pleasures, to avoid frivolities, to reject superfluous occupations, to reject talkativeness, and ceaselessly to strive after that one thing that alone is necessary.[79] And so Jeremiah advises: *Break up anew your fallow ground, and sow not upon thorns: Be circumcised to the Lord, and take away the foreskins of your hearts.*[80]

Exaltabor in gentibus, I will be exalted among the nations, that is, I, the Only-begotten of God, and the Savior of the world will be acknowledged by the Gentiles, and will be honored by the preaching of the Apostles, according to that foretold by Isaiah: *They to whom it was not told of him,*

---

76 Zech. 6:13b.
77 2 Cor. 5:19a.
78 *Cf.* Prov. 4:23: *With all watchfulness keep your heart, because life issues out from it.*
79 *Cf.* Luke 10:42.
80 Jer. 4:3b–4a.

have seen: and they that heard not, have beheld.[81] And again: *All the ends of the earth shall see the salvation of our God.*[82] And yet again: *Glorify the Lord in instruction. From the ends of the earth we have heard his praises, the glory of the Just One.*[83] And through another prophet, Christ says: *For from the rising of the sun even to the going down, my name is great among the Gentiles.*[84] Of which Micah foretells: *He shall be magnified even to the ends of the earth.*[85] *Et exaltabor in terra,* and I will be exalted in the earth, that is, in the Jewish people at the end of this age.[86] For when the fullness of the Gentiles enters, then all of Israel will become saved. For the blindness and captivity of the Jews will last even to the end of the world according to this: *The end thereof shall be waste, ... and the desolation shall continue even ... to the end.*[87] Close to the end of the age they will convert with the coming of Elijah in the manner that the Lord said: *Behold I will send you Elijah the prophet, before the coming of the great and dreadful day of the Lord; and he shall turn the heart of the fathers to the children, and the heart of the children to their fathers: lest I come, and strike the earth with anathema.*[88]

45{46}[12] The Lord of armies is with us: the God of Jacob is our protector.

Dominus virtutum nobiscum; susceptor noster Deus Iacob.

45{46}[12] *Dominus virtutum nobiscum: susceptor noster Deus Iacob;* the Lord of armies is with us: the God of Jacob is our protector. This verse, which we have already seen satisfactorily explained, is repeated on account of the sweetness and dignity of its significance.

---

81   Is. 52:15b.
82   Is. 52:10b.
83   Is. 24:15b–16a.
84   Mal. 1:11a.
85   Micah 5:4b.
86   Rom. 11:25: *For I would not have you ignorant, brethren, of this mystery, (lest you should be wise in your own conceits), that blindness in part has happened in Israel, until the fulness of the Gentiles should come in.* "The glorious Messiah's [second] coming is suspended at every moment of history until his recognition by 'all Israel.' for 'a hardening has come upon part of Israel' in their 'unbelief' toward Jesus.... The 'full inclusion' of the Jews in the Messiah's salvation, in the wake of 'the full number of the Gentiles,' will enable the People of God to achieve 'the measure of the stature of the fullness of Christ,' in which 'God may be all in all.' CCC § 674 (quoting or citing Rom. 11:12, 20–26; Matt. 23:39; Luke 21:24; Eph. 4:13; 1 Cor. 15:28).
87   Dan. 9:26b, 27b.
88   Mal. 4:4–6.

See how full this Psalm is with sacramental mystery, in which faith is strengthened, hope in God is made firm, fortitude is excited, the early Church is explained, the grace of Baptism is commended, the benefits of God are recalled, the Incarnation of Christ is pointed out, the faithful are invited to the consideration of the divine works, the divine power is preached, and the sweet and paternal admonition of God is contained, the magnificence of the Savior is preached, and then the first and great and most sweet benefit of God is returned to, namely his Incarnation: and with this benefit, the Psalm finishes, so that in no way it may be consigned to being forgotten. Let us strive, therefore, most devoutly to sing this Psalm which is so fruitful and beautiful.

PRAYER

GOD OF JACOB AND LORD OF HOSTS, destroy the bows of our adversaries, and shatter their most wretched arms against us so that by sweeping away war by your strength we might unceasingly be still and know that you are God.

Deus Iacob et Domine virtutum, arcum nobis adversantium contere, et eorum arma nequissima contra nos confringe: ut tua virtute ablatis bellis, perenniter tibi vacemus, et videamus quoniam tu es Deus.

Psalm 46

ARTICLE LXXXIX

EXPOSITION OF THE FORTY-SIXTH PSALM:
OMNES GENTES, PLAUDITE MANIBUS.
O CLAP YOUR HANDS, ALL YOU NATIONS.

46{47}[1]   *Unto the end, for the sons of Korah. A Psalm.*

In finem, pro filiis Core. Psalmus.

HE TITLE OF THIS PSALM IS: 46{47}[1] *IN finem, pro filiis Core, psalmus David; unto the end, for the sons of Korah, a Psalm of David*, whose meaning is clear from the expositions of the preceding titles. And the Prophet [David] in this Psalm invites the faithful to acclaim the Ascending Christ, and to the praise of the Lord for his benefits, and it says:

46{47}[2]   *O clap your hands, all you nations: shout unto God with the voice of joy.*

Omnes gentes, plaudite manibus; iubilate Deo in voce exsultationis.

46{47}[2] *Omnes gentes*, O all you nations converted to the faith, *plaudit manibus, clap your* hands: that is, with all your heart exult, so that from the fullness of interior joy the exterior members may be extended up to the honor and praise of God, and the interior cheerfulness expressed, as the Apostle [Paul] teaching Timothy said: *Lifting up pure hands, without anger and contention.*[1] And Jeremiah, *Lift up*, he says, *your hands,*[2] *and he will have mercy.*[3] Or [we might understand it] thus: *Clap your hands*, that is, praise and honor God with good works. For this is the best kind of praising the Most High: with virtuous acts to venerate his majesty. For this reason it is written: *Who is a wise man, and endued with knowledge among you? Let him show, by a good manner of life, his*

---

1   1 Tim. 2:8b.
2   Lam. 2:19b.
3   Lam. 3:32a.

work in the meekness of wisdom.[4] *Iubilate Deo, shout out [with joy] unto God,* that is, ineffably praise him to the glory of God, *in voce exsultationis, with the voice of joy,* that is, with the mouth's open joyful expression. For jubilation (*iubilus*) is the inexpressible joy of the heart, which is unable to be completely hidden nor can it be expressed in its fullness.[5] The Prophet [David] therefore wishes that our soul might conceive such a praise of God that is unable to be explained with the mouth.

46{47}[3] *For the Lord is high, terrible: a great king over all the earth.*

Quoniam Dominus excelsus, terribilis, rex magnus super omnem terram.

46{47}[3] *Quoniam Dominus excelsus, for the Lord is high,* that is incomprehensible, sublime, and immense; *terribilis, terrible,* since he is the infallible Judge, strict and just; *rex magnus super omnem terram, a great king over all the earth: for all things are in your power,*[6] and all elements are subject to him. Regarding this excellence the holy Job states: *He is higher than heaven, and what will you do? He is deeper than hell, and how will you know? The measure of him is longer than the earth, and broader than the sea. If he shall overturn all things, or shall press them together, who shall contradict him?*[7] And again: *The pillars of heaven,* he says, *tremble, and dread at his beck.*[8] And elsewhere the divine word says: *Behold the*

---

4 James 3:13. E. N. I have replaced the Douay-Rheims's "conversation" with "manner of life" as a translation of *conversatione*. Throughout this translation *conversatio* has been translated as "manner of living," or "way of life."
5 E. N. *Iubilus enim est inexpressibile gaudium cordis, quod nec occultari potest in toto, nec exprimi valet ex integro.* Denis's definition of *iubilus* (jubilation) appears to be derived from the Gloss which, as quoted by St. Thomas Aquinas in his commentary on Psalm 46, is: *Iubilus est ineffabile gaudium, quod nec taceri potest, sed non potest exprimi, quia excedit comprehensionem.* "Jubilation is ineffable joy which cannot be kept silent, but cannot be expressed, because it exceeds comprehension." The inadequacy of words is expressed by the series of tones sung by monks on the last vowel of a text without words, which is called a *iubilus*, and which in the *Breviarium in Psalmos* attributed to St. Jerome (Ps. 32, PL 26, 915) is defined as follows: *Iubilus dicitur, quod nec verbis, nec syllabis, et nec litteris, nec voce potest erumpere, aut comprehendere quantum homo Deum debeat laudare.* "*Iubilus* is said for that which neither by words, nor syllables, nor letters, nor speech can express or comprehend as to how much man ought to praise God." With *iubilus* we enter into mystical, contemplative praise of God, into that realm of the Spirit which praises God "with unspeakable groanings." Rom. 8:26.
6 Esth. 13:9a.
7 Job 11:8–10.
8 Job 26:11.

heaven, and the heavens of heavens, the deep, and all the earth, and the things that are in them, shall be moved in his sight, the mountains also, and the hills;... and when God shall look upon them, they shall be shaken with trembling.[9] But how great and free and powerful a king God is over all the earth is expressed where the Lord says to Job: *Where were you when I laid up the foundations of the earth? Tell me if you have understanding. Who has laid the measures thereof?... And who has stretched the line upon it? Or upon what are its bases grounded?*[10]

This part can also fittingly be explained in this manner: *for the Lord Jesus, who is the prince of the kings of the earth; is high,* for according to his divinity he is equal to the Father, but according to his humanity God gives him a name which is above ever other created name, namely to be the mediator between God and man,[11] as the Apostle [Paul] states it, *God has exalted him, and has given him a name which is above all names;*[12] *terrible,* because of the future judgment, as he himself attested: *And there shall be signs in the sun, and in the moon, and in the stars; and upon the earth distress of nations, by reason of the confusion of the roaring of the sea and of the waves; men withering away for fear, and expectation of what shall come upon the whole world...; and then they shall see the Son of man coming in a cloud, with great power and majesty.*[13] See how truly and immeasurably terrible is Christ, who has power to destroy both body and soul in hell.[14] *A great king over all the earth*: that is, Jesus Christ with the whole world turned toward him is the great and most powerful king, in the manner that Balaam prophesied: *A star shall rise out of Jacob, and a man shall spring up from Israel... and he shall possess Edom.*[15] By the word "Edom" is designated the Gentiles. Whence other translations [of Num. 24:18] have: "And all the earth will be in his possession." For which reason Christ through the prophet Malachi says: *My name is dreadful among the Gentiles.*

46{47}[4] He has subdued the people under us; and the nations under our feet.

Subiecit populos nobis, et gentes sub pedibus nostris.

---

9   Ecclus. 16:18–19.
10 Job. 38:4–6a.
11 E. N. 1 Tim. 2:5: *For there is one God, and one mediator of God and men, the man Christ Jesus.*
12 Phil 2:9.
13 Luke 21:25–27.
14 Matt. 10:28.
15 Num. 24:17b-18a (Edom is sometimes written Idumea).

46{47}[4] *Subiecit populos nobis, et gentes sub pedibus nostris; he has subdued the people under us, and the nations under our feet.* This is the voice of the Apostles or the early Church by which Christ has subjected the people, that is, the Jews converted to the faith, and the believing Gentiles: indeed God wishes the whole world to be subject to the Church militant;[16] and those not subject [to him through the Church] will be eternally tormented, in the way that Isaiah says about the Church: *For the nation and the kingdom that will not serve you, shall perish.*[17]

46{47}[5] *He has chosen for us his inheritance the beauty of Jacob which he has loved.*

Elegit nobis haereditatem suam; speciem Iacob quam dilexit.

Next, the of Church of the elect, recalling the great benefits of God, says: 46{47}[5] *Elegit nobis hereditatem suam, he has chosen for us his inheritance*: that is, Christ decreed to give us heavenly goods, not earthly goods, the happiness of eternal life, not prosperity of a mundane life; and he desired more to make us heirs of God, even his joint heirs,[18] than to give us temporal goods which are common to the good and to the evil.[19] Thus he chooses us, that is, to our salvation, his inheritance, that is, eternal happiness, namely, *speciem Iacob, the beauty of Jacob*, that is, the beauty of the elect, of the supplanting vices,[20] *quam, which* Jacob, or those designated by Jacob, God *dilexit, has loved*. For God also loved holy Jacob, as Malachi confessed: *Was not Esau brother to Jacob? And I have loved Jacob, but have hated Esau.*[21] Christ also has loved the elect

---

16 "[A]s Jesus Christ came into the world that men 'may have life, and have it abundantly' [John 10:10], so also has the Church for her aim and end the eternal salvation of souls, and hence she is so constituted as to open wide her arms to all mankind, unhampered by any limit of time or place." DS 3166 (Leo XIII, *Immortale Dei*). See also footnote 44-123.
17 Is. 60:12a.
18 Rom. 8:17a: *And if sons, heirs also; heirs indeed of God, and joint heirs with Christ.*
19 Denis draws on St. Augustine's distinction that eternal goods are goods common only to the good, whereas temporal goods are common to the good and evil. "For one thing are goods found nowhere but with the good, and another are goods which are common with the good and the evil. The goods which are not found except among the good are piety, faith, justice, chastity, prudence, modesty, charity, and others of this kind. The goods which are common with the good and evil, are money, honor, power of this age, administration, and the health of the body." Sermon 311, 12, 11, PL 38, 1418.
20 For Jacob as the "supplanter" of vices, *see* footnote 43-103.
21 Mal. 1:2–3.

signified by Jacob, in the manner that we read in Revelation: *He who has loved us, and washed us from our sins in his own blood.*[22] And so the inheritance of God, by which God chooses to give to the elect is *the beauty of Jacob*, that is, it is the highest adornment and most beautiful grace of the elect, since it is the height of their perfection. For which reason it is said in a Psalm above: *I have loved, O Lord, the beauty of your house,*[23] that is, the blessedness of the heavenly homeland.

46{47}[6] *God is ascended with jubilee, and the Lord with the sound of trumpet.*

Ascendit Deus in iubilo, et Dominus in voce tubae.

46{47}[6] *Ascendit Deus, God is ascended*, that is, the Only-begotten of God, Jesus Christ, above all the heavens, *in iubilo, with jubilee*, that is, in ineffable praise and joy both of his own as well as of the holy multitude that saw him ascend, and of the holy men who, seeing him ascend, said: *The Lord who is strong and mighty: the Lord mighty in battle; and the Lord of hosts, he is the King of Glory:*[24] concerning which I fully pondered about in the exposition of the twenty-third Psalm.[25] Indeed, Christ with jubilation in his own heart ascended, saying to the holy angels: *I, that speak justice, and am a defender to save.*[26] Also about the Apostles and the others who saw Christ ascending it is written: *And he led them as far as Bethany, . . . and he blessed them, . . . and he was carried up to heaven; and they adoring went back into Jerusalem with great joy, . . . praying and blessing God.*[27] *Dominus in voce tubae, the Lord with the sound of a trumpet*: that is, Christ ascended with a trumpet-like voice of the consoling angels to his disciples, according to that which is written in Acts: *And while they were beholding him going up to heaven, behold two men* (that is two angels in the form of men) *stood by them in white garments, who also said: Men of Galilee, why stand you looking up to heaven?*[28] Or [we might understand it this way], *the Lord* ascended *with the sound of a* trumpet, that is, with his own sonorous and loud

---

22 Rev. 1:5.
23 Ps. 25:8a.
24 Ps. 23:8b, 10b.
25 E. N. See Article LV (Psalm 23:8, 10) in Volume 1. There Denis speaks of the three questions of the three hierarchies of angels to the ascending Christ, and his three responses: Ps. 23:8b, 10b; Is. 63:1b; and Is. 63:3a.
26 Is. 63:1b.
27 Luke 24:50–53.
28 Acts 1:10-11a.

voice, for (as Luke says) *lifting up his hands, he blessed them ... and he departed from them.*[29] And many other and sublime things did he say to his disciples when about to ascend, as is related in Acts.[30]

46{47}[7] *Sing praises to our God, sing: sing praises to our king, sing.*
Psallite Deo nostro, psallite; psallite regi nostro, psallite.

46{47}[8] *For God is the king of all the earth: sing wisely.*
Quoniam rex omnis terrae Deus, psallite sapienter.

Since therefore it is so, O all the faithful, 46{47}[7] *Psallite Deo nostro, sing praises to our God*, namely, to Jesus Christ, the Creator, the Savior, and our Judge, *psallite, sing*, that is, praise him with good works; *psallite regi nostro, sing praises to our king*, namely Christ, who rules heaven and earth, and does not abandon his Church, *psallite, sing.* 46{47}[8] *Quoniam rex omnis terrae Deus, for God is the king of all the earth*: that is, Christ is the Lord of the entire world to all those who believe in him. Whence he said to the Apostles: *You shall be witnesses unto me in Jerusalem, and in all Judea, and Samaria, and even to the uttermost part of the earth.*[31] And the Apostle [Paul] said: *In these days God has spoken to us by his Son, whom he has appointed heir of all things.*[32] *Psalliter sapienter, sing wisely*: that is, with an interior relish of the mind and with a heartfelt relish, offer the words of the Psalm, praise and honor God, not with an inconstant and arid heart. Since as the bodily sense of taste distinguishes, tastes, and savors the individual particularities of food, so does the interior sense of taste of the soul attend to, taste, and savor each individual word of the Holy Spirit. To sing in this way is truly to sing wisely: because wisdom may be said to be like a flavorful knowledge.[33] But some sing and pray foolishly. Of these the Lord through the Prophet [Isaiah] says: These

---

29 Luke 24:50b, 51b.
30 Acts 1:3–8.
31 Acts 1:8b.
32 Heb. 1:2.
33 E. N. Denis has *sapientia dicitur quasi sapora scientia*. More commonly, the medieval etymology, derived from St. Isidore and found, for example, in St. Thomas's *Summa Theologiae*, is that *sapientia quasi sapida scientia*, "wisdom is like a savory knowledge." ST, IIaIIae, q. 45, art. 2, arg. 2. The bishop William of Auvergne (1180/90–1249) accepted both, as he defines wisdom (*sapientia*) as *sapida seu sapora scientia*, a savory or flavorful knowledge. Guillermi Parisiensis, *Operum summa divinarum humanarum rerum difficultates profundissime resolvens* (1516), fol. 75. All these Latin words have derivatives in English, so we could say with William of Auvergne, sapience is a sapid or saporous science.

people honor *me with their lips; but their heart is far from me.*³⁴ And such praise without prayer is unfruitful, according to the Apostle [Paul]: *If I pray in a tongue,... but my understanding is without fruit.*³⁵ And so he adds: *I will pray with the spirit, I will pray also with the understanding; I will sing with the spirit, I will sing also with the understanding.*³⁶ And that which is salubrious and fruitful he expresses by appending: *But in the church I had rather speak five words with my understanding... than ten thousand words in a tongue.*³⁷ Let us apply ourselves, therefore to *sing wisely*: since that applies with much greater force to us solitaries the more we possess purity of mind in a manner greater than others. Or [we can see it] thus: *Sing wisely*, that is, praise and worship Christ, not only as man, but also as true God, according to that which the Apostle [Paul] says, *And if we have known Christ according to the flesh*, still *now we know him no longer.*³⁸

46{47}[9] *God shall reign over the nations: God sits on his holy throne. Regnabit Deus super gentes; Deus sedet super sedem sanctam suam.*

46{47}[9] *Regnavit Deus super gentes, God shall reign over the nations,* those turned toward him by faith and worship. *Deus sedet super sedem sanctam suam, God sits on his holy throne,* that is, Christ sits at the right hand of the Father in the throne of majesty. Or [alternatively], *sits upon his holy throne*, that is, in the mind of all the blessed in heaven, according to that Psalm that we find later on: *You that sit upon the Cherubim, shine forth.*³⁹ Whence the Prophet [Daniel] says: *I beheld till thrones were placed, and the Ancient of days sat... his throne like flames of fire,* that is, the holy angels:⁴⁰ of whom in a subsequent Psalm is written, *Who makes our angels spirits: and your ministers a burning fire.*⁴¹ Indeed, so does the Apostle [Paul] state using this verse: *He that makes his angels spirits, and his ministers a flame of fire.*⁴²

---

34 Is. 29:13a.
35 1 Cor. 14:14.
36 1 Cor. 14:15.
37 1 Cor. 14:19.
38 2 Cor. 5:16.
39 Ps. 79:2b.
40 Dan. 7:9.
41 Ps. 103:4.
42 Heb. 1:7.

46{47}[10] *The princes of the people are gathered together, with the God of Abraham: for the strong gods of the earth are exceedingly exalted.*

Principes populorum congregati sunt cum Deo Abraham, quoniam dii fortes terrae vehementer elevati sunt.

46{47}[10] *Principes populorum congregati sunt cum Deo Abraham, the princes of the people are gathered together, with the God of Abraham.* This commonly is explained in this manner: *The princes of the people,* that is, certain out of the leaders of the people, such as the Centurion and other converted princes, *are gathered together with the God of Abraham,* that is, are joined with Christ, who is the God of Abraham, through faith. But it seems more agreeable and more proper to be explained as referring literally of the Apostles, of whom Christ in the Gospel says, *Blessed are the eyes that see the things which you see;*[43] and again, *To you it is given to know the mystery of the kingdom of God;*[44] and also, *The children of the bridegroom cannot mourn as long as the bridegroom is with them.*[45] For they bodily conversed with the God of Abraham in the world, that is, with the Incarnate Son of God; and they came upon that most precious pearl, which is how Christ in the Gospel referred to himself.[46] And this exposition is more in line with the literal sense, and corresponds with the fact that in the feasts of the birth of the Apostles these aforementioned words are sung of the Apostles in the place of the antiphon.[47]

Quoniam dii fortes terrae, for the strong gods of the earth, that is, the holy Apostles through the excellence of the deifying grace, and by producing gods of the earth (that is, of men),[48] ruling and instructing, and, in a

---

43   Luke 10:23b.
44   Luke 8:10a.
45   Matt. 9:15a.
46   Matt. 13:45–46.
47   E. N. Denis is arguing from *lex orandi, lex credendi* that the liturgy uses the first part of Ps. 46:10 as an antiphon in the feasts celebrating any feast involving the birth of an Apostle (*In Nataliciis Apostolorum*), which means that the Church's liturgical selection of this antiphon as applying to the Apostles should be given great weight in choosing the more agreeable exposition, thus "with a single antiphon unlocking whole abysses of Scripture!" Frederick William Faber, *The Blessed Sacrament* (London: Burns & Oates 1861), 4.
48   E. N. This, of course, is a reference to the doctrine of "divinization" or *theosis*, which is the transforming result of sanctifying grace on the soul and its glorification in heaven. As St. Athanasius succinctly and famously put it: *Ipse siquidem homo factus est, ut nos dii efficeremur,* Αὐτὸς γὰρ ἐνηνθρώπησεν, ἵνα ἡμεῖς θεοποιηθῶμεν. "Indeed, he became man so that we might become gods." *De Incarnatione,* 54, 3, PG 25, 192. It should be understood that there is no absorption into the Godhead nor

manner of speaking, saving them, *vehementer elevati sunt, are exceedingly exalted*: for they received the *first fruits* of the Holy Spirit,[49] both with respect to the gifts of sanctifying grace and charisms, and by these they were constituted princes over all the earth, as has been addressed in another Psalm.[50] But if we want to know how exceedingly exalted are the strong gods of the earth, that is, the holy Apostles, let us think about what Christ said to them in the Gospel: *Whose sins you shall forgive*, he said, *they are forgiven them; and whose sins you shall retain, they are retained.*[51] And again: *You, who have followed me, in the regeneration, when the Son of man shall sit on the seat of his majesty, you also shall sit on twelve seats judging the twelve tribes of Israel.*[52] And also: *You are the light of the world; and, You are the salt of the earth.*[53] And yet again: *Behold, I have given you power to tread upon serpents and scorpions, and upon all the power of the enemy: and nothing shall hurt you.*[54] And again: *Raise the dead, heal the sick, cleanse the lepers, cast out devils.*[55] Whence, Isaiah exceedingly marveled foreseeing such and so many future Apostles, saying: *Who are these, that fly as clouds, and as doves to their windows?*[56] For they flew as the clouds, sublimely contemplating, quickly running throughout the world, and loftily preaching. Regarding these we are able to apply that which is in Lamentations: *Whiter than snow, purer than milk, more ruddy than the old ivory.*[57] Indeed, the Apostles were whiter than snow because of the splendor of the wisdom with which they were infused; they were purer than milk because of the innocence and cleanliness of life; they were more ruddy than old ivory because of

---

do we become God when we obtain the beatific union and participate in God's life: "Such union takes place when God performs on the soul this sovereign mercy, wherein all the things of God and of the soul become one in a participative transformation; and the soul appears more like God than soul, yet still it is God by participation, though it is true that its natural being, though it is transformed, is as distinct from God's as it was before, even as a stained glass window is distinct from the ray that is giving it resplendence. San Juan de la Cruz, Subida del Monte Carmelo (Barcelona: Juan Roca y Bros 1883), 73 (translation mine).

49 Rom. 8:23a.
50 Ps. 44:17b: *You shall make them princes over all the earth.* See Article LXXXVII (Psalm 44:17). For the difference between the graces known as *gratia gratum faciens* (sanctifying grace) and *gratia gratis data* (charisms), see footnote 44-40.
51 John 20:23.
52 Matt. 19:28.
53 Matt. 5:14a, 13a.
54 Luke 10:19.
55 Matt. 10::8.
56 Is. 60:8.
57 Lam. 4:7.

the ardor of divine and fraternal charity. With merit, therefore, they are called gods of the earth, for they were teachers and judges of men, and prelates with excellent wings. Whence the Lord said to Moses: *Behold I have appointed you the god of Pharaoh.*[58]

See how this Psalm of brief eloquence is truly charming, beautiful, sweet, and full of meaning, in which with such repeated succession we are roused to praise God: for five times are we reminded in it to sing to God.

PRAYER

GOD, KING OF ALL THE EARTH, SITTING upon your holy throne, elect us to be your inheritance, so that reigning with you in eternal glory, and aided by you, we may rejoice before you with joy unspeakable and glorified, who with the same God the Father and Holy Spirit live and reign for ever and ever.

Rex omnis terrae Deus, sedens super sedem sanctam tuam, elige nos tibi in hereditatem: ut tecum regnantes in aeterna gloria, te praestante exsultemus coram tem laetitia inenarrabili et glorificata: qui cum eodem Deo Patre et Spiritu Sancto vivis et regnas in omnia saecula.

---

58 Ex. 7:1. In one of his sermons, St. Thomas Aquinas states: "Dionysius said in his *Heavenly Hierarchies* that nothing is more divine than to be cooperators with God, and when you preach for the salvation of souls, or when you do other good works, then you cooperate with God. Hence God said to Moses (Ex. 7:1): I have appointed you the god of Pharaoh." *Homo quidam erat dives,* pars 2.

Psalm 47

ARTICLE XC
EXPOSITION OF THE FORTY-SEVENTH PSALM:
MAGNUS DOMINUS ET LAUDABILIS NIMIS.
GREAT IS THE LORD, AND EXCEEDINGLY TO BE PRAISED.

47{48}[1] *A Psalm of a canticle, for the sons of Korah, on the second day of the week.*
Psalmus cantici. Filiis Core, secunda sabbati.

PLACED BEFORE THIS PSALM NOW BEING expounded is this title: 47{48}[1] *Psalmus cantici, filiis Core, secunda sabbati; a Psalm of a canticle, for the sons of Korah, on the second day of the week*: that is, this Psalm which is called a canticle because it deals with divine things in which alone true and holy rejoicing is to be had, applies to the sons of Korah, that is, the imitators of the Crucified;[1] *on the second day of the week*, that is, treating of those things that pertain to the second day of the week [two days after the Sabbath]. For in the first day following the Sabbath, God made heaven and earth and divided the light from the darkness:[2] and by this is mystically understood the day of the Lord's Resurrection, in which Christ created all things. But the second day of the Sabbath or of the week he made the firmament,[3] by which spiritually is designated the founding of the Church, which after Christ's resurrection, with the coming of the Holy Spirit, was founded and confirmed by Christ.[4] And it is of this founding of the Church that this Psalm we will see literally is about.

47{48}[2] *Great is the Lord, and exceedingly to be praised in the city of our God, in his holy mountain.*
Magnus Dominus et laudabilis nimis, in civitate Dei nostri, in monte sancto eius.

---

1 See Article LXXX (Psalm 40:1) and *see also* footnote 40-3 for an explanation of the relationship between Korah and Calvary.
2 Gen. 1:1, 4.
3 Gen. 1:7.
4 Acts chp. 2.

The Prophet [David] therefore says that which the mystery of Christ most excellently clarifies, **47{48}[2]** *Magnus Dominus et laudabilis nimis; great is the Lord, and exceedingly to be praised*: which may be addressed to the whole Trinity, or to any one of the divine Persons, yet because of what follows it is especially applicable to Christ. For he is a great Lord, indeed boundless and *exceedingly to be praised*, even unto infinity. For whatever goodness a thing may have, it is to that extent praiseworthy. Since, therefore, the nature of God is boundless and pure goodness, it is clear that he is infinitely praiseworthy, and that a creature is neither worthy nor sufficient to be able to praise him. For this reason, elsewhere is written: *The Lord is terrible, and exceeding great,*[5] *the Almighty is above all his works.*[6] *Glorify the Lord however much you can, for he will yet far exceed:*[7] *for he is above all praise.*[8] *In civitate Dei nostri, in the city of our God*, that is, in Jerusalem, the city designated for divine worship, which the evangelist Matthew calls the *holy city*;[9] especially though *in monte sancto eius, in his holy mountain*, that is, in the temple built on Mount Moriah,[10] or the higher location of this city. Or, *in his holy mountain*, that is, in the Cenacle, in which Christ observed the Last Supper with his Apostles.[11] For the site of the Cenacle was upon that mountain, not far from the temple. And so Christ is said to be *great and exceedingly to be praised* in the just-mentioned *city* and the *mountain* because he especially demonstrated his majesty and praiseworthiness in that city, as will be made clear. Because that which we read in Matthew: *When Jesus was come into Jerusalem, the whole city was moved, saying: Who is this? And the people said: This is Jesus the prophet, from Nazareth of Galilee.*[12] But most of all the majesty and praise of Christ appeared in the *holy mountain* of that *city*, that is, in the temple and the Cenacle: for in the temple he performed many miracles, as the Evangelist Matthew there adds: *And there came to him the blind and the lame in the temple; and he healed them.*[13]

---

5 Ecclus. 43:31a.
6 Ecclus. 43:30b.
7 Ecclus. 43:32a.
8 Ecclus. 43:33b.
9 Matt. 27:53.
10 2 Chr. 3:1.
11 Luke 22:12.
12 Matt. 21:10–11.
13 Matt. 21:14.

47{48}[3] *With the joy of the whole earth is mount Sion founded, on the sides of the north, the city of the great king.*

Fundatur exsultatione universae terrae mons Sion; latera aquilonis, civitas regis magni.

47{48}[3] *Fundatur exsultatione universae terrae,* with the joy of the whole earth... *is founded*: that is, the holy city Jerusalem is built to the great joy of all believers in the whole world: for in it was the early Church of Christ, and the Catholic faith began first in it through the preaching of the Apostles, and from there the faith of Christ was spread throughout all mankind. For which reason there is written in Isaiah: *The law* (no question meaning anything else but the Gospel) *shall come forth from Sion, and the word of the Lord from Jerusalem.*[14] From this also arose a great joy to all the Gentiles converted to Christ, according to that which we read in Paul who said to the Jews: *To you it behooved us first to speak the word of God: but because you reject it, and judge yourselves unworthy of eternal life, behold we turn to the Gentiles,* and so forth. *And the Gentiles hearing it, were glad, and glorified the word of the Lord.*[15] This also was said by an angel to the shepherds: *I bring you good tidings of great joy, that shall be to all the people: For, this day, is born to you a Savior.*[16] For this birth was first foretold publicly in Jerusalem. *Mons Sion,* Mount Sion, which is on one side of Jerusalem, *latera aquilonis, on the sides of the north,* that is, that part opposite the mount, is *civitas regis magni, the city of the great king,* that is of God most high. For a city is constituted from the extremities of its parts; and, at the same time, the parts are accepted as being the same as the whole.[17]

Now this part can also be explained in a spiritual sense, and it comes to almost the same thing. *Great is the Lord, and exceedingly to be praised, in the city of our God,* that is, in the Church militant, which by faith and grace is founded *in his holy mountain,* that is, in Christ, who is the great mountain, because of the eminence of all his divine gifts. Of which is written in Daniel: the *stone* that was *cut out of a mount without hands* created a great mountain *and filled the whole earth.*[18] Or [alternatively] *in his holy mountain*

---

14 Is. 2:3b; Micah 4:2b.
15 Acts 13:46, 48a.
16 Luke 2:10–11a.
17 E. N. In other words, any part within the boundary of a city can be considered to be as part of the city or being in the city as a whole.
18 Dan. 2:34a, 35b. Dan. 2:34–35: *Thus you saw until a stone was cut out of a mountain without hands: and it struck the statue upon the feet thereof that were of iron and of clay, and broke them in pieces. Then was the iron, the clay, the brass, the silver,*

is the same thing as what was said immediately before, *in the city of our God*: for the Church of Christ is a great mountain because of the height of grace. For which reason Isaiah writes of it: *In the last days the mountain of the house of the Lord shall be prepared on the top of mountains, and it shall be exalted above the hills, and all nations shall flow unto it.*[19] By the term *in the last days* is understood the time of grace and the evangelical law, which is the final and ultimate law. And so this time was the *mountain* of the Lord, that is, the Church of Christ, in the summit of the mountain, that is, more sublime in gifts and graces of the Holy Spirit than the Synagogue and the church all the elect who have been from the beginning of the world until the coming of Christ.[20] Or *mountain home of the Lord* is called *mount Sion*:[21] which during the time of Christ was at the peak of the mountain, that is, higher than mount Sinai and mount Tabor, not because of the location of the place, but because of the presence and preaching and miracles of Christ, which in mount Sion, that is, in the temple and in the home of the cenacle where he appeared, preached, and did great miracles: especially in the cenacle or room, in which he entered with the doors closed, in which he consecrated his Body and Blood, in which he also sent the Apostles the Holy Spirit by a visible sign, giving them clear knowledge of all languages and of the divine Scriptures.[22] *Fundatur exsultatione universae terrae, with the joy of the whole earth... is founded*: that is, the early Church founded and established by Christ is to the joy of all the faithful. For due to the fact that the early Church received such a large amount of grace and power from Christ, the whole world was converted to Christ: and as a result of that conversion the elect rejoiced. *Mount Sion*, that is, the people converted from the Jews, *on the sides of the north*, that is, the Gentiles, those sluggish with vices, those weak in affection, and those cold in good works. For the north is a frozen region, just like it states in Ecclesiasticus, *The cold north*

---

and the gold broken to pieces together, and became like the chaff of a summer's threshing floor, and they were carried away by the wind: and there was no place found for them: but the stone that struck the statue, became a great mountain, and filled the whole earth.
19 Is. 2:2.
20 The notion that the Church is as old as Adam and in some form pre-existed Christ is well-established, though perhaps not as widely known as it ought to be. A succinct treatment of the Church during the ante-Messianic times, with reference to the Fathers of the Church, can be found in Henri de Lubac, *The Splendor of the Church* (San Francisco, Ignatius Press, 1986), 58–65.
21 E. N. *Mons domus Domini*, the "mountain home of the Lord," is found in Micah 4:1: *And it shall come to pass in the last days, that the mountain of the house of the Lord (mons domus Domini) shall be prepared in the top of mountains, and high above the hills: and people shall flow to it.*
22 John 22:26; Matt. 26:26 *et seq.*; Acts 2:1–4.

wind blows, and the water is congealed into crystal.[23] This therefore is the *city of the great king*, that is, the Church of Christ: for in Christ as *a chief corner stone* are joined both Jews and the Gentiles so as to constitute one city or temple in which God by grace dwells.[24] Of this temple Zechariah has written: *Behold a man, Orient* (that is, Messiah) *is his name; ... and he shall build a temple to the Lord*, that is, the Church militant, ... *and the counsel of peace shall be between them both*,[25] that is, between the *mountain* and the *sides of north* according to the exposition we have just related. And this is what the Apostle [Paul] says: *That which you were at that time without Christ ... and without God in this world, now ... in Jesus Christ, who some time were afar off, are made nigh by his blood. For he is our peace, who has made us both one, and breaking down the middle wall of partition, the enmities of his flesh, making void the law of commandments contained in decrees, so that he might make the two in himself into one new man, making peace ... by the Cross, killing the enmities in himself.*[26]

47{48}[4]   *In her houses shall God be known, when he shall protect her.*

   Deus in domibus eius cognoscetur cum suscipiet eam.

47{48}[5]   *For behold the kings of the earth assembled themselves: they gathered together.*

   Quoniam ecce reges terrae congregati sunt, convenerunt in unum.

47{48}[6]   *So they saw, and they wondered, they were troubled, they were moved.*

   Ipsi videntes, sic admirati sunt, conturbati sunt, commoti sunt.

47{48}[7]   *Trembling took hold of them. There were pains as of a woman in labor.*

   Tremor apprehendit eos; ibi dolores ut parturientis.

---

23   Ecclus. 43:22a.
24   Eph. 2:20–21. E. N. "Christ instituted this new covenant, the new testament, that is to say, in his Blood, calling together a people made up of Jew and Gentile, making them one, not according to the flesh, but in the Spirit. This was to be the new people of God." DS 4122 (VII, *Lumen Gentium*, 9). "Often, the Church has also been called the *building* of God [1 Cor. 3:9]. The Lord himself compared himself to the stone that the builders rejected but that was made into the cornerstone. [Matt. 21:42] ... This edifice has man names to describe it ... especially, the holy *temple*." DS 4110 (VI, *Lumen Gentium*, 6).
25   Zech. 6:12–13.
26   Eph. 2:12–16.

47{48}[8] *With a vehement wind you shall break in pieces the ships of Tarshish.*

In spiritu vehementi conteres naves Tharsis.

47{48}[9] *As we have heard, so have we seen, in the city of the Lord of hosts, in the city of our God: God has founded it for ever.*

Sicut audivimus, sic vidimus, in civitate Domini virtutum, in civitate Dei nostri: Deus fundavit eam in aeternum.

47{48}[4] *Deus, God in domibus eius, in her houses,* that is, by the citizens or the inhabitants of Jerusalem, *cognoscetur, cum suscipiet eam, shall be known, when he shall protect her,* that is, when by his grace he will call her to faith and to such great glory. For Christ was acknowledged by Simeon and Anna and many others in the city of Jerusalem. Or [alternatively]: *in her houses,* that is, in the particular Churches or by the single faithful of Christ, *he shall be known, when he shall protect her,* that is, when he will so illuminate the Church so that it might be recognized by all, in the manner that is foretold by Isaiah: *The earth is filled with the knowledge of the Lord, as the covering waters of the sea.*[27]

But the inhabitants of Jerusalem were led to acknowledge Christ to be born by the coming of the three Magi in Jerusalem arriving and asking, *Where is he that is born king of the Jews?*[28] And so there is added: **47{48}[5]** *Quoniam ecce reges, for behold the kings,* namely, the three Magi, *congregati sunt, have assembled themselves* bodily, *convenerunt in unum, they gathered together* spiritually, namely in one faith and with the intention to adore the Christ that was born. **47{48}[6]** *Ipsi, they,* that is, the inhabitants of Jerusalem, namely, Herod and the chiefs of the priests, and many others, *videntes sic, so... saw,* the Magi come with such a retinue and glory, *admirati sunt, conturbati sunt; they wondered, they were troubled,* that is, they were disturbed because of anxiety, *commoti sunt, they were moved* to ill-will; **47{48}[7]** *tremor apprehendit eos, trembling took hold of them,* for Herod feared the loss of his reign, and from this other Jews feared it would provoke great persecutions. Whence we read: *King Herod hearing this, was troubled, and all Jerusalem with him.*[29] Or [we might understand it] thus: *They,* that is, the three Magi, *so... saw* the star appear to them, and thereafter to disappear, and again to appear, *they wondered, they were troubled* by sorrow, when the star disappeared; *they*

---

27 Is. 11:9b.
28 Matt. 2:2a.
29 Matt. 2:3.

were moved to question where Christ would be born; *they were moved*, that is, a reverential fear entered into their minds—from the fact that the Holy Spirit had revealed to them[30]—and they recognized the child whom they saw and adored him as the true God. Whence with fear and with greatest reverence they offered him gifts, according to that which Isaiah had foreseen: *Kings shall see, and princes shall rise up, and adore for the Lord's sake* your God. This also can be understood of all the princes of the earth that have converted to the faith. *Ibi*, there, namely in the land of Judah, *dolores ut parturientis, there were pains as of a woman in labor*: because of the mothers of infants which were killed by Herod, so much were they afflicted by the death of their children that it was as if they were in labor. 47{48}[8] *In spiritu vehementi, with a vehement wind*, that is, in an impetuous anger, *conteres, you shall break in pieces*, O Lord God, that is, you will allow Herod to burn up, *naves Tharsis, the ships of Tarshish*. For Herod seeing that the Magi had eluded him became furiously angry; and he caused that the ships of Tarshish be destroyed because he heard that by them the Magi had returned to their own home.[31]

Then the Prophet [David] says in the person of the early Church, in which he saw fulfilled the mysteries of Christ, or of all Christians who with faith reflect upon the deeds of Christ: 47{48}[8] *Sicut audivimus, as we have heard* in the divine Scriptures, *sic vidimus, so we have seen* with the eyes of our mind or body, *in civitate Domini virtutum, in the city of the Lord of hosts*, namely, *in civitate Dei nostri, in the city of our God*, that is, in Jerusalem, for in it Christ appeared as was foretold by the Prophets. Or [an alternative interpretation], *in the city of the Lord of hosts*, that is, in the Church, which is the *city of* God, who is the Lord of hosts, that is, of the angels. *Deus fundavit eam, God has founded it*, that is, the Church, *in aeternum, forever*; for the faith of the Church will last even unto the end of the world, in the manner that Christ told his Apostles in the person of the Church: *Behold I am with you all days, even to the consummation of the world.*[32]

---

30 E. N. 1 Cor. 12:3b: *No man can say Lord Jesus, but by the Holy Ghost.*
31 "Arnobius the Younger (*ca.* 460) was the first to connect the ships of Tarsus of Psalm XVIII with Herod and the Magi, and to suggest that the return of the Magi was by ship. Anselm of Laon (1050–1117) made an exhaustive compilation from previous commentators, and added that the "Kings returned by ship to Persia, and that Herod, in a fury, burned these ships after their return." Marcia R. Rickard, "The Iconography of the Virgin Portal at Amiens," Gesta 22, no. 2 (1983), 147–57, 151 (citing to Arnobii Iunioris, *Psalmus XLVII, Commentarium*, PL 53, 391 and Anselmi Laudunensis, *Enarrationes in Matthaeum*, 11, PL 152, 1254–57).
32 Matt. 8:20b. E. N. It is the Apostles who received Christ's declaration who were in the person of the Church, just like the Apostle John received Christ's "Behold your mother!" in the person of the Church (John 19:27).

47{48}[10] *We have received your mercy, O God, in the midst of your temple.*
Suscepimus, Deus, misericordiam tuam in medio templi tui.

47{48}[10] *Suscepimus, we have received,* O *Deus,* God the Father, in the day of Purification,[33] *misericordiam tuam, your mercy,* that is, Christ your Son most mercifully sent and born, of whom you said through Isaiah, *My salvation is near to come;*[34] and again, *I will give salvation in Sion, and my glory in* Jerusalem;[35] *in medio templi tui, in the midst of your temple,* for then the blessed Virgin offered Christ in the temple, and Simeon received him in his arms, and the holy Anna confessed the same, and speaking about him *to all that looked for the redemption of Israel,* as we read in Luke.[36]

And this presentation of Christ in the temple the prophet Malachi clearly predicted. For speaking in the person of Christ, he said *Behold, I send my angel, and he shall prepare the way before my face:*[37] and this certainly is a prediction of the precursor of Christ.[38] And therefore it continues with the coming of Christ, *And presently the Lord, whom you seek, and the angel of the testament, whom you desire, shall come to his temple.*[39] Moreover, the prophet Haggai beautifully speaks of the same thing. For when he had said, *The desired of all nations shall come,* he immediately added, *And I will fill this house with glory, says the Lord.*[40] And to those knowing the Scriptures it is certain that this speaks of the temple in Jerusalem built after the return from the Babylonian captivity: to which reconstruction Zechariah himself encouraged the Jews.[41] And of the glory of this temple is later stated: *Great shall be the glory of this last house more than of the first, says the Lord.*[42] But the excellence in the structure of the temple built later than the temple built by Solomon was none other but that one in which Christ in his own person would appear, teach, and perform miracles. For elsewhere [it is stated that] this latest temple was as nothing in reputation compared to the first temple built by Solomon. Consequently, those who had seen the first temple passionately

---

33 The Day of Purification (of Mary) is the day that Jesus was presented at the Temple, forty days after his birth.
34 Is. 56:1b.
35 Is. 46:12b. E. N. Denis replaces "Israel" with "Jerusalem," which departs from the Sixto-Clementine Vulgate, but is consistent with the Antiphon for the Third Sunday of Advent which takes its wording from an older Latin variant.
36 Luke 2:22 *et seq.*
37 Mal. 3:1a.
38 E. N. It is a reference to John the Baptist.
39 Mal. 3:1b.
40 Hag. 2:8.
41 Ezra 5:1, 2; 6:14.
42 Hag. 2:10.

mourned as the second temple was being built;[43] but those that had not seen [the first temple] rejoiced greatly. From this one can see the clear argument that the Messiah king has already come and appeared in that temple which has now for a long time been destroyed by the Romans.[44]

47{48}[11] *According to your name, O God, so also is your praise unto the ends of the earth: your right hand is full of justice.*

Secundum nomen tuum, Deus, sic et laus tua in fines terrae; iustitia plena est dextera tua.

47{48}[11] *Secundum nomen tuum, Deus, sic et laus tua in fines terrae; according to your name, O God, so also is your praise unto the ends of the earth*: that is, according to your greatness or the majesty of your name, the news of your sublimeness has extended far and wide, and your dignity has been published, and reverence is exhibited towards you in all the parts of the world. For the worship of latria is to be given to God to whom alone it ought to be given: and so according to his name he ought everywhere be honored, since no one is able to praise, love, or honor him to the degree that he is worthy. And this is why the Lord himself protested to Isaiah: *I will not give my glory to another, nor my praise to graven things.*[45] But that God is to be praised according to his name to the ends of the earth the Prophet [Isaiah] expresses right away, adding: *Sing to the Lord a new song, his praise is from the ends of the earth.*[46] And again: *They shall give glory to the Lord, and shall declare his praise in the islands.*[47] The apostle Paul declaring this be fulfilled, said, writing to the Gentiles: *You turned to God from idols, to serve the living... God.*[48] *Iustitia plena est dextera tua; your right hand is full of justice*: that is, your gracious presence, your kindly protection, or your propitiation, O Lord, is full of equity. For in a later Psalm is written, *The Lord is just in all his ways*:[49] for when he has

---

43 Ezra 3:12–13.
44 E. N. Denis is saying that—because the second temple was manifestly less glorious than the temple built by Solomon—the only possible excellence relating to the second temple prophesied by Haggai 2:10 had to be the visitation of the Messiah King. Since the second temple has been destroyed, it means that the presence of the Messiah King—that which made the second have glory "more than the first"—has been fulfilled. Otherwise, the temple would have been destroyed without Haggai's prophesy being fulfilled.
45 Is. 42:8.
46 Is. 42:10a.
47 Is. 42:12.
48 1 Thess. 1:9b.
49 Ps. 144:17a.

pity on the ungodly, he does so justly as a result of his goodness, because he is so good that he himself is just even to do good to the unworthy and to have mercy upon the ungrateful. And when he gives grace to the good, he is just both on his part and on the part of the just. Or [we may understand it thus]: *Your right hand is full of justice*: that is, you yourself are utter justice, with respect to those who in the day of judgment will be at your right hand, to whom you will say, *Take possession of the kingdom prepared for you from the foundation of the world.*[50]

47{48}[12] *Let mount Sion rejoice, and the daughters of Juda be glad; because of your judgments, O Lord.*

Laetetur mons Sion, et exsultent filiae Iudae, propter iudicia tua, Domine.

47{48}[12] *Laetetur mons Sion, let mount Sion rejoice*, that is, the early Church in mount Sion, instituted and illumined, as has already been made clear, *et exsultent filiae Iudae, and the daughters of Juda be glad*, that is, all of the successors of the first faithful, or all the children of the Church, who are the daughters of Juda, that is, the children of the confession of divine praise and one's own fault.[51] For the holy prophets customarily designate by the name daughters, whether in the singular or in the plural, the entire people. Whence Isaiah says: *Come down, sit in the dust, O virgin daughter of Babylon;*[52] and Zechariah, *Rejoice greatly, O daughter of Sion;*[53] and Zephaniah, *Rejoice with all your heart, O daughter of Jerusalem.*[54] In this place the name daughters of Sion is understood to be the entire people of the faithful. Therefore these exult *propter iudicia tua, Domine; because of your judgments, O Lord*: whereby you will be merciful to whom you wish, and you will harden whom you wish;[55] whereby you will save the just, and damn the ungodly; whereby you will leave behind nothing disordered; whereby in the present life you distinguish the good from the evil and divide up grace, promise, and merit, and in the future you will separate the same by place and reward. And these judgments of God are God himself judging all things, or the effects of divine justice.

---

50 Matt. 25:34.
51 E. N. On the distinction between confession of praise and the confession of fault or sin, *see* footnote 27-49.
52 Is. 47:1a.
53 Zech. 9:9a.
54 Zeph. 3:14b.
55 *Cf.* Rom. 9:18: *He has mercy on whom he will; and whom he will, he hardens.*

47{48}[13] *Surround Sion, and encompass her: tell you in her towers.*

Circumdate Sion, et complectimini eam; narrate in turribus eius.

47{48}[13] *Circumdate Sion, surround Sion*: that is, defend the Church of Christ with word and deed, scandalizing, perverting, or oppressing no one, but protecting, confirming, and venerating the faith and the faithful with all your powers so that what Habakkuk says may be fittingly apply to all of you: *I will stand upon my watch, and fix my foot upon the tower: and I will watch, [to see what will be said to me, and what I may answer to him that reproves me].*[56] In this way the most sacred Isaiah surrounded Sion when he said: *I am upon the watchtower of the Lord, standing continually by day: and I am upon my ward, standing whole nights.*[57] This most prominently applies to the prelates of the Church. *Et complectimini eam, and encompass her*: that is, with heartfelt affection love the Church and all its members. *For he that loves his neighbor has fulfilled the law: love therefore is the fulfilling of the law.*[58] For this reason, Christ said: *A new commandment I give unto you: That you love one another, as I have loved you, that you also love one another.*[59] And again: *By this shall all men know that you are my disciples, if you have love one for another.*[60] *Narrate in turribus eius, tell you in her towers*, that is, announce to the princes and the prelates of the faithful the doctrine of Christ, O preachers of the word of God, so that they might live and might govern others according to the precepts of Christ. According to this Paul said to the tower of the Church, that is, the pastors of others: *Take heed to yourselves, and to the whole flock, wherein the Holy Ghost has placed you bishops, to rule the church of God, which he has purchased with his own blood.*[61] And Peter: *The ancients...I beseech...feed the flock which is among you,...being made a pattern of the flock from the heart.*[62]

47{48}[14] *Set your hearts on her strength; and distribute her houses, that you may relate it in another generation.*

Ponite corda vestra in virtute eius, et distribuite domos eius, ut enarretis in progenie altera.

---

56 Hab. 2:1. The part in brackets replaces Denis's "etc."
57 Is. 21:8.
58 Rom 13:8b, 10b.
59 John 13:34.
60 John 13:35.
61 Acts 20:28.
62 1 Pet. 5:1–3.

450   DENIS THE CARTHUSIAN : *Commentary on the Psalms : Volume 2*

47{48}[15] *For this is God, our God unto eternity, and for ever and ever: he shall rule us for evermore.*

Quoniam hic est Deus, Deus noster in aeternum, et in saeculum saeculi; ipse reget nos in saecula.

47{48}[14] *Ponite corda vestra in virtute eius, set your hearts on her strength*: that is, apply your minds to knowing and to imitating perfection, or the charity of the Church, so that you might be members of the Church that are alive and worthy, and not useless servants, lest you be cast out *into the exterior darkness;*[63] *et distribuite domos eius, and distribute her houses*, that is, put in order those sons of the Church, and assign everyone to his proper office: so that, as the Apostle says, *all things may be done decently, and according to order;* [64] and so everyone may walk *worthy of the vocation* to which he was called.[65] Whence Moses said: *You shall not take nor remove your neighbor's landmark, which your predecessors have set in your possession.*[66] Which can be stated more plainly in this ordinary way: *Pass not beyond the ancient bounds which your fathers have set.*[67] And Dionysius [the Areopagite] often states that the holy angels in no manner presumed to do something other than that which has been pre-determined for them by the divine law. And let us therefore keep custody of our order and let each one do that which is incumbent upon him; let him not occupy himself with those things that do not pertain to him, for in no other way will he be able to have a true and stable peace.

And so do this, O teachers and other leaders, *ut enarretis in progenie altera, that you may relate it in another generation*, that is, since you instruct your successors when they may hearken to your praiseworthy lives and your saving doctrine. And what they ought to say to their posterity is added: **47{48}[15]** *Quoniam hic, for this*, that is, Christ who for us was Incarnate and suffered his Passion, *est Deus, is God* of all things as Creator, *Deus noster, our God*, as our Savior, *in aeternum et in saeculum saeculi, unto eternity, and for ever and ever*, that is, in the present age and in the future without end; *ipse reget nos in saecula, he shall rule for us evermore*, that is, as long as we exist. For Christ rules us through sacred Scripture, by which we are taught what we ought to do; also by the guardian angels, and also by his vicars, the pastors of the Church;

---

63   Matt. 25:30a.
64   1 Cor. 14:40.
65   Eph. 4:1.
66   Deut. 19:14a.
67   Prov. 22:28.

and also by the grace and gifts poured out by the Holy Spirit, by which in all things we know that God is pleased. For this reason the book of Wisdom says: *She conducted the just through the right ways, and showed him the reign of God.*[68] And that which is already stated in this verse is promised to the Church of Christ elsewhere: *Give praise, O daughter of Sion: shout, O Israel: be glad, and rejoice with all your heart, O daughter of Jerusalem. The Lord has taken away your judgment, he has turned away your enemies.... The Lord your God in the midst of you is mighty, he will save: he will rejoice over you with gladness, he will be silent in his love.*[69]

See this Psalm, in the profundity of its plenary sense,[70] how copiously and splendidly it describes the mystery of Christ and the beginnings of the Church.

PRAYER

LORD, WHO ARE GREAT AND EXCEEDINGLY worthy to be praised in all your creatures, in your mercy receive us who are sighing for you; place our hearts in your virtue: and you, our God, who in perfect Trinity live and reign as God, rule us in the everlasting age.

Qui es magnus Dominus et laudabilis nimis in omnibus creaturis tuis, suscipe nos ad te respirantes in misericordia tua; pone corde nostra in virtute tua: et tu, Deus noster, rege nos in aeterna saecula, qui in Trinitate perfecta vivis et regnas Deus.

---

68 Wis. 10:10a.
69 Zeph. 3:14–16.
70 E. N. Denis speaks here of the *sensum plenus*, the full sense, of the Psalm. This is a nod to the so-called *sensus plenior* or "fuller sense" of Scripture. This *sensus plenior*, though tied to the literal text, is "that additional deeper meaning, intended by God, but not clearly intended by the human author, which is seen to exist in the words of a biblical text (or group of texts, or even a whole book) when they are studied in the light of further revelation or development in the understanding of revelation." Raymond E. Brown, *The Sensus Plenior of Sacred Scripture* (Baltimore: St. Mary's University, 1955), 92. "The plenary sense is the prolongation and deepening of that fullness of the literal sense already present in the original wording, and so it brings to the literal sense its authentic value." St. Augustine, *Exposition of the Psalms (1-32)* (Hyde Park, NY: New City Press 2000), 37 (Michael Fiedrowicz, intro.).

Psalm 48

ARTICLE XCI

EXPOSITION OF THE FORTY-EIGHT PSALM:
AUDITE HAEC, OMNES GENTES.
HEAR THESE THINGS, ALL YOU NATIONS.

48{49}[1] *A Psalm of a canticle, for the sons of Korah, on the second day of the week.*
Psalmus cantici. Filiis Core, secunda sabbati.

THE TITLE OF THIS ELUCIDATING PSALM IS this: 48{49}[1] *In finem, filiis Core, psalmus; unto the end, a Psalm for the sons of Korah:* that is, this present Psalm is unto the end, that is, directs us towards Christ and true happiness; it pertains to the *sons of Korah,* that is, the imitators of Christ that have been slain, who following Christ disdain temporal prosperity and seek the true beatitude of the heavenly homeland. For this Psalm speaks against those who, when some adversity occurs to them, they then are scandalized and fall; but when all things are succeeding prosperously for them, they glorify God. Of these persons the Savior says: *When they hear, they receive the word with joy: and these have no roots; for they believe for a while, and in time of temptation, they fall away.*[1] The cause for these persons falling away Christ identifies in another place: *The cares of the world, and the deceitfulness of riches, and the lusts after other things entering* into the heart *choke the word, and it is made fruitless.*[2] And of these things is also written in Malachi: [for therein it is related that] you said:[3] *Vain is he that serves the Lord; and what profit is it that we have kept his ordinances, and that have walked sorrowful before the Lord? Wherefore now we call the arrogant people happy, indeed, they that work wickedness are built up.*[4]

48{49}[2] *Hear these things, all you nations: give ear, all you inhabitants of the world.*

---

1 Luke 8:13.
2 Mark 4:19.
3 E. N. The change to second person is in the original text.
4 Mal. 3:14–15. E. N. I have departed from the Douay-Rheims somewhat.

> Audite haec, omnes gentes; auribus percipite, omnes qui habitatis orbem.

48{49}[3] *All you that are earthborn, and you sons of men: both rich and poor together.*

> Quique terrigenae et filii hominum, simul in unum dives et pauper.

48{49}[4] *My mouth shall speak wisdom: and the meditation of my heart understanding.*

> Os meum loquetur sapientiam, et meditatio cordis mei prudentiam.

48{49}[5] *I will incline my ear to a parable; I will open my proposition on the psaltery.*

> Inclinabo in parabolam aurem meam; aperiam in psalterio propositionem meam.

Against these speaks the Prophet [David], setting forth in advance the reward, so as to render us attentive, and says: 48{49}[2] *Audite haec, hear these things*, which follow, *omnes gentes, all you nations*, for they regard the salvation of all of you, the ignorance of which will not excuse you; *auribus percipite, give ear* [with the ear] of heart and body, *omnes qui habitatis orbem, all you inhabitants of the world*, that is, all mankind. 48{49}[3] *Quique terrigenae et filii hominum; all you that are earthborn, and you sons of men*. It repeats the same thing frequently, so that it might cause us to be fully apprehensive. *Simul in unum dives et pauper, both rich and poor together*, for I will propose to you a common good. 48{49}[4] *Os meum loquetur, my mouth shall speak* in this Psalm *sapientia, wisdom*, that is, news of divine things. For some things of God and of true happiness, which is eternal life, are addressed in this Psalm. *Et meditatio cordis mei, and the meditation of my heart* will speak by the bodily mouth *prudentiam, understanding*, that is, moral knowledge. For other things looked at in this present Psalm relate to moral formation, as will become clear. 48{49}[5] *Inclinabo in parabola aurem meam, I will incline my ear to a parable*: that is, to understand hidden any mystical inspirations and the transmitted writings of other Saints metaphorically (*parabolice*), I will apply my talents. Whence in Ecclesiasticus we have this stated: *The wise men will seek out the wisdom of all the ancients, and will be occupied in the prophets.*[5] *Aperiam in psalterio, I will open . . . on the psaltery*, that is with the present

---

5   Ecclus. 39:1.

Psalm of this book, which is called the Psalter, *propositionem meam, my proposition*, that is, that which I have conceived in my heart. Or [we can understand it this way], *on the psaltery*, that is, with good works, so that I not only say that which will be said with mouth and tongue, but with deed and in truth. It is necessary that life should agree with doctrine. For he who is disdainful of his life is also contemptuous of instruction.

Up until this point is the introduction: and indeed unless that which follows was not exceedingly notable, the Prophet David would by no means have led with such a remarkable prologue.

48{49}[6] *Why shall I fear in the evil day? The iniquity of my heel shall encompass me.*

Cur timebo in die mala? Iniquitas calcanei mei circumdabit me.

Beginning the narration, he proposes a question: **48{49}[6]** *Cur timebo in die mala? Why shall I fear in the evil day?* That is, what is it that can be a cause for fear for me in the day of judgment? Or why will I then fear if I do not now do penance? And this question is proposed in the person of all people, most especially of sinners. And he responds: *Iniquitas calcanei mei; the iniquity of my heel*, that is, my deeds (for by heel or foot is denoted one's path or way of life or deeds), *circumdabit me, shall encompass me*, that is, indeed, they will be cast before me, and they will surround me. For in the day of judgment man will be accused by the devil, by the angels, and by his own conscience: indeed also by the Judge himself, in the manner that the Lord said through Malachi: *I will come to you in judgment, and will be a speedy witness against sorcerers, and adulterers, ... and them that deceive and oppress the poor, and have not feared me.*[6] And Isaiah said: *Behold the name of the Lord comes from afar, his wrath burns, and is heavy to bear: his lips are filled with indignation, and his tongue as a devouring fire. His breath as a torrent overflowing even to the midst of the neck, to destroy the nations unto nothing.*[7] This therefore is the cause of fearing the future judgment, for the iniquity of our deeds will then encompass us. For which reason in Revelation it says: *Their works follow them.*[8] And the Savior says: *Amen I say to you; but except you do penance, you shall all likewise perish.*[9] The day

---

6 Mal. 3:5. Denis has replaced the hireling in his wages, the widows, the fatherless, and the stranger with the all-inclusive word *pauperem*, poor.
7 Is. 30:27–28a.
8 Rev. 14:13b.
9 Luke 13:5.

of judgment is called evil, not from the malice of fault, since it will be a day of most just recompense, the most judicious discrimination, and the most strict examination; but from the malice of punishment, because there will be much evil of punishment in it, in the manner that Zephaniah attests: *That day is a day of wrath, a day of tribulation and distress, a day of calamity and misery, a day of darkness and obscurity, a day of clouds and whirlwinds, a day of the trumpet and alarm.*[10] See how horrid and most horrible is that day, whose horror the Prophet took such care to explain with so many names.

48{49}[7] *They that trust in their own strength, and glory in the multitude of their riches.*

Qui confidunt in virtute sua, et in multitudine divitiarum suarum gloriantur.

48{49}[7] *Qui confidunt in virtute sua*, they that trust in their own strength, that is, who presume to be able to save themselves by their own strength, and place their hope in worldly, natural, or bodily powers, and not in the mercy and the grace of the Creator, *et in multitudine divitiarum suarum gloriantur*, and glory in the multitude of their riches, that is, inordinately rejoicing in their possessions or in their own merits and righteousness, not returning thanks to the giver of all things, but delighting in themselves as if they had not received anything and spurning others. Let such as these fear, for in the evil day they will not have the strength to avoid that which follows next.

48{49}[8] *No brother can redeem, nor shall man redeem: he shall not give to God his ransom.*

Frater non redimit, redimet homo: non dabit Deo placationem suam.

48{49}[9] *Nor the price of the redemption of his soul: and shall labor forever.*

Et pretium redemptionis animae suae. Et laborabit in aeternum.

48{49}[10] *And shall still live unto the end.*

Et vivet adhuc in finem.

---

10   Zeph. 1:15–16a.

48{49}[8] *Frater non redimit, no brother can redeem,* that is, no person related by blood or other kinsman will be able to deliver another in the day of judgment, according to that which is protested by the Lord in Ezechiel: *When a land shall sin against me,... I will destroy man and beast out of it. And if these three men, Noah, Daniel, and Job shall be in it, they shall deliver their own souls by their justice, ...but they shall deliver neither sons nor daughters.*[11] And again, the same Prophet says: *The justice of the just shall be upon him, and the wickedness of the wicked shall be upon him.*[12] Since, therefore it is so, *Redimet homo? Shall man redeem?* It asks a question, so it should be understood in this sense: If a kinsman or brother will not be able to redeem a sinner, much less will a mere man — that is, anyone who is a stranger, or only remotely or distantly related — be able to redeem another. Whence also elsewhere the Lord said: *If Moses and Samuel shall stand before me, my soul is not towards this people.*[13] *Non dabit Deo placationem suam, he shall not give to God his ransom*: that is, in the day of judgment the sinner will not be able to placate God, for after death is clearly not the place for prayers or obtaining merit, nor is repentance fruitful then, according to that which Christ intimated of the foolish virgins who were late in coming and were saying, *Lord, Lord, open to us,* to which he responded, *Amen I say to you, I know you not.*[14] Indeed, this life is the way to future life: therefore the means of meriting and demeriting ceases with this finite

---

11 Ez. 14:13–14, 16a. In his *Commentary on Ezechiel,* Denis, relying on St. Jerome, explains why the triumvirate of Noah, Daniel, and Job are selected: "Because Noah with his prayers was not able to prevent the flood, and Daniel also was unable by his tears to mitigate the captivity of the Jews, and Job was unable to redeem from death his sons and daughters, for whom he daily sacrificed." Doctoris Ecstatici D. Dionysii Cartusiani, *Opera Omnia,* Vol. 9 (Montreuil: 1900), 473. If these men most worthy to pray for those less worthy were unsuccessful in their prayers, then it follows that us lesser mortals can redeem no brother.
12 Ez. 18:20b.
13 Jer. 15:1a. E. N. In his *Commentary on Jeremiah,* Denis explains the choice of Moses and Samuel. They were chosen "because we read in the Old Testament these two to have entreated for their adversaries. Indeed, one assailed by his people to stone him (Ex. 17:4), yet he also prayed 'forgive them this trespass.' (Ex.32:31). The other was driven away from ruling (1 Sam. 8:5), and nevertheless said: 'far from me be this sin against the Lord, that I should cease to pray for you.' (1 Sam. 12:23)." Relying on St. Jerome, Denis concludes: "We read of these of holding back the anger of God against the people, and to avert an already impending judgment." Doctoris Ecstatici D. Dionysii Cartusiani, *Opera Omnia,* Vol. 9 (Montreuil: 1900), 135–36. So Jeremiah is saying that even if these two great intercessors were present, God will not change his judgment.
14 Matt. 25:11b, 12b.

life, and so it leads unto to the other life; but by death man reaches the term of movement.[15] Whence the Damascene:[16] *What to the angel is a fall*, he says, *is to men death*. **48{49}[9]** *Et pretium redemptionis animae suae, nor the price of the redemption of his soul*: that is, the sinner after death is unable to bring forth satisfaction to rescue his soul from the owed punishment.

See how terrible God is after death, who before death awaits so mercifully, as Isaiah says: *Therefore the Lord waits that he may have mercy on you*.[17] No one of us should trust in his virtue, no one in his wisdom, no one should glory in his merits, lest he become that which the prophet Jeremiah said: *Your arrogance and the pride of your heart have deceived you*.[18] Also that of Isaiah: *Woe to you that are wise in your own eyes*,[19] who again says: *Your wisdom and your knowledge, this has deceived you*.[20] But also of those glorying in spiritual riches, John says in Revelation: *Because you say: I am rich, . . . and have need of nothing: and know not that you are wretched, and miserable, and poor, and blind, and naked*.[21] But with regard to the rich, to those glorying in bodily riches, it is said in Luke: *Woe to you that are rich: for you have your consolation*.[22]

Thereafter he addresses the punishment of the evil—who will be damned in the final judgment. *Et laborabit in aeternum, and he shall labor forever*: that is, the ungodly will be eternally afflicted, and they will be tormented with the most dreadful punishments, in the manner that is written: *He shall be tormented with fire and brimstone in the sight of the holy angels . . . ; and the smoke of their torments shall ascend up for ever and*

---

15   E. N. Denis uses the words *in termino motus*, "at the term of movement," which means that the soul has reached the term or end of being able to change; it is fixed in the state it was in at the time of death.

16   E. N. St. John of Damascus. See footnote 32-4. Denis states: *quod angelo est casus, hoc hominibus est mors*, meaning that the sin of the wicked angels caused their irreversible and instant fall (sin and fall were instantaneous); that irreversible fall for men is not at sin, but at death, since before death man can repent; but if he dies in unrepentant mortal sin (if he does not die in a state of sanctifying grace), a man's death, like an angel's fall, results in instantaneous and irreversible damnation. The reference is to John of Damascus's *De Fide Orthodoxa*, II, 4: *Post lapsum enim nulla ipsis poenitentia est, uti nec hominibus post mortem*. "After the fall there is no possibility [to the angels] of repentance for them, just as after death there is none for men." PG 94, 877–78.

17   Is. 30:18a.
18   Jer. 49:16a.
19   Is. 5:21a.
20   Is. 47:10a.
21   Rev. 3:17.
22   Luke 6:24.

ever: neither have they rest day nor night.²³ 48{49}[10] *Et vivet adhuc in finem*, and shall still live unto the end, that is, his natural life will never be done away with, although he will long for it to be done away, but he will eternally live in a state of nature so that he may unceasingly persevere in punishment. For this reason John says: *In those days men shall seek death, and shall not find it: and they shall desire to die, and death shall fly from them.*²⁴ And this is not discordant with that which we read elsewhere: *Death shall be chosen rather than life by all that shall remain of this wicked kindred.*²⁵ For although according to the philosophers all being naturally desires to be, and all living things naturally have a desire to live, yet the reprobate in hell will desire not to be and not to live: for the natural appetite arising from the sensitive or intellective appetite will be overcome by the vehemence of misery. But that which has already been said of the sinner, *he shall labor forever and shall still live unto the end*, accords to that which is written in Daniel regarding the reprobate, *They shall awake from the dust . . . unto reproach, to see it always.*²⁶ O how great the misery, and how hateful will it be, always to be, and never to be well, eternally to remain, and for no other reason except to be eternally compelled to feel torments! Whence, because of such an unhappy state so replete with punishment, the evil in hell unceasingly blaspheme the true and holy God, as we read in Revelation, *They gnawed their tongues for pain, and they blasphemed the God of heaven, because of their pains and wounds.*²⁷

48{49}[11] He shall not see destruction, when he shall see the wise dying: the senseless and the fool shall perish together: And they shall leave their riches to strangers.

Non videbit interitum, cum viderit sapientes morientes. Simul insipiens et stultus peribunt; et relinquent alienis divitias suas.

48{49}[12] And their sepulchers shall be their houses forever. Their dwelling places to all generations: they have called their lands by their names.

Et sepulchra eorum domus illorum in aeternum, tabernacula eorum in progenie et progenie; vocaverunt nomina sua in terris suis.

---

23 Rev. 14:10-11a.
24 Rev. 9:6.
25 Jer. 8:3a.
26 Dan. 12:2.
27 Rev. 16:10b-11.

48{49}[11] *Non videbit interitum, he shall not see destruction*, that is, the sinner will not reflect upon the fact that after temporal death he is menaced by the possibility of being in eternal death with the wicked, *cum viderit sapientes, when he shall the wise*, that is, the informed and virtuous men, *morientes, dying* bodily, just like all others also die. For many of those that appear, as relates to the present bodily state, good and evil, wise and foolish, will equally pass through death, supposing that there is no other life but the present one. Of these persons [and their reasoning] we find written in the book of Wisdom: *No man has been known to have returned from hell. For we are born of nothing, and after this we shall be as if we had not been.*[28] *Come therefore, and let us enjoy the good things that are [present, and let us speedily use the creatures as in youth.]*[29] And elsewhere: *Let us eat and drink; for tomorrow we shall die.*[30]

Simul insipiens, the senseless... together, that is, they not knowing divine things, but living diabolically, *et stultus, and the fool*, that is, he neither knowing nor doing good deeds, *peribunt, shall perish*, with perpetual death, as the Apostle [Paul] says: *He who knows not, shall not be known.*[31] *Et relinquent alienis divitias suas, and they shall leave their riches to strangers*, that is, the senseless and the fool will distribute their possessions to strangers. Whence of the sinners mentioned above is said: *He stores up: and he knows not for whom he shall gather these things.*[32]

48{49}[12] *Et sepulcra eorum, domus illorum in aeternum; and their sepulchers shall be their houses forever*: that is, the ungodly in accordance with their lack of belief have reckoned that they would never rise again from the earth, but they would be forgotten deep within the earth, because they do not believe that which we read in Daniel: *Those that sleep in the dust of the earth, shall awake;*[33] and that which holy Job confesses, *I know that my Redeemer lives, and in the last day I shall rise out of the earth.*[34] *Tabernacula eorum in progenie et progenie, their dwelling places to all generations*: that is, the houses built by the ungodly remain for their succeeding generations. For they built for themselves sometimes great palaces in order that they might remain in the memories of men for as long as those structures last. For because they do not hold there

---

28   Wis. 2:1b–2a.
29   Wis. 2:6. I have added the part in brackets referred to by Denis by "etc."
30   Is. 22:13b.
31   1 Cor. 14:38a.
32   Ps. 37:7b.
33   Dan. 12:2a. The verse continues: *some unto life everlasting, and others unto reproach, to see it always.*
34   Job 19:25.

to be a future life after this one, they desire at least to remain in the memories of men. And so is added, *vocaverunt nomina sua in terris suis, they have called their lands by their names*, that is, they have labored to leave to posterity some memorial so that they do not consign themselves to oblivion. Whence in Genesis the sons of men said: *Come, let us make a city and a tower, the top whereof may reach to heaven: and let us make our name famous through all the earth.*[35]

48{49}[13] *And man when he was in honor did not understand; he is compared to senseless beasts, and is become like to them.*

Et homo, cum in honore esset, non intellexit. Comparatus est iumentis insipientibus, et similis factus est illis.

48{49}[13] *Et homo cum in honore esset, non intellexit; and man when he was in honor did not understand*: that is, the sinner since he is made in the image of his Creator does not give heed to his own dignity, or live rationally, nor desire heavenly and angelic beatitude, but he immerses himself in temporal and carnal things, not allowing reason to prevail over his passions. And so *comparatus est iumentis insipientibus, he is compared to senseless beasts,* he has become *like the horse and the mule, who have no understanding,*[36] *et similis factus es illis, and is become like to them,* following the impetus of concupiscence and the impulse of vices, and neither the command of reason nor the censor of divine law. Of such men the Lord says in Genesis: *My spirit shall not remain in man forever, because he is flesh.*[37] For he does not fulfill that which the Lord said: *The lust thereof shall be under you, and you shall have dominion over it.*[38] O how many are the prelates and teachers today, and indeed many others, who do not understand their own honor, but act most dishonestly before God and live repulsively and carnally before God, and are ungrateful and rebellious to God!

48{49}[14] *This way of theirs is a stumbling block to them: and afterwards they shall delight in their mouth.*

Haec via illorum scandalum ipsis; et postea in ore suo complacebunt.

---

35 Gen. 11:4.
36 Ps. 31:9a.
37 Gen. 6:3a.
38 Gen. 4:7b.

48{49}[15] *They are laid in hell like sheep: death shall feed upon them. And the just shall have dominion over them in the morning; and their help shall decay in hell from their glory.*

Sicut oves in inferno positi sunt: mors depascet eos. Et dominabuntur eorum iusti in matutino; et auxilium eorum veterascet in inferno a gloria eorum.

48{49}[14] *Haec via illorum, this way of theirs,* that is, this just mentioned conceit and evil manner of living, is the way or the operation of the ungodly, *scandalum ipsis, is a stumbling block,* that is, leading them to fall and to eternal death. For it is the occasion of ruin and damnation to those in such a life. Whence Solomon said: *The way of the wicked is darksome: they know not where they fall.*[39] *Et postea in ore suo complacebunt, and afterwards they shall delight in their mouth*: that is, after they have amassed riches and have dealt themselves temporal goods, they will be pleased among themselves, mutually blessing, praising, and flattering themselves: just like it is said in an earlier Psalm, *For the sinner is praised in the desires of his soul;*[40] and in a later one, *They have called the people happy, that have these things.*[41] For these glory when *they have done evil, and rejoice in most wicked things.*[42] And yet they are most miserable, and they deceive each other, as the Lord gives witness to in Isaiah: *O my people, they that call you blessed, the same deceive you, and destroy the way of your steps.*[43] **48{49}[15]** *Sicut oves in inferno positi sunt, they are laid in hell like sheep*: that is, in the manner that sheep suddenly and improvidently are led to death and slain, so evil men will be quickly and unexpectedly condemned. *For when* (as Paul says) *they shall say peace and security; then shall sudden destruction come upon them.*[44] For which reason Christ exhorts: *Watch you, therefore, for you know not when the lord of the house comes: in the evening, or at midnight, or at the cockcrowing, or in the morning, lest coming all of a sudden, he find you sleeping.*[45] And, *Watch you, therefore, praying at all times, that you may be accounted worthy to escape all these things that are to come, and to stand before the Son of man.*[46] *Mors depascet eos, death shall feed upon them*: that is, that

---

39 Prov. 4:19.
40 Ps. 9:24[10:3].
41 Ps. 143:15a.
42 Prov. 2:14.
43 Is. 3:12b.
44 1 Thess. 5:3a.
45 Mark 13:35–36.
46 Luke 21:36.

pain of hell, which is more bitter than death, will be the food of the impious and the damned: so just like eating food fills one up, so they will be filled with perpetual punishments; and as through food a soul is preserved in being, so infernal punishments will keep the unjust in being, always tormenting them, yet never consuming them. Whence the Lord says in Jeremiah: *Behold I will feed them with wormwood, and will give them gall to drink.*[47]

Et dominabuntur eorum iusti in matutino, and the just shall have dominion over them in the morning: that is, the elect in the blessed resurrection shall prevail over the unjust. For *they shall stand with great constancy against those;*[48] and, the Saints *shall judge nations, and rule over people.*[49] For at that time the wicked will in no way be able to oppose the Saints, nor will they be able to diminish their happiness, nor to ascend to them, or to look upon their glory. But the just, if it pleases them, will be able to descend to the damned, to perceive their misery, and most justly to revile them.[50] *Et auxilium eorum veterascet in inferno a gloria eorum, and their help shall decay in hell from their glory*: that is, the fortitude and space and all relief which the ungodly have in the present life in fleeting and perishable things will entirely perish, and, just like an old tattered rag they will disappear in hell, and they will be disabused from the presumption and vain joy which they had in this world: because at that point in time nothing will be of any use to them, as the book of Wisdom has them complaining: *What has pride profited us? Or what advantage has the boasting of riches brought us? All those things are passed away like a shadow.*[51] And this is what the Lord most terribly says to sinners through Ezechiel: *Behold I have clapped my hands at your evils. Shall your heart endure, or shall your hands prevail ill the days which will bring upon you? And I will gather you together and will burn you in the fire of my wrath.*[52]

---

47 Jer. 23:15a.
48 Wis. 5:1a.
49 Wis. 3:8a.
50 E. N. Denis uses the verb *insultare*, to insult or revile, and so goes beyond the supplement to the *Summa*, which says that the blessed in glory will have no pity on the damned. *[B]eati qui erunt in gloria nullam compassionem ad damnatos habebunt.* ST, IIIa (Supp.), q. 94, art. 2, co. The blessed are allowed to see the sufferings of the damned, so that the "beatitude of the saints may be more pleasing to them, and so that they may render greater thanks to God for it." *Id.* q. 94, art. 1, co.
51 Wis. 5:8–9a.
52 Ez. 22:13a, 14a, 21a.

48{49}[16] *But God will redeem my soul from the hand of hell, when he shall receive me.*

Verumtamen Deus redimet animam meam de manu inferi, cum acceperit me.

48{49}[16] *Verumtamen Deus redimet animam meam de manu inferi, but God will redeem my soul from the hand of hell,* that is, from the cause and the deservingness of falling into the punishments of hell, that is, from mortal sin and servitude to the devil, *cum acceperit me, when he shall receive me,* that is, when he will deal graciously and mercifully with me, forgetting vices and infusing grace. Or [we can understand it thus]: He *will redeem... from the hand of hell,* that is, from all the power of the devil and the punishments of hell, when he will receive me into an immortal and impassible state, namely, in the day of judgment, when he will say to the just: *Come you blessed of my Father.*[53]

48{49}[17] *Be not afraid, when a man shall be made rich, and when the glory of his house shall be increased.*

Ne timueris cum dives factus fuerit homo, et cum multiplicata fuerit gloria domus eius.

48{49}[18] *For when he shall die he shall take nothing away; nor shall his glory descend with him.*

Quoniam, cum interierit, non sumet omnia, neque descendet cum eo gloria eius.

48{49}[17] *Ne timueris, be not afraid,* with a human and turbulent fear, *cum dives factus fuerit homo, when a man shall be made rich,* in temporal and sensible goods, *et cum multiplicat fuerit gloria domus eius, and when the glory of his house shall be increased,* that is, fame, honor, delight, strength, prosperity, and such similar things, which are often conceded to the reprobate in this world. **48{49}[18]** *Quoniam cum interierit, non sumet omnia, for when he shall die, he shall take nothing,* that is, none of those things will he be able to take with him; *neque descendet, nor descend with him* to the punishments of hell, *cum eo, with him* already dead and judged, *gloria eius, his glory,* that is, his temporal and mundane prosperity. Whence the Apostle [Paul] says: *For we brought nothing into this world: and certainly we can carry nothing out.*[54] And holy Job says:

---

53 Matt. 25:34b.
54 1 Tim. 6:7.

The rich man when he shall sleep shall take away nothing with him: he shall open his eyes and find nothing; poverty like water shall take hold of him.[55] For this reason Solomon commands: *Whatsoever your hand is able to do, do it earnestly: for neither work, nor reason, nor wisdom, nor knowledge shall be in hell, where you are hastening.*[56] And again: *When the wicked man is dead, there shall be no hope any more.*[57]

48{49}[19] *For in his lifetime his soul will be blessed: and he will praise you when you shall do well to him.*

Quia anima eius in vita ipsius benedicetur; confitebitur tibi cum benefeceris ei.

48{49}[19] *Quia anima eius in vita ipsius benedicetur*, *for in his lifetime his soul will be blessed*: that is, therefore you ought to fear when a man has been made rich, for a soul is not blessed by God because of riches, but because of his justice, which, if you do not possesses, you are not divinely blessed. Or [we can understand it in this manner]: *In his lifetime his soul will be blessed*, that is, the sinner in the present life is blessed and praised in the present life by flatterers and vain men, as it was said in an earlier Psalm, *For the sinner is praised in the desires of his soul: and the unjust man is blessed.*[58] [In understanding this verse,] we can also take the part for the whole, namely, the soul for the whole man. *Confitebitur tibi*, *and he will praise you*, that is, to give you thanks, O Lord, this he will do, and he will praise you, *cum benefeceris ei, when you shall do well to him*, that is, when all things occur at his nod, when he does not hold back adversity, when he prospers temporally. But is there any sin to confess to the Lord in prosperity? Doesn't the Apostle [Paul] say, *Thanks be to God for his unspeakable gift?*[59] And again: *Blessed be God . . . who comforts us.*[60] And Isaiah: *I will remember the tender mercies of the Lord, the praise of the Lord for all the things that the Lord has bestowed upon us.*[61] Why is it, therefore, that the just and pleasing deeds of men are appropriated now by the impious, except that the just man both in prosperity and adversity praises the Lord, but the wicked man only in prosperity? And, therefore, the praise or the giving thanks of a wicked man does not arise

---

55 Job 27:19–20a.
56 Eccl. 9:10.
57 Prov. 11:7.
58 Ps. 9:24[10:3].
59 2 Cor. 9:15.
60 1 Cor. 1:3–4a.
61 Is. 63:7a.

from divine charity, but out of self-love or natural love, namely, because naturally man loves himself. For it is natural to praise and to love one's benefactor. If, however, a man were to love himself with a love ordained to God, then in all events he will give thanks to the divine dispensation, and he will glory in adversity, inasmuch as through it he is cleansed of sin, and joined to grace, conformed to Christ, and led to eternal happiness. Therefore, we remain fixed in the Lord whatever befalls us. If he withdraws spiritual consolation, if he does not increase graces in accordance with our desires, if temptations oppress and are multiplied, our hope in the Lord will remain unmoved, and we do that which is in us, without ceasing, sighing, calling upon, and beseeching God.

48{49}[20] *He shall go in to the generations of his fathers: and he shall never see light.*

Introibit usque in progenies patrum suorum; et usque in aeternum non videbit lumen.

48{49}[20] *Introibit usque in progenies patrum suorum; he shall go in to the generations of his fathers*: that is, the sinner when he dies will be gathered together with the reprobate in hell, who are his fathers because he has followed their works. For generations are of two kinds: one of the good and another of the wicked. And so in the manner that is frequently found in sacred Scripture, the just are said to be gathered together into the fathers, or into their people, that is, to be added to the society of the elect; but the evil, when they die, they are added to the generation or the society of the damned. Indeed, it is precisely written: Israel *came to mount Hor*, and the Lord said to Moses: *Let Aaron go to his people.*[62] *Usque in aeternum non videbit lumen, and he shall never see light*, that is, he will never see the glory of the blessed in heaven, which is consistent with this, *Let the wicked be removed lest they see the glory of God.*[63] And Job of such men says: *Let mercy forget him: may worms be his sweetness.*[64] *God has given him a place for penance, and he abuses it unto pride.*[65] For in hell there is no redemption,[66] but weeping and

---

62 E. N. Denis is using the instance of Aaron "going to his people" in Numbers 20:22-24, which is a clear euphemism for his death, as an instance of this Scriptural manner of speaking to support his interpretation of Ps. 48:20.
63 Is. 26:10b (LXX). This departs from the Sixto-Clementine Vulgate.
64 Job 24:20a.
65 Job 24:23a.
66 This terse statement is found in the Catholic Office of the Dead (third Nocturn of Matins): *Peccantem me quotidie, et non poenitentem, timor mortis conturbat me. Quia*

gnashing of teeth,[67] and palpable darkness;[68] never will the condemned be able to rise up to the light of grace and the brightness of glory.

48{49}[21] *Man when he was in honor did not understand: he has been compared to senseless beasts, and made like to them.*

Homo, cum in honore esset, non intellexit. Comparatus est iumentis insipientibus, et similis factus est illis.

48{49}[21] *Homo cum in honor esset, non intellexit. Comparatus est iumentis insipientibus, et similis factus est illis; man when he was in honor did not understand: he has been compared to senseless beasts, and made like to them.* This verse, which we see has already been satisfactorily explained,[69] is repeated because of the beauty and utility of its sentiment.

See how this Psalm so beautifully reproves temporal prosperity and glory and demonstrates the future torments of the ungodly, and how beautifully it expresses the ignobility and blindness of the sinning soul, and how it unfolds the future dominion of the just. Let us endeavor, therefore, to despise all temporal things, to cast off the flowery world[70] with all of its delights and vanities, for *the world passes away and the concupiscence thereof.*[71] And, as Isaiah asserts, *All flesh is grass, and all the glory thereof as the flower of the field; the grass is withered, and the flower is fallen.*[72] And let us prepare ourselves unceasingly for the happiness of death, which can be fearlessly expected, and can be received with joy by him who loves nothing carnal, worldly, or transitory, but who

---

in inferno nulla est redemptio, miserere mei, Deus, et salva me. "Sinning daily, and not repenting, the fear of death disturbs me. For in hell there is no redemption, have mercy on me, O God, and save me."

67 Matt. 8:12; 13:42, 50; 22:13, etc.

68 E. N. *palpabiles tenebrae*, "touchable/palpable darkness," a darkness so thick one can feel it. This is one of the so-called "nine torments of hell," along with fire (*ignis*), intolerable cold (*intolerabile frigus*), undying worms (*vermes immortales*), intolerable stench (*fetor intolerabilis*), cutting whips (*flagra caedentium*), palpable darkness (*tenebrae palpabiles*), the confusion (or shame) of sins (*confusio peccatorum*), horrible sight of the devils (*horribilis visio deamonum*), and fiery chains (*ignea vincula*).

69 E. N. See Ps. 48:13.

70 L. *Florentem mundum*, the "flowery world," is an expression found in Pope St. Gregory the Great's sermon regarding the martyrs of Campagna at the Church of Sts. Nereus and Achilles: *Sancti isti ad quorum tumbam consistimus, florentem mundum mentis despectu calcaverunt.* "These saints upon whose tomb we stand trampled upon the flowery world with disdain of mind." *Hom. in Ev.* 28, 3, PL 76, 1212.

71 1 John 2:17a.

72 Is. 40:6b–7a.

with the entirety of his affection seeks heavenly things, and supremely desires the holy and blessed God, the most sweet fountain of all holy happiness, efficaciously thinking that which the most wise Solomon did: *Man knows not his own end: but as fishes are taken with the hook, and as birds are caught with the snare, so men are taken in the evil time, when it shall suddenly come upon them.*[73]

PRAYER

CHRIST, O MERCIFUL REDEEMER, WHO for the salvation of the world hung innocent on the wood of the Cross, and by dying called back the people of your saints to the rule of heaven: we beseech you, by the operations of your mercy through which you will accept us, redeem our souls from the hand of hell, and cause them to receive a share of the blessed resurrection.

Pie redemptor Christe, qui pro salute mundi in ligno crucis innocens pependisti, et moriendo populum Sanctorum ad imperium revocasti caelorum: tuae, quaesumus, miserationis operatione, quum nos acceperis, animas nostras de manu inferi redime, atque eas partem beatae resurrectionis fac obtinere.

---

73 Eccl. 9:12.

Psalm 49

ARTICLE XCII

EXPOSITION OF THE FORTY-NINTH PSALM: DEUS DEORUM DOMINUS LOCUTUS EST. THE GOD OF GODS, THE LORD HAS SPOKEN.

49{50}[1] *A Psalm for Asaph. The God of gods, the Lord has spoken: and he has called the earth. From the rising of the sun, to the going down thereof.*

Psalmus Asaph. Deus deorum, Dominus, locutus est, et vocavit terram a solis ortu usque ad occasum.

THE TITLE OF THIS PRESENT PSALM IS BRIEF, namely: **49{50}[1]** *Psalmus Asaph, a Psalm for Asaph.* Now, according to Jerome and Hebrew teachers, Asaph was a prophet and the author of this Psalm. But according to Augustine, David is the author of this Psalm, and he ascribed it to Asaph as a cantor, because he was one of the principal cantors assigned to the temple by David.[1] Also, according to Cassiodorus, Asaph is placed here on the title because of the interpretation given his name: for its interpretation is congregation. And this Psalm deals with the congregation of the faithful. And so this Psalm is full of the mystery of Christ, speaking of the institution of the new law and the cessation of the Old Testament, and the two comings of Christ, and many other things.

And therefore the Prophet says: *Deus deorum Dominus, the God of gods, the Lord,* that is Christ, the only-Begotten of God, the true God of the angels, and of men, the Lord of the saints, *locutus est, has spoken* to us in his very self through assumed flesh, as the Apostle [Paul] says: *In these days has spoken to us by his Son.*[2] In the manner that the Son of God was promised by Isaiah: *Therefore my people shall know my name in that day: for I myself that spoke, behold I am here.*[3] Now the holy angels and virtuous men are called gods because they participate in the divine perfection in a most excellent way, and of such gods Moses says: *You shall not speak ill of the gods.*[4] And the Savior said, *He called them gods to*

---

1 1 Chr. 25:1-2.
2 Heb. 1:2a.
3 Is. 52:6.
4 Ex. 22:28a.

*whom the word of God was spoken.*⁵ *Et vocavit terram, and he has called the earth,* that is, Christ by himself and through his disciples called men to the faith and to his worship. And this, *a solis ortu usque ad occasum; from the rising of the sun, to the going down thereof,* that is, *their sound went forth to all the parts of the earth.*⁶ And Christ elsewhere said: *Be converted to me, and you shall be saved, all you ends of the earth.*⁷ And: *Going therefore, teach you all nations; baptizing them in the name of the Father, and of the Son, and of the Holy Spirit.*⁸ Which elsewhere is stated more clearly: *Go into the whole world, and preach the gospel to every creature.*⁹

49{50}[2] *Out of Sion the loveliness of his beauty.*

Ex Sion species decoris eius.

49{50}[2] *Ex Sion specie decoris eius, out of Sion the loveliness of his beauty:* that is, the first beauty and brightness of the evangelical law or of the human nature of Christ and his divinity was preached and was made public out of Mount Sion and the holy city of Jerusalem. For already in the preceding Psalms explanations have been given regarding how the evangelical law was instituted by Christ in the day of the Last Supper and Pentecost, or other particular times, in Mount Sion; and how first the Resurrection and the Gospel were preached in Jerusalem, in the way that was predicted by Isaiah, *The law shall come forth from Sion, and the word of the Lord from Jerusalem.*¹⁰ And from that giving and institution of the new law, Jeremiah most openly prophesized: *Behold,* he says, *the days shall come, says the Lord, and I will make a new covenant with the house of Israel, and with the house of Juda; and I will write my laws in their heart.*¹¹

49{50}[3] *God shall come manifestly: our God shall come, and shall not keep silence. A fire shall burn before him: and a mighty tempest shall be round about him.*

Deus manifeste veniet; Deus noster, et non silebit. Ignis in conspectu eius exardescet; et in circuitu eius tempestas valida.

---

5   John 10:35a. On men as "gods," and the notion of *theosis* or divinization, *see* footnote 46-48.
6   Ps. 18:5a.
7   Is. 45:22a.
8   Matt. 28:19.
9   Mark 16:15.
10 Is. 2:3b.
11 Jer. 31:31, 33b.

49{50}[3] *Deus manifeste veniet, God shall come manifestly.* Here the Prophet touches upon the second coming of Christ, which will be in majesty and glory, as the first one was in humility and punishment. For because Christ first came so as to be judged and to suffer, it was fitting that his first coming should in some way be hidden: *for if they had known it, they would never have crucified the Lord of glory.*[12] But because the second coming of Christ is so that the world might be judged, therefore for that very reason the second will be manifest to all. This is the reason why Christ said to the Jews: *Hereafter you shall see the Son of man sitting on the right hand of the power of God, and coming in the clouds of heaven*[13] *with great power and majesty.*[14] And: *For as the lightning that flashing from under heaven shines unto the parts that are under heaven, so shall the Son of man be in his day.*[15] *Deus noster,* our God, namely, Jesus Christ, who is true God, eternal, immeasurable, and supersubstantial; *et no silebit, and shall not keep silence* in the second coming as in the first. For in the second coming he will scrutinize all things, he will carry out judgment, and he will inflict punishment. But in the first coming he did not carry himself so, according to that which is asserted in the Gospel: *God sent not his Son into the world, to judge the world, but that the world may be saved by him.*[16] And this is what he himself said through Isaiah: *I have always held my peace, I have I kept silence, I have been patient, I will speak now as a woman in labor: I will destroy, and swallow up at once.*[17] And through Amos: *Behold, I will screak under you as a wain screaks that is laden with hay; and flight shall perish from the swift, and the valiant shall not possess his strength, neither shall the strong save his life.*[18]

Ignis in conspectus eius exardescet, a fire shall burn before him. As first the world perished through flood, so will it at the last days perish by the fire of conflagration which will consume the earth and sea, will cleanse the air, and will set afire sinners during the judgment and at the same time roll out the rendered sentence; and he who possesses heat and smoke will descend into hell to the degree he has them, but the one who is fixed

---

12   1 Cor. 2:8b.
13   Matt. 26:64b.
14   Luke 21:27b.
15   Luke 17:24. I have replaced the Douay-Rheims's "lightening" with "flashing" for the Latin *coruscans.*
16   John 3:17.
17   Is. 42:14.
18   Amos 2:13–14. E. N. I did not have the heart to change this quaint translation as found in the Douay-Rheims: it means I will squeak under you as a wagon squeaks that is laden with hay.

in brightness and light will ascend to the heights.[19] According to Basil,[20] it is believed also that the fire of conflagration will ascend as high as the waters of the flood, namely fifteen cubits above all the mountains.[21] And of this fire of which it now speaks, it says a fire shall burn *before him*. For it will precede the descent of Christ and will last even until the end of the judgment.[22] *Et in circuitu eius, round about him,* namely, the judgment of Christ, will be *tempestas valida, a mighty tempest,* that is, a prodigious noise, a vehement lamentation, bewailing, and weeping. For the ungodly, seeing the coming and scattering Judge, will be troubled with a horrible fear, saying: *Mountains: cover us; and to the hills: fall upon us,*[23] *and hide us from the face of him that sits upon the throne and from the wrath of the Lamb.*[24] Of that horrible tempest of that day, we find written in Joel: *Let all the inhabitants of the land tremble: because the day of the Lord comes, ... a day of darkness ... the like to it has not been seen from the beginning, nor shall be after it ... Before the face thereof a devouring fire, and behind it a burning flame.*[25] *All faces shall be made like a kettle.*[26] *At their presence the earth has trembled, the heavens are moved: the sun and moon are darkened, and the stars have withdrawn their shining.*[27]

---

19 "In the Apostolic writings we are told that the end of the world will be brought about through a general conflagration, which, however, will not annihilate the present creation, but will change its form and appearance (2 Peter 3:10–13; cf. 1 Thessalonians 5:2; Apocalypse 3:3, and 16:15)." McHugh, John, *The Catholic Encyclopedia.* Vol. 8. (New York: Robert Appleton Company, 1910) (s.v. "General Judgment").
20 E. N. St. Basil the Great (*ca.* 330–379 AD). One of the Cappadocian Fathers, Basil was bishop of Caesarea. Because he drafted some monastic rules, he is known as the Father of Eastern Monasticism. Moreover, because of his great sanctity and the quality of his writings, St. Basil is also regarded as a Doctor of the Church.
21 Gen. 7:20. On the notion of the fires of conflagration being fifteen cubits higher than the mountains covered by the flood waters, *see* ST III (Supp.), q. 74, art. 4, s.c. where St. Thomas finds the authority for this notion by referencing a gloss on 2 Thess. 1:8.
22 E. N. *See* ST IIIa (Supp.) q. 74, art. 7, co.
23 Hosea 10:8b; Luke 23:30; *Cf.* Rev. 6:16a.
24 Rev. 6:16b.
25 Joel 1b–3a.
26 Joel 2:6b. An *olla* is a pot or a jar, here translated as kettle. As Denis describes its significance in his *Commentary* on Joel 2:6, "pots (kettles) placed upon fire are similar to each other. For in the manner that such pot (kettle) is stained with soot and blackened, so the faces of the Jews with fear and tears will appear as if on fire, according to that found in Lamentations: *Their face is now made blacker than coals, and they are not known in the streets.* (Lam. 4:8a). Doctoris Ecstatici D. Dionysii Cartusiani, *Opera Omnia,* Vol. 10 (Montreuil: 1900), 135–36.
27 Joel 2:10.

49{50}[4] *He shall call heaven from above, and the earth, to judge his people.*

Advocabit caelum desursum, et terram, discernere populum suum.

49{50}[5] *Gather together his saints to him: who set his covenant before sacrifices.*

Congregate illi sanctos eius, qui ordinant testamentum eius super sacrificia.

49{50}[4] *Advocabit caelum desursum, he shall call heaven from above*: that is, Christ coming to the judgment will convoke and bring with him all citizens of the heavenly homeland, namely the holy angels, and all the blessed, who also will appear visibly then to all, according to Gregory.[28] Whence in Zechariah we read: *The Lord my God shall come, and all the saints with him. And it shall come to pass in that day, that there shall be no light, but cold and frost*, that is, a *mighty tempest* (as is stated [in the earlier verse]). For Christ also will come at night. This is what is said in Isaiah: *The Lord will enter into judgment with the ancients of his people, and its princes.*[29] Whence also Jude says: *Now of these Enoch also, the seventh from Adam, prophesied, saying: Behold, the Lord comes with thousands of his saints to execute judgment upon all, and to reprove all the ungodly for all the works of their ungodliness, whereby they have done ungodly, and of all the hard things ... spoken against* the Lord.[30] *Et terram, and the earth*: that is, Christ will call to judgment the inhabitants of the earth, namely, all men, most especially those who by the fire of conflagration will be consumed, but also all whose bodies will be raised again.[31] For which reason it is stated in the Gospel: *The hour comes, wherein all that are in the graves shall hear the voice of the Son of God.*[32] *Discernere populum suum, to judge his people*: that Christ will summon therefore heaven and earth since he will separate his people from all those present, that is, [he will distinguish] between the elect and the reprobate, and at that place he will separate by place and reward the sheep from the goats, gathering his wheat into his barn, but burning the chaff with unquenchable fire.[33] Whence the Lord says: *I will gather together all nations, and will*

---

28 Reference is to Pope St. Gregory the Great (540–604 AD), but I could not locate the reference. *Cf.* ST IIIa (Supp.), q. 89, art. 3, co.
29 Is. 3:14a.
30 Jude 14, 15.
31 E. N. Denis is distinguishing between those whose death will be caused by the conflagration and those who had died before the conflagration.
32 John 5:28.
33 *Cf.* Matt. 25:32–33; 3:12.

bring them down into the valley of Josaphat, and I will plead with them there ... for there I will sit to judge the nations round about.[34]

But because this bringing forward will be done through the ministry of the angels (for they will collect together the ashes of the bodies rising again, and they will carry the risen to judgment), therefore consequently he says to the angels: **49{50}[5]** *Congregate illi, gather together,* that is to the judgment of Christ, *sanctos eius, his saints,* who with holiness served him in this life that they might obtain due and complete mercy, and that they might cling to their Head in eternity. Whence Christ professes with regard to himself: *The Son of man shall send his angels, and they shall gather out of his kingdom all who have caused others to stumble, and them that work iniquity, and they shall cast them into the furnace of fire.*[35] And again: *At the end of the world, the angels shall go out, and shall separate the wicked from among the just.*[36] And so, *gather together his saints to him, qui ordinant testamentum eius super sacrificia, who set his covenant before sacrifices,* that is, they who in the Church militant regulate how the divine commandments regarding oblations and sacrifices are to be executed. For although Christ himself prescribed a sacrifice to be offered as much in the New as [sacrifice had been enjoined] in the Old Testament, yet he did not determine all the methods and rites by which it ought to be done; but this he relinquished to the ordinance of the Saints, which he decreed would be completed by the Holy Spirit, as a great many things regarding the office of the Mass are prescribed and ordered by the holy Fathers.

49{50}[6] *And the heavens shall declare his justice: for God is judge.*

Et annuntiabunt caeli iustitiam eius, quoniam Deus iudex est.

49{50}[5] *Et annuntiabunt caeli iustitiam eius,* and *the heavens shall declare his justice*: that is, the holy angels, and perfect men, who in the day of judgment will judge with Christ as his assistants, will approve and praise the judgment of the Judge and the recompense that he will give each one. And this they will do, *quoniam Deus iudex est, for God is judge,* that is, because they will know that he who judges neither deceives nor is able to be deceived, nor is he a respecter of persons, nor does he dissimulate in anything, since he is God for whom it is impossible to fall into error and injustice. But if a judge were to be a pure creature, it would not seem so safe to approve of his justice, because a creature is

---

34 Joel 3:2a, 12b.
35 Matt. 13:41–42a. E. N. I have departed from the Douay-Rheims.
36 Matt. 13:49.

able to err and to deceive. Or [we can understand this verse thus]: *And the heavens declare*, that is, the Apostles and the other holy preachers leading a heavenly life on earth [declare], *his justice*, that is, the precepts and counsels of Christ, throughout the orb of the earth. And to either of these explanations one is able to refer to that said in Revelation by the saints prophetically declared: *Great and wonderful are your works, O Lord God Almighty; just and true are your ways, O King of ages. Who shall not fear you, O Lord, and magnify your name?*[37] And again: *Yea, O Lord God Almighty, true and just are your judgments.*[38]

49{50}[7] Hear, O my people, and I will speak: O Israel, and I will testify to you: I am God, your God.

Audi, populus meus, et loquar Israel, et testificabor tibi. Deus, Deus tuus ego sum.

Then it moves to the institution of the evangelical law, and the Savior, who in the unity of person is God and man, says: **49{50}[7]** *Audi, populus meus; hear, O my people*: that is, with the ear of the heart and the body listen, O Jews, who were the peculiar people of God, as Moses wrote, *The Lord your God has chosen you, to be his peculiar people of all peoples that are upon the earth*;[39] *et loquar, and I will speak* perfect doctrine. *Israel, et testificabor tibi; O Israel, and I will testify to you.* The title "my people" he repeats, calling them "Israel," because they were born from the seed of Jacob, whom the angel called Israel.[40] For Israel is often the name that designates the entire Jewish people, such as when the Lord says to Pharaoh: *Israel is my son, my firstborn. I have said to you: Let my son go, that* he *might sacrifice to me.*[41] Also morally [that is, tropologically], by Israel is understood also the Church militant, or any individual man contemplating God. Christ therefore says: *Israel, I will testify to you*, that is, O sons of Israel, to whom I was specially sent, hear, *and I will testify to you*, that is, by word, power, and miracles I will affirm that which follows: *Deus, Deus tuus ego sum; I am God, your God.* For Christ in his own person preached to the Jews, and he often asserted himself to be God. Whence it is written: *the Jews sought the more to kill him, because he did not only*

---

37 Rev. 15:3–4.
38 Rev. 16:7.
39 Deut. 7:6.
40 Gen. 32:28.
41 Ex. 4:22b–23a. Denis has *ut sacrificet mihi* instead of the Sixto-Clementine's *ut serviat mihi*, "that he may serve me."

break the sabbath, but also said God was his Father, making himself equal to God.⁴² And when the Jews said to him, *Who are you?* He responded: *The beginning, who also speak unto you.*⁴³ And this Christ also confirmed by miracles. For this reason he said: *If I do not the works of my Father, believe me not; But if I do, though you will not believe me, believe the works.*⁴⁴

> 49{50}[8] *I will not reprove you for your sacrifices: and your burnt offerings are always in my sight.*
>
> *Non in sacrificiis tuis arguam te; holocausta autem tua in conspectu meo sunt semper.*

49{50}[8] *Non in sacrificiis tuis arguam te, I will not reprove you for your sacrifices*: that is, for the omission of the legal sacrifices I will not reprehend you in the time of the new law and grace, for they will then cease; *holocausta autem tua in conspectus meo sunt semper, and your burnt offerings are always in my sight.* The negation which is placed in the first part of the verse is repeated here, as in the verse of the preceding Psalm, wherein it was said: *He shall not give to God his ransom, and the price of the redemption of his soul,* that is, not the price of his soul.⁴⁵ And therefore, it is [to be understood] in this sense: just as *I will not reprove you for your* omitted *sacrifices,* so *your* legal *burnt offerings* are no longer acceptable to me. Now how sacrifice and holocaust differ, and on the manner and the time of their cessation, is stated in sufficient length in the exposition of the thirty-ninth Psalm, whose beginning is, *With expectation I have waited for the Lord.*⁴⁶

> 49{50}[9] *I will not take calves out of your house: nor he goats out of your flocks.*
>
> *Non accipiam de domo tua vitulos, neque de gregibus tuis hircos.*
>
> 49{50}[10] *For all the beasts of the woods are mine: the cattle on the hills, and the oxen.*

---

42 John 5:18.
43 John 8:25.
44 John 10:37–38a.
45 E. N. This is already done by the translator of the Douay-Rheims. Denis is saying that the negative of the first clause of Ps. 49:8 applies also to the second clause, so it should be read: *and your burnt offerings are NOT always in my sight.*
46 E. N. See Article LXXVIII (Psalm 39:7).

Quoniam meae sunt omnes ferae silvarum, iumenta in montibus, et boves.

49{50}[11] I know all the fowls of the air: and with me is the beauty of the fields.

Cognovi omnia volatilia caeli; et pulchritudo agri mecum est.

49{50}[12] If I should be hungry, I would not tell you: for the world is mine, and the fulness thereof.

Si esuriero, non dicam tibi: meus est enim orbis terrae, et plenitudo eius.

49{50}[13] Shall I eat the flesh of bullocks? Or shall I drink the blood of goats?

Numquid manducabo carnes taurorum? Aut sanguinem hircorum potabo?

49{50}[9] *Non accipiam,* I will not take, in the time of the new law, *de domo tua vitulos, neque de gregibus tuis hircos;* calves out of your house, nor goats out of your flocks, so that they might be offered in the way as they were offered in the Old Testament, although other means of offering will be available to the ministers of the Church or the poor for the sake of God and the support of life. 49{50}[10] *Quoniam meae sunt omnes ferae silvarum,* for all the beasts of the woods are mine, that is, the wild animals, *iumenta in montibus et boves,* the cattle on the hills and the oxen, that is, the domestic animals. For I have created all things. 49{50}[11] *Cognovi omnia volatilia caeli,* I know all the fowls of the air of those that fly: and so it is not necessary that they be made present in the sight of my temple. *Et pulchritude agri mecum est,* and with me is the beauty of the field, that is, all the fruitfulness and the adornments of the earth are known to me, and reside within my power: whence I do not need the sacrifices that were of the fruits of the earth. 49{50}[12] *Si esuriero, non dicam tibi;* if I should be hungry, I would not tell you: not that God in his nature ever hungers; but it [must be understood] in this sense: If it was arranged by me, that I might want food or drink, I would not have need to make such a thing known to you, or to request from you anything; *meus est enim orbis terrae et plenitudo eius,* for the world is mine, and the fullness thereof: just as it is said in a Psalm above, *The earth is the Lord's and the fullness thereof.*[47] But regarding this, the error is spread

---

47 Ps. 23:1.

about which says that God either did not create the inferior things or that he does not know them particularly and distinctly, nor exercise providence over them.[48] **49{50}[13]** *Numquid manducabo*, shall I eat, I the eternal and unchangeable God, *carnes taurorum, the flesh of bullocks*, which are offered, *aut sanguinem hircorum*, or... *the blood of goats* that are immolated *potabo, shall I drink*, I the incorporeal God, who am in myself fully perfect and full? Of course not.

49{50}[14] *Offer to God the sacrifice of praise: and pay your vows to the most High.*

Immola Deo sacrificium laudis, et redde Altissimo vota tua.

Since, therefore, this is so, O Catholic Church, **49{50}[14]** *Immola Deo*, offer to God the Father, and the whole Trinity, *sacrificium laudis, the sacrifice of praise*, that is, the Sacrament of the Body and Blood of Christ, which is in and of itself the awaited, received, and ultimate sacrifice, in which all the benefits of God are gathered together, our sins are cleansed, and God is most highly honored; *et redde Altissimo vota sua, and pay your vows to the most High*, that is, fulfill your promises, those either of your Baptism,[49] or those upon your receipt of Orders, or other promises: for (as the Scriptures say) *an unfaithful and foolish promise displeases him.*[50] And so also Jonah: *I will pay whatsoever I have vowed for my salvation* (he says) *to the Lord.*[51]

---

48 E. N. Denis is likely referring to the Epicurean and Stoic denials of God's particular Providence, that is, their denial that God is intimately concerned and involved in the governance of the world, the acknowledgment that, as inscrutable as it might be, "There's a special providence in the fall of a sparrow. If it be now, 'tis not to come; if it be not to come, it will be now; if it be not now, yet it will come. The readiness is all." Shakespeare, *Hamlet*, 5.2.219-23. *Cf.* Matt. 10:29. "By his providence God protects and governs all things he has made, 'righting mightily from one end of the earth to the other, and ordering all things well' [Wis. 8:1]. For 'all are open and laid bare to his eyes' [Heb. 4:13], even those things that will be done by the free action of creatures." DS 3003 (Vatican I). We might also reflect upon the admonition of denying such Providence: *Neque dicas coram angelo: Non est providentia; ne forte iratus Deus contra semones tuos dissipet cuncta opera manuum tuarum.* "Say not before the angel: There is no providence: lest God be angry at your words, and destroy all the works of your hands." Eccl. 5:5.
49 E. N. The promises made at baptism are: (1) to renounce Satan, all his works, and all his pomps, and (2) acceptance of the Creed. *Haec est fides nostra. Haec est fides Ecclesiaea, quam gloriamur, in Christo Iesu Domino nostro.*
50 Eccl. 5:3b.
51 Jonah 2:10b.

ANOTHER (MORAL) EXPOSITION

And so this part [of the Psalm], because the literal understanding is plain, can be expounded upon in a moral sense so as to be instructive to any one of us, so [that it can be understood] in this sense: *Hear, O my people*, who obtain their name from me, Jesus Christ, that is, Christian, for whose redemption I allowed myself to be killed; *and I will speak* to you through internal inspiration, through the preachers of the Church, through the study of sacred Scripture. *O Israel*, whose *conversation is in heaven*,[52] *beholding the glory of the Lord with open face*,[53] *and I will testify to you*, that *I am God, your God*, who chose you from eternity, and called you to the faith, and have provided unceasingly for your salvation. *I will not reprove you for your sacrifices*, that is, your interior and exterior sacrifices are pleasing to me, are accepted of themselves, and not by figure.[54] *And your burnt offerings*, that is, your oblations, which are inflamed by the fire of divine love, namely, the abnegation of your own will, patience in adversity, interior mortification of spirit, and the daily taking up of the Cross, fervent prayer, and such similar things, *are always in my sight*, that is, will be to me unceasingly pleasing, will not be consigned to oblivion, but will be rewarded with eternal beatitude. Whence also the angel told the most blessed centurion Cornelius: *Your prayers and your alms are ascended for a memorial in the sight of God.*[55] And John says: *The smoke of the incense of the prayers of the saints ascended up before God from the hand of the angel.*[56] *I will not take ... out of your house*, that is, from your heart, which is the home of your thoughts, *calves*, that is, insolent movements, or disobedient and unstable affections and desires, which arise petulantly and restlessly, with the resemblance of bull calves. Hence, therefore, is written elsewhere: *Woe ... you that sleep upon beds of ivory, and are wanton on your couches;*[57] and *Woe you that devise that which is unprofitable, and work evil in your beds.*[58] *Nor he goats out of your flocks*, that is, of the number of your deeds that I will not accept, I will not have grace cheapened by simulation or hypocrisy, which, in the

---

52 Phil. 3:20a.
53 2 Cor. 3:18a.
54 E. N. *Figurativa*, figuratively. What Denis means is — unlike the sacrifices under the Old Law, which were *figures* of the internal sacrifices that please God — the internal sacrifices, the sacrifices of the heart, are what please him *directly* and *immediately*.
55 Acts 10:4b.
56 Rev. 8:4.
57 Amos 1a, 4a.
58 Micah 2:1a.

manner of male goats, pretend severity and hardness on the outside, but within have succumbed to vanity. For this reason, it is written: *Dissemblers and crafty men provoke the wrath of God.*[59] *For all the beasts of the woods,* that is, all of the souls fleeing worldly and carnal softness, and keeping up the hard labors of penance, *the cattle,* that is, they who carry above them the yoke of the divine precepts, *on the hills,* that is, in the perfection of virtue, *and the oxen,* that is, the preachers, and the spiritual cultivators of others' hearts. *I know,* through approbation and spiritual dwelling, *all the fowls of the air,* that is, those spurning the things of the earth and who are at leisure for heavenly things, who *take shall take wings as eagles,*[60] so that they might fly like the angels; *and... beauty of the fields,* that is, the perfection of the heart, and of exterior manner of life, of an exemplary character, or of probity of life in general, which are the fields of the prelates of the Church, *are with me,* that is, by the unlikeness of fault are not far away from me, but are delightful to me. *If I should be hungry, I would not tell you.* Hunger and desire, if they are properly understood, are by no means appropriate to God, for they involve a lack and absence of some good.[61] But God is said to hunger for our justice, and to desire our salvation and perfection, because, as far as is in him, he is most ready to bestow to every single person grace, for he does not will the death of a sinner,[62] nor does he rejoice in the destruction of the living.[63] Hence in an earlier Psalm is said: *The king shall greatly desire your beauty.*[64] And in Deuteronomy we read this: The Lord said to Moses: *Who shall give them,* namely the children of Israel, *to have such a mind, to fear me, and to keep all my commandments at all times, that it may be well with them...forever?*[65] It will be in this sense, therefore, *If I should be hungry,* that is, if I should desire the

---

59 Job. 36:13a.
60 Is. 40:31a.
61 E. N. Strictly speaking, God cannot be said to hunger since hunger necessarily means the lack of some good. And God lacks nothing. God is absolutely self-sufficient.
62 *Cf.* Ez. 18:23: *Is it my will that a sinner should die, says the Lord God, and not that he should be converted from his ways, and live?*
63 *Cf.* Wis. 1:13: *For God made not death, neither has he pleasure in the destruction of the living.*
64 Ps. 44:12a. "When the sinner co-operates with actual grace, the Holy Ghost enters his soul and confers on it a brightness and beauty which claim the friendship of God. This indwelling beauty of the soul is due to the presence of the Holy Spirit and is called 'sanctifying grace.'" Francis Spirago, *The Catechism Explained* (New York: Benziger Brothers, 1899), 211. Sanctifying grace is also known as *gratia gratum faciens,* the grace *which makes us pleasing* to God.
65 Deut. 5:29.

spiritual advance and perfection of one of my intellectual creatures, *I would tell you not*, that is, I would not need to request help from you in order that I might guide my desire to its effect; *for the world is mine*, that is, for the whole Church diffused around the world subsists in my power, *and the fulness thereof*, that is, the universal perfection of grace and the virtue of all the faithful is mine, for it is given, preserved, and brought to consummation by me: and so in me, by me, and from me, I am powerful enough to perfect and save whomsoever I will, and I do not need to make this known to another. And as the sins of men do not injure me, so their salvation is of no profit to me. Therefore, I do not desire the salvation of anyone by reason of any need in me, and if I hunger for the salvation of the elect, I have no need to disclose this to you. This is what is stated in the divine sermon: *If you sin, what shall you hurt him?.... And if you do justly, what shall you give him?... Your wickedness may hurt a man that is like you: and your justice may help the son of man.*[66]

Shall I eat the flesh of bullocks? That is, shall I, God, who love the humble, have delight (which is the refreshment of the mind) in the abstention of the proud? By no means. For such I say through Isaiah: *Behold in the day of your fast your own will is found.*[67] *Or drink the blood of goats?* That is, shall I take pleasure in the apparent mortification of the hypocrite? Indeed not, for in the Gospel I said: *When you fast, be not as the hypocrites.... But you, when you fast, anoint your head and wash your face, so that you appear not to fast to men.*[68] *Offer to God the sacrifice of praise*, that is, the giving of thanks in adversity and prosperity, ascribing to him all good, so that you might fulfill that which has been brought up before [in an earlier Psalm], namely, *I will bless the Lord at all times, his praise shall be always in my mouth.*[69] *And pay your vows to the most High*, that is, pour out your desires before God, and do not just beseech him in every distress, in the way that the wise and just man in Ecclesiasticus does: *He will give his heart to resort early to the Lord that made him, and he will pray in the sight of the most High.*[70]

---

66 Job 35:6–8.
67 Is. 58:3b. E. N. In Isaiah, the merit in a man's fast or abstention may be selfishly motivated, and, though he may delight in food, he may also take delight in in fasting. Whereas God, who has no needs to fulfill (*Deus nullius indiget*, God lacks nothing), will take no delight in abstaining from the proud, even though he delights in the humble.
68 Matt. 6:16–18a.
69 Ps. 33:2.
70 Ecclus. 39:6.

49{50}[15] *And call upon me in the day of trouble: I will deliver you, and you shall glorify me.*

Et invoca me in die tribulationis; eruam te, et honorificabis me.

49{50}[16] *But to the sinner God has said: Why do you declare my justices, and take my covenant in your mouth?*

Peccatori autem dixit Deus: Quare tu enarras iustitias meas? et assumis testamentum meum per os tuum?

49{50}[16][71] *Peccatori autem*, but to the sinner, persevering in sin and not relinquishing the will to sin through repentance, *dixit Deus*, God has said, the incarnate Son of God, of himself and through his prophets: *Quare tu enarras iustitias meas? Why do you declare my justices?* That is, how is it that you dare to preach the word of God, and to teach others that which you yourself do not do? *Et assumis testamentum meum per os tuum, and take my covenant in your mouth?* That is, you presume to proclaim the holy and immaculate law of God through your defiled mouth? For this Christ has said through Isaiah: *This people draw near me with their mouth, and with their lips glorify me, but their heart is far from me*,[72] and in vain do they worship me. It is also precisely this scripture that sets forth Christ to be true God, rebuking the Pharisees and saying: Well has Isaiah prophesied of you, saying, *This people honors me with their lips: [but their heart is far from me]*.[73] Whence in Ecclesiasticus it says: *Praise is not seemly in the mouth of a sinner*.[74]

What then is to be done by the sinner who is obligated to celebrate [Mass] or to preach? If he does that which is incumbent upon him [e.g., says Mass], he sins;[75] and if he does not do it, he sins because he neglects his duty: and so he appears to be in a dilemma (*perplexus*). And the response [to this is] that no one is ever in a dilemma:[76] for in such

---

71 E. N. Denis does not provide commentary on Psalm 49:15.
72 Is. 29:13a.
73 Matt. 15:7–8. E. N. The part in brackets replaces the "etc." in the text.
74 Ecclus. 15:9.
75 E. N. The celebrant at Mass must take communion from the elements he consecrated at that Mass to complete the sacrifice of the Mass, something he cannot do if in mortal sin, for to take communion in mortal sin is to commit the mortal sin of sacrilege. See Reginald Garrigou-Lagrange, O. P., *The Priest in Union with Christ* (Westminster, MD: The Newman Press 1954), 72 (G. W. Shelton, S. T. L., trans.).
76 E. N. St. Thomas observes that no innocent person will ever confront a dilemma in a strict sense (*perplexus simpliciter*), that is, one will never confront a situation where, through no fault of one's own, one confronts a situation where any choice made is sinful. However, it is possible that prior sins or culpable failure to form one's

an event [*i.e.*, in a true dilemma] it is impossible to avoid sin. [But in this example] the unworthy priest or preacher is not in a dilemma because he is able to do penance, and by changing his intention [by repenting and confessing his sin] he may carry out without sin the divine office. Yet so long as he remains in sin he does better, generally speaking, in not exercising [his duty to celebrate Mass]; because in exercising [his duty to celebrate Mass] he sins mortally.[77] However, in other divine matters, namely, in the canonical Hours, it is better for any sinner obligated to undertake the Hours to fulfill than to omit. For by not fulfilling [his obligation], he sins mortally, inasmuch as he is acting against a precept of the Church; but he does not sin mortally if he fulfils [his obligation] outside of the state of grace, for there is not a requirement of precept to fulfill [the obligation] in that state of salvation or grace, as there is a special precept with respect to being in a state of salvation for the celebration and administration of the sacraments of Christ and the divine word, so that any priest who dispenses unworthily any of the sacraments of Christ sins mortally.

49{50}[17] But you have hated discipline: and have cast my words behind you.

Tu vero odisti disciplinam, et proiecisti sermones meos retrorsum.

49{50}[18] If you did see a thief you did run with him: and with adulterers you have been a partaker.

Si videbas furem, currebas cum eo; et cum adulteris portionem tuam ponebas.

---

conscience could place one in a situation where whatever one chooses is sinful. This is a self-caused dilemma, a dilemma in a weak sense because it is "unavoidable" in a weak sense (*perplexus secundum quid*). See *De Veritate*, q. 17, art. 4; ST IaIIae, q. 19, art. 6; IIIa, q. 64, art. 6. For an example of such self-caused dilemmas, *see* Graham Green's *The Heart of the Matter*. Yet these dilemmas in a weak sense can present horrendous moral cul-de-sacs. For a horrendous example of a dilemma in a weak sense caused by prior sinful action, see Andrew M. Greenwell, "Artificial Limbo: The Moral Quandary of Frozen Embryos," https://www.catholic.org/news/national/story.php?id=46916.

77   E. N. Denis is saying that the sin incurred by not saying Mass, a sin of omission, is less grievous than the sin incurred by a priest, who is in a state of mortal sin, saying Mass and partaking in sacrilegious communion. This reflex principle appears to draw from the *Summa Theologiae* of St. Thomas, where it states that because sins of commission contain an affirmative act contrary to virtue whereas sins of omission a simple negation, "simply and absolutely speaking, a transgression [sin by commission] is a graver sin than omission." ST IIaIIae, q. 79, art. 4, c. This is only generally true, and not true in every case, "as there are some cases where an omission may be more grave than some transgression."

49{50}[17] *Tu vero, but you O sinner, odisti disciplinam, have hated discipline,*[78] that is, instruction and correction and the owed punishment for your excesses, and so it is written of them: *They have hated him that rebukes in the gate.*[79] Against which Solomon admonishes: *My son, reject not the correction of the Lord: and do not faint when you are chastised by him.*[80] Who elsewhere also says: *Poverty and shame to him that refuses instruction: but he that yields to reproof, shall be glorified.*[81] And in another place: *He that rejects instruction, despises his own soul: but he that yields to reproof possesses understanding.*[82] And the same danger exists in disregarding the discipline of the prelates and of God, for the prelates are the vicars of God. For this reason the Savior says of these sorts of people [that do not regard the teaching of the prelates]: *He that hears you, hears me; and he that despises you, despises me.*[83] And that great and holy prelate Moses said to the sons of Israel: *Your murmuring is not against us, but against the Lord.*[84] If, therefore, we wish to be saved, let us love the discipline of God and of our superiors, for it is written: *The man that with a stiff neck despises him that reproves him, shall suddenly be destroyed.*[85] *Et proiecisti sermones meos restrorsum, and [you have] cast my words behind you,* that is, you have not submitted to my precepts, but you have placed your will before my will. 49{50}[18] *Si videbas furem, currebas cum eo; if you did see a thief, you did run with him,* likewise thieving, or favoring and cooperating with the one thieving, *et cum adulteris portionem tuam ponebas, and with adulterers you have been a partaker,* making yourself a consort and a participant of their vices. For it is a kind of spiritual theft when man usurps the honor and glory that is due God alone; and he who takes common counsel with such theft stains himself according to this, *He that has fellowship with the proud, shall put on pride.*[86]

---

78 E. N. The reader should keep in mind the etymology of the English word "discipline." While it often connotes notions of chastisement or reproof, it also contains positive notions of the Latin *disciplina* which is instruction, teaching, learning, knowledge. A disciple (*discipulus*) is, after all, a student, a pupil, and follower.
79 Amos 5:10a.
80 Prov. 3:11.
81 Prov. 13:18.
82 Prov. 15:32.
83 Luke 10:16a.
84 Ex. 16:8b.
85 Prov. 29:1a.
86 Ecclus. 13:1b.

49{50}[19] *Your mouth has abounded with evil, and your tongue framed deceits.*

Os tuum abundavit malitia, et lingua tua concinnabat dolos.

49{50}[20] *Sitting you did speak against your brother, and did lay a scandal against your mother's son.*

Sedens, adversus fratrem tuum loquebaris, et adversus filium matris tuae ponebas scandalum.

49{50}[19] *Os tuum abundavit malitia,* your mouth has abounded with evil, that is, with illicit words, *et lingua tua concinnabat dolos,* and your tongue framed deceits, that is, false words put together so as to defraud others. This is evident from the fact that 49{50}[20] *Sedens,* sitting in the seat of pestilence, *adversus fratrem tuum,* against your brother, that is, against your neighbor, *loquebaris,* you have framed false, stabbing, detracting, and rancorous words; *et adversus filium matris tuae,* and against your mother's son, namely of the Church or of your actual mother in the flesh, *ponebas scandalum,* did lay a scandal, furnishing an occasion of ruin or a stumbling block by an untempered word or deed, all of which is against the admonition of the Apostle [Paul], where he says: *Let us not therefore judge one another anymore. But judge this rather, that you put not a stumbling block or a scandal in your brother's way. Destroy not him ... for whom Christ died.*[87] Also the Savior: *Woe to that man by whom the scandal comes.*[88] There is nevertheless a certain scandal of the Pharisees (*scandalum Pharisaeorum*), that arises out of malice and blindness of the scandalized, not from the defect of scandalization: and such cannot be always avoided. For, as the evangelist attests, when the disciples said to Christ, *Do you know that the Pharisees, when they heard this word, were scandalized?*[89] He responded: *Let them alone: they are blind, and leaders of the blind.*[90] But the scandal of the little ones (*scandalum pusillorum*) is to be avoided: indeed, sometimes certain things that are not evil, or even certain good things not required, must be set aside lest the little ones be scandalized, as the Apostle said: *If meat scandalize my brother, I will never eat flesh.*[91] For he who is scandalized is a "little one": for the perfect are not scandalized, according to Jerome; nor do they cause

---

87   Rom. 14:13, 15b.
88   Matt. 18:7b.
89   Matt. 15:12b.
90   Matt. 15:14a. E. N. As St. Thomas puts it, as to this "scandal of the Pharisees," our Lord teaches that it is "to be contemned." ST IIaIIae, q. 43, art. 7, co.
91   1 Cor. 8:13a.

scandal, according to Thomas.[92] Let us, therefore, zealously apply ourselves that we might be examples to each other.

49{50}[21] *These things have you done, and I was silent. You thought unjustly that I should be like to you: but I will reprove you, and set before your face.*

Haec fecisti, et tacui. Existimasti inique quod ero tui similis: arguam te, et statuam contra faciem tuam.

49{50}[21] *Haec, these* evil things, *fecisti, you have done,* O sinner, *et tacui, and I was silent.* For Christ frequently waits a long time and does not immediately seek judgment. *Existimasti inique, quod ero tui similis? You thought unjustly that I should be like you?* That is, because of my long-suffering patience you suppose that I will not take notice, or I will be well disposed toward, your sins, and I will not inflict upon you just punishment? *Arguam te, I will reprove,* either before death or at the time of death, and most especially in the day of general judgment,[93] *et statuam contra faciem tuam, and set before your face,* that is, I will expose in a manifest way your sins to you, and I will require from you an accounting of all your works, both upon the hour of your death as well as in the last day.

49{50}[22] *Understand these things, you that forget God; lest he snatch you away, and there be none to deliver you.*

Intelligite haec, qui obliviscimini Deum: nequando rapiat, et non sit qui eripiat.

49{50}[23] *The sacrifice of praise shall glorify me: and there is the way by which I will show him the salvation of God.*

---

92 E. N. The perfect are not scandalized (suffer passive scandal): ST, IIaIIae, q. 43, art. 5, co. *See also* St. Thomas, *Super Matt.*, cap. 18 l. 1 ("The perfect are not scandalized"). The perfect do not give scandal (active scandal). ST, IIaIIae, q. 43, art. 6, s.c. & co.
93 E. N. "Each man receives his eternal retribution in his immortal soul at the very moment of his death, in a particular judgment that refers his life to Christ: either entrance into the blessedness of heaven-through a purification [Purgatory] or immediately [Heaven],— or immediate and everlasting damnation [Hell]." CCC § 1022. "The Last Judgment will come when Christ returns in glory." CCC § 1040. "Whosoever... says there is neither a resurrection (μήτε ἀνάστασιν/*neque resurrectionem*) nor a judgment (μήτε κρίσιν/*neque iudicium*), he is the first-born of Satan (πρωτότοκός ἐστι τοῦ σατανᾶ/*primogenitum es Satanae*)." St. Polycarp, Epistle to the Philippians, 7, PG 5, 1019.

Sacrificium laudis honorificabit me; et illic iter quo ostendam illi salutare Dei.

49{50}[22] *Intelligite haec, understand these things,* that is, reflect upon them in a most profound way, *qui obliviscimini Deum, you that forget God,* you not attending to his precepts, nor thinking of his horrible judgment, nor attending to his glorious promises; *nequando rapiat, lest he snatch you away,* that is, lest God extract you from this life at some time when you are unprepared, unexpectedly to present you at his tribunal, *et non sit qui eripiat, and there be none to deliver* you of his just judgment. For no one is able to redeem a person who dies in mortal sin, unless through some special grace that person would be brought back to his earlier state.[94] **49{50}[23]** *Sacrificium laudis, the sacrifice of praise:* of which has already been spoken of [in the verse of this Psalm that said] *offer to God the sacrifice of praise,*[95] *honorificabit me, shall glorify me,* for it is *per se* accepted; *et illic iter, and there is a way,* that is, by such sacrifice, that is, in the praise to God reverently offered is the way, *quo ostendam illi, by which I will show you,* the one immolated in such a sacrifice, *salutare Dei, the salvation of God,* that is, Christ, the Savior of the human race. For by the sacrifice of praise we come upon the vision of Christ in the present by faith and face-to-face in the future. Indeed, the most optimal way to acquire beatitude is the praise of God, according to that which the Lord asserted in another place: *Whosoever shall glorify me, him will I glorify.*[96]

See how admirable is the virtue of this Psalm, how fruitful is its knowledge. And who is able to express its praise? In this [Psalm] the goodness of the first coming of the Lord and Savior is described so

---

94 E. N. Denis is referring to what we contemporaneously refer to as near-death experiences which were recorded in the middle-ages. A couple of examples of such stories of people dying in mortal sin, "as if by error their souls were taken from their body," but who are snatched out of hell and restored to life can be found in the fourth book of St. Gregory the Great's *Great Dialogue* (chapter 36), where he states that this situation is not an error, but a great grace, a warning: (*non error, sed admonitio est*): *Superna enim pietas ex magna misericordiae suae largitate disponit, ut nonnulli etiam post exitum repente ad corpus redeant, et tormenta inferni, quae audita non crediderant, saltem visa pertimescant.* "For it is a supernal kindness from [God's] great largesse of his mercy, that he disposes that some after their [soul's] sudden exit suddenly return to their bodies, and the torments of hell, which they had heard of but not believed, they having seen it with their eyes may fear." Gregory gives an example of a Spanish-born monk named Peter who died in mortal sin, saw hell, and was brought back to life and transformed his life. He also gives an example of a merchant doing business Constantinople named Stephen who died while there. PL 77, 381.
95 E. N. Ps. 49:14.
96 1 Sam. 2:30b.

beautifully, because the God of gods himself has spoken to the world, inviting all men to his faith;[97] and, in addition, the terror of the future judgment or his second coming is so terrifyingly explained in it; and many other things are most brilliantly sung about in it. Let us endeavor, therefore, so to follow the humility, poverty, and piety of the Christ of the first coming, so that in his second coming we may be found worthy to see his majesty and glory and justice without fear. Let us propose with the eye of our mind, and in our hearts let us vigorously picture, the quality of the future judgment — how horrendous it will be to see the burning elements, the battle-array of angels, the faces of demons, the most monstrous bodies of the reprobate, the rending of the highest heavens, the yawning of the earth, the Judge in a rage, and to await the inevitable sentence of eternal damnation, and to see before oneself the sempiternal torment being made ready. If we consider this and similar things in a solicitous way, then without doubt in the day of such horror we will stand secure and rejoicing.

PRAYER

DIRECT UPON US, O LORD, EYES OF MERCY, and in the day of tribulation, deliver us with the power of your arm, so that we might also honor you and we might devoutly offer to you a sacrifice of praise for our deliverance.

Dirige, Domine, super nos oculos misericordiae, et in die tribulationis, potentiae tuae brachio nos erue: ut et te honorificemus, ac pro nostra liberatione sacrificium tibi laudis devote immolemus.

---

97 E. N. In referring to Christ's faith, Denis is using an objective genitive (faith in Jesus, the Catholic Faith) and not a subjective genitive (faith of Jesus). Christ did not have faith in the ordinary sense, since his human nature enjoyed the beatific vision from the first moment of his existence as man. For more on this topic, *see* footnote 20-23 in Volume 1.

Psalm 50

ARTICLE XCIII

EXPOSITION OF THE FIFTIETH PSALM:
MISERERE MEI, DEUS, SECUNDUM, &c.
HAVE MERCY UPON ME, O GOD, ACCORDING, *&c.*

50{51}[1] *Unto the end, a Psalm of David,*

In finem. Psalmus David,

50{51}[2] *When Nathan the prophet came to him after he had sinned with Bathsheba.*

In finem. Psalmus David, cum venit ad eum Nathan propheta, quando intravit ad Bethsabee.

THE TITLE DECLARING THIS PSALM IS: **50{51}** [1] *In finem. Psalmus David; unto the end, a Psalm of David,* **50{51}** [2] *cum venit ad eum Nathan propheta, quando intravit ad Bethsabee; when Nathan the prophet came to him after he had sinned with Bathsheba.* Now this title is clear to one who knows the history according to the second book of Samuel: in which is narrated the manner David engaged in adultery with the wife of Uriah; and after it, namely, after the death of Uriah, when David led her into marriage; it was then that Nathan came to David and disclosed to him so great a crime.[1] And David becoming aware of the committed crime grieved most vehemently, and out of his heartfelt repentance, wrote this Psalm. In this [Psalm] (in his own person, or any profoundly penitent person) he speaks with the greatest feeling, prays most humbly, and pours forth most ardent words. For so great is the virtue and the dignity of this Psalm, that language fails in praising it.

50{51}[3] *Have mercy on me, O God, according to your great mercy. And according to the multitude of your tender mercies blot out my iniquity.*

Miserere mei, Deus, secundum magnam misericordiam tuam; et secundum multitudinem miserationum tuarum, dele iniquitatem meam.

---

1 2 Sam. chps. 11, 12.

Therefore, he says: **50{51}[3]** *Miserere mei, Deus, secundum magnam misericordiam tuam; have mercy on me, O God, according to your great mercy.* O salutary word, O only counsel, O singular refuge! When the sinner may not know what to do, where to go, to whom he ought to turn, this remains to him the only solace, the complete refuge, and the most prudent counsel, that he say: *Have mercy on me, O God, according to your great mercy.* When a man is oppressed by the huge weight of his own wickedness, when a man is terrified by the excessiveness of his ingratitude, when a man is consumed with the multitude and magnitude of his sin, this alone remains, that he say: *Have mercy on me, O God, according to your great mercy.* For this reason it is written: *As we know not what to do, we can only turn our eyes to you.*[2]

And so two things in particular ought to be weighed by the penitent, indeed, any praying wayfarer, namely, his own misery and the divine mercy. Out of the consideration of his misery he may quickly turn to prayer, and he may humble himself and accuse himself; but from the consideration of the mercy of God he may catch his breath, he may grab hold of the hope of forgiveness, and may invoke God with unceasing trust. For if the sinner pondering the enormity of his vices thinks only of divine justice, it may be that he will more likely despair than pray, in the manner that befell Cain, who said: *My iniquity is greater than that I may deserve pardon.*[3] And [in the manner of] the traitor Judas, who when he said, *I have sinned in betraying innocent blood, ... went and hanged himself with a noose,*[4] *and burst asunder.*[5] Nevertheless, the sinner ought to consider the divine justice, so that he may know to fear and to correct himself; and also the divine power, so that he may know that it is not possible for him to avoid or to resist it; and also the divine wisdom, so that he may know that he is unable to hide from it. But since the consideration of these things strikes the guilty conscience with nothing else but horror and sorrow, it remains that he may turn toward extraordinary mercy of God, and from his contemplation of it he may receive consolation and trust. Whence the blessed Job, considering the omnipotence, wisdom, and justice of his Judge, turned himself to his extraordinary mercy, and said: *Man cannot be justified compared with God; and if he will contend with him, he cannot answer one for a thousand. Although I should have any just thing, I would not answer to him, but would make*

---

2   2 Chr. 20:12b.
3   Gn. 4:13.
4   Matt. 27:4–5. In quoting Matt. 27:5, I have replaced the Douay-Rheims "halter," which translates *laqueo*, with "noose."
5   Acts 1:18a.

supplication to my judge. And if I would justify myself, my own mouth shall condemn me.... Although I should be simple, even this soul shall be ignorant.[6]

And so the sinner in the sight of the most high Judge who scrutinizes all things, recollecting himself, and trembling at the enormity of his sins, considering also that the strictness of divine justice will not be able to tolerate them, nor that they can be hid from the eye of the divine wisdom, nor that he will be able to resist the divine power, fleeing to the extraordinary mercy of the kindly Creator, he may say: *Miserere me, Deus, have mercy on me, O God*: that is, because I am miserable, and you are merciful, therefore have mercy on me, having compassion, not being indignant; overlooking, not taking vengeance; giving aid, not deserting. Do not will to show the power of your justice in me, lest I be found a vessel of dishonor or of wrath fitted for destruction, but [will to show the] abyss of your clemency, so that I might be a vessel of mercy fitted for salvation.[7] *Enter not into judgment with your servant,*[8] nor recompense me *according* to my *sins;*[9] but because I am greatly miserable (for sins are what make the sinner miserable), and you are greatly merciful, therefore, *Have mercy, O God, secundum magnam misericordiam tuam, according to your great mercy*: which—since it is boundless—infinitely exceeds all my misery; just like, therefore, the expanse of the sea will absorb a drop of water as if it were nothing, so the immensity of your mercy, O Lord, will consume and eternally blot out all my misery.

Et secundum multitudinem miserationum tuarum, dele iniquitatem meam; and according to the multitude of your tender mercies, blot out my iniquity.[10] God is naturally merciful (*misericors*), and it is his property always

---

6 Job 9:2b–3; 15, 20a, 21a.
7 Cf. Rom. 9:21–23: *Or has not the potter power over the clay, of the same lump, to make one vessel unto honor, and another unto dishonor? What if God, willing to show his wrath, and to make his power known, endured with much patience vessels of wrath, fitted for destruction, that he might show the riches of his glory on the vessels of mercy, which he has prepared unto glory?*
8 Ps. 142:2a.
9 Ps. 102:10a.
10 E. N. In this Dionysian excursus on mercy, we run smack dab into the problem that Edmund Hill, O. P. described as follows: "*Misericordia*, it scarcely needs saying, appears... often in the Bible. Two other Latin words appear frequently in its company, the related noun *miseratio*, usually in the plural *miserationes*, and the related verb *misreor*. The first weakness of the English 'mercy' is shown by the fact that it does duty... for all three of these Latin words.... More seriously, in the Bible these three Latin words represent three Greek words (fairly consistently), namely *misericordia/ eleos, mireor/eleeo*, and *miserationes/oiktirmoi*; and further these three Greek words represent (fairly consistently) three Hebrew words, respectively ḥesed, ḥanan, and raḥamin. So the divine revelation on this point was first conveyed by the use of at

to have mercy (*misereri*) and to spare (*parcere*). For this reason, it is written, *For you only are merciful (pius)*.[11] Now the mercy (*miseratio*) of God, actively signified, is the mercy (*misericordia*) of God, according to which he actually has mercy (*miseretur*). And though, in God himself, the mercy (*misericordia*) of God and his mercifulness (*miseratio*) are one and simple, still the mercies (*misericordiae*) of God are said to be many, and his mercies (*miserationes*) a great number, because of their diversity and the multitude of their effects. But the tender mercy (*miseratio*) of God passively understood is the effect of his mercy (*misericordiae*). And so, therefore, in this sense. *According to the multitude of your tender mercies*, that is, according that you are able to have mercy (*misereri*) in many ways and through various kinds of aid; according to this, *blot out my iniquity*, because you have the power to provide help through infinite ways and unfailing kinds of aid: and thus, I pray, that you may show me the *multitude of your tender mercies*. Or [we might understand it] thus: *According to the multitude of your tender mercies*, that is, since you have had mercy (*misertus es*) to many saints in the past and repentant sinners, according to this I beseech that you apply to me your multiform mercy (*misericordiam*), and that you blot out from my soul the sins of omission and commission. I do not pray, O Lord, that you do to me according to the multitude of my merit, but *according to the multitude of your tender mercies* remove my iniquity. And this is what Daniel asks for: *For your own sake, ... incline your ear, O my God, ... for it is not for our justifications that we present our prayers before your face, but for the multitude of your tender mercies (miserationibus). O Lord, hear; O Lord, be appeased; ... do not delay.*[12] Finally, never is mortal sin blotted out unless [sanctifying or habitual] grace is infused. This means, therefore, that he who prays that his iniquities be taken away implicitly requests that he be filled with grace.[13]

---

least three wholly distinct words from three separate roots; reduced in Greek to three distinct words, but from only two separate roots; reduced in Latin to three words from one root; reduced to English to one word." Edmund Hill, O. P., *The Quality of 'Mercy'*, New Blackfriars, Vol. 46, No. 538 (April 1965), p. 411. The problem being practically insurmountable left me no choice but to have the Latin words in parentheses.
11 Rev. 15:4a. E. N. I have modified the Douay-Rheims which reads, *For you only are holy*, where "holy" translates the Latin *pius*. The Latin word *pius* is notoriously difficult to translate. Generally, in the translation of these Commentaries, it has been translated as "kindly" with reference to God, and "pious" or "devout" with reference to man. Here, however, it is clear that Denis views it as a synonym with "merciful."
12 Dan. 17b, 18b, 19a.
13 E. N. Mortal sin and being in a state of sanctifying grace are mutually exclusive, so that mortal sin can be defined as the state of lacking sanctifying grace (*gratia gratum faciens*) and lacking sanctifying grace as being in a state of mortal sin.

50{51}[4] *Wash me yet more from my iniquity, and cleanse me from my sin.*

Amplius lava me ab iniquitate mea, et a peccato meo munda me.

50{51}[4] *Amplius lava me ab iniquitate mea, wash me yet more from my iniquity,* that is, through the infusion of your grace cleanse my soul from the stain that it incurred while sinning, and grant to me internal compunction[14] and the fountain of tears, by which I might be washed from the filth of vices, in the way it is prescribed for me: *Wash your heart from wickedness.*[15] *Et a peccato meo munda me, and cleanse me from my sin,* remitting the punishment and fault, and adorning the mind with the resplendence of grace and virtue. For sins beat down and stain my soul, and make it similar to the devil and dissimilar to the holy Trinity, and obstruct from it all the good of your grace; as the prophet Jeremiah said, *your sins have withheld good things from you;*[16] and Isaiah, *Your iniquities have divided between you and your God, and your sins have hid his face from you.*[17] Whence in the book of Job we read: *Is it a great matter that God should comfort you? But your wicked words hinder this.*[18] Therefore, O Lord, because Isaiah witnessed, *this is all the fruit, that the sin thereof should be taken away,*[19] I pray, *wash me from my iniquity,* so that what is written of you may be fulfilled in me: *He will send his fury in no more, because he delights in mercy; he will turn again, and have mercy on us: he will put away our iniquities: and he will cast all our sins into the bottom of the sea.*[20] Fulfill also in me that which you promised through Isaiah to those seeking you: *If your sins be as scarlet, they shall be made as white as snow: and if they be red as crimson, they shall be white as wool.*[21]

50{51}[5] *For I know my iniquity, and my sin is always before me.*

Quoniam iniquitatem meam ego cognosco, et peccatum meum contra me est semper.

---

14 E. N. "I would rather feel compunction, than to know its definition." Thomas à Kempis, *The Imitation of Christ*, I, 1, 3. "Pray, therefore, humbly to the Lord that he may give you the spirit of compunction, and say with the Prophet: 'Feed me, O Lord, with the bread of tears and give me to drink in tears without measure.'" *Id.* I, 21, 5.
15 Jer. 4:14.
16 Jer. 5:25b.
17 Is. 59:2.
18 Job. 15:11.
19 Is. 27:9a.
20 Micah 7:18b–19.
21 Is. 1:18b.

And so I ask to be made clean from sin, **50{51}[5]** *Quoniam iniquitatem mea ego cognosco, for I know my iniquity.* I do not hide it, nor do I make excuses for myself, nor do I blame it on demons or on others, but I confess my sins. Since the confession of evil or the recognition of sins is the beginning of good, pardon me, and commence and renew the spiritual life in me. If you, therefore, desire to obtain mercy, acknowledge your sin, do not spot the splinter in the eye of your brother, but see the log that is in your own eye,[22] and say that which is written: *I have sinned, and indeed I have offended, and I have not received what I have deserved.*[23] Here the Lord through Jeremiah said to those making excuses for themselves: *I will contend with you in judgment, because you have said: I have not sinned.*[24] If, however, you want to know what is the true way to recognize your own sins, listen to Manasseh praying and saying: *I have sinned, O Lord, I have sinned, and I acknowledge my iniquities. I beg praying to you: do not destroy me together with my iniquities.*[25] *Et peccatum meum contra me est semper, and my sin is always before me,* that is, it always displeases me, and I detest it. Other versions [of the Scriptures] have, *coram me est semper, always before me,* and the rest [of the verse] is the same. For the sense is: I always hold up that [sin] which is in my consideration, and I examine it, since I mourn it.

50{51}[6] *Against you only have I sinned, and have done evil before you: that you may be justified in your words and may overcome when you are judged.*

Tibi soli peccavi, et malum coram te feci; ut iustificeris in sermonibus tuis, et vincas cum iudicaris.

50{51}[7] *For behold I was conceived in iniquities; and in sins did my mother conceive me.*

Ecce enim in iniquitatibus conceptus sum, et in peccatis concepit me mater mea.

---

22 Matt. 7:4–5.
23 Job 23:27b.
24 Jer. 2:35b.
25 E. N. The lovely apocryphal Prayer of Manasseh is not part of the Canon of Scripture (though St. Jerome included it in his Vulgate, and it is frequently included as an Appendix in Catholic Bibles). Purporting to be the penitential prayer of King Manasseh of Judah, it was probably written in the second century B. C. Manasseh, guilty of idolatry, was captured by the Assyrians and held captive (2 Kings. 21:1–18; 2 Chr. 33:1–13). While he was held prisoner, Manasseh begged forgiveness, as reflected in this lovely prayer, which led to his freedom and his rejection of idolatry. (2 Chr. 33:15–17).

50{51}[6] *Tibi soli peccavi, against you only have I sinned*: for all sin is against your law in some way; sin against one's neighbor or one's self does not find the reason of its sinfulness in itself, except to the extent it is in origin contrary to, or dissonant with, the order of your wisdom and justice, because you are the measure, cause, and fountain of all universal holiness. *Et malum coram te feci, and have done evil before you,* that is, with you present and knowing all things, I am not afraid to do evil: and in this I aggravate my wrongdoing, for with so little concern do I regard your presence. *Ut iustificeris in sermonibus tuis, et vincas cum iudicaris; that you may be justified in your words, and may overcome when you are judged.* Commonly, among the expositors something is implied [by them] in this place, such, "Pardon me," or "Have mercy on me." So that we may read it in this sense: *Against you only have I sinned, and have done evil before you,* and I plead that you might pardon me [for my sins], that you might have mercy, so that you *may be justified,* that is, you might find me just and true, *in your words,* wherein by the mouth of the holy Prophets you have promised forgiveness to the penitent, such as this: *I will heal their breaches, I will love them freely: for my wrath is turned away from them.*[26] *And you may overcome,* that is, you may exceed and rise above others in justice, *when you are judged,* that is, during the time when your judgment is made known to others, and by this they judge that you have done well and rightly and justify your judgment.[27]

But I judge it better to imply nothing: indeed, if we view things rightly, no implication will be seen [to be understood or needed]. For we need to follow the exposition of the Apostle [Paul]. And the Apostle introduces and asserts [in his epistle] to the Romans these words [of this Psalm] in this manner: *But God is true; and every man a liar, as it is written, That you may be justified in your words, and may overcome when you are judged.*[28] It is therefore clear that, according to the intent of the Apostle, holy David introduced these words in this sense: that God justifies us out of our iniquity, and overcomes [our iniquity] when he judges. And this more clearly appears from the words of the Apostle that follow: for he adds, *But if our injustice commend*

---

26 Hosea 14:5.
27 E. N. That is, it will be apparent to all in the final judgment as God is seen to judge — even the damned, and certainly by the elect — that God is a just judge: for the elect will be justified (in a state of grace) and so merit heaven whereas the reprobate (those not in a state of grace) will deserve hell and damnation. Therefore, in a manner of speaking, and certainly not strictly speaking, God will be "judged," and he will be found just.
28 Rom. 3:4 (quoting Ps. 50:6).

*the justice of God, what shall we say?*²⁹ It should be noted, however, that to be justified, to be glorified from our sins, and to overcome [them] when judged by God can be understood in two ways. The first, causally (*causaliter*)³⁰ and directly: and in this sense it [the statement that our sins cause God's justice and hence our righteousness] is not true. Secondly, occasionally (*occasionaliter*) ³¹ and indirectly or consecutively: and in this sense it is true,³² as the Apostle has proposed. And however much the first exposition is plausible [in a literal sense], this [latter one] proposes the more literal sense [and so is in my opinion superior]. And so [this verse] has this sense: *To you only have I sinned and have done evil before you, that* from this occasionally and consecutively *you may be justified in your words*, by which you said through the Prophets that no man is without sin, but all men to be liars³³ in word or by deed, or some other vice: for as is written in the book of Job, *No one is clean from defilement.*³⁴ Or [an alternative explanation], *In your words* by which you damn and punish sinners, but [by which] you save and glorify the just. For my evil is ordered to the good by you, that is, [my evil] is justly punished or mercifully forgiven, redounding to your glory: in the way acknowledged in Augustine's *Enchiridion*;³⁵ indeed, in all things your justice and power shine upon all falsehood and are to be trusted.

---

29 Rom. 3:5a.
30 L. *Causaliter*, causally is said when something is the cause of its form, as, for example, the sun causally is hot.
31 L. *Occasionaliter*, occasionally, is not to be understood in its ordinary sense. It means that something is the *occasion* but not the cause of something happening. "So the fall of St. Peter proceeded *occasionally* from his entry into the home of Caipahas." Expositio Terminorum Philosphicorum (Ghent 1824), 92 (s.v. "causaliter" "occasionaliter").
32 E. N. It is in this *occasional* sense that the *felix culpa*, the "happy fault" of Adam in the *Esxultet* sung at the Easter Vigil is to be understood: *O felix culpa quae talem et tantum meruit habere redemptorem*, "O happy fault that *merited* such and so great a Redeemer." Sin does not "merit" a Redeemer *causatively*, though can be said to "merit" a Redeemer *occasionally*, that is, by providing the occasion for it.
33 *Cf.* Ps. 115:11b: *Every man is a liar*.
34 E. N. *Nemo mundus a sorde*. This is not in the Sixto-Clementine Vulgate, but is nevertheless a concise summary of the Scripture Denis cites, namely Job 15:15, 25:4. Job 15:15: *Behold among his saints none is unchangeable, and the heavens are not pure in his sight*. Job 25:4: *Can man be justified compared with God, or he that is born of a woman appear clean?* The phrase is from Job 14:4 from the Latin translation of the Greek Septuagint.
35 E. N. *Enchiridion*, 24, 96, PL 40, 276. "It is not to be doubted God to do good even in allowing that some do evil. For he does not allow [evil] except by just judgment, and certainly all that is just is good."

To address [this subject] more fully, the previous words can be explained four ways. And we have already expounded upon two of them. Now the third way is exposited: *Against you alone have I sinned, and have done evil before you, that you may be justified in your words,* that is, seeing that you may appear just consecutively *(consecutive)* or concomitantly *(concomitanter)*[36] in the words by which you promised to become incarnate from my seed.[37] For while I am said to sin thereby [that is, by the human seed, since in sin my mother conceived me], and yet you nevertheless fulfill that which you promised, it is clear that it is not on account of my merits, but because of your justice whereby you carry out the promise and assume human nature from my root *(ex stirpe mea), and may overcome* others in equity,[38] *when you are judged* by a people to whom you ought not to fulfill the promise because of the enormity of my sins.[39]

The fourth interpretation is thus: *Against you alone have I sinned, and have done evil before you, that you may be justified,* that is, since you alone are truly proved good by your own words, *and may be overcome*

---

36 L. Here *consecutive*, translated into English as consecutively, has a meaning different than the ordinary usage of its English derivative (one thing following after another). Here *consecutive* or consecutively means that something is the property or quality of another thing; thus consecutive to being a man is the ability to laugh, because it is a quality of man to be risible because of his rational nature. Something occurs *concomitanter* or concomitantly to another when one thing does not flow from another, yet it is so conjoined to it that they require each other's existence or presence. The existence of one necessarily requires the existence of the other. Thus the corruption of one thing is concomitant to the birth of another, the taking of wealth from a man makes the man taking them rich and concomitantly makes the one whose goods are taken poor.

37 E. N. Broadly, the "promise" and the reference to the "seed," is to Gen. 3:15, the so-called *protoevangelium*, or "first gospel," where God, speaking to the serpent, says, "I will put enmities between ... your seed and her [the human] seed," implying thereby that the Messiah would come from human seed, thereby further implying the Incarnation of the Word. But in a more focused sense (since the Psalm is David's voice) it is David's seed: "Jesus Christ ... which he had promised before by his prophets, in the holy Scriptures, concerning his Son, *who was made to him of the seed of David according to the flesh*." (Rom. 1:1–3). So what Denis is saying is that although David has sinned in his seed (in sin his mother conceived him), yet from this seed he had promised to overcome sin.

38 E. N. As the verse in a Medieval hymn states: *Impleta est veridica iam natum prophetia nam ex stirpe Davidica en oritur Maria.* "Truly was fulfilled the prophecy for, lo! The just born infant comes forth from Mary out of the Davidic branch."

39 E. N. According to Denis's interpretation, David is suggesting that by his sin he has made himself and his seed or his Davidic line unworthy of the Messiah, specifically, that the Lord should became incarnate by assuming a human nature from the Davidic line. He therefore feels he may have threatened the salvation of mankind which is unworthy of being saved because of their sins anyway.

when you are judged that you should have done this or done that.⁴⁰ Or [an alternative explanation]: since you, who lived without deceit or fault, were judged by Pilate and the Jews to be put to death,⁴¹ and you suffer so because of all my sins; and thus by means of a chains of events [I set in motion] you are judged for my sins.⁴²

After this the Prophet [David] recalls the fragility and mortal inclination of nature arising from fault, since by these he may summon and incline God toward mercifulness and forgiveness, according to that which God himself promised to Noah in Genesis: *I will no more curse the earth for the sake of man*, he said, *for the imagination and thought of man's heart are prone to evil from his youth.*⁴³ And David therefore says: **50{51}[7]** *Ecce enim in iniquitatibus conceptus sum, for behold I was conceived in iniquities*: it is as if he said, well does it become you to have mercy upon me a weak sinner, for — look at me — I am conceived in vice, *et in peccatis concepit me mater mea, and in sins did my mother conceive me*. Since the tinder (*fomes*) of sin is inborn in me,⁴⁴ it is not much of a surprise that I have fallen into sin.

---

40   E. N. That is, the contemporaries of Christ judged his teachings, his actions, and his identity, some believing different things of him and believing he should have acted in this way or that. That is, all human judgments of Christ (by the Pharisees, for example) will be found wanting and Christ alone will be seen proved by his own words.

41   Matt. 27:26.

42   E. N. There is an ambiguity here. Denis uses the word *pateris*, which could be translated "you make manifest" or "you expose" all my sins. But it can also be translated as "you suffer" or "you endure." Since the focus is on the Passion of Christ as he is confronting the Jews and Pilate, and not the final judgment, I have opted with the latter.

43   Gen. 8:21.

44   E. N. The fomes (tinder, fuel) of sin — the *fomes peccati* — may be defined by drawing from St. Thomas's *Summa Theologiae*. It is a tendency in us that deviates from reason, consists in a rebellion of the lower powers against reason, the "sting (or thorn) of the flesh" (2 Cor. 12:7), a "blemish of the flesh," which inclines us to sensuality and sin. In itself, it is not sin, but a punishment for the loss of original justice; however, if it is acted upon, it leads to sin, to transgressions of the divine law. It is because of the fomes of sin that "the flesh lusts against the spirit." (Gal. 5:17) This inclination is directed to one's private good (egotism), and so neglects both God and one's neighbor. It has been imposed upon us as a just punishment for Adam's original sin. It is equivalent to concupiscence. It can, however, be resisted and overcome by grace and the Holy Spirit, and so presents us with an occasion of virtue and merit. Neither Jesus nor Mary suffered the fomes of sin. ST, IIIa, qq. 15, 27, q. 39, art. 5. "The fomes is nothing but a certain inordinate, but habitual, concupiscence of the sensitive appetite, for actual concupiscence is a sinful motion. Now sensual concupiscence is said to be inordinate, in so far as it rebels against reason; and this it does by inclining to evil or hindering from good. Consequently, it is of the essence of the fomes to incline to evil, or hinder from good." ST IIIa, q. 27, art. 3, co.

But in what way can man be conceived in iniquities, when the subject of sin and virtue can be nowhere but in the soul or an intellectual essence, which is not then infused in the human body at the time of conception?[45] Again it might be asked how he is conceived in iniquities when he is only conceived in original sin, which is but one sin just as original justice was but one virtue. The response to this [the first question] is that original sin is transferred with the seed (*semine*); yet it is not in the seed (*semine*) as in a subject, but as in origin (*radice*):[46] and therefore, since the seed is so infected, the soul is immediately defiled and contaminated with original sin when it is infused. An example of this [which can be used as an analogy] is the seed of a leper. For the leper generates nothing but lepers, and he transfers leprosy with the seed; but for all that, it [the leprosy] is not in the seed as in a subject, but as in origin: but once the soul is infused immediately the offspring contracts leprosy from the contamination of the seed.[47] To the second [question] we answer that original sin formally is one, namely, the lack of original justice that belonged to it; but materially it is many, because of the four wounds of the soul following original sin, which are ignorance, malice, weakness, and concupiscence, as we have said above.[48]

Third, we might ask in what way the parents transmitted original sin even though in Baptism the original sin is remitted through the merits of the Lord's Passion.[49] The response is that it [original sin] is remitted with respect to the guilt of punishment or stain, but not entirely as to the fomes or inclinations [toward sin], however much they might be weakened.[50] But then it might be more boldly asked in what way this sin can be transmitted to all persons, since the marital coupling is

---

45 E. N. On the matter of ensoulment, Denis appears to have accepted St. Thomas's theory (based upon Aristotelian science, which was then generally accepted) for a development of the soul in the embryo, first vegetative (*nutritiva*), followed by animal (*sensitiva*), finally by a human component (*intellectiva*). Since, according to this science, the embryonic soul at conception would be vegetative and so would not have an intellectual component, Denis asks how the embryo can be said to be "conceived in sin," since sin implies a creature with intellect.

46 E. N. "According to the Catholic Faith, we are bound to hold (*est tenendum*) that the first sin of the first man is by way of origin (*originaliter*) transmitted to his descendants." ST IaIIae, q. 81, art. 1, co.

47 The leper analogy is taken from ST IaIIae, q. 81, art. 1, co.

48 E. N. See Article XXV (Ps. 7:7) in Volume I.

49 E. N. Denis assumes both parents are baptized, and therefore free of original sin. How can they who are free of original sin through baptism conceive a child in original sin? That is the questions he seeks to answer.

50 E. N. ST IaIIae, q. 81, art. 3, ad 1.

able to be free of any sin, indeed to be even virtuous and meritorious,[51] which is commanded by the Apostle [Paul] who says, Let the husband render the debt to his wife, and the wife ... to the husband (but no sin, or a sin inseparably connected, is commanded [by St. Paul in exhorting this]); similarly to the extent it is an act of religion;[52] thirdly, inasmuch as it is an act of the sacrament. The response [to this question] is that the parents do not transmit original sin as if they are the personal and proximate cause of its generation, or because in that conjugal joining they always or inevitably sin, but on account that they proceed from a marred root [or origin]. Indeed, this means a child incurs original sin in a manner different from the way original justice is obtained; he does not have it [original sin] insofar as he was *born* from the first parents, but from the fact that it is *propagated* by the first parents,[53] both as seminal reasons (*rationem seminalem*) and as a corrupt substance (*corruptam substantiam*).[54]

50{51}[8] *For behold you have loved truth: the uncertain and hidden things of your wisdom you have made manifest to me.*

Ecce enim veritatem dilexisti; incerta et occulta sapientiae tuae manifestasti mihi.

---

51 "Since no act proceeding out of a deliberate will is indifferent, ... the matrimonial act is always either sinful or meritorious for the person who is in a state of grace. For if the matrimonial leads to virtue, either of justice, so that the [marital] debt be rendered, or of religion, that they may procreate children for the worship of God, it is meritorious." ST IIIa (Supp.), q. 41 art. 4, co.
52 E. N. In his *Commentary on First Corinthians* (7-1, 1 Cor. 7:1–9 [329]), St. Thomas states: "[I]t should be noted that the conjugal act is sometimes meritorious and without any mortal or venial sin, as when it is directed to the good of procreation and education of a child for the worship of God; for then it is an act of religion; or when it is performed for the sake of rendering the debt, it is an act of justice. https://isidore.co/aquinas/SS1Cor.htm.
53 "If anyone asserts that this sin of Adam, which is one in origin and is transmitted by propagation, not by imitation, and which is in all men, proper to each ... let him be anathema." DA 1513 (Council of Trent).
54 Seminal reasons. The concept of the potentiality in creation was called *logoi spermatikoi* (λόγοι σπερματικοὶ) by the Stoics—in Latin *rationes seminales*. Though usually referred to incipient and inchoate creation, here Denis adapts it to the "seed" of Adam to explain the transmission of original sin. He seems to be alluding to St. Augustine's *On the City of God*: "For all of us were [potentially] in that one [Adam], when all of us were that one [Adam]... There were not yet singly created and distributed forms [souls, since the soul is the form of the body], in which singly we were to live, but there was then a seminal nature (*natura seminalis*) from which we might be propagated (*propagaremur*)." *De Civ. Dei*, 13.14, PL 41, 386.

50{51}[8] *Ecce enim veritatem dilexisti, for behold you have loved truth.* It is as if he said: "Because you love truth, I confess my own fault without excuse; and because I do that which pleases you, it becomes you to be favorably disposed to me." Whence the Savior said: *You shall know the truth, and the truth shall set you free.*[55] God most certainly loves the truth: for similarity is the cause of love.[56] Because God is by nature true, even essentially uncreated truth, it follows that he naturally loves truth. *Incerta, the uncertain,* that is, future contingencies: which properly include prophecy, and to foresee is proper to God, according to Isaiah: *The things that are to come,* announce to us, *and we shall know that you are gods;*[57] *et occulta sapientiae tuae, and hidden things of your wisdom,* that is, the profound and high mysteries of the Godhead and the most-high Trinity, and Christ's Incarnation, Passion, Resurrection, and Ascension, *manifestasti mihi, you have made manifest to me,* by the illumination of the Holy Spirit, more clear, more pure, and more fully than other prophets: for I received from the Holy Spirit everything that I have written (*conscripsi*) in this book not through symbolic illuminations or through sensible forms, but through anagogical irradiation, that is, by intelligible and internal illuminations without the sensible representations of forms.[58]

50{51}[9] *You will sprinkle me with hyssop, and I shall be cleansed: you will wash me, and I shall be made whiter than snow.*

Asperges me hyssopo, et mundabor; lavabis me, et super nivem dealbabor.

50{51}[9] *Asperges me,* Domine, *hyssopo;* O Lord, *you will sprinkle me with hyssop.* In the book of Leviticus we read of the manner that the Lord ordered the cleansing of the leper by sprinkling with hyssop so that he might become clean.[59] Since, therefore, he says, *you will sprinkle me with hyssop,* he describes himself as if he had incurred spiritual leprosy, from which he asks to be cleansed by the aspersions with hyssop, that is, by the contrition of humble repentance. For hyssop is a little plant, adhering by its roots in rocky places, [and is useful in] driving away and healing inflammation of the lungs. And so penance is signified by

---

55 John 8:32.
56 S. T. IaIIae, q. 27, art. 3, co. "Similitude, properly speaking, is the cause of love."
57 Is. 41:23a.
58 *See* Article I, Volume 1, where Denis treats of the levels or grades or prophecy and identifies this one as the supreme grade of prophecy.
59 Lev. 14:2–7.

it: which [penance] is founded upon Christ (who is called a rock),[60] and it heals pride of the heart, and it causes men to regard themselves inconsiderable and small in their own eyes. *Et mundabor, and I shall be cleansed* from interior stain. *Lavabis me, you will wash me*, that is, with a spiritual ablution through the infusion of grace, *et super nivem dealbabor, and I shall be made whiter than snow*, that is, through a spiritual cleansing I will be made more resplendent in attire and radiance than snow is white. For spiritual purity exceeds in every way bodily purity. And this is what the Lord said through Ezechiel: *And I will pour upon you clean water, and you shall be cleansed from all your filthiness.*[61] Of this sprinkling, cleansing, and washing the Savior also said: *When you fast anoint your head, and wash your face, that you appear not to men to fast.*[62] And elsewhere: *Anoint your eyes with eyesalve (collyrio), that you may see.*[63] Or [we can understand it] thus: *You will sprinkle me with hyssop*, that is, with faith and the fruit or merits of the Blood of Christ: by which faith and sprinkling alone are saved the saints of the Old Testament; *and I shall be cleansed*: for by the merits of the Blood of Christ we [of the New Testament] are cleansed from all fault. *You will wash me* in the fountain of Baptism: which refers especially to the Catechumens;[64] *and*

---

60 1 Cor. 10:4: *And all drank the same spiritual drink; (and they drank of the spiritual rock that followed them, and the rock was Christ).*
61 Ez. 36:25a.
62 Matt. 6:17–18a. The relationship between this cite and Denis's argument is not readily apparent. The relationship can be understood by referring to Denis's comments on this verse in his *Commentary on Matthew*: "And *your face*, that is, your conscience, *wash*, that is, from all corrupt intention and all stain, as is counseled by Jeremiah: *Wash your heart from wickedness ... that you may be saved.* (Jer. 4:14a) And Isaiah says: *Wash yourselves, be clean, take away the evil of your devices*." Doctoris Ecstatici D. Dionysii Cartusiani, *Opera Omnia*, Vol. 11 (Montreuil: 1900), 84. In other words, Jesus was counseling *interior or spiritual contrition, and interior penance*, and not external manifestations of it which — if exclusive — lead to hypocrisy or spiritual showboating.
63 Rev. 3:18b. Here also the relationship between this cite and Denis's argument is not apparent. Turning to Denis's *Commentary on Revelation* on this verse we find the explanation: "*Anoint your eyes with eyesalve (collyrio), that you may see.* By eyesalve — which is produced from the earth, which at first irritates the eye, and then cleanses it of the noxious humor, and so effects a clearer vision — is represented the contrition of the heart or compunction, which excites (embitters) the mind through the sorrow for sin, and cleanses it from the squalor of vice, elicits tears, and leads to illumination. By this eyesalve the eye of the heart is anointed, so long as it feels true remorse before God, and so we see in the light of grace, and recognize our defects." Doctoris Ecstatici D. Dionysii Cartusiani, *Opera Omnia*, Vol. 14 (Montreuil: 1901), 256.
64 E. N. The catechumens are, of course, not yet baptized. Hence the verse refers in the future to their being cleansed by the waters of Baptism. "Holy Baptism is the basis of the whole Christian life, the gateway to life in the Spirit (*vitae spiritualis*

I shall be made whiter than snow: because in Baptism all sin is taken away according to this [Scripture], *Baptism saves us, not the putting away of the dirt of the flesh, but the examination of a good conscience towards God.*[65]

50{51}[10] *To my hearing you shall give joy and gladness: and the bones that have been humbled shall rejoice.*

Auditui meo dabis gaudium et laetitiam, et exsultabunt ossa humiliata.

50{51}[10] *Auditui meo*, to my hearing, exterior and interior, *dabis gaudium*, you shall give joy of the forgiveness of sins, *et laetitiam*, and gladness of the restoration of grace. Literally, God gave the holy David this joy and this gladness when through the prophet Nathan and through internal inspiration, he promised forgiveness and restored grace.[66] We also receive from God joy and gladness when we console ourselves through sacred Scripture, saying to him: *If the wicked do penance for all his sins which he has committed, ... I will not remember all his iniquities that he has done.*[67] And again: *Return and live,*[68] for I do not wish the death of the sinner, but that he be converted and live.[69] And this does not differ from that which the Savior affirms: *It is not the will of your Father, who is in heaven, that one of these little ones should perish.*[70] For this reason we find elsewhere: *God made not death, neither* does he take delight *in the destruction of the living.*[71] And so he pours forth great joy upon us, since he is so ready, indeed he most readily offers to fill with grace according to that which he himself has borne witness to: *Everyone that asks, receives,*

---

ianua), and the door which gives access to the other sacraments. Through Baptism we are freed from sin and reborn as sons of God; we become members of Christ, are incorporated into the Church and made sharers in her mission: 'Baptism is the sacrament of regeneration through water in the word.'" CCC § 1213 (citations omitted).
65 1 Pet. 3:21a. E. N. I have replaced "filth" which translates *sordium* with "dirt," since filth carries with it moral connotations, and St. Peter is clearly speaking here of the superficial cleaning of the body, the *sacramentum tantum* of Baptism, and not Baptism's *res et sacramentum* or *res tantum*.
66 2 Sam. 12:13: *And David said to Nathan: I have sinned against the Lord. And Nathan said to David: The Lord also has taken away your sin: you shall not die.*
67 Ez. 18:21–22.
68 Ez. 18:32b.
69 *Cf.* Ez. 18:23: *Is it my will that a sinner should die, says the Lord God, and not that he should be converted from his ways, and live?*
70 Matt. 18:14.
71 Wis. 1:13. Denis has *delectator* (take delight) instead of the Sixto-Clementine Vulgate's *laetatur* (take joy or pleasure).

and he that seeks, finds: and to him that knocks, it shall be opened.[72] And again: *Your Father from heaven gives the good Spirit to them that ask him.*[73] And also through the hidden instinct[74] of the Holy Spirit God gives us joy and gladness: for (as the Apostle [Paul] says) *the Spirit himself gives testimony to our spirit, that we are the sons of God.*[75] And again: *He has given the pledge of the Spirit in our hearts.*[76] *Et exsultabunt ossa humiliata, and the bones that have been humbled shall rejoice.* The name of the part is referring to the whole,[77] so that it [should be understood] in this sense: "I, a sinner and penitent, who even to the humiliation of my bones — or the bowing down, genuflection, or prostration of my body — humble myself." Or [alternatively]: *The bones that have been humbled rejoice,* that is, the interior gladness from its fulness redounds into my body, and the bones of my body exhibit unmistakable signs of my interior joy. For just like *a sorrowful spirit dries up the bones,*[78] so does a spirit of joy fatten and gladden the bones. Or [yet another way of looking at it]: *The bones that have been humbled,* that is, the virtues of my soul[79] — which before repentance were oppressed, put to sleep, and idle, but after repentance joyfully and fervently begin to operate, because *where sin abounded,* grace also abounds[80] — *shall rejoice,* are put into motion joyfully and with strength.

50{51}[11] Turn away your face from my sins, and blot out all my iniquities.

Averte faciem tuam a peccatis meis, et omnes iniquitates meas dele.

50{51}[11] *Averte,* turn away, O Lord, *faciem tuam,* your face, that is, your consideration, *a peccatis meis,* from my sins, and forget them, that is, hold yourself out in the manner of a forgetful person in not returning vengeance and in forgiving. And this most certainly the most kindly God

---

72 Matt. 7:8b; Luke 11:10.
73 Luke 11:13b.
74 E. N. On St. Thomas's notion of the "instinct" of the Holy Spirit, *see* footnote 34-86.
75 Rom. 8:16.
76 2 Cor. 1:22b.
77 E. N. In other words, this is a synecdoche, where a part of something refers to the whole, such "all hands on deck," where "hands" means sailors.
78 Prov. 17:22b.
79 E. N. The "bones" are frequently used to refer to the virtues in Scripture. *See* footnote 33-72.
80 Rom. 5:20b.

freely does, if you look upon, ponder, lament, correct, and avoid your sins; otherwise, he will do to you that which he did to those persevering in sin by the prophet Amos who said: *The Lord has sworn... Surely I will never forget all their works.*[81] Hence, of the negligent and those not lamenting their own evil doings the Apostle [Paul] says: *Do you despise the riches of his goodness, and patience, and longsuffering? Do you not know that the benignity of God leads you to penance? But according to your hardness and impenitent heart, you treasure up to yourself wrath, against the day of wrath, and revelation of the just judgment of God.*[82] And so, O Lord, *turn away your face*, that is, the reproach of your justice, *from my sins*, so that you may not withdraw grace in the presence or glory in the future from me because of their demerit; *et omnes iniquitates meas dele*, and blot out all my iniquities, remitting their punishment and the fault,[83] and receiving me into your friendship as if I had never sinned.

50{51}[12] *Create a clean heart in me, O God: and renew a right spirit within my bowels.*

Cor mundum crea in me, Deus, et spiritum rectum innova in visceribus meis.

50{51}[13] *Cast me not away from your face; and take not your holy spirit from me.*

Ne proiicias me a facie tua, et spiritum sanctum tuum ne auferas a me.

50{51}[14] *Restore unto me the joy of your salvation, and strengthen me with a perfect spirit.*

Redde mihi laetitiam salutaris tui, et spiritu principali confirma me.

50{51}[12] *Cor mundum crea in me, Deus; create a clean heart in me, O God*: that is, fashion and begin in me a spiritual existence and one able to earn merit by the creation of grace.[84] For *blessed are the clean of heart, for they shall see God.*[85] In fact, cleanliness of the heart ought to be the final

---

81 Amos 7:7.
82 Rom. 2:4–5.
83 For the difference between fault of sin and punishment for sin, see footnote 21-146 in Volume I.
84 On grace being the principle of the supernatural (spiritual) life and merit, see footnote 36-120.
85 Matt. 5:8.

end of all our exercises, according to that which Solomon admonished: *With all watchfulness keep your heart.*[86] And if you desire to receive true purity of heart, then so repeat, meditate upon, reflect, plead, and draw forth this verse in your mind and mouth as you draw in your breath through your nose. For great and of ineffable virtue is this verse and the next one. *Et spiritum rectum innova, and renew a right spirit,* that is, pour in anew the Holy Spirit, *in visceribus meis, within my bowels,*[87] that is, in the most intimate part of my soul, giving grace, wisdom, charity, and the other virtues and the gifts of the Holy Spirit. **50{51}[13]** *Ne proiicias me, cast me not away* because of my sins, *a facie tua, from your face,* that is, from the countenance of your kindness and from your preservation; *et spiritum sanctum tuum, and your holy* spirit, that is, the gracious dwelling and merciful presence of the Holy Spirit, *ne auferas a me, take not...from* me, but conserve me in good. **50{51}[14]** *Redde mihi laetitiam salutaris tui, restore unto me the joy of your salvation,* that is, the joyful contemplation of Christ, in whom subsists the salvation of all men. For as a result of his fault, David was seen to have lost this for a time, and to have sent away the prophetic spirit. Whence, he was unable to see the enormity of his own sin. Because *wisdom will not enter into a malicious soul,*[88] we also by sinning send it away. And so for its restitution, increase, and preservation we ought unceasingly to pray. *Et spiritu principali, and with a perfect spirit,* that is, the Holy Spirit, *confirma me, strengthen me,* establish my heart in his grace: for as the Apostle [Paul] said, *It is best that the heart be established with grace.*[89] For no one is *crowned, except he strive lawfully;*[90] nor will he be saved, unless he *persevere unto the end:*[91] for none of this is possible, except to him that God confirms with the Holy Spirit.

See the most blessed David evidently demonstrates in this verse the faith and mystery of the supermostglorious Trinity. For by the name of God, he designates the Father; by the name of the right, perfect, and holy spirit, he designates the Holy Spirit; and by the name salvation, he sets forth the Son, of whom Peter said, *Neither is there salvation in any other.*[92] Similarly, the prophet Isaiah clearly reveals Trinity of divine persons, when the Lord says through him: *[I am he,] I am the first, and*

---

86 Prov. 4:23a.
87 On the meaning of bowels (*viscera*) in this context, see footnotes 29-49 and 41-86.
88 Wis. 1:4a.
89 Heb. 13:9a.
90 2 Tim. 2:5.
91 Matt. 10:22b; *cf.* Matt. 24:13.
92 Acts 4:12a.

I am the last.[93] And shortly after this *first* and the *last* is added: *And now the Lord God has sent me, and his spirit.*[94] There by *first* and *last* is understood Christ, who in Revelation says, *I am the Alpha and Omega, [the first and last,] the beginning and the end;*[95] and again, *I am the First and the Last, and I was dead, and behold I am living forever and ever, and I have the keys of death and hell.*[96] Since, therefore, Christ has been sent by the Lord [God the Father] and invokes his Spirit, the mystery of the Trinity is most clearly demonstrated.

50{51}[15] *I will teach the unjust your ways: and the wicked shall be converted to you.*

Docebo iniquos vias tuas, et impii ad te convertentur.

50{51}[15] *Docebo iniquos vias tuas, I will teach the unjust your ways*: that is, once grace has been conceded by you to me, I will communicate to others, and I will devote myself to lead others by my example to saving repentance, and I will exhort them to observe the divine precepts. This applies to holy David as much as it does to the princes of the people: indeed it seems to apply to everyone in a certain way, according to this, *As every man has received grace, ministering the same one to another: as good stewards of the manifold grace of God.*[97] For this reason Paul says: *Brethren, and if a man be overtaken in any fault, you, who are spiritual, instruct such a one in the spirit of meekness, considering yourself, lest you also be tempted.*[98] Hence Dionysius [the Areopagite] says that of all the divine perfections, the highest is to be a cooperator of God in the restoration of the soul to the First Principle.[99] *Et impii ad te convertentur, and the*

---

93 Is. 48:12b. E. N. Denis does not have the part in brackets in the Latin text, but it seems required by the Trinitarian argument, otherwise the Father is left out of the picture.
94 Is. 48:16b.
95 Rev. 22:13. E. N. The part within brackets is added though it is not in Denis's text. It would seem to have been warranted by his argument.
96 Rev. 1:17-18a.
97 1 Pet. 4:10. St. Thomas Aquinas quotes 1 Pet. 4:10 in his *Commentary on the Gospel of John*: "Because [the Apostle] Thomas had not been with the others, the other disciples told him, *We have seen the Lord.* This was by the divine ordinance that what one receives from God should be shared with others: *As every man has received grace, ministering the same one to another.*" *Super Io.,* cap. 20 l. 5.
98 Ga. 6:1.
99 E. N. [O]*mnium divinarum perfectionum altissima est, Dei cooperatorem exsistere in reductione animarum ad primum principium.* The reference appears to be to Pseudo-Dionysius's *Celestial Hierarchy* c. 3. However, this appears to be a synthesis of

wicked shall be converted to you, from my teaching: which is powerfully meritorious because it is written: *He who causes a sinner to be converted from the error of his way, shall save his soul from death, and shall cover a multitude of sins.*[100] And Daniel says: *They that are learned shall shine as the brightness of the firmament: and they that instruct many to justice, as stars for all eternity.*[101] But who is so worthy to be so divinely illuminated that he may be suitable to inform others? The most illustrious Isaiah gives to us the answer when he says: *Whom shall he teach knowledge? And whom shall he make to understand the hearing? Them that are weaned from the milk, that are drawn away from the breasts,*[102] that is, those who avoid carnal delights and sensual pleasures, and are able to take hold of strong meat;[103] though living in the flesh, not walking according to the flesh,[104] nor giving access to the vanities of the world. For we see many who are very-well prepared for the instructing others, yet they accomplish little or nothing at all because they spout off their own ideas, and not those of the Holy Spirit; and they speak with cold, arid words, and not with pointed, penetrative, and warm ones. To each of these, the Apostle said: *Are you confident that you yourself are a guide of the blind, a light of them that are in darkness, an instructor of the foolish, a teacher of infants, [having the form of knowledge and of truth in the law.] You therefore that teach another, teach you not yourself?*[105] *Do you that make your boast of the law, by transgression of the law dishonor God?*[106]

50{51}[16] *Deliver me from blood, O God, God of my salvation: and my tongue shall extol your justice.*

Libera me de sanguinibus, Deus, Deus salutis meae, et exsultabit lingua mea iustitiam tuam.

---

the Dionysian principles in that chapter by Denis, and not a direct quote, and its analogous application to man to arrive at the conclusion that the highest perfection is cooperating with God in bringing back souls to him.
100 James 5:20.
101 Dan. 12:3.
102 Is. 28:9.
103 Heb. 5:14. E. N. In the segue from the milk of Is. 28:9 to strong meat of Heb. 5:14, it helps to have the intermediation of Heb. 5:13, which ties the two together: Heb. 5:13-14: *For every one that is a partaker of milk, is unskillful in the word of justice: for he is a little child. But strong meat is for the perfect; for them who by custom have their senses exercised to the discerning of good and evil.*
104 *Cf.* 2 Cor. 10:3.
105 Rom. 2:19–21a. E. N. The part in brackets replaces Denis's "etc."
106 Rom. 2:23.

50{51}[17] *O Lord, you will open my lips: and my mouth shall declare your praise.*

Domine, labia mea aperies, et os meum annuntiabit laudem tuam.

50{51}[16] *Libera me de sanguinibus, deliver me from blood,* that is, from my past, present, and future sins, *Deus, O God,* of all, *Deus salutis meae, God of my salvation,* in whose power consists my salvation, from whom all my perfections proceeds and all the good of my soul depends; *et exsultabit, and I shall extol,* that is, with exultation shall I sing and say, *lingua mea iustitiam tuam, my tongue … your justice,* that is, the just is the judgment by which you condemn the obstinate, have mercy on the repentant, hear those who pray, bestow the abundance of your grace to those turning towards you with all their heart, and justify the sinner confessing his own sins. **50{51}[17]** *Domine, labia mea aperies; O Lord, you will open my lips,* that is, from interior devotion and grace you will make my lips burst forth in acts of good utterances, so that I might speak at the prompting of the Holy Spirit, and not be induced through my own self. For *he that speaks of himself, seeks his own glory.*[107] *Et os meum annuntiabit laudem tuam, and my mouth shall declare your praise*: because then truly worthily will I praise, if my lips are opened by you, in the manner that you say elsewhere: *Open your mouth, and I will fill it.*[108]

50{51}[18] *For if you had desired sacrifice, I would indeed have given it: with burnt offerings you will not be delighted.*

Quoniam si voluisses sacrificium, dedissem utique; holocaustis non delectaberis.

50{51}[19] *A sacrifice to God is an afflicted spirit: a contrite and humbled heart, O God, you will not despise.*

Sacrificium Deo spiritus contribulatus; cor contritum et humiliatum, Deus, non despicies.

Then David asserts the reason why it was becoming for God to be forgiving. **50{51}[18]** *Quoniam si voluisses sacrificium, for if you had desired sacrifice* under the Law, *dedissem utique, I would indeed have given it,* a sacrifice for the satisfaction of my departures [from the law]; but *holocaustis,*

---

107 John 7:18a.
108 Ps. 80:11b. Denis has *aperi,* "open," a different reading from the Sixto-Clementine Vulgate's *dilata,* "spread out."

burnt offerings that are legal and figurative *non delectaberis, you will not be delighted*. For the sacrifices of the Old Law did not contain grace, nor were they accepted for themselves (*per se*), but only to the extent of the devotion of the one offering.[109] And so by it God was not able to be placated except by him who had grace before the sacrifice or at least during it. Whence it says in the scripture in Genesis: *The Lord had respect to Abel, and to his offerings*.[110] For he respected first the offeror, and then the offering. And so David longed to receive grace before the offering of the sacrifice or during it. And so also any of the [Christian] faithful can says these words with respect to himself: because if he desires to please God, there also remains in the New Testament a legal sacrifice,[111] and it might be offered by the Christian for the satisfaction [of sins]. 50{51}[19] *Sacrificium Deo spiritus contribulatus, a sacrifice to God is an afflicted spirit*: that is, the soul lamenting and sorrowing for sins is to God an acceptable sacrifice: for it offers itself to God, and of its own will subjects itself to him so as to do and to suffer those things that are pleasing to God. Hence, Ecclesiasticus proposes: *It is a wholesome sacrifice to take heed to the commandments, and to depart from all iniquity*.[112] And Baruch: *The soul that is sorrowful for the greatness of evil it has done, and goes bowed down, and feeble, and the eyes that fail, and*

---

109   E. N. For the objective nature of the Sacrifice of the New Law — the bloody Sacrifice of Christ and the unbloody representation of that Sacrifice in the Mass — which works *ex opere operato*, and not subjectively *ex opere operantis*, as did the sacrifices of the Old Law, see footnote 39-33.
110   Gen. 4:4b.
111   E. N. The "legal sacrifice" Denis refers to as "remaining," is the "sacrifice of the New Law." "It was fitting that the sacrifice of the New Law (*sacrificium novae legis*) instituted by Christ should have something more, namely, that it should contain the one who suffered (*ipsum passum*), not merely in signification or figure, but also in very truth." ST, IIIa, q. 76, art. 1, co. The fact that the Sacrifice of the Mass, in contradistinction with the sacrifices of the Old Law, works *ex opere operato* does not nullify or excuse the role of the participant. Indeed, given the reality of the Sacrifice, it demands *more* of the offeror or recipient. In other words it does not remove the need for subjective grace and devotion. "Grace is given *ex opere operato*, when, the proper dispositions being supposed in the recipient, it is given through the ordinance; it is given *ex opere operantis*, when, whether there be outward sign or no, the inward energetic act of the recipient is the instrument of it.... [T]he Sacrifice of the Mass benefits the person for whom it is offered *ex opere operato*... but it benefits him more or less, *ex opere operantis*, according to the degree of sanctity which [he] has attained, and the earnestness with which he offers it." St. John Henry Newman, *Lectures on Certain Difficulties Felt by Anglicans in Submitting to the Catholic Church* (London: Burns & Lambert, 1850), 72.
112   Ecclus. 35:2.

the hungry soul gives glory and justice to you the Lord.[113] *Cor contritum et humiliatum, Deus, non despicies; a contrite and humbled heart, O God, you will not despise,* as is witnessed by Isaiah: *To whom shall I have respect, but to him that is poor and little, and of a contrite spirit, and that trembles at my words?*[114] And Job says: *He that has been humbled, shall be in glory . . . and the innocent shall be saved.*[115] And Ecclesiasticus: *The prayer of him that humbles himself, shall pierce the clouds.*[116]

50{51}[20] *Deal favorably, O Lord, in your good will with Sion; that the walls of Jerusalem may be built up.*

Benigne fac, Domine, in bona voluntate tua Sion, ut aedificentur muri Ierusalem.

50{51}[21] *Then shall you accept the sacrifice of justice, oblations and whole burnt offerings: then shall they lay calves upon your altar.*

Tunc acceptabis sacrificium iustitiae, oblationes et holocausta; tunc imponent super altare tuum vitulos.

LITERAL EXPLANATION

50{51}[20] *Benigne fac, Domine, in bona voluntate tua Sion, et aedificentur muri Ierusalem; deal favorably, O Lord, in our good will with Sion, that the walls of Jerusalem may be built up.*[117] This verse along with the one which follows, will first be explained literally; and it should be understood in this sense:[118] *O Lord, in your good will* where you promised to me that my son Solomon would build to you a temple,[119] *deal favorably with Sion*, that is, in your kindness fulfil in mount Sion that which you have promised, namely that upon it will be built a temple in your name; *and that the walls of Jerusalem may be built up*, that is, the walls of the temple or the walls of the city, which David saw in the spirit often being destroyed. 50{51}[21] *Tunc*, then, that is, the temple having been

---

113 Baruch 2:18.
114 Is. 66:2b.
115 Job. 22:29–30a.
116 Ecclus. 35:21a.
117 E. N. Denis's variant has *et* (and) instead of *ut* (that), reading, ". . . with Sion *and* the walls . . ." rather than ". . . with Sion, *that* the walls . . ."
118 E. N. This is in the person of David, i.e., David speaking.
119 2 Sam. 7:12–13.

built, *acceptabis sacrificium iustitiae, shall you accept the sacrifice of justice,* which justly will be offered to you, *oblationes, oblations,* which are not totally consumed by fire, *et holocausta, and whole burnt offerings,* which are entirely consumed by fire; *tunc imponent, then shall they lay,* in the temple, *vitulos, calves,* for according to the law, a calf was the animal suitable to be offered.

MORAL EXPLANATION

But morally it is explained thus: *Deal favorably, O Lord, in our good will,* by which you promise always grace to men, so long as they turn back to you, *Sion,* that is, the Church militant, seeing you by faith, and you conserving it in the faith and grace of Christ, *and the walls of Jerusalem may be built up,* that is, the prelates of the Church, who are the protectors, or the walls and supports, of others. These, therefore, spiritually build up, that is, that they may be confirmed in the advancement of virtue and grace, in the way that the Apostle [Paul] said, *Keep the things that are of edification one towards another;*[120] and, *Let every one of you please his neighbor unto good, to edification.*[121] Or [alternatively]: *The walls of Jerusalem may be built up,* that is, the two people of the Jews and the Greeks assembling together in the one faith of the Church, as the Apostle said: *For there is no distinction of the Jew and the Greek.*[122] *Then shall you accept* in the Catholic Church *the sacrifice of justice,* that is, the sacrifice of praise and of the Eucharist, *oblations* of prayer and of alms, and of exterior things, *and burnt offerings,* that is, of their own will unadulterated and freely-willed abnegations, those, that is, who offer themselves totally in the divine worship, holding as contemptible all other things, and holding back nothing for themselves. *Then shall they lay... upon your altar:* which is the humanity of Christ, by which all our duties and services (*officia*) are made acceptable;[123] *calves,* that is, themselves, following in his [Christ's] path, and mortifying themselves every day following his example, as the Apostle attests: *With all confidence... shall Christ be magnified in my body, whether it be by life or by*

---

120 Rom. 14:19b.
121 Rom. 15:2.
122 Rom. 10:12a.
123 E. N. I have translated *officia*, "offices," a Latin word difficult to translate with one English equivalent, especially when the context uses it in its broad sense. It can include duty, favor, service, ceremonial observance, compliance, obligation, office, employment. I have therefore translated it with two words: duties and services.

death. For to me, to live is Christ, and to die is gain.¹²⁴ Or [alternatively]: *They shall lay calves upon your altar*, that is, in the faith of the Church they will offer to you divine praises: as is written by Hosea: *We will render the calves of our lips.*¹²⁵

ANAGOGICAL EXPLANATION

Finally analogically it is expounded thus: *Deal favorably, O Lord, in your good will with Sion*, that is, the Church triumphant contemplating you face-to-face, *and the walls of Jerusalem may be built up*, that is, the fall of the evil angels may be repaired by the salvation of the elect of mankind.¹²⁶ Then, when, namely, *when that which is perfect is come*,¹²⁷ most especially after the day of the general judgment, when the walls of the heavenly Jerusalem will be completely rebuilt,¹²⁸ [the Jerusalem] *which is our mother*,¹²⁹ of which glorious things are said¹³⁰ (would also that they might also worthily desire it): *then*, I say, O Lord, *shall you accept the sacrifice of justice*, that is, perpetual praises and most pure and perfect *oblations*, in which all the blessed in the heavenly homely will completely offer themselves to you, remaining always inavertibly¹³¹ turned and fixed in you; *and burnt offerings*, that is, perfect acts of charity. For the saints in the heavenly homeland perfectly fulfill the precept of loving God which they were unable to do while they were in the wayfaring state: and these acts of charity are called burnt offerings because

---

124 Phil 1:20–21.
125 Hosea 14:3b.
126 E. N. It is the common opinion that the number of fallen angels is to be made up by men who are saved. For example, St. Augustine in his *Enchiridion de Fide, Spe, et Caritate*, IX, 29 states: "And so it pleased God, Creator and governor of the universe, that because the whole multitude of the angels had not perished by deserting him, those who perished would remain perpetually in perdition; but those who had persisted [by being loyal] through the desertion should forever rejoice at the most certain knowledge of their future happiness. But he would supplant that portion of the angelic society diminished by the diabolic ruin by that repaired portion of the other rational creation, which was found in men, because it had totally perished through both original and personal sins and punishments." PL 40, 246.
127 1 Cor. 13:10a.
128 *Cf.* Amos 9:11: *In that day I will raise up the tabernacle of David, that is fallen: and I will close up the breaches of the walls thereof, and repair what was fallen: and I will rebuild it as in the days of old.*
129 Gal. 4:26: *But that Jerusalem, which is above, is free: which is our mother.*
130 *Cf.* Ps. 86:3: *Glorious things are said of you, O city of God.*
131 E. N. This word frequently used by Denis means it cannot be averted, deflected, moved. See footnote 29-67.

by them intellectual creatures are entirely released into the divine love. *Then shall they lay... upon your altar*, that is in the empyreal heaven,[132] the *calves* of lips, as has been already explained; or [alternatively], *calves*, that is, themselves, because inflamed with the divine fire of love, they dissolve, and they are entirely transformed in God.[133]

See how we have been taught by this most excellent Psalm, which not only instructs us by the sense of its words, but it also greatly teaches us by the example of its author. For who is able to presume of himself, when he sees the author of this Psalm, the holy David, after the attainment of such divine gifts, to have fallen so gravely, not only into adultery, but also into the act of homicide? He when at a young age lived a life so perfect and humble, willed not to slay, or even grant permission to wound, his enemy,[134] but returned good for evil, snatching from death him who with all his strength was laboring to kill him, who subdued a lion and a bear, who cut down a giant, who received so many and so momentous sacred revelations, now in old age overthrown by such a monstrous sin.[135] And so, who is able to lose hope when he hears an adulterer and murderer to have fallen from such perfection? Let us apply ourselves, therefore, beloved, to truthfully do penance with the holy David, and in all things embrace an unsimulated humility: for (as Pope Leo said) the entire discipline of Christian wisdom does not consist in the abundance of words, or in clever disputing, or in the eagerness of praise and glory, but in true and voluntary humility; which the Lord Jesus, with all fortitude both chose and taught for all of us from the womb of his Mother even unto his execution on the Cross.[136] And again: All victory, it says, of the Savior who overcame the devil and the world was conceived in humility and was accomplished with humility. Whence Christ asserts: *Unless you be converted, and become as little children, you shall not enter into the kingdom of heaven. Whosoever therefore*

---

132 E. N. The highest of all heavens. On the empyrean or empyreal heaven, see footnote 19-11 in Volume 1.

133 E. N. Note Denis does not mean that we are entirely transformed into God in some sort of annihilation, but that we are entirely transformed or divinized in God. "We shall see and possess God; we shall be united to Him in an intimate manner, but we shall ever retain our distinct personality and individuality." F. J. Boudreaux, S. J., *The Happiness of Heaven* (London: Burns & Oates 1881), 21.

134 1 Sam. 24:5-8; 26:7-12. E. N. David would not kill Saul when he had the opportunity, nor allow Abisai to kill him.

135 1 Sam. 17:34-36; 49.

136 E. N. This follows closely, indeed almost verbatim, with Pope St. Leo the Great's Sermon 37, 3 (Epiphany, 7, 3). PL 54, 258.

shall humble himself as this little child, he is the greater in the kingdom of heaven.[137] To which, after this dwelling in exile, the almighty Creator, three and one, who is above all things God sublime and blessed, may immediately lead us. Amen.

PRAYER

MERCIFUL GOD, TURN AWAY YOUR FACE from our sins, and blot out all our iniquities before your sight; wash us from our injustice so that, cleansed by the gift of your grace, we may remain always in a manner of living holy and pleasing to you.

Miserator Deus, faciem tuam a peccatis nostris averte, et omnes in conspectu tuo iniquitates nostras dele; lava nos ab iniustitia nostra, ut dono gratiae tuae emundati, in sancta ac tibi placita conversatione semper maneamus.

*End of the Commentary
of the
First Fifty Psalms*

---

137 Matt. 18:3–4.

ABOUT THE TRANSLATOR

ANDREW M. GREENWELL IS A MARried Catholic layman, with three children and four grandchildren. He is a civil trial and appellate lawyer based in Corpus Christi, Texas, who has written articles for Catholic Online and for a number of years wrote a blog on the natural moral law called *Lex Christianorum*. He has translated works from German, Latin, French, and Italian into English. He is a member of the Latin Mass Community at St. John the Baptist Church in Corpus Christi, Texas. Angelico Press is publishing his translations of all of Denis the Carthusian's works on the Mass and the Eucharist.

www.ingramcontent.com/pod-product-compliance
Lightning Source LLC
Chambersburg PA
CBHW021421070526
44577CB00001B/5